ENCYCLOPEDIA
Science
SUPPLEMENT
1970

1

ENCYCLOPEDIA
Science
SUPPLEMENT
970

A synthesis of art and technology: the picture on the cover, entitled *Eclipse*, was created at California Computer Products, Inc., by using a computer and a microfilm plotter. Originally done in black and white as a test pattern for the plotter, the picture was later colored by hand. Variations of the design can be created by instructing the computer to change the diameter, add or delete lines, and so on. In less than a second the changes are displayed by the plotter. This technique — called computer graphics — has practical as well as esthetic applications.

ISBN 0-7172-1501-6

Library of Congress Catalog Card Number: 64-7603

CONTENTS

  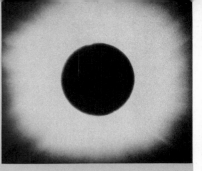

CONTRIBUTORS

TOM ALEXANDER   SOME BURNING QUESTIONS ABOUT COMBUSTION; SCIENCE REDISCOVERS GRAVITY
Associate Editor, *Fortune*

BERNARD ASBELL   CAN WE SURVIVE THE MADDING CROWD?
Educational consultant; free-lance writer, author: *When FDR Died, The New Improved American*

ISAAC ASIMOV   IS THERE INTELLIGENCE OUT THERE?
Professor of Biochemistry, Boston University; noted author of numerous books and articles

C. LORING BRACE   THE ORIGIN OF MAN
Associate Professor of Anthropology, University of Michigan

WALTER B. CHARM   WORKING THE *GLOMAR CHALLENGER*
Institute of Marine and Atmospheric Sciences, University of Miami

PETER T. CHEW   RESCUING THREATENED ANIMALS
Staff writer, *The National Observer*

CLARENCE COTTAM   PESTICIDE POLLUTION
Director, Welder Wildlife Foundation, Sinton, Texas

V. G. DROZIN   CYBERNETICS
Professor of Physics, Bucknell University

LOUIS C. FARON   THE INCA
Chairman, Department of Anthropology, State University of New York at Stony Brook

IRWIN K. FEINSTEIN   THE BINARY NUMERAL SYSTEM
Professor of Mathematics, University of Illinois at Chicago Circle

WEBB GARRISON   PAIN
Clergyman; author of numerous books on religion and science

PHILIP GOLDSTEIN   HOW TO DO AN EXPERIMENT
Chairman (retired), Department of Biology, Abraham Lincoln High School, Brooklyn, New York

THOMAS J. GRADEL   THE CASHLESS SOCIETY
Staff, RCA Information Systems Division

EDMUND F. GREKULINSKI   AN ODYSSEY IN PAPER; PLATE TECTONICS
Associate Editor, *The Book of Popular Science and Encyclopedia Science Supplement*

KATHERINE HARAMUNDANIS   Coauthor, THE MOON
Supervisor, Star Catalog Project, Smithsonian Astrophysical Observatory

TOM HERMAN   EXOTIC INVADERS BRING WOE TO FLORIDA
Staff reporter, *The Wall Street Journal*

LOU JOSEPH   IS A THUMB FOR SUCKING?
Assistant Director, Bureau of Public Information, American Dental Association

J. PETER KANE   INSTANT REPLAY
Video Consultant, Ampex Corp.

PETER R. KANN   THE DANIS OF JIWIKA
Staff reporter, *The Wall Street Journal*

MORLEY KARE
Professor of Physiology, University of Pennsylvania

BIONICS

GERSHON KINGSLEY
President, Kingsley Sound Inc.

Coauthor, ELECTRONIC MUSIC

MORT LA BRECQUE
Staff writer, *The Sciences*

POLYWATER

CHARLES LINCOLN
Staff, *Popular Electronics* magazine

CASSETTES

J. R. MACDONALD
Senior Curator of Vertebrate Paleontology, Los Angeles County Museum of Natural History

DEATH TRAP OF THE AGES

WILLIAM H. MATTHEWS III
Author, *Fossils: An Introduction to Prehistoric Life*

DIGGING FOR FOSSILS

STEVEN MOLL
Assistant Editor, *Encyclopedia Americana*

RETURN TO THE MOON

RICHARD M. NIXON
President of the United States

CLEANING UP OUR ENVIRONMENT

CECILIA PAYNE-GAPOSCHKIN
Senior Scientist, Smithsonian Astrophysical Observatory

Coauthor, THE MOON

BENJAMIN H. PEARSE
Writer, Editorial Services Division, U.S. Office of Education's Office of Information

THE BOY CANNOT READ . . .

JOHN E. PFEIFFER
Science writer; author, *The Emergence of Man*

VISCERAL LEARNING

JACQUES PICCARD
Oceanographer and deep-sea explorer

DRIFTING IN A SILENT WORLD

TED J. RAKSTIS
Free-lance writer

SENSITIVITY TRAINING

ROBERT REINHOLD
Staff writer, *The New York Times*

SCIENTISTS ISOLATE A GENE

ROGER REVELLE
Director, Center for Population Studies, Harvard University

THE WORLD FOOD SUPPLY

TOM SHACHTMAN
Writer, National Geographic Society

ART AND THE COMPUTER

ISRAEL SHENKER
Staff writer, *The New York Times*

THE REMARKABLE EFFECTS OF L-DOPA

DIANE SHERMAN
Free-lance writer; author, *About Canals and You and the Oceans*

FUN WITH FIBONACCI

HUGH SPITZER
Staff reporter, *The Wall Street Journal.*

METHADONE THERAPY FOR HEROIN ADDICTS

GUNTHER STENT

Department of Neurobiology, Harvard Medical School

THE 1969 NOBEL PRIZE FOR PHYSIOLOGY AND MEDICINE

CLAYTON R. SUTTON
Free-lance writer

BUILDING HOMES WITH BUILDING BLOCKS

JENNY ELIZABETH TESAR   THE FIGHT AGAINST RUBELLA;
PORTRAIT OF MARS;
THE SOVIET YEAR IN SPACE

Associate Editor, *The Book of Popular Science* and *Encyclopedia Science Supplement*

WERNHER VON BRAUN   AFTER APOLLO, WHAT?

Deputy Associate Administrator for Planning, National Aeronautics and Space Administration

JOHN WATTS   Coauthor, ELECTRONIC MUSIC

The New School for Social Research

DAVID WEBSTER   DOES HOT WATER FREEZE
FASTER THAN COOL WATER?

Educational consultant; author, *Brain Boosters* and *Snow Stumpers*

SUSAN WERNERT   THE CHEMICALS YOU EAT

Science editor and free-lance writer

PHILIP WYLIE   AGAINST ALL ODDS, THE BIRDS HAVE WON

Noted author (*Generation of Vipers*) and longtime conservationist leader

PATRICK YOUNG   THE LUNAR ROCKS

Staff writer, *The National Observer*

ANTHROPOLOGY
AND ARCHAEOLOGY

CONTENTS

On the warpath. The Danis of New Guinea live a Stone-Age existence, which until recently was based largely on intertribal warfare and cannibalism.

From Robert Gardner's film *Dead Birds*

3

REVIEW OF THE YEAR-ANTHROPOLOGY AND ARCHAEOLOGY

Anthropology. The age of man on earth, once measured in thousands of years, has been pushed into the millions of years as anthropologists make find after find pointing to a far greater antiquity for humanity than had previously been demonstrated. Although there are disputes among anthropologists as to whether particular specimens are representative of apelike men or manlike apes, the consensus is that an age of 4 million years for true man is not excessive, and that further research might easily double this age.

In August 1969, a well-preserved skull attributed by anthropologist Louis B. Leakey to *Homo habilis,* a small-statured, slender ancestor of *Homo sapiens* (modern man) was found in Olduvai Gorge in Tanzania, and was assigned an age of 2 million years. Teeth and jaws of manlike beings to which an age of 4 million years was given were excavated in southern Ethiopia earlier in the year by an expedition from the University of Chicago. Two lower jaws and 40 teeth found in the basin of the lower Omo River were stated by Professor F. Clark Howell, chairman of the university's anthropology department, to extend the evolutionary history of the man ape *Australopithicus* much further into the past than was previously suspected. After examination of fossil teeth and jaws which had lain in collections of the Calcutta Museum and the British Museum for many years, Drs. Elwyn L. Simons and David R. Pilbeam, both of Yale University, assigned them to a manlike homonid that lived in India and Africa between 8 million and 15 million years ago. Meanwhile, use of radiocarbon dating and other methods of determining age of anthropological specimens gave dates of considerable antiquity to specimens found in the Americas. In 1914 the bones of a woman were found in one of the La Brea tar pits near Los Angeles. Associated with these human remains were bones of a giant condor and other extinct creatures. Despite apparent evidence of age, the skeleton was pronounced that of a modern Indian by Dr. Ales Hrdlicka of the U.S. National Museum, who was convinced that man had not reached the Americas earlier than 2,000 years ago. Researchers at the Los Angeles County Museum of Natural History announced in December 1969 that the skull had been tested by means of radioactive carbon in the bone, and was found to be 9,000 years old — more than four times as old as Dr. Hrdlicka had stated. Radiocarbon dating also established an age of 17,000 years for a skull — also that of a woman — found in 1933 near Laguna Beach, California.

Since skin disintegrates whereas bone does not, anthropologists have usually had to guess about the details of appearance of the primitive men whose remains they have found. But a prehistoric burial site found in August 1969, near Santander, in northern Spain, gave researchers a good picture of a dead adult who had been interred some 30,000 years ago. A fine clay silt, seeping into the grave, filled in the cavities where the skin had been, thus preserving the appearance of this Stone Age man, who had been buried with game animals at his head and feet, possibly as provender for his journey into the afterworld.

Archaeology. A strange complex of structures, including stone-lined passages and chambers and a large, flat eight-ton stone resembling a sacrificial altar, has been known for many years near North Salem, New Hampshire and variously attributed to Colonial farmers and Viking settlers. The New

England Antiquities Research Association has been seeking evidence of a connection between "Mystery Hill" and similar structures in the Mediterranean area. During an excavation in May 1969, stone tools and charcoal were found near one of the walls. Radiocarbon dating of the charcoal gave a date of 2995 ± 180 years B.P. (before the present), or approximately 1000 B.C., making the structure one of the oldest known in North America. Further investigations are being carried on to try to determine the origin and cultural characteristics of the presently unknown builders of Mystery Hill and other such sites in New England.

The Fertile Crescent — that region in the Middle East closely associated with the Tigris and Euphrates rivers — was long regarded as the site of the Biblical Garden of Eden. As the birthplace of such early nations as Babylonia and Assyria, the Crescent has been a favorite research area for generations of archaeologists, who have long been convinced that the art of agriculture began there about 7500 B.C. Recently, however, an expedition from the University of Hawaii, headed by Dr. Wilhelm G. Silheim II, has determined that the oldest domesticated seeds yet discovered come from a cavern called Spirit Cave in northern Thailand, near the Thai-Burmese border. Radiocarbon dating has set the age of grain found there at approximately 9700 B.C. Other finds in the vicinity included bronze axes used about 1500 B.C., and the husks of cultivated rice that was grown about 3500 B.C. — long before that crop was known in either China or India.

Now that all of Jerusalem is in Israeli hands, as a result of the 1967 six-day war, archaeologists such as Dr. Nahum Avigad are working in regions not previously accessible to them; they are uncovering evidence of the razing of Jerusalem and the destruction of the Second Temple by the Romans in A.D. 70, the date of the Diaspora, or dispersion of the Jews. Several rooms, one apparently used as a pharmacy and the other as a carpentry shop, have been found; both show evidence of intense heat from the burning of the Jewish quarter by the Romans, who had orders to level the spot as though it had never been inhabited. Coins dating between A.D. 66 and A.D. 70 were found in the ruins. Also discovered on a nearby wall was a depiction of a menorah, or seven-branched candlestick — perhaps the one that was used in the temple. The only remaining portion of the temple is that wall known for centuries as the Wailing Wall. Also in Israel, Dr. Beno Rothenberg of Tel Aviv University reported finding evidence of a people who lived in the southern Sinai desert about 4000 B.C. and who were subservient to King Suhare of Egypt.

One of the most famous statues of antiquity was the Aphrodite of Cnidus, which stood in a circular, Doric-style temple on a peninsula in Turkey that reaches out into the Aegean Sea. The statue was carved by Praxiteles in the 4th century B.C.; although it was copied many times, the original has been mysteriously lost. Excavations at Cnidus during 1969, directed by Professor Iris C. Love of Long Island University, revealed the outlines of the temple and marble fragments which may have been from the statue itself. Further work is planned at the site with the possibility that the statue itself might be buried there, as an incentive.

A chair that has traditionally been venerated as having been used by St. Peter, who died in Rome around A.D. 65, has been shown to be no older than the ninth century. An archaeological commission set up by the Vatican to determine the facts about the ancient chair reported that it was apparently the coronation throne of Charles the Bald, Roman emperor and king of the West Franks, who was crowned in A.D. 870 and died in 877. Radiocarbon dating and tree-ring tests were applied to the chair in ascertaining its date.

THE DANIS OF JIWIKA*

How New Guinea Tribe and
Dutch Missionary Lead
a Strange Existence

BY PETER R. KANN

FATHER VERHAVEN is nestled in his favorite armchair, engrossed in a Leon Uris novel. His neighbors, who dropped by as usual after dinner, are equally absorbed.

One elderly gentleman, spear scars across his chest, is concentrating on pulling hairs out of his groin with tweezers fashioned from a reed. Another guest is spreading a bit of beauty balm — pig's grease mixed with ashes — on his shoulder-length hair. A third visitor is busily tightening the vine binding on his stone axe. And a fourth neighbor is tapping his fingernails against his axe in perfect time to the static emanating from a shortwave radio. "Wa Wa Wa Wa," says the older gentleman, informing the group that he is happy and contented.

It is a very typical cool, clear evening in this mountain village, which is about as

* Reprinted from *The Wall Street Journal*, August 28, 1969.

remote from the twentieth century as man can get.

Jiwika, a jumble of several score thatch huts, lies under a mountain wall toward the eastern end of the Grand Baliem Valley in the rugged interior of the vast Indonesian-administered territory of West Irian, which makes up the western half of the South Pacific island of New Guinea.

No more cannibalism

The Grand Baliem is a glorious green valley some 40 miles long and 10 miles wide surrounded by jagged peaks ranging up to 16,500 feet. It was first sighted by plane only during World War II, and the first white man to enter the valley was a Dutch missionary who did so only 12 years

Native of the Grand Baliem. Aircraft and shortwave radios have put these people in tenuous contact with the outside world. But life remains as it has been for centuries.

Photos, The Permanent Mission of the Republic of Indonesia to the U.N.

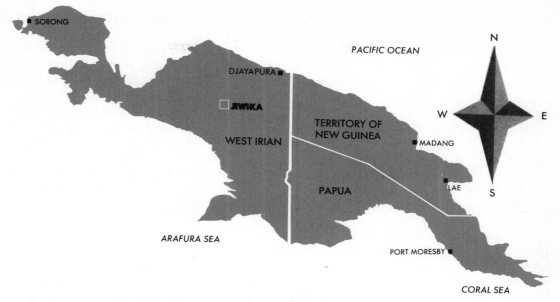

New Guinea, showing region where the Danis of Jiwika live.

ago after a 2-month trek through virgin wilderness. He discovered that the valley was inhabited by black-skinned Dani tribesmen — some 70,000 by current estimate — living a Stone Age existence based largely on intertribal warfare and practicing cannibalism.

Largely through the efforts of several dozen missionaries like Father Verhaven, a Dutch Franciscan priest, there have been some changes here in the past decade. Cannibalism no longer is practiced in the Grand Baliem (though 2 missionaries venturing into a neighboring valley were killed and eaten 2 years ago). There has been no major war in the valley since 1966, when 60 men from the Jiwika area were killed by spears and arrows in combat with tribesmen across the valley. The shortwave radios and single-engine Cessna aircraft of the missionaries have put the Baliem in tenuous contact with other parts of West Irian and thus, very tenuously indeed, with the outside world. Some primary schools, primitive medical clinics and very small-scale farming cooperatives also have been established.

But, as Father Verhaven readily admits, the changes have not yet run deep, and in most respects life in the Baliem remains the same as it has been for centuries.

Kirimo dresses up

With few exceptions, the Danis dress as they always have. The men wear only cowrie-shell necklaces, bird-feather bracelets, penis sheaths (long gourds that extend upward to the shoulders where they are attached by a vine) and a thick coating of pig's grease and ashes smeared over the entire body. The women, hair shaved close to the scalp, wear either short grass skirts (if unmarried) or tightly bound reeds around their midsection (if married). All women go barebreasted, but are scrupulously modest about covering their backs with nets. "Modesty" also characterizes the men, who are mortified if their sheaths ever slip off.

A few men in Jiwika have tried Western clothes, but generally not for long. On one wall of Father Verhaven's three-room thatch house hangs a photo of Kirimo, a young Dani warrior, outfitted in full Western attire and looking like a dapper African diplomat.

The photo delights Kirimo, who since has returned to traditional Dani undress. He discarded pants when a prospective father-in-law vetoed him, says Father Verhaven, "because the tribal elders looked upon him as some sort of hippie."

The Dani diet consists nearly exclusively of sweet potatoes, which are grown on small plots interlaced by irrigation canals. The Danis occasionally eat rats, insect grubs, or birds unlucky enough to be hit by hunters' wobbly, featherless arrows. And, of course, the Danis have sometimes eaten each other. There is no big-game hunting here or anywhere in West Irian, animal life consisting mostly of rodents, a few small marsupials and some large birds, like the ostrich-size cassowary.

The importance of pigs

Pigs, probably introduced to New Guinea by Portuguese explorers who landed on the coast in the 16th century, provide the main, though infrequent, source of meat. But pigs are far more important than simply a source of protein.

A man's status and wealth are measured by the number of pigs he owns and, to a lesser extent, the number of wives he keeps. Wives are definitely secondary. If a man has many pigs, he naturally needs some wives to take care of them and therefore trades a few piglets for a bride or two. The great Dani leader Kuralu keeps 17 wives and more than 100 pigs, awesome statistics to other warriors. Pigs generally are eaten only on ceremonial occasions such as funerals or at the Great Pig Feast, which occurs every 4 or 5 years, at the discretion of Kuralu and other leaders.

The Danis have no formal rulers. Rather, they venerate "important men," like Kuralu, for their military prowess, knowledge of tribal ritual and force of personality.

The Danis have little fear of anything alive, but they do live in deathly terror of the ghosts of dead friends and relatives, and they spend much time trying to placate bothersome ghosts. For instance, the Dani funeral ritual includes chopping off the fingers of young girls. The fingers are then wrapped in leaves and placed in trees as an offering to the ghost of the deceased.

The death of an important man may require several dozen fingers, while the death of a poor old lady may merit only 1 or 2. The fingers are hacked off with a stone axe, and no anesthetic is used, but young girls nevertheless seem to consider

themselves honored to be chosen. There are few girls in Jiwika older than 10 who have more than 5 fingers, and some older women have none at all.

Dani housing is curious as well. Women and children live in small thatch huts, which their menfolk periodically visit. But the men sleep and spend most of their time in special "men's houses," round thatch structures, one to a village, with a downstairs social room and an upper loft for communal sleeping.

To enter, one crawls through a small hole to find a half dozen men squatting around glowing coals in a tight, airless, virtually pitch-black room. The smell is overpowering: a combination of pig-grease body coating, smoke from the chimneyless fire, crude tobacco, and long-unwashed bodies. In one corner are gourds of pig's grease and "holy vegetables" to be used in some future ceremony. Bows and arrows and stone axes are stacked against one wall. There is an implement made of hardwood and twisted vine for starting the fire. Several men are playing miniature reed mouth harps, which make a single-toned, twanging sound.

The holy stones

In another corner are the village's most prized possessions: holy stones wrapped in layer upon layer of leaves and bark. The stones are unwrapped only on great ceremonial occasions, and a visitor's request to see one stirs excited whispering. Finally one stone is slowly and reverently uncovered. It is a smooth, flat, black rock about six inches long. It evidently possesses great powers. After the visitor examines it, he is told by one older man: "Now you will grow very big potatoes." The stone is carefully rewrapped, and the warrior who handled it meticulously dusts off his fingers with a sacred bird feather.

Conversation in the men's house is mostly of war, of great battles passed down as legends and of more-recent battles in which these warriors participated. The termination — or at least temporary cessation — of such warfare has left a great void in the living pattern and psyche of the

The Danis dress as they have for centuries. These women wear either short grass skirts or tightly bound reeds around their midsections; their backs are covered with nets.

Dani men. Warfare used to occupy nearly all their time and energies. Now they live only on memories. They are bored.

Even the possession of spears has been banned by the largely absentee Indonesian administration, though the ban is hardly effective. One warrior leads a visitor through a maze of huts, pulls a 15-foot spear out of a thatch roof and begins an impromptu enactment of a battle. He stalks an imaginary foe through the brush, flings the spear, portrays the victim writhing in anguish, then the victim's wailing kinsmen, and closes with the triumphant war dance of the victor. By the end, he is jumping up and down, shaking the spear in near frenzy.

Warfare in the Baliem is of several sorts. The Danis are divided into scores of village confederations that in turn are grouped into a dozen grand alliances. The first type of conflict takes place within a confederation and generally amounts to little more than a brawl, perhaps over a contested piglet. It rarely culminates in killing.

Rained-out wars

The second sort is a feud between two confederations, often involving surprise spearing raids that can result in serious, though still small-scale, bloodshed. Finally, there are the major wars between alliances. Until recently these were a never-ending fixture of Dani life. Each alliance was constantly at war, though every decade or so, like musical chairs, there would be a switching of enemies.

Actual combat, however, is sporadic and highly ritualized. The prearranged battles take place on traditional battle-fields and involve tribesmen of all ages. The prime warriors defend a narrow front line, separated from the enemy by a twenty-yard no-man's-land. From this range they fling spears and shoot rickety arrows, which generally are dodged and shot back again. Older warriors sit to the rear, smoking and chanting incantations to the ghosts. Children stand behind and cheer while the women bake sweet potatoes for the lunch break. There are frequent rest periods, and at dusk, or at the first drop of rain, the battle is discontinued and rescheduled for another day. If a warrior has the misfortune to be captured, he may be roasted and eaten by his captors. Such cannibalism is part of the ritual of war rather than a source of dietary sustenance.

Wars are fought not for political domination, property or ideology, but rather as a sort of sport and as a response to the omnipresent ghosts. Thus if a warrior from alliance A is killed, his ghost will haunt his kinsmen until they have killed a warrior from alliance B, which then must kill another warrior from A, and so on.

While there has been no major conflict in the Baliem for three years, Father Verhaven and others fear it will recur. The tribesmen of the Jiwika area still owe

9

a blood debt to their rival alliance as a result of the 1966 war.

"The bloodletting will have to be balanced out eventually. The people here know this, and they live in fear of it," says the Father.

Jiwika lies in a particularly favorable position in the valley, for in the mountain just above the village is a salt pool, the only source of salt in the Baliem. Some Danis must walk forty miles to reach it; from Jiwika it is only a few hours' hike.

One sets out for the salt pool accompanied by six warrior-guides, dressed only in their sheaths, which, amazingly, remain in place as the men hop up and down the steep, rocky trail like mountain goats. The guides, Kirimo among them, point out spots of interest along the way. An odd-shaped, rounded rock is a "laki-laki" (boy) long ago turned to stone. A small cleft in another rock is the footprint of a famous warrior who long ago jumped down from a mountaintop. "We cannot jump that far anymore," explains Kirimo.

A small waterfall is pointed out as a place of great danger. "Many deaths have taken place here," Kirimo says. How many people have died here? he is asked. "Only one old woman," he says disdainfully, but then adds with great emotion, "many, many pigs."

The salt pool is a shallow pond fed by a spring running out of a nearby cliff. Wading in the pool are a dozen women with pendulous breasts and the ever-present nets shielding their backs. They submerge banana stalks in the pool until they soak up the salty water. The spongy stalks are then carried down the mountain trail and later are laid out to dry in the sun at home. The water evaporates, leaving the valuable grains of salt. While the women slave in the murky water, the men sit on rock ledges, smoking and toying with their stone axes. Dani women do most of the hard work in this society and are treated a good deal less solicitously than pigs.

On Sunday morning

Dani men, however, do fear women on one account: There's an ancient legend that an angry woman will put a mouse down a man's throat while he's asleep, and the mouse will eat out his heart. And women practice some "magic" unknown to the men: There's a root or herb taken by Dani women that apparently acts as a birth-control "pill."

Back in Jiwika, it is Sunday morning, time for Mass. Father Verhaven's straw church is crowded with Dani parishioners, men squatting on mats to one side, women on the other. Of perhaps a hundred churchgoers, only about a dozen are clothed. The air is thick with the smell of pig's grease. Only a handful of the people are baptized Catholics. The rest have come out of curiosity, out of respect for Father Verhaven, or just because Sunday Mass is the village's major weekly event. This doesn't bother Father Verhaven, who seeks no "instant conversions."

After Mass, Father Verhaven doffs his priest's robe, and the whole congregation moves up the path to his house. Here Father Verhaven assumes another of his vital roles, that of village shopkeeper. The villagers bring in sacks of sweet potatoes and a few other vegetables, which are weighed and exchanged for hand mirrors, fishhooks, razor blades and other small objects flown in by the mission Cessna. The plane may later carry some of the produce on to coastal mission stations several hundred miles away, where the native diet consists almost exclusively of sago. Such trade isn't economical for the mission service, but it teaches the Danis they don't live completely in a mountain vacuum. And Father Verhaven doesn't believe in simply giving things away: The concept of a fair bargain is important.

Indonesian and United Nations officials in Djayapura, capital of West Irian, talk of long-range economic-development plans for the Baliem Valley: stimulating sugar and tobacco production, introducing poultry, even building dirt roads across the valley and flying in a few old trucks or buses for transportation. But, for the foreseeable future, the twentieth century is not likely to swallow up the Danis.

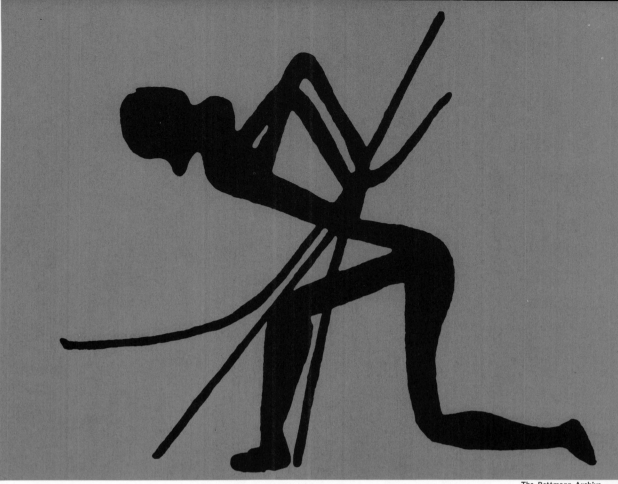

THE ORIGIN OF MAN*

The Species with a Culture

BY C. LORING BRACE

MORE than a century ago when Darwin published *On the Origin of Species,* it was authoritatively assumed by those who had not read the book that he was chiefly concerned with the origin of man. He actually mentioned the word *man* only once in the epoch-making work, and then in a cryptic sentence on the last page. But such is the strength of popular assumption that the title has been consistently misquoted. The popular press still refers to his book as *The Origin of the Species,* and *the* species is assumed to be man. This example typifies man's timeless fascination with himself, as well as his

* © *Natural History,* 1970

propensity for repeating misinformation about himself — a universal quality that may have been best summed up by the acerbic Ambrose Bierce early in the twentieth century when he defined man as "an animal so lost in rapturous contemplation of what he thinks he is as to overlook what he indubitably ought to be."

But what is man? What was he in the past, and what has allowed him to survive to the present? If these questions are answered, we can contemplate, perhaps with alarm, the basis for what is to come.

Central to any definition of man, and the key to his evolutionary success, is a phenomenon not immediately visible when specimens of the creature are scrutinized. This phenomenon is what the anthropologist calls culture. It includes not only the high points of art, music, and literature, but also all those things that re-

11

12

This picture shows, from left to right, skulls of a gorilla, a primitive Australian, and a modern European. The Australian skull is a little larger than the African skulls mentioned below, but much like them in shape.

American Museum of Natural History

sult from the cumulative efforts of other people and previous generations. Tools, the traditions regulating their use, vital information, and language itself — all are included in the concept culture. Man is not just an animal that possesses culture, but an animal that cannot survive without it. Men could not exist if each had to discover anew the control of fire, the manufacture of clothing and shelter, the sources of edible sustenance, and the guidelines for workable interpersonal relationships, to say nothing of the mechanics, electronics, chemistry and physics on which human life depends today. These elements of culture are a cumulative continuation of simpler counterparts in the past.

In the beginning, our ancestors, like other animals, must have been faced with the problem of surviving without the aid of culture. So much of culture is perishable or intangible that there is no way to determine when culture as a cumulative phenomenon began. Nonperishable cultural elements have an antiquity of about 2 million years in Africa. The cultural tradition of which they are a part continues without break, expanding to occupy the tropical and temperate parts of the Old World about 800,000 years ago, and ultimately developing into all the cultures in the world today.

From this we postulate an African origin for all mankind. The existence of crude stone tools in Africa 1.5 million to 2 million years ago allows us to suppose the existence of culture at that time. Our guess suggests that the possessor of this culture could not have survived without it; therefore, he deserves the designation *man* — however primitive and crude he might have been.

We further postulate that culture existed a long time before the initial appearance of recognizable stone tools. This is speculation, but not idle speculation, because we could not otherwise account for the transformation of ape to man. Although small in quantity, supporting evidence exists in the form of skeletal material. Fossilized remains, including skulls, jaws, teeth and a few other skeletal pieces have been found in association with the oldest known stone tools both in Olduvai Gorge in East Africa and in the Transvaal of South Africa. Since the discovery of these fossils in 1924, argument has continued over their status: ape? man? human ancestor? extinct side line? Brain size was within the range of that for the large modern anthropoid apes, but these early hominids walked erect on two feet as does modern man. Molar teeth were of gorilloid size, but the canines did not project beyond the level of the other teeth.

Despite continuing arguments over whether the balance of traits was on the human or simian side, it is apparent that the survival of these early hominids depended on a distinctly non-apelike adaptation. Bipedal locomotion did not enable hominids to escape predators by rapid flight. Neither could these hominids seriously threaten to bite a potential predator. Contrast this with such modern ground-dwelling primates as baboons and gorillas where the enlarged canine teeth of the males represent formidable defense weapons. We can guess that these early hominids depended for survival on something not visible in their anatomy, and our guess is that they used hand-held tools.

Possibly they defended themselves with the crude hunks of worked stone found at the sites where their skeletal remains have been discovered, but more likely they relied on pointed sticks. To use a rock as a defensive weapon requires close contact with the attacking creature, while the defender probably preferred to face his tormentor from the far end of a pointed stick. Not only is the pointed stick a simple and effective weapon — devisable with a minimum of manufacturing effort — but it can also double as a digging tool. Edible roots and bulbs are a substantial part of the diet of baboons that live today in the savanna, an environment typical of the areas inhabited by the earliest hominids. The addition of a simple digging stick of the kind used by the surviving hunting and gathering human groups — and probably by the early hominids — could easily double the baboons' food supply.

The huge, worn molars of the early hominids indicate that they relied on gritty, uncooked vegetables for subsistence. Unlike any other primate's, their canine teeth are functionally indistinguishable from their small incisors. Assuming that the remote hominid ancestor had enlarged canine teeth like all other primates, then the creatures associated with the stone tools in East and South Africa 2 million years ago belonged to a line in which the selective pressures needed to maintain large canines had been suspended for a long time. Cultural means of defense must have existed long before the earliest stone tools.

PREHISTORIC WEAPONS AND TOOLS

OLD STONE AGE (PALEOLITHIC)

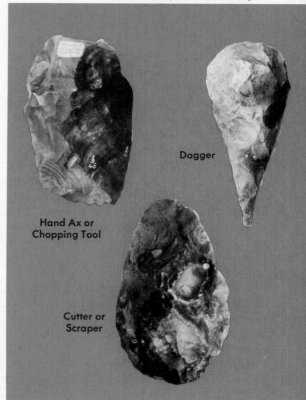

Hand Ax or Chopping Tool

Dagger

Cutter or Scraper

NEW STONE AGE (NEOLITHIC)

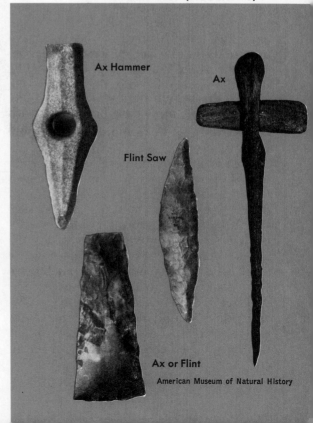

Ax Hammer

Ax

Flint Saw

Ax or Flint

American Museum of Natural History

Within the last 3 years jaws and teeth have been found in southwestern Ethiopia that are so like the Olduvai and Transvaal finds that they must be related. Their antiquity, however, extends back nearly 4 million years, and no stone tools are associated with them. The canine teeth in the fragmentary remains are not enlarged, leaving us to infer that defensive weapons must have been used some 4 million years ago — 2 million years before the earliest stone tools existed.

Reliance on hand-held weapons for defense (and perhaps also for food getting) did not automatically convert apes into men, but it altered the forces of selection so that evolution in the human direction was a consequence. For one thing, occupation with tool wielding reduced the locomotor role of hands. Legs and feet, as a result of natural selection, assumed the entire burden of locomotion. Tools usurped the defensive role of canine teeth, and, with an accumulation of mutations, these teeth were reduced. The vast majority of mutations interfere with the development of the structures that depend on their control, but usually these "deleterious mutations" are eliminated by selection. When selection is reduced or suspended — as when tools reduced the defensive role of teeth — the reductive mutations simply accumulate in the ongoing gene pool of the population. The structure controlled by the genes — the canine teeth, for example — eventually fails to achieve the full development once characteristic of the remote ancestral population.

Early in hominid development, when defensive weapons were not well developed, those charged with the task of defense, the males, must have been substantially more rugged than those less concerned with defensive activities, the females. Among terrestrial primates where a culture with weapons plays no defensive role, males tend to be much larger and stronger than females. Baboons, gorillas and other ground-dwelling primates are good examples. Fossil fragments hint that this must have been the case for the earliest hominids as well. The difference in robustness of specimens from the early levels of Olduvai Gorge, the Transvaal and now from Omo in southwest Ethiopia has led some scholars to suggest that two different species of hominid — one small and slender, the other large and robust — shared the same habitat. However, now that we can demonstrate a time span of nearly three million years for the early hominids, it makes better ecological and evolutionary sense to explain the differences in size as sexual dimorphism — male-female difference — in a single species of early hominid.

The taxonomy of these earliest hominids continues to be debated. Genera such as *Australopithecus, Paranthropus, Zinjanthropus, Homo* and others have been suggested, and even more species tentatively recognized. Whatever the taxonomic designation, these early hominids, except for their reliance on learned behavior and on hand-held tools for defense

Before primitive man had fire or recognizable tools and weapons, he attacked wild animals by stoning them.

American Museum of Natural History

From *The Search for the Tassili Frescoes* by Henri Lhote. Copyright © 1959 by E. P. Dutton Co., Inc. Reproduced by permission of the publishers.

A Stone Age rock painting in the Sahara. Created thousands of years before the existence of written records, such art provides clues to the cultures of primitive man.

and food getting, lived more like apes than humans.

The evidence from Olduvai Gorge in East Africa shows that crude stone tools were added to the limited cultural repertoire toward the end of this long early hominid phase — a period I prefer to call the australopithecine stage. These tools belong to the incipient part of a tradition of butchering large animals in the Middle Pleistocene. At the end of the Lower Pleistocene, however, they occur mainly with the fossilized remains of immature animals. We can guess that this records the beginning of the adaptive shift that was largely responsible for the development of *Homo sapiens,* a shift related to the development of hunting as a major subsistence activity.

In the Middle Pleistocene, somewhat less than a million years ago, man emerges as a major predator. This adaptation is unique among the primates, and it is not surprising that many of the physical, behavioral, and physiological characteristics that distinguish man from his closest animal relatives are related to this adaptation. While we cannot make direct behavioral or physiological tests on fossils, we can make inferences based on their anatomy, on their apparent ecological adaptation, and on conditions observable in their modern descendants.

Anthropologists generally agree that the men of the Middle Pleistocene are properly classified as *Homo erectus.* The first specimen to be discovered was classified in the genus *Pithecanthropus* at the end of the nineteenth century. While we no longer accept this generic designation, pithecanthropine remains a convenient, nontechnical term for Middle Pleistocene hominids.

Brain size was twice that of the preceding australopithecines and two thirds that of the average modern man. With the absence of a specialized predatory physique, natural selection probably encouraged the evolution of intelligence. While brain size had increased, the size of the molar teeth had reduced, although they were still quite large by modern standards. This reduction may have been related to the shift from a rough vegetable diet to one with a large proportion of meat. Meat, needing only to be reduced to swallowable pieces, requires far less mastication than starches, which begin the process of conversion to simple sugars by mixing with salivary enzymes through extensive chewing.

Evidence, although fragmentary, also suggests that bipedal locomotion in its modern form was perfected at this time, the Middle Pleistocene. While man's mode of locomotion may not be speedy, it requires an expenditure of relatively little energy. To this day, primitive hunters employ the technique of trotting persistently on the trail of an herbivore until it is brought to bay, often many days later.

15

Several correlates of this hunting life are suggested. Man, reflecting his primate heritage, is relatively night-blind and must therefore confine his hunting activities to the daytime. A tropical mammal (and physiologically man is still a tropical mammal) pursuing strenuous activities in broad daylight is faced with the problem of dissipating metabolically generated heat. The hairless human skin, richly endowed with sweat glands, is unique among terrestrial mammals of much less than elephantine size, and I suggest that this developed under the selective pressures of regular big-game hunting early in the pithecanthropine stage.

The elimination of the hairy coat by natural selection left the skin exposed to the potentially damaging effect of the ultraviolet component of tropical sunlight. The obvious response was the development of the protective pigment melanin. Consequently the Middle Pleistocene ancestors of all modern men were probably what in America today is called black.

The conversion of this being into what is technically known as *Homo sapiens* requires only the further expansion of the brain from the pithecanthropine average of 1,000 cubic centimeters (actually well within the range of modern variation) to the average today of 1,400 cc. Fragmentary fossil evidence suggests that this transition had taken place by the beginning of the Upper Pleistocene, about 120,000 years ago. Men at that time — referred to as Neanderthals — still had an archaic appearance. In general these early representatives of *Homo sapiens* were more muscular and robust than their modern descendants — particularly the males. Jaws and teeth were large, especially the front teeth, which, from their wear patterns, evidently served as all-purpose tools.

Since the first appearance of *Homo sapiens* in his Neanderthal form, human evolution has been characterized by a series of reductions. Whenever human ingenuity made life easier, there was a relaxation of the forces of selection, and these reductions followed. More effective hunting techniques lessened the burden on the hunter's physique, and an eventual reduction in muscularity was the result. Manipulating tools lessened the stress on the anterior teeth, and the consequent reduction of these and their supporting bony architecture converted the Neanderthal face into modern form. In parts of the world where manipulative technology is a late phenomenon, such as aboriginal Australia, faces and teeth have remained large. Where clothing was developed for survival in northern climes, the significance of protective skin pigment was lessened, and the consequent reduction produced the phenomenon that is euphemistically called white.

The only thing that has not been reduced is the number of human beings. We cannot even guess at the population density of the australopithecines. Throughout the Middle Pleistocene, the archaeological record suggests a fairly constant population for the hunting pithecanthropines. Evidently the population increased dramatically with the Neanderthal form of *Homo sapiens*. The diversification of food resources and the increase in cultural complexity that accompanied the first appearance of modern *Homo sapiens* just under 35,000 years ago also signaled another sharp jump in population. This set the stage for the tremendous population growth made possible by the development of agriculture after the end of the Pleistocene 10,000 years ago.

Thus did *Homo sapiens* emerge — a manifestation of ecological imbalance, literally shaped by the consequences of his own impact upon the world. His fate, too, will be shaped by his future impact on the world — the result of his numbers and his actions. Malthus sounded the alarm nearly two centuries ago, but few listened to his warning. One who did was Ambrose Bierce, who added in his definition of man that "his chief occupation is extermination of other animals and his own species, which, however, multiplies with such insistent rapidity as to infest the whole habitable earth. . . ."

AN ODYSSEY IN PAPER

The Voyage of the *Ra*

BY EDMUND F. GREKULINSKI

Right: the *Ra* shortly after it was launched in May 1969. Below: the papyrus boat is moved from its construction site. It was dragged across the desert on wooden tracks, as it might have been done by the ancient Egyptians.

UPI

Wide World

Far and few, far and few
Are the lands where the Jumblies live;
Their heads are green, and their
   hands are blue,
And they went to sea in a sieve.

From The Jumblies by Edward Lear
(1871)

THE above is an example of a "nonsense" poem. But the idea of going to sea in a sieve has turned out to be not so nonsensical; certain people have apparently been doing it for centuries.

"Any water pouring over the strange wash-through Inca reed boats just ran through their bottom and out, making scooping and bailing unnecessary. . . . To the modern generations they have become symbolic of a primitive past, something leaking like a sieve and therefore unfit for ocean travel." So the Norwegian anthropologist Thor Heyerdahl, of *Kon Tiki* fame, describes the strange reed boats

of the sixteenth-century Inca Indians. The Spanish conquistadors encountered these craft off the coast of Peru; some were quite large, rivaling the Spanish ships in size.

Reed boats have sometimes been called "paper boats." In ancient times, reeds, in particular, papyrus, were the raw materials from which paper was made.

Many twentieth-century authorities were convinced that reed boats and rafts were basically unseaworthy and unsuitable for long voyages. They felt that materials such as reeds would soon fill with water, rot and sink beneath the waves.

Thor Heyerdahl, however, became convinced that the truth was otherwise. He studied the reed boats surviving among certain primitive peoples today in Africa, Latin America and the Pacific. He also surveyed archaeological remains. Heyerdahl concluded that reed craft could safely navigate the seas and that they had, in fact, been the chief agents in the spread

17

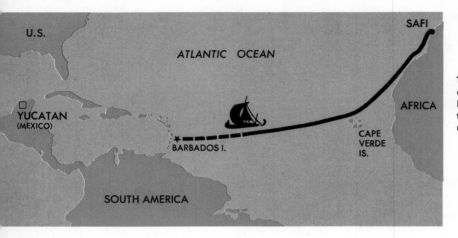

The *Ra* left Safi, Morocco, destined for the Yucatan Peninsula. But the craft had to be abandoned about 600 miles east of Barbados.

of past cultures from one hemisphere to another.

Heyerdahl was especially impressed by certain cultural similarities among the early peoples of the African, Latin-American and Pacific areas. He decided that features such as stone architecture, sun worship and solar calendars did not develop independently in these places but were carried from one area to another by people journeying in vessels of reed.

Winds and currents are favorable for westward journeys across the Atlantic, from the Old World to the New World. Scholars long before Heyerdahl believed that ancient Asian or African sailors, such as Phoenicians, Carthaginians or Egyptians, visited the Americas long before the Europeans of a later period. There are Mayan and Aztec legends of bearded white men — "gods" — from the east, who brought them civilization.

Heyerdahl decided to make a transatlantic voyage in a reed boat to prove his thesis. Using ancient Egyptian representations of reed craft as a guide, he had a large boat constructed in Egypt, near the Great Pyramids. The material was papyrus reeds from the Ethiopian segment of the Nile River. The builders were 3 craftsmen from central Africa, where reed boating is still practiced on Lake Chad. The men tied huge bundles of papyrus into a crescent-shaped vessel nearly 50 feet long, about 15 feet wide and weighing about 13 tons. A wickerwork mat, or

deck, was constructed over the bottom; a wickerwork cabin was built on this mat. The entire craft resembled a huge, elongated basket. A cotton sail on a wishbone-shaped mast, plus a dozen oars for rowing and steering, provided the motive power. The vessel was not entirely primitive: stowed aboard were a radio, a life raft and diving gear.

With its international crew of 7 men, the strange vessel, named the *Ra* after the ancient Egyptian sun god, set sail on May 25, 1969, from the Atlantic port of Safi in western Morocco. They hoped to reach the Mexican coast in 40 to 60 days.

Trouble soon beset the voyagers. Storms and waves badly damaged the *Ra*. In spite of heroic repair efforts by the crew, the ship had to be abandoned on July 19, about 600 miles east of the West Indian island of Barbados. The men had traveled 2,700 miles before leaving the *Ra* and boarding a modern vessel that had been summoned by radio.

In spite of the technical failure, Heyerdahl believes that the voyage was a success. The reeds never disintegrated or became waterlogged. In fact, Heyerdahl thinks that had they followed the designs of the ancient Egyptian craftsmen more closely, the *Ra* would never have foundered. Going to sea in a "paper sieve" is not so nonsensical after all.*

* *Editor's note:* On May 17, 1970, Heyerdahl and his crew left Safi on *Ra II* in a second attempt to prove that Egyptians could have crossed the Atlantic several thousand years ago.

THE INCA

Princes of the Peruvian Highlands

BY LOUIS C. FARON

Incan treasure: a silver portrait jug of the period following Pizarro's conquest (when native art tended to reflect the Spanish influence).

Wide World

THE Inca are an Indian people who maintained a vast South American empire until it was destroyed by Spanish conquerors in the 16th century. The Inca were originally a tribe, or small state, of Quechua-speaking Indians who lived in the central Andean highlands of what is now Peru. (The name *Inca* is the Quechua word for "prince" or "male of royal blood.") In approximately A.D. 1400 they rose from relative social and cultural obscurity to conquer eventually 10 million aboriginal inhabitants of the present nations of Peru, Ecuador, Bolivia, western Argentina and the northern half of Chile. In turn, they were conquered by a handful of Spaniards under the leadership of Francisco Pizarro.

The modern Quechua-speaking Indians of the Peruvian highlands number about six million. Highly conservative of ancient traditions and largely ignorant of contemporary national conditions, problems, and aspirations, they constitute a potentially tremendous cultural force that, as yet, is almost untapped.

The rise of Inca culture

The development of Inca cultural beliefs and social organization is the product of age-old local evolution in the general area of Cuzco, their capital city and, today, the urban center of a Peruvian political department of the same name.

Origin of the Inca state. Inca genealogical history traces back, often in mythological fashion, to A.D. 1200. Archaeological and even historical evidence for the Cuzco region provides additional information about Inca culture before the

Inca became a political and economic power in Peru.

The Inca were only one of a number of small societies that had developed a statelike organization approximately two centuries before the Spanish conquest. Other states, such as the Chimu, which built the 11-square-mile city of Chan Chan on the north coast of Peru, were politically and culturally more advanced. Archaeological evidence shows without doubt that the Inca were latecomers in overall cultural sophistication in the central Andean region, but archaeological data as well as Spanish written descriptions of the Inca empire attest to its consummate social and political achievement less than 100 years before the arrival of the Europeans on the northern coast of Peru.

Most historical information is contained in Spanish chronicles, some of which were gleaned from Inca officials, and in the writings of the Hispanicized Inca noble Garcilaso de la Vega. These works describe the short and successful history of Inca contests for power and, eventually, their territorial control, first around Cuzco and, later, throughout the Andean area and even into the jungles of extreme western Brazil and eastern Bolivia. There are no records of the dynastic marriages that served to consolidate and preserve the political and military gains of the Inca. It is known, however, that one of the most influential of the Inca emperors, Pachacuti, married the daughter of a neighboring chief for the purpose of gaining a strong military ally; this suggests that the Inca were somewhat prepared to understand the feudal mentality of their Spanish conquerors.

Expansion of the Inca empire. Pachacuti was a magnificent military leader and imperial organizer who instructed his son Topa to succeed him in such a way that it is difficult to decide who may have been the more astute ruler. Pachacuti extended the small Inca state from the area around Cuzco north along the highlands to a point directly east of Lima. His conquests reached south to the vicinity of Lake Titicaca, the highest freshwater lake

The University
Museum, Philadelphia

Incan pottery exhibits a high degree of technical skill. Here, a stone llama from Peru.

of its size in the world, around whose margins lived the Aymará Indians.

The Inca conquered the Aymará early in their empire-building period. By that time, between approximately 1438 and 1463, the Inca had established themselves as rulers in the southern and central highlands of Peru. Pachacuti's son Topa aided him in expanding the Inca state, which between 1463 and 1471 conquered territories as far north as Quito, Ecuador. Around 1471, Pachacuti relinquished command to Topa, who conquered lands as far south as the Maule River in central Chile, subdued the Chimu kingdom in the north of Peru, and put down several rebellions in the Cuzco area. Topa also attempted to extend the empire into the forested region of southern Chile and into the dense jungles east of the Andes, but failed in the face of difficult battle conditions and tenuous supply lines.

Topa died in 1493 and was succeeded by his son Huayna Capac, who also excelled in his generalship of Inca armies. Huayna Capac conquered the lowland area of Ecuador in the vicinity of what is today the city of Guayaquil. He also quashed several rebellions in the newly formed empire and defeated the Guaraní Indians (Chiriguano), who had attacked the Argentine border of the Inca empire. Huayna Capac died in 1527.

Francisco Pizarro arrived with troops in Tumbez in 1532. In the five years between Huayna Capac's death and Pizarro's conquest, the Inca empire was wracked by civil war. The internal warfare made it

An Incan aryballus. A cord passed through the handles enabled a person to carry the vase on his shoulders.

easier for Pizarro's troops to subjugate the peoples of the central highlands, province by province. This conquest was completed by 1538.

At the height of its power Inca culture extended far and wide along both highland and coastal regions, reaching as far north as the border of Colombia and south to central Chile. Imperial expansion and territorial control depended on a social and economic base, which in the case of the Inca was one of the most highly developed in the New World.

The Inca economy

The Inca empire was dependent upon the agricultural production of the millions of common people who inhabited the Andean region. Farming had been the basic means of subsistence of these village people for more than 2,000 years. During that time many agricultural innovations were developed to support an ever-increasing population, by far the densest in all of South America.

Principal crops. By Inca times, more than 40 varieties of domesticated plants were grown in the central Andes. Many were probably developed in the region, while others, such as root and vegetable crops, were borrowed from non-Andean peoples. Maize (corn) was domesticated in Mexico about 7,000 years ago, while manioc (cassava) seems to have had a tropical lowland origin.

The crops grown in any single valley depended mainly on altitude. For example, at the highest altitudes, potatoes constituted the principal crop, as they do today; *quinoa* (a grain) was also grown at high altitudes as well as at sea level. Above 12,000 feet, only about a half dozen crops were generally grown. As many as two dozen different crops were cultivated in the warm coastal valleys, where maize rather than potatoes was the staple crop.

The Inca traded regionally-specialized crops within the empire, bringing to the high mountain areas such temperate and tropical foods as sweet potatoes, beans, chili peppers, peanuts, tomatoes, and avocados. Trade of this type was rigidly controlled by state officials.

Use was made of many wild plants and of both domesticated and wild animals, although hunting and gathering were relatively unimportant compared to agriculture. Hunting weapons were slings, bolas, clubs, and nets for catching birds. Fishing was also unimportant, except on Lake Titicaca and at favored points along the coast.

Food habits. Food was rather simply prepared, usually by boiling in pottery vessels or by roasting. The most common fare consisted of soups and stews, as it still does, and bread made from maize flour and cooked in ashes. Some meat was preserved by sundrying (*charqui* or "jerked" meat), and potatoes were frequently dried and frozen (*chuño*). Grain was stored in large urns or in adobe silos and prepared for use as needed by stone grinding. Plates and cups were used in eating and were made of pottery, wood, or metal.

Domesticated animals were llamas, alpacas, dogs, guinea pigs, and ducks. Llamas were seldom eaten but were very important pack animals, providing wool for weaving clothes and being used as sacrificial animals in religious ceremonies. Alpacas were kept only for their very fine wool. Dogs were pets and scavengers but were sometimes eaten as well as used in religious sacrifice. Guinea pigs provided a steady meat supply for the village Indians. Ducks were also eaten.

Irrigation. The use and maintenance of farmland and the production of food surpluses required vast effort, both intellectual and physical. In addition to the seasonal, arduous field labor of digging up the land (plows were unknown in pre-Spanish times) and breaking clods of earth, the Inca built and maintained irrigation canal networks. Irrigation canals are a dominant feature of the Peruvian landscape today as are the terraced fields in the steepsided highland basins. Irrigation systems and terraced fields developed in the central Andean region during many centuries, and their extension and elaboration correlate with increasing population density and the need to expand the basis of food production. Some irrigation systems run for many miles and cover entire valleys. Frequently, entire mountainsides have been transformed into networks of terraced fields linked by a massive system of irrigation canals.

Irrigation is needed throughout most of Peru because of a long dry season (on the coast there is virtually no rain at all). Terracing slopes serve to increase level land areas and minimize soil erosion. Early systems of canals and terraces were rather simple, probably the work of family groups. As political states arose, the construction of such systems became public works controlled by governments. In Inca times, control was still more rigid and encompassing, and a system of enforced labor gangs (*mita*) was devised to expand and maintain these and other public works.

Labor drafts. The rulers of the Inca empire controlled agricultural production and drafted laborers to meet the various needs of the state and the church. The commoners, however, were allowed to have sufficient time to perform farm work, even though they also had to perform services for the state and the church on buildings, roadways, bridges, in textile and ceramic factories, in mines, and in military service.

The agricultural cycle began in the villages in August, when men and women were summoned by their local leader, the *curaca*, to prepare the fields belonging to the church and those of the state. This was a festive kind of labor, in the sense that work was done in large gangs to rhythmic chanting; food and *chicha* (a kind of cider) were given to the workers. After the work was done on church and state lands, individual household plots were prepared in much the same way. Work gangs made a round of the village's fields until all work was done. Again there was a festive air, and food and drink were dispensed by the head of the family whose fields were prepared in this cooperative manner.

Similar arrangements characterized all phases of the agricultural cycle until the crops were finally harvested in common and stored in the granaries of the church, the state, and in private dwellings.

Jorgen Bitsch — Pix

An Indian peasant, as in ancient times, herds his llamas past the walls of the Sacsahuamán fortress near Cuzco. Typical of Inca architecture, the massive stones of the fortress walls were fitted by joints and required no mortar.

In time of food shortage, doles were made to the common people.

Buildings and roads. A large part of the labor of village Indians went into the construction of public buildings, which were built by *mita,* or corvée, labor drafts summoned by the government on a regular, orderly basis. The Inca also had full-time specialists, such as architects and masons, who designed buildings and other projects and supervised work.

The Inca did excellent stonework. They moved out stones weighing several tons on rollers and ramps, fashioning them with such tight-fitting joints that no mortar was needed to hold them together. There are examples of this architecture in the city of Cuzco, the fortress of Machu Picchu, and elsewhere in highland Peru.

Road building, which was integral to Inca economy and to political and military organization, was well executed and extensive. Roads linking all parts of the empire were built and maintained by *mita* laborers from the villages along their route. There was rapid courier service along these roads performed by runners who served 15 days *mita* in this work. A main road ran the length of the highland part of the empire and another, parallel road, ran along the coast. Transverse roads connected the longitudinal roads at strategic points. It was possible for relay runners to bring fresh fish from the coast to the emperor's table in highland Cuzco in two days, which is faster than today's ordinary bus service.

Other industries. Supporting the Inca economy were factories producing woolen cloth of many kinds and grades, including coarse llama, fine alpaca, still finer vicuña, and even the hair (wool) of bats. The spinning and weaving were performed by women on three different kinds of looms — belt, horizontal, and vertical. Specialists wove the finest cloth for the royalty, such as tapestries and intricate goods to which feathers and beaten metals were added. Pottery was generally of a beautiful quality, fine-grained and almost metallic in hardness, highly polished and painted. Metallurgy involved a great many metals, although copper was the most widely used. Copper and bronze were made into weapons and tools; gold, silver, and *tumbago* (an alloy of copper and gold) were reserved for luxury goods used by nobles and by priests in religious ceremonies. In all, Inca craftsmanship was excellent.

Village life

Village life in the Andes was deeply affected under Inca conquest and administration. The Inca language, Quechua, became the official language and took root so quickly that, by the time the Spaniards began recording native languages, most of the local, non-Inca dialects were forgotten.

Most pre-Inca villages seem to have grown in shape and size as a result of local population expansion and without planning. They were irregular in shape. The Inca enforced relocation and village planning, in which villages were systematically laid out and people were given better access to their fields. Houses were made from either field stones or adobe. They were thatched and usually rectangular in form. They were often built in a compound; a wall surrounded a cluster of houses which were probably occupied by an extended family group of close relatives. Household furniture was scant, consisting typically of a clay stove, clay cooking ware, wooden spoons, stools and woolen sleeping blankets that were simply placed on the earth floor.

Village land was owned, as was all land in the empire, by the Inca emperor; it was merely allocated to families for their use in farming and herding. The Inca government carefully marked the boundaries of all village fields. This was essential to their system of taxation by *mita,* or labor draft. Moving field boundary markers was punishable by death. Each family was apportioned land according to its needs as determined by the number of family members. As a household increased or decreased in size, it was either given more land or had land taken from it.

Mita workers were selected on a decimal basis and apportioned equally over

The University Museum, Philadelphia

A kero (wooden cup) from Peru. The inlaid design on this Incan artifact is lacquered.

the empire under the Inca system of taxation-by-service. Among the commoners, manufacturing specialists and personal servants of the nobles were exempt from the labor draft and enjoyed other advantages. Nobles and priests were not subject to taxation in any form.

Social organization. Although few accurate details remain about Inca village social organization, some general features are known or are probable. Villages tended to be endogamous; that is, villagers married one another rather than contracting marriage with persons from other villages. Villages were made up of several patrilineal, extended families that maintained their own fields. Marriage was permitted between first cousins, if the woman were destined to become the man's principal wife; nobles were permitted to marry their half-sisters, and the emperor made one of his full sisters his principal wife. The number of wives a man had was an indication of his social status. Most of the ordinary Indians were monogamous out of economic necessity.

The Inca community was called *ayllu,* a localized kin group in which members traced descent patrilineally, that is, through a male line back to a common male ancestor. The *ayllu* was originally a landowning group that redistributed fields among its several families according

to their needs, a custom that antedates the Inca systematization of village planning and land redistribution in the 15th and 16th centuries.

Villages were composed of two or more *ayllus,* usually called "upper" and "lower," in a dual organization, the details of which remain unknown. The Inca also had an age-grade system of 12 ranks, in which persons passed from one social status to another according to their age. This custom was used by the Inca government for census taking and tax levies *(mita).* The most important age-grade was that of married adult, fully responsible worker, and taxpayer.

Clothing. A breechclout was worn at the age of 14 and was a symbol of manhood. Both men and women wore woolen clothing (cotton on the coast), sleeveless tunics for men and wraparound dresses for women. Both men and women wore long cloaks, sandals, headbands, and jewelry. Nobles wore large earplugs, bracelets of gold and silver, and metal disks around the neck and on the forehead, as well as garments made of the finest materials. Soldiers decorated themselves with necklaces of human teeth. Special feathered costumes were worn at religious ceremonies, and men painted their faces during religious and mourning ceremonies and in time of war. Dress and ornamentation were indexes of social status among the Inca.

Political organization

The Inca empire was divided into four territorial divisions with their center in Cuzco. The quartering was done by Pachacuti in the 1430's for administrative purposes. Each division had its own provinces and capital, but as the empire grew in size the four sectors became disproportionate in size, shape, and population.

The emperor. At the apex of the Inca empire was the emperor, the absolute ruler by divine right and the descendant of the sun-god. The emperor had many wives and many children who enjoyed positions of great privilege. Each emperor built and furnished in Cuzco a new palace befitting his exalted status in life and serving as his perpetual shrine and tomb after death.

The death of an emperor was an occasion for nationwide funeral ceremonies and mourning. His body was preserved and wrapped in cloth and cared for by his descendants. It was displayed in the sacred square in Cuzco during important public festivals. Some of the emperor's wives and retainers were put to death by strangulation and interred with him in his palace. The deceased emperor was attended by servants in much the same ceremonious manner that he was treated during his life.

The emperor's descendants in the male line composed the royal *ayllu* and served as his court of topmost administrators and advisers, attending him with elaborate ritual respect. The imperial successor was publicly named by the emperor from among his many sons. The importance of public recognition may be seen in the case of Huayna Capac's son, Huascar, who was named as successor on Huayna Capac's deathbed. Because this was not done in public, Atahualpa, who was Huascar's half-brother, made the claim that Huayna Capac had divided the empire between them. At the time,

Atahualpa was in command of a strong army in Quito (Ecuador) and was thus able to contest Huascar's claim and emerge victorious. Huascar's capture in battle and his death occurred at about the time that the Spaniards arrived in the city of Cajamarca in the northern highlands of Peru.

The administrative class. Each territorial unit was governed by an official who resided in Cuzco and had under his command *curacas,* local leaders who resided in the provinces. *Curacas* were ranked according to the number of tax-paying Indians they controlled, based on a decimal system of reckoning — 10,000, 5,000, 1,000, 500, and 100. The office of *curaca* became hereditary and remained in the same family, passing from father to son, as the thoroughly bureaucratized Inca empire attained a peak of stability before the arrival of the Spaniards in the first half of the 16th century.

Administrative officers took very detailed headcounts in their precincts, continually revising census figures to accord with births and deaths. These censuses were the basis for taxation in the form of labor drafts and enforced military service. Census records were kept by officials on knotted string devices called quipu, which

These fine Incan sculptures are done in silver. From left to right, they represent an alpaca, a llama and a human being.

A view of Macchu Picchu, the ancient citadel of the Inca. The city stands high in the Andes, 50 miles from Cuzco. Abandoned by the Inca after the Spanish conquest in the 16th century, the city was rediscovered in 1911 by Hiram Bingham.

Allyn Baum — Rapho Guillumette

are still used by highland Indians in keeping accounts of llama and sheep.

The *curacas* made up the bulk of the provincial administrative class. Their children were formally educated in Cuzco, to assume administrative roles when they reached adulthood. The *curacas* were exempt from taxation and were handsomely rewarded for their services. They were made "Incas-by-Privilege," which means that although they were not of the Inca tribe itself (and therefore not "Incas-by-birth"), they were accorded similar status as a reward for their loyalty and administrative services.

Inca nobility, therefore, was composed of Incas-by-Birth and Incas-by-Privilege and, at the time of the Spaniards' arrival on the north coast of Peru, a hereditary aristocracy had begun to form. As the empire expanded there was an increasing need for administrators, who came to number in the thousands. Talent and loyalty were sought out and rewarded by promotion and gifts of wealth and generally by admission to the growing aristocracy.

By the time of the Spanish conquest, the Incas-by-Privilege far outnumbered those born to the Inca tribal lineages. This was a consequence of the need for more and more administrative officers in the far-flung empire. There were two categories of nobles — those who belonged to the 11 royal lineages of the Inca tribe and those who were incorporated into the administrative hierarchy. The Incas-by-Privilege came from the tribes adjacent to or near the Inca stronghold of Cuzco. Many men from these tribes governed distant provinces. Those who remained in or near Cuzco made up the highest nobility and were assigned the most important posts.

The commoners. Shoring up the empire were millions of commoners who provided agricultural products, labor and military service. Women as well as men were rigidly controlled by the Inca state. Most women were allowed to marry fellow villagers and lead ordinary domestic lives. Some women, as young girls, were selected for special lives and were called "chosen women," mainly because of their beauty and health. They were assigned to convents for special training. After a 4-year period of training some were given to nobles as secondary wives, some were assigned to a temple of the sun and remained virgins for life, and some were sacrificed on ritual occasions.

Religion of the Inca

Religious ideology as expressed in ritual ceremonies tended to permeate Inca life. Stress was laid on ritual performances rather than on mysticism. Most attention was given to the supernatural increase of crops and animals and to the health and well-being of the people. Animal and human sacrifice were part of the ritual life. Animal sacrifice was the

The sun temples at Pachá-camac, Peru. This major religious center was located in the Lurín Valley about 11 miles south of Lima. The temples are actually artificial hills with terraces; the walls are made of sunbaked clay.

American Museum of Natural History

most common form and usually involved slitting the animal's throat and burning the corpse at a shrine. Human victims such as the chosen women were strangled, after which their throats were cut or their hearts cut out.

The Inca had a large pantheon of deities. At the apex was Viracocha, the Creator, who was thought to have a human form and who was represented in icons in a number of temples. He was believed to live in the sky and to command a host of lesser supernatural beings who looked after the welfare of human beings.

Next in rank to Viracocha were the sky-gods. The most important of these was Inti, god of the sun and founder of the Inca royal lineage. Inti was also believed to be human in form. He was felt to be a guardian of crops and was of great importance in agricultural ritual. Following in importance were the deities of thunder, various star constellations, moon, earth, and sea, the latter three being represented as females. The god of thunder regulated rainfall and was therefore of vital importance to farming. The goddess of the moon (wife of the sun-god) was important because she was linked with the periodicity associated with women and thus with the regulation of the agricultural cycle and the festival calendar.

Among the stars there were several constellations that looked out for human welfare by guarding plants and animals. The goddesses of earth (agriculture) and

sea (fishing) were of considerable importance in the Inca ritual calendar.

Scattered throughout the central Andean region were innumerable shrines or sacred places called *huacas*. The majority of these were stones and springs, although many hills, caves, houses and other natural and man-made objects were also sacred. Places associated with the emperor were sacred, as was the city of Cuzco as a whole. Snow-capped mountains were and still are very sacred objects.

The Inca Indians believed in many evil spirits. However, very little has been recorded about their attributes. Most descriptions of spirits are of those helpful to mankind — spirits who were supplicated for their help in life and after death. There were many temples in which, among other things, the spirits of the dead were propitiated and sacred objects retained and cared for by priests. Of the innumerable Inca *huacas,* only the most important ones were attended by priests and other specialists such as diviners, sacrificers, caretakers and virgin women.

Sorcery and countersorcery were (and still are) prevalent in the Andean region. It was believed that sorcerers could cause illness and other misfortunes. Both public ceremonies led by priests, and private ceremonies led by shamans, were considered effective means of combating human misfortune. Many supernatural beliefs of the past are still widely held among highland Peruvian Indians.

ASTRONOMY

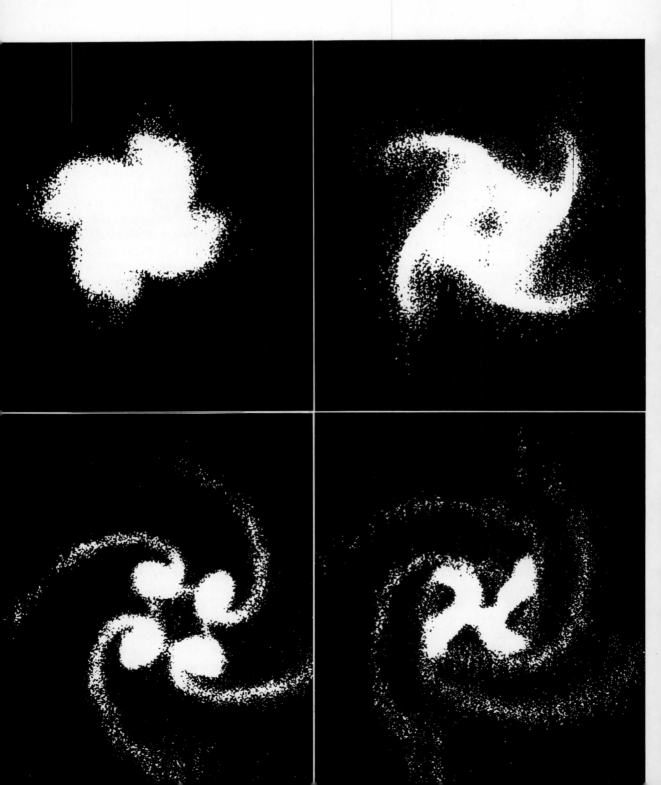

CONTENTS

Scenes (in sequence) from the first computer motion picture showing the birth of a galaxy and its early evolution. This computer model permits an experimental approach to the study of stellar systems.

Columbia University

REVIEW OF THE YEAR-ASTRONOMY

To the layman, the starry night sky looks much as it did to his ancestors thousands of years ago.   But modern astronomers and physicists have a very different concept of the universe than did their ancient predecessors — or their counterparts of only ten years ago.   The decade of the 1960's revolutionized astronomy and cosmology.   It saw the discovery of quasars and pulsars; the general acceptance of the big bang theory of the universe's origin; the voyage of men to the moon and their return to earth with lunar rocks and soil; and the apparent detection of gravity waves.   New and improved astronomical instruments opened more windows to the sky. Artificial satellites carried men's "eyes" above the troublesome veil of the earth's atmosphere, revealing new wonders about the heavens.   Instruments landed on the moon and the planet Venus, providing answers to many of man's questions about those bodies.

Pulsars.   Astronomers generally agree with Dr. Martin Schwarzschild of Princeton University that pulsars are "a third fundamental class of stars: neutron stars." (The other classes are ordinary stars and white stars.)   By the end of 1969, 46 pulsars were known.   In general, the pulse rates of these pulsars are slowing down.   This slowing is believed to be caused by the progressive energy loss of the pulsars; they simply spin more slowly as time goes by.   Other regular variations in pulse rates may be due to the orbiting of planetary bodies around pulsars.   These planets, or companions, exert gravitational effects on the pulsars that periodically alter their radiation output.   But irregular and sudden increases in the pulsation, and therefore rotation, rates of pulsars have recently been discovered by scientists at Princeton and Cornell Universities.   These are difficult to explain except as possible "starquakes."   That is, sudden changes in the shape of the pulsar and the distribution of its matter could produce such fluctuations in the pulsation rate.   An increasing number of astronomers and physicists believe that pulsars are the sources of gravitational waves.   They may also generate most of the high-energy cosmic rays that pervade the universe.   Cosmic rays consist mostly of subatomic particles which have been accelerated by energies thousands to millions of times more powerful than those produced in the mightiest "atom-smashers" built by man.   Pulsars may be energetic enough to generate and accelerate cosmic particles that, in turn, move from galaxy to galaxy at speeds approaching that of light (186,000 miles a second).

Not all space radiation comes from pulsars.   Many kinds of celestial objects, both visible and invisible, emit rays both seen and unseen.   Among the most peculiar are the X-ray sources; these may or may not be optical (light-emitting) stars.   In mid-1969, a pair of American Vela satellites detected a tremendous X-ray flare in the sky between the constellations Lupus and Centaurus; the intensity of the radiation tapered off in the following two weeks.   X rays are highly energetic forms of radiation and bespeak unusual cosmic and atomic events when they occur.   Gamma rays are even more powerful.   They occur almost everywhere in space along with cosmic-ray particles and are in fact a component of cosmic radiation.   In 1969, after ten years of searching, the first point source of gamma rays in space was discovered, in the constellation Sagittarius.   It is not yet certain whether this source is a conventional star or a pulsar.

Quasars. A decade has passed since the first quasar was discovered in 1960. But these objects continue to puzzle scientists. Many astronomers think these extremely bright and energetic starlike masses are billions of light years from earth. They must be incredibly large — millions of times the size of our sun — to be seen from so far away. Yet quasars display characteristics, such as rapid changes in overall radiation, that imply comparatively small sizes. This leads some astronomers to doubt that the quasars are so far from our solar system. As if to add to the confusion, astronomers at the California Institute of Technology have found a group of objects that exhibit characteristics of both quasars and galaxies. They are fantastically brilliant and distant, like quasars, but they also have gaseous haloes or spiral arms, like many galaxies. Is there an evolutionary relationship between quasars and galaxies? Are the newly-discovered objects a "missing link" between the two?

Gravitation. According to Albert Einstein's theories of relativity, gravitation could take the form of radiating waves. But, say the theories, these waves would be so weak as to be virtually undetectable. Dr. Joseph Weber of the University of Maryland has spent more than ten years trying to identify these gravity waves. In 1968 he reported possible success; by early 1970 his expanded findings were called "just fantastic" and "utterly wild" by fellow physicists. Dr. Weber's apparatus consists of large solid aluminum cylinders, suspended in such a manner that they are supposedly unaffected by forces other than gravitation. When gravity waves pass through them, the cylinders oscillate. Gravity waves may be generated by the motions of very massive or dense bodies in space. Such waves may also be produced by the collapse of a massive star. In January 1970, Dr. Weber reported that two hundred "significant events" had been recorded during the second half of 1969. Approximately two thirds of these events appear to have originated from the center of our galaxy. The signals were so strong and occurred so frequently that some astronomers question that they were caused by gravitational waves; one scientist suggested they may have been caused by a form of wave unknown to man.

Cosmochemistry. Water, ammonia and, most recently, formaldehyde have been found to exist in interstellar space. Formaldehyde, composed of two hydrogen and an oxygen atom bonded to carbon, is the most complex molecule ever discovered in space. Together with water and ammonia it implies the possible existence of methane, a hydrocarbon which unfortunately cannot be detected with radio telescopes. All of these compounds play a role in the formation of living matter, notably protein. Thus scientists speculate that the raw materials of life existed in huge interstellar clouds prior to the formation of presently-existing stars and planets. Many astronomers believe that these clouds spin and contract to form stars and planetary systems. Any gases found in the clouds could thus be expected in the planetary atmospheres. Water molecule radio emissions observed with a radio telescope at Maryland Point, Maryland, indicate that scientists may be witnessing just such a "birth." These emissions seem to originate from rings of gas and dust that are rapidly spinning and condensing toward a central object.

The solar system. Lunar samples brought back to earth by Apollos 11 and 12 show a surprising degree of complexity. They indicate that the moon is at least as old as the earth; yet it underwent an entirely different kind of development. Laser reflectors left on the moon by the astronauts have enabled scientists to measure earth-to-moon distances to an accuracy of ±6 inches. Seismometers have detected moonquakes and meteorite impacts.

The most surprising seismic data resulted from the planned crash impact on the moon of the Apollo 12 lunar module. "It is as though someone struck a bell in the belfry of a church, and it kept reverberating for 30 minutes," said Dr. Maurice E. Ewing of Columbia University's Lamont-Doherty Geological Observatory . (A similar reaction occurred when the spent third stage of Apollo 13's Saturn V booster crashed onto the moon in April 1970.)

Data telemetered from Mariners 6 and 7 and from Veneras 5 and 6 provided new insights concerning surface and atmospheric conditions on Mars and Venus. Photographs taken by the Mariner craft, which flew past Mars on July 31 and August 5, 1969, respectively, revealed the presence of two previously unknown types of topography: chaotic terrain and featureless terrain. The Venera probes, which entered the Venusian atmosphere in May 1969, confirmed beliefs that Venus is an inhospitable planet. Its dense atmosphere, consisting largely of carbon dioxide, obscures a surface where temperatures may reach 1,000° F. and pressures reportedly average more than 1,470 pounds per square inch.

Early in 1970 scientists used NASA's Orbiting Astronomical Observatory 2 (OAO–2) to study a newly discovered comet. The comet, Tago-Sato-Kosaka, was named for the three Japanese amateur astronomers who discovered it in October 1969. The most abundant element in the universe is hydrogen, but pure hydrogen produces most of its light in the far ultraviolet regions of the spectrum. This radiation, called Lyman alpha radiation, does not penetrate the earth's atmosphere. OAO–2, above the obscuring density of the atmosphere, gave man his first look at a comet in the light of hydrogen Lyman alpha. Data showed that the head of Tago-Sato-Kosaka is surrounded by a huge glowing cloud of hydrogen — a cloud as large as the sun! Ultraviolet radiation from other molecules was also found with OAO–2. Such information, coupled with ground-based observations, should enable scientists to determine more accurately the amount of mass ejected from the comet and to learn more about the comet's composition.

Since 1964 the Smithsonian Institution's Astrophysical Observatory of Cambridge, Massachusetts, has operated the Prairie Network, a system of 16 automatic camera stations in the Midwest. The network was designed to record falling meteorites. On January 3, 1970, two of the cameras photographed the fiery streak left by a meteorite as it plunged to the earth. From these photographs scientists calculated the estimated point of impact. On January 9, the 21.6-pound meteorite was found within a half mile of the predicted site. This rapid recovery made it possible for scientists to study short-lived radioactive substances in the meteorite. The photographs also enabled scientists to calculate the meteorite's orbit. It was found that the iron-rich rock orginated in the asteroid belt, which lies mostly between the orbits of Mars and Jupiter. This was the second time that a meteorite had been tracked back to its source. The first time was in 1959, by Czech astronomers. That meteorite also originated in the asteroid belt.

A meteorite discovered in France several years ago shows tracks of what California Institute of Technology scientists believe are particles generated by the decay of plutonium 244. To our knowledge, this radioactive element is man-made and does not occur naturally. But perhaps it once did; its short lifetime of 118 million years would not have permitted it to survive from any period earlier than this length of time.

UFO's. In December 1969, the U.S. Air Force ended Project Blue Book, its 22-year investigation of unidentified flying objects.

"They *seem* friendly."

IS THERE INTELLIGENCE OUT THERE?*

Or Is Man Alone in the Universe?

BY ISAAC ASIMOV

UNTIL recently, mankind was sure it was not alone in the universe. Other intelligences? Of course! Every culture believed in a variety of all-knowing gods and demons, of spirits and angels, of jinn and fairies and little people, of goblins and gnomes and elves. And every one of these species of intelligence was believed greater than man — stronger and longer-lived. Of all the intelligent beings in the universe, we viewed ourselves as the weakest and least knowing.

But we did consider the earth to be alone in the universe. About the earth might be crystalline spheres that made music, together with hosts of little stars, but earth was the only actual world of its sort anywhere.

* Reprinted from RCA *Electronic Age*

Then look what happened!

The earth was dethroned from its high place. It came to be viewed as a planet like the other planets circling the sun. The stars, we grew to realize, were really other suns. With every advance in astronomy, we found the universe to be larger than we had previously believed. The planets, it turned out, were millions of miles away; the nearer stars were trillions of miles away; farther stars were quintillions of miles away, sextillions. . . .

The universe seemed incredibly vast and incredibly empty. The stars filled it in the way that three scattered dust specks would fill New York's Madison Square Garden. We were riders on one of those specks lost in nothingness, for, at the same time that the universe expanded beyond all knowledge, most of the spirits vanished from our beliefs. These other intelligences — from demons to leprechauns — now exist only in fantasies and children's books. In the whole universe, as far as we know, we are the only intelligent life.

Or are we? In our own solar system, there is no world fit for us to live on comfortably except earth. On some of the other planets of this system, perhaps there may be life-forms as complicated as bacteria, but no more complex than that. Conceivably, there might also be life in chemical and physiological forms utterly unfamiliar to us, but we have no evidence to support this theory, no guidelines as to what the "utterly unfamiliar" might be, no way of talking about it.

On the other hand, in other systems, in other families of planets circling other stars, there conceivably might be worlds as comfortable as earth — habitable worlds. Perhaps on these worlds there may be life-forms as complex as our own. We don't know. Perhaps we may never know. But we can do a bit of speculating.

To begin with, how many stars are there? Our own sun is part of the Milky Way galaxy, a vast conglomeration of some 135 billion (135,000,000,000) stars. There are other galaxies, too, perhaps as many as 100 billion of them. These other galaxies are incredibly distant, and we may as well concentrate on our own. Surely, 135 billion stars are enough to begin with.

Of course, not every star is suitable for the development of life, if it has a planetary system. It would seem life doesn't develop very quickly, judging from the case of our own earth. A planet must form, settle down, and develop complicated chemicals, simple life-forms and then more-complex ones. Finally, an oxygen-containing atmosphere must slowly be created by the action of living things.

It was only about 600 million years ago, at which time the earth was 4 billion years old and creatures as complex as shellfish already had evolved, that our oxygen atmosphere was formed. And it was only about 300 million years ago that life advanced out of the seas to penetrate and conquer the land areas of the earth.

During all the time that life was developing, the sun had to, and apparently did, deliver light and warmth to our planet at a steady rate. Life, after all, is a delicate thing, and what might have been a mere hiccup of irregularity in the lifetime of the sun would have been sufficient to wipe out life on earth.

Astronomers know enough now to be able to tell a great deal about a star from

The Bettmann Archive

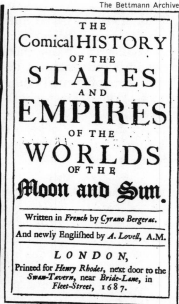

An illustration and the title page from a 1687 edition of a novel by Cyrano de Bergerac, the French dramatist and novelist whose works were precursors of modern science fiction. Seated in a space capsule, the hero leaves on an "extraordinary voyage" to the moon and sun.

In 1835, the New York *Sun* reported that astronomer Sir John Herschel had discovered these creatures on the moon. The convincing hoax included descriptions of tiny bison, horned bears and four-foot-tall lunar humanoids with "wings composed of a thin membrane lying snugly along their backs."

The Bettmann Archive

the analysis of the light it emits. Some stars are too dim and cold to serve as sources of enough heat and light for life to develop at any point within their planetary systems. Some are too hot. Others are at a stage in their development where they are undergoing rapid alteration. Still others are of kinds that will never settle down for 4 billion years of uninterrupted steadiness of delivery of light and warmth. All this can be deduced from the light sent us by the stars. Fewer than 1 star in 8 are warm enough and steady enough to possess planets that can develop life, but even so that leaves 17.5 billion suitable stars in our galaxy alone.

Still, just because a star can serve as an energy source that is steady enough for the development of life on one or more of its planets doesn't necessarily mean that it has planets at all. How many stars have planets anyway? Up to 30 years ago, the most common theory of planetary formation involved near collisions of 2 stars. Gravitational pull was supposed to have yanked material out of each passing star, and from that material the planets formed. But there have been so few near collisions between the widely spaced stars of the Milky Way in all the time the galaxy has existed that only a handful of near-misses could have taken place. According to that view, our own sun and the star that nearly

collided with it might own the only planetary systems in all the galaxy.

In the 1940's, new information and ideas caused astronomers to change their minds. It began to seem very likely that every forming star leaves behind clouds of gas and dust that gradually condense into planets. If this is true, then just about every star has a planetary system. In fact, planets outside the solar system actually have been detected. Some of the nearer and smaller stars show wobbles in their motions that can be due only to the gravitational pull of large planets. If there are 17.5 billion stars that deliver energy in sufficient quantities and with adequate reliability, then there are 17.5 billion planetary systems where life might possibly be incubated.

To be sure, not every planet would do. Some would be too close to a sun and too hot, some too far from it and therefore too cold. Some would have orbits that were too elongated, or periods of rotation that were too slow, or tippings of axes that were too extreme. In all these cases, there would be periods when extremes of cold or heat would be too great for life to exist. Judging from the manner in which planets are distributed in our own solar system, it isn't likely that there will be more than 1 habitable planet for each star and sometimes not any. Making a few rough esti-

35

mates and a few guesses, Stephen H. Dole of the Rand Corporation has argued that, of the stars suitable for life, only 1 in 27 would possess a planet on which life of the form familiar to us could take shape. Even so, this still means that in our galaxy alone there are roughly 650 million planets that are capable of developing life under conditions similar to those on earth.

But would life develop on those planets? Or is life just a superlucky accident that has taken place only on earth? Actually, it is possible to attempt an answer to these questions through experimentation in the laboratory. Data gathered by astronomers concerning the general chemical makeup of stars and of the dust and gas scattered through the space between the stars tell us something about the nature of the material out of which the earth was originally formed. This, combined with our basic knowledge of physics and chemistry, makes it possible to reason out what the earth may have been like chemically when it first settled down into its planetary shape. The consensus is that its atmosphere was composed originally of a mixture of ammonia and methane. The action of the ultraviolet light of the sun slowly turned such an atmosphere into nitrogen and carbon dioxide. Finally,

the action of life-forms replaced carbon dioxide with oxygen and gave us our present nitrogen-oxygen atmosphere. If this line of reasoning is correct, then life must have formed at a time when our atmosphere was still in its primitive state, perhaps when it was still ammonia-methane.

Beginning in the early 1950's, chemists attempted to trace the course of biochemical evolution experimentally. They started with a sterile mixture of chemicals similar to that believed to have existed in the earth's primordial oceans and atmosphere. That mixture was subjected to a source of energy that was analogous to lightning or to the ultraviolet radiation of the sun. The simple chemicals in the mixture absorbed the energy and combined to form more-complicated chemicals of the sort that play parts in certain chemical reactions in living tissue. Mixtures of these more-complicated chemicals were used as a starting point, and yet-more-complicated chemicals were formed, still like those in living tissue.

By the end of the 1960's, the basic building blocks of those all-important chemicals of life — the proteins and nucleic acids — had been formed in this manner. The net result of 20 years of experimentation seems to show that random combinations and recombinations of the common chemicals present in the primordial earth produce substances closer and closer to the makeup of living things. No chemicals are formed that seem to indicate

Both photos: The Bettmann Archive

Lunar life is portrayed in these illustrations from G. Melies' *Trip to the Moon* (1902). We now know that the moon is void of life. But do such creatures live elsewhere in the universe?

some direction of development away from the basic chemistry of known life-forms.

Life, then, seems to have resulted from movement along the chemical line of least resistance. Given certain chemicals to begin with plus a supply of energy, life must form. No other direction of chemical change could have taken place with anything like equal probability.

If this is so, then we might suspect that on any planet like earth — one with a similar chemical makeup and exposed to the radiation of a sun like our own — life must form and possibly might do so within a billion years. Following this line of reasoning, we can conclude that, in our galaxy alone, there are not only 650 million planets capable of bearing life, but 650 million planets that do bear life.

But what kind of life?

Ah, there at last we are totally stuck. We cannot say. It is impossible, so far, to experiment with organic evolution as we have been doing with chemical evolution. Life develops inevitably, but where matters will go from there remains a mystery.

We know, to a certain extent, what has taken place in organic evolution on earth, but are we typical? May not earth be a most unusual exception? Might not life ordinarily remain at the one-celled stage, so that earth is a curious anomaly where, alone in all the galaxy, large multicelled creatures have formed? On the other hand, other planets might have developed elaborate organisms, within 100 million years of the origin of life, with evolution racing on from there to superintelligence. If this is true, earth may be a lonely primitive exception.

How can we say for sure whether intelligence has developed on other worlds? We can't, but we can still speculate.

Suppose earth is a typical or average life-bearing planet. It took some 4.5 billion years of existence before intelligent life formed, and this might be just about the span of time required on other worlds as well. Those earthlike planets that are older than earth would have developed intelligent life long ago. On younger planets such life would not yet have evolved. If earth is of an average age for a planet of our galaxy, then we might suppose that intelligence has developed on a little more than ½ of the life-bearing planets: 325 million of them.

At the rate at which intelligent species advance their technology, any world that is even a few hundred thousand years ahead of us would be incredibly advanced. We might expect 325 million such "supercivilizations" in our galaxy. If so, why haven't they made themselves known to us? Why can't we detect beams of radio signals that they may be sending out? Why don't they visit us?

Let us suppose these 325 million planets are evenly spaced throughout the galaxy. Since about 90 per cent of all the stars of the galaxy are far off in its central nucleus, that is where 9 out of 10 of the intelligences would be. The remaining 10 per cent would be out in the spiral arms, where we are.

If this is so, then, on the average, 90 light-years would separate neighboring civilizations in the spiral arms. It takes a beam of light traveling at 186,281 miles a second — the maximum speed possible in this universe — 90 years to traverse a distance of 90 light-years. If a spaceship launched from earth were traveling at a speed of merely 18,000 miles a second, it would take nearly 1,000 years to reach the nearest outside intelligence. To send detectable beams of light or radio waves over that distance would require tremendous amounts of power. And communication would be extremely complicated, since each set of signals would require 180 years for the round trip.

This is the chief reason that I remain skeptical about reports that flying saucers may be ships piloted by extraterrestrial intelligences. That those intelligences exist I consider conceivable; that they might wish to visit earth is also conceivable. However, I cannot believe that repeated trips from star to star would be made without any serious attempt to establish contact. Surely any intelligent organisms capable of making an interstellar flight would be so far beyond us technologically as to have no need for fearing contact. Lack of contact would mean only that we didn't interest them. But then, if we are so retarded in comparison with them that they see no point in making contact, why should so many flying saucers visit us?

To me, it seems that if any intelligent race were to plan an extraterrestrial voyage, it would choose targets with the greatest care, in view of the investment of time and energy that would be necessary. I suspect that no advanced civilization would consider earth worth even a single trip, though if a ship were to pass us en route to somewhere else, we might be subject to casual, distant observation.

It is possible that we have never been visited because although the galaxy is full of life, it is void or almost void of intelligence. Suppose the earth has not followed the typical course of organic evolution. Perhaps the development of human-level intelligence here on earth was a sheer accident of the most extraordinary kind. After all, there is no real reason to assume that intelligence is the inevitable consequence of organic evolution, as life is of chemical evolution. Intelligence doesn't even seem to have much survival value.

Mammals, with all their intelligence, aren't doing so well as insects, so far as sheer survival is concerned. The highly intelligent elephant, for example, isn't as hardy as the quite unintelligent cockroach. What really count in survival are sheer fecundity (the ability to have many young) and the ability to eat almost anything. Man's early survival under conditions where the apes did poorly is very likely due to the fact that men would eat virtually anything whereas apes required specialized diets.

Of course, once an intelligent creature passes a certain point — becomes capable of taming fire, perhaps — he will advance to control his environment and will therefore come to dominate his planet. But is it perhaps inevitable that, in so doing, the intelligent creature eventually will discover nuclear power and destroy himself in war? Is it inevitable that the intelligent creature will strip his planet of habitability by consuming part of its resources and polluting the rest? We might argue that man is a freak among intelligences in this respect. Other intelligent creatures on other planets, we might speculate, are not so combative or competitive as man. I certainly hope this is true, but it is also possible to argue that, without a strong streak of combativeness and generally aggressive instincts, no intelligent creature can manage to win the struggle for survival that is necessary before "This is my property" can be stamped on a whole planet.

In either instance — if intelligence does not develop in the course of organic evolution except through the most unusual accident, or if intelligences that do develop generally commit suicide within a million years — there may possibly be no other intelligences in the entire galaxy. In this case, if we ever play a game of cosmic "knock-knock," there will be no one to answer, "Who's there?"

And if this is so, then surely it is more important than ever that we beat the game: that somehow we must learn, before it is too late, how not to commit suicide through nuclear war, overpopulation and overpollution. After all, the whole galaxy may be ours — all those millions of rich planets that bear life but not intelligence. Let us live to inherit them.

" 'Insects,' murmured Cavor, 'insects.' " This illustration is from H. G. Wells' *The First Men in the Moon* (1901).

The Granger Collection

THE MOON

A Survey of What We Know
about Earth's Satellite

BY CECILIA PAYNE-GAPOSCHKIN
and KATHERINE HARAMUNDANIS

The rugged, cratered surface of the far side of the moon, photographed from the Apollo 10 lunar module. Were these craters formed by meteorites or by volcanic action?
NASA

THE moon, circling the earth under the pull of gravity, passes across our sky once every 24 hours. Since the dawn of history, man has been fascinated by the moon; he has spun legends about it and has used it in many ways. In prehistoric times, for example, primitive man observed the phases of the moon and, in some societies, used these phases to form a calendar. In the western world, obvious surface markings on the moon were called "the man in the moon"; in China these markings were called "the mortar and pestle and the hare."

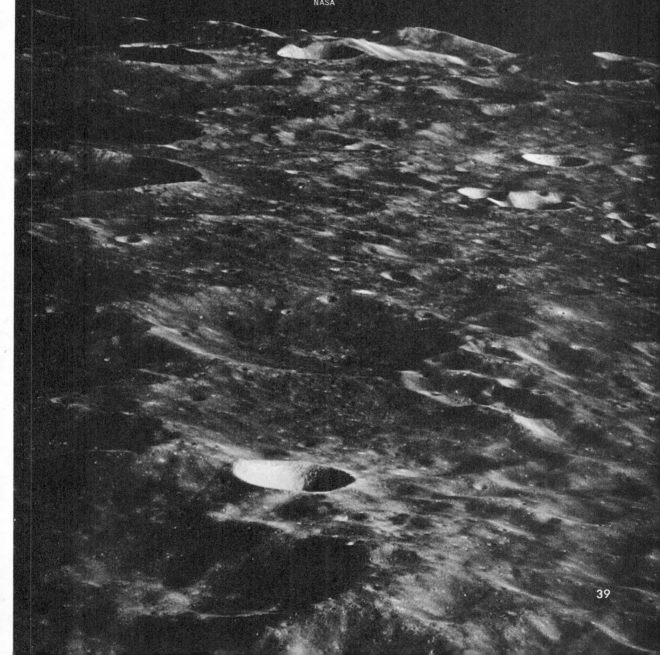

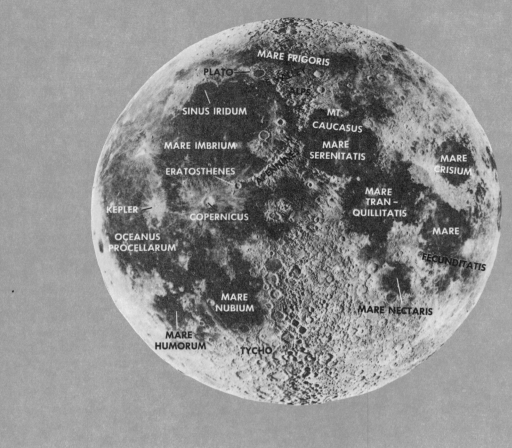

MARE FRIGORIS
PLATO
ALPS
SINUS IRIDUM
MT. CAUCASUS
MARE IMBRIUM
MARE SERENITATIS
ERATOSTHENES
MARE CRISIUM
KEPLER
COPERNICUS
MARE TRAN-QUILLITATIS
OCEANUS PROCELLARUM
MARE FECUNDITATIS
MARE NUBIUM
MARE NECTARIS
MARE HUMORUM
TYCHO

Lick Observatory

Major features of the lunar surface are labeled on this photograph of the full moon. The dark, flat-looking regions are called *maria* ("seas"), although they contain no water. The light-colored areas have rough textures and contain mountain ranges. Thousands of craters dot the surface, especially near the south pole. Notice the rays that radiate from craters such as Copernicus.

When Galileo first turned his telescope on the moon in 1609, he saw its surface in considerable detail. He recognized mountains and large dark areas, which he called *"maria"* because he thought they might be seas. (*Maria* is the Latin word for "seas.") The word *"maria"* is still used, although we know now that there are no visible bodies of water on the moon. As larger telescopes were made, more and more details were noticed and mapped. Beginning in the 1960's, artificial satellites and manned spacecraft were launched from the earth to pass near the moon or land on it. Pictures obtained by these vehicles have revealed the surface in extraordinary detail.

An observer gazing at the moon can distinguish light and dark areas. The light areas are generally uplands, and the dark areas low-lying flat regions. Many features are seen to throw shadows on the lunar surface. These shadows can be used to estimate the heights of the features. The telescope also shows bright streaks, radiating from some craters. These *rays* do not throw shadows and are therefore not raised features. Dark, meandering riverlike features, called *rills,* are probably surface cracks, but no water flows in them. There also are the myriads of craters, which range from huge rings like Bailly with a diameter of 186 miles to tiny pockmarks a foot or less across.

Size of the moon

In order to measure the size of the moon, we must find out how far away it is.

This is done with the same methods that are used by surveyors. The angular direction to the moon is measured from two widely separated places on opposite sides of the earth, at the same time. Since we know the distance between the two points of observation, the average distance to the moon can be calculated by simple trigonometry. The average distance is 238,857 miles. The diameter of the moon is 2,161 miles, about $\frac{1}{4}$ that of the earth. Other planets in our solar system have satellites, some of which are larger than ours, but our moon is the largest with respect to its primary. The largest satellite of Jupiter (Ganymede) is only $\frac{1}{27}$ the size of Jupiter; Titan, the largest satellite of Saturn, is $\frac{1}{25}$ the size of Saturn.

The mass of the moon, which is measured by its gravitational effect on the earth, is $\frac{1}{81}$ of the earth's. Its volume is $\frac{1}{50}$ of the earth's; hence the moon is less dense than the earth. If we take the density of water as 1, then the earth's density is 5.5, or $5\frac{1}{2}$ times that of water. The moon's density is 3.3 on this scale. Actually, the moon is about as dense as the rocks on the earth's surface and is probably made of similar materials. One possible explanation of the lower overall density of the moon may be its lack of a dense metallic core, such as the earth has.

Phases of the moon

Anyone who looks at the moon notices that its apparent shape changes from night to night, and runs through a complete cycle in about a month. These changes of shape, the *phases* of the moon, are caused by the changing relative positions of moon, sun and earth. When the moon is directly in line between the sun and the earth, the sun is shining on the far side of the moon; this phase is known as *new moon.*

As the moon goes around the earth and moves out of the sun-earth line, the illuminated part becomes visible to us as a thin crescent, which increases, or *waxes,* night after night. When the line from earth to moon makes an angle of 90° with the line from earth to sun, we see half the moon's face illuminated; this phase is called *first quarter.* When earth, moon and sun are again in line, with sun and moon on opposite sides of the earth, we see the whole face of the moon illuminated. This phase is the *full moon.* Thereafter, the moon *wanes,* and the illuminated surface grows smaller. When the direction from earth to moon again makes an angle of 90° with the direction from earth to sun, we again see half the moon's face illuminated (the *last quarter*), and the crescent continues to wane until new moon is reached again. Between the quarters and new moon, the shape of the illuminated portion of the moon is called a *crescent.* Between the quarters and full moon, the shape of the illuminated disk is described as *gibbous,* that is, not fully circular.

The crescent moon, 24.3 days after new moon. The horns, or cusps, of the crescent moon always point away from the sun. The line between the light and dark areas is called the terminator.

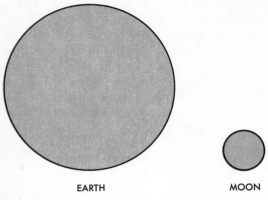

EARTH   MOON

Comparative sizes of the earth and moon. The earth's diameter is 7,927 miles; the moon's is 2,161 miles, about ¼ that of the earth. Its volume is 1/50 of the earth's.

The line that separates the illuminated and dark portions of the moon is known as the *terminator.* The crescent moon, whether waxing or waning, has horns, or *cusps,* which always point away from the sun. Near the time of new moon it is often possible to see the whole disk of the moon faintly illuminated ("the old moon in the new moon's arms"). The light by which we see this phenomenon is sunlight that has been reflected back to the moon from the bright surface of the earth.

The photographs taken of the various phases show that although the illuminated area changes, we always see virtually the same side of the moon. This is because the moon is gravitationally locked to the earth, and makes one rotation on its own axis in nearly the same time it takes to

make one revolution around the earth. However, it should not be forgotten that the sun shines on all sides of the moon in turn during the cycle of phases, while we see only the illuminated portion that faces us.

The months: synodic and sidereal

Several different kinds of month are recognized by astronomers. The simplest one is the *synodic month,* or *lunation,* the interval from one new moon to the next new moon (29½ days). This, however, is not the time taken by the moon to make one complete orbit around the earth. The moon falls behind because of the earth's motion around the sun, which carries the earth about 1/12 of the way around its orbit between lunations. The orbital period of the moon, known as the *sidereal month,* is 27⅓ days; therefore it is nearly 2 days shorter than the synodic month. Because it is gravitationally locked to the earth, the moon rotates on its axis once in a sidereal month.

Orbit of the moon

The motion of the moon is far from simple and has presented a challenge to the ingenuity of astronomers for several centuries. The orbit is not circular; it does not lie always in the same plane; and its shape and position relative to sun and earth are continually changing. For these reasons, that part of the moon seen from the earth varies slightly, so that over a period of time we can view 59 per cent of the

The moon's phases. The disks inside the orbit show the phases as seen from the earth.

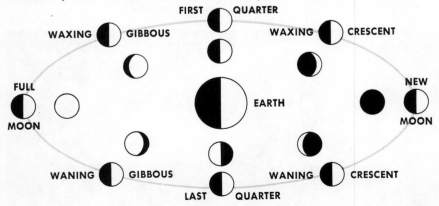

FIRST QUARTER

WAXING GIBBOUS   WAXING CRESCENT

FULL
MOON   EARTH   NEW
MOON   MOON   SUN

WANING GIBBOUS   WANING CRESCENT

LAST QUARTER

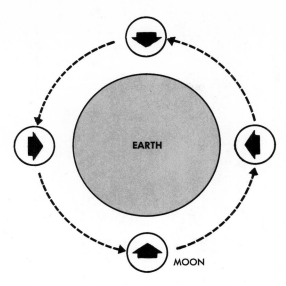

As the moon revolves around the earth, the same side always faces our planet. This occurs because the moon's period of rotation on its axis is the same as its period of revolution around the earth: 27 days, 7 hours and 43 minutes. This orbital period of the moon is called the sidereal month. This is not the same as the time from one new-moon phase to the next new-moon phase. That is nearly 2 days longer and is called the synodic month.

moon's surface from a place of observation on the earth. The changes in the moon's orbit run in cycles; because of this, the visible surface of the moon undergoes rocking motions, or *librations,* which bring small areas near the edges of the observable disk into view. Several decades elapse before all possible areas are visible to viewers on earth. Today, with manned spacecraft, astronauts are obtaining detailed close-up photographs of even the far side of the moon.

Eclipses of the sun and the moon

By a happy accident, the size of the moon as seen from the earth is almost exactly the same as the size of the sun as seen from the earth. This is an extraordinary coincidence, because the sun is about 64 million times the volume of the moon. If the orbit of the earth around the sun and the orbit of the moon around the earth were in exactly the same plane, the moon would pass exactly across the face of the sun at every new moon. Thus there would be an eclipse of the sun once a month. Similarly, at every full moon the

shadow of the earth would fall on the moon, and there would be a total eclipse of the moon once a month.

But the moon's orbit is inclined, on the average, by about 5° to that of the earth. This means that the moon can come in front of the sun only near the position where the two orbits intersect (the *nodes*). When a new moon occurs very near the node, the moon will pass exactly across the face of the sun, and there will be a *total eclipse* of the sun. Farther from the node, the moon will cover only part of the sun's face (a *partial eclipse*). Because neither the moon's nor the earth's orbit is circular, the distances from earth to moon and sun are not constant. As these distances vary, so do the apparent sizes of sun and moon. Thus on some occasions, the moon may not cover the entire solar disk, allowing a thin rim of sunlight to be visible around its edge (an *annular eclipse* of the sun).

An eclipse of the sun is visible only from the small portion of the earth on which the moon's shadow is cast. The shadow moves rapidly across the surface of the earth, and total eclipses last a couple of minutes or less, as seen from one station. The prediction of the times at which such eclipses will occur involves elaborate calculations which must take into account the complexities of the moon's motion.

An eclipse of the moon takes place when the moon passes through the shadow cast by the earth. They must therefore occur at the time of full moon, when the moon is near the node. There is usually an eclipse of the moon two weeks before or after an eclipse of the sun. At a total eclipse of the moon, the moon is wholly within the earth's shadow and no sunlight falls on it. When the moon is not wholly within the shadow, there is a partial eclipse. Unlike solar eclipses, lunar eclipses are seen from every part of the earth where the moon is visible at the time.

The tides: spring and neap

There are 2 high tides for every passage of the moon across a meridian (a

44

north-south line) of the earth, principally because of the gravitational pull of the moon on the ocean waters. In the course of a month there are 2 *spring tides* (when the range of the tide is largest) and 2 *neap tides* (when the range is smallest). At the spring tides the pulls of sun and moon are in the same line; at the neaps, they make an angle of 90° with one another. Therefore the spring tides occur at full and new moon; the neaps, at the quarters. In a particular locality the tide may peak some time after the passage of the moon across the local meridian because of the inertia of the ocean waters and the variations of the local coastline.

Tides are not confined to the oceans: they occur in every body of water, in the atmosphere and also in the earth itself. Earth tides are not so large as the ocean tides, because the earth is essentially a solid elastic mass. Just as the moon raises tides on the earth, the earth raises tides on the moon.

The brightness of the moon

The moon has no light of its own, but shines by reflected light. The percentage of light reflected by the moon is known as its *albedo*. On the average the moon reflects only 7 per cent of the sunlight that falls vertically upon it. As there are many bright and dark areas on the moon, some areas reflect more light than this, and some less. All the light by which we see the moon comes from the sun, either directly or after reflection from the earth (*earthshine*). The surface of the earth is a much better reflector than that of the moon. The albedo of the earth can be found by measuring the brightness of earthshine and is found to be 35. This means that the earth reflects 35 per cent of the sunlight that falls on it, largely because its atmosphere contains so many clouds. Although the moon is the second brightest object in the sky, it sends us only two millionths as much light as the sun.

Temperature of the moon's surface

When it is midday on the moon, with the sun directly overhead, the temperature

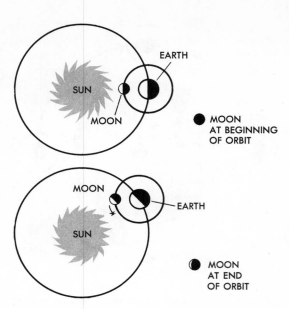

The synodic month. Top: as the moon moves around the earth, the earth moves around the sun. Bottom: by the time the moon has completed 1 orbit, the earth has moved along its orbit. Thus the moon is not between the sun and earth. It will take almost 2 more days before the moon is between the 2 bodies and we again have a new moon.

is 212° F.; at lunar midnight the temperature drops to about −240° F. This difference, so much greater than the temperature extremes known on earth between midday and midnight, is mainly due to the moon's lack of atmosphere. An atmosphere acts as a blanket and prevents excessive cooling and heating. It should also be remembered that the lunar day (interval between successive lunar midnights) is the time taken by the moon to make a complete rotation relative to the sun; it is therefore equal to 27⅓ of our days. The lunar surface therefore has longer intervals in which to heat up and cool down than does the surface of the earth in the course of a terrestrial day and night.

Direct evidence that the moon has no atmosphere is obtained by watching an *occultation,* that is, the passing of a star behind the moon. If the moon had an atmosphere, the star would fade gradually, but it always vanishes abruptly and reappears as abruptly at the moon's other edge.

It is not surprising that the moon has no appreciable atmosphere, because gravity at its surface is only one sixth of that at the surface of the earth, and this is not enough to retain most gases at its surface. Small amounts of gas have been seen to exude from certain points on the moon's surface, but they must have been quickly lost into space.

Topography of the moon

The largest features on the moon, and the only ones that can be readily seen with the naked eye, are the *maria*. They are darker than the rest of the surface, and are flat areas strewn with small boulders and pocked with craters. Many are surrounded by mountain ranges. The largest is Mare Imbrium, about seven hundred miles across. The Latin names of the *maria*, such as Mare Serenitatis, Mare Fecunditatis and Mare Tranquillitatis, were assigned in 1651 by the Italian astronomer Giovanni Riccioli. It is remarkable that all the *maria* but one are on the side of the moon facing the earth. Among the *maria*, the most curious is Mare Orientale, situated on the *limb* of the moon (the edge of the moon's disk) and surrounded by three great circular mountain ranges. It is generally thought that the *maria* are hardened lavas that were caused to flow by the impact of large bodies colliding with the moon.*

The moon's surface is very heavily pocked with *craters* of all sizes. They are circular, with raised rims, and some have central peaks. Many craters overlap with other craters, and may occur within the *maria* and on the mountain chains. Some craters appear to be filled with lava, others to be partially buried in dust flows. In the photographs of the great crater Aristarchus, both types of flow may be seen. Aristarchus has a central peak, and its floor seems to be filled with lava. The crater nearby is very shallow and has been nearly obliterated by a dust flow. A number of much smaller bowl-shaped craters dot the area.

Very large craters are often called "walled plains," because they enclose fairly level surfaces, which may be light in color, like the lunar uplands, or dark, like the *maria*. The crater wall, or rampart, is roughly circular and has often been designated as a circular mountain range.

Editor's note: Other authorities, however, believe the lavas flowed through the moon's own internal processes, much as on earth.

These close-up photographs of the lunar surface were taken by Apollo 11 astronaut Neil A. Armstrong. By studying these pictures, and the rocks themselves, scientists hope to gain an understanding of the processes that have shaped and modified the surface of the moon since its formation billions of years ago.

Photos, NASA

Left: a 2½-inch-long stone embedded in powdery surface material. The small, glazed pits on the stone's surface are thought to have been made by micrometeorite impact. Above: clumps of variously colored lunar-surface powder.

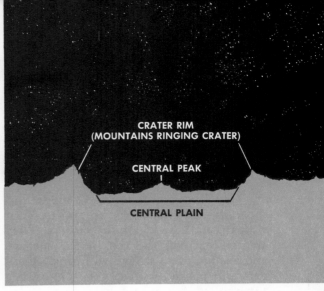

CRATER RIM
(MOUNTAINS RINGING CRATER)

CENTRAL PEAK

CENTRAL PLAIN

NASA

Left: the Schmidt crater, located at the western edge of Mare Tranquillitatis. It has a diameter of 7 miles. Right: cross section of a common type of crater. Mountains on its rim slope down gently on the outside, steeply on the inside. Smaller mountains may rise from the flat central plain.

However, the wall is often low in comparison with the surrounding land and even in comparison with the enclosed surface, or crater floor. The diameters of the largest craters reach nearly two hundred miles. Some craters, however, are very deep, so deep, in fact, that their bottoms are always in shadow. Still other craters are mere pits in the lunar surface, with little or no raised rim surrounding the central depression.

On the earth there are two major types of crater: the volcano and the impact crater. Volcanic craters have steep sides and often a central rise or knob. Crater Lake in Oregon is a good example. Impact craters, such as the Meteor Crater in Arizona and the Chubb Crater in Canada, are shallower relative to their diameters and do not usually possess central peaks. Impact craters can be very much larger than volcanic craters: the southeastern shore of Hudson Bay may be the remainder of a great impact crater.

Both types of crater can probably be recognized on the moon. There is little doubt that the moon's surface has been heavily bombarded by meteoritic bodies over a long period of time. This bombardment has probably produced not only a large percentage of the craters but also the *maria*. The great dust splash extending halfway around the moon from the huge crater Tycho is clear evidence that it is an impact crater. A large impact crater usually has many small impact craters near it, which were probably formed by the debris thrown out by the original impact. The boulders found in the vicinity of impact craters have a similar origin.

A possible example of a volcanic crater on the moon is Aristarchus. Many small changes have been recorded near it, and quite possibly gases emerge from it on occasion. It has a pronounced central peak and what appears to be a lava-filled floor.

Lunar *rays* are lunar features that extend radially outward from certain craters such as Tycho and Copernicus. They appear lighter than the surrounding terrain principally because they reflect light better. This is probably because they are made of very finely divided particles. The reflectivity of particles depends largely on their average size, finer particles reflecting light more brilliantly under vertical illumination than coarse ones.

Rills are narrow, riverlike valleys made visible by shadows cast into them. They may be cracks in the surface, or possibly canyons formed by ash flow from volcanoes. Some are twisted and tortuous, and some are associated with chains of craters. Some of the straight rills seem to be associated with settling phenomena around the *maria*. Others may have been furrowed by boulders rolling downhill.

The *mountains* of the moon form large, rugged chains principally concentrated around the *maria*. Their heights can be measured by the length of the shadows which they cast; the highest, the Leibnitz Mountains, attain a height of 26,000 feet. In proportion to the diameter of its parent body, this is really higher than Mt. Everest on earth (29,000 feet). Heights on the moon are measured relative to a nearby low-lying area on its surface, whereas heights on earth are measured with respect to sea level, a height about halfway between highest and lowest points on the earth's surface. Lunar mountains seem to have been thrust up as a result of impact rather than formed by folding of rocks as has been the case with many mountains on the earth.

A mountainous feature known as the Straight Wall, in the Mare Nubium, south of the lunar equator, appears to be a 60-mile-long line of cliffs produced by faulting. A gigantic crack in the lunar surface has caused the development of a cliff face 800 feet high.

Naming the features on the moon

When the telescope was first turned on the moon, the principal *maria* and mountain chains were named by early observers. The *maria* were given fanciful Latin names, and many mountain chains were called after well-known mountains of Europe. Since that time, advances in observational techniques have revealed more and more detail, and thousands of features have been named. The International Astronomical Union now has the responsibility for assigning names, a task that has been enormously increased by the recent observations of the far side of the moon. Major craters have been named most usually after astronomers or scientists, but other prominent individuals, such as Jules Verne, a nineteenth-century author, and Plato, a Greek philosopher, have also been commemorated.

Origin and history of the moon

The history of the moon is bound up with the history of the whole solar system, which is believed, from several independent estimates, to be about 4,500,000,000 years old. There are two principal theories concerning the origin of the moon. The first considers that the moon was once part of the earth and was separated from the earth either by tidal forces or by the gravitational attraction of a passing star. It was drawn out from that gap in the earth's crust that is now filled by

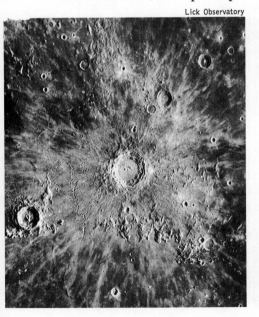

Lick Observatory

Left: the crater Copernicus. The bright streaks radiating from the crater are rays. Scientists believe these rays consist of finely divided, highly reflective particles which may be debris thrown out of the crater at the time it was formed.

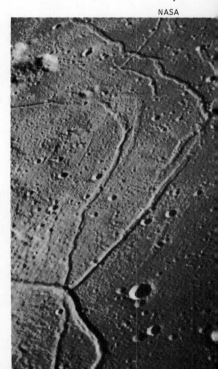

NASA

Right: rills such as these are cracks in the lunar surface. Some are very tortuous, like meandering rivers; others are quite straight. Their origin is in dispute: some scientists believe they were formed by ash flows from volcanoes; other scientists believe they were formed by water; still others think the rills were formed by the collapse of lava tunnels.

the Pacific Ocean, according to one important view.*

The second theory assumes that the earth and the moon were formed at about the same time from the agglomeration of cold material then circulating about the sun. Similar processes are invoked for the origins of the other planets and their satellites. In the first theory, it is assumed that the original material was hot, and formed bodies that are now cooling. The second, on the other hand, pictures the formation of the earth, the moon and the other bodies of the solar system from cold materials, some of which are now heating up as a consequence of internal pressure and radioactivity.**

According to the second hypothesis, the moon is about as old as the earth — about 4,500,000,000 years. But no doubt the lunar features vary in age, just as earth features do. That the moon at one time during its history underwent extensive development can be seen by a mere glance at its face. Close observation of the moon since the invention of the telescope has revealed very few signs of anything much happening there in recent times. However, signs of volcanic activity and perhaps radioactive glows seem to indicate that the moon is not really such a dead world after all. The present topography, plus the damage that has apparently been inflicted on its features, certainly means that a lot did happen to the moon in the past.

If the moon once did have an atmosphere and running water, as some authorities believe, then a history somewhat like the earth's must have taken place until air and water vanished. But despite such an event, erosion is still possible on an airless globe. Alternate extreme heating and chilling of rock will crack and flake it. Collisions with asteroids and meteorites pulverize the surface and perhaps release

volcanic forces. Movements and sliding of rock masses down slopes will cause damage. Even the strong radiation from space may disrupt the lunar crust. There certainly is plenty of detritus, as satellite investigations show. The accumulated ravages of countless centuries of small-scale erosion look impressive. So much so, that persons are tempted to attribute them to tremendous catastrophes, as was the fashion with regard to spectacular earth features in the early days of geologic study. Nevertheless, because of the slow pace of erosion on the moon, experts tend to agree that the moon preserves many ancient features that have long since vanished on the earth.

Lunar exploration by satellite

Artificial earth satellites have added a new dimension to the study of the moon. The first satellite to circle the moon in 1959 sent back pictures of the far side. Later satellites (the Ranger series) took close-up pictures of the lunar surface in much greater detail than had ever been possible from the earth, transmitting their pictures until the last instant before impact. Soft landings made by the Surveyor series permitted probing of the lunar surface, and showed that much of the moon is covered with granular, sandlike material. These probes indicated that the moon's surface was firm enough for exploration by manned vehicles.

Lunar Orbiters have photographed in fine detail every portion of the lunar surface, both near and far sides. They have also provided additional data, from analyses of the perturbations of their orbits, concerning the internal structure of the moon. From the analysis thus obtained, it has been verified that the moon is not a perfect sphere, but bulges toward the earth, as had earlier been suspected from studies of lunar motion.

Conditions for the lunar explorer

The view of the moon, as described by Apollo astronauts, gives us an idea of what the lunar explorers encounter. The moon presents a forbidding landscape in

* *Editor's note:* Recent evidence tends to discount the view that the Pacific Ocean basin was the moon's birthplace. It seems the moon has been the earth's companion for many hundreds of millions and perhaps billions of years. At such an early time, there was no Pacific Ocean as we understand it today, especially in light of the possibility that the continents have been drifting around the earth's surface in various directions for countless centuries.
** *Editor's note:* A third theory states that the moon is a former planet that was captured by the earth.

BIRTH OF THE MOON: THREE BASIC THEORIES

EARTH

1 — According to one theory, the moon was once part of the earth. It was separated from the earth by tidal forces or by the gravitational attraction of a passing star. This happened billions of years ago.

MOON

2 — Another theory assumes that the earth and the moon were formed at about the same time from the agglomeration of gas, dust and other particles then circulating about the sun.

3 — The third theory suggests that the moon was formed somewhere else in the solar system. As it passed near the earth, it was captured by the earth's gravity.

MOON

EARTH

various shades of gray. No color enlivens the landscape; even the sky is black. Without an atmosphere there can be no wind, no rain and no weather. There can be no sound, and no living things. In the sunshine the temperature is that of boiling water, but without the blanket of an atmosphere, a step into the shadow brings one to a temperature far below freezing. There are no beautiful sky colors at sunset and sunrise, and no twilight. Like the blue sky, these earthly beauties depend on our atmosphere, and on an airless body they are simply absent.

For these reasons a lunar explorer needs protection, not only against lack of air, but against extremes of temperature. Equally important, he must be protected against the incessant bombardment by cosmic and other rays and particles, and the effects of ultraviolet radiation. On the earth we are shielded from the deleterious effects of strong solar and cosmic rays by our atmosphere and the earth's magnetic field. But the lunar explorer has no such natural protection: the moon is without an atmosphere and has an extremely weak magnetic field.

Since gravity at the moon's surface is $\frac{1}{6}$ that on the earth, all weights on the moon are diminished by a factor of 6. A man who weighed 180 pounds on earth would weigh about 30 pounds on the moon, and with the same muscular effort would be able to jump 6 times as high or lift 6 times as great a weight as on earth. This compensates to some extent for the weight of the equipment that he has to carry to protect himself from the severe conditions. Similarly the launching of a rocket from the surface of the moon would require only $\frac{1}{6}$ of the thrust required to launch the same rocket from the earth's surface. This makes the return journey of an astronaut from the moon and its vicinity easier.

In some cases, his diminished weight works to the disadvantage of the lunar explorer. This occurs if he uses his weight to operate a lever or use a shovel.

Complete weightlessness is experienced by astronauts in flight, and techniques have been developed to combat the problems involved. All our natural functions are conditioned by our normal gravitational environment, as are the operations of many instruments that must be used in such explorations.

The earth as seen from the moon

A man standing on the moon sees the earth as a disk 2½ times the size of the moon seen from the earth. Because of its high albedo, the surface of the earth has 5 times as much reflecting power as the surface of the moon. Also, because of its greater apparent size, the full earth sends about 31 times as much light to the lunar observer as the full moon sends to us. To him our clouds look brilliantly white, the oceans dark blue, and the continents almost uniformly purplish brown.

Because the moon and earth are gravitationally locked, a lunar observer does not see the earth rise or set. If he is on the near side of the moon, the earth is always visible, and if he is on the far side of the moon, he cannot see the earth at all.

When the observer on the moon is at lunar midnight, he sees a "full earth," completely illuminated, unless the moon is directly in line between sun and earth. In that case he observes an eclipse of the earth by the moon at the same time when earth observers see a solar eclipse. When the observer is at lunar midday, and the sun is directly behind the earth, he observes "new earth." If the sun is completely eclipsed by the earth, the earth would be seen surrounded by a bright halo caused by the sunlight scattered in the earth's atmosphere. Conditions for such an eclipse are very similar to those for a solar eclipse seen from the earth, but the track of totality on the moon would be 2½ times as wide. Because the apparent size of the earth is so much larger than that of the sun when seen from the moon, a lunar observer can never witness the beautiful solar corona or Baily's beads, which are such striking features of a total solar eclipse for us. Even if the apparent size of the earth were small enough to cover the solar disk as does the moon, the earth's atmosphere would inhibit the formation of either the "diamond ring" or Baily's beads, since these also depend largely on the fact that the moon has no atmosphere.*

Like the moon seen from the earth, the earth seen from the moon passes from "new earth" through crescent, gibbous and full phases, and back again to "new earth." These changes take the same time as the corresponding changes in the moon seen from the earth, and run through a full cycle in one lunation.

The moon as an observing station

From the point of view of the astronomer, the moon would be an ideal site for a telescope. The useful size of telescopes on earth is limited on the one hand by our atmosphere, which blurs optical images and limits the kinds of light waves reaching the earth. On the other hand, the engineering problems presented by the construction and operation of large and heavy instruments in the gravitational field of the earth are formidable. In the absence of an atmosphere, the detail that a telescope can record is limited only by the optical properties of the instrument. The smaller value of gravity on the moon would make it possible to operate larger instruments than are feasible on the earth. A lunar observing period for optical instruments would be a half month long, followed by a similar period in sunlight. Weather would never interfere with observing schedules, but instruments would have to be well protected to withstand the lunar extremes of temperature. Many advantages of lunar-based telescopes are shared by orbiting telescopes, which would not only be in a situation of reduced gravity, but actually of weightlessness. Such orbiting satellites would also be free from any atmosphere.

* *Editor's note:* Baily's beads are the blobs of light produced by the rough surface of the moon as it passes across the sun's disk. They are caused by sunlight shining through lunar valleys and peaks along the edge of the moon's disk. The "diamond ring" is a great ring, or halo, of sunlight that appears momentarily when the moon covers the solar disk during an eclipse. It reappears briefly just as the moon begins to "leave" the sun, on the opposite side of the solar disk. When such a solar eclipse is observed from the moon, earth-based observers witness a lunar eclipse.

Souvenir from the moon: a large microbreccia. This is a rock composed of fragmental material. Note the glass-lined pits on the rock's surface.

NASA

THE LUNAR ROCKS*

Scientists Report Exciting Discoveries

BY PATRICK YOUNG

SELENE, the moon goddess of ancient Greece, is a very old lady — at least 4.6 billion (4,600,000,000) years. Yet men still argue over her harsh and aged beauty. The moon, it seems, still retains much of its mystery.

Scientists gathered for four days in January 1970 to offer some explanations and theories of the lady's mysterious face and features. It was the National Aeronautics and Space Administration's (NASA) first lunar-science conference, and the more than 850 scientists heard detailed reports on the lunar rocks and soil collected in July 1969 by Apollo 11 astronauts Neil Armstrong and Edwin "Buzz" Aldrin during man's first moon landing.

And they puzzled and argued as well over what the scientific finds meant in terms of the moon's internal composition, its geological history, and its origin.

Many discoveries

The scientists heard, among many significant discoveries, that:

* Reprinted by permission from *The National Observer*, January 12, 1970

● The moon is at least 4.6 billion years old, and the lava flow that forms the Sea of Tranquility, where Neil Armstrong landed the lunar module *Eagle,* is about 3.6 billion years old. The oldest rock found at Tranquility Base was formed 4.4 billion years ago, 1 billion years before the oldest-known earth rock.

● The lunar topsoil, or regolith, in the immediate vicinity of Tranquility Base ranges in depth from 10 to 18 feet. Readings from seismometers left by both the Apollo 11 and 12 crews indicate that beneath this topsoil, at least in the relatively smooth lunar seas, there is a layer of enormous boulders and rocky rubble to a depth of at least 12 miles.

● The lunar surface at Tranquility Base was extremely hot 3.6 billion years ago, a minimum of 2,160° Fahrenheit, and this molten mass extended as deep as 62 miles. The heating may have come from deep inside the moon, or resulted from a huge meteor smashing onto the surface; the scientists disagreed on the cause.

● No lunar water was found in the lunar samples, nor any indication that some form of life once existed on the lunar surface. "If NASA wants to put a permanent base on the moon, they better cart all the water up on their backs, because they aren't going to find any," predicted Dr. Gordon G. Goles of the University of Oregon in Eugene.

• At least 68 of the 92 natural elements present on earth, and probably all, definitely exist on the moon. Scientists identified over 30 minerals in the lunar samples; more than 2,000 are known on earth. Three of these minerals are not found naturally on earth, nor are they regarded as valuable.

• Precious minerals such as gold and silver do exist, but in "small quantities." "The amount is much too small to finance the space program," said Dr. Edward Anders of the University of Chicago. One scientist reported finding small rubies in one of the core samples taken by Buzz Aldrin. About 98 per cent of the gold on the lunar surface apparently comes from meteorites that strike the moon.

• Meteorites fall on the moon at an average rate of 1,000 tons a year and make up about 2 per cent of the lunar soil. Carbon meteorites are the most common on the moon, and apparently in the universe.

• Glass beads, formed at high temperatures, were found mixed in the lunar soil. Many of these are pitted and scarred by ancient gas bubbles and meteorite impacts. "Some of the moon samples look like golf balls," said Dr. Joseph V. Smith of the University of Chicago.

• Studies of solar particles trapped in lunar rocks show that the pattern of the sun's solar flares and sunspots has been the same for several million years. "That doesn't, perhaps, surprise anyone, but this is the first direct experimental evidence that this is true," said Dr. James R. Arnold of the University of California at San

Left: a crater on the surface of a glass bead. The crater was probably caused by a micrometeorite. Meteorites hit the moon at an average rate of 1,000 tons a year and make up about 2 per cent of the lunar soil. (Photograph enlarged 100 times actual size.)

NASA

General Electric

Right: by etching fragments of lunar material, scientists have discovered that the rocks are riddled with tracks left by cosmic rays, charged particles that bombard the moon from outer space. The arrow points to a typical cosmic ray track.

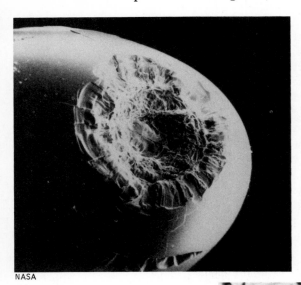

Diego. Added Dr. Robert M. Walker of Washington University in St. Louis: "One of the interesting features of the moon is that it preserves the history of the sun. This makes it possible to study the history of the sun almost to the formation of the solar system."

• Laser beams bounced off a reflector left at Tranquility Base have measured the distance of the moon from the earth, which varies more than 31,000 miles over a month's time, to within one foot of accuracy. Prelaser measurements were accurate to within one quarter of a mile.

• Preliminary analysis, conducted by scientists at NASA's Lunar Receiving Laboratory, indicates that the 45 moon rocks returned by Apollo 12's crew are generally younger than the Apollo 11 samples. However, at least one rock from the Sea of Storms dates back 4.6 billion years. "Maybe what we are learning is that the moon has been a geologically active body with several periods of lava flows," said Dr. Anders. NASA began handing samples of Apollo 12 lunar material to scientists for detailed investigation early in February 1970.

The Apollo 11 findings are based on studies made of 17.6 pounds of lunar rocks and dust, divided among 142 scientific teams in the United States and 8 foreign countries. Each team received only tiny samples. Dr. Gerald J. Wasserburg of the California Institute of Technology in Pasadena drew an understanding laugh when he spoke of his group's "wanton destruction of two grams of lunar material."

A small fragment from a moon rock designated number 17 posed an unexpected problem for Dr. Arnold and his colleagues of the University of California. They first had to determine which part of the rock had lain exposed on the lunar surface before they could conduct their studies of solar particles.

One morning Dr. Arnold found a note on his desk parodying the television show *Mission: Impossible*: "Your mission, Jim, should you decide to accept it, is to find the surface of rock 17. This rock will self-destruct in 78 days."

Photographs taken with a scanning electron microscope. Above: this lunar fragment has been enlarged 3,300 times. Note the dust fragments on its surface. Below: a glassy spherule, enlarged 6,600 times. The spherule's shape indicates that it underwent prior melting. It may have been created when a meteorite hit the moon, melting lunar material and splashing it long distances.

Both photos, General Electric

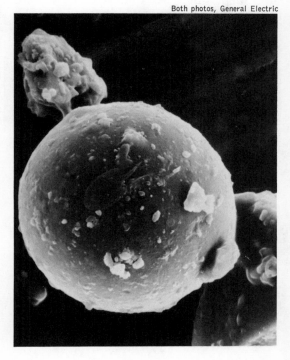

A rich lode of information

A sense of excitement and a sense of history pervaded the meeting. They existed among the men who presented the results of their investigations and among those who came to listen and learn as well. Many expressed the feeling, too, that the lode of information was too rich to digest in a few days or even weeks.

"I really wish that NASA would let us have a three-month moratorium on experiments and let us closet ourselves in our offices and read the 147 papers that have come out of this meeting," one scientist said.

There was surprisingly close agreement on many of the detailed findings presented, such as the presence and percentage of the various elements found in the lunar samples. But many investigators offered their raw data without discussion or explanations for their findings, and some expressed outright bemusement.

The reports certainly did not settle the fundamental questions of how the moon was formed; whether it has a molten core as does earth; and whether the lunar craters were formed by volcanic action or the impact of meteors. This was not surprising. As one researcher said, "We have only sampled, only scratched the surface of the moon."

Dr. M. Gene Simmons of the Massachusetts Institute of Technology, who doubles as chief scientist at NASA's Manned Spacecraft Center, was asked which major lunar theories had been solidly interred by the Apollo 11 findings. "It is almost certain," he replied solemnly, "that the moon is not made of green cheese."

Nevertheless, some scientists viewed the amassed data and reached strikingly opposite views on the same subject. The tektite-origin controversy is one example.

Tektites are 700,000-year-old glassy stones found strewn across earth in a giant pattern from southern Africa to the Philippines. Some theorists argue that the tektites were, by some mechanism, flung through space from the lunar surface to rain down upon earth. Others say their origin is terrestrial.

Dr. John O'Keefe III of NASA's Goddard Space Flight Center in Greenbelt, Maryland, supports the first theory. "If they come from the moon, which I rather think the evidence was helpful on, then they have to come from something like a lunar volcano," he said in one discussion. "I've made a few computations and that looks reasonable."

Dr. O'Keefe's view, however, got a blunt rejection from Dr. Robert N. Clayton of the University of Chicago's Enrico Fermi Institute. "We see nothing coming to the earth from the moon," he said.

There were some phenomena mentioned here that seemed, at times, tossed out to provoke discussion. Thomas Gold, astronomer from Cornell University, pinpointed one such lunar mystery.

Dr. Gold noted that the lunar surface is composed of soft material and that the pattern of many rocks shows they have been ejected from craters. "There can be no question that at the time they fell that each of these objects would have left a substantial scar in this soft material into which it fell," he said.

But there is no visual evidence: no shallow trench as when a stone is thrown into soft beach sand; no tiny mound of material in front of the rocks.

"It is absolutely clear that a process has taken place on the surface which fills in the trench and takes away the piled-up dust that it must have caused," Dr. Gold said. "And yet, even for rocks that are only two inches above the moon surface, the tops are absolutely clean. Now that process, we don't understand. But it is there." Other scientists saw a simple answer. Meteorites striking the surface over millions of years, they argued, could fill the trenches, smooth out piled-up dust, and clean off the rocks' tops.

The Apollo 11 moon material has provided some interesting answers and posed even more interesting questions. "When we come back for the next conference," says Dr. Smith of the University of Chicago, "I think we will find some basic changes in our thinking about the moon."

THE MOON AND ITS ROCKS

In 1969, man first set foot on another heavenly body. He returned to earth with priceless treasures: rocks, soil, glasslike beads. On these pages are close-ups of some of these magnificent lunar souvenirs.

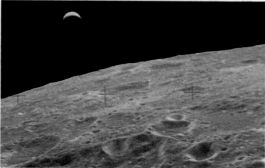

All photos NASA

This colorful microsection of an igneous rock contains three minerals: clinopyroxene (colored areas), plagioclase (grayish areas) and ilmenite (black areas).

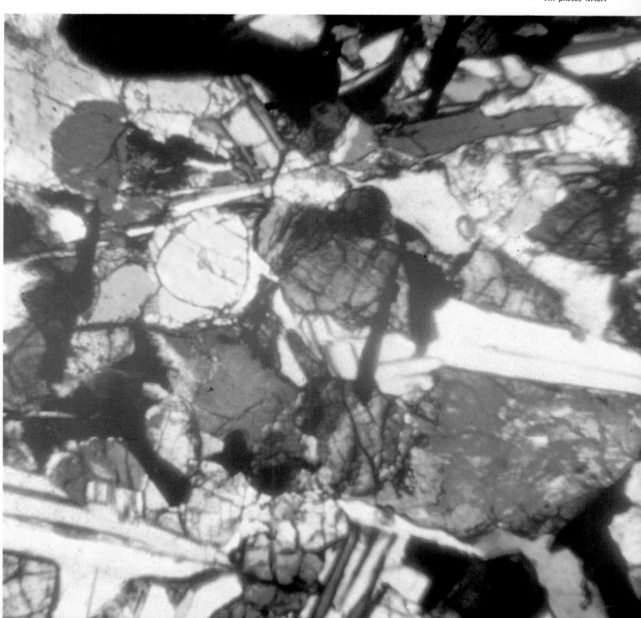

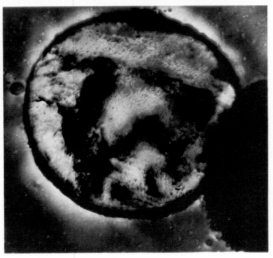

Close-up of a lunar rock. At least one specimen brought back by the astronauts is 4,600,000,000 years old, thus apparently dating back to the formation of the solar system.

Right: The colors in these two thin sections of lunar rock are caused by the interaction of polarized light with the crystalline structure of the various minerals. Each color usually represents a different mineral.

Below: In this sample, the yellow and reddish orange mineral is pyroxene, the black is ilmenite and the whitish blue is plagioclase (a type of feldspar).

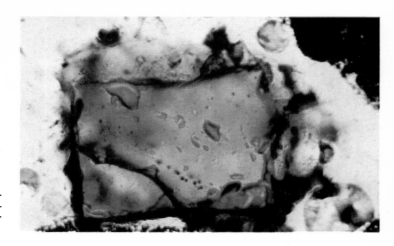

Right: Photomicrographs of thin sections are used to identify the minerals in the rocks and to study their crystalline structures.

Below: A microscopic view of glass spherules found in lunar soil. Scientists believe these beads were formed under extremely high temperatures, perhaps as a result of meteorite impacts.

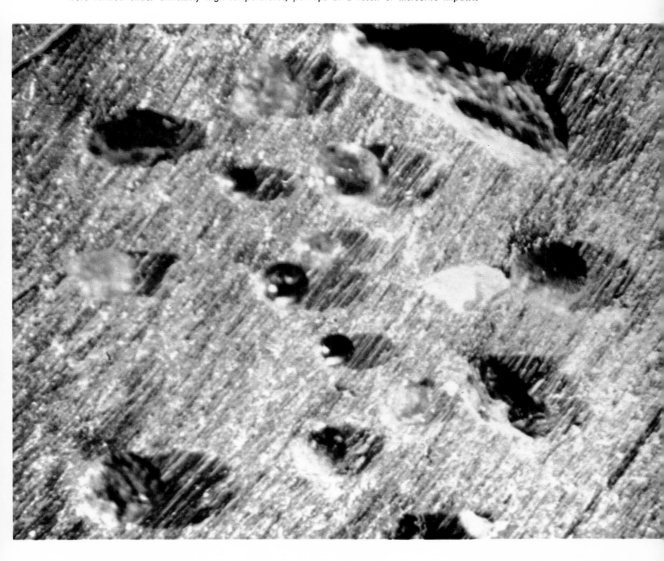

Right: Undisturbed lunar sediment, photographed as a core tube is opened. The material resembles silty sand, with scattered rock fragments, glass spherules and highly reflective aggregates of glass.

Below: Examining a moon rock at the Manned Spacecraft Center's Lunar Receiving Laboratory in Houston, Texas. Traces of gold and three new minerals were found in the Apollo 11 specimens.

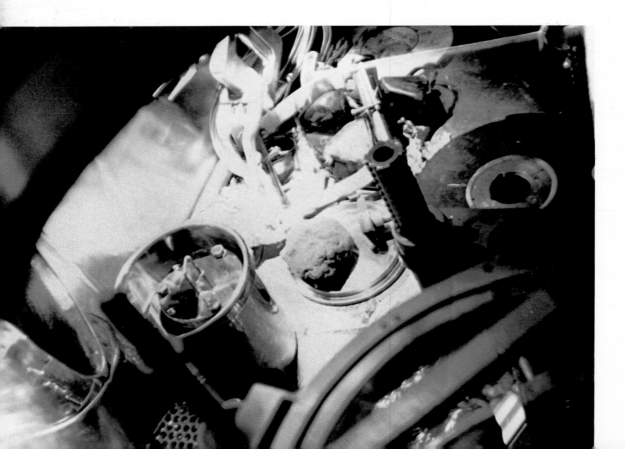

DARKNESS AT NOON

Millions Watch Solar Eclipse

Photos, NASA

The series of five photographs taken by U. S. satellite ATS 3 shows the moon's shadow (predominant dark spot among the clouds) moving northeastward across the earth. Below: the March 1970 eclipse as seen at Miahuatlan, Mexico. The moon totally blocked out the sun for 3 minutes, 28 seconds.

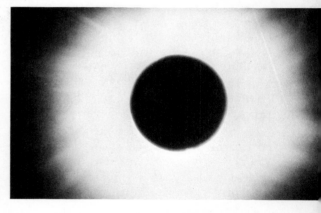

"ZEUS, the father of the Olympic Gods, turned midday into night, hiding the light of the dazzling Sun; and sore fear came upon men."

So wrote the Greek poet Archilochus in the seventh century B.C. Today a solar eclipse rarely inspires fear in mankind; men know that the light of the sun is hidden not by an angry god but by the moon as it comes between the earth and the sun.

The fear has been replaced by curiosity — and the realization that a total eclipse provides a unique opportunity to study various scientific phenomena. What causes sudden changes in the solar radiation received by the earth? How is the temperature of the earth's atmosphere affected? How do animals react to the sudden twilight?

On March 7, 1970, a total solar eclipse was visible in an 85-mile-wide path from the mid-Pacific, across southern Mexico, along the East Coast of the United States and in the Atlantic east of Canada's Maritime Provinces. The moon's shadow raced over the surface of the earth at about 1,500 miles per hour. Thus, at any one place, the total eclipse lasted only 2 to 3 minutes. Scientists had spent hundreds of hours preparing to collect data during these few minutes.

Most of the experiments sponsored by NASA observed eclipse effects on the earth's atmosphere and ionosphere. The highlight of the NASA studies was the launching of 31 sounding rockets from Wallops Station, Virginia. These carried out investigations in 3 areas: meteorology, solar physics and ionospheric physics. The information obtained by the rockets

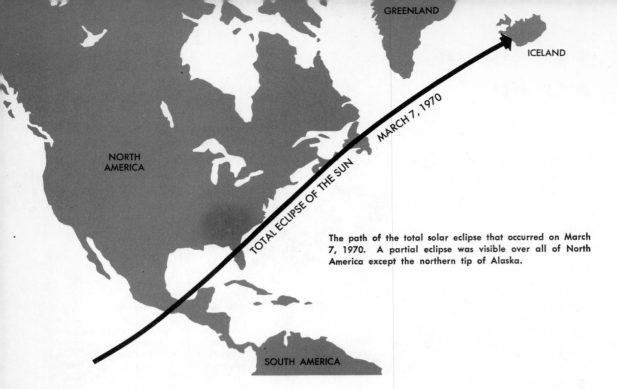

GREENLAND

ICELAND

NORTH AMERICA

MARCH 7, 1970

TOTAL ECLIPSE OF THE SUN

SOUTH AMERICA

The path of the total solar eclipse that occurred on March 7, 1970. A partial eclipse was visible over all of North America except the northern tip of Alaska.

is being compared with data from ground observations made in Virginia and near Oaxaca, Mexico.

Seven NASA spacecraft also transmitted data on the eclipse. These included Mariner 6, which was 235 million miles from earth — on the opposite side of the sun.

In Georgia's Okefenokee Swamp, scientists observed the eclipse's effect on the "local inhabitants": raccoons, birds, foxes and so on. As the light faded, the temperature in the swamp dropped, and the barometric pressure rose slightly. The raccoons settled down to sleep; the foxes began cleaning themselves; and mosquitoes began biting "just as they do at dusk," said biologist Andrew J. Olsen of the Fernbank Science Center in Atlanta, Georgia.

Near Oaxaca, Mexico, Drs. Arcadio Poveda and Manuel Mendez of the National University of Mexico tried to repeat experiments done during a 1919 eclipse; if successful they would confirm Einstein's theory of general relativity.

Hundreds of astronomers from around the world set up experiments in the Oaxaca area. The site was favored by scientists because the total eclipse lasted

3 minutes and 28 seconds: the longest along the eclipse's land path. Scientists from Kitt Peak National Observatory in Arizona photographed the border between the sun's chromosphere (its lower atmosphere) and the corona (the sun's outer, or upper, atmosphere); they hoped to learn why the corona has such an extremely high temperature (1 million degrees or more). Other observers recorded polarization variations within the corona. The expedition from the Soviet Union used a radio interferometer to measure solar radio emissions. They hoped to determine which emissions originated from sunspots.

The inhabitants of this rugged region are Zapotec Indians. Their lives are far different from those of the highly educated, worldly scientists who invaded their villages. Most were curious and enthusiastic about the visitors and the eclipse that brought them to Mexico. But among some of the Zapotecs, old superstitions remain, and the eclipse was a bad omen. As darkness came to Oaxaca, some individuals probably agreed with the sentiments expressed in Homer's *Odyssey:* "And full of ghosts is the porch and full the court, and the Sun has perished out of heaven, and an evil mist hovers over all."

SCIENCE REDISCOVERS GRAVITY*

Suddenly,
an Exciting Frontier
of Research

BY TOM ALEXANDER

The Granger Collection

Sir Isaac Newton (1642–1727) proved that the natural force that causes apples to fall from a tree also holds the planets in their orbits.

IT PROBABLY was not a fish, a wise observer once remarked, that first noticed the existence of water. With somewhat the same kind of obliviousness to what is present all around him, man has paid rather little attention to the convenient gravitational arrangements whereby he keeps his feet on the ground. Gravity was a major preoccupation, to be sure, in the brilliant seventeenth-century awakening of physical science, culminating in the work of Sir Isaac Newton. But with the conspicuous exception of Albert Einstein, the great scientists of subsequent generations found

* Reprinted from the December 1969 issue of *Fortune* magazine by special permission; © 1969 Time Inc.

little new to say about gravity. In this century, Einstein's work aside, fundamental physics has primarily focused upon the domain of the very small — molecules, atoms and elementary particles — where the influence of gravity is negligible. For many years gravity research was left largely to amateur theorizers and antigravity buffs, plus a smaller body of theorists in general relativity. But just in the past few years all this has changed. Almost suddenly, gravity has become an exciting frontier of science. One consequence is a notable migration of other types of scientists and graduate students into the fields of astronomy, astrophysics, cosmology and relativity research.

Radio telescopes are among the most important tools of astronomers. This giant parabolic dish — one type of radio telescope — is at Arecibo, Puerto Rico.

Cornell University

That advances in technology depend upon advances in science is an oft-noted truth, but the reverse also holds. The new interest in gravitation stems from new means of probing further into gravity's special domain, the domain of the very large. In recent years, sensitive electronic detectors and high-altitude probes have greatly broadened the spectrum of observation into the radio, infrared, ultraviolet, X-ray and gamma-ray regions. It turns out that the old astronomy's optical telescopes furnished deceptively placid pictures of our universe: the new "full-color" views show it to be much more dynamic and mysterious than was ever suspected. Most of this newly detected dynamism appears to be the work of gravity.

Great waves from unknown sources

The first of the startling new mysteries, discovered by radio astronomers in 1963, were the "quasi-stellar sources," or "quasars." Quasars are astronomical objects that appear to be so far away and yet to radiate so intensely across the void as to persuade astronomers that utterly unfamiliar processes must be involved in the production of their energy. Then, a few years later, came the discovery of "pulsars": other starlike radio sources that flashed on and off at intervals approaching the precision of the best clocks on earth.

Most astrophysicists now think that both quasars and pulsars involve some manifestation of a phenomenon called "gravitational collapse."

More recently still have come reports, still controversial, that actual waves of gravitational radiation are sweeping over the earth from mighty but previously undetected events in space. If the evidence can be believed, it suggests that grand-scale destruction of matter is taking place at a rate so rapid as to raise questions about how our galaxy can still endure.

Gravity is 1 of the 4 elementary forces that, physicists say, account for all of the known phenomena in nature. Two of them, gravity and electromagnetism, are familiar in everyday manifestations; the other 2, the so-called "strong" and "weak" forces, operate only inside the atom. Improbable as it may seem to anyone who has ever taken a hard fall or dropped a heavy object on his foot, gravity is by far the weakest of the 4 forces.

The most powerful is the straightforwardly named strong force, which holds together the particles making up atomic nuclei. In some way not understood, it also probably determines the nature and size of these particles themselves. Next in strength is electromagnetism, about a hundredth as strong as the strong force. The most important role of electromagnetism in our world is to confine the negatively charged electrons in their complex orbital patterns around the positively charged nucleus. These patterns determine most of the properties of matter, such as hardness, color and chemical behavior; hence the world of ordinary experience is largely shaped by electromagnetic force. Next in descending order of strength is the weak force, which appears to play a role at both the nuclear and atomic levels, modifying the behavior of the first 2 forces and causing radioactive decay. The weak force is only a trillionth as strong as electromagnetism. But feeble as it is, the weak force is still a trillion trillion trillion times stronger than gravity.

In view of gravity's weakness, it seems contradictory that the vast universe is shaped largely by this force. For all their immensely greater strength in their own spheres of action, the other 3 elementary forces are subject to severe limitations that do not apply to gravity. The strong and weak forces, as noted, have very short range: they are confined to the atom, to the world of the very small. Electromagnetism has infinite range, but it rarely intrudes its full might into our visible world. Since the number of negative electric charges here on earth equals the number of positive charges, the two kinds of charge tend to cancel each other at dimensions larger than the atom. Gravity, too, is a force of infinite range, and so far as anyone knows it is never canceled out by anything. It is quite unlike the other forces in that its effectiveness accumulates as larger and larger masses are involved. In the world of the very large, therefore, gravity rules. It has the whole universe for a kingdom.

Arena of the forces

Some scientists suspect that gravity is a more fundamental aspect of nature than the other forces. John A. Wheeler, a physicist-cosmologist and eminent teacher at Princeton, remarks that gravity is "a kind of master field. It creates the arena in which all the other forces live and move and have their being."

Everything in nature both exerts gravitation and is affected by it, not only all forms of matter but all forms of energy as well. The relationship between energy and gravitation emerges from Einstein's theory of relativity. It means, for instance, that if you wind a watch, the wound watch will be infinitesimally heavier — and hence will exert more gravitational force — than an unwound watch, because of the energy stored in the mainspring in the form of electromagnetic pressure between atoms. To use another illustration, the application of force (or energy) to an object to increase its speed also increases its mass (or weight). The effect is unimpressive — for practical purposes, indeed, it is negligible — until the speed becomes a significant fraction of the speed of light. But at the speed of light itself, the mass of any object would be infinite. Again, the added mass due to increased speed is "real" mass in the sense that it exerts additional gravitational pull on other objects.

Mass is the only property of matter that makes any gravitational difference — the more mass, the more gravity. But mass is also the measure of an object's inertia, or resistance to being moved by force. Since the gravitational force acting upon any object is precisely proportional to that object's mass (and therefore to its inertia), gravity accelerates all bodies equally, no matter what their mass. This proportional relationship between gravity and mass and between mass and inertia — the "principle of equivalence," it is called — was recognized in the seventeenth century, by Galileo and Newton among others, but no one grasped its full significance until Einstein made it a basis for his theory of general relativity, which he proposed in 1916.

Earlier, in 1905, he had proposed his theory of special relativity, which basically excluded from consideration both gravity and inertia, and dealt only with bodies in uniform motion, where there is no acceleration and therefore no need to consider inertia. General relativity is simultaneously a theory about gravity and an at-

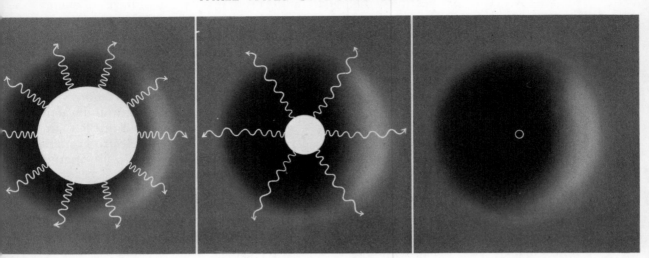

THREE FATES OF DYING STARS

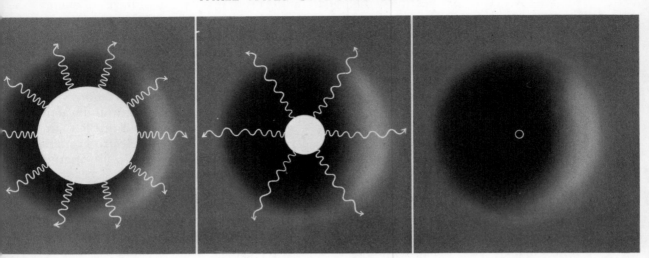

Any star must eventually burn up by thermonuclear fusion and undergo gravitational collapse. Theorists predict various possible "deaths" for stars, depending on their mass. Smallish stars — roughly the size of our own sun — will collapse only as far as the white-dwarf stage, where repulsion forces between electrons halt the collapse (left above). The entire mass is concentrated into a sphere the size of the earth. In the illustration, the depression surrounding the star is meant to represent the space "curvature" caused by the star's gravity.

A larger star will continue to collapse until its atoms are compressed into neutrons (middle). The neutron star's gravitational field will be so powerful that light waves and other radiation must struggle to escape, the result being a shift to lower frequencies, as indicated by the wiggly lines.

With a still larger star, the collapse proceeds farther resulting, according to theory, in a "black hole" (far right). In this strange outcome, matter utterly disappears, leaving its gravitational field behind as a permanent pit of curved space. The star also leaves behind a kind of relativistic ghost of itself, indicated by the white circle — the "gravitational radius." Within this radius, the field is so strong that light and other energy can never emerge. From just outside the radius, a small amount of energy will, in theory, continue to leak away forever.

tempt to extend special relativity to encompass accelerated motion. Though it has never suffered an experimental defeat, general relativity has far less evidence to back it up than special relativity (which has achieved almost the status of a law of nature), mainly because the weakness of the gravitational force makes experimentation difficult. The peculiarities of general relativity are evident only when immensely powerful concentrations of gravitation are present.

Pulsars, quasars and the sources of gravitational waves, most astrophysicists suspect, do involve great concentrations of gravity. Hence these phenomena may eventually provide a laboratory for the testing of general relativity. By the same token, scientists know that they will need general-relativity theory (or one of the variations that have been proposed) in try-

ing to grasp what is taking place. Comments physicist Kip S. Thorne of the California Institute of Technology: "In our solar system, for instance, general relativity's deviations from Newtonian nature are usually less than one part in a million. But in the case of things like the sources of gravitational radiation, general relativity is the entire story. If you use Newtonian theory, you're just 100 per cent wrong."

Round and round in the pit

The mind's propensity to invent new "forces" to explain phenomena it doesn't understand has littered the history of science with superseded notions. An example is the centrifugal "force" of repulsion, which Newton explained away as merely the tendency of moving objects to follow straight rather than curved paths.

The force that Einstein explained away was gravity. Instead of regarding it as a simple force that reaches out and pulls things toward massive objects, he suggested, we could more fruitfully think of gravity as a distortion or curvature in the space around objects — curvature that gives the illusion of attraction.

It is hard to visualize curved three-dimensional space except through mathematical formalisms, but two-dimensional analogues can help. Imagine, for instance, a large frame — like a large picture frame laid flat — over which a thin, tough sheet of rubber is tightly stretched. The two-dimensional upper surface of this sheet can be regarded as a stand-in for the three-dimensional volume enclosing, say, our solar system. If a cannonball were to be placed in the middle, the indentation it made would represent, in a limited way, the "curvature" that the sun's gravitational field imparts to space. Similarly, several ball bearings of various sizes could be arranged around this fancied sun to represent planets and moons. These would all roll into the sun's pit unless they were given just enough motion to keep them rolling round and round, like motorcyclists racing around a steeply banked motordrome. (An absence of friction must be assumed if these "planets" are going to stay in "orbit.") Such an analogue can go a long way in simulating the complex motions of celestial bodies and, for that matter, space vehicles plying our solar system.

When a star runs out of fuel

Along with its new picture of the universe, general relativity contains some startling predictions that have been receiving more and more attention in recent years, mostly as a result of the new astronomical discoveries. Even as far back as the thirties, a few physicists began using relativity theory to ponder what the outcome might be when a star ran out of fuel and began to collapse. With the discovery of quasars, these speculations suddenly took on increased interest. Puzzled by the question of where quasars got their

energy, physicists began looking at gravitational collapse as a possible explanation. The results have not only provided powerful hints as to what is taking place in some of the recent astronomical discoveries, but have also been the springboard into what is currently the most exciting topic of pure physical theory — "black-hole physics."

Stars, it seems, are mortal and do eventually die. Like our own sun, the stars are balls of immensely hot vaporized matter held together by their own gravitational force. Because of the heat and pressure, elements are undergoing self-sustaining nuclear fusion — similar to the hydrogen-bomb reaction. In turn, it is the expansive force of the heat produced by this fusion that balances the gravitational attraction and gives the star its size. But after billions of years, when the fuels are largely consumed, the star begins to contract. As it does so, its inner gravitational attraction increases, at a rate of 2 per cent for every 1 per cent of contraction, tending to cause it to contract still more. Theory predicts 1 of 3 outcomes: white dwarf, neutron star or black hole.

The first white dwarf was identified in 1844 after astronomers detected a wobbling motion of Sirius, which because of its nearness is the star that appears brightest from the earth. Trying to account for the wobble, astronomers finally spotted a tiny, dim companion near Sirius. The two were circling each other, and from the gravitational influence the dwarf had upon its neighbor, scientists were able to compute its stupendous density.

To turn into a white dwarf, theory tells us, is the fate of a small star that at the end of its collapse has a mass no greater than 1.4 times that of our own sun. If the mass is larger, up to twice that of the sun, the buildup of gravitational forces is so strong as to collapse atoms entirely and convert them into neutrons. Associated with this gravitational process, computations suggested, was the likelihood that huge amounts of energy would be liberated, perhaps enough to blast the outermost layers of the star's material out into space in a supernova-like explosion. The unexploded remnant would be a hard core of tightly packed neutrons — in effect, an atomic nucleus several miles in diameter and weighing billions of tons per cubic inch.

Until a few years ago, scientists had small hope of ever actually spotting such neutron stars; theory said they would glow too dimly. But in the summer of 1967, Jocelyn Bell, a young graduate student at Mullard Radio Astronomy Observatory at Cambridge University, first noticed the sharp, incredibly precise pulses of radio energy that signaled the existence of pulsars. Subsequently the imaginative Austrian-born astrophysicist Thomas Gold and others proposed that pulsars might actually be neutron stars. Calculations indicated that neutron stars, if they existed, would in all likelihood be spinning extremely fast, perhaps rotating several times a second. The explanation is the well-known law of conservation of angular momentum: just as a whirling figure skater whirls much faster when she pulls in her arms and legs, so any spin a star might have would be tremendously magnified when it underwent collapse. Gold imagined that such a star might emit energy from some spot on its surface in much the same way as the sun emits energy from sunspots. The combined effect might be a beam sweeping the heavens, a beam we would detect as pulsations.

The Crab's convulsions

Such speculations revived interest in neutron-star theory. Since it was thought that such a star might be at the core of a supernova explosion, radio-astronomy observatories began searching the Crab nebula. The Crab, a brilliantly glowing, crab-shaped cloud of gas some 6,000 light-years distant from earth, is the result of an explosion that Chinese and Japanese astronomers saw and recorded in the year 1054. It is the nearest supernova man is known to have witnessed. The National Radio Astronomy Observatory at Green Bank, West Virginia, reported pulsations in the vicinity of the Crab in the fall of 1968, and not long afterward the Arecibo Ionospheric Observatory's giant radio telescope in Puerto Rico pinpointed a pulsar flickering away smack in the middle of the crablike cloud. The Crab's pulsar is the most rapidly pulsing one yet found — 30 pulses per second. Moreover, the pulsation rate is perceptibly slowing down (by 37 billionths of a second per day). These characteristics lend support to the idea that it is a neutron star of comparatively recent origin whose spin is decreasing because of the dragging effect of all the energy it is emitting.

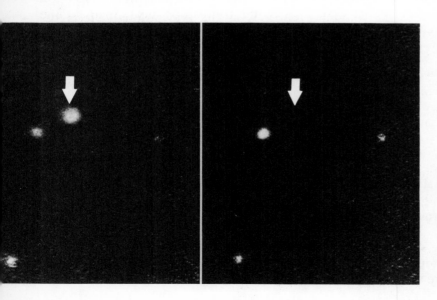

Now you see it (far left), now you don't (left): a pulsar in the Crab nebula. Is this source of energy a neutron star spinning at tremendous speeds?

Lick Observatory

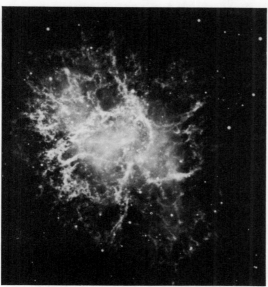

Mount Wilson and Palomar Observatories

The Crab nebula, remnant of a great stellar explosion.

Electromagnetism and the strong force — the forces involved in ordinary nuclear reactions on earth — can never convert more than 1 per cent of mass into energy, mainly in the form of heat, light, and various other forms of radiation. In a neutron-star collapse, gravity converts up to 10 per cent of a star's mass into energy, which appears as the supernova's light and other electromagnetic radiation, plus gravity waves and neutrinos (massless particles, virtual seeds of pure energy, that travel through the universe at the speed of light). Some theorists suspect that under certain conditions of gravitational collapse virtually all of the matter might be converted into radiation or neutrinos.

To a bizarre end

What eventually halts the collapse of white dwarfs is the opposition of electromagnetism; the strong force plays the same role for the neutron star. The strong force is peculiar in that while it acts as a force of attraction over part of its range, it becomes in its innermost regions a force of repulsion. So as the collapsing star becomes very dense, the strong force counteracts the gravitational force.

But, according to theory, if the star reaches the later stages of collapse with a mass greater than twice that of the sun, no countervailing forces can stop the collapse. Quite the contrary, the effect of any countervailing force would only be to hasten the collapse. To appreciate this, one has to understand that Einstein's mass-energy equivalence is to be taken quite literally: any form of energy or pressure is a source of gravitational force just as is any form of matter. In the case of very large collapsing stars, where the full panoply of relativistic effects is unleashed, the electromagnetic and strong-force pressures at work trying to stop the collapse only add that much more gravitational attraction. In such a tightening spiral of inevitability, physicists see no way out but for the collapse to proceed to a bizarre and paradoxical end.

To return to the elastic-sheet analogue, it is as if the sphere in the center kept getting smaller and smaller in volume without getting proportionately lighter in weight. It would exert increasing pressure, and the depression around it would get deeper and, especially near the center, steeper. With an infinitely small, infinitely dense particle and an infinitely tough "space," the depression would presumably become infinitely deep.

If theory can be believed, the final outcome of this process in nature is a "black hole" in space into which matter can be said to have vanished, leaving, however, all its gravitational effects behind. The black hole would act as a kind of hungry vortex into which other objects — and even other energies, such as light — would be drawn, and all their properties ironed away into additional curvature of space. Because of the energy bound up in its gravitational field, it would hold itself intact and attract and be attracted by other astronomical bodies, swallowing up anything that came too close. Needless to say, no black hole has ever been spotted telescopically, but several scientists are now urging a special program to search for them out in the reaches of the universe by looking for gravitational effects not otherwise explainable.

In spite of all the seeming implacability of the relativistic equations leading to black holes, many theorists are uncomfortable. In the first place, they look with deep suspicion upon any calculations that end up with infinities, as these do. Such calculations almost inevitably lead to paradoxes. In the late stages of black-hole collapse, moreover, general relativity runs head on against the deepest and most cherished foundations of quantum theory. Along with special relativity itself, quantum theory has proved to be one of man's most successful formulations in its ability to predict and inspire new discoveries about nature.

Quantum theory and general relativity look at nature from two different standpoints. Quantum theory looks at the world of the very small and sees there a world of graininess — of discrete quantities such as energy, spin, charge, and momentum — that can occur only in multiples of basic units. General relativity, by contrast, looks out upon a world of the very large and sees there nothing but a smooth continuum of values, a vast gravitational curvature that pervades and shapes the universe.

As for black holes, the collapse of matter into infinite density is very disturbing from the standpoint of quantum theory. The substance of all quantum theory's cherished conservation laws, in fact, precludes the outright destruction of most categories of elementary particles — together with their properties of spin, charge and so forth — except through a process of annihilation that always involves their antiparticles. Still, quantum theory is based upon empirical evidence gained in comparatively tame experiments here on earth. And quantum theory, too, is flawed by its own chain of mathematical logic that eventually leads to distressing infinities like those that plague the logic of the black holes. One such flaw concerns the nature of ordinary electrons, which, if one could believe the inescapable but obviously erroneous implications of pure quantum theory, would appear to have infinitely great energy and mass.

Despite these apparent contradictions, few scientists would aver that either quantum theory or relativity is wrong. It is thought instead that both must be incomplete, missing some essential facts about nature. The incompleteness must lie somewhere in the interface between the macro-world and macro-energy and the micro-world and micro-energy. A happy simile of Wheeler's likens the world of general relativity to the surface of a great ocean whose long gentle swells are like the gravitational curve of space. The quantum world begins after the swells have rolled up into shallows and curled and finally broken into the individual droplets and froth that represent the elementary particles of matter and their indivisible quantum properties. The nature of the shallow-water behavior and the "surface tensions" that cause the droplets to form has constituted the most pressing unfinished business of fundamental physics for the past quarter of a century. Some physicists suspect that the swells of general relativity will break into the droplets of quantum theory somewhere at the end stages of gravitational collapse, in the peculiar physics of black holes. Observes Wheeler: "The issue of the final state of the black hole is one of the most important problems in the history of physics."

Plunged into disarray

If recent evidence can be believed, the astrophysicists may have acquired a new form of astronomy, one well suited for watching the process of gravitational collapse. Still, this new evidence is not an unmixed blessing, because it may have destructive implications for conventional ideas about the universe. In June 1969 a paper appeared in the journal *Physical Review Letters* claiming discovery of gravity waves. The author of the paper was Joseph Weber, an experimental physicist from the University of Maryland. Weber, fifty, is a slight, wiry, mild-mannered former electrical engineer who turned to physics in 1950. He has spent some 11 years in the single-minded pursuit that led to his June paper.

Joseph Weber with one of the "antennas" he used to detect gravitational radiation. The cylinder, made of aluminum, is 5 feet long and 2 feet in diameter. It weighs 1½ tons.

University of Maryland

In that paper he reported that, on at least 17 occasions in the first 3 months of 1969, what appeared to be bursts of gravitational radiation swept over the earth from somewhere deep in space. Having improved his experimental techniques since that time, Weber is now recording this phenomenon about once a day. For a time the sun was his primary suspect as the source for these waves. But in October 1969 he told the New York Academy of Sciences that they may be emanating from the direction of the center of our galaxy.

Weber's announced discovery of gravity waves plunged the science of astrophysics — hardened as it was to shocks of new discovery — into a disarray more severe than that caused by quasars and pulsars. The problem is not that gravitational waves might exist; general relativity predicts that such waves should occur when matter is disturbed. In the two-dimensional space analogue, one would expect that ripples or tremors might flow across the surface when heavy bodies collide or undergo abrupt movements. Similarly, electromagnetic waves, including light, radiate away through space from charged objects that collide or undergo acceleration. But theory says that gravitational waves should be very weak compared with electromagnetic waves. A tremendously energetic process would be required to transmit a detectable wave over interstellar distances. Before Weber published his paper, most astrophysicists would have bet against his finding any trace of gravity waves with present-day technology. Their genuine respect for his thoroughness as an experimenter was mingled with admiring pity for anyone who would dedicate so much of his working life to so futile a quest.

Dr. Weber discusses some of his evidence of gravitational radiation. When a gravity wave passes through one of the aluminum cylinders, a distortion is produced. This can be changed to an electrical impulse by quartz crystals fused to the side of the cylinder. The electrical impulse is then recorded on a graph.

Both photos University of Maryland

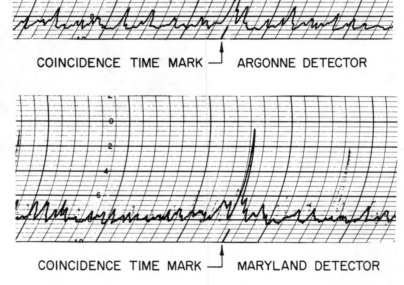

COINCIDENCE TIME MARK ⅃ — ARGONNE DETECTOR

COINCIDENCE TIME MARK ⅃ — MARYLAND DETECTOR

Dr. Weber has 2 large detectors, 1 at Argonne National Laboratory, the other in Maryland. A telephone line transmits the output of the Argonne detector to Maryland. The outputs of the 2 detectors are thus recorded together. Note the coincidence of detection shown here. The probability that such a coincidence is accidental is very slight — and Weber has observed more than 200 such "events."

Tiny signals in the noise

In principle, Weber's apparatus is simple, consisting mainly of a pair of similar gravitational "antennas," 1 located on the Maryland campus, and the other at the Atomic Energy Commission's Argonne National Laboratory near Chicago. Each antenna is a huge cylinder of solid aluminum, about 5 feet long and 2 feet in diameter, weighing several thousand pounds. To each cylinder are fastened piezoelectric crystals that function like ultrasensitive microphones to pick up motions of the bar.

Weber's calculations said that a wave of gravitational radiation should set up alternating movements of elongation and compression in the bar. These movements would be tiny, amounting to no more than a few hundredths of the diameter of an atomic nucleus. Ordinarily, such signals would be masked by "noise," namely, other motions caused by passing trucks, wind, earth tremors, stray electrical disturbances, or simply the thermal motion of the bar's own molecules. Thus Weber's apparatus is not only a tour de force of signal detection but also a tour de force of shielding from extraneous noise. A further safeguard is to count as gravity signals only those signals recorded more or less simultaneously by both antennas. While no other known effect should cause the simultaneous disturbance of 2 such antennas spaced 600 miles apart, a certain amount of extraneous noise is always present. Hence, Weber's experiments ultimately boil down to a controversial statistical exercise in determining the odds for and against simultaneous occurrence of "signals" on the 2 bars as a result of pure chance. But by now many eminent scientists have examined Weber's techniques and his statistics with great care and are at a loss to explain his results except in terms of gravitation.

For so much gravitational radiation to be detected on the earth would suggest that even within our own galaxy there are immense, irregularly occurring processes unknown to other forms of astronomy. One process might be the gravitational collapse of a star in our galaxy and its subsequent explosion into a supernova. The last known supernova in our galaxy, however, occurred nearly 400 years ago.

Another hypothesis is that stars may be collapsing totally into black holes. But our galaxy's stars would have to be collapsing on a daily basis to account for Weber's "signals." There is no reason to believe that we live in a special time of stellar suicide, so the black-hole explanation leads to the puzzle of how, after billions of years, any stars have survived.

Weber's recent tentative conclusion that the source of the waves lies near the center of our galaxy raises other possibilities. Clouds of interstellar dust hide our own galaxy's center, but in other, distant galaxies that man can see (though only dimly), the centers appear to be much more densely packed with stars than the outer regions. The density could be so high, some scientists speculate, that stars are actually colliding, or passing closely

and tearing one another apart. Such events could also generate gravitational waves.

No matter what the mechanism, if present theories are correct the energy needed to generate detectable waves would be so immense as to involve the annihilation of great quantities of matter. Again, this raises the question of how the process can keep going.

A use for the moon

"If Weber is right," sums up Patrick Thaddeus of NASA's Goddard Institute for Space Studies, "this may prove to be one of the great scientific discoveries of all time. But its potential impact upon all our established ideas is all the more reason why it must be examined with the greatest possible caution." Adds University of California mathematician-physicist Rainer K. Sachs, speaking wryly as a gravity theorist: "Perhaps we're easier to convince than other people because we've been working so long in a field where we've always been looked down upon for never having experimental results."

In any event, theorists may not have to agonize much longer. Weber's announcement has galvanized other experimenters, notably here and in the Soviet Union, to attempt to duplicate his findings. In the forefront is Stanford University's experimental virtuoso William M. Fairbank, who has pioneered in applying the peculiar properties of matter chilled to extremely low temperatures to a wide variety of difficult experimental tasks. Fairbank and his colleague, William O. Hamilton, propose to immerse an entire aluminum gravitation antenna in a bath of liquid helium at temperatures near absolute zero, thus eliminating most of the masking thermal noise. Meanwhile, Weber, who has struggled so many years in the face of skepticism and marginal funding for his difficult line of work, has still more ambitious ideas. He thinks that if the moon were properly instrumented — by astronauts, perhaps — it would make a superb antenna for gravity waves.

BEHAVIORAL
SCIENCES

CONTENTS

Woodstock, 1969: a weekend of music and togetherness. The youthful crowd of 400,000 was noted for its spirit of cooperation, widespread use of drugs and lack of violence.

Ken Regan — Camera 5   69

REVIEW OF THE YEAR-
BEHAVIORAL SCIENCES

Intelligence. Is intelligence inherited or determined by one's environment? Few scientists believe it's an "all or none" situation; most researchers feel both are factors in determining IQ. But "environmentalists" stress the importance of environmental factors while "behavioral geneticists" believe genetic factors are the more important. The controversy made the front pages in 1969 when Dr. Arthur R. Jensen, an educational psychologist at the University of California, published a lengthy article in which he argued that inheritance is much more important than environment. He based his conclusions on the results of numerous intelligence tests administered to individuals who had a variety of racial, social, educational and economic backgrounds. Jensen noted that (a) the more closely related people are, the more similar are their IQ scores, and (b) black children generally score lower on IQ tests than white children. He concluded that genetic determinants cause the lower IQ scores of black children. Critics questioned the validity of Jensen's position, pointing out, for example, that (a) IQ tests are often culturally unfair, having a white, middle-class orientation; (b) a study of identical twins raised in different environments showed that their average IQ differences were greater than the average differences between black and white populations; and (c) a recent study showed that, in some cases, the low IQ scores of ghetto children were traceable to prenatal vitamin deficiencies.

Among the general public, there is increasing opposition to IQ testing in the public schools. New York City and Washington, D.C., stopped using group IQ tests several years ago. Early in 1969, primary schools in Los Angeles stopped using such tests after parents charged that the test results caused the schools to incorrectly classify many Mexican-American children as retarded (when 47 of these youngsters were retested in Spanish, their "average IQ" increased 13 points). "If all kids enjoyed the same environment," says Earl S. Schaefer, research psychologist for the National Institute of Mental Health, "IQ tests would be a good measure of genetic potential. But they don't, so IQ is a deceptive thing. The tests actually reflect skills acquired in the society—and lower-class children don't get these skills."

Violence. Another characteristic that seems to be associated with the individual's environment is violence. According to the National Commission on the Causes and Prevention of Violence, a number of social conditions lead to violence. These include inadequate education and job opportunities for the poor, lack of interest in the concerns of youth, and the national prosperity, which generates violence in people who feel they are not sharing in the wealth. In its final report, the commission said: "The way in which we can make the greatest progress toward reducing violence in America is by taking the actions necessary to improve the conditions of family and community life for all who live in our cities, and especially for the poor who are concentrated in the ghetto slums."

Dr. Philip G. Zimbardo, a Stanford University research psychologist, has suggested that the pressures of urban life are transforming Americans into potential assassins. The anonymity of big-city life, the feeling of powerlessness and the mobility of people all contribute to a process he calls "deindividuation." In a study of vandalism, Dr. Zimbardo and a colleague left unlicensed cars near university campuses in 2 middle-class areas, 1 in Palo Alto, California, the other in the Bronx section of New York City. In Palo Alto, the car remained untouched for more than a week. The Bronx car, attacked 23 times within 3 days, became a "battered useless hulk of metal."

Drug addiction. Why are so many of our youth "turning on" with marihuana, amphetamines and heroin? Many experts agree with Dana L. Farnsworth, director of University Health Services at Harvard: "The peer-group influences surrounding high-school and college students have a very strong effect on their behavior. Drug use — to further creativity, to obtain self-understanding or even just to produce new experiences or 'kicks' — has assumed the pro-portions of an initiation rite. . . . Loss of confidence in parents, teachers, physicians and institutions such as school and church is so widespread that many young people often feel that they have no one to turn to but the mem-bers of their own peer group for setting standards of behavior and for ac-ceptance as individuals. Thus a student is placed under extraordinary pressures to go along with the group, often greater than he can withstand. He may feel that there is no reliable way to establish his own identity except through the enhancement of his own experiences and feelings. Many young people do not even care if the drugs they use are harmful; having no goals and unable to visualize themselves as moving into the present adult world, they feel that there is no future and whatever happens to them is applicable and operative only at the present moment."

Brendan Sexton, program coordinator for Encounter, a rehabilitation center for drug addicts in New York, says: "The problem is one of a whole society and an entire life-style, shared by young and old alike. . . . We take Dexedrine for fatness, Seconal to sleep, Miltown to get us to work, Valium to get through school, alcohol for social lubrication, and the little gentle blue pill for such upsets as a bad golf game or a wedding." It is the older generation, says Mr. Sexton, that has shown youth how drug usage can help one escape reality and the hassles of everyday life.

Psychotherapy. Victims of mental illness, especially long-term patients, often have their abnormal patterns of behavior "rewarded" by people, doctors included, who humor the patients' delusions. This is wrong, according to psychologists who believe in reinforcement therapy, or operant conditioning. These psychologists believe that responses that are followed by rewards will increase. Therefore, only "good" responses should be rewarded. For example, a withdrawn patient who makes an effort to talk with others receives certain rewards, such as extra food, candy or spending money; if he withdraws into silence, these amenities are withheld. Approximately fifty institutions in the United States are using reinforcement therapy. Practitioners can point to an impressive number of improvements in patients; many individuals who underwent such therapy have been released from mental institutions and now lead "normal" lives. Some psychologists, however, are not convinced; they claim that these results are superficial and that the genuine illnesses of the patients have not been eliminated.

Manic-depression. In April 1970, the Food and Drug Administration ap-proved the use of lithium carbonate for treatment of manic-depressive psychosis. The drug, which is widely used in other nations, effectively treats the manic phase of the illness; the mechanism is unknown. The only other methods of treatment — electric shock and heavy doses of tranquilizers — have a number of disadvantages.

IS A THUMB FOR SUCKING?*

Linus Thinks So, but

Some Doctors Disagree

BY LOU JOSEPH

* Reprinted by permission from *Today's Health*, published by the American Medical Association

THE parents of Linus probably aren't worried about his thumb-sucking. At his age it's cute. And Linus will never grow up.

But as a real thumb-sucking child grows older, his parents begin to nibble on pencils and gnaw on their fingernails when he doesn't quit.

This vexing habit — thumb-sucking, that is — not only worries parents but also generates considerable discussion and sometimes outright controversy among child-health experts.

The pediatrician may advise the parents to forget the thumb-sucking for the present as it probably will work out all right. The family physician may say that it is better to tolerate the thumb-sucking habit than to rear a frustrated child. The orthodontist may warn the parents that persistent thumb-sucking will cause malocclusion. And the psychiatrist may urge the parents not to break the habit even if it creates a malocclusion, because "crooked" teeth are less harmful and easier to correct than a mental problem.

Most dentists and pediatricians absolve intermittent thumb-sucking in infancy of any abnormality. But there is general agreement in the dental profession that prolonged and intensive thumb-sucking past the time the first permanent teeth erupt — at five to six years of age — can lead to misshapen mouths and displaced teeth.

"Perhaps no other single factor has been responsible for so much concern to both parents and dentists as thumb-sucking," says Dr. Kyrle W. Preis, professor of orthodontics at the University of Maryland Dental School. "In many cases, particularly with children under two years of age, much of this worry is needless, provided the child is under capable supervision." The mere fact that a child sucks his thumb does not mean that all the ills attributed to persistent thumb-suckers will follow. Intermittent sucking has very little or no appreciable effect upon the teeth or tissues.

"Thumb-sucking is very common in infancy, but generally is discontinued by two or three years of age," says Doctor Preis. "The further continuation may be an indication of a general emotional immaturity."

Dr. Clifford L. Whitman of Hackensack, New Jersey, a clinical professor of dentistry in the division of orthodontics at Columbia University School of Dental and Oral Surgery, explains infantile thumb-sucking as an outgrowth of the basic suckling instinct for receiving nourishment from the mother's breasts.

"Sucking is a normal habit but with our modern ways of living, breast feeding [which takes longer than bottle feeding] has unfortunately become a thing of the past," he says. "Years ago, mothers knew that babies need something additional to suck on whether it be sugar in cloth, bacon rind, a pacifier, or even a large bone which cannot be swallowed. These provide the infant with the necessary and normal sucking from which he derives pleasure and satisfaction. Lack of provision for sucking has resulted in the all-American hobby of thumb sucking or finger sucking."

"The creation of a euphoric state — a feeling of well-being — is important in early life," says Dr. T. M. Graber, an orthodontist in Kenilworth, Illinois. "Sucking appears to satisfy this need to a large extent. Pediatricians today emphasize the need of adequate time for nursing." The hand-to-mouth movement is normal in infancy and into the second and third year, he says; to advise parents to break up this needed reflex-like mechanism during this time ignores the basic physiology of infancy.

Infantile sucking is among a group of innate reflexes which includes grasping, eye movements, and those related to hearing and phonation. The sucking serves the physical development of the infant. It brings a better blood supply to the muscles of the head, face, and probably the brain itself, thus contributing to the growth of these areas. Sucking also has a marked effect on the development of the jaw, which is ill-defined before birth and is in part remodeled after birth. The jaw begins to show its adult configuration under the influence of the muscle pressure that is produced during activities such as sucking, mastication (chewing), and swallowing.

By four months of age, there is an acquired change in the sucking activity. Thumb-sucking and nursing now represent two separate activities, each occurring appropriately and independently. Sucking is the innate reflex, but systematic thumb-sucking is acquired.

The view that sucking is important because it provides the baby with a feeling of pleasure and security is shared by many pediatricians. "Any infant should be allowed the gratification of thumb-sucking because he will be faced by much frustration as he grows older," says Dr. Paul Tracy of Park Ridge, Illinois, a past president of the Chicago Pediatric Society. "So why take away something from him that gives him some means of gratification in earlier years?" He agrees with the dental profession that the habit should be relinquished between the ages of three and four years because it may lead to malocclusion or other oral problems. But he feels that the danger of developing orthodontic problems in chronic thumb-suckers may well be overrated.

Thumb-sucking is often an alternative to prolonged bottle sucking in infants seeking relief from abdominal discomfort, says Dr. Eugene F. Diamond, professor of pediatrics at Stritch Medical School of Loyola University in Chicago. "An infant suffering from colic will have a special urge to suck his thumb. I would rather see a baby suck his thumb because on the bottle he may gulp in air, complicating his stomach disorder."

After the second year, the thumb-sucking habit may appear only at bedtime. A return to thumb-sucking may occur during the next two years as the youngster begins to watch television and the mental strain created by the excitement and suspense of the program plus the extended period of physical inactivity combine to encourage the thumb-to-mouth response. One solution here might be to encourage children to do some handwork while they watch television.

The real problem arrives if thumb-sucking persists after the first permanent teeth erupt when the child is five or six. Ridicule, shaming, punishment, slapping the hands, or pulling the thumb away often cause an intensified reaction that fixes the habit more firmly. This treatment will not break the habit; it will break the spirit. The underlying cause and the emotional insecurity may show up in other, perhaps worse, ways.

Dr. Sigmund Freud differentiated the need to suck from the need for nourishment and viewed thumb-sucking as a pleasurable stimulation of the erogenous zone of the lips and mouth. He considered thumb-sucking in an older child as a symptom of an underlying psychological disturbance, and warned that interfering with that disturbance which serves to reduce the anxiety associated with the habit is likely to produce serious symptom substitution, such as stuttering and antisocial tendencies in the child.

Freud's conclusions conflict sharply with some recent findings. Dr. Park O. Davidson, associate professor of psychology at the University of Calgary, found just the opposite to be true about symptom substitution. "Actually it appears as if forcefully stopping thumb-sucking decreases the likelihood of more serious habits developing." He notes that the behavioral-therapy approach he utilized in the study failed to demonstrate any consistent psychological abnormalities. And arresting the habit with a specially designed dental appliance failed to produce any significant increase in alternative symptoms. "These results support the behavior-therapy interpretation of thumb-sucking as a simple habit and fail to support the psychoanalytic interpretation of thumb-sucking as a symptom of psychological disturbance," he says.

A different opinion is expressed by Dr. Ner Littner, a leading child psychiatrist in Chicago. He sees thumb-sucking in an older child as a nonspecific symptom of emotional tensions and as a defense

The creation of a euphoric state. Thumb-sucking is a common habit in infancy but should be relinquished between the ages of three and four. Some doctors think pacifiers are preferable to thumb-sucking: a child will stop sucking a pacifier much more quickly than a thumb, they say.

mechanism to get rid of such tensions. Doctor Littner, who is director of the child-therapy training program of the Chicago Institute for Psychoanalysis and a past president of the American Psychiatric Association, compares thumb-sucking to a safety valve for letting off emotional steam. "Do not block this safety valve even if it means risking a dental problem," he warns. Many older children, despite their thumb-sucking, experience no more than the normal frustrations of growing up. Therefore, if the habit appears by itself, one should not be too concerned about it. "However," says Doctor Littner, "in some cases thumb-sucking is part of the total package of a disturbed child which includes stealing, setting fires, and tearing clothing."

A sampling of views on the thumb-sucking problem would be incomplete if no mention is made of a controversial device commonly known as the pacifier. Damned for decades as a cause of diarrhea and even death itself, the pacifier today is the subject of kind words from the mouths of many dentists.

Says one orthodontist, "Pacifiers were frowned upon until recently, but thank goodness, they are being used again." If the thumb-sucking tendency is present at birth, a pacifier may solve the problem because a child will stop using a pacifier more quickly than the thumb or finger, he says. With infants suffering from cardiac disorders, the pacifier may be the only way to stop constant crying, thus preventing possibly fatal overexertion.

A number of orthodontists recommend the use of a physiologically designed pacifier for all children as they teethe and at other times to supplement the nursing exercise. They feel that such a pacifier coupled with the use of an "anatomic" nipple for nursing bottles "will greatly reduce the need and desire of the infant for supplemental sucking exercise and turning to the finger and thumb between meals and at bedtime." The anatomic nipple is designed to simulate the shape of the mother's nipples.

Not all pediatricians share the new enthusiasm for pacifiers, and often urge their use be restricted to "problem" babies. Doctor Tracy of the Chicago Pediatric Society is totally opposed to pacifiers. He compares them to the pep pills and tranquilizers that are so commonly used by today's adults.

Thumb-sucking can displace teeth, but this is not always so. In a child with normal occlusion, whose thumb-sucking lacks force and persistence and is of short duration, little or no damage may ensue. However, the child with an unstable dentition, who sucks long and hard, can produce considerable damage. The trio of factors — duration, frequency and intensity — coupled with an analysis of the oral-growth pattern, can enable the dentist to predict the potential damage to the dentition. Other factors that cannot be overlooked are the compensatory muscular changes of the lips and tongue which will accompany the movement of front teeth as the thumb-sucking continues.

What is the dentist's responsibility to the family, when during examination deformation of the dental arches is discovered and thumb-sucking is identified as the villain?

He will suggest one of several methods aimed at terminating the habit. First, of course, he will attempt to seek the full cooperation of both the child and parents. If he decides to choose the motivational approach, he may give the youngster calendar charts to mark down thumb-sucking days and stars for days without thumb-sucking. He may call the youngster on the telephone to remind him of his promised cooperation in attempting to break this potentially harmful habit.

Other methods include painting the thumb with a bitter-tasting lotion; sedative pills to control restlessness at bedtime; bandaging the thumb; mittens; boxing gloves; and elbow cuffs. One orthodontist uses splints which his young patients must fasten to their thumbs with tape. Every day the youngster does not take off the splints to suck his thumb, he receives a gold star. Still other methods utilize either fixed or removable dental appliances to keep the thumb out of the mouth.

Richard E. Jennings, a pedodontist (dentist specializing in treatment of children) at the University of Texas Dental Branch in Houston, takes a somewhat critical view of a dental appliance. It may solve the oral problem, but isn't that treating only the symptom and not the causes? he asks.

He offers this advice to parents who are worried about their offspring's thumb-sucking problem: "Before three years of age, sucking is a normal behavior for the majority of children. Past age three, it rapidly passes out of the child's repertoire as an instrument for emotional stability."

Do not punish, censure, nag or shame your child, he says, because it will tend to create a greater need for the anxiety-relieving thumb-sucking pattern. Treatment must be directed toward correcting the total situation.

Ernest T. Klein, a Denver orthodontist, gives perhaps one of the best rationalizations of thumb-sucking when he says: "Basically, we all are thumb-suckers if we analyze our oral habits. We live in a time of great stress, and most of us seek assurances of security, although not so obviously as children. We like the feeling of cigarettes, pipes, cigars, pencils, and chewing gum in our mouths. We miss these sucking devices if we try to give them up; therefore, let us practice tolerance toward these children and understand their desire for security."

Paul Fusco

SENSITIVITY TRAINING*

Fad, Fraud or New Frontier?

BY TED J. RAKSTIS

HIGH on a mountainside overlooking the Pacific Ocean in central California, 25 strangers gather at the Esalen Institute for a five-day adventure into "self-discovery." At the outset, several members of the group are openly hostile. But after a week of nude sulphur baths, dream analysis and

* Reprinted by permission from *Today's Health*, published by the American Medical Association

pull-no-punches dialogues, the onetime adversaries warmly embrace and leave filled with at least temporary love for each other and the world.

In a Chicago suburb, 65 people walk in off the street and pay $6 each to attend a three-hour "microlab" conducted by an amateur psychologist who assures them that they will "find a beautiful feeling, a sense of being connected to their fellow

Paul Fusco

77

man." They touch one another's faces, grope around while blindfolded, and lie in a circle and ramble on about the happiest moment in their lives.

And in Boston, a dozen hard-bitten businessmen meet for three days under the guidance of an expert in group dynamics. Following a test to measure their attitudes toward group inclusion, affection and the need to control, one executive's profile nails him as a corporate tyrant. A subordinate tells him: "It's no wonder we can't communicate on the job — you're uptight and you bug everyone around you."

In one form or another, all these people are undergoing sensitivity training, an anything-goes human relations movement whose major precepts are "do your own thing" and "tell it like it is." Sensitivity training sessions also are known as encounter groups, personal growth labs, T-groups ("T" for training), awareness experience, confrontation groups, training laboratories, organizational development and, collectively, the human potential movement. Whatever it may be called, the phenomenon is attracting hundreds of thousands of Americans of all ages to programs run by persons who may be either skilled professionals or rank amateurs.

The tangle of sensitivity training nomenclature suggests that not even the experts can clearly define it. It incorporates elements of psychiatry, sociology, philosophy, education, religion and community organization, and its practitioners number people from these and other fields. Depending upon his professional background and personal bias, each person who conducts a sensitivity group has a different focus.

Most sensitivity sessions, however, share several common attributes. The programs are designed to place people in a group situation. Through a mixture of physical contact games and no-holds-barred discussions about each other's strengths and failures, each group member hopefully will feel less constricted. He will become more open, readily able to understand himself and others. If he is a member of an organization, it may enable him to become a more persuasive and influential participant in group decisions.

But these goals can be achieved only if the person is willing to accept the rules of the group and its trainer. He must *want* to be sensitized and must be prepared to deal with the frank criticism that the group may engender. Unless he is willing to "open up," he will be wasting his time and may run the risk of psychological punishment. In short, sensitivity training is not for everyone.

Skeptics and supporters

Sensitivity training has been around since 1947, when three social psychologists formed an organization bearing the cumbersome title of National Training Laboratories Institute for Applied Behavioral Science (NTL). Yet only in the past few years has the movement really begun to explode. "Growth centers," emulating the highly experimental work of Esalen Institute, now are found throughout the nation, and countless independent entrepreneurs are running sessions that seek to "turn on" participants through sensory awareness rather than drugs.

During a time when Americans are torn with conflict and beset by fear, loneliness, and alienation, many are searching for something of meaning. Says Thomas Bennett, Ph.D., director of graduate studies for George Williams College and a fellow of NTL: "In our culture, it's extremely difficult to find experiences with other people which provide a degree of freedom and intimacy and a real opportunity to deal with persons at a fairly intense level. A lot of that has led to the growth in sensitivity training."

The supporters of sensitivity training call it a new frontier in social psychology, a means of making people more innovative, honest, trusting, and free. It is not a form of psychoanalysis, they say, but a significant outgrowth of adult education rooted in emotions rather than intellect. Numerous organizations — corporations, universities, churches, government agencies — view it as a method of helping people break the communication barrier.

Skeptics term it "the acidless trip" or "instant intimacy." Right-wing political groups have tried to link sensitivity training with Communism, brainwashing, and sexual promiscuity. More responsible critics, including some in the medical profession, question the wisdom of stripping a person's emotions to the core in a group setting. They challenge the use of unskilled trainers, the frequent absence of pre-screening to keep psychotics out of the programs, and the problem of returning to an essentially insensitive world after an emotion-charged group experience.

The sensitivity training boom has come so quickly and assumes so many forms that most of the experts have been caught off guard. Neither the American Psychiatric Association nor the American Psychological Association has an official position, and the American Medical Association's Council on Mental Health offers this middle-of-the-road viewpoint:

"Although sensitivity training is an issue of current concern, it is not an accepted part of medical practice. The Council believes that the procedures employed are not well enough defined to lend themselves to objective evaluation. It urges that particular caution be taken against participating in sessions conducted by leaders who are not professionally trained and qualified, in view of reports of psychotic and neurotic sequelae [consequences]."

It is difficult, however, to define "qualified trainer." At present, there are no laws controlling trainer certification. National Training Laboratories, based in Washington, D.C., with several branch offices across the nation, has the most stringent standards. NTL requires that its trainers have a Ph.D. or master's degree in psychology, social work, or one of the other related "helping professions" and that trainer candidates take advanced laboratory training. But NTL represents only one branch of the field. Some "trainers" have virtually no education whatever. Says one: "Who needs a degree? I know I'm a good trainer because I've got a 'gut' feeling for people."

The motivations of persons enrolling in sensitivity groups vary as widely as the caliber of the trainers. Some are making an honest attempt to discover themselves; others want a quick emotional "high" and a chance to meet members of the opposite sex; many attend only because their job requires it. A few use it as a cheap substitute for group psychotherapy. Oron P. South, Ph.D., director of the Midwest Group for Human Resources, a division of NTL, warns: "This is learning, not therapy. It is not intended for sick people, but for the 'normal neurotic' who wants to get more out of his relations with people."

A variety of programs

Just as the quality of programs and trainers defies easy categorization, "sensitivity training" in itself is an omnibus label that means little. Despite the profusion of names and the frequent overlapping of techniques, there are really three distinct styles.

One is the encounter group, sometimes called a "personal growth lab," which focuses on the individual and seeks to instill in him a sense of self-awareness. Since it relies heavily on non-verbal ("touch and feel") methods, this is actually sensitivity training in the most commonly accepted use of the term.

The T-group, an older method, uses more verbal exercises and emphasizes the "here and now" — the relationship of each group member to what is happening in the group at that particular time. It allows the participant to know what others think of him, to be granted the wish once expressed by the Scottish poet Robert Burns: "Oh wad some power the giftie gie us To see oursels as others see us!"

A third basic form is a T-group offshoot known as organizational development. Somewhat less personal than either the encounter session or the T-group consisting of strangers, its goal is to help members of an organized body — a business, school, or church — learn to work better as a team.

There also are several different time lengths for sensitivity programs. The

Michael Alexander

shortest form is a three-hour "microlab." More often, encounter or T-group labs run from two days to two or more weeks, and yet another version is the "marathon," a continuous, exhaustive session that may last for 24 or 48 consecutive hours. Because of the emotional and physical fatigue that may result, NTL and most other responsible training groups usually avoid the marathon.

Esalen Institute, at Big Sur, California, developed the encounter method. Founded in 1962 by Michael Murphy, a 39-year-old psychology graduate of Stanford University, Esalen attracts some 25,000 awareness seekers each year to Big Sur and a branch in San Francisco. At Big Sur, the site of a former health spa, 75 people pay $60 each to attend weekend meetings, and 25 more spend up to $175 on in-depth, five-day sessions.

The Esalen pilgrims are a mixed lot — business and professional people, teachers, movie stars, housewives, hippies. Unlike NTL, Esalen conducts no programs for organizations. "You do things in a personal growth lab that you could never try with a bunch of IBM executives," explains Stuart Miller, Ph.D., the Institute's vice president.

Philosophy, psychology, the meditative aspects of Eastern religions — these and dozens of other approaches are tried at Esalen. "Our techniques demand the total involvement of participants and, like the experiences of an LSD trip, are intensely personal and extremely difficult to describe in conventional language," says Murphy. Miller further terms Esalen as "experiential and experimental, a forum for the exploration of human potential."

The Esalen enrollee may find himself hugging strangers of both sexes, pounding pillows to release aggressions, telling the group his deepest secrets, acting out all the characters in his dreams, or taking an imaginary trip through his own body and relating the experience. William C. Schutz, Ph.D., one of the Institute's leading figures, says that the goal is to find "joy," and, appropriately, he has written a book titled *Joy*.

The most controversial phase of the Esalen program has been its mixed nude bathing, an idea conceived in 1967 by Paul Bindrim, a Los Angeles psychologist who has his own growth center at Palm Springs, California. Bindrim, who emphasizes that his approach is totally nonsexual, explains: "If a participant disrobes physically, he might gain the freedom to also disrobe emotionally."

Persons who have gone to Esalen often say they were wary and nervous when the sessions began. The most antagonistic members of some groups frequently find Schutz placing them in a situation of direct physical or verbal confrontation. In most cases, the hostility melts into trust or even affection. By the end of a week, says one writer who entered Esalen full of doubt, "I found myself hugging everyone, behaving like the idiots I had noticed on first arriving."

Esalen has 15 full-time associates on its staff. Ten have advanced degrees, but several never have graduated from high school. "We consider experience, talent, and creativity far more important than formal education," says Stuart Miller. Similarly, the outsiders who come to Esalen to conduct workshops may be psychotherapists, historians, Hindu mystics, or LSD apostles.

Some 90 growth centers — Miller calls them "little Esalens" — have sprung up across the United States. A year ago, there were only 40, and five years ago they were almost unknown. Among them are Kairos, in San Diego; Oasis, in Chicago; Espiritu, in Houston; and the Center for the Whole Person, in Philadelphia. Many were founded by persons trained at Esalen and closely follow the Big Sur methods.

A number of solo practitioners also are operating encounter groups. One such man is Jorge Rosner, a Chicagoan who tries to help people overcome their "mini-fears" through weekly three-hour "Adventures Into Being" at a place called The Center. Rosner, a product of Esalen, admits that he has no degree but feels that his background in experimental theater qualifies him as a trainer.

"In this field, a college education is not important," he maintains. "People with degrees get too hung up on intellectual aspects. Psychiatrists, particularly, are used to working with people on a one-to-one basis and can't get with it in a group situation."

Esalen and its disciples are part of the freewheeling, eclectic West Coast encounter movement. The East Coast school, exemplified by National Training Laboratories, is more scientific, oriented toward research and organizational work, insistent upon education and experience in its trainers. NTL is the father of the T-group.

In a sense, the T-group is as unstructured as the encounter group. There is no agenda; the leader lets the group swing on its own momentum. The session revolves around the "here and now" rather than the "then and there." Group members, usually 10 or 12 in number, often know each other only by their first names. Their occupations, home problems, and childhood experiences are irrelevant. What matters is what is happening within the group.

Like encounter groups, T-groups often play many nonverbal games. People may shout, crawl around the floor, chant arm in arm, or hug each other. But there also is considerable talk, centered upon how the group is behaving. For those who enjoy cocktail banter, a T-group experience can be painful. Masks are torn away and emotions exposed; a person may face a torrent of comments like, "I perceive that you're acting phony," or "You're a nonperson; you really turn me off."

The T-group has a peculiar lingo, a mixture of hippie talk and social science jargon. People are always "hungup" or "uptight," trying to discover "where I'm at." They don't talk; they "have a dyad." In one exercise, half the group listens to the others and then gives its impression of what it has heard. But this is not talking and criticizing — it is known as "input" and "feedback." (Some sophisticated T-groups get "feedback" through videotaped replays.)

Despite the esoteric terminology, the T-group to some extent shares with its cousin, the encounter group, a basic disdain for intellectual solutions. Trainers speak about a need to elevate the "affective domain" over the "cognitive domain," to trust the senses more and the intellect less. A common T-group remark is: "Don't *think — feel!*"

The T-group theory is that criticism will develop honesty, self-understanding, and trust in others. However, it also can result in conflict, and for this reason a

A CIRCLE OF LOVE

What kind of a person am I?
What kind of a person are you?
How can we communicate?

Through a mixture of meditation, physical contact and no-holds-barred conversation, these participants in sensitivity sessions hope to understand themselves and their fellow-man better. They look at this new frontier in social psychology as a means of becoming more innovative, honest, trusting . . . and free.

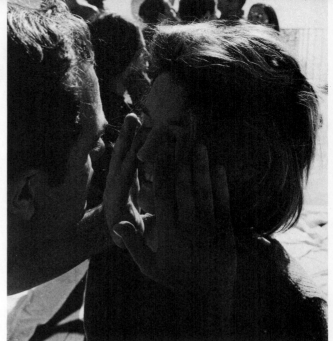
Michael Alexander

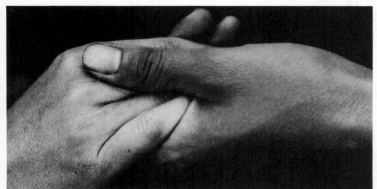
Paul Fusco

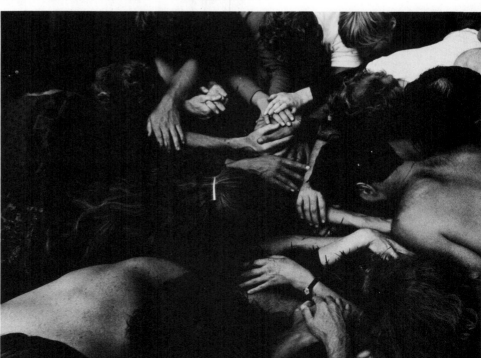

82

Paul Fusco

Michael Alexander

Paul Fusco

skilled trainer is a requisite. Jerry Spiegel, an active NTL trainer in Chicago, observes: "In most cases, a poor trainer will simply create a dull group. But there's always the chance that two people will really get into a major conflict — or that a participant may be on the verge of real emotional difficulty — so the trainer must be prepared to intervene. T-group training is like fire. It can warm the house and make it comfortable, or it can burn the damn thing down."

Besides drawing together an assortment of strangers, the T-group also can be used as a training tool for homogeneous groups. Spiegel's wife, Eleanor, who also is an NTL trainer, has been involved in working with a series of all-female T-groups where the major emphasis has been issues of femininity. The techniques range from the more nonverbal aspects of sensitivity training to written tests that evaluate such perceptions as the need for affection. Many NTL trainers also conduct sessions for married couples, single people, and family groups.

Nearly 75 per cent of the work of most NTL trainers is with organizations, and business has become a strong booster of T-group learning, which it sometimes terms organizational development. Among the companies that have sponsored programs for their employees are General Electric, Standard Oil of New Jersey, Syntex Laboratories, Humble Oil and Refining, and Texas Instruments. One of the corporate pioneers is TRW, Inc., a Cleveland aerospace contractor that has offered training to executives in its four divisions since 1963. Some companies force their employees into T-groups. TRW makes attendance optional, yet about 90 per cent of those who are eligible accept.

"You've got to make T-group instruction voluntary," says Thomas A. Wickes, Ph.D., director of personnel development for TRW and an NTL trainer. "This program is not for everyone, and the guy who is compelled to attend is likely to resist. He may even suffer emotional damage. We also give our men three or four 'checkout' points when they can

drop out. T-groups make our men more human executives. But, unfortunately, those who benefit the most are the ones who need it the least . . . and vice versa."

Many companies have discovered that T-group experience enables executives to talk matters out more freely. In an era in which the autocratic and arbitrary rule of a few men at the top of the corporate pyramid has given way to consensus decisions made by committees, the T-group is designed to bring forth the best skills that each man can contribute.

One T-group conceptualization describes personality traits and shows that most people fall into one of three categories — the "Tough Battler," the "Friendly Helper," and the "Objective Thinker." The lesson is that any decision-making group needs each of these types if it is to function as a representative body. Through T-groups, companies have uncovered men who are highly valuable but who previously were never noticed and thus never consulted.

Besides helping to build functional management teams, business has found the T-group useful in reducing potential employee conflict. When Scott Paper Company hired 30 disadvantaged persons — primarily black — for its plant in Chester, Pennsylvania, it put 300 workers through 16 hours of T-group training to help them understand the problems of slum-dwellers. Company officials later said that the program averted what could have been an explosive transition.

Schools have employed the T-group for similar purposes. In Pontiac, Michigan, a community filled with racial tension, the school board recently allocated $25,000 for a program for parents, students, teachers, and administrators throughout the school system. After black students boycotted Proviso East High School in Maywood, Illinois, early in 1969, NTL was called in to organize a teacher-student lab. "The NTL project opened up lines of communication so that students and teachers began talking to each other," notes one Proviso East teacher. "Things came out in the open."

State and municipal bodies — including the police forces in Los Angeles, Houston, and Grand Rapids, Michigan — have experimented with T-groups. Some physicians are trying it as a means of improving patient relationships, and the University of Alabama Medical Center recently began an organizational program for some 100 medical personnel. Many people in the creative arts, notably the theater, have turned to T-groups and encounter programs.

A number of churchmen also are adopting the technique. In Chicago, for example, the Rev. Owen F. McAteer, associate pastor of St. Dorothy's Catholic Church, has organized a group of 25 priests and nuns and set up sensitivity training under the auspices of the Archdiocese of Chicago. "The program is helping nuns and priests to communicate better with their parishioners, to come down a bit off their pedestals," says Father McAteer. "This can be one of the most effective of all methods to achieve the goals of Christianity."

As sensitivity training spreads throughout America, attitudes polarize. Proponents call it one of the major learning discoveries of this century, but opposition develops on many fronts. It has become a prime target of the same ultraconservative groups that oppose sex education in the schools, such as the John Birch Society and the American Independent Party. A Chicago group called Let Freedom Ring recently issued a manifesto branding sensitivity training as "a Communist brainwashing technique" and "a grotesque, mind-bending program." Yet not all the critics are of this fanatical breed; even responsible medical men are troubled by abuses.

At a school district in Jackson, Michigan, a sensitivity training program that mixed teachers with teen-agers became so controversial that the Michigan State Medical Society launched a statewide study. The Society's Committee on Mental Health, in probably the strongest statement yet issued by a major American medical body, concluded that sensitivity training is acceptable only when conducted by professionals in the field of mental health.

"These programs are being run by unskilled and unqualified lay individuals," declares Benjamin Jeffries, M.D., a Detroit psychiatrist who is chairman of the committee. "As a result, participants are experiencing emotional problems beyond their capacity to control. I personally feel that the only people who should be doing this type of training are psychiatrists, psychologists, and psychiatric social workers."

The medical profession is sharply divided over whether encounter and T-groups actually constitute psychiatry in disguise. Howard P. Rome, M.D., senior consultant and professor of psychiatry at the Mayo Graduate School of Medicine and a member of the AMA Council on Mental Health, feels that sensitivity training is outside the field of medicine.

"People in the behavioral sciences other than psychiatry are most valuable in conducting these programs," Doctor Rome asserts. "With the nation facing a critical health manpower shortage, we must use all available resources."

NTL officials state that less than one per cent of the persons who have been in their sessions have suffered psychological damage and that most of those already had emotional problems. Although most reputable trainers try to screen out persons with psychiatric disorders, some occasionally slip through. When an unqualified trainer is presiding, the problem can become acute.

The vice president of one Midwest corporation suffered a complete mental breakdown in a T-group and was forced to enter a hospital. In New York, a mentally ill woman enrolled in a growth center and soon started to organize her own sessions. And in Evanston, Illinois, after an untrained high school teacher tried to sensitize his students, one girl went into screaming hysterics and a boy later was found wandering the streets in a stupor.

"Sensitivity training can all too easily become insensitivity training," contends

Dana L. Farnsworth, M.D., director of health services for Harvard University and chairman of the AMA Council on Mental Health. "There can be great danger for the person who has psychotic difficulties or who is involved in any sort of acute crisis."

Moreover, laboratory training is viewed by most experts as essentially a program for adults. In many communities, some of the strongest opposition to T-groups has come after teachers participated with youths and trainers utilized some of the more deeply personal techniques of sensitivity training. "When teen-agers are involved, you've got to be very careful in what you do," says NTL trainer Jerry Spiegel. "A T-group is a learning process, not a way to get an emotional kick."

Perhaps the greatest potential danger occurs when an inexperienced person who has been "turned on" at a session tries to help others find the same route. So far, there is little evidence of outright fraud in the sensitivity training field, but there is a proliferation of misguided do-gooders. A number of teachers, for example, have been known to begin programs for their students on the basis of a single weekend's encounter experience. Their intentions may have been honest, but the results sometimes were disastrous. As Doctor Farnsworth puts it: "Compassion without competence soon becomes quackery."

Another major problem is the inability of many people to cope with an insensitive society once they have left the sanctuary of the group. The T-group hangover has been particularly troublesome for business. A *Wall Street Journal* survey of companies sponsoring T-groups reported that many persons have returned to their jobs disillusioned with office policies and personnel, tried for a more open environment, and then were either fired or quit in frustration. Although a T-group may alter an individual's personality, it is likely to have little effect upon the organization he works for.

The encounter session or T-group can become an emotional crutch for the person who finds it difficult to adjust to the world around him. "You see a number of people coming back year after year; they're called T-group bums," says Morton A. Leiberman, Ph.D., associate professor of psychiatry at the University of Chicago. "They have a strong need for this kind of relatedness and they aren't getting it outside in real life."

The potential of T-groups

There is also mixed opinion over whether people derive any meaningful long-term benefits from laboratory training. Although NTL claims that two thirds of the persons who have taken T-group instruction have improved their skills, there as yet are no scientific studies to support this. It is highly doubtful whether sensitivity training can conquer both heredity and environment and create a new person, but it can make him think and perhaps modify his behavior.

"T-groups can't change your personality," Jerry Spiegel observes. "However, they can make you acutely aware of the impact you have on others — and their impact on you. The training session furnishes you with the information, the sort of things your friends won't tell you. What you do with that information is up to you."

For good or ill, sensitivity training appears to be more than a mere passing fad. In its more bizarre forms, as a means of providing thrill-seekers with a quick emotional jolt, it may fade into obscurity once the novelty has worn off and the publicity has subsided. But as a means of learning to cope in a group, of discovering and capitalizing upon hidden inner strengths, its potential appears limitless.

"Sensitivity training will settle down and find its rightful place," Doctor Rome predicts. "Hopefully, we will see the day when instruction in human relations will be as much a part of the school curriculum as the three R's. When properly used, sensitivity training can help to educate our young people to live in a pluralistic society as better, more understanding citizens. It can be a powerful tool in creating a better world."

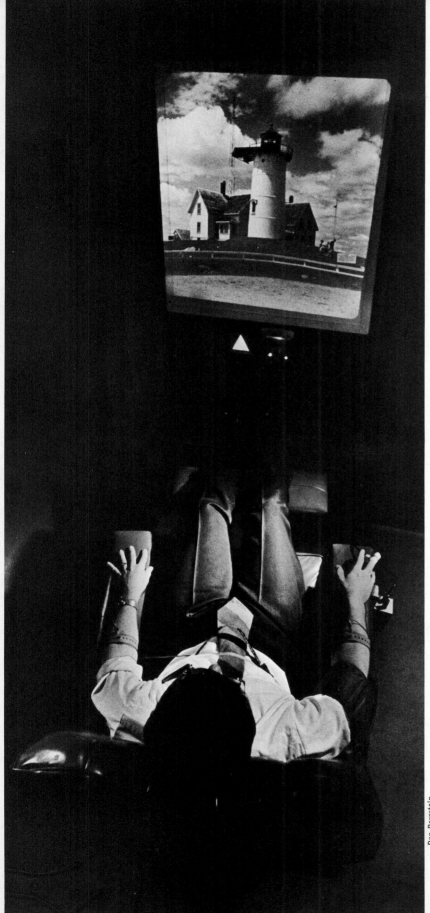

VISCERAL LEARNING*

A New Human Faculty?

BY JOHN E. PFEIFFER

Dan Bernstein

* Reprinted by permission from *Think* Magazine, published by IBM, Copyright 1969 by International Business Machines Corporation.

WE ARE not surprised when a man improves his marksmanship on a rifle range by noting how far he comes from hitting the bull's-eye and readjusting his aim accordingly. But it is something else again to discover that man may be able to adjust his blood pressure by similar practice — or regulate his heart rate, kidney function, blood flow, intestinal and stomach contractions, brain-wave rhythms, and so on.

Rapidly expanding experiments and studies indicate that he may well be capable of doing these things — that he possesses untapped, yoga-like powers of self-discipline, amounting almost to the discovery of a new human faculty: a high order of "visceral learning."

Although this work is still at an experimental stage, clinical trials at leading medical centers have already yielded important results. It may not be long before systematic self-control of internal processes will supplement or replace drugs and surgery in treating certain forms of heart disease, epilepsy and other ailments. Healthy persons may benefit as well as patients. One day, for example, desk-bound business executives may be able to keep in top physical condition by controlling their own blood pressure and heart rate instead of jogging or doing setting-up exercises.

Significant theoretical advances may also result. The more we know about visceral learning, its possibilities and limitations, the better we will understand the causes of psychosomatic illness and the complex interactions between body and mind.

Breakthroughs have come swiftly in recent years, due in large measure to the pioneer experiments of Neal E. Miller at Rockefeller University in New York. For nearly two decades the sixty-year-old psychologist has been waging and is now winning a battle against an old and firmly held notion about learning.

Most of his colleagues have traditionally believed that we become better marksmen and acquire other skills because our skeletal muscles — those which move our limbs, shoulders, eyes, and so on — are under voluntary control, under the control of the highest brain centers. But, in this view, the practice-makes-perfect principle does not apply to the activities of internal organs. They are controlled by lower centers of the "autonomic" or involuntary nervous system, centers supposed to work automatically and independently of the will. Feats such as those achieved by yogis, who have long regulated heart rates and other visceral processes to enhance their powers of concentration, were regarded as a sort of "cheating." The Hindu mystics, according to the majority view, were producing these effects indirectly, by relaxing their skeletal muscles, which in turn produced the internal changes. Direct control was considered physiologically impossible.

Disproving this dogma turned out to be a formidable task. The main problem was the force and prevalence of sheer disbelief. Miller needed help, and over a period of many years no help was forthcoming. At one point things looked brighter for a while, because a new assistant joined the laboratory with the understanding that he would devote half his time to research on visceral learning. But he kept putting it off week after week for two years, concentrating entirely on other projects.

"I couldn't really blame him," Miller says. "You can't expect a man to gamble his time, or possibly his career, on a series of seemingly fruitless animal tests. In his case and others, the notion that visceral learning was impossible was too strong. It's better to let people work on something they have faith in."

Even when a volunteer stepped forward in the summer of 1962, there were obstacles and letdowns. In fact, for many months it looked very much as if the skeptics were right. But Jay Trowill, a graduate student, had unusual perseverance as well as faith. He needed both. Three years of intensive and often discouraging animal research lay ahead. His project involved devising a way of teaching the control of heart rates. Trowill ran into a succession of complications knotty enough to discourage nine out of ten workers.

Trowill spent about a year and a half simply trying to find the right experimental animal. In the beginning he devoted most of his time to dogs and cats, but, for various technical reasons, neither species proved suitable. Rats represented another possibility, but as usual there were catches. For one thing, demonstrating direct control of heart rates and other visceral functions calls for the ruling out of possible indirect effects due to the action of skeletal muscles. This can be done with injections of the ancient South American arrow poison, curare, a drug that paralyzes these muscles without affecting the muscles of the heart and most other internal organs. The difficulty was that curare paralyzes breathing muscles, thus demanding some form of artificial respiration — and a standard method of artificially respirating small animals such as rats had not been developed.

That problem was solved as the result of a chance observation. One morning Miller noticed that a member of his own research group, Eric Stone, working on an entirely different project, had improvised a simple artificial lung using, of all things, a toy balloon. The balloon is cut so that a wide end can be slipped over the rat's face; the mouthpiece is attached to a small pumplike device which forces air in and out of the animal's lungs.

Trowill adopted the makeshift-mask technique and promptly ran head on into further problems. Rats, like people, learn best when they know they are doing well — but how do you reward a paralyzed animal? The answer involved careful and precise brain surgery. Trowill learned to implant electrodes in rat brains, specifically in nerve clusters located near the base of the brain. Studies conducted during the past 15 years show that these clusters operate as "pleasure sites." When they are stimulated by electrical signals flashed to

Leo V. DiCara

In this apparatus, a free-moving rat is trained to change its blood pressure in the rewarded direction. The reward may be direct electrical stimulation of a rewarding area of the brain. Or the rat's reward may be escape from a mild electric shock.

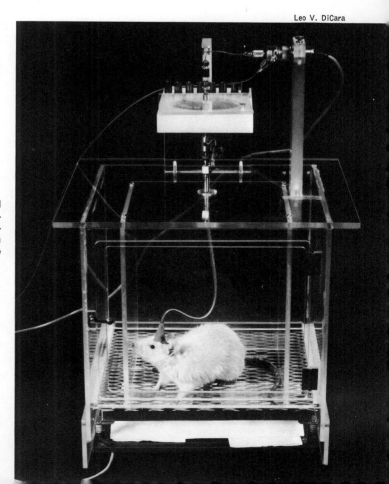

the implanted electrodes, the animal has sensations of intense satisfaction.

Finally, the young investigator had to teach himself some applied electronics. He needed a kind of robot monitor — equipment that would pick up regular electrical pulses produced by contracting heart muscles, recognize brief periods of faster-than-average and slower-than-average heart rates, and automatically trigger the device that transmits pleasure signals to the brain. According to Trowill, who is now studying rewards and brain stimulation at the University of Massachusetts, "I had trouble finding a good timing device. The United States was shooting rockets at the moon, but we hadn't developed a timer that would work accurately under the conditions of the experiments I wanted to conduct."

Wired for pleasure

One day, while thumbing through an equipment catalog, Trowill found a device that would do, and from then on he began obtaining promising results. But he still had to contend with the skeptics: "My biggest problem was psychological. It was very discouraging when prominent investigators visited the laboratory, looked at my work, and said 'Very nice. Let us know when you find something interesting.' I thought I already had something interesting, but they weren't satisfied. They had read that it couldn't be done. That's the power of the published word."

Trowill's immobilized, wired-for-pleasure, and electronically monitored rats were soon performing according to expectations. Every time their heart rates increased spontaneously, the robot apparatus went into action, flashing signals to the brain so that the rats received their reward: intense feelings of pleasure. Of course, the animals didn't know what they were doing. But they knew what they liked, namely more of the same, and the only way they could get this was by increasing their heart rates.

That is exactly what they did, although how they did it remains to be explained. After about an hour of training,

15 out of 19 rats tested increased their heart rates by an average of 5 per cent, or some 20 beats per minute. (The average rat heart rate is about 400 beats per minute.) Furthermore, 15 out of 17 rats rewarded for decreasing their heart rates achieved changes of the same magnitude in the opposite direction.

This crucial experiment was completed 3 years ago, and things have been sizzling ever since. The heart-rate changes were small but definite and statistically significant, sufficiently so to indicate the possibility of visceral learning and encourage more-extensive tests. Students and assistants joined in a research drive that is still in high gear, and has involved studies of more than a thousand rats and the use of at least as many multicolored balloons. Working 14 to 16 hours a day, 7 days a week, has been common during peak periods; on occasion workers spent as much as 20 consecutive hours adjusting instruments and keeping tab on the rats' performance. "I live right across the street," one investigator told me. "It's the only way you can do this work and still keep your wife."

The hard work paid off. Miller and Leo DiCara, his chief assistant, improved on Trowill's results by continually "raising the ante." That is, as soon as a rat increased or decreased its heart rate by a certain amount, say 20 beats per minute, no further rewards were provided until it attained further changes at still higher levels of 25 or more beats per minute. In this way, they gradually reached a point where they could produce changes of about 20 per cent in either direction, so that a rat with a starting heart rate of 400 beats per minute could be trained to attain slow rates of about 320 and fast rates of 480.

Similar results were obtained for other visceral responses. Rats spurred on by the prospect of increased rewards learned to control the activity of their intestines, increasing or decreasing contractions by up to 40 per cent; double or halve the rate at which their kidneys produced urine; raise or lower their blood pressure; and regulate the amount of blood flowing in their stomach walls. They also learned to change the firing or signaling rates of nerve cells in their brains, producing a predominance of fast or slow brain waves depending on how they were rewarded.

Learning and "good form"

These and other experiments reveal that visceral learning is not only possible, but that in many ways it resembles the process we go through in acquiring any basic skill. A novice learning to play golf or drive a car does not coordinate all at once. At first he makes awkward and unnecessary motions. In swinging the club or shifting gears he has difficulty building individual actions into a single smooth sequence. True economy of effort — what we call good form — comes with increasing practice.

There is also a kind of "good form" in visceral learning. Some rats being trained to increase or decrease intestinal contractions, for example, may also alter another function such as heart rates by small amounts. But the effect is least marked in the best learners, and usually diminishes with continued training. In fact, one of the most impressive general findings is that internal processes are subject to highly precise and specific controls. When practice has been completed, one and only one function, the rewarded function, is learned. An animal trained to lower its blood pressure will show no significant changes in heart rate or blood flow in its stomach walls. More significant, rats have learned to dilate blood vessels in their right ears but not in their left ears, and vice versa, indicating a degree of selective control which surprised even Miller.

As far as studies of human capabilities are concerned, Miller's hunch has long been that "people are at least as smart as rats," a reasonably safe assumption which subsequent studies have confirmed. Work is just beginning, but possibilities are hinted at in cooperative research conducted by Miller's group and physicians at the nearby Cornell Medical Center. A typical study involved a man suffering

from abnormally fast heart rates, 95 to 100 beats per minute compared with a normal average of 70 or so. The patient sat in an easy chair, with wires running from his chest and leg to a monitoring device that recorded his heart rate. Doctors told him that they were trying to train him to slow down his heart, and that whenever a slight deceleration occurred spontaneously he would hear a beeping tone. He needed no further information and no special reward: the desire to achieve a healthier heart rhythm was incentive enough.

Unlike the rats, the man knew what he was supposed to do. But aside from relaxing, which has no appreciable effect in such cases, he had no idea of how to go about it. He simply tried to make the beeps as frequent and long-lasting as possible, and somehow this worked. "It's something like learning to serve in tennis," Miller explained. "What you think you're doing may be quite different from what you're actually doing. But you are aware of results, and that sort of feedback helps you improve with practice."

The patient made some improvement during the very first session, which lasted an hour. After 3 weeks and 30 sessions, the end of his experimental training period, his heart rate had dropped to a low-normal figure of about 65 beats per minute. Follow-up studies have not been completed for this case, but Bernard T. Engel of the National Institutes of Health has produced similar results by similar training methods, and reports that beneficial effects have lasted for as much as 2 years.

Further studies are proceeding at the Harvard Medical School where David Shapiro, Bernard Tursky and their associates have spent more than 6 years investigating reward techniques in the control of visceral functions. Currently, some of the most important tests involve blood-pressure changes among healthy as well as ailing persons.

I had an opportunity to observe one of the tests during a recent visit to their laboratory. I watched through a one-way mirror from a room crammed with electronic gear, a computerized monitoring system. The system was busy automatically runing an experiment under way in the next room, where a student volunteer sat in front of a screen about the size of a small blackboard.

After long and difficult trial and error, experimenters had devised a system for monitoring blood pressure — utilizing an ordinary blood-pressure cuff in combination with a complex bank of electronic logic modules — which permits the recording of and therefore the reinforcement of blood-pressure changes at each successive heartbeat.

With the volunteer tied into this system, a red light flashed, and there was a beeping tone. Then the image of a scantily-clad girl, or a landscape, or dollar signs, appeared on the screen before him and vanished after a brief 5-second exposure. The light-tone signal indicated that his blood pressure had fallen slightly; the image was his reward.

The student, like the rats in Miller's tests, did not know what he was doing. He had simply been instructed to make the signal and the images appear as often as possible. During the next 40 minutes or so, he saw a succession of different images, and by the end of that period his systolic blood pressure had fallen from 119, which is about normal for a young adult, to 114.

Visceral teaching machines

On the basis of tests involving more than 50 healthy volunteers, the Harvard investigators are now conducting systematic studies of high-blood-pressure patients. In these cases, as in the cases of patients with abnormally fast heart rates, no special reward has been necessary, other than the prospect of being able to help themselves. So far, pressure reductions of up to 10 per cent in a single 45-minute session have been common, and one patient has already succeeded in lowering his systolic pressure from 180 to 155.

Pioneer experiments in therapeutic training also include efforts to relieve digestive disorders, inflammation of the colon and related conditions by teaching patients to control the so-called "involuntary" intestinal muscles. Control of the brain offers particularly interesting possibilities. For example, one mark of epilepsy is electrical "explosions" in the brain, the sudden firing of many nerve cells at once — and these bursts of cerebral activity appear as large "spikes" or sharp deflections of recording pens on brain-wave machines. Research indicates that certain patients can be trained to reduce the number of such spikes in their brains, a finding that raises the hope of reducing the number and severity of their attacks.

There has been an increase in such studies, an increase which has become particularly noticeable within the past eight months or so with news of results being obtained by Miller and his associates at Rockefeller University. Investigators at the State University of New York, Williams College, McGill University in Montreal, the University of Tennessee, and other institutions are applying similar techniques to wider and fuller explorations of visceral learning. Meanwhile the man chiefly responsible for the current research boom looks ahead to the coming of a new breed of health devices, "visceral teaching machines" about the size of hearing aids.

"Wearing such a unit," Miller explains, "a patient or a person who wants to avoid becoming a patient, say a busy executive, could practice visceral control at home or on his way to work. A sharp tone might indicate that his heart rate or blood pressure was on the rise, and he could train himself to counteract such effects by stopping the tone. Electronic self-monitoring devices may help us play a more direct role in controlling our own health."

The Rockefeller investigator is also concerned with the nature of the learning process, and its relationship to disease. He and his colleagues are using rats in an effort to create relatively sophisticated "models" of conditions that affect human beings. For example, psychological factors may be involved in certain forms of

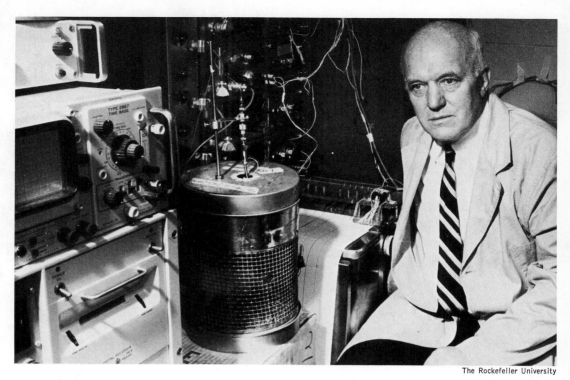

Professor Neal E. Miller of The Rockefeller University with the apparatus used in his laboratory to record and reward changes in a rat's blood pressure.

high blood pressure. Some patients, long before coming down with the disease, have episodes of irregular pressure levels, periods when readings dip and rise for no obvious reason. Then suddenly the blood pressure levels hit a high and tend to stay there. If this sequence of events can be produced experimentally, say by subjecting rats or other laboratory animals to stress, scientists may learn how to treat and perhaps prevent similar conditions in people.

Another animal model may have even-more-far-reaching implications. Psychiatrists, Freudian and otherwise, have long emphasized the fact that what happens to us during childhood may influence how we behave for the rest of our lives — and much of that behavior involves visceral functions. A boy afraid of going to school may exhibit a wide range of symptoms, from stomachaches, headaches and palpitations to faintness and pallor. But which symptoms develop into a set lifelong pattern may depend on the reactions of his parents.

The uses of stomachaches

If they happen to be particularly upset by their son's stomach pains (perhaps because of their own "visceral" personalities) and tend to play down the other effects, they will "reward" or reinforce the specific symptoms whenever they occur. They will decide that he is sick and ought to stay home, and he will learn the uses of stomachaches not only during his school days but throughout life whenever he finds himself under stress. Obscure muscular pains, low backache and stiff neck, constipation, fainting spells and other difficult-to-treat ailments may often be traced to such early conditions and conditioning.

Miller believes that it may be possible to reproduce analogous behavior among young rats, starting at weaning age (about twenty days). If he succeeds, psychiatrists will have fresh clues to the causes and treatment of neuroses and psychosomatic disorders. Even more significant, the new insights may bring about major changes in family relationships, child rearing and education.

Reversal of letters is one type of reading disability. This exercise at the blackboard shows the boy what is wrong with his lettering.

THE BOY CANNOT READ...*

He Has Dyslexia, a Common Problem among Children

BY BENJAMIN H. PEARSE

THE New Year burst upon the National Institutes of Health in Bethesda, Maryland, with a ringing of telephone bells and a blizzard of more than 15,000 letters inspired by a small item in a syndicated newspaper column that read as follows:

"Dear Ann Landers: Our middle son, age 10, is an unhappy child. This boy has always done poorly in school, and we were at a loss to understand why. The teachers complain that he daydreams in class, doesn't pay attention, and misses at least half of what is going on. His grades show it.

"Last week it came to my attention that the boy cannot read. I was shocked. How he managed to fool everyone is beyond me. His English teacher suggested that he might have dyslexia, which she described as a disorder of the brain that can be corrected. Do you know anything about this? Does this mean that my child is retarded? Can you help me?" It was signed, "Reader."

Miss Landers' reply assured the worried parent that children with dyslexia are not retarded and actually often have above-average intelligence. She explained that while the cause was uncertain the disorder was frequently discovered because

Benyas-Kaufman/Black Star

a child had trouble reading. She concluded: "I suggest you write to The Advisory Committee on Dyslexia and Related Reading Disorders, NIH Building 31, Bethesda, Md. 20014."*

The thousands of inquiries inspired by that modest item added fuel to the fires of debate, controversy and misconception that have surrounded this educational culprit identified medically more than fifty years ago but rediscovered recently as a problem of considerable prevalence. The committee was preparing a report for publication. But the staff marked time long enough to reply to "Reader" and the myriad other parents similarly agitated.

"When a child fails to read satisfactorily," Charles A. Ullmann, director of the committee staff, explained, "parental concern is natural and desirable. The question is not only *what* to do but *how* to do it.

"The child with mild reading difficulties often can be helped in the classroom where the teacher usually can count on health services or education specialists to provide consultation on learning diffi-

* Originally titled "Dyslexia," this article is reprinted from the April 1969 issue of *American Education,* published by the U.S. Office of Education

* The committee formally completed its work in August 1969.

culties and to correct visual, hearing or other health conditions. But the child with more severe reading difficulty may be suffering from a combination of factors, such as a long-standing handicap in vision or hearing, limited general ability, emotional maladjustment or poor schooling."

Dr. Ullmann pointed out that reading requires a child to perceive information through the sense organs, to process it through the brain, and to express the results in terms of language or behavior. Some children experience reading difficulties for which a clear explanation is not yet available. But comprehensive physical and psychological examinations are among the first steps to be taken to determine whether the problem stems from the way the child sees or hears letters, syllables or words, whether it involves his thought processes, or the verbal or physical expression he is called upon to make.

"The extent to which severe reading disorders may be overcome, and the difficulty involved, varies with each case," Dr. Ullmann says. "But early diagnosis is undoubtedly a most important factor. The child whose problem is not recognized until he has already experienced long-term failure in school is usually saddled with a psychological block which may be aggravated by the tension arising from lack of parental understanding at home. Termed lazy or stupid by his teacher and parents, the child tends to accept their word and cease all efforts to improve."

Just what is this thing that, for want of a better name, is known as dyslexia? The word is a compound of the Greek prefix *dys* (bad, ill or difficult) and *lexia* (word). But a committee of noted medical and educational specialists in the field of learning problems meeting in New York three years ago was unable to agree on a definition after a whole day of discussion. Later, a conference on dyslexia and related reading disorders, held at Southwest Texas State College at San Marcos and sponsored by the U.S. Office of Education, reached this conclusion:

"First, we should not permit semantics to dissipate our time and energies. . . . If you prefer some other term, use it, with the understanding that you are talking about the kind of child who cannot unscramble auditory and/or written symbols which reach the brain so that they have the same order-pattern and meaning which they have for others. . . . Second, . . . we should remember that our purpose is to determine what should be done about the disability, rather than what to name it. . . ."

The pressing need for determining what should be done about the disability is obvious from the response to the syndicated column and from the statement of former Secretary of Health, Education, and Welfare Wilbur J. Cohen when he established the National Advisory Committee in August 1968:

"Investigators now estimate that reading disorders are more widespread than

Some children have difficulty with order patterns. This youngster tries to put the doll's arms and legs in the right places.

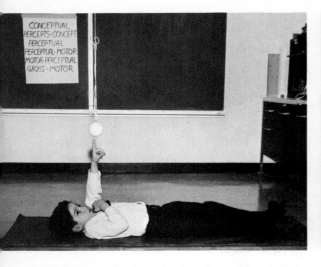

Developing eye-hand coordination: the reclining youngster follows the suspended moving ball with his eyes and, upon direction, taps it with his finger. Variations include standing and following the ball's movement with a finger.

Practicing visual-motor activities. The boy in the center turns the wheels, identifying directions as indicated by arrows on the backs of the wheels. The boy on the left uses a flashlight to spell words on the moving wheels.

was formerly assumed — affecting to a greater or lesser degree up to as many as 20 per cent of schoolchildren. The ability to read is becoming increasingly necessary for every person growing up in America today."

The Department of Health, Education, and Welfare now supports more than three hundred programs dealing with this problem and related learning disorders, most of them conducted at colleges and universities throughout the country. The programs being administered by the Office of Education are distributed in the fields of research, training, and diagnosis and treatment. Several Office of Education bureaus are involved in studying aspects of the problem. All the programs conducted by the Children's Bureau deal with training, and the programs under the National Institute of Child Health and Human Development concentrate on research. The National Institute of Mental Health, the National Center for Chronic Disease Control, and the National Institute of Neurological Diseases and Stroke also share in the joint effort.

Notwithstanding the widespread disagreement as to a precise definition of dyslexia, it is generally recognized that the

disability appears in two forms. One of these, primary or developmental dyslexia, is endogenous (internally caused), and reflects a neurological malfunction not indicated by any sign or history of brain injury. The other, secondary or reactive dyslexia, is exogenous (externally caused) and reflects an emotional disturbance, or the results of environmental factors, deprivation or distortion in early language experience.

There is a consensus, too, that the causes of dyslexia usually overlap so that single causative factors can seldom be isolated. The reading disability is the final result of multiple causes that are interactive. The primary disability, for example, often gives rise to reactions in school and at home that strengthen and prolong the original cause. The case of a boy in Natchez, Mississippi, illustrates the prime importance of early diagnosis of dyslexia.

Jimmy, a fifth grader, was becoming a problem to his teacher and parents when he realized he could not go on to the sixth grade with his class. He did well in his other subjects but could only read at the third-grade level. As the school term neared its close, he became moody and withdrawn. He walked with his head

As he draws bilateral circles, the youngster is developing eye-hand coordination, directionality and peripheral vision. His eyes are directed between the circles as he draws them. (Therapist in these photos: Cynthia Kallen.)

Photos both pages Maimonides Medical Center

Some children have difficulty in recognizing shapes. This boy traces triangles with a flashlight. Related activities include walking along a triangle taped to the floor, and drawing triangles with the template (right of center).

down, seldom looked at his teacher when she spoke to him, doodled instead of studying, and resented the slightest correction. One morning, Jimmy was brought to the classroom crying softly in his father's arms. That's when his teacher decided to do something about it.

The parents, the teacher learned, were at a loss to understand Jimmy's behavior. His homelife didn't seem to be the culprit: a sister was doing well at the same school. But he kept to himself, spending most of his time in his room alone, or silently watching television. His parents were somewhat impatient, suspecting Jimmy was merely sulking, but they were anxious to cooperate. At the teacher's suggestion, the father took Jimmy to the Child Development Center at the University of Mississippi at Jackson, a two hours' drive from Natchez. The boy was given a series of tests designed by Charles L. Shedd, head of the Reading Disability Clinic at the University of Alabama Medical College, and his trouble was diagnosed as a "specific perceptual-motor disability," Dr. Shedd's way of saying dyslexia.

From the medical point of view, dyslexia is a neurological ailment which

bears no more relation to intelligence than, say, color blindness. There is evidence that the condition has a physiological basis and is hereditary, being transmitted by a dominant gene and by either parent. However, it seems to occur more often in boys than girls, although statistics to establish a definite ratio are as yet not comprehensive enough to be conclusive.

Neurologists suspect that there may be some lack of synchronization between the brainstem and the thalamic system, and possibly some involvement affecting the "firing" of the electric impulses in the nervous system. One moment an impulse may get through the nerve paths normally, and a moment later an impulse from the same stimulus may not get through at all, giving the impression that the youngster is daydreaming, and requiring that the stimulus be repeated or modified or the child's position be changed.

To many educators, however, the term dyslexia is less descriptive than "reading disability," partly because it has been used in so many magazine and newspaper articles to describe a single type of ailment characterized by the reversal of letters and numbers that look alike — p and b, b and d, 6 and 9 — both in reading and writing. That type happened to be the one that afflicted Jimmy. But it is only one of the many types of reading disabilities.

The examinations to detect and correctly identify these reading disabilities vary from one diagnostic or treatment center to another but follow a general pattern. Jimmy's started with a standard oral IQ test in which his score was spotty: high in some areas, low in others. His performance was poor on a series of tests on reading aloud and writing, and he scored below his mental-age level on the draw-a-man test. Asked to draw the best picture of a man that he could, he traced the bare outline of the head, body, arms and legs without filling in facial features or details of clothing, such as collar, tie, pockets or buttons.

To test his sense of direction, 50 stick figures, some facing toward, some away from Jimmy and with their arms variously in the up, down or horizontal position, were held up for 1-second intervals while he marked their positions on his scorecard. More than 20 errors indicated he had trouble with "directional discrimination." In another visual test, he was given a sheet of paper and asked to copy 12 figures such as squares, diamonds, and circles, some with internal markings. His circle looked more like an egg. His square and diamond were misshapen, and the lines did not meet at the angles. Instead of arranging them in rows, as they were on the chart, he drew them helter-skelter on his paper.

IQ and reading and writing tests merely confirmed that his deficiencies were not due to lack of intelligence. The draw-a-man and the copy-a-figure tests were to determine how well he could distinguish internal detail. The result indicated that Jimmy was able to distinguish the general outline of a figure (a man) but not internal details (features and clothing). This explained why he had trouble telling the difference between an "o" and an "e." His failure to close the angles of the figures showed he couldn't distinguish an "o" from a "u," and the distortion showed he confused a whole word such as "told" with, say, "both" because in general outline they looked alike to him. Drawing the figures at random on his paper suggested lack of mental organizing ability.

The directionality tests were designed to reveal any confusion in right-left discrimination, a common characteristic of children with reading difficulties. We live in a right-handed world, and ability to distinguish left from right is particularly important in reading, where the text invariably proceeds from left to right. One of the indicators in Jimmy's case was his confusion between "b" and "d" and even between words, "was" and "saw." There were several more tests as a result of symptoms revealed in a discussion with Jimmy's father, who told of the boy's difficulties not only in school but at home and in his relations with neighborhood youngsters. Jimmy was only one of many Natchez children who were having severe reading problems, and in the fall of 1967 the Natchez-Adams County public-school system obtained from the U.S. Office of Education a grant of nearly $500,000 under title III of the Elementary and Secondary Education Act to conduct a 3-year program of instruction.

"When we started our center," says Director Joyce Jones, "Dr. Shedd helped us examine the 60 children with the lowest reading scores. Forty some were classified as having severe reading disabilities and formed our first classes.

"We had one class for second, third, and fourth graders and another for fifth, sixth, and seventh graders. They kept on with their regular work in other subjects, but in reading they all started from scratch with the 'APSL Approach to Literacy,' which Dr. Shedd designed."

APSL stands for "Alphabetic Phonetic Structural Linguistic," a multisensory method in which the student learns by seeing, saying, hearing, and feeling, first the letters of the alphabet and later, families of words. On the book's first left-hand page is a large letter "A" in script. A dot in the upper right quadrant indi-

The walking beam helps to develop body coordination. These pictures were taken at the Lafayette Clinic near Detroit, Michigan.

Both photos Benyas-Kaufman/Black Star

Right: The instructor's steadying hand helps a boy find his balance. Most experts agree that purposeful, coordinated body movements must be achieved before a child can master more complex learning skills.

cates where the child should start tracing the letter, and 15 tiny arrows show the path he should follow counterclockwise around to the starting dot again, then downward to complete the turn to the next letter.

As the child sees the letter, he pronounces it aloud so that he hears himself and others around him making the short "A" sound. At the same time, he traces the letter, following the arrows with his index finger so that he also feels the letter. Then he uses a piece of fine sandpaper to "draw" the letter on, so that he really feels how it is formed.

On the opposite page of the book are small and capital letters of the alphabet in script and print and the first word family, consisting of "a" and "at." The next two pages in the same pattern add "p" and "h" to make more word families. Gradually the child learns — with the aid of arrows to stress reading from left to right — to read such complicated phrases as "A fat cat sat" and "Pat a hat, Mat." When he reaches page 32 and can read "Tod had a duck in a box" and "Josh put the fox on the dock," he graduates to the next book, which has long vowels and consonant combinations such as "bl" and "cl."

To improve their motor coordination, the children attend classes in folk dancing and practice jumping rope, marching to music, playing ball, shooting baskets, and forward passing. These "play" sessions have a psychological purpose as well. The youngsters may never

When a youngster can slip a cylinder into its proper spot, he is on his way to mastering normal order patterns.

Benyas-Kaufman/Black Star

learn to excel at games or sports, but usually they can acquire enough skill to take part without embarrassment. Right-left confusion can be most mortifying on the dance floor.

The process is arduous but, in the long run, effective. At the end of the first year, 15 of the 43 in the first group returned to their former classrooms, and the average reading improvement for the entire group was measured at 2 years and 1 month.

Jimmy? He's been able to keep up with his other work and is now in the seventh grade with his reading score practically up to the sixth-grade level. Life at home is back to normal now, and he feels sure he'll be able to read all those eighth-grade books by the time he gets there.

The magnitude of the job of coping with the nation's reading disabilities has more or less dictated the approach being followed by the Office of Education's Bureau of Education for the Handicapped, according to the director, Associate Commissioner James J. Gallagher. If the 20 per cent figure used by former Secretary Cohen in estimating reading-disability prevalence turns out to be correct, it means that practically 1 schoolchild out of 5 is affected. This suggests that between 8 and 10 million children in the elementary and secondary schools need help. There are not enough centers or clinics in the country, Dr. Gallagher explained, to examine so great a number of children.

"Our bureau naturally is interested in the etiology — the medical cause — of learning problems, which include reading disability," he says. "And we welcome any advances made in that field and put them into practice. However, our job is primarily educational. We are more concerned with the symptoms than with the cause of learning disabilities, which constitute one of the major causes of children's handicaps. For that reason, BEH is concentrating research not on discovering the causes of these learning difficulties but on methods of dealing with them and, preferably, not in clinics or centers but in

Benyas-Kaufman/Black Star

Children who lack a sense of direction may be helped by this activity: crawling through a tunnel. Many youngsters are in need of such remedial training.

the neighborhood school. Its training is designed to develop specialists and, in addition, eventually to familiarize all teachers with the symptoms so that children can be attended to at the earliest possible stage.

"If a child has trouble reading in the first grade," Dr. Gallagher says, "he's likely to have it in the second grade, too. Teachers are quite likely to struggle along with poor readers in the lower grades, especially if they are doing well in their other subjects. But that is the best time to diagnose the problem, before it is complicated by frustration and emotional overtones."

The daydreaming and inattention mentioned in the letter to Ann Landers are two of the telltale symptoms that teachers are learning to watch for. The moody, shamefaced air, the distracted doodling, and the sensitiveness to criticism displayed by Jimmy are also common. So are hyperactivity, squirming, fidgeting, cracking the knuckles, tapping on the desk, and various types of motor awkward-

ness, stumbling, or inability to keep time. Children get mixed up playing "Peas Porridge Hot." Girls can't jump rope, and boys miss hitting a pitch "by a mile." Lack of left-right dominance may be a symptom; many perceptual-motor cases come from families in which left-handedness or ambidexterity occurs frequently. Slurring or mispronouncing words that sound somewhat alike may be another indication of reading disability.

The benefit of early diagnosis of reading disability was stressed in the report of a project headed by Dr. Eli Z. Rubin and being carried out in a suburb of Detroit by staff from the Lafayette Clinic. The project deals with retraining procedures for emotionally handicapped children who have many of the perceptual and motor deficiencies characteristic of poor readers. Many of the evaluative tests and corrective procedures actually are the same, since reading problems are an integral part of learning difficulties. Dr. Rubin reported among his findings that skills not only can be improved with training, but that the earlier the training begins the more likely it is that positive benefits will result.

101

BIOLOGY

CONTENTS

Spotted cats such as the cheetah and leopard are facing extinction. One conservation group has asked women to pledge not to buy coats made from the skins of these and other endangered species.

Norman Myers — Salmer   **103**

REVIEW OF THE YEAR-
BIOLOGY

Biologists continue to move closer to the core of life itself. In 1969, a
monumental accomplishment: the isolation of a single gene. During the year
work also proceeded on the isolation and synthesis of the basic substances of
life, and the laboratory duplication and explanation of human life processes.
More of the details of the system of life on earth were elucidated, and the
life of earth organisms in space was studied minutely, if somewhat briefly, in
the biosatellite program.

Molecular and cellular biology. One of the most significant biological
achievements of recent times occurred in 1969 when a team of scientists at
Harvard Medical School, headed by Dr. Jonathan Beckwith, isolated a single
gene (the basic unit of heredity). This feat will make it easier for researchers
to isolate other genes and to proceed into the steps of RNA synthesis in the
cell. But the achievement was described by one of the scientists as work that
might "loose more evil than good" on mankind: implications for possible
genetic control are myriad. The Harvard team isolated the lac operon gene.
This gene regulates the production of beta-galactosidase, an enzyme that
breaks down lactose. The men chose two bacteriophages (viruses which
multiply inside bacteria) that would infect the bacterium *Escherichia coli* and
incorporate the bacterium's lac operon gene (and some other gene segments)
into their own genetic material. The DNA of the two phages was then
isolated; a single strand of DNA was obtained from each sample. Each of the
strands contained a matching portion of the lac operon gene; when the strands
were joined, a whole coiled lac operon gene was formed, with the rest of
the DNA remaining separate. This excess DNA was destroyed enzymatically,
leaving the lac operon gene.

Gamma globulin, a complex molecule containing 1,320 amino acids, is one of
the defensive substances synthesized by the body when a foreign substance
invades. In 1969, the complete structure of this antibody was deciphered by
a group of Rockefeller University scientists headed by Dr. Gerard M. Edelman.
Gamma globulin is the first antibody to be deciphered and is the most complex
molecule to be deciphered thus far. It was already known that gamma
globulins consisted of four chains of amino acids; it took Dr. Edelman 3½
years to determine the sequence of the amino acids in these chains and to
locate the chemical bonds that hold the chains together. Dr. Edelman
discovered that the chains are formed in sections, or homologues, that are
quite similar. The sequences of some of these homologues seem to vary from
one antibody to another, while others do not vary. This discovery has important
genetic implications concerning the production of antibodies in the body.

Biochemists at the University of Wisconsin and the University of Rochester
have clarified the mechanism by which vitamin D operates in the body.
(Vitamin D is needed for normal growth and maintenance of bone.) By
studying calcium release from fetal rat bones and calcium transport in the rat
intestine, the scientists determined that a substance called 25-hydroxy-
cholecalciferol (25-HCC), a metabolite of vitamin D, is the active principle of
the vitamin. In order for vitamin D to produce its calcium mobilizing and
intestinal calcium transport effects in the body, it must be converted to 25-HCC.
At present, the liver appears to be the only place in the body where a significant

amount of vitamin D is converted to 25-HCC. There is still a possibility, according to Dr. Hector F. DeLuca of the University of Wisconsin, that 25-HCC may be converted to still another active principle in the tissues of the body where it is to act; present study is pursuing this line. Hopefully, this work will lead to a more rapid and reliable agent for treating diseases such as low blood calcium.

An important advance in the diagnosis and treatment of thyroid disorders was made by Baylor University College of Medicine scientists with their isolation and synthesis of the hormone TRF (thyrotropin releasing factor). This substance causes the pituitary gland to release thyrotropin, which then stimulates the thyroid gland to release thyroid hormone. TRF is produced in the hypothalamus, a small area at the base of the brain. The Baylor team, headed by Dr. Roger C. L. Guillemin, isolated the TRF from sheep brains and found that its structure consists of only three amino acids. The scientists tested the activity of both synthetic and natural TRF by injecting it into rodents; a rise in thyroid function was observed. Scientists believe that other releasing factors also exist in the brain. These factors, which also act on the pituitary, would control the production of growth and sex hormones. These other factors are also believed to originate in the hypothalamus and thus isolation of TRF should pace the way for identification of the other releasing factors.

In August 1969, the three-dimensional structure of insulin was announced by Nobel Laureate Dorothy C. Hodgkin of Oxford University in England. Her research group used X-ray crystallography to determine the structure of this hormone. This process involved bombarding insulin crystals with X rays. Electrons within the insulin molecules diffracted the X rays. By measuring the intensity and direction of the scattered X-ray particles, it was possible to map electron densities within the molecule. This, in turn, enabled the scientists to compute the arrangement of the molecule's atoms and thus its three-dimensional form. Dr. Hodgkin's group found that the insulin molecule consists of 2 chains of amino acids: a B chain of 30 amino acid subunits in a distorted U-shape with an A chain of 21 amino acid subunits nestled inside it.

In continuing fertilization studies, scientists at Cambridge University in England have apparently succeeded in the laboratory fertilization of a large number of human eggs. In early 1969 they reported that they were able to fertilize 18 out of 56 eggs. The scientists cultured human oocytes (egg cells) in the lab and then added human spermatocytes (sperm cells) to the culture. They were able to observe the penetration of sperm into the layers of the egg cells (an egg was considered fertilized when the sperm reached the zona pellucida of the egg).

Classification. An infrequent addition was made to the ordered system that classifies all the known animals of the world. This was the addition of a 28th phylum, Gnathostomulida, a group of delicate marine worms. Although the first species of this new grouping was described in 1928, the description was not published until 1956. Since then 10 genera and 43 species have been found attached to silts in shallow waters along coastlines throughout the world. The Gnathostomulida are difficult to observe because they reach only ½ millimeter (0.04 inches) in length and can be recognized only when they are alive. They need little oxygen and can survive under stagnant conditions.

A deep-sea animal whose existence was first reported in the 1870's was seen this year for the first time in its habitat on the ocean floor. The organism is a long-stemmed polyp of the family Umbellulidae. A special deep-sea camera photographed the tentacled animal at a depth of 15,900 feet in the Atlantic Ocean. The organism is related to sea anemones and living corals and, like these, lives attached to the ocean floor, unable to change its site.

Animal communication. In January 1970, a strange thing happened in Florida: 200 false killer whales swam onto the shore at Fort Pierce and beached themselves. When marine patrolmen towed a number of the whales out to sea, the 1,500-pound animals swam right back to the beach. After a second attempt the following day, the towed whales remained in the water and headed out to open water. But approximately 150 whales could not be saved and had to be buried. Dr. J. R. White of the Miami Seaquarium gave several possible explanations for the whales' behavior. Whales will beach themselves when the herd leader is ill or if the whales are infected; however, no sign of infection was detected in the blood of six of the beached whales. Secondly, echo-location signals used by the whales for navigation do not echo when they are aimed through shallow water toward a shelving beach; the whales think they are headed into open sea when they actually are headed for land. A third possibility is that the whales became disoriented in the shallow water, panicked and swam onto the beach.

Space biology. On July 28, 1969, a 14-pound male macaque monkey named Bonny was launched aboard Biosatellite 3 into a circular orbit 220 miles above the earth. The mission was to last 30 days but 8½ days after lift-off the flight was halted when Bonny became abnormally sluggish. The monkey died within 12 hours of recovery, apparently from adverse effects of weightlessness. A preliminary report said that Bonny had lost 20 per cent of his body weight through fluid loss caused by sweating and then by diuresis, which seemed to occur because of the redistribution of blood due to weightlessness in space. Because Bonny was monitored for 33 types of physiological information, a great deal was learned from the mission in spite of its premature end.

Ecology. Massive destruction of living coral in the coral reefs of the South Pacific is causing alarm among biologists. The perpetrator of this destruction is *Acanthaster planci,* the Crown of Thorns starfish. A 16-armed echinoderm about 2 feet in diameter, the Crown of Thorns has a voracious appetite — with a preference for living coral. It spawns twice a year, producing about one million eggs each time. The starfish was quite rare for decades; its population was controlled by natural enemies, especially the triton snail and living coral (which eats the larvae of the starfish). Why the sudden "population explosion"? The exact cause is not known, but the following explanations have been proposed: recent dredging and channel building in the area have killed the organisms that feed on the Crown of Thorns larvae; DDT and residual radiation from atomic tests may have had some effect; and demand by shell collectors for the beautiful triton shells may have decreased the number of this starfish enemy. By late 1969 the Crown of Thorns had invaded Australia's Great Barrier Reef (destroying more than 100 square miles of living coral), Guam (90 per cent of the coral had been destroyed along a 24-mile section), Borneo, Fiji, Palau, Wake, Midway and Saipan, among others. Since coral protects many of these islands from oceanic erosion and also forms many of the islands, the consequences of this invasion are widespread. The natural environment, including the supply of marine life that the islanders eat, is being destroyed. Marine scientists are working to determine the cause of the starfish invasion and to develop methods of combating the animals. One method currently being used is to inject fatal doses of formalin into the starfish. Using this method a 4-man team on Guam once killed 2,589 starfish during a 4-hour period.

SCIENTISTS ISOLATE A GENE*

Major Step in Hereditary Control

BY ROBERT REINHOLD

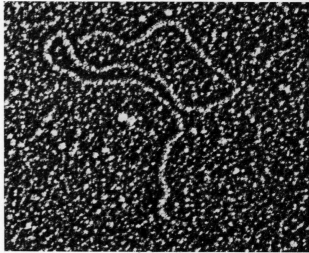

Dr. Lorne MacHattie, Harvard Univ.

A gene, the basic unit of heredity, isolated and photographed for the first time. The magnification was not determined. The calculated length of the gene is 1.4 microns.

"THIS is a very significant achievement," said Dr. Philip C. Hartman of Johns Hopkins University, an authority in the field.

"It's one of those things other scientists take pleasure in reading about," remarked Dr. Sol Spiegelman of Columbia University, a leading microbiologist.

The two men were commenting on a major advance in microbiology: the basic chemical unit of heredity, the gene, had been isolated from an organism for the first time by a team of scientists at Harvard Medical School.

The feat, considered a major one by other scientists, paves the way for detailed study — and possibly eventual control — of the complex and little-understood process by which genes determine tangible living traits. The team was headed by Dr. Jonathan R. Beckwith, 33 years old.

In spite of the significance of the feat, scientists were hardly surprised. It was the logical next step in a series of dramatic events that has revolutionized the science of biology since the basic chemical stuff of heredity was identified 25 years ago as deoxyribonucleic acid (DNA), a complex molecule present in the nuclei of all living cells.

It was a small segment of this substance that the Harvard group isolated from a common intestinal bacterium called *Escherichia coli*, or *E. coli*. The material represented the gene that controls the ability of the bacterium to metabolize, or use for fuel, a sugar known as lactose.

Because the gene came from such a lowly organism, the Harvard techniques cannot readily be applied to human or other complex organisms. However, the work has major implications for higher life because there is growing evidence that all living things, from the lowest single-celled bacterium to human beings, receive their traits by fundamentally the same mechanism.

For this reason, the achievement probably brings much closer the day — less than 25 years away by some estimates — when it will be possible to cure human diseases or change inborn traits by injecting new genes into people. Because such methods could be misused, many scientists view this prospect with considerable ambivalence.

An elegant experiment

The Harvard work, the experimental details of which were published in November 1969 in the journal *Nature*, was performed during the summer of 1969.

In an experiment that other scientists called "elegant," the term they apply to a sophisticated experiment that cuts to the heart of a complex conceptual problem with great simplicity, the Harvard team focused on the lactose gene, one of the largest and most thoroughly studied. It is one of 3,000 genes on the *E. coli* chromosome, the rod-shaped cell structure that bears the hereditary material.

They extracted the gene by using viruses as intermediary carriers. To do this they relied on the now classic techniques for which 3 American scientists — Max Delbruck, Alfred D. Hershey and Salvador E. Luria — were awarded the 1969 Nobel Prize for Physiology and Medicine.

These techniques are based on the fact that bacteria are infected by certain viruses, called phages. Phage particles enter the bacterial cells, pluck out small bits of the cell's genetic material (the DNA) and multiply.

The Harvard scientists used 2 such phages, known technically as lambda-plac*5* and phi-80plac*1*, both of which contain the lactose gene picked up from *E. coli* cells, along with several other, unwanted genes. The 2 phages differ mainly in the sequences of chemical units that make up the lactose gene. These sequences face in opposite directions, which was the key to the experiment.

The DNA in each of these phages is double stranded, shaped something like a twisted ladder, the rungs of which consist of chemically complementary pairs.

By treatment with special chemicals, these strands were unwound and separated. Then 2 strands, 1 from each phage, were brought together in a test tube. Since only the lactose genes were opposite mirror images of each other, and therefore complementary, they immediately came together and formed a new double strand.

The remaining, unwanted gene segments could not find complementary partners and hung on as loose, single-stranded ends. These ends were then dissolved by treating with a special enzyme, or biological catalyst, that affects only single-stranded DNA.

The result was a purified segment of bacterial DNA that was responsible for only 1 genetic function, which is the ultimate definition of a gene. Large enough to be photographed with an electron mi-

croscope, it measured 1.4 microns, or .000055 inches, in length.

Many scientists have been working on the gene-purification problem for some time, using a variety of approaches. Until now, they had succeeded only in isolating 3 or 4 genes together.

It was important to obtain a single pure gene so that its action and the action of other cell components on it could be studied without other genes present to complicate the situation.

The most immediate practical significance of the feat is its implications for understanding the mechanisms by which genes are controlled. The broad outlines of these mechanisms were sketched by 2 French scientists, François Jacob and Jacques Monod, whose efforts were rewarded by a Nobel Prize. The inner biochemical and biophysical workings of the process, however, remain to be elucidated.

The French scientists advanced the theory, now substantially verified, that genes are controlled by a negative mechanism. That is, they are kept turned off by a "repressor" until another substance, an "inducer," comes along and disengages the repressor, thus allowing the gene to express itself.

Thus a gene consists of 3 elements, together called an operon. The elements are a "promoter" that produces the repressor; an "operator" that starts the gene operating but is normally dampened by the repressor; and a "structural" portion, which is placed into action by the operator and does the main work of the gene. It does this by directing the production of cell proteins which in turn govern cell reactions and the formation of protoplasm, the cellular material. The proteins, thus, specify genetic traits.

Operon isolated

Therefore what Dr. Beckwith and his team did was to isolate the lactose operon. The "lac operon," as it is called, controls the bacteria's ability to metabolize lactose by governing the production of an enzyme, called beta-galactosidase, which chews up the sugar. Enzymes are proteins.

The achievement clears the path for a detailed study of the workings of the Jacob-Monod mechanism in the test tube under controlled conditions. A variety of experiments is possible, not only with the lac operon but with other bacterial genes, now that the techniques are perfected.

For example, it should be possible to zero in on the mystery of where on the gene the repressor binds to prevent its function, as well as where and how the gene directs protein formation. Such knowledge may permit scientists to turn genes on and off at will.

In addition, the purified gene could be used to study the chemical products of a gene in action uncontaminated by the products of other genes. Ultimately it may also be possible to pin down the exact sequence of chemical units that make up individual genes.

It is generally believed that the operator is the crucial site for the regulation of protein production. Recently other scientists at Harvard University isolated the repressor substance. Now that the gene has also been isolated, the effect of the repressor can more readily be studied.

Genes operate by first producing a substance called ribonucleic acid (RNA), which acts as a messenger, carrying the genetic information of the DNA to the site of protein manufacture in the cells.

Other steps possible

With a purified gene now available, it should be possible in the test tube to measure with great precision the nature of the RNA produced and follow the complex steps of protein production.

If scientists can determine the sequence of chemical units in individual genes, this may someday enable them to "manufacture" genes artificially to compensate for genetic deficiencies.

The genetic-control mechanisms have attracted the attention not only of basic scientists like the Harvard team, but also medical men. It is widely thought that diseases like cancer are fundamentally cases of the genetic-control mechanisms having broken down.

All of this has broad implications for "genetic engineering," the intervention in hereditary processes to instill desired new traits or to eliminate unwanted ones.

Misuse feared

As yet, the methods are not perfected, but biologists speak confidently of someday infecting humans with viruses that carry new genes in order to cure hereditary diseases, such as hemophilia. But some also fear the same ability could be turned to destructive purposes by an unscrupulous government.

Such fears have caused much unease among scientists, including Dr. Beckwith and his associates, Dr. James A. Shapiro; Dr. Lorne A. MacHattie; Lawrence J. Eron, a student; Dr. Garret M. Ihler and Dr. Karen Ippen.

"The more we think about it, the more we realize that it could be used to purify genes in higher organisms," said Dr. Beckwith, a molecular geneticist, who wears a dark beard, a Caesar-style haircut and flare-bottom trousers. "The steps do not exist now, but it is not inconceivable that within not too long it could be used, and it becomes more and more frightening — especially when we see work in biology used by our Government in Vietnam and in devising chemical and biological weapons."

Dr. Shapiro concurred. "The work we have done may have bad consequences over which we have no control," he said, drawing a parallel to the development of atomic energy. "The use by the Government is the thing that frightens us."

Not all scientists agree with them. Dr. Joshua Lederberg, the Nobel Prize-winning geneticist at Stanford University, has consistently argued that the potential medical benefits of genetic manipulation outweigh the risks of misuse for political purposes.

The Harvard experiment was supported by grants from the American Cancer Society, the Jane Coffin Childs Memorial Fund for Medical Research, the National Institutes of Health and the National Science Foundation.

An oil-saturated duck, barely able to move because of a thick coating of crude oil, struggles on a California beach.

UPI

BEWARE OF MAN

Water and Shore Birds Fight for Survival

A LOON, caught in the sticky black oil, dies as its respiratory system becomes clogged. On the nearby shore, a cormorant, trying to clean its oil-soaked feathers, dies from ingesting the lethal goo.

A grebe, which regularly eats up to five pounds of fish daily, consumes the DDT in the fishes' bodies. Eventually the high DDT level in its body causes the grebe to die of nerve poisoning.

A tern, eating shellfish found in mud flats, dies from poisons in the shellfish — poisons that originated in a chemical plant that dumps its wastes into a nearby river.

A hungry whooping crane is forced to leave the wildlife refuge where its numbers have slowly increased. Dredging operations upstream from the refuge have killed the sea animals that compose the whooping crane's diet. There is no other suitable habitat for the bird. Though hungry, it dies not of starvation but from a shot fired by a careless hunter.

A flock of ducks bypass the bay where once they spent the winter. The grasses, snails and crabs that lived there have been replaced by a tract of homes; the once-fresh water is now being polluted by raw sewage from the new homes.

These examples illustrate some of the tragic consequences of man's growing population and advancing technology.

The water and shore birds of North America are valuable components of a healthy, balanced wildlife community. Their economic value — in luring people to seaside resorts, for example — is great.

Their esthetic value to man is immeasurable. What is more elegant than the flight of a flock of swans, their powerful wings moving slowly as they pass northward across the evening sky? What is more graceful than a flamingo, with its long curving neck and its pink plumage? What is more pleasurable than recognizing the "qualk" of an eastern green heron or the "kuk-kuk-kuk" of a pied-billed grebe?

If man wishes to continue to share this planet with birds, he must reverse the trends that threaten their extinction.

It is essential that he keep certain areas free from the influences of civilization. Many birds require specialized habitats for nesting or for year-round residence. The development of wildlife refuges, national parks and local nesting areas should be strongly encouraged.

Man must stop polluting the environment with poisonous herbicides, pesticides and factory wastes. He must clean up his sewage and stop using rivers and ocean beds as places to dump his garbage.

And he must educate his fellowmen to the dangers of the paths we have followed for too long. This task is of major importance. "It's so difficult to make people understand the seriousness of the threat," says ecologist David M. Gates. "They don't realize how much we've lost already. They don't realize that we live in a closed system, that the air and water, the plants and animals are being irreparably damaged and there are no replacements."

110

WATER AND SHORE BIRDS OF NORTH AMERICA

Russ Kinne, National Audubon

Birds are surely among the most beautiful of our wildlife. Their spectacular colors, intricate feather patterns, charming songs and delightful behavior have given pleasure to all of us. The birds of our waters and shores are loved by all who have seen a heron standing guard near its nest, heard the calls of wild geese flying overhead, watched a sandpiper race along the water's edge or fed a pair of mallards in the community pond. On these pages we look at some of the most popular water and shore birds. Above: A pair of wood ducks (Aix sponsa); they can be found throughout temperate North America.

The somewhat comical looking Atlantic puffin (Fratercula arctica) has a large sculptured bill. It is found along the North Atlantic coast.

The brown pelican (Pelicanus occidentalis) has a wingspread up to seven feet. Its range is mainly tropical, extending northward only as far as the coasts of California and the Carolinas.

Young American egrets (Casmerodius albus egretta). These gregarious birds can be found as far north as southern Canada, but they retreat to warmer climes for the winter season.

Cy La Tour

Red-necked grebes (Colymbus grisegena) are shy birds during nesting season. They are found on the lakes in the prairies and spruce forests of Canada and the northern United States.

Cleveland P. Grant

Helen Cruickshank, National Audubon

The slender-billed white ibis (Eudocimus albus) nests in the southern United States and southward into South America. Its diet consists largely of crayfish.

Common terns (Sterna hirundo) nest in central and eastern Canada southward to the Gulf of Mexico. The young begin to fly when they are about one month old.

The red-backed sandpiper (Erolia alpina) nests in the Arctic and winters on the U.S. coasts. During the spring it has a distinctive red back and a black belly.

The plumage of the least bittern (Ixobrychus exilis) matches the reedy marshes where it lives. This small member of the heron family is found from South America to southern Canada.

This jaunty-looking bird is the red-whiskered bulbul. A native of India, it has become a pest in southern Florida where it feeds on mangoes and avocados.

EXOTIC INVADERS BRING WOE TO FLORIDA*

Walking Catfish, African Snails and Giant Toads Thrive in Area

BY TOM HERMAN

PEOPLE around Miami don't know whether to laugh or cry. But then, what would you do if you were being invaded by giant African snails, Asian walking catfish, red-whiskered bulbuls and giant toads?

* Reprinted from *The Wall Street Journal*, January 14, 1970.

This giant toad (*Bufo marinus*) has sacs of highly toxic poison on its back. The animal can squirt drops of the poison up to a distance of two feet.

111

Unlikely as it may sound, just such an invasion is occurring. "Miami has never been more exciting," says one positive-minded local official.

The snail invasion started when a few of the snails were brought from Hawaii, probably 3 or 4 years ago. "As near as we can tell, a youngster brought 2 or 3 of them back in his pocket," says a spokesman for the Florida Department of Agriculture and Consumer Services. "Evidently he got tired of them and let them go." Now there are thousands of them.

The snails turned out to be giant African snails, which can grow to as much as a foot in length — and which reproduce prodigiously. Moreover, they seem to eat almost anything.

In September 1969, startled residents of North Miami discovered hordes of giant snails creeping over their yards and houses, munching away at lawns, trees and ornamental plants — and even chewing the paint off houses in search of the calcium they need for their shells.

Billions of descendants

The Department of Agriculture and Consumer Services moved into the 14-square-block area of North Miami where the outbreak occurred, spreading poison pellets on lawns and gathering up as many snails as it could find. As of December,

it had collected 15,667, of which 5,480 were dead as an apparent result of the poison.

But, one official says, "those snails can lie dormant for months and then reproduce like hell. So if we miss one, we may have the same problem again in no time." Indeed, a single snail can lay 600 eggs a year — and one scientist calculates that its descendants could theoretically number in the billions within a few years.

Walking catfish also are undergoing a population explosion — as are the red-whiskered bulbuls and the giant toads, known to scientists as *Bufo marinus.*

The catfish, which attain lengths as great as two feet, are particularly pesky because as they increase in number they gobble up large quantities of food in the city's waterways, leaving little for popular game fish. Officials say fishing in Biscayne Bay and in Miami's canals has suffered as a result.

Unlike the giant snails, the catfish are nearly impossible to exterminate, according to one official. "Poison one lake or canal, and those clever catfish just simply walk to another," he says.

Actually, naturalists say the catfish doesn't exactly walk. Instead, as one explains it, the fish "creeps along like an infantryman sneaking under barbed wire, using its fins for knees and elbows." The

walking catfish has a primitive lung that enables it to absorb oxygen from the atmosphere. Thus it can stay alive for long periods out of water.

John W. Woods, chief of fisheries for the Florida Game and Freshwater Fish Commission, says walking catfish were brought into Florida by tropical-fish enthusiasts. It's believed, he says, that they escaped when breeders tried to raise them in backyard pools — and the fish simply walked away.

A Federal offense

Since January 1, 1970, it has been a Federal offense to buy or sell walking catfish. But there is a thriving black market in which they sell for up to $10 apiece.

The red-whiskered bulbul is a bird, a cardinal-size native of India. Several years ago a small flock escaped from a local bird importer, and now the birds have multiplied to a population of several hundred.

Bird watchers are delighted, but growers of mangoes and avocados are up in arms because the birds delight in eating their products before they have a chance to harvest them.

The bufo toads, natives of South America, evidently were imported deliberately from the Caribbean to control a beetle that attacks sugarcane, according to Vernon Ogilvie, a biologist for the state

Florida Dept. of Agriculture and Consumer Services

The giant African land snail (*Achatina fulica*) is hermaphroditic, having both male and female reproductive organs. It reproduces at a fantastic rate; theoretically, one snail could produce 8,000,000,000 descendants in 3 years.

Game and Freshwater Fish Commission. "But," he says, "what they're really controlling is our dogs and other toads."

The bufo toads, which are 6 inches high and can be 18 inches long with legs extended, eat smaller toads. They don't attack dogs, but they have sacs of highly toxic poison on their backs. The poison is released when dogs attack them.

"Hundreds of dogs have died," says Mr. Ogilvie. He says he saw one Doberman pinscher die within 45 minutes after it bit a bufo toad. The dog died while it was being taken to a veterinarian.

"The catfish are walking," say Floridians on rainy nights. About 1 foot long and weighing 1 pound when fully-grown, the fish can walk 4 or 5 feet a minute over wet ground. It does this by balancing on the tough spine of its dorsal fin, arching its back and dragging its tail forward. Normally the fish takes in oxygen through its gills. However, a rudimentary lung located behind the gills enables it to breathe air while it is out of water.

Charles L. Trainor

BIONICS

Simulating the Functions of Living Things

BY MORLEY R. KARE

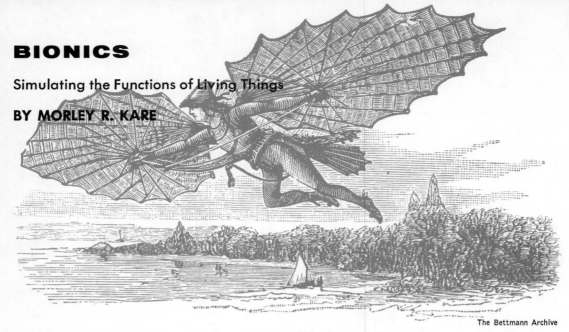

The Bettmann Archive

By wearing wings and a tail, man once tried to imitate the majestic flight of birds.

A SPARROW swoops through the air. Adjusting swiftly for flight speed and wind, it lets down its "landing gear" just in time to stop precisely on a twig. How does this bird make all the calculations and accomplish the feat so deftly? Most airplanes, even with pilots' compartments filled with instruments, still need long landing fields.

If we were to place a piece of rotting meat in a stream, it would soon be covered with invertebrates such as *Planaria* that are directed to the meat by their chemical senses. Many fish, with taste buds on the outside of their bodies, can demonstrate even more impressively a sensitivity for chemical stimuli. How do these animals perceive the chemical, and how do they track it down?

These questions are of special interest to researchers in an area of scientific technology called bionics (*bio,* from the Greek word for "life," and electro*nics*). Bionicists attempt to solve technical problems by the application of mechanical and electrical mechanisms comparable to those found in nature. They design and develop machines and instruments that to some extent mimic, or simulate, the reactions and behavior of living organisms.

Although the name bionics was coined as recently as 1960, the subject to which it refers has interested man for hundreds of years. Early inventors of flying machines, for example, tried to imitate biological examples by building their unsuccessful flying machines with flapping wings; some models even included a covering of chicken feathers. Levers such as crowbars and bottle openers are applications of mechanisms found in the skeletal systems of animals. More recently, an optical ground-speed indicator for airplanes was designed by mimicking a beetle's response to moving light patterns. And an understanding of the function of the visual system of the horseshoe crab has suggested a means of creating a television image with sharper contrast than any previously produced television system.

The scope of bionics

The field of bionics overlaps or approaches other comparatively new disciplines. It is closely related to cybernetics — the science of control and communicaton systems in animals and machines. It merges with cyborg (from *cyb*ernetic *orga*nism) — the mechanical, electronic and biomedical techniques used to improve the performance of the human body. Bionics is related to robotics — the design of robots, or machines that resemble men or animals or that perform some of their functions. Then there is the possibility of creating life in a test tube; that is, synthetic biological molecules or even protoplasm.

Finally, bionics is related to the abstract (not actual or mechanical) simulation of life processes by means of computers or mathematical models. For example, biomathematicians have made computer models of systems in the human body, including the respiratory, nervous and circulatory systems. Information about a particular system is fed into a computer, which determines the relationships between the various components of the system, and analyzes the ways in which their actions are controlled. Mathematical models representing each of the theories are developed, and the computer determines which of these models best simulate the function of the system. Such abstract models may lead to bionic applications. For example, a simple mechanical model of a nerve has been developed from such a study; based on a steel tube and water bath, it is able to simulate various nervelike phenomena.

In this article, we will restrict ourselves to mechanical, chemical and electronic simulation of biological reactions.

Approaching a problem

A simple example will serve to illustrate bionic techniques. In building a submarine, designers wish to determine the most efficient shape for the hull. The bionic approach to this problem consists of studying organisms that exhibit the desired characteristic of moving through water with the least amount of resistance. We know that fish meet this requirement and that sharks and dolphins are fast, efficient swimmers and could serve as models for the shape of our hull. The answer given to engineering by the biological model may not be simple and straightforward. For example, after a group of engineers determined the muscle power, size and shape and calculated the theoretical speed of the fast-swimming dolphin, it was determined that this aquatic animal's observed speed was ten times its capacity to produce energy. The explanation is thought to rest upon the rubbery skin of the dolphin, which tends to reduce the drag of the water flowing along its surface. Thus it would seem that an actual imitation of the elastic covering of the dolphin might increase a submarine's velocity. This information has also been considered for airplane coverings and the inside coatings of pipelines.

The lesson to be gained is that engineers must do more than superficially copy nature. They must determine the crucial principles that account for the specific characteristic: the why and how in the construction of an organism. Of primary importance in the flight of a bird is the shape of the rounded leading edge and the thin, tapered trailing edge of the wing; the feathers are not so important.

Many of the basic characteristics of living organisms suggest that there are new and more fundamental approaches to old engineering problems. At present, for example, we use heat to generate steam; this steam drives a turbine that drives an electric generator. It would be more efficient to convert the heat directly into electrical energy. It is known that certain microorganisms will generate electrical potentials in the process of breaking down organic waste products such as garbage. Might a properly designed garbage dump yield significant amounts of electrical power?

The study of animal senses

It is the sensory mechanisms of animals that have attracted the most interest among bionicists. In the past it was assumed that simpler forms of animal life had less complex sense organs than man. It is now abundantly evident that this is not invariably the case. Some animals with nervous systems less developed than man's have certain sensory capabilities that exceed our own. A dog can hear sounds in ranges beyond those discernible to the human ear. A bird has an acute sense of visual detail; it can better discriminate objects than can a human being. A butterfly, using sense organs on its feet, can detect minute concentrations of sugar; man is unable to taste such small amounts of this substance.

Not only do many organisms surpass our abilities in sensory modes similar to our own, but they possess types of perception unknown to man. An African fish, *Gymnarchus niloticus,* possesses special organs that generate a weak electric field around the fish. Any object that enters this field causes a disturbance; a change of 1/5,000,000 of a volt can be detected by the fish.

Perhaps the most studied of the senses not found in man is the echo-location system of the bat. This system is akin to the principle of radar and sonar. The bat emits short shrieks of sound, which sweep or scan over a range of frequencies, too high for a human to hear. These are reflected from obstacles and return to be heard by the bat. In natural surroundings, the bat locates moths and other insects by means of this echo ranging. Moths, in their turn, can detect the high-frequency shrieks with a pair of tiny hearing mechanisms, each consisting of only two cells. When the moth detects a bat-like sound, it begins to fly erratically, rapidly changing directions and seeking ground or other cover. This behavior

General Electric

By means of an advanced control system, this four-legged "walking machine" mimics and amplifies the movements of its operator. The operator's arms control the unit's front legs; his legs control the rear legs of the machine.

can be observed in the summer by attracting moths to a light and shaking a set of keys. Some of the metallic sounds of the keys mimic those of the bat, thus provoking the moth's defensive flight pattern.

While man's senses are often downgraded when compared with those of some animals, they are, nevertheless, of interest to bionicists. Under ideal conditions man can perceive a wire one eighth inch in diameter at a distance of a half mile. He can detect some odors when they are present in only a fraction of a millionth of a

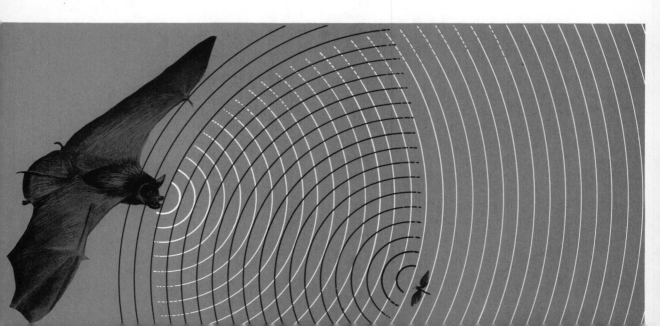

This electronic device "sees" like a real frog's eye. The display panel held by the engineer on the left shows what the simulated eye is seeing. Compare it with the disk held before the device by the man on the right. The location of the disk on the "frog's eye" is the same as on the display panel.

RCA "Electronic Age"

gram. He can hear sounds so low that his eardrums vibrate through a distance of less than the diameter of a hydrogen atom.

Body mechanics

Although bionicists have been most interested in sensory mechanisms, there are equally important engineering lessons to be learned from a study of other biological systems. There is the internal-gland cooling system of a fowl; the double-barreled pump in the proboscis of a mosquito; the bioluminescence of a firefly; the nutrient-distribution system in plants.

Studies of insect flight reveal that these animals are equipped with tiny hairs

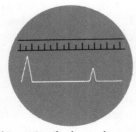

Tracking aircraft by radar, a bionic application of the bat's echo-location system. As a transmitter (left) sends out a searching pulse, it also sends out a locking pulse to the receiving set. The range indicator (above) shows a deflection from the locking pulse and a second, smaller deflection from an echo pulse.

to sense speed; the leading edges of their wings are slotted and able to detect turbulent airflow. It was also found that insects obtain the greatest lift on the flat wing surfaces when they are close to stalling speed. Airline pilots flying between San Francisco and Hawaii, in efforts to conserve fuel during the 2,700-mile journey, discovered the same principle some thirty years ago.

Applications of bionics

A number of mechanical and electrical principles found in living organisms have been used to improve man-made devices or to invent new ones. Pumps, levers and bellows are inventions in which man has unknowingly simulated animal mechanisms. Applications in the design of airplanes, submarines and other machines have already been mentioned.

The eye of a frog reacts primarily to small moving objects such as insects. But it is also very sensitive to the bluish parts of the light spectrum. It is believed that this adaptation enables the frog to jump toward water when danger threatens (water reflects blue light waves). Military and aerospace engineers have developed a radar system based on the optics of a frog's eye. It can detect planes, missiles and spacecraft better than ordinary radar, which is too often "confused" by acci-

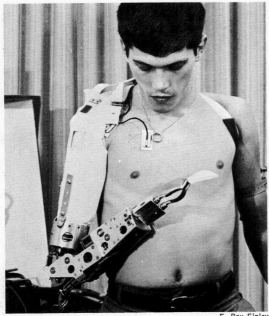

F. Ray Finley

This artificial arm simulates the actions of a real arm. When the man tenses certain body muscles, tiny electrical currents are produced. These currents activate the arm.

dental intrusions such as clouds, rain and birds.

Medical applications include a small, portable sonar apparatus built into a special cane for the blind. Using echolocation, the sonar detects obstacles in the person's path. The resulting changes in the sonar sound are heard by the person, thus enabling him to walk more freely.

Studies of the nature of muscular contraction and of the relationships between muscles and nerves have led to the construction of an electronic arm. This artificial arm operates through signals from the brain, in much the same manner as a normal arm. The arm is powered by a battery which, in turn, is activated by electrodes attached to the skin over muscles in the chest, back and shoulder that control arm motion. If, for example, the person wishes to open a door, electrical impulses for the necessary movement travel from the brain to nerves in the muscles. Here the impulses are picked up by the electrodes, which amplify and transmit them to an electronic box in the arm. The incoming signals indicate the type of move-

ment wanted by the brain; the electronic instrumentation activates motors in the arm, which then carry out the orders.

In a system called Visilog, the distance-judging ability of an eye is simulated in an instrument within a moving vehicle. This device detects the vehicle's approach to a solid object by the apparent change in the texture of the solid's surface as it becomes larger in the field of view. The device can compute the rate of approach from these textural impressions; it then slows the vehicle accordingly.

In some cases, man's machines far surpass living things in power, speed and adaptability. In other cases, they are woefully inferior. The biological cell, for example, is a miracle of complex functions in a microscopic package. Man's attempts at miniaturizing his devices are almost laughable in comparison.

There are limits on the usefulness of biological models for engineering-system designs. For example, no animal uses the wheel as a mechanism to propel itself. Had the inventors of the automobile been purely imitative bionicists, they would have incorporated a system of mechanical legs into their machines.

The purpose of bionics is to look for, and simulate, systems, techniques and devices in the world of plants and animals. The ultimate bionic development would encompass all the abilities of the nervous system of a living organism. It would be capable of modifying its operation to meet the demands of the environment; it would be capable of "learning" to cope with changes; it would have the capacity of self-repair; and it would be able to receive, store and intelligently use information.

As human society becomes more and more complex, new ideas for devices are needed in an ever-increasing number to keep in step with the changing mode of living. There is ample incentive to encourage engineers to study the self-adaptive and self-organizing systems found in nature; we can expect that this systematic combination of physical science and biology will be a fruitful union of benefit to all mankind.

Caltech   UPI   Wide World

Max Delbrück   Alfred D. Hershey   Salvador E. Luria

THE 1969 NOBEL PRIZE FOR PHYSIOLOGY AND MEDICINE*

BY GUNTHER STENT

WITH the award of the 1969 Nobel Prize for Physiology and Medicine to Max Delbrück of the California Institute of Technology, Salvador E. Luria of the Massachusetts Institute of Technology, and Alfred D. Hershey of the Carnegie Institution of Washington, 3 men are honored at last who, 30 years ago, began to transform the landscape of classical Mendelian genetics into the latter-day "molecular" Crick-Watsonian scene. This long delay in bestowing the ultimate accolade upon the 3 prime movers of molecular genetics is only too comprehensible from the purview of the Nobel Prizes. Indeed, to Nobelologists it must come as a surprise that this award was made at all, since neither Delbrück's nor Luria's name is associated with any of the kinds of spectacular breakthrough discoveries for which the prize is almost always given, and Hershey's best-known experiment represented merely an independent confirmation of an inference

* Reprinted from *Science,* Vol. 166, pages 479–481, October 24, 1969. Copyright 1969 by the American Association for the Advancement of Science.

drawn by others 8 years before. That is not to say that these men have remained obscure and unappreciated until the present. On the contrary, all 3 are widely revered, but the basis of their fame is elusive and difficult to explain to strangers (and even to molecular geneticists under 30). In order to set forth the peculiar nature of Delbrück's contribution, his friends and colleagues (including Luria and Hershey) published a collection of autobiographical essays, *Phage and the Origins of Molecular Biology,* on the occasion of his 60th birthday. These essays give a much better overall picture of the significance of this Nobel Prize than can be provided in this brief appreciation.

From physics to genetics

Max Delbrück was born in Berlin in 1906, the scion of a well-known German family whose members included bankers, clerics, and savants, among them Delbrück's father Hans, the famous historian of war. Delbrück studied physics in Göttingen, in the wake of the revolution

119

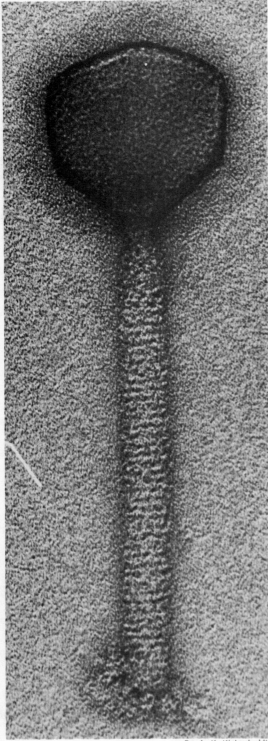

Dr. A. K. Kleinschmidt

A bacteriophage, enlarged to 845,000 times its actual size. The head consists of DNA surrounded by a protective protein membrane. The tail consists of a protein sheath surrounding a hollow central core.

brought about by the development of quantum mechanics. Later he went as a postdoctoral fellow to Niels Bohr's Copenhagen laboratory at a time when Bohr was working out the philosophical implications of the fundamental changes which the new physics had brought to the conception of the nature of physical law. Bohr then believed that the general notion of complementarity, of which Werner Heisenberg's "uncertainty principle" is but an example, ought to have important epistemological consequences also for other scientific domains, especially for biology. In particular, Bohr thought that, for the ultimate understanding of life itself, some fundamental complementarity relation holding for living aggregates of matter must first be found, and that this finding would devolve from the discovery of some deep paradox presented by life. Delbrück was profoundly influenced by Bohr's "Copenhagen spirit." He returned to Berlin to become an assistant to Otto Hahn and Lise Meitner, but in his spare time he joined a discussion group led by the Russian geneticist N. W. Timofeeff-Ressovsky. As a result of this contact, Delbrück published a paper in 1935 in which he pointed out that genetics is that domain of biology in which Bohr's anticipated complementarity relation is most likely to be found, because the long-term stability of the tiny gene bids fair to embody a deep paradox. In fact, Delbrück decided to do full-time work in genetics and went to the California Institute of Technology (Caltech), where Thomas Hunt Morgan and his school then reigned over classical genetics. Delbrück thus left his employers Hahn and Meitner just before they discovered uranium fission. Contrary to his expectation, Delbrück did not take up work with any of the standard experimental materials of classical genetics at Caltech, but instead joined Emory L. Ellis in a study of phage reproduction. In collaboration with Ellis he designed the one-step growth experiment, publication of which in 1939 marked the beginning of modern phage research. This experiment showed very clearly that after the phage, or bacterial virus, particle infects its bacterial host cell, there elapses a half-hour latent period during which the parental phage multiplies to yield an issue of several hundred progeny. Delbrück realized that the phage-infected bacterium represents the ideal experimental system for studying self-replication, the evident capacity for self-replication being the most mysterious and, hopefully, paradoxical aspect of the gene. And since the small size of the phage particle is of about the same order of magnitude as that which in the late 1930's had been estimated to be the size of the gene, Delbrück thought it should not be too difficult to work out just how, during that half-hour latent period, the parent phage manages to give rise to its progeny.

The American phage group

In 1940, at a meeting of the American Physical Society in Philadelphia, Delbrück happened to meet Salvador Luria, then recently arrived in America as a refugee from war-torn Europe. Luria, born in 1912 in Turin, had studied medicine in Italy. The outbreak of World War II found him working in Paris at the Pasteur Institute, where he (like the 1965 laureate André Lwoff) had learned the techniques of phage research from Eugene Wollman. Upon the fall of France, Luria fled to Marseilles, whence he managed to sail for the United States. He has described his meeting with Delbrück in these terms: "After a few hours of conversation and a dinner with Wolfgang Pauli and G. Placzek, during which the talk was mostly in German, mostly about theoretical physics, mostly above my head, Delbrück and I adjourned to New York for a 48-hour bout of experimentation in my laboratory at the College of Physicians and Surgeons." Delbrück and Luria had found that they were both interested in the same fundamental problem (though Luria denies having had much use for such romantic ideas as paradoxes), and with their first meeting there had come into being the American Phage Group, whose members were united by the common goal of solving the enigma of self-replication. One of the first recruits was Thomas F. Anderson, in collaboration with whom Luria obtained an electron micrograph of phage particles in 1942. This picture confirmed Helmut Ruska's first report of the year before; that phage particles consist of a round head and a thin tail. Just as the birth of genetics is considered to have taken place in 1865

This electron microphotograph shows two bacteriophages (arrows) infecting a bacterial cell. Only the phages' nucleic-acid molecules (DNA) enter the bacterium; the protein coats remain outside. The DNA causes the bacterium to produce new phages. Thus it is the sole genetic material of the bacteriophages.

Manfred E. Bayer

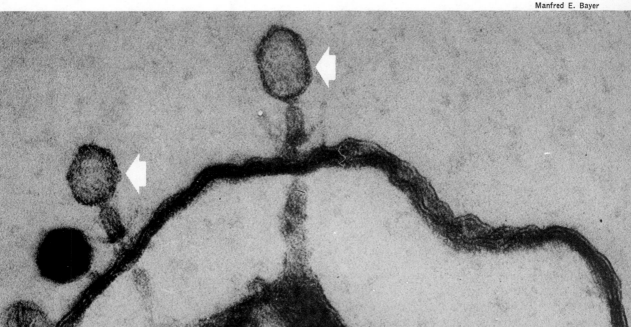

122

upon the appearance of Gregor Mendel's paper reporting the conclusions he had drawn from his crosses of the garden pea, so the birth of bacterial genetics can be dated as of 1943, when Luria and Delbrück published a joint paper in which they showed that the appearance of phage-resistant variants in cultures of phage-sensitive bacteria represents the selection of spontaneous bacterial mutants. This conclusion was contrary to the then current teachings of bacteriology, which, according to Luria, was "the last stronghold of Lamarckism." Luria and Delbrück were not the first to study bacterial mutation, any more than Mendel was the first to cross plants for the study of heredity. But with their paper Luria and Delbrück did for bacterial genetics what Mendel had done for general genetics — namely, showed for the first time what kind of experimental arrangements, what kind of data analysis, and, above all, what kind of sophistication is needed for obtaining meaningful and unambiguous results. Whereas it did not announce any striking or unexpected result, their paper became the standard by which all later papers were measured.

While he was working on the manuscript of that paper, Delbrück (then an instructor of physics at Vanderbilt Univer-

sity) was paid a visit by Alfred Hershey. When returning the manuscript to Luria, Delbrück reported that Hershey "drinks whiskey but not tea. Simple, to the point, likes living in a sailboat for three months; likes independence." Born in 1908, in Lansing, Michigan, Hershey did his undergraduate work in chemistry at Michigan State College. He then went to Washington University, St. Louis, where he studied under J. Bronfenbrenner, one of the first bacteriologists to have taken up the study of phages in America, shortly after their discovery in Europe during World War I. Upon meeting Delbrück in 1943, Hershey became another charter member of the nascent Phage Group and began to address himself to the kind of genetic problems in which Delbrück and Luria were interested. In 1945 both Hershey and Luria demonstrated the occurrence of spontaneous phage mutants. And in the following year Delbrück and Hershey independently discovered the existence of genetic recombination in phage, a process which had been previously thought to be reserved for more evolved, sexually reproducing forms of life. (Delbrück actually believed at first that he had discovered specifically induced mutations rather than recombination, and it was Hershey and his student

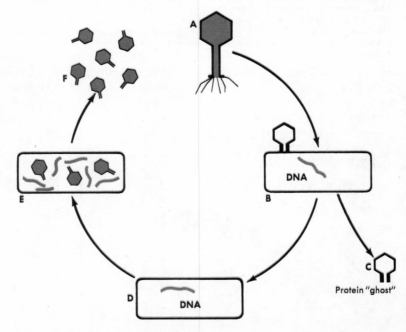

Hershey's "blendor experiment" demonstrated that only the DNA of a phage invades a bacterial cell (B). When the culture is placed in a mixer and shaken, the protein coat separates from the bacterial wall (C). The bacterium can then be removed from the liquid solution (D). The DNA causes the bacterium to produce new phages (E). When the bacterial cell bursts, a new generation of phages is released (F).

Raquel Rotman who later showed that phage recombination corresponds formally to meiotic crossing-over by chromosomes of higher organisms. These findings gave the start for phage genetics, whose ultimate refinement by Seymour Benzer a few years later led to reform of the classical concept of the gene.

The genetic material

By 1950 Anderson had shown that the phage head is a proteinaceous bag stuffed with DNA and that the phage attaches itself to the surface of its bacterial host cell by the tip of its proteinaceous tail. According to Hershey, it was an appreciation of these facts that "literally forced" him and his assistant Martha Chase to perform their celebrated "blendor experiment" in 1952. This experiment showed that, upon infection, the phage DNA is the only, or at least the principal, phage component to enter the host cell, the bulk of the phage protein remaining outside, beyond the cell wall. This discovery showed that DNA, rather than protein, is the genetic material of the phage, in complete harmony with the demonstration by Oswald T. Avery, Colin M. MacLeod, and Maclyn McCarty in 1944 that DNA is the genetic material of bacteria. The Hershey-Chase experiment made a tremendous impact in its time and focused attention on DNA as a carrier of hereditary information. The fundamental problem of phage self-replication could now be restated in terms of two functions of the phage DNA: an autocatalytic function by means of which the DNA reproduces itself, and a heterocatalytic function by means of which the DNA directs the synthesis of phage proteins. Upon learning the result of the Hershey-Chase experiment, James D. Watson, a student of Luria's, intensified his collaborative efforts with Francis H. Crick to find the structure of DNA, efforts which were to be crowned with success in the very next year. And with this development molecular genetics, which accounts for heredity in terms of nucleotide base sequences, had become established as a separate discipline whose frame of reference clearly transcends that of billiard-ball-gene classical genetics.

By 1953, the Phage Group counted dozens of members and Delbrück was beginning to lose interest. For, with the discovery of the DNA double helix, it seemed likely that the eventual solution of the problem of self-replication would not lead to any deep paradoxes and hence would fail to uncover any new complementarity relations (the self-complementary nature of the DNA double helix is not, of course, the kind of complementarity that Bohr had been talking about), and so Delbrück turned his attention to sensory perception, on which he has been working ever since. Luria and Hershey, however, continued to make important research contributions to the further growth of molecular genetics, which has meanwhile blossomed into an elephantine academic discipline.

What will Max think?

No recitation of the research accomplishments of these 3 laureates can, however, give an adequate account of the real role they have played in the growth of molecular genetics. Although it would be difficult to imagine 3 personalities more unlike than those of Delbrück, Luria, and Hershey, they have one trait in common — total incorruptibility — and it is just this trait of their personalities that these 3 men managed to impose on an entire scientific discipline. Undoubtedly Luria and Hershey would agree that, in the personality department, it was Delbrück who actually wielded the greatest influence. For Delbrück managed to become a kind of Gandhi of biology who, without possessing any temporal power at all, was an ever-present and sometimes irksome spiritual force. "What will Max think of it?" had become the central question of the molecular biological psyche. Thus the award committee for the Nobel Prize for Physiology and Medicine is to be congratulated for its wisdom in recognizing the contributions of 3 men who have made molecular biology not merely a nice place to visit but also a good place to work.

EARTH SCIENCES

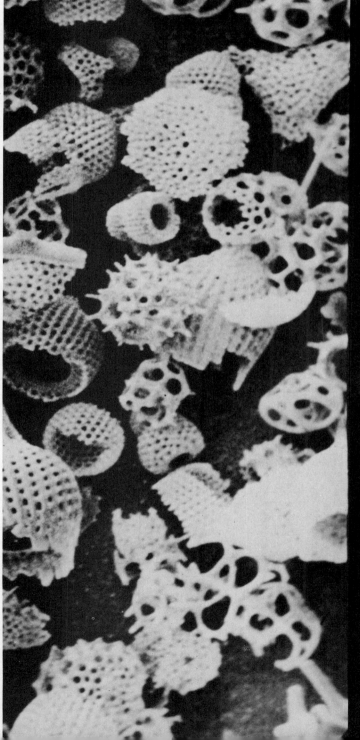

CONTENTS

These skeletons of Radiolaria (magnified 100 times) were found in sediment cores taken 9,383 feet below the ocean's surface in the western Pacific.

Scripps Institution

REVIEW OF THE YEAR- EARTH SCIENCES

Seismology.   Earthquakes continue to scourge mankind.   In October 1969 a quake, registering 8 on the 12-degree Modified Mercalli Intensity Scale, destroyed the town of Banja Luka in Yugoslavia.   Many people predicted that an earthquake in April 1969 would cause the state of California to disappear into the sea.   This major quake did not occur, but the state was shaken by several tremors during the year.   Some seismologists are concerned that the tremors could be forerunners of a severe quake.   On the other hand, these relatively minor shocks may have relieved the strains that had been building up in the earth — strains that could have been released more suddenly in a disastrous earthquake.   With increasing density of world population, a strong quake could destroy many lives and much property.   Seismologists are therefore anxious to predict earthquakes with far more accuracy than they can at present.   New and improved instruments and techniques are being used to monitor the slight movements and changes in rocks that may presage an earthquake.   Such changes include alterations in resistance to electric current, gas emissions, very slow movements along cracks in the ground, and slight tilts in the level of the rocks and the ground.

Evidence is now conclusive that man himself can cause earthquakes.   Any large-scale engineering project may disturb the ground, straining and even cracking the rocks.   This, in turn, may cause the ground to shift along a system of fractures.   Tremors and even a large earthquake may follow.   For example, it is believed that the filling of a reservoir in India caused a December 1967 earthquake that killed about two hundred people.   Atomic explosions such as the Nevada test blasts during the past few years also cause detectable ground tremors.   Because of this, numerous scientists and other citizens objected to the October 1969 underground test explosion of a 1.2-megaton hydrogen bomb on Amchitka Island off Alaska.   However, although low-level aftershocks were recorded, no earthquake or tidal wave occurred, and there was no evidence of movement along the fault that bisects the island.   Some seismologists, such as Dr. Louis C. Pakiser, head of the National Center for Earthquake Research, believe that atomic and conventional explosions might be used to prevent serious earthquakes: they might relieve strains that could otherwise lead to disastrous quakes.

New developments supporting the theory of continental drift have improved man's understanding of earthquake distribution on a worldwide scale.   The crust of the earth is apparently divided into huge, stable sections, or plates. Each plate bears a number of continents or parts of continents, together with adjoining portions of the ocean floor.   These plates move very slowly, covering vast distances over long periods of time.   The plates are bounded by deep cracks, or faults, in the earth; it is along these that movement takes place.   As two plates move apart, lava flows out of the cracks and hardens, adding to the edges of the plates.   Where one plate moves over a second plate, old rocks are absorbed.   It is in these cracked and faulted zones that earthquakes occur.

Natural resources.   Man's quest for mineral riches continues at a great pace.   The earth's resources will be studied by means of unmanned Earth Survey Satellites circling the globe.   These satellites will contain remote-sensing instruments such as infrared cameras, radar and magnetic detectors.

They will be able to map large areas of the earth within a few feet of accuracy, providing weather information, tracking large schools of fish, indicating deposits of ores and oils, accurately predicting harvests, and so on.

The offshore petroleum industry has grown rapidly since its modest beginning in 1948. Improved equipment and technology are enabling firms to search for oil and natural gas in ever deeper waters. Geologists have discovered what may prove to be valuable petroleum deposits in the sea floor off the coast of West Africa, off the North Slope of Alaska and off the shores of Japan. New and potentially rich oil fields are being opened in Siberia and Alaska. American and British companies have leased vast tracts of land for exploitation on Alaska's North Slope. The major problem will be transporting the petroleum from this Arctic wilderness to populated areas. Long pipelines may have to be constructed; shipping the oil in tankers through the ice-choked Northwest Passage has met with limited success.

Oceanography. Scientific exploration of the ocean is providing a wealth of exciting information. Vessels such as the *Glomar Challenger* and the *Oceanographer* have shed new light on the mysteries of the sea and the sea bottom. A new drilling technique has enabled the *Glomar Challenger* to drill 2,500 feet into the sea floor, in water depths as much as 17,000 feet. The extracted cores of rock and sediment have indicated that the oldest known rocks under the sea are no more than 140 million years old. The oldest known land rocks are well over 3,000,000,000 years in age. Thus the ocean floor is comparatively young; this lends support to the theory that the floor is produced by the motion of the earth's crustal plates as they drift and separate along the surface of the globe.

In April 1969, Project Tektite I came to a successful conclusion. For 60 days, 4 marine scientists lived in submerged chambers 47 feet below the water's surface off St. John Island in the United States Virgin Islands National Park. The project was basically a test of human skills and endurance in a suboceanic environment; television cameras and microphones enabled land-based behavioral and biomedical scientists to observe the aquanauts. Data from Tektite I indicate that man can survive in an undersea environment for long periods of time without major changes in physiological functions. And he can be performing useful work.

When they surfaced on August 14, 1969, south of Nova Scotia, Swiss oceanographer Jacques Piccard and his 5-man crew in the submarine *Ben Franklin* had completed a month-long underwater tour of the Gulf Stream. Leaving Florida on July 14, the 50-foot, 146-ton submarine drifted 1,500 miles along this underwater "river" at depths as great as 2,000 feet. The men were surprised at the small number of fish in the stream and at the lack of a deep scattering layer (a belt of plankton and other organisms present in almost all parts of the ocean). Surface waves do not affect the deep waters, but still there was movement: wide internal waves moved the vessel up and down, once even pushing it up to the surface.

An impressive array of surface and submarine research vessels is being designed and built. In September 1969, RCA announced that it is developing an unmanned sailboat that can be sent by remote control to any spot on the ocean and stay there for up to a year without a mooring. Called SKAMP, for Station Keeping And Mobile Platform, the buoylike vessel could be equipped to chart ocean currents, monitor surface weather, serve as a navigating station and so on. General Electric's Bottom-Fix is a system designed to house men and equipment at depths of 12,000 feet or more. The system will consist of spherical modules, each 12 feet in diameter; these can be assembled in a variety of configurations. Small models of these modules have successfully completed test dives to 12,000 feet. The United States Navy is developing a new class of submarines called Deep Submergence Rescue Vehicles. These vessels will have computerized guidance and control systems enabling precise underwater rendezvous and docking maneuvers. Thus the vessels could be used to carry men and supplies to permanent laboratories on the sea bottom.

Meteorology. A series of hurricanes in 1969 brought death and destruction to the Caribbean, the Gulf of Mexico and the southern regions of the United States. The most vicious storm was hurricane Camille; her 200-mile-per-hour winds whipped up huge tidal waves and created more than a hundred tornadoes. She was responsible for more than 250 deaths and caused property damage estimated at more than $1,000,000,000. Pass Christian, on Mississippi's Gulf Coast, was among the hardest hit: at least 70 per cent of the city was destroyed or heavily damaged by the storm. After sweeping across Mississippi, Camille headed east, crossing the Appalachians and causing heavy floods in Virginia and West Virginia before moving out to sea.

Meteorologists involved in Project Stormfury have been hoping to learn how to tame hurricanes. By dropping silver-iodide crystals near the eye of a storm, scientists hope to distribute heat through the storm, thus weakening the uprush of hot air that causes a powerful chimney effect near the eye. In August 1969 the men had their first real success. They seeded hurricane Debbie, causing the wind to drop briefly from 113 to 78 miles an hour. At present, only hurricanes far from land are selected for this operation. But Robert H. Simpson, director of the National Hurricane Center in Miami, speculated that "in five years time we'll probably set up operations for regular seeding of all hurricanes threatening the continent." During the past two winters, researchers from the Environmental Science Services Administration (ESSA) have been seeding snow clouds in the Lake Erie area. Radar checks indicate that silver iodide thins the clouds, causing the snow to be spread over a larger area.

Computers are being used to improve weather forecasting. The computers are fed data on past and current weather observations; they predict tomorrow's weather on the basis of what happened in similar situations in the past. Another approach is to program computers with mathematical data that represent ideal atmospheric conditions — so-called simulated weather patterns. These simulated situations are then compared with actual weather observations being made; the computer's comparison results in a forecast of what will probably happen. Unfortunately today's computers are too slow and have very limited capacities — they cannot make accurate weather forecasts quickly enough. Faster, more versatile computers are being designed to do the job in the future.

In April 1969, NASA launched Nimbus 3, a satellite equipped with infrared sensors that enable it to measure temperature and other atmospheric properties. Its orbit carries it over North America and Europe as well as vast stretches of the Atlantic and Pacific where weather observations by conventional means have been very limited. Other satellites played an important part in BOMEX (Barbados Oceanographic and Meteorological Experiment), an American project that studied interactions of the atmospheric and oceanic systems in tropical and subtropical waters. The project, which ran from May to August 1969, involved ships, airplanes, balloons, blimps, buoys and satellites. Detailed measurements of the sea and air were taken in a "column" that extended from the ocean floor, three miles down, up into the atmosphere to an altitude of twenty miles.

PLATE TECTONICS

New Theory
Revolutionizes Geology

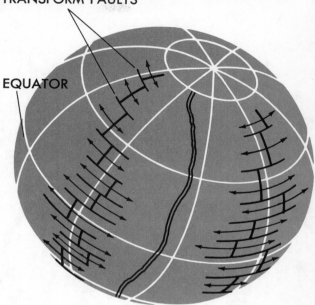

TRANSFORM FAULTS

EQUATOR

BY EDMUND F. GREKULINSKI

THE modern theory of continental drift holds that the continents have slowly drifted over the earth, moving thousands of miles from the locations they once occupied. Many geologists, in fact, believe that all the present-day continents were once part of one or two gigantic landmasses. These supercontinents, which existed more than 200 million years ago, slowly broke apart and eventually gave rise to our present continents.

Deep faults, called transform faults, form steplike patterns on the edges of plates. These faults indicate the travel paths of the plates. The rate of travel is indicated by the arrow's length; note that the rate of travel, or sea-floor spreading, is greatest near the equator.

Below: The Atlantic floor, showing the mid-Atlantic ridge and the transform faults that cut across it. It is at this ridge that new ocean floor is formed. As the plates on either side move apart, liquid rock rises to the crust's surface and solidifies.

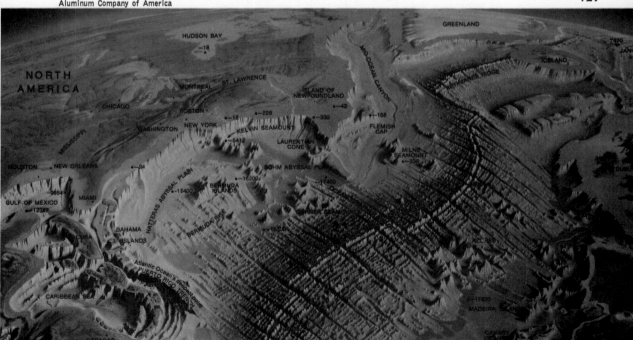

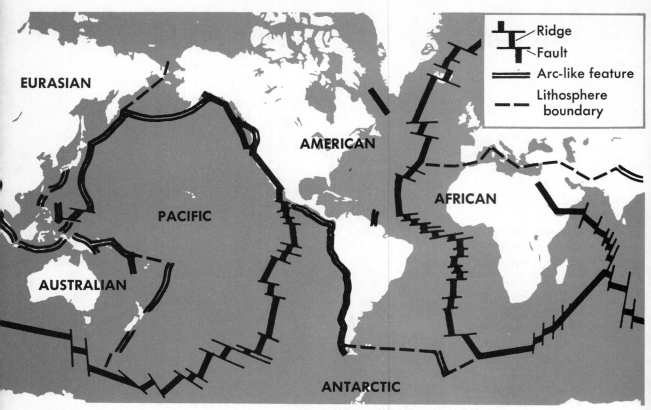

This map shows the six major tectonic plates and the geologic features that separate them. It is at the systems of rifts and ridges that the plates slowly drift apart. The arclike features occur in regions where plates are pushing against each other, or colliding. These regions are characterized by earthquakes, volcanic action, faulting and folding.

Only in recent years have scientists accumulated sufficient evidence to explain why and how this may have happened. To understand the process, we must first consider the earth's structure (according to current theory).

The outermost layer of the earth is called the lithosphere. This rigid rock layer consists of the thin, outer crust and the upper part of the mantle. (The mantle forms much of the earth's interior; it is composed of compressed rock material that may be in a solid, plastic and at times liquid state. It surrounds the dense metallic core that is the earth's center.)

The lithosphere is approximately 60 miles thick. Directly underneath it is a mantle layer called the asthenosphere. The rock material in this layer is hot, soft and relatively weak. It responds to motions of the lithosphere by flowing and has a thickness of a hundred miles or more.

Broad-scale movements

Many geologists currently believe that the lithosphere is geographically divided into 6 major slablike sections, called tectonic plates, plus a number of smaller ones. These plates contain the continents and adjoining portions of the ocean floors. It is the relative movements of these plates, toward and away from each other, that shift the continents — not any individual motions of the continents. The soft asthenosphere yields to the plate movements, enabling the latter to take place.

The boundaries of the plates are marked by certain major geologic features whose origins have long puzzled scientists. These features include the following:

(1) rifts and ridges
(2) fold mountains
(3) island arcs
(4) transform faults.

Running mainly across the ocean bottoms of the world, often down their geographic middle lines and squarely between a pair of continents, is a generally connected system of rifts and ridges. These rifts and ridges represent deep cracks (faults) in the earth's crust and are thought to be places where two or more adjacent plates are drifting away from each other. Here, liquefied material from the mantle rises to the surface of the crust, solidifying into new rock to replace what is drifting away. The general location of a rift with respect to the involved plates does not change, because the new liquefied rock hardens more or less symmetrically on both sides of the rift. The fresh rock on one side of the rift becomes part of the tectonic plate on that side; the same thing happens on the other side of the rift to the other plate. And, as the plates move apart, the new rocks move away from each other, and the process repeats itself.

Another feature is the fold mountains, so called because they were formed by the crumpling of rock layers by gigantic forces acting on the crust of the earth. Long chains of such mountains — for example, the Andes of South America — may run along one edge of a continent and may indicate the boundary of a tectonic plate.

The island arcs are a third feature bounding plates. An island arc consists of an arched chain of islands lying some distance off the coast of a continent. Typical examples are the Aleutians, the Japanese islands, the East Indies and the West Indies. The islands are rugged and volcanic, often being shaken by earthquakes and cracked by faults. Off the convex, oceanic side of an arc is a trench in the sea floor, an ocean deep, that is several miles in depth.

The fold mountains and island arcs represent regions where tectonic plates are pushing against each other, or colliding. The edges of the colliding plates become crumpled into mountain ranges. In the case of the island arcs, the collision process is more extreme, because the leading edge of one plate is pushing beneath the leading edge of the opposed plate and is enter-

CROSS SECTION OF THE EARTH

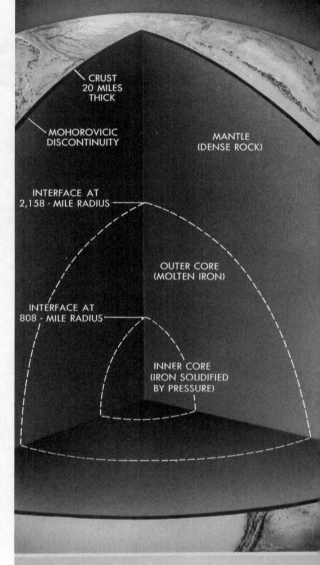

From the surface of the earth to the center of the planet is a distance of about 3,950 miles (6,360 km). The weight of the overlying material produces pressures of about 54.5 million pounds per square inch (50.3 grams per sq cm) at the center. The diagram below indicates the dimensions of the major divisions of the earth: a core of iron (in both a solid and a molten state), a mantle of iron and dense rock, and a thin outer crust of complex and varied rock materials.

CRUST 20 MILES THICK

MOHOROVICIC DISCONTINUITY

MANTLE (DENSE ROCK)

INTERFACE AT 2,158 - MILE RADIUS

OUTER CORE (MOLTEN IRON)

INTERFACE AT 808 - MILE RADIUS

INNER CORE (IRON SOLIDIFIED BY PRESSURE)

Geophysicists may sometimes make another division of the outer portion of the earth. Thus, a rigid lithosphere consisting of the crust and the upper mantle is said to float on a softer, more deformable lower portion of the mantle.

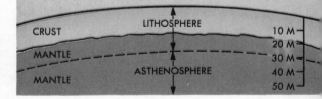

CRUST
MANTLE
MANTLE

LITHOSPHERE
ASTHENOSPHERE

10 M
20 M
30 M
40 M
50 M

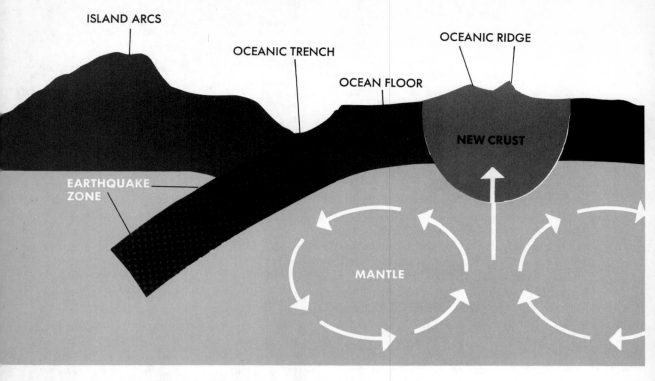

This diagram illustrates sea-floor movements and mantle convections associated with such movements. At a ridge, two plates drift apart and new crust is formed. At a trench near island arcs, one plate moves beneath another; almost all major earthquakes originate in such a region.

ing the mantle. This accounts for the existence of the ocean deep near the islands — the crust is downbuckled there. If the rocks of the plate reach a sufficient depth into the mantle, they will "melt" or "dissolve" into the latter.

Thus, a tectonic plate is being "manufactured" at the rift, which marks its trailing, or rear, edge. It is being "unmade" at an island arc or mountain range, which marks its leading, or front, edge.

Inch by inch

The combination of asthenosphere, rifts, faults and island arcs in theory allows, even perhaps causes, the tectonic plates to move around for thousands of miles. The rate of movement is slow, averaging a few inches each year.

This movement is complicated by the presence of deep faults, called transform faults, that cut across and even offset the rifts and ridges into steplike patterns. These cross-rift faults indicate the travel paths of the plates. The horizontally overlapping segments of adjacent plates slide past each other along the transform-fault surfaces, parallel to the lines of the faults.

You can approximate this situation by interlocking the fingers of your hands. The hands represent two adjacent plates moving away from each other. Slowly pull your hands apart. They slide along the lateral edges of the fingers, edges that represent the transform-fault surfaces. In the case of the earth, the "fingers" are constantly "growing" because new rock is being added to the plates as they drift apart.

The movements of the plates along faults — in ocean bottoms, mountains and island arcs — accounts for the many earthquakes and volcanic eruptions that occur along and near the borders of tectonic plates. In comparison, conditions are quite stable toward the geographic interior of a plate, such as the eastern and

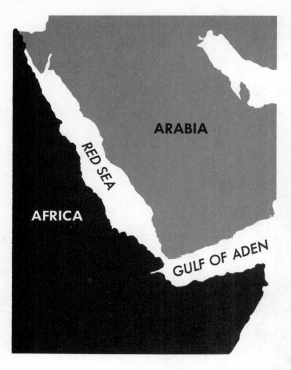

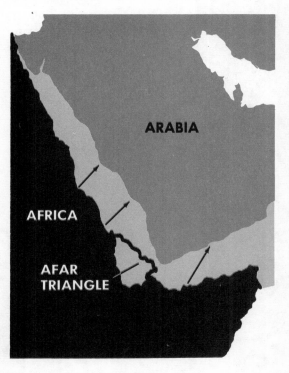

New bodies of water. Above: The Red Sea-Gulf of Aden area as it is today. But 20 million years ago Arabia was joined to Africa. Below: Note the remarkable fit of the present-day shorelines when they are superimposed. The part of Ethiopia that is overlapped — the Afar triangle — has some characteristics of an ocean floor and is probably younger than the other land areas shown here.

central portions of the North American mainland.

Three major theories

The causes of plate movement are still in dispute, but scientists have proposed a number of theories to account for the process. The oldest and, until recently, the most commonly accepted one is the convection-current theory. This theory proposes that the mantle is the site of vast heat (convection) currents that rise through the rock, move along the bases of the plates and drag the latter along the earth's surface, and then sink back into the mantle. The oceanic rifts are the places where the currents rise and spread the ocean floor apart. The island arcs are sites where the currents descend and drag some of the plates down with them.

A more recent theory considers gravity to be the mainspring of plate tectonics. The leading edge of a plate tends to be pulled down into the asthenosphere because of the plate's weight. The rest of the plate follows along, pulling itself away from another plate. The plate slides into the mantle until it stops at a "bottom" defined by a high-density condition that does not permit the plate to sink any farther.

A third theory suggests that the absorption of water by oceanic rocks swells the latter. The resulting strains crack the rocks, developing a system of rifts, ridges and transform faults. According to this view, the swelling pushes the plates apart at the rifts and shoves them together at the mountains and island arcs.

Whatever the cause, geologists continue to accumulate evidence to support the theory of plate tectonics. The theory is of major importance; for the first time, science has a single unifying concept that explains much of the geologic activity on our planet. Geology is now undergoing a revolution similar to that which occurred in biology during the fifties and sixties. As marine geologist Henry W. Menard writes: "Ideas are changing, and new puzzles present themselves even as the old ones are solved. The only certainty is that the subject will never be the same again."

DEATH TRAP OF THE AGES*

The Animals of Rancho la Brea

BY J. R. MACDONALD

IMPERIAL MAMMOTH

illus., Arthur J. Anderson

THE quiet of the basin is shattered by trumpets of fear and rage as the great imperial mammoth struggles to free himself from the deadly pool of asphalt. Pacing the solid bank and snarling at each other, small packs of sabertooths and dire wolves wait for the end — and an evening meal. Overhead, great teratorns circle on their 12-foot wingspread in the patient vultures' death watch.

One sabertooth, bolder — or perhaps hungrier — than the rest, leaps toward the struggling mammoth. He lands on its side, slips, and catches himself with his front claws, but his hind quarters sink into the pool. The teratorns continue to circle; struggling animals are not for them.

Rancho la Brea claims two more victims. Later, when their struggles cease, one of the teratorns, settling on a carcass, dips a wing into the pool and becomes additional bait for this self-perpetuating trap.

Between 10,000 and 40,000 years ago, near the end of the Ice Age, this was an often-repeated scene on what is now the "Miracle Mile" section of Wilshire Boulevard, just east of Beverly Hills, California. Today, the sticky asphalt still oozes to the surface through natural fissures in the rocks. No longer do sabertooths, dire wolves or mammoths come to drink water covering sticky pools; today there are only sparrows, pigeons and cottontails.

Europeans first took note of this site on August 3, 1769, when Caspar de Portola wrote, "The 3rd, we proceeded for three hours on a good road; to the right of it were extensive swamps of bitumen which is called *chapapote*. We debated whether this substance, which flows melted from underneath the earth, could occasion earthquakes."

Trapped the thirsty

For thousands of years these swamps of asphalt have been fed by springs of oil, and in the slightly moister climate of the late Ice Age they were covered with water which lured thirsty animals to their doom.

* Reprinted by permission from *National Wildlife*

Coming to drink in the area, these went to the pools, where a misstep entangled them in sticky asphalt. Their struggles and cries attracted predators and scavengers which, in turn, became entangled in the asphalt, adding more bait to the trap.

Near the end of the Ice Age, the Los Angeles basin looked very much as it did when the first Europeans came to California. The rainfall averaged only a few inches or more a year, the native trees crept a little farther down the hillsides and out onto the plain to form a savanna, and the sky was hazy, not with smog but with fog and haze trapped by the temperature inversion that often holds eye-burning smog in the basin today.

The wildlife, however, was completely different. The only way to picture North America in the geologic past is to think in terms of those magnificent pictures of African game taken in the 1920's and 1930's. The species were different but the great herds of herbivores and packs of stalking carnivores looked much the same.

Herbivores outnumber carnivores

In any animal community the herbivores, eaters of grass and leaves, make up the great bulk of population. Since a carnivore such as a mountain lion requires one deer every week or ten days for food, obviously there must be many more deer than mountain lions. This economy normally prevailed in the geologic past, but at Rancho la Brea the ratio is reversed.

There, carnivorous mammals outnumber the herbivores ten to one, and among birds, 75 per cent are hawks, eagles, falcons, condors or vultures. Vast numbers of carnivorous animals were attracted to the asphalt pools by the sight of an easy meal and, in turn, became trapped themselves. So sabertooths, dire wolves and coyotes are the most common fossils in the pits.

What was the fauna of the Los Angeles basin at the end of the Pleistocene epoch? Millions of bones preserved in asphalt at Rancho la Brea give us a wide window into this segment of geologic time.

There were no dinosaurs. Dinosaurs became extinct at the end of the Cretaceous period, nearly 70 million years before the first drop of sticky oil bubbled to the surface at Rancho la Brea.

The North American fauna of today or, rather, the pre-European fauna of North America, is a direct descendant of the late Ice Age fauna. Slow decline and elimination, rather than catastrophic extinction, have removed many of the larger and some of the smaller mammals and birds from the fauna. Africa and southeastern Asia retain much of their Pleistocene faunas; Europe and northern Asia lost their Pleistocene faunas by slow extinction, and later the job was finished by man.

In the New World, man certainly had little to do with faunal decline until the arrival of Europeans. If Stone-Age hunters in Africa could not eliminate the Pleistocene fauna, there is no reason to believe North American aboriginal hunters,

with no better tools, could bring about the extinction of large animals here.

Mammoths were 13 feet tall

Certainly the most spectacular mammals at Rancho la Brea were great mammoths and slightly smaller mastodons. Arriving in North America near the beginning of the Ice Age, mammoths quickly spread throughout the continent and diversified into many species. Two species roamed Southern California. The larger was the imperial mammoth (*Mammuthus imperator*), which sometimes stood 13 feet high at the shoulder. The scarcity of mammoths in the asphalt pits may be due to their greater strength, greater intelligence or smaller numbers.

Mastodons and their near relatives were earlier immigrants to the New World, entering near the end of the Miocene epoch about 15 to 20 million years earlier. Smaller than mammoths, with elongated heads and occasionally small

CONDOR-LIKE VULTURE

SABER TOOTH CAT

FOX

IMPERIAL MAMMOTH

Arthur J. Anderso

tusks on lower jaws, *Mammut americanus* is an even rarer fossil at Rancho la Brea.

To those familiar with American and African wild animals, ground sloths seem the most bizarre animals of the time. Standing slightly over 4 feet high when walking on all fours, these massive, bulky animals made their way into North America from South America just before the Pleistocene when the 2 continents were rejoined after 60 million years of isolation. The strange construction of the sloths' feet and limbs gave them their unusual gait.

Their ancestors were South American tree sloths which had become adapted for hanging upside down from branches. When some were forced out of forests onto the plains, they readapted for ground living, but their twisted feet did not become straightened again. Instead, they retained the "curl" developed by their ancestors. Thus, the ground sloth walked on the knuckles of his front feet and the outer sides of his back feet. This stance caused modification of the limb bones which makes them unique among mammals.

There were three genera of sloths in the Rancho la Brea area, but some paleontologists believe this was not their normal habitat. Perhaps the ones trapped in the asphalt were passersby who just stopped for a drink.

Bones of the North American camel

The only other exotic herbivore in the fauna was the camel (*Camelops hesternus*) which had a body about like that of the modern camel, but with somewhat longer legs. We don't know if there was a hump or not, since humps are adaptations for desert living which would not be needed in the areas where New World camels lived. It is not generally known, but the camel is a native of North America, and a fairly recent emigrant into Eurasia. The earliest known camel dates back 40 million years, into the late Eocene of the Rocky Mountains.

The other large herbivores are familiar to all of us — horses, bison and deer. The bison was somewhat larger than the modern species, and there were a few giant *Bison latifrons*, whose horns had a span nearly twelve feet long, measured along the curve.

Many of the carnivores inhabit the modern forest and plain: foxes, badgers, skunks, weasels, mountain lions, lynx, black bears and grizzly bears. These have changed little since the late Pleistocene and, perhaps, if we had their entire carcasses to study we might find they differed from their modern counterparts only at the subspecies level.

The carnivore which seems strangest to us is the sabertooth, *Smilodon californicus bovard*. The last survivor of a very successful lineage, this animal is little understood by the nonpaleontologist and is misnamed in the popular tongue.

The largest known assemblage of sabertooths came from Rancho la Brea. Through the years, they must have flocked in vast numbers to feed on animals trapped in the asphalt. Paleontologists don't agree on whether sabertooths made their living by hunting active prey. In the Rancho la Brea area they hunted the weak, the young, the dying, the sick and the old. Their relatively weak hind legs, their massive forelegs, and their great sabers were well-suited for dispatching the weak and cutting up carrion.

Nonscientists and pseudoscientists often state that the sabertooth (usually called "sabertooth tiger" even though a tiger is a modern biting cat with stripes, not even in the same animal family as sabertooths) grew longer and longer sabers until they became so long the animal could no longer open his mouth to feed! This is supposed to prove that evolution works against itself and that evolutionists don't know what they are talking about. This is absurd!

The truth is that 35 million years ago, at the beginning of the Oligocene epoch, there were fully-developed sabertooths, some with sabers relatively longer than *Smilodon's!* All the sabertooths were well adapted for their way of life, and their design was frozen almost as soon as they appeared. It is said imitation is the sincerest form of flattery, and in the case of saber-tooths, it must be so. Several times during the age of mammals, lineages of true cats adapted to this mode of life and became "false sabertooths." In South America, where all mammalian carnivores were marsupials (animals that carry their young in pouches) there was a marsupial sabertooth which nearly out-sabered northern hemisphere types.

The best known captive

The sabertooth, perhaps, symbolizes Rancho la Brea to most people, not only because of its numbers, but because of its exotic form and its (perhaps unwarranted) reputation as a mighty hunter.

Outnumbering sabertooths were dire wolves (*Canis dirus*). Packs of them roamed Southern California by the thousands. Slightly smaller than the northern timber wolf, the dire wolf ranged through North America during the late Pleistocene. Fossils have been found as far east as Kentucky and as far south as the Valley of Mexico. Leg proportions indicate it was not as swift a runner as the modern timber wolf, and thousands of specimens in the asphalt pits suggest the great packs were scavengers when given the chance.

The common coyote also ranged the Los Angeles Basin and frequented Rancho la Brea. Minor differences separate it at the subspecific level from the living species, our familiar western singer.

Two carnivores stand out in the fauna because of their great size, although few individuals are known. The great cat (*Panthera atrox*) structurally resembled the jaguar, although the males were nearly 1/4 larger than the largest living cats. Ranging North America during the closing days of the Ice Age, this magnificent species was certainly the mighty hunter of its day.

Exceeding the great cat in size was the short-faced bear (*Arctodus simus*). On all four feet it stood a foot higher than modern grizzly bears and was larger and more massively built than the Kodiak bear. Its teeth suggest a more carnivorous habit than that of any living bears.

The huge birds

With two exceptions, the birds of Rancho la Brea would seem familiar to all but the most highly-trained observer. Many of the species or their close relatives are still living nearby today. The two exceptions are the La Brea stork, unknown in California today, and the huge condor-like vulture (*Teratornia merriama*).

Teratorns were the largest known late Pleistocene flying birds, having wingspreads of 12 feet or more. The number of these scavengers found in the pits makes one think at times the sky was clouded with circling teratorns. Long thought to have been the largest flying bird, *Teratorn merriami* is known to have been exceeded by the late Pliocene through Pleistocene species *Teratornis incredibilis* which may have had a wingspread of 17 feet.

"The Death Trap of the Ages" was a place that would offend the eyes, the ears and the nose. The vast numbers and kinds of animals roaming the area would have made it a nature lover's paradise, although the accelerated pace of death in the pools of asphalt would sicken the humanitarian. However, the existence of this trap has given us an unparalleled view into a small area in the geologic past, which will probably never be excelled.

Today, the center of Rancho la Brea is a county park, named for the donor of 23 acres, Captain G. Allan Hancock. It is also a National Park Service Natural History Landmark. Many of the pits have been filled but others are fenced to protect pets and children from the still active asphalt seeps. The Los Angeles County Museum of Natural History administers the park. It maintains a display in an observation pit with attendant tour guides and it is developing a display of fiber glass reconstructions of the extinct animals of the area.

There are now reconstructions of 3 mammoths and 2 sabertooths. Eventually it is hoped to have about 60 reconstructions in a recreated Pleistocene environment available for the instruction of the public.

A MOST SIGNIFICANT DISCOVERY

Antarctic Team Reports Major Fossil Find

U.S. Navy

Drs. David Elliot and Edwin Colbert looking at a fossilized bone in the rocks at Coalsack Bluff. Numerous fossils of temperate-climate organisms have been found in this region.

LATE in 1969, a team of geologists working at Coalsack Bluff in Antarctica's Queen Alexandra Range discovered a very important fossil: part of a skull from a reptile named Lystrosaurus. The discovery of this skull followed reports of other important fossil finds in Antarctica. Comparison of these fossil remains with those found in other parts of the world provided important evidence of the former existence of a great southern continent known as Gondwanaland.*

Early fossil finds

Scientists have long known that Antarctica formerly had a temperate climate; the land was once covered by lush vegetation that gradually sank into swamps, becoming compressed into rock. Fossils of ferns (*Glossopteris*) and other plants were found as early as 1911, during Captain Robert Falcon Scott's expedition to the South Pole. The British leader and his party perished on the return trip, but specimens were found with their bodies by a search party in 1912. Scott's party had discovered beds of coal, containing fossil leaves, in the mountain wall bordering the Beardmore Glacier not far from the present camp at Coalsack Bluff.

The first fossil bone of a land-living vertebrate was found late in December 1967 by Peter J. Barrett of Ohio State University's Institute of Polar Studies. The bone was subsequently identified as part of the jaw of a labyrinthodont amphibian — an animal that resembled an overgrown salamander.* The bone was found among plant fossils in an ancient sediment-filled stream bed near Beardmore Glacier. Other fossils of these animals, which lived about 200 million years ago, have been found in South Africa and Australia; until Dr. Barrett's discovery, however, there had been no evidence of the existence of a vertebrate animal that lived on land or in fresh water and was common both to Antarctica and to other continents. The labyrinthodont could not have swam to Antarctica; it was unable to survive in salt waters. Nor could it have existed in a cold climate; it was a tropical animal.

In 1968, insect fossils were discovered for the first time in Antarctica. This find was made at the Carapace Nunatak, about 100 miles from McMurdo Station and roughly 300 miles from the site of the current paleontology work.

---

* This huge land mass is believed to have fragmented; the segments drifted apart, forming the continents in the Southern Hemisphere.

* Some members of this extinct group of amphibians gave rise to reptiles and, thus, to all higher four-footed animals. They are so named because of the intricate, labyrinthine foldings of their tooth enamel.

Coalsack Bluff

The 1969 discoveries and collections were made at Coalsack Bluff, so named by New Zealanders because of its coal seams. The camp there was established by a United States Navy construction crew, part of the Naval Support Force that provides logistics support for the scientific activities in Antarctica. Aircraft equipped with skis flew in supplies and equipment during November 1969, following a reconnaissance mission during which the scientists selected the site of their camp.

The camp consists of four Jamesway huts, which have prefabricated wooden floors and frames covered with insulated canvas. From the base camp the scientists shuttle to work areas by helicopter.

The camp is in a mountainous, heavily glaciated area about midway between McMurdo Station and the South Pole, in the area of the Queen Alexandra Range. The scientists plan to work in various areas within about 100 miles of the Coalsack Bluff camp.

The scientists were flown to the camp on November 22, 1969; they began their field investigations the next day. It was then that the first fossil discoveries were made.

Several types of vertebrates

The first bones were discovered by Dr. David H. Elliot of Ohio State University in an ancient sandstone riverbed atop Coalsack Bluff. A group of vertebrate paleontologists then began a systematic exploration of the exposure. They included Dr. Edwin H. Colbert, Curator of Vertebrate Paleontology at the American Museum of Natural History, in New York; Mr. James Jensen of Brigham Young University, Provo, Utah; Mr. William J. Breed of the Museum of Northern Arizona, in Flagstaff; and Mr. Jon S. Powell of the University of Arizona, Tucson.

During the initial stages of what will be an intensive collecting program, various types of vertebrate fossils were discovered. These included fossil bones of

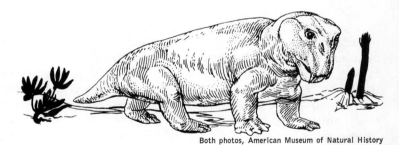

Lystrosaurus was a small reptile whose fossilized remains have been found in South Africa, Asia and, most recently, Antarctica. (The sketch is from Dr. Colbert's *The Age of Reptiles*.)

Both photos, American Museum of Natural History

Below: *Lystrosaurus* remains found in the Coalsack Bluff area. The find is important evidence in support of the theory of continental drift.

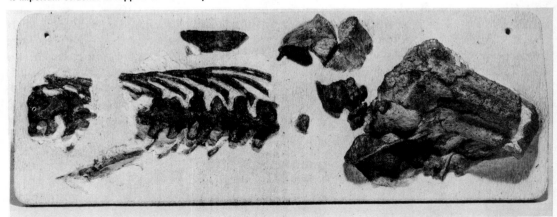

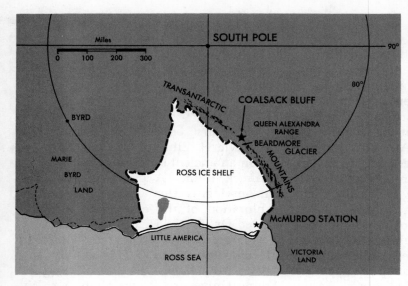

The Coalsack Bluff camp was located in the mountainous, heavily-glaciated area of the Queen Alexandra Range. The scientists worked in the area during November and December, when the sun's rays warmed the Bluff for long hours each day.

both amphibians and reptiles. The amphibians were labyrinthodonts; the reptile finds included the remains of thecodonts. Thecodonts were ancestors of the dinosaurs. The only evolutionary descendants of these creatures living on earth today are crocodiles and alligators and, through a more complex evolution, birds.

Then: Lystrosaurus. According to Dr. Colbert's book, *The Age of Reptiles,* this hippopotamus-like reptile "had a peculiarly-shaped skull, with the nostrils high on the skull, between the elevated eyes. This almost surely indicates aquatic habits. . . ."

Lystrosaurus is considered an index fossil; this means it can be used to establish the age of a particular deposit. Index fossils have three important characteristics. These are:

(1) They are found in relatively large numbers.

(2) They were common during one small period of the earth's history, after which they became extinct.

(3) They are easily recognized.

Lystrosaurus is known to have lived about 200 million years ago. Fossil remains of these 2- to 4-foot-long reptiles have been found in Asia and South Africa — and now in Antarctica. Could they have developed independently on these separate continents? Could they have developed in one place and swam to the other continents? Most scientists agree that the answer to both questions is no.

Continental drift

Soon after the Coalsack Bluff fossil bed was discovered, scientists there sent a report to the National Science Foundation. They clearly indicated the importance of the find:

"This discovery is of great significance to students of earth history. During recent years the so-called theory of continental drift has received increasingly favorable attention from geologists and other students of the history of the earth. This theory, developed in detail more than fifty years ago, supposes that the present continents are remnants of a once supercontinent, or perhaps two such continents, that fragmented, the separate pieces then slowly drifting across the face of the globe to their present positions. If this theory is valid, Antarctica was once part of a great southern land mass known as Gondwanaland.

"The presence of fresh-water amphibians and land-living reptiles in Antarctica, some 200 million years ago, is very strong evidence of the probability of continental drift because these amphibians and reptiles, closely related to backboned animals of the same age on other continents, could not have migrated between continental areas across oceanic barriers."

DRIFTING IN A SILENT WORLD*

Voyage of the *Ben Franklin*

BY JACQUES PICCARD

THE Gulf Stream, the surging river that rushes out of the Gulf of Mexico, bringing warmth and life-sustaining temperatures to the coasts of North America and Eu-

rope, is not merely one flood of water but several swirling, colliding, meandering torrents tumbling northward.

This marine phenomenon at great depths moves at less than two knots south of Cape Hatteras, North Carolina, then picks up speed as the current gallops away

143

The *Ben Franklin* and her crew are given a watery welcome by a fireboat as they enter New York Harbor after completing their 30-day underwater drift in the Gulf Stream. Two Coast Guard cutters escorted the yellow-and-white submarine to her pier.

All photos Grumman

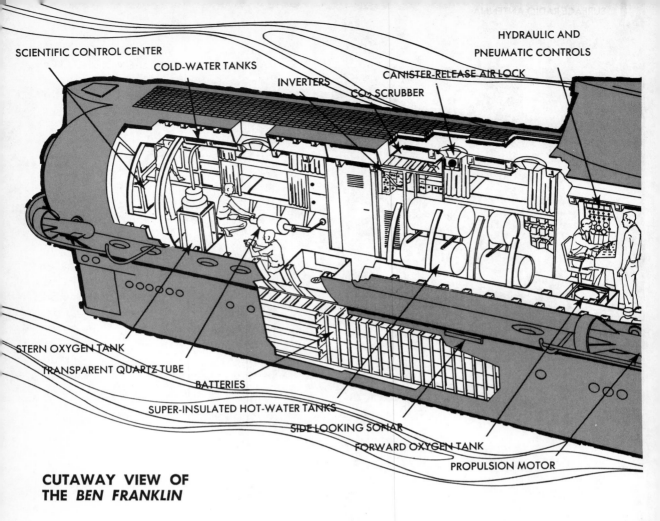

SCIENTIFIC CONTROL CENTER
COLD-WATER TANKS
INVERTERS
CO_2 SCRUBBER
CANISTER-RELEASE AIR LOCK
HYDRAULIC AND
PNEUMATIC CONTROLS

STERN OXYGEN TANK
TRANSPARENT QUARTZ TUBE
BATTERIES
SUPER-INSULATED HOT-WATER TANKS
SIDE LOOKING SONAR
FORWARD OXYGEN TANK
PROPULSION MOTOR

CUTAWAY VIEW OF THE *BEN FRANKLIN*

from the coast toward northern Europe. There is a paucity of fish life and no deep, scattering layer of plankton — the minute marine organisms, lowest rung on the ladder of fish life — in the stream, probably attributable to the warmth of the water. What plankton is encountered is strongly attracted by artificial light.

These are some of the apparent preliminary findings of a 30-day submerged drift, completed on August 14, 1969, which I led with 5 companions in the submersible *Ben Franklin*. During our transit of some 1,500 miles, we have first proved that man can indeed drift silently for more than 4 weeks, and that the special design I prepared for the *Ben Franklin* met all of the tests for which she was conceived.

The object of our inquiry, the Gulf Stream, is a vast and mysterious phenome-

non, much, much too complex to be plumbed in a 30-day expedition. But we do know that this combination of rivers in the sea, a three-dimensional movement of water, has great implications for weather determination, for shipping, for the fishing industry and as a basis for general knowledge of the oceans.

Twenty-seven days under surface

As I began to sketch out this account of my voyage we had already passed 27 days under the surface of the Atlantic. More than 1,200 miles had been explored as we were pushed along by the stream, expending practically no electrical energy, save for the powerful searchlights that we use from time to time to illuminate our environment.

After leaving the coast of Palm Beach, Florida, we drifted in a wonderful tran-

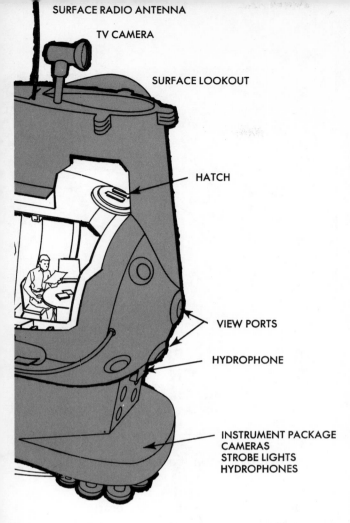

SURFACE RADIO ANTENNA

TV CAMERA

SURFACE LOOKOUT

HATCH

VIEW PORTS

HYDROPHONE

INSTRUMENT PACKAGE
CAMERAS
STROBE LIGHTS
HYDROPHONES

tion to the water around the vehicle. We were part of the ideal research platform for listening to the infinite variety of noises in the sea. Being completely silent ourselves, and appearing motionless to the fish who were also drifting in the current and were therefore unaware of it, we could in no way disturb the environment or frighten the sea life away.

Writing these thoughts, nearing the end of our voyage, how would I describe our home away from home? From the outside she is a small, yellow and white submarine, a cylinder with hemispheres for ends and 29 viewports scattered around on all sides. The keel, ballast tanks and 4 electric motors are suspended outside, providing extreme maneuverability for the boat.

Inside, 2 main platforms for working and observation, 1 at either end, are connected by a gangway some 35 feet long. Along this aisle are carefully arranged bays of electronic equipment, bunks, a shower, our galley and the oceanographic laboratory.

The inside of our boat is quite comfortable. In the forward hemisphere is a round table and seats — our wardroom. Without moving, I can peer at the sea through 12 portholes. Sixteen other viewports are distributed around the hull, and 1 is equipped with a device for taking samples of plankton.

One porthole is a mere foot above my pillow in my bunk. When I am reclining there my view can extend as far as the clarity of the water will allow. On one occasion I could distinguish the surface waves in this manner as we cruised at a depth of 330 feet, a remarkable exception.

The existence of these many portholes, with the possibility of looking in virtually every direction, is a principal characteristic of the mesoscaph and distinguishes her from naval or combatant submarines.

These were our link with the outside. They also aroused the curiosity of the fish and squid, and we could often see them looking inside at us, their strange new neighbors. Once a small squid came and

quility — quieter than any oceanographic laboratory had ever been. Between 600 and 2,000 feet, protected from the surface waves and tempests and also from the thousands of small, daily preoccupations of modern life, we were able to dedicate ourselves entirely to the study of the sea in which economists have placed so much importance for the feeding of mankind in the year 2000.

Never had a group of oceanographers been able to live so intimately with the inner sea, and still we have the impression that we had barely begun to penetrate its problems, so immense is the world beneath the waves.

Comfortable quarters

The drifting approach we employed had the advantage of producing complete silence and complete immobility in rela-

146

attached itself to the windowsill above my bunk, and we observed each other in complete tranquility.

I am remembering now the evening of July 14. It is about 6:30, and we are off the coast of Palm Beach. We are approaching the dive site, the point where we will flood the ballast tanks and dive underneath the waves and begin our journey. The bottom is more than 600 feet below us. Rapidly we open the hatch, descend into the vehicle, and gently ease the hatch shut behind us. For an instant I cogitate: Who are we, the 6 men in a sealed underwater galleon?

Aside from myself, first, there is the captain. A Grumman Aerospace Corporation employee for 2 years, a former U.S. Navy submariner, at 30 the youngest among us, Donald J. Kazimir has solid experience with the sea.

His principal aide, and mine as well, is a Swiss, Erwin Aebersold, the pilot of the *Ben Franklin*. A pilot of planes first, he is trained for instrument flying. He has worked for me for 7 years, a precision-minded technologist.

Two oceanographers

We have 2 oceanographers on board: Frank Busby, a young, sporty graduate of Texas A. & M., a civilian employee of the U.S. Naval Oceanographic Office, who knows perhaps more about research submersibles than any other living man.

Kenneth Haigh is the other oceanographer. An exchange scientist from the British Royal Navy to the U.S. Navy, he is a specialist in echo sounding: he is our universal earphone. Only one thing ruffled Ken during the trip, and this was the inclusion in our menu of freeze-dried tea in powder form (and I side with him).

The final crewman is Chester May, a National Aeronautics and Space Administration engineer. In 1972, NASA will put into earth orbit a big space laboratory, where successive scientist crews will stay for several weeks. NASA must know how the scientists will live on board the orbiting station. Of great importance are answers to questions such as "What will be

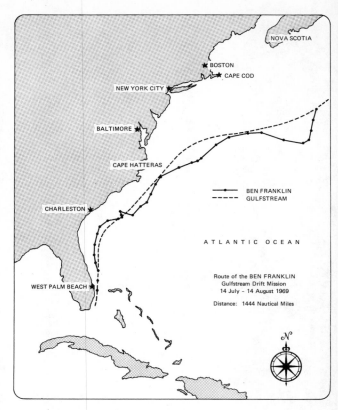

the biological life on board?"; "What about microbes, bacteria and viruses?" Chet May is our life engineer.

He has placed in strategic locations 3 cameras that will freeze our actions every 2 minutes for the duration of the trip. The resultant 64,800 photographs will help plot the course and direction of NASA's future space-station configuration.

Under each mattress Chet has placed a counter that will tell him how much "sack time" we log. On the floor, counters record our steps, and at regular intervals he takes samples of our skin, swabs from the sink, the floor and the portholes. He then retreats to his work area and begins cultivating colonies of bacteria in his collection of Petri dishes.

Mission highlights

Since it is neither possible nor practical to describe every moment of every day for the full mission, I would share with you some of the highlights:

July 16. All during the night the *Franklin* has drifted slowly at about 600

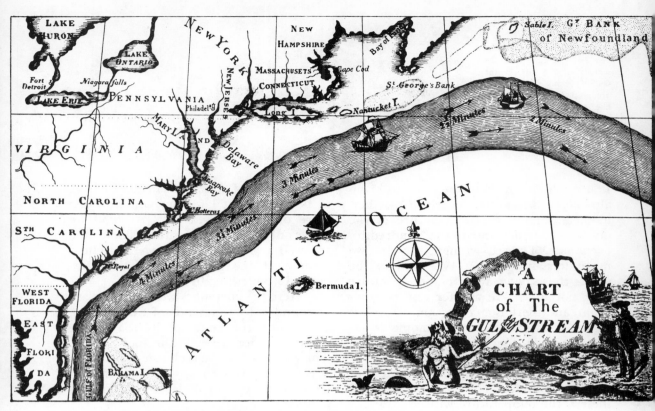

The submarine *Ben Franklin* was named in honor of Benjamin Franklin, the first person to study the section of the Gulf Stream where the submarine drifted. This map was drawn in 1770.

feet. Nothing has been moved to adjust her stability. Everything is fine; we are at a point 60 miles southeast of Cape Kennedy. We send a message to the Apollo 11 crew, a few hours before they leave for the moon. At 9:32 A.M. we hear—indirectly by way of radio and underwater telephone — the countdown and departure of the most fantastic expedition ever undertaken by man.

Outside, our searchlights are off. However, it is still clear, but there is no contrast. Everything is gray, or blue-gray, and because we have no point of reference (there are no fish or squid visible), we cannot gauge how far we can see. Plankton is too small or too transparent to be seen.

July 18. At the beginning of our fourth day, as usual, we receive our position as determined by the *Privateer* [a Navy surface support ship]. We mark the point on the chart. We count the miles. Our speed is good. But wait. Suddenly

Below: The basic specifications of the *Ben Franklin*. The power was supplied by 378 lead acid batteries.

General Specifications

Displacement	295,000 pounds
Length	48 feet, 9 inches
Beam	18 feet, 6 inches
Height	20 feet
Operational Depth (maximum)	2,000 feet
Collapse Depth	4,000 feet
Submerged Speed (maximum)	4 knots
Life Support	6 men for 6 weeks
Payload (nominal)	5 tons (mission dependent)
Total Power	756 KWH

One of the surprises of the *Ben Franklin* drift was the scarcity of sea life in the Gulf Stream. Shown here are salp (transparent jelly-like creatures joined in a chain), a school of tuna and a crab.

Frank, who has marked the chart and who also keeps an eye on his electrical thermometer giving the temperature of the outside water, accurate to two hundredths, exclaims, "They're wrong! Or did we misunderstand them? We cannot be where they say we are. The temperature does not fit." We ask for our position again, and there is a correction. Frank is right. Navigation by thermometer [as originated by Benjamin Franklin] is a reality.

We prepare tonight for a new descent to the bottom. Frank declares, "450 meters, the temperature will be 7.15° C." At times like this we ask ourselves why he is here, when he knows all the answers already. But it was just for that reason that I chose the Gulf Stream and not some unknown current for study. When the base is relatively well established, every new bit of data can be integrated into the system and become useful.

At 5 o'clock I open the valves of our variable ballast tank for descending.

Every pound of water taken in will have to be blown out later on, and we must spare our compressed air. At 6:30 we arrive only 30 feet above the sea floor. We are well equilibrated and well oriented because of the guide rope that is suspended from our craft.

Here the current is weak, and we are surrounded by thousands of tiny shrimp, euphausids, the same species that is the main food for several kinds of whales. The water is very clear, clearer in fact than at 600 feet. And the temperature is 7.18° C., a mere .003 of a degree off Frank's prediction.

On the sea floor are a few crabs 4 to 6 inches in diameter. A few fish; a sea anemone slowly moving its tentacles; a small fish darting away from the claws of a crab — all this we witness from our floating observation station.

Fifty explosions heard

In the middle of the night, the *Privateer* detonates a series of small charges,

Jacques Piccard, underwater explorer and developer of the *Ben Franklin*. His father, Auguste Piccard, also a scientist and explorer, invented the bathyscaph.

minute after minute. Fifty explosions are triggered, and 50 times we hear the muffled report and the various echoes. Fifty times the waves arrive to be recorded with precision on the magnetic tapes.

Before going to sleep, Chet is looking for new bacteria, counting old ones and feeding them. Up to now he can report that the situation is under control.

July 19. I stay at the window until 5 A.M., with searchlights on, 2 cameras nearby, ready for any event. Nothing is to be seen except a few plankton, already well known to us.

The assault occurred at 6:09, at 827 feet down.

As a matter of fact, it was really an attack, short, precise. The swordfish was about 5 or 6 feet long. Another one was waiting for him at the limit of our visibility. The combatant rushed forward and apparently tried to hit our porthole, missing it by a few inches. Then he circled around for several minutes, close to the boat. Content that his domination of this portion of his realm was not threatened, he joined his friend and left, never to be seen again.

This attack is extremely strange, like science fiction. It is interesting too, because last year another swordfish attacked another submersible, the *Alvin*. We were probably considered an underwater monster, and our portholes were thought to be eyes. But why, I wonder, such an attack, and what courage for such a fish to take on a 130-ton submarine!

July 20, Sunday. There is no weekend underwater. The watches succeed the watches. The work has to be done as usual. A Bible is on board. During the day we wait with impatience for the news of the moon landing. The message arrives finally at 4:20 P.M., and it is short and precise, without any comment. "Two Americans have landed on the moon."

So that is all we are to learn about the most beautiful technical achievement ever made by mankind. Save for some 800 million Chinese and Albanians, we are perhaps the only people on earth not to have witnessed this historic event on our television screens. We must wait 3 weeks to enjoy the moment vicariously.

Water-propelled creature

Tonight I saw at my porthole a big salp, a sea creature perhaps 10 inches long and 2 to 3 inches in diameter. I could see it swimming, ejecting water from within itself to propel itself in circles through the water.

The mesoscaph is well equilibrated, following her course. The Gulf Stream is not regular, however, and it has internal waves of wide amplitude, 60, sometimes 100 or more feet. When we are in them, we go up and down in the stream. Every time, we have to fix our eyes on the depth gage, ready to quickly flood or blow the variable ballast tanks, lest one of these waves send us too close to the surface or too near the bottom.

August 11. The day after tomorrow at 8:30 P.M. we will have completed a full 30 days adrift. Over 5 million measurements of temperature, salinity, speed of sound and depth have been recorded. About 1,000 explosions with their multiple echoes have been recorded on magnetic tapes. The contents of the seawater, principally its chlorophyll and various minerals, have been measured regularly several times a day. The earth's gravity has also been measured during a total of 23 hours.

During these 730 hours of our drift, covering close to 1,500 miles, we have sped along at an average of 2 knots; we have measured ambient light for several hundred hours; and we individually and collectively spent many hundreds of hours at the portholes. We feel we know intimately several species of plankton, little sea animals that at first elicited great interest, but that are now greeted with indifference, including the comment of one crewman who reported, "Nothing to see; always the same old stuff."

The fauna has certainly been less numerous than we expected. We saw a few schools of fish but did not find the deep scattering layer [of plankton], that belt of sea life that plays havoc with echo sounders and sonar equipment. We had so much hoped to study this phenomenon, and the Navy provided special, sophisticated equipment for our experiments.

Only once [July 25] has the current rejected us. We then came back to the surface and without opening the hatch, in order to preserve our life-science experiments for the full 30 days, were towed by the *Privateer* back into the middle of the stream.

All the data that we gathered will be diligently studied and interpreted in the laboratories of Grumman, the Navy and NASA. They will be published along with the pictures we took, for nothing is classified on this mission. The sea is owned by everybody.

We did not miss a thing. Chet's colonies remained under control, and no poisons were detected in the atmosphere within the boat. The [dehydrated and freeze-dried] food was, if not tasty, very well studied as far as calories and protein and vitamins were concerned.

August 15. On board the Coast Guard cutter *Cook Inlet.* The voyage ended yesterday at 8 A.M. without incident. Fortune smiled on us right up through the last day.

The unexpected speed of the stream after passing Cape Hatteras raised one minor problem. Our charts, anticipating a termination point many miles farther west, seemed until the last few days to be inadequate. Suddenly, just as the plot of our course was about to jump into the margin, the Gulf Stream obligingly drove us almost due north, skimming the end of the chart until we surfaced.*

The life experience of the voyage was fascinating, and it was marked throughout by congeniality. Aebersold was later to remark: "We began the mission as six men, we ended it as six friends."

The final results of our journey must await detailed analysis of the millions of water readings — several made every 2 seconds during the journey — by the automatic and scientist-operated equipment placed on board. This, too, must be coordinated with the findings and synoptic measurements carried out along the route of our mission by the surface support ship *Privateer* and her crew of ocean scientists.

We must scrutinize the stereophotographs taken by our cameras of the ocean floor, and the pictures taken by those 3 "peeping tom" cameras that every 2 minutes photographed the crew during the entire voyage. The physical oceanographic findings, the physiological-psychological "readout" and the full implications for future ocean research are still to come.

We can also state categorically that we have unlocked more questions about the Gulf Stream than our journey answered. Each of the crew realizes that there is a great deal more to learn and that others will come along and build upon the basic information generated by the Gulf Stream Drift Mission, until a better understanding of the stream is gained.

I foresee these future oceanographic missions patterned on the lines of ours, perhaps of two weeks' or ten days' duration, focusing on segments of the Gulf Stream, using the *Ben Franklin* or new vehicles similar in capability to her. Unlike our voyage, which was underwritten almost entirely by Grumman, future expeditions will most likely be supported in total or major part by government funds.

The significance of the oceans for all mankind, coastal nations and landlocked ones alike, is too great for quibbling over money or support.

The interpretation of the data we obtained, in correlation with those gained from the *Privateer,* will guide scientists who one day will decide the place and the conditions of a possible new mission.

The Gulf Stream has been deeply studied, and a few secrets have been uncovered. But it will probably always shield the majority of its mysteries from mankind.

Thus is the law of universal science. The deeper you delve into it, the more you realize that it is endless, limitless, infinite.

---

* *Editor's note:* The *Ben Franklin* surfaced about 300 miles off the coast of Halifax, Nova Scotia.

Space Science & Engineering Center, Univ. of Wisconsin

"In throwing wide the horizons of space, we have discovered new horizons on earth."

Richard M. Nixon

DEEP-SEA EXPLORATION

The ocean, brilliantly blue, teeming with life and covering nearly three fourths of our planet, is mankind's last frontier on earth. In a variety of projects, we are beginning to delve into the mysteries of this vast "horizon."

G.E. Ocean Systems Projects

Perhaps the most significant survey of the sea bottom is the Deep Sea Drilling Project. Cores of sediment recovered by the drilling ship, Glomar Challenger, are providing exciting data on the age and structure of the ocean floor.

At a drilling site (right), a sonar beacon is dropped to the ocean floor where it emits signals used in positioning the ship. The drilling assembly is rigged up and lowered into the ocean. When it touches the ocean floor, power is turned on, and the drill bit starts to penetrate the sediment. The expedition has drilled to depths of more than 3,300 feet below the ocean floor. Below: day's end.

Photos this page, Scripps Institution of Oceanography

The drilling crew assembles the drilling tools. Sediments have been recovered from deposits three miles underneath the ocean surface. They have provided confirmation of sea-floor spreading and, in the words of Dr. Maurice Ewing of Columbia University, opened "a new era in the science of geology."

Exploring the Gulf Stream. On July 14, 1969, the research submarine Ben Franklin (right) and her 6-man crew slipped beneath the ocean's surface off the Florida coast. One month and 1,444 nautical miles later, she surfaced, having silently drifted along the mysterious Gulf Stream.

Grumman Aerospace Corp.

Mining the riches of the seas. A number of operations are under way to recover minerals from the oceans. One company has begun to mine manganese nodules (below). It is estimated that there are at least 90,000,000,000 tons of these nodules on the ocean bottoms. Here, the nodules are brought aboard the research vessel R. V. Prospector (left) in wire dredge baskets (below, left).

Three photos Deepsea Ventures, Inc.

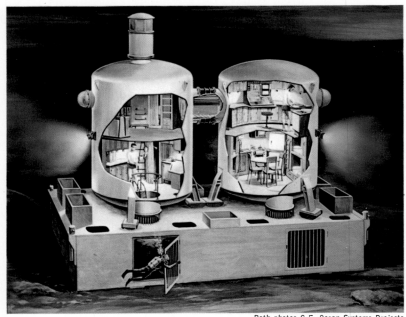

On February 15, 1969, 4 aquanauts began a 60-day underwater mission entitled Project Tektite. Living in a double-domed habitat (left) on the ocean floor in Virgin Islands National Park, the men moved freely from their dry "home" into the surrounding waters.

The coming years. Engineers have designed a number of deep-sea habitats and vehicles which will be tested in the early 1970's. Below: Bottom-Fix, a planned project for housing men and equipment at 12,000 feet or deeper.

Both photos G.E. Ocean Systems Projects

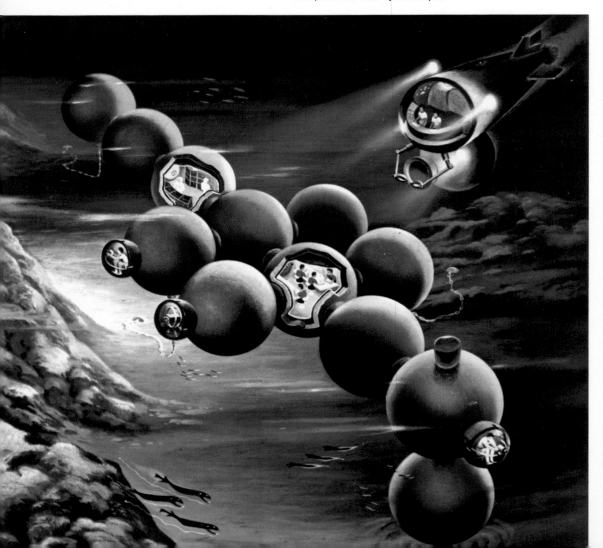

WORKING THE "GLOMAR CHALLENGER"*

Drilling Holes in the Ocean Floor

BY WALTER B. CHARM

Don Marszalek

Microfossils such as this can be used to identify the age of sediment brought up in core samples. These foraminifera (*Globotruncana*) lived 72 to 90 million years ago.

THE size and structure of the ocean basins have always been, literally, the deepest of mysteries. In the years since the first weighted rope was flung overboard to measure the depth of deep water, many improvements have been made in the tools of marine exploration. Yet, until recently, the sediment layers beneath the deep ocean floor were still beyond the reach of geological sampling. Geologists could only scratch the topsoil of the ocean basins with corers and dredges. The new drilling vessel *Glomar Challenger*, which can drill through several thousand feet of sea bottom in over 20,000 feet of water, therefore represents a significant extension of geology's reach.

My first view of the *Glomar Challenger* was from the window of a taxi caught up in the unbelievable traffic of Rio de Janeiro on a late Friday afternoon. As we threaded our way through the trucks and buses, the 200-foot-high drill tower came into view, projecting high above anything in the dockyard. I was expecting a large vessel, but not one of such imposing structure. I thought back to May 1964, when I boarded a small drilling vessel that was scheduled to drill 6 holes into the continental shelf off Jacksonville, Florida, 1 hole to be drilled in the then unheard-of depth of 3,000 feet of water. Because that first venture into deep-water drilling was a success and recovered enough material

* Reprinted by permission from *Sea Frontiers,* copyrighted 1969 by The International Oceanographic Foundation, 10 Rickenbacker Causeway, Virginia Key, Miami, Florida 33149

to provide a tremendous impetus to the study of the deep basins, I was now about to depart as one of 14 scientists on the fourth Atlantic leg of the Deep Sea Drilling Project, on a 2-month cruise on a ship capable of drilling in over 6 times that depth.

Changing parties

After the initial confusion of being assigned to cabins and learning how to get around the vessel, the activity around me began to take on some semblance of order. Roughnecks were loading equipment and supplies with the big cranes. The scientists who had just completed Leg III — from Dakar, Africa, to Rio — were still working on the samples and preparing the reams of data to be shipped to labs all over the United States. Leg III had been very successful and the core recovery was high.

Because the ship's entire crew and scientific party changes after every leg, there is a period of laboratory orientation for the incoming scientists and technicians. When the wireline brings the core up from the ocean floor, the work has just begun. Unlike the majority of research vessels, where the cores are stored on the ship and all the routine analysis is done at the shore-based laboratory, *Glomar Challenger* has facilities for all the necessary

151

analysis right aboard. The ship arrives at the shore lab with most of the routine work completed. There is, of course, much information left to be obtained by specialists, and their specially requested samples are sent out following every leg.

During the shipboard orientation period both the technicians and scientists are given instructions on shipboard treatment of cores. When the drill crew recovers a 30-foot core, it is cut into 5-foot workable sections and tightly capped. It is then run through a variety of analyses that enables the scientists to obtain as much information about the ocean floor as possible. These tests appear confusing and difficult at first, but the routine is soon established and everything then goes smoothly.

The ultimate tool

As a research vessel the *Glomar Challenger* is in a class by herself. She is extremely stable at sea and her mechanical

equipment is the finest. The quarters are clean and comfortable. She would appear to be the ultimate tool of marine geology.

But deep-sea drilling is still a new technique and there are many factors that are not entirely understood by the drilling engineers. Although some of the equipment was designed especially for the Deep Sea Drilling Project, and some taken from the Mohole project, the majority of the drilling machinery used aboard the ship is essentially the same type used on the land-based or off-shore drill rigs. The continuous movement of the vessel makes it very difficult for the driller to know what is really happening on the bottom. Special antiroll tanks dampen much of the rolling motion, but there is still the problem of pitching. No one actually knows what the thousands of feet of drill pipe are doing while hanging suspended from a vessel. Is it being snapped around and bent by the current and ship movement, or is it hanging straight down with little movement? Sometimes the driller feels the drill bit smashing up and down in the hole, crushing the sediment instead of drilling it. Two telescoping drill pipes

Atlantic Leg IV of the Deep Sea Drilling Project is mapped below. Site 26 marks the Vema Fracture Zone where sediment from the Amazon River was found. At Site 27 the sediments were similar to those exposed on nearby Barbados.

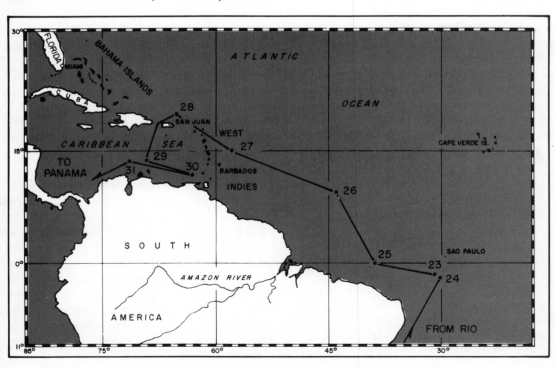

called bumper subs help reduce this action but it still happens when the sea is rough.

Recovery still uncertain

The biggest problem facing both ocean and land-based drilling is what to do when the bit on the end of thousands of feet of pipe wears out. The usual procedure is to pull up the pipe, change the bit, and go back down to continue where the drilling stopped. This "round trip" can easily be done on land, but the movement of the ship makes it almost impossible to reenter the same hole through miles of water and tricky currents. Some engineer will have to come up with a method of removing a worn drill bit and adding a new one without pulling up all the pipe. Various National Science Foundation contractors are investigating retractable bits and down-hole motors. These are also of great interest to the off-shore oil industry.

Core recovery also presents problems. Most ocean sediments are soft enough to be cut with a knife. This is especially true of the top 100 feet. As one goes deeper, the sediment becomes compacted under the weight of the sediment above it. Core recovery is usually higher in soft than in hard sediment, but is still inconsistent. While coring in the same material, a 30-foot core may be followed by a disappointing 2-foot one. Improved coring technology and familiarity with the deep-ocean sediments themselves will greatly improve recovery.

Holding station

The *Glomar Challenger* is placed in position over the drilling pipe by extra side propulsion propellers called thrusters, which are controlled by computers. This system will hold the vessel's position in winds up to 50 knots and waves as high as 20 feet. The whole operation is dependent on a transponding sound beacon placed on the ocean floor, which sends a pulse to the ship's computer. If this beacon stops sending the signal (and this has happened), the vessel has to be controlled

Above: 20,000 feet of drill pipe lie in racks aboard the *Glomar Challenger*. Thirty-foot standard lengths are joined to make "triples" 90 feet long. The racked pipes are capped (second photo) to avoid damage to their threaded ends. Below: UCLA student Tom Collins measures the velocity of sound through a core sample. The ship has full laboratory facilities, enabling scientists to study the cores as soon as they are recovered. The cores come up in clear plastic tubes, which aids in handling and examination.

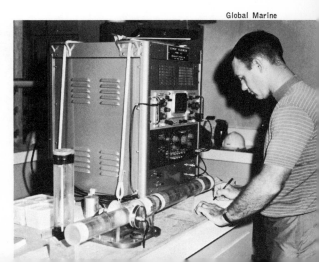

manually. If the drill pipe is not too deep into the sediment, it can probably be pulled out and recovered. Otherwise there is a good chance that the ship will move, causing the drill string to break and leaving all the pipe twisted like spaghetti on the bottom. (This also has happened.) Research into the design of deep-ocean positioning beacons is now being carried out by private and government laboratories. In the near future telemetering beacons and buoys will do many jobs that now require expensive ships, time and equipment.

Book of the past

As with most pioneer operations, few of the original problems are really solved. Instead, new data breed new problems. One important task on Leg IV was to sample certain layers below the ocean floor called reflecting layers, known to occur in the North Atlantic. They have been recorded seismically, but very rarely sampled because they are buried beneath hundreds of feet of ocean floor. Plans were also made to sample the deep igneous rocks underlying the sediments. It was hoped that the rocks could be sampled in areas where the sediment cover was thin. Although many reflections were seen on the seismic records, they proved elusive to the drill bit. It was not until site 29 in the central Caribbean that a thick million-year-old chert layer was successfully drilled and cored. It was very similar to reflecting layers found on previous legs in the North Atlantic Ocean Basin and off the west coast of Africa. This suggests that the Caribbean Sea and the North Atlantic Ocean were closely associated in the geologic past. The chert layer has not been found in the South Atlantic Ocean, indicating that this may be a separate geologic province.

For many years paleontologists have been trying to obtain a deep-sea core long enough to enable them to piece together the entire history of the Cenozoic era, which extends from the present to 63 million years ago. The Caribbean Sea was thought to be an ideal place to find this sequence, for it has been relatively free of major thrusts or dislocations of the earth's crust and the sediments in the Venezuelan Basin are uniform and undisturbed. But when the cores came on board the expected fossils were absent. This absence was caused by a little-understood phenomenon called calcium carbonate compensation. At certain depths in the ocean (carbonate compensation depths) the calcium carbonate that composes the shells of the important microfossils dissolves. This depth varies in time and place. Although the expected fossils were absent at some of the Caribbean sites, one site yielded a good section from the present to the middle Miocene (20 million years ago). By the time all the proposed holes are drilled, the paleontologists may be able to piece together their book of the past.

Amazon gold at sea

Other discoveries were more exciting. At site 26, the Vema Fracture Zone, an area 600 miles out into the Atlantic off Brazil, the drill string penetrated 2,000 feet into a deep basin of sediment that surprisingly turned out to be of Pleistocene age, probably formed during the last 500,000 years. When we examined the sediment closely, we found not only the remains of terrestrial plants, but traces of the rare minerals gold, topaz, tourmaline and aquamarine, which are characteristic of Brazil. Apparently the basin has been filled by Amazon River material carried by currents out to this distant location in the Atlantic. This demonstrated that turbid flows can travel greater distances than expected and that they are important in deep sediment deposition.

At another site close to Barbados we encountered deep sediments similar to those exposed on that island. If they are in fact identical, then this is the first time that an outcropping formation on land has been sampled in place in the deep ocean floor. It would mean that Barbados was uplifted 3 miles from the bottom of the Atlantic, creating a sheer cliff that, were it visible in air, would be more spectacular than the Grand Canyon.

WEATHER-SATELLITE SCOREBOARD

The First Ten Years

APRIL 1, 1970, marked the tenth anniversary of the launch of the first American weather satellite. Since the initial launch, 22 additional weather satellites, plus 2 Applications Technology Satellites (ATS) carrying meteorological cameras, have been successfully launched by the United States, providing nearly continuous space observation of this planet's weather phenomena.

The chart below, provided by the Environmental Science Services Administration (ESSA), briefly summarizes the first decade of weather satellites.

SATELLITE	LAUNCH DATE	USEFUL LIFE (DAYS)	PICTURES TRANSMITTED
TIROS 1	4/1/60	89	22,952
TIROS 2	11/23/60	376	36,156
TIROS 3	7/12/61	230	35,033
TIROS 4	2/8/62	161	32,593
TIROS 5	6/19/62	321	58,226
TIROS 6	6/19/63	389	68,557
TIROS 7	12/21/63	1,809	125,331
TIROS 8	12/21/63	1,287	102,463
TIROS 9	1/22/65	1,238	88,892
TIROS 10	7/1/65	730	79,874
ESSA 1	2/3/66	861	111,144
ESSA 2	2/28/66	1,480	126,288
ESSA 3	10/2/66	241	92,076
ESSA 4	1/26/67	110	27,129
ESSA 5	4/20/67	1,037	86,715
ESSA 6	11/10/67	755	64,154
ESSA 7	8/16/68	338	39,953
ESSA 8	12/15/68	471*	46,073*
ESSA 9	2/26/69	398*	54,793*
NIMBUS 1	8/28/64	27	27,100
NIMBUS 2	5/15/66	978	210,000
ATS 1	12/7/66	1,209*	9,420*
ATS 3	11/5/67	877*	369,249*
NIMBUS 3	4/14/69	351*	281,175*
ITOS 1	1/17/70	67*	20,800*

*Still operating as of March 31, 1970.

ENVIRONMENTAL SCIENCES

CONTENTS

"Behind the complex predictions and obscure language, beyond words like ecology, environment and pollution, there is a simple question: do we want to live or die?"

John V. Lindsay

REVIEW OF THE YEAR-
ENVIRONMENTAL SCIENCES

The end of the sixties marked a turning point in the public's attitude toward its environment. The change was well expressed by a participant in a 1969 conference sponsored by the conservationist Sierra Club: "Two years ago we were considered way-outs. Nobody knew what conservation meant. Now we find ourselves right in the middle of what's happening." The reasons for the change were all too apparent. People could no longer ignore or avoid the adverse side effects of modern living. As the former Secretary of Health, Education, and Welfare, John W. Gardner, said in October 1969, "we get richer and richer in filthier and filthier communities, until we reach a final state of affluent misery — Croesus on a garbage heap."

Oil pollution. "Environment" and "ecology" became emotionally-charged words largely as a result of the blowout of an oil well off Santa Barbara, California, in January 1969. The uncontrolled flow of oil fouled miles of beachfront, killed seals, sea lions and countless birds, and caused a decline in the number of fish and other sea organisms in the area. This was only 1 of 17 major oil spills (worldwide) in 1969. ◆ In February 1970, three incidents greatly increased the cry for governmental action against the oil polluters. On February 4 a tanker ran aground off Nova Scotia; oil from the leaking ship polluted at least 20 miles of Canadian coastline. On the 13th a tanker ran aground off Tampa, Florida, spilling oil that spread across the bay and onto beaches. But the public cry was loudest when an intense fire broke out on a Chevron oil platform over the Gulf of Mexico on February 10. Oil poured out of the damaged pipes. The resulting slick threatened wildlife preserves and Louisiana's shrimp and oyster industries. At least 1 of the 8 wells that contributed to the leak lacked required safety equipment. ◆ On April 3, 1970, President Nixon signed a Water Quality Improvement Act, which makes oil polluters liable for all cleanup costs "without regard to whether any such act or omission was or was not negligent."

Water pollution. A wide variety of waste materials is reaching surface waters in increasing quantities. As Charles C. Johnson, Jr., of the U.S. Public Health Service said in a speech in March 1969, "many of these are extremely complex and are unaffected by present water and waste-water treatment procedures. Some, such as pesticides and oil-refinery wastes, have been shown to be toxic or carcinogenic. We know little about the identification and measurement of these compounds in drinking water, and we have little knowledge of their long-range health effects." ◆ Numerous polluted bodies vie for the title, "Exhibit A." Perhaps the 1969 winner of so dubious an award is the Cuyahoga River, which flows through Cleveland, Ohio. For years, Ohio residents had jokingly called the sludge-filled river a fire hazard. In June 1969 the joke was no longer funny. An oil slick on the water ignited, and flames spread along the river, causing 2 bridges to catch fire. The Cuyahoga River empties into Lake Erie, a lake "threatened with death," according to Dr. Barry Commoner of Washington University. ◆ Nations along the Rhine River — the "sewer of Europe" — are discussing emergency measures to prevent or minimize future pollution of this 820-mile waterway. Concern reached a peak after a June 1969 incident: in the German segment of the river, 40 million fish died. The cause of death was never completely explained. ◆ An alarming report by the U.S. Marine Laboratory at Sandy Hook, New Jersey, has dramatically illustrated the consequences of using the ocean as a garbage dump. For 40 years, New York City wastes have been dumped in the waters off Sandy Hook. Today the 20-square-mile area, once teeming with sea life, is a "dead sea."

Pesticides. Americans use 800 million pounds of synthetic organic pesticides each year. These substances have been a major factor in achieving the nation's high productivity and food quality and in eradicating disease-carrying insects and other pests. But mounting evidence indicates that some pesticides, in particular the chlorinated hydrocarbons, are more harmful than beneficial. The chlorinated hydrocarbons include DDT and dieldrin; these pesticides, noted for their toxicity and longevity, accumulate in soil, in water, and in the fatty tissues of animals. Especially large amounts are found in predatory animals — and occasionally in man. In May 1969, toxicologist Dr. Goran Lofroth of Stockholm University in Sweden announced that breast-fed babies throughout the world were ingesting about 2 times the amount of DDT compounds recommended as a maximum daily intake by the World Health Organization (0.7 milligrams). Growing concern of health officials and conservationists over the harmful effects of DDT finally led a number of states and nations to ban or restrict the use of this chemical.

Air pollution. In a May 1969 speech, Charles Johnson said that "toxic matter is released into the air over the United States at a rate of more than 142 million tons a year, or ¾ of a ton for every American." The relationship of air pollution and respiratory diseases is by now evident. And other perils are indicated by recent studies. Chemist Robert Shapiro of New York University has discovered that sulfur dioxide, a major air pollutant and food additive, causes a "drastic" change in the basic structure of the chemicals of heredity and therefore may cause mutations and cancer in humans and other living organisms. According to Dr. John R. Goldsmith of California's Department of Public Health, carbon monoxide can greatly reduce the blood's oxygen-carrying capacity. This may cause various circulatory diseases. For example, Dr. Goldsmith explained that "the damaged heart of the coronary patient is not able to compensate adequately for this reduced oxygen supply, and the result could be a fatal disruption in the cardiac rhythm." Increasing concentrations of lead are another area of concern. "It has been demonstrated by previous work that long-term increases in atmospheric lead will result in predictably higher blood lead levels in the exposed population," said Dr. Tsaihwa J. Chow, a geochemist at the Scripps Institution of Oceanography. "Because of the well-known toxicity of lead, the health hazard of increasing lead pollutants in the environment cannot be ignored." In February 1970, major car manu-facturers said that many of their 1971 models would be designed to burn unleaded fuel; oil companies have begun to market leadless gas.

Solid wastes. Discarded automobiles, old newspapers and telephone books, tin cans, nonreturnable bottles — all add to the growing problems of solid-waste disposal. In the past 20 years the U.S. population has grown 30 per cent; the amount of solid wastes has increased 60 per cent. The solution, ecologists say, is to use these wastes wisely so that they benefit the environment, not damage it. Such recycling would often be expensive, but, as ecologist David Gates says, "we're poisoning our world and we can't afford not to spend the money as soon as possible." Treated sewage could be used in irrigating farmlands, used paper could be reprocessed into newsprint, and so on. But equally important, according to many environmentalists, is the reassessment of our national and personal priorities. Is an ever-increasing gross national product desirable? Are our demands for high-powered cars, convenience packaging and a multitude of electrical gadgets justifiable? Ecocide — the murder of the environment — is everybody's business.

Chas. Addams; © 1969 The New Yorker Magazine, Inc.

"Now maybe they'll be moved to do something about water pollution!"

CLEANING UP OUR ENVIRONMENT*

The Fight against Pollution

BY RICHARD M. NIXON

LIKE those in the last century who tilled a plot of land to exhaustion and then moved on to another, we in this century have too casually and too long abused our natural environment. The time has come when we can wait no longer to repair the damage already done, and to establish new criteria to guide us in the future.

The fight against pollution, however, is not a search for villains. For the most part, the damage done to our environment has not been the work of evil men, nor has it been the inevitable by-product either of advancing technology or of growing population. It results not so much from choices made, as from choices neglected; not from malign intention, but from failure to take into account the full consequences of our actions.

* The full text of the message President Nixon sent to the United States Congress on February 10, 1970

Quite inadvertently, by ignoring environmental costs we have given an economic advantage to the careless polluter over his more conscientious rival. While adopting laws prohibiting injury to person or property, we have freely allowed injury to our shared surroundings. Conditioned by an expanding frontier, we came only late to a recognition of how precious and how vulnerable our resources of land, water and air really are.

The tasks that need doing require money, resolve and ingenuity — and they are too big to be done by government alone. They call for fundamentally new philosophies of land, air and water use, for stricter regulation, for expanded government action, for greater citizen involvement, and for new programs to ensure that government, industry and individuals all are called on to do their share of the job and to pay their share of the cost.

Because the many aspects of environmental quality are closely interwoven, to consider each in isolation would be unwise. Therefore, I am today outlining a comprehensive, 37-point program, embracing 23 major legislative proposals and 14 new measures being taken by administrative action or Executive Order in 5 major categories:

(1) water-pollution control
(2) air-pollution control
(3) solid-waste management
(4) parklands and public recreation
(5) organizing for action.

As we deepen our understanding of complex ecological processes, as we improve our technologies and institutions and learn from experience, much more will be possible. But these 37 measures represent actions we can take *now,* and that can move us dramatically forward toward what has become an urgent common goal of all Americans: the rescue of our natural habitat as a place both habitable and hospitable to man.

Our polluted waters

Water pollution has three principal sources: municipal, industrial and agricultural wastes. All three must eventually be controlled if we are to restore the purity of our lakes and rivers.

Of these three, the most troublesome to control are those from agricultural sources: animal wastes, eroded soil, fertilizers and pesticides. Some of these are nature's own pollutions. The Missouri River was known as "Big Muddy" long before towns and industries were built on its banks. But many of the same techniques of pest control, livestock feeding, irrigation and soil fertilization that have made American agriculture so abundantly productive have also caused serious water pollution.

Effective control will take time, and will require action on many fronts: modified agricultural practices, greater care in the disposal of animal wastes, better soil-conservation methods, new kinds of fertilizers, new chemical pesticides and more widespread use of natural pest-control techniques.

A number of such actions are already under way. We have taken action to phase out the use of DDT and other hard pesticides. We have begun to place controls on wastes from concentrated animal feedlots. We need programs of intensified research, both public and private, to develop new methods of reducing agricultural pollution while maintaining productivity. I have asked The Council on Environmental Quality to press forward in this area.

Meanwhile, however, we have the technology and the resources to proceed *now* on a program of swift cleanup of pollution from the most acutely damaging sources: municipal and industrial waste.

Municipal wastes. As long as we have the means to do something about it, there is no good reason why municipal pollution of our waters should be allowed to persist unchecked.

In the four years since the Clean Waters Restoration Act of 1966 was passed, we have failed to keep our promises to ourselves: Federal appropriations for constructing municipal treatment plants have totaled only about one third

162

of authorizations. Municipalities themselves have faced increasing difficulty in
selling bonds to finance their share of the
construction costs. Given the saturated
condition of today's municipal bond markets, if a clean-up program is to work it
has to provide the means by which municipalities can finance their share of the
cost even as we increase Federal expenditures.

The best current estimate is that it
will take a total capital invesment of about
$10 billion ($10,000,000,000) over a 5-year
period to provide the municipal waste-
treatment plants and interceptor lines
needed to meet our national water-quality
standards. This figure is based on a recently completed nationwide survey of the
deficiencies of present facilities, plus projections of additional needs that will have
developed by 1975 to accommodate the
normal annual increase in the volume of
wastes, and to replace equipment that can
be expected to wear out or become obsolete in the interim.

This will provide every community
that needs it with secondary waste treatment, and also special, additional treatment in areas of special need, including
communities on the Great Lakes. We
have the industrial capacity to do the job
in 5 years if we begin now.

To meet this construction schedule, I
propose a two-part program of Federal assistance:

• I propose a Clean Waters Act with
$4 billion to be authorized immediately,
for fiscal 1971, to cover the full Federal
share of the total $10 billion cost on a
matching-fund basis. This would be allocated at a rate of $1 billion a year for the
next 4 years, with a reassessment in 1973
of needs for 1975 and subsequent years.

By thus assuring communities of full
Federal support, we can enable planning
to begin *now* for all needed facilities and
construction to proceed at an accelerated
rate.

• I propose creation of a new Environmental Financing Authority (EFA),
to ensure that every municipality in the
country has an opportunity to sell its
waste-treatment-plant-construction bonds.

The condition of the municipal bond
market is such that, in 1969, 509 issues
totaling $2.9 billion proved unsalable. If
a municipality cannot sell waste-treatment-plant-construction bonds, EFA will
buy them and will sell its own bonds on
the taxable market. Thus, construction
of pollution-control facilities will depend
not on a community's credit rating, but
on its waste-disposal needs.

Providing money is important, but
equally important is where and how the
money is spent. A river cannot be polluted on its left bank and clean on its
right. In a given waterway, abating *some*
of the pollution is often little better than
doing nothing at all, and money spent on
such partial efforts is often largely wasted.

Present grant-allocation formulas —
those in the 1966 Act — have prevented
the spending of funds where they could

Plain Dealer Photo — Mitchael J. Zaremba

In July 1969, Cleveland's Cuyahoga River caught fire, burning
with such intensity that two railroad bridges, including that
shown here, were severely damaged. The river is so polluted
that it contains no visible life,
not even the leeches and sludge
worms that are usually plentiful
in waste-filled waters.

produce the greatest results in terms of clean water. Too little attention has been given to seeing that investments in specific waste-treatment plants have been matched by other municipalities and industries on the same waterway. Many plants have been poorly designed and inefficiently operated. Some municipalities have offered free treatment to local industries, then not treated their wastes sufficiently to prevent pollution.

To ensure that the new funds are well invested, five major reforms are needed. One requires legislation; the other four will be achieved by administrative action.

• I propose that the present, rigid allocation formula be revised, so that special emphasis can be given to areas where facilities are most needed and where the greatest improvements in water quality will result.

Under existing authority, the Secretary of the Interior will institute four major reforms:

• Federally assisted treatment plants will be required to meet prescribed design, operation and maintenance standards, and to be operated only by State-certified operators.

• Municipalities receiving Federal assistance in constructing plants will be required to impose reasonable users' fees on industrial users sufficient to meet the costs of treating industrial wastes.

• Development of comprehensive river-basin plans will be required at an early date, to ensure that Federally assisted treatment plants will in fact contribute to effective cleanup of entire river-basin systems. Collection of existing data on pollution sources and development of effluent inventories will permit systems approaches to pollution control.

• Wherever feasible, communities will be strongly encouraged to cooperate in the construction of large regional treatment facilities, which provide economies of scale and give more efficient and more thorough waste treatment.

Industrial pollution. Some industries discharge their wastes into municipal

In 1968, 15.2 million fish were killed by water pollution in the United States. Municipal and industrial pollution were the main causes (6.9 and 6.3 million, respectively).

systems; others discharge them directly into lakes and rivers. Obviously unless we curb industrial as well as municipal pollution our waters will never be clean.

Industry itself has recognized the problem, and many industrial firms are making vigorous efforts to control their waterborne wastes. But strict standards and strict enforcement are nevertheless necessary, not only to ensure compliance, but also in fairness to those who have voluntarily assumed the often costly burden while their competitors have not. Good neighbors should not be placed at a competitive disadvantage because of their good-neighborliness.

Under existing law, standards for water-pollution control often are established in only the most general and insufficient terms: for example, by requiring all affected industries to install secondary-treatment facilities. This approach takes little account of such crucial variables as the volume and toxicity of the wastes actually being discharged, or the capacity of a particular body of water to absorb wastes without becoming polluted. Even

Cleaning up after the polluters. Right: raking oil-soaked hay along the surf line of Santa Barbara Harbor (February 1969). The oil washed ashore after an offshore well began leaking. Below: one of the thousands of volunteers who tried to save birds caught in an oil slick that resulted from the rupture of a tanker in Tampa Bay, Florida (February 1970).

UPI

Wide World

more important, it provides a poor basis for enforcement: with no effluent standard by which to measure, it is difficult to prove in court that standards are being violated.

The present fragmenting of jurisdictions also has hindered comprehensive efforts. At present, Federal jurisdiction generally extends only to interstate waters. One result has been that as stricter State-Federal standards have been imposed, pollution has actually increased in some other waters: in underground aquifers and the

oceans. As controls over interstate waters are tightened, polluting industries will be increasingly tempted to locate on intrastate lakes and rivers — with a consequently increased threat to those waterways — unless they too are brought under the same strictures.

I propose that we take an entirely new approach: one that concerts Federal, State and private efforts; that provides for effective nationwide enforcement; and that rests on a simple but profoundly significant principle: the nation's waterways belong to us all, and neither a municipality nor an industry should be allowed to discharge wastes into these waterways beyond their capacity to absorb the wastes without becoming polluted.

Specifically, I propose a seven-point program of measures we should adopt *now* to enforce control of water pollution from industrial and municipal wastes and to give the states more effective backing in their own efforts.

• I propose that State-Federal water-quality standards be amended to impose precise effluent requirements on all industrial and municipal sources. These should be imposed on an expeditious timetable, with the limit for each based on a fair allocation of the total capacity of the waterway to absorb the user's particular kind of waste without becoming polluted.

• I propose that violation of established effluent requirements be considered sufficient cause for court action.

• I propose that the Secretary of the Interior be allowed to proceed more swiftly in his enforcement actions, and that he be given new legal weapons including subpoena and discovery power.

• I propose that failure to meet established water-quality standards or implementation schedules be made subject to court-imposed fines of up to $10,000 per day.

• I propose that the Secretary of the Interior be authorized to seek immediate injunctive relief in emergency situations in which severe water pollution constitutes an imminent danger to health or threatens irreversible damage to water quality.

• I propose that the Federal pollution-control program be extended to include all navigable waters, both inter- and intra-state, all interstate groundwaters, the United States' portion of boundary waters, and waters of the Contiguous Zone.

• I propose that Federal operating grants to State pollution-control-enforcement agencies be tripled over the next 5 years — from $10 million now to $30 million in fiscal year 1975 — to assist them in meeting the new responsibilities that stricter and expanded enforcement will place upon them.

The air we breathe

Air is our most vital resource, and its pollution is our most serious environmental problem. Existing technology for the control of air pollution is less advanced than that for controlling water pollution, but there is a great deal we can do within the limits of existing technology — and more we can do to spur technological advance.

Most air pollution is produced by the burning of fuels. About half is produced by motor vehicles.

Motor vehicles. The Federal Government began regulating automobile emissions of carbon monoxide and hydrocarbons with the 1968 model year. Standards for 1970-model cars have been made significantly tighter; this year, for the first time, emissions from new buses and heavy-duty trucks have also been brought under Federal regulation. In future years, emission levels can and must be brought much lower.

The Secretary of Health, Education, and Welfare is today publishing a notice of new, considerably more stringent motor-vehicle-emission standards he intends to issue for 1973 and 1975 models — including control of nitrogen oxides by 1973 and of particulate emission by 1975.

These new standards represent our best present estimate of the lowest emission levels attainable by those years.

Effective control requires new legislation to correct two key deficiencies in the present law:

a) Testing procedures. Under present law, only manufacturers' prototype vehicles are tested for compliance with emission standards, and even this is voluntary rather than mandatory.

I propose legislation requiring that representative samples of actual production vehicles be tested throughout the model year.

b) Fuel composition and additives. What goes into a car's fuel has a major effect on what comes out of its exhaust, and also on what kinds of pollution-control devices can effectively be employed. Federal standards for what comes out of a car's engine should be accompanied by standards for what goes into it.

I propose legislation authorizing the Secretary of Health, Education, and Welfare to regulate fuel composition and additives.

With these changes, we can drastically reduce pollution from motor vehicles in the years just ahead. But in making and keeping our peace with nature, to plan only one year ahead or even five is hardly to plan at all. Our responsibility now is also to look beyond the seventies, and the prospects then are uncertain.

Based on present trends, it is quite possible that by 1980 the increase in the sheer number of cars in densely populated areas will begin outrunning the technological limits of our capacity to reduce pollution from the internal-combustion engine.

I hope this will not happen. I hope the automobile industry's present determined effort to make the internal-combustion engine sufficiently pollution-free succeeds. But if it does not, then unless motor vehicles with an alternative, low-pollution power source are available, vehicle-caused pollution will once again begin an inexorable increase.

Therefore prudence dictates that we move now to ensure that such a vehicle will be available if needed.

I am inaugurating a program to marshal both government and private research with the goal of producing an unconventionally powered, virtually pollution-free automobile within five years.

• I have ordered the start of an extensive Federal research and development program in unconventional vehicles, to be conducted under the general direction of the Council on Environmental Quality.

• As an incentive to private developers, I have ordered that the Federal Government should undertake the purchase of privately produced unconventional vehicles for testing and evaluation.

A proposal currently before the Congress would provide a further incentive to private developers by authorizing the Federal Government to offer premium prices for purchasing low-pollution cars for its own use. This could be a highly productive program once such automobiles are approaching development, although current estimates are that, initially, prices offered would have to be up to 200 per cent of the cost of equivalent conventional vehicles rather than the 125 per cent contemplated in the proposed legislation. The immediate task, however, is to see that an intensified program of research and development begins at once.

One encouraging aspect of the effort to curb motor-vehicle pollution is the extent to which industry itself is taking the initiative. For example, the nation's principal automobile manufacturers are not only developing devices now to meet present and future Federal emission standards, but are also, on their own initiative, preparing to put on the market by 1972 automobiles that will not require and indeed must not use leaded gasoline. Such cars will not only discharge no lead into the atmosphere, but will also be equipped with still more effective devices for controlling emissions — devices made possible by the use of lead-free gasoline.

This is a great forward step taken by the manufacturers before any Federal regulation of lead additives or emissions has been imposed. I am confident that the petroleum industry will see to it that suitable nonleaded gasoline is made widely available for these new cars when they come on the market.

Stationary-source pollution. Industries, power plants, furnaces, incinerators — these and other so-called "stationary sources" add enormously to the pollution of the air. In highly industrialized areas, such pollution can quite literally make breathing hazardous to health, and can cause unforeseen atmospheric and meteorological problems as well.

Increasingly industry itself has been adopting ambitious pollution-control programs, and state and local authorities have been setting and enforcing stricter antipollution standards. But they have not gone far enough or fast enough, nor, to be realistic about it, will they be able to without the strongest possible Federal backing.

Without effective government standards, industrial firms that spend the necessary money for pollution control may find themselves at a serious economic disadvantage as against their less conscientious competitors. And without effective Federal standards, states and communities that require such controls find themselves at a similar disadvantage in attracting industry, against more-permissive rivals. Air is no respecter of political boundaries: a community that sets and enforces strict standards may still find its air polluted from sources in another community or another state.

Under the Clean Air Act of 1967, the Federal Government is establishing air-quality-control regions around the nation's major industrial and metropolitan areas. Within these regions, states are setting air-quality standards (permissible levels of pollutants in the air) and developing plans for pollution abatement to achieve these air-quality standards. All state air-quality standards and implementation plans require Federal approval.

This program has been the first major Federal effort to control air pollution. It has been a useful beginning. But we have learned in the past two years that it has shortcomings. Federal designation of air-quality-control regions, while necessary in areas where emissions from one state are polluting the air in another, has been a time-consuming process. Adjoining states within the same region often have proposed inconsistent air-quality standards, causing further delays for compromise and revision.

There are no provisions for controlling pollution *outside* of established air-quality-control regions. This means that even with the designation of hundreds of such regions, some areas of the country with serious air-pollution problems would remain outside the program. This is unfair not only to the public but to many industries, since those within regions with strict requirements could be unfairly disadvantaged with respect to competitors that are not within regions.

Finally, insufficient Federal enforcement powers have circumscribed the Federal Government's ability to support the states in establishing and enforcing effective abatement programs.

It is time to build on what we have learned and to begin a more ambitious national effort. I recommend that the

"On a clear day you can see forever. . . ." But blankets of smog (above) increasingly hide the valley below the San Bernardino Mountains. Aided by onshore winds, smog is blown up into the mountains to damage forests in its path. Right: Forest Service researchers have found some ponderosa pine trees are more susceptible to smog injury than others. The tree at left is dying while the one at right appears quite tolerant.

U.S. Forest Service

Clean Air Act be revised to expand the scope of strict pollution abatement, to simplify the task of industry in pollution abatement through more-nearly-uniform standards, and to provide special controls against particularly dangerous pollutants.

• I propose that the Federal Government establish nationwide air-quality standards, with the states to prepare within one year abatement plans for meeting these standards.

This will provide a minimum standard for air quality for all areas of the nation while permitting states to set more-stringent standards for any or all sections within the state. National air-quality standards will relieve the states of the lengthy process of standard-setting under Federal supervision, and allow them to concentrate on the immediate business of developing and implementing abatement plans.

These abatement plans would cover areas both inside and outside Federally designated air-quality-control regions, and could be designed to achieve any higher levels of air quality which the states might choose to establish. They would include emission standards for stationary sources of air pollution.

• I propose that designation of interstate air-quality-control regions continue at an accelerated rate, to provide a framework for establishing compatible abatement plans in interstate areas.

• I propose that the Federal Government establish national emissions standards for facilities that emit pollutants extremely hazardous to health, and for selected classes of new facilities which could be major contributors to air pollution.

In the first instance, national standards are needed to guarantee the earliest possible elimination of certain air pollutants which are clear health hazards even in minute quantities. In the second instance, national standards will ensure that advanced abatement technology is used in constructing the new facilities, and that levels of air quality are maintained in the face of industrial expansion. Before any

emissions standards were established, public hearings would be required involving all interested parties. The states would be responsible for enforcing these standards in conjunction with their own programs.

• I propose that Federal authority to seek court action be extended to include both inter- and intrastate air-pollution situations in which, because of local non-enforcement, air quality is below national standards, or in which emissions standards or implementation timetables are being violated.

• I propose that failure to meet established air-quality standards or implementation schedules be made subject to court-imposed fines of up to $10,000 per day.

Solid-waste management

"Solid wastes" are the discarded leftovers of our advanced consumer society. Increasing in volume, they litter the landscape and strain the facilities of municipal governments.

New packaging methods, using materials that do not degrade and cannot easily be burned, create difficult new disposal problems. Though many wastes are potentially reusable, we often discard today what a generation ago we saved. Most bottles, for example, now are "nonreturnable." We reprocess used paper less than we used to, not only adding to the burden on municipal sanitation services but also making wasteful use of scarce timberlands. Often the least expensive way to dispose of an old automobile is to abandon it — and millions of people do precisely that, creating eyesores for millions of others.

One way to meet the problem of solid wastes is simply to surrender to it: to continue pouring more and more public money into collection and disposal of whatever happens to be privately produced and discarded. This is the old way; it amounts to a public subsidy of waste pollution. If we are ever truly to gain control of the problem, our goal must be broader: to reduce the volume of wastes and the difficulty of their disposal, and to encourage their constructive reuse instead.

To accomplish this, we need incentives, regulations and research directed especially at two major goals: a) making products more easily disposable—especially containers, which are designed for disposal; and b) reusing and recycling a far greater proportion of waste materials.

As we look toward the long-range future — to 1980, 2000 and beyond — recycling of materials will become increasingly necessary not only for waste disposal but also to conserve resources. While our population grows, each one of us keeps using more of the earth's resources. In the case of many minerals, more than half those extracted from the earth since time began have been extracted since 1910.

A great deal of our space research has been directed toward creating self-sustaining environments, in which people can live for long periods of time by reprocessing, recycling and reusing the same materials. We need to apply this kind of thinking more consciously and more broadly to our patterns of use and disposal of materials here on earth.

Many currently used techniques of solid-waste disposal remain crudely deficient. Research and development programs under the Solid Waste Disposal Act of 1965 have added significantly to our knowledge of more efficient techniques. The Act expires this year. I recommend its extension, and I have already moved to broaden its programs.

I have ordered a redirection of research under the Solid Waste Disposal Act to place greater emphasis on techniques for recycling materials, and on development and use of packaging and other materials that will degrade after use: that is, which will become temporary rather than permanent wastes.

Few of America's eyesores are so unsightly as its millions of junk automobiles. Ordinarily when a car is retired from use it goes first to a wrecker, who strips it of its valuable parts, and then to a scrap processor, who reduces the remainder to scrap for sale to steel mills.

The prices paid by wreckers for junk cars often are less than the cost of transporting them to the wrecking yard. In the case of a severely damaged or "cannibalized" car, instead of paying for it the wrecker may even charge towing costs. Thus the final owner's economic incentive to deliver his car for processing is slight, nonexistent or even negative.

The rate of abandonment is increasing. In New York City, 2,500 cars were towed away as abandoned on the streets in 1960; in 1964, 25,000 were towed away as abandoned; in 1969, more than 50,000.

The way to provide the needed incentive is to apply to the automobile the principle that its price should include not only the cost of producing it, but also the cost of disposing of it.

I have asked the Council on Environmental Quality to take the lead in producing a recommendation for a bounty payment or other system to promote the prompt scrapping of all junk automobiles.

The particular disposal problems presented by the automobile are unique. However, wherever appropriate, we should also seek to establish incentives and regulations to encourage the reuse, recycling or easier disposal of other commonly used goods.

I have asked the Chairman of the Council on Environmental Quality to work with the Cabinet Committee on the Environment, and with appropriate industry and consumer representatives, toward development of such incentives and regulations for submission to the Congress.

Parks and public recreation

Increasing population, increasing mobility, increasing incomes and increasing leisure will all combine in the years ahead to rank recreational facilities among the most vital of our public resources. Yet land suitable for such facilities, especially near heavily populated areas, is being rapidly swallowed up.

Plain common sense argues that we give greater priority to acquiring now the lands that will be so greatly needed in a few years. Good sense also argues that the

Federal Government itself, as the nation's largest landholder, should address itself more imaginatively to the question of making optimum use of its own holdings in a recreation-hungry era.

• I propose full funding in fiscal 1971 of the $327 million available through the Land and Water Conservation Fund for additional park and recreational facilities, with increased emphasis on locations that can be easily reached by the people in crowded urban areas.

• I propose that we adopt a new philosophy for the use of Federally-owned lands, treating them as a precious resource — like money itself — which should be made to serve the highest possible public good.

Acquiring needed recreation areas is a real-estate transaction. One third of all the land in the United States — more than 750 million acres — is owned by the Federal Government. Thousands of acres in the heart of metropolitan areas are reserved for only minimal use by Federal installations. To supplement the regularly appropriated funds available, nothing could be more appropriate than to meet new real-estate needs through use of currently owned real estate, whether by transfer, sale or conversion to a better use.

Until now, the uses to which Federally-owned properties were put have largely been determined by who got them first. As a result, countless properties with enormous potential as recreation areas linger on in the hands of agencies that could just as well — or better — locate elsewhere. Bureaucratic inertia is compounded by a quirk of present accounting procedures, which has the effect of imposing a budgetary penalty on an agency that gives up one piece of property and moves to another, even if the vacated property is sold for 10 times the cost of the new.

The time has come to make more rational use of our enormous wealth of real property, giving a new priority to our newly urgent concern with public recreation — and to make more imaginative use of properties now surplus to finance acquisition of properties now needed.

• By Executive Order, I am directing the heads of all Federal agencies and the Administrator of General Services to institute a review of all Federally-owned real properties that should be considered for

Symbol of an affluent and wasteful society. Americans junked seven million cars in 1968. These cars pile up in junk yards or simply lie abandoned on streets. Some method of "recycling" wornout automobiles must be found.

UPI

other uses. The test will be whether a particular property's continued present use or another would better serve the public interest, considering both the agency's needs and the property's location. Special emphasis will be placed on identifying properties that could appropriately be converted to parks and recreation areas, or sold, so that proceeds can be made available to provide additional park and recreation lands.

• I am establishing a Property Review Board to review the GSA reports and recommend to me what properties should be converted or sold. This Board will consist of the Director of the Bureau of the Budget, the Chairman of the Council of Economic Advisers, the Chairman of the Council on Environmental Quality and the Administrator of General Services, plus others that I may designate.

• I propose legislation to establish, for the first time, a program for relocating Federal installations that occupy locations that could better be used for other purposes.

This would allow a part of the proceeds from the sales of surplus properties to be used for relocating such installations, thus making more land available.

• I also propose accompanying legislation to protect the Land and Water Conservation Fund, ensuring that its sources of income would be maintained and possibly increased for purchasing additional parkland.

The net effect would be to increase our capacity to add new park and recreational facilities by enabling us for the first time to use surplus-property sales in a coordinated three-way program: a) by direct conversion from other uses; b) through sale of currently owned properties and purchase of others with the proceeds; and c) by sale of one Federal property, and use of the proceeds to finance the relocation and conversion costs of making another property available for recreational use.

• I propose that the Department of the Interior be given authority to convey surplus real property to state and local governments for park and recreation purposes at a public-benefit discount ranging up to 100 per cent.

• I propose that Federal procedures be revised to encourage Federal agencies to make efficient use of real property. This revision should remove the budgetary penalty now imposed on agencies relinquishing one site and moving to another.

As one example of what such a property review can make possible, a sizable stretch of one of California's finest beaches has long been closed to the public because it was part of Camp Pendleton. Last month the Defense Department arranged to make more than a mile of this beach available to the State of California for use as a state park. The remaining beach is sufficient for Camp Pendleton's needs; thus the released stretch represents a shift from low-priority to high-priority use. By carefully weighing alternative uses, a priceless recreational resource was returned to the people for recreational purposes.

Another vast source of potential parklands also lies untapped. We have come to realize that we have too much land available for growing crops and not enough land for parks, open space and recreation.

• I propose that instead of simply paying each year to keep this land idle, we help local governments buy selected parcels of it to provide recreational facilities for use by the people of towns in rural areas. This program has been tried but allowed to lapse; I propose that we revive and expand it.

• I propose that we also adopt a program of long-term contracts with private owners of idled farmland, providing for its reforestation and public use for such pursuits as hunting, fishing, hiking and picnicking.

Organizing for action

The environmental problems we face are deep-rooted and widespread. They can be solved only by a full national effort embracing not only sound, coordinated planning, but also an effective follow-

Reynolds Metals Co.

What can we do? There are numerous "eco-activities" that can be performed by individuals or local school and community groups. Here are two examples. Above: Los Angeles teen-agers load bags filled with discarded aluminum cans to take them to a reclamation center where they are worth half a cent each. Right: old car tires are used in an experiment to stop soil erosion along Minnesota's Rum River. Local students furnished the labor and later planted trees inside the tires.

USDA Soil Conservation Service

through that reaches into every community. Improving our surroundings is necessarily the business of us all.

At the Federal level, we have begun the process of organizing for this effort. The Council on Environmental Quality has been established. This Council will be the keeper of our environmental conscience, and a goad to our ingenuity; beyond this, it will have responsibility for ensuring that all our programs and actions are undertaken with a careful respect for the needs of environmental quality. I have already assigned it major responsibilities for new program development, and I shall look to it increasingly for new initiatives.

The Cabinet Committee on the Environment, which I created last year, acts as a coordinating agency for various departmental activities affecting the environment.

To meet future needs, many organizational changes will still be needed. Federal institutions for dealing with the environment and natural resources have developed piecemeal over the years in response to specific needs, not all of which were originally perceived in the light of the concerns we recognize today. Many of their missions appear to overlap, and even to conflict.

Last year I asked the President's Advisory Council on Executive Organization, headed by Mr. Roy Ash, to make an especially thorough study of the organization of Federal environmental, natural-resources and oceanographic programs, and to report its recommendations to me by April 15. After receiving their report, I shall recommend needed reforms, which will involve major reassignments of responsibilities among Departments.

For many of the same reasons, overlaps in environmental programs extend to the Legislative as well as the Executive branch, so that close consultation will be necessary before major steps are taken.

No matter how well organized government itself might be, however, in the final analysis the key to success lies with the people of America.

Private industry has an especially crucial role. Its resources, its technology, its demonstrated ingenuity in solving problems others only talk about — all these are needed, not only in helping curb the pollution industry itself creates but also in helping devise new and better ways of enhancing all aspects of our environment.

I have ordered that the United States Patent Office give special priority to the processing of applications for patents that could aid in curbing environmental abuses.

Industry already has begun moving swiftly toward a fuller recognition of its own environmental responsibilities and has made substantial progress in many areas. However, more must be done.

Mobilizing industry's resources requires organization. With a remarkable degree of unanimity, its leaders have indicated their readiness to help.

I will shortly ask a group of the nation's principal industrial leaders to join me in establishing a National Industrial Pollution Control Council.

The Council will work closely with the Council on Environmental Quality, the Citizens' Advisory Committee on Environmental Quality, the Secretary of Commerce and others as appropriate in the development of effective policies for the curbing of air, water, noise and waste pollution from industrial sources. It will work to enlist increased support from business and industry in the drive to reduce pollution, in all its forms, to the minimum level possible. It will provide a mechanism through which, in many cases, government can work with key leaders in various industries to establish voluntary programs for accomplishing desired pollution-control goals.

Patterns of organization often turn out to be only as good as the example set by the organizer. For years, many Federal facilities have themselves been among the worst polluters. The Executive Order I issued last week not only accepts responsibility for putting a swift end to Federal pollution, but puts teeth into the commitment. I hope this will be an example for others.

At the turn of the century, our chief environmental concern was to conserve what we had — and out of this concern grew the often embattled but always determined "conservation" movement. Today, "conservation" is as important as ever. But no longer is it enough to conserve what we have: we must also restore what we have lost. We have to go beyond conservation to embrace restoration.

The task of cleaning up our environment calls for a total mobilization by all of us. It involves governments at every level; it requires the help of every citizen. It cannot be a matter of simply sitting back and blaming someone else. Neither is it one to be left to a few hundred leaders. Rather it presents us with one of those rare situations in which each individual everywhere has an opportunity to make a special contribution to his country as well as his community.

Through the Council on Environmental Quality, through the Citizens' Advisory Committee on Environmental Quality, and working with governors and mayors and county officials and with concerned private groups, we shall be reaching out in an effort to enlist millions of helping hands, millions of willing spirits— millions of volunteer citizens who will put to themselves the simple question: "What can I do?"

It is in this way — with vigorous Federal leadership, with active enlistment of governments at every level, with the aid of industry and private groups, and above all with the determined participation by individual citizens in every state and every community — that we at last will succeed in restoring the kind of environment we want for ourselves, and the kind the generations that come after deserve to inherit.

This task is ours together. It summons our energy, our ingenuity and our conscience in a cause as fundamental as life itself.

AGAINST ALL ODDS, THE BIRDS HAVE WON*

Conservationists Win an Important Battle

U.S. Dept. of the Interior, National Park Service

BY PHILIP WYLIE

IT SEEMED the only logical, sensible course of action. Thirty-nine square miles were purchased in central south Florida; $13 million was spent; a landing strip for training flights was constructed. Florida desperately, obviously, needed a new jetport; the site beside Everglades National Park was eminently reasonable: within swift reach of the booming cities on both coasts, once expressways were constructed.

Yet it is not to be. The startling fact, rumored for weeks, was confirmed by President Nixon in January 1970: No Federal funds would be granted for a jetport in the Everglades. The port, with its satellite industries and residential developments, would have to be built elsewhere.

And all to save an apparent wasteland — a superswamp, an endless sea of shallow-water saw grass — from the pollution of jet sound and jet contrails, from the attendant on-ground sewage and industrial waste. All to save a 1.4 million-acre megabog, an infinite nothing where those tourists who are forced to stop for a tire change get out of their cars in wary dread. For the Everglades is known to abound in horrors, in alligators, poisonous snakes, clouds of mosquitoes and huge, biting flies.

Natural assets and wildlife preserves have been rescued before, just before the

bulldozers moved in. But what was new here was the magnitude of the work already done, the money spent, the solid expectations suddenly rejected. What was novel was that the Nixon fiat had been made against tremendous commercial investment and popular demand and need: in the face of the jetport, its hotels and supermarkets and other cultural artifacts that would attract the whole world of air travelers and become 50 or 500 times as great a source of profits and taxes as the million or so tourists who now visit the Everglades each year.

What was portentous was the precedent: Had an example been set? Would the conservationists, the champions of ecology, outnumbered by perhaps 100 to 1, slandered for years as "fanatics who care more for birds than for people" — would these enemies of progress gain the upper hand?

The victory, of course, is not total. The existing landing strip will be used for training flights until a new site is found. The ecological effect of such flights is unforeseeable. Yet, the President's announcement is a start, and more than a start for those who have fought the jetport: the men and women who were fascinated by the incredible birdlife in the Glades; the others interested in conserving game to shoot at; those who hoped simply to preserve swatches of wilderness for the eyes of posterity; and those who understood the unique ecology of south Florida's Glades, yet found it difficult to

U.S. Dept. of the Interior

A victory for baby egrets (left). Conservationists, through great pressure on government officials, stopped construction of a jetport six miles north of Everglades National Park (above).

communicate their knowledge to anybody else.

One logical argument the jetport opponents had been able to summon up was easily expressed. The aquifer from which the urban sprawl of coastal cities draws water might have been polluted by the development. These many-trillion-gallon stores of groundwater lie only one hundred feet below the porous rock of south Florida. Already, this natural storage cistern had been diminished by saltwater incursions, caused by activities such as canal digging and drilling.

On the other side, it was pointed out that, even if the groundwater became contaminated, there was an alternative supply to the north. Yet the threat to a vital water source was not easily talked away.

But all such arguments, and the alarums of bird lovers and hunters alike, might have gone for naught without the fast-growing American opposition to environmental pollution in general. It has made ecology big today. It has been said that every congressman has become an ecologist overnight, though few could have defined the word a year ago. Now it has political clout, even though congressman and layman alike find the conception beyond their perception.

The relationship of life-forms to their environment? It can be rattled off the tongue, but it still eludes the mind.

The Everglades are, ecologically, unique on the planet and extremely complex. A map of Florida will show why. The southern 1/3 of the peninsula will be marked "Everglades." This vast wetland is, in fact, 3 kinds of swamp. The northmost begins at Lake Okeechobee, a shallow body of tepid fresh water more than 700 square miles in area. The lake is (or was) the "head" of the Everglades supply of slow-flowing water, aptly called a "river of grass" by author Marjorie Stoneman Douglas.

This first segment of the Glades is the Big Cypress Swamp, though all the big trees save a sample owned by the Audubon Society have been cut, and most of the cypress was always stunted and small, though often very old. Next comes the saw-grass region, the swamp that gave its name to the whole, an interminable prairie of brownish "grass" standing in shoal water, as a rule, and broken only by jungle domes called hammocks. The saw grass is not grass but an abrasive sedge, and a man trying to bull through it would soon be stripped of clothing and of skin.

The third swamp is a mangrove forest, the largest on earth, where labyrinthine waterways twist and branch and open into secret lakes. Mangrove is literally impassable for any distance, as its tentacle-like roots and stiff, entwined branches stand in slow-moving water that

175

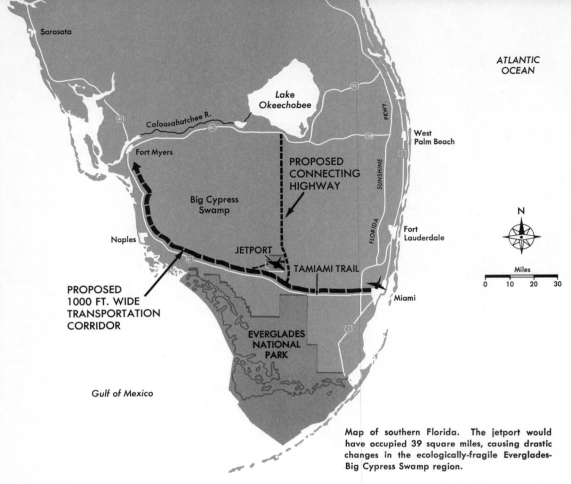

Map of southern Florida. The jetport would have occupied 39 square miles, causing drastic changes in the ecologically-fragile Everglades-Big Cypress Swamp region.

becomes brackish, then salty and, finally, the sea. All 3 swamps compose the Everglades — and it occupies the whole peninsula from edge to edge, a swamp of more than 5,000 square miles soaked by a river that is the world's slowest, shallowest and, since man has tinkered with it, perhaps the least dependable.

A slightly tilted cookie tray

Nothing anywhere on earth is even physically similar. Southern Florida is like a very slightly tilted cookie tray, with low, coastal edges where dunes and outcrops of oolite, a soft, limy rock full of fossil shells, are elevated enough for building. The cities and satellite towns string down both coasts to the place where the statewide "river" begins to merge with seawater, now the oceanfront of the park. The hammocks that interrupt the saw grass are caused by such oolite emergences. Some are miles long, others the size of a carousel, and they support trees of many

sorts, including West Indian species and most of what is left of the once-abundant mahoganies.

It is possible, of course, to build in the Glades. Many developments already encroach on them. The vast wasteland could be turned into a megalopolis with modern machinery. Excavating fill for building sites would merely leave large stretches of water canals and lakes, an effect that could rival Venice and be huge enough for 10 million inhabitants or more. And if the Everglades were to vanish beneath an aquatic supercity, humanity could exist without missing a thing, save for a few lowly creatures.

Why guard such a priceless region from so rich a potential when, especially, the coastal strips are already solid walls of cement, and the pressure of local population is desperate? With 20-odd million tourists shoving, too!

Why halt progress, especially when progress has already played havoc with the wet wilderness and may yet destroy it, the national park included? The Army Corps of Engineers has constructed enormous "water conservation" areas to the north, diked megaponds that store the rainy season's deluge for urban and agricultural use. These reservoirs were made to prevent flooding, also, and they have, so far, failed to supply the park with sufficient water in dry periods to sustain its flora and fauna.

The impounded water has drowned deer in the thousands. And fresh water needed to sustain the Glades and to maintain groundwater capacity for the million or so people now in south Florida runs off, mostly, to the sea, far north of the useful points.

A recent close call

Those "conservation areas" nearly killed the park in a recent drought. Loss of a national park would have been a "first" both for the engineers and for the citizens of the United States. Lucky rains supervened.

The mucklands south of Okeechobee sustain sugarcane and winter vegetable enterprises. They are another hazard. The first farmers to see the black, friable soil thought it as fertile as the dark earth of the Midwestern prairies. It wasn't. Pure humus, leached of minerals, it requires heavy fertilization, and, as it is kept dry by ditching and canals, it oxidizes — literally burns up and blows away — so the drainage systems must be deepened constantly until bedrock is reached, in a decade or two. As the digging deepens, salt water intrudes from the surrounding seas. Salt water also intrudes wherever canals have been excavated. So south Florida, like Southern California, may eventually have to get its water from upstate.

Water conservation by immense impoundments to the north has also resulted in periods of diminished brackishness in the park and the mangrove expanses. Many fish and various crustacea depend on freshwater dilution for breeding. Drought halts the fresh mix, and breeding suffers. But commercial fisheries can fail, and have failed, without great public loss, and some sport fish breed elsewhere.

So there is nothing indispensable about the Everglades. The long struggle to make a good sample of the wonderland a national park was opposed by multitudes on general principles. They could not think of any commercial value for the Glades, but it was land and so should be open to private purchase. There was tannic acid in the maze of creeks and lakes but not in a commercially recoverable form.

It was not very effective to point out that thousands of ecological niches existed in the vastness, places where plants of a single species grew and only there, or that many life-forms were present but as yet unknown to science and that the wild scene was beyond imagining: the egrets and ibises, ducks of every sort, water turkeys and real turkeys, panthers, foxes of a special breed, herons and gallinules, deer, bear, otters and endless sorts of flowers, orchids, air plants, poisonous trees and snakes.

It was almost useless to assert that this cornucopia of living wonders, if preserved, might someday supply the natural source of new and priceless drugs, for one example of the sane and possible. Such a not-too-far-out suggestion would be derided by drug manufacturers, who would assert that every natural drug from quinine to penicillin had been synthesized, a rebuttal that overlooks the fact that these miracle remedies were first found in nature.

The inevitable reaction: So what?

You could lead a supposedly informed citizen into the Audubon Society's Corkscrew Swamp and show him native hibiscus in bloom and cypress bigger around than a dining-room table, and you could spend as much time as he would allow pointing out the rare, the gorgeous, the irreplaceable and the possibilities for all men in these, but his reaction would be: So what?

Trees are lumber, and a quagmire is a stinking breeder of pests. Prairies are to plough; rivers are for sewage and waste disposal; lakes are for dumping and transport and boating fun; scenery that lies over ore or petroleum deposits is to be removed or drowned in guck; and all swamps, of course, are for draining. This is land improvement, and, unfortunately, even those who oppose it usually do so for superficial reasons: to watch birds or hunt them.

The Everglades do not make a vital contribution to man's essential environment. The tremendous swamp is only a minor sample of wild environs that must be preserved if man is to continue his existence. The antipollution motif perhaps tilted the scale against that jetport. And even as an antipollution ruling, it is poorly stated.

What man must see, what this Everglades effort visualizes, is the essential human right to an environment free of pollution. Unless man gains that right, his pursuit of life, liberty and happiness will soon be impossible.

Most Americans are now urban dwellers, and the great majority of these are ecological ignoramuses. They are wary when they step off paved surfaces, and they have no idea of the names of trees and wild flowers, let alone the animals, in the nearest wood. That state of mind bodes ill for the human future, for it is blank and even hostile toward the world on which man depends: the algae in the sea he calls slime, but which provides his breathable air; the flashing minnows, which mean a creek is viable.

And so man's chances are enhanced by that trifle, a clean breeze. Men want to banish the pollutants they can smell, hear, feel or detect by smarting nostrils. But who realizes that if all the sense-perceived contaminants were gone, the job would be about one per cent complete?

The lesson of the Everglades

Man's great illusion continues. Nature cannot be conquered or controlled by man, as men believe, because man is not in charge of it and never will be. Who is in charge of wind and rain, of green plants and photosynthesis, of birds, insects, the

seven seas? Nobody. Nature is in charge, exclusively and forever. The Everglades offer a textbook illustration of what mankind has not yet begun to face: nobody owns anything, and all anyone has is the use of his presumed possessions.

That is the ecological law. It is true for Communists as for capitalists, for disadvantaged peoples as for the affluent and industrial societies. And it is absolute.

We do not own the Everglades or any part of that strange land, even if we have a deed to it. We are allowed its use. All we do own is what our individual skins contain. To save them we must save whatever chains of life are essential to our own.

The value of the Federal decision against a jetport rests in the symbol of the act. If the symbol is understood, its worth will be immeasurable. For man is soon going to be compelled to forego countless multi-billion-dollar opportunities and change his plans for even more, not to gain a specific if obscure end of swamp salvage but for a greater though a scarcely comprehensible reason.

If all the ecologists could pool all they know and add all the data from every science, they would be unable to say what life-forms and life systems are essential for man's survival. We know too little about the intricate, living understructure supporting our species to risk losing any wild living form, weed or pest or predator, lest one break in the planetary, life-sustaining system be fatal.

There never was a guarantee by nature that man should survive for any particular time. And there are many points in the natural order of beings where a lost or broken system may result in an inexorable act of nature fatal to man.

There are X numbers of similar niches and wild lands that may have an indispensable function for man. The problem is, we don't know them; it is the major, formidable, overwhelming problem in the whole business. We don't know. We would probably continue to live and thrive, to the extent we are thriving, if we paved over the Everglades. But the emphasis is on "probably."

UPI

EARTH DAY, 1970

Earth Day in New York. For two hours, thousands of people replaced buses and cars on fashionable Fifth Avenue. Will these people act to avert an environmental catastrophe?

The First National Environmental Teach-in

PEOPLE will long remember April 22, 1970. But for what? Was it a landmark in the awakening of an ecological ethic among Americans? Did it galvanize people into a long-overdue commitment to clean up their environment, cut out their conspicuous waste of their nation's resources, and ease their heavy dependence on the fuels, ores and proteins other nations need if they are to develop?

Or did Earth Day merely provide an easy catharsis for millions of students and adults who will soon grasp at some new fad?

The answers will turn on how fully Earth Day's environmental happening helped Americans to realize that *people,* not machines, are the root of our ecological troubles. *People* consume the enormous amounts of electricity generated by power plants. *People* have enjoyed a half-century love affair with the automobile.

The Population Reference Bureau points out that the number of Americans is increasing at a rate of over two million a year. More and more Americans, the bureau says, demanding a higher and higher material standard of living are the

major reasons for urban sprawl; the loss of open spaces, watersheds and plant cover; the air pollution from millions of automobiles, factories and private homes; the destruction of estuarine ecosystems and freshwater lakes; and countless exploitations of our common, life-sustaining environment.

Alvaro Garcia-Peña, acting president of the bureau, said: "If we truly want a high standard of living for ourselves and our children, we must achieve a very slow rate of population growth — perhaps zero growth. We must also curb our economic-growth mania. Either we make these sacrifices, or we will face a continuing destruction of other forms of life and growing dangers to man himself."

Such changes in attitude and behavior demand more from people than the attention given a passing fad. Can we do it? When the last lecture was given on Earth Day, the last automobile engine buried, the last demonstration ended, did we commit ourselves to environmental reform? Or did we retire to our all-electric homes and wonder what new happening tomorrow would bring?

179

SOME BURNING QUESTIONS ABOUT COMBUSTION*

Where There's Fire, There's Smoke

BY TOM ALEXANDER

CIVILIZATION has been formed in the crucible of fire. Combustion, or the rapid chemical reaction of oxygen with carbon, has propelled human advancement. But Prometheus' presumptuous gift of fire to man is calling down a punishment not anticipated by the ancients. For where there's fire, there's smoke.

Fossil fuels that accumulated over hundreds of millions of years are being converted to gas and ash in a combustive gluttony that began a century ago. In the United States, the tonnage of these fuels consumed now doubles every twenty years. All this combustion — the internal combustion of transportation and the external combustion of industries, power plants, home heating, and incineration — is by far the principal contributor to the dirtiness of cities and the foulness of air. Still, if pollution is the brother of affluence, concern about pollution is affluence's child. Air pollution is not a recent invention: some nineteenth-century cities with their hundreds of thousands of smoldering soft-coal grates coughed amid a richer and deadlier smog than any modern city can concoct. But while in some ways air pollution is not so bad as it used to be, it threatens to get a lot worse than it is unless society revises the traditional orientation of engineering toward efficiency and economy.

The best antipollution intentions come up against certain gritty realities. The hunger for energy seems insatiable.

* This material is part of a book, *The Environment: A National Mission for the Seventies,* by the Editors of *Fortune;* it has been published by Harper & Row. Copyright 1970 Time Inc.

Combustion of fossil fuels — particularly coal and petroleum products, which are the worst polluters — is likely to increase for quite some years to come, probably reaching several times present levels by the end of the century. The only courses left open, then, appear to be cleaning up combustion and substituting noncombustive modes of energy production. Whichever course society chooses — or even if it chooses to do nothing — men will pay a higher price for their energy.

By-products of combustion make up roughly 85 per cent of the total tonnage burden of air pollutants in the United States. Most of the emissions commonly classified as pollutants are not inherent in combustion, but are rather the results of inefficient burning or impure fuels. The pollutants fall into two main types, particles and gases. The particles include fly ash, which is an unburnable mineral fraction of ordinary coal; soot, which is burnable but unburned carbon; and lead, the unburnable additive in gasoline. Less visible but more damaging are the gases. These include sulfur dioxide (SO_2), a product of the combustion of coal or oil that contains sulfur; carbon monoxide (CO), emitted when insufficient oxygen is present during combustion; and various oxides of nitrogen, products of very high combustion temperatures. A great many complex hydrocarbon compounds also result from incomplete combustion.

Sometimes it rains acid

Few would quarrel with the view that air pollution is aesthetically objectionable. Numerous studies confirm it to be an economic drain upon society as well. Government economists at the National Air Pollution Control Administration in North Carolina have taken several routes to arrive at admittedly broad-brush estimates that air pollution costs U.S. citizens between $14,000,000,000 and $18,000,000,000 a year in direct economic loss.

The potpourri of airborne particulates is the main cause of soiling — whether of shirt collars or of office buildings. But sulfur dioxide accounts for

UPI

most of the damage to materials and much of that to agriculture. SO_2 combines with oxygen and then with moisture to form sulfuric acid. Sometimes this takes place in the lungs of animals, sometimes on the leaves of plants, sometimes in droplets of rainwater and sometimes simply in the atmosphere where the acid persists as a fine, floating mist. The atmosphere of many industrialized areas is more corrosive to metals and other materials than sea air.

Under the influence of sunlight, several of the hydrocarbons react with the oxides of nitrogen to form ozone and a variety of complex organic compounds. Many of these "photochemical" substances are particularly damaging to plants. Because of the prevalent photochemical smog, leafy crops such as lettuce and spinach can no longer be grown in parts of Southern California.

Sulfur dioxide has been implicated as the cause of many deaths in several air-pollution disasters, including those in the Meuse Valley in Belgium in 1930, in Donora, Pennsylvania, in 1948, and in London in 1952. These occurred when atmospheric temperature inversions combined with low wind ventilation to trap coal smoke over populated areas. Few doubt that any of the pollutants, not just SO_2, are harmful in concentration. The real question concerns the hazards of the long-term, low-level exposures encountered in everyday life. A great many studies strongly suggest that SO_2 is a cause or intensifying agent in various respiratory ailments even without inversion situations. The gas seems to do its worst in conjunction with particle pollutants, which can carry the SO_2 deep into the lungs and hold it there against sensitive tissue.

Similar evidence is also building up against nitrogen dioxide as a contributing cause of respiratory ailments. Carbon monoxide, a well-known poison, has been measured at toxic levels in the streets of certain cities. Hydrocarbons and ozone are implicated in the eye-irritating smogs typical of Los Angeles and other sunny cities. Some animal experiments suggest that hydrocarbons also cause lung cancer.

But the medical evidence against most air pollutants is far from conclusive. Even in the most polluted areas, citizens still breathe air whose contaminants are many times less concentrated than the pollutants in a lungful of tobacco smoke — and it took years to establish a tight case against cigarettes. After one surprising series of experiments, an independent laboratory under contract to the electric-power industry has found that guinea pigs that have spent their life breathing an atmosphere with a fairly high concentration of SO_2 seem to live longer than guinea pigs breathing pure air.

The missing greenhouse

One combustion product that worries some scientists a great deal is not usually classified as a pollutant. This is carbon dioxide (CO_2), which unlike CO, SO_2 and the rest, is an inevitable result of carbon combustion. Hundreds of millions of tons of CO_2 are discharged into the atmosphere each year. Though CO_2 constitutes less than $\frac{1}{10}$ of 1 per cent of the earth's atmosphere, the amount has increased roughly 25 per cent during the past 100 years or so, and is expected to increase another 25 per cent by the year 2000. CO_2 probably poses no direct threat to health, but quite a few scientists maintain that in the long run it may prove to be the most important pollutant of them all.

In theory, at least, an increase in atmospheric CO_2 should tend to raise the average worldwide temperature. The CO_2 acts like the glass in a greenhouse in trapping heat near the earth's surface. Accordingly, it is sometimes argued, the continued buildup of CO_2 will inescapably lead to calamitous overheating of the earth. Despite the theory, however, the average worldwide temperature has actually registered a slight drop since 1940. To account for this puzzling phenomenon several meteorologists are pointing suspiciously at another combustion product, suspended particulate matter, or smoke. Careful measurements indicate that the global atmospheric "turbidity" — or murkiness — has indeed increased over the past century, and thus could have offset the CO_2's "greenhouse effect." The particles not only shade the earth, but also act as "condensation nuclei" to promote cloud formation and so further reduce the amount of solar energy reaching the earth. Some meteorologists have even begun to worry in advance about the widespread operation of supersonic transport planes, because their release of condensation nuclei at high altitudes might greatly increase the cirrus cloud cover over much of the earth.

Whether the climate gets warmer or cooler, the implications are serious. Man and his institutions everywhere are critically adjusted to just the climatological conditions that prevail. Remarkably little is known about the interactions between earth and atmosphere, but it may well be that the nature of our environment is such that relatively small perturbations could trigger latent instabilities. Taken individually, the various inflictions that man imposes upon his environment may be tolerable; but in combination, they could work to disastrous effect. For instance, the expected exponential increase in worldwide combustion could combine with man's widespread destruction of the vegetation that removes CO_2 from the atmosphere. This, in turn, could lead to a world warming trend. Since water's capacity to absorb CO_2 decreases as the water gets warmer, the result might be still more CO_2 in the atmosphere and further warming from greenhouse effect, and so on.

Where time and space are lacking

In terms of sheer tonnage the automobile is the prime U.S. air polluter, contributing about 40 per cent of the 200 million tons of emissions that human activities put into the air in a year. The wide range of demands upon automotive engines — both cold and hot starting, high and low speeds, rapid acceleration, idling — entails compromising both combustion efficiency and fuel purities. Share of nationwide tonnage, to be sure, does not tell

Taxi drivers exhale for science. This Columbia University project monitors the drivers' breath and blood samples to measure the amount of CO absorbed into their bloodstreams.

all the story. Given enough time and space to do its job, nature can cleanse the air of almost anything. Pollution is still very much the special bane of places where the time and space are lacking: where there is high traffic density, for example, or where people live too close to smokestacks. Much of the automobile pollution is discharged in open country where nature has a chance to work. Moreover, the auto emits little SO_2.

While efforts to find a substitute for the internal-combustion engine have captured much recent attention, probably the most productive approach to the problem of auto pollution for a couple of decades at least will prove to be what the auto companies have been maintaining: cleaning up the present internal-combustion engine or its fuel, or both. Despite intensive and expensive efforts, no one yet appears to have come close to devising a marketable alternative propulsion system that can do more than nibble at the edges of the national problem. No prospects are in evidence for inexpensive, lightweight batteries or fuel cells that could supply the combined range, speed, and hill-climbing ability that Americans will probably continue to demand. Several planners have pointed out another objection to battery propulsion: if most Americans were to drive electric autos, the power for charging the batteries would doubtless have to be drawn from the electric-utility system. This would mean something like a doubling of electric-power capacity and immense additional air pollution from power plants.

Neither the steam engine nor the gas turbine looks like a panacea at present either. It is probably no fluke that the internal-combustion engine won out during the evolution of the automobile. In spite of centuries of engineering attention, steam systems are still heavy and complicated in comparison with internal-combustion engines. Because they operate under more uniform conditions, gas turbines emit less carbon monoxide and hydrocarbons than piston engines per pound of fuel. But gas turbines burn more fuel per mile, especially in city traffic.

Even if alternative modes of propulsion do emerge, the sheer economic, political and social inertia represented by all the institutions that have grown up to feed and care for conventional automobiles would seem to preclude a sudden shift. Happily, the near-term problems posed by the internal-combustion engine appear to be somewhat less pressing now that they did a year or so ago. Federal auto-emission standards, which were first applied to 1968 models and will become increasingly more stringent through at least 1975, have already begun to have discernible effects. The inevitable CO_2 aside, Federal authorities estimate that auto-pollutant tonnages, which totaled about 80 million tons per year in 1968, will be reduced to about 75 million tons this year and will continue to decline. If new exhaust standards that the government is pushing are adopted, the emissions should drop to about 55 million tons per year in 1985. After that, however, with continued increases in the number of cars and car-miles, the levels may begin to climb again. Adoption of some of the contemplated standards will hinge upon the development of a workable device — such as an afterburner — that would complete the combustion of unburned components of exhaust.

For the near term, at least, this process of modification will be less costly in either money or performance than alternatives to conventional internal-combustion engines. Conceivably, however, with sufficient attention to development, a respectable alternative could emerge. One possible approach is a "hybrid" vehicle with electric propulsion and a small combustion engine used to charge the batteries, but only in open country. Because this engine would turn at constant speeds and be equipped with exhaust afterburners, it would emit only a tiny fraction of the pollutants now put forth by the conventional engine.

The power predicament

The most nagging problems of pollution and pollution-control policy for the future appear destined to spring from the electric-power industry. Though electric-power generation now produces only 13 per cent of the total pollutant tonnage, it accounts for more than 50 per cent of the sulfur dioxide, about 27 per cent of the oxides of nitrogen, and nearly 30 per cent of the particulates. Present trends indicate that soft-coal consumption by electric utilities will increase by a factor of roughly $3\frac{1}{2}$ between now and the year 2000. This projection reflects anticipated demand for electric power as well as the great economic inertia provided by long-life coal-burning plants that are already built or committed. Nuclear energy's role will rapidly increase, but its rate of growth will be restrained by limitations in manufacturing capacity and by practical policies — in the electric-power industry and in government — of maintaining both a competitive alternative to nuclear power and a viable coal-mining industry — a large, labor-intensive activity that cannot be turned on and off with ease. While implying no inevitability, the projection for coal points to the magnitude of the air-cleaning tasks ahead. If sulfur dioxide and dioxides of nitrogen are of concern now when electric utilities emit some 25 million tons of these pollutants a year, how much worse will the problem be when they burn $3\frac{1}{2}$ times as much coal?

Reducing air pollution. Above: this jet has been equipped with modified engines that emit virtually no smoke on take-off. Below: this plane, with standard engines, emits large amounts of exhaust smoke (unburned carbon particles).

United Air Lines

Since coal disappeared years ago from the cellars of most houses, Americans have come to think of it as old-fashioned. But coal still provides most of the energy propelling the U.S. economy. While estimated reserves of oil, gas, and uranium are reckoned in terms of a few decades, coal reserves are apparently ample for centuries.

The roughly $1,000,000,000 the electric-utility industry has spent so far for controlling air pollution has gone mostly into filters and electrostatic precipitators for removing particulate matter, and partly into premium prices paid for fuels with low sulfur content, including desulfurized oil and natural gas. For the future control of gaseous emissions most people in the industry would prefer to rely upon these measures, plus tall smokestacks. Tall stacks, industry spokesmen say, would permit the emissions from even very large plants to be adequately diluted before reaching the ground. One appealing quality of tall stacks is that compared with alternatives they are cheap, costing considerably less than other control devices to put in and nothing to operate. But outside the industry there is sharp disagreement about the effectiveness of tall stacks, especially as more and more generating plants dot the landscape. Great Britain has been equipping power plants with tall stacks, and one apparent consequence is that Scandinavian countries across the North Sea are occasionally pelted by rains and snows with a high content of sulfuric acid.

For control of sulfur dioxide, Federal authorities would prefer removal of sulfur before the fuel is burned, or removal of sulfur dioxide from the flue gas. Both oil and certain kinds of coal can be desulfurized at an additional cost of about 10 per cent. Already a great deal of desulfurized oil is being sold in cities, New York, for example, that have imposed stringent standards on SO_2 emissions. Potentially, at least, SO_2 could be removed from stack gases through any of a variety of approaches. Each of these approaches is likely to be expensive, adding somewhere between 10 and 20 per cent to the cost of generating power, compared with about 1 per cent for the tall-stack approach. The actual penalty for sulfur removal depends upon a number of variables difficult to quantify. In terms of capital outlay, the cheapest method involves injection of limestone into the combustion flame, where it combines with oxides of sulfur to form a solid, calcium sulfate. Calcium sulfate in copious quantities — 1,100 tons per day from, say, a 1,000-megawatt power plant — would present an expensive waste-disposal problem and, if not carefully managed, a potential water-pollution problem as well.

Other methods of SO_2 removal involve higher capital and operating costs but yield as a by-product either sulfur or sulfuric acid that might be sold to offset some of their cost. By the 1990's, however, power generation might produce these chemicals so abundantly as to wreck the market for either. In this case they too would become costly liabilities. Even now, while U.S. sulfur producers are busy extracting some 12 million tons a year, fossil-fuel burners are putting more than 16 million tons into the atmosphere.

Stamping out fire

Imposition of stringent and expensive controls on pollutants from combustion of coal or oil would no doubt lead to broader use of alternative fuels and would also hasten the emergence of alternatives to the combustion process itself. One alternative fuel is natural gas, which has little sulfur content and in burning emits smaller quantities of oxides of nitrogen and hydrocarbons than coal, oil or gasoline. Some urban generating plants now operate part time on gas. A number of enthusiasts envision a large future for compressed natural gas as a motor fuel. But natural gas is the least abundant of the fossil fuels, and this fact alone will limit its role largely to the requirements for residential heating.

Proper economic inducements — including stricter emission standards — would also make the gasification of coal attractive. Relatively pollution-free, coal gas would necessarily cost a lot more than its thermal equivalent in solid coal, but its use as a fuel might prove cheaper than the other technological approaches to cleaning up coal combustion.

Noncombustive means of generating electricity have a long history: at one time, indeed, the term "generator" called up in the public mind an image of dams and water turbines. But hydroelectric power, which amounts to about 12 per cent of total installed capacity in the United States, is already approaching full exploitation here, as in most other industrialized nations. A number of other clean and noncombustive technologies, including geothermal power, tidal power and solar power, are under development, but their potential uses appear to be limited to certain regions or special applications.

Fuel cells can produce electricity directly from a variety of substances. The use of hydrocarbon fuels, such as natural gas, entails — as always — emission of carbon dioxide. But other fuel-cell reactions do not even produce CO_2. With pure hydrogen and oxygen, the by-product is nothing more objectionable than water. Other possible fuels are hydrazine and reformed ammonia, both compounds of nitrogen and hydrogen, which react with oxygen to produce electricity plus nitrogen and water. Though the potential cost of some of these fuels could approach that of coal, fuel cells will be far too expensive for widespread use until the cost — especially of their catalysts — can be brought down. Costs of catalysts now range about $2,400 per kilowatt of generating capacity. This compares with *total* costs of about $100 per kilowatt of capacity for steam power plants.

The fear of a nuclear neighbor

Ultimately it seems inevitable that nuclear reactions will largely supplant combustion reactions in the production of electric power, especially in the very large central generating stations that are increasingly the fashion. Right now, though, nuclear energy is being slowed by some fundamental problems, aside from high cost and slow deliveries. One particular difficulty is the fear that leads citizens to prefer a fossil-fuel plant as a neighbor to a nuclear plant. A lot of concern has been voiced about radiation, including the possibility of such substances as iodine 131 finding their way into food chains and hence into the bodies of human beings. But actual measurements seem to show that the radioactive substances normally emitted by nuclear plants are virtually undetectable in the surrounding environment. Some nuclear plants actually emit less radioactivity than many fossil plants. Assuming that a continuing increase in electric-power demand is inevitable and a choice must be made, the evidence available suggests that nuclear plants pose less threat to the environment and to human well-being than fossil plants.

A valid objection to nuclear power is the thermal pollution that present-day plants pour into rivers and streams. To prevent their fuel elements from melting, nuclear plants produce steam at a lower temperature than fossil-fuel plants. This means that for an equivalent amount of electricity nuclear plants produce more steam. After passing through the turbines, the steam must be rapidly condensed: otherwise the power plant could not operate efficiently. To accomplish this condensation, the power plant draws large volumes of cooling water from a stream, pumps them through a condenser and then returns them to the stream. The warmed-up water discharged by a nuclear plant is at about the same temperature as that from a fossil-fuel power plant, but there is about 40 per cent more of it. By 1980, nuclear plants alone will require about one eighth of the total volume of streamflow in the United States for cooling. Possible remedies include paying a penalty in generating efficiency by operating with less coolant volume; discharging the heat far out at sea; channeling the warmed water to cooling towers that discharge heat into the atmosphere; or, finally, putting the heat to use for space heating or industrial purposes. A bonus of the last approach is that it would reduce the burden of pollutants from combustive activity. By the mid-1980's the thermal problem should be moderated by the introduction of other kinds of reactors, notably breeder reactors. Breeders can operate with high-temperature fuel elements. The result is higher thermal efficiency and less discharge of waste heat.

As things stand now, there is reason for concern about the adequacy of the reserves of cheap nuclear fuel. Reasonably assured reserves of uranium in the United States would be insufficient to last beyond the 1980's if nuclear technology were limited to present types of reactors. More uranium will no doubt be discovered, but there is no way of knowing how much or what it will cost to find and mine. Worries about fuel, however, should vanish for practical purposes with the development of the breeder reactor, which will create more fissionable fuel than it consumes. Even so, the fast breeder under development now is a difficult and skittish device, the safe operation of which may require expensive safeguards and so keep the price of electricity high.

The ultimate energy source

In the past year, scientists have gained renewed encouragement over the prospects for controlled nuclear fusion. The new optimism comes from experimental evidence — mostly obtained by Soviet scientists — apparently indicating that the long-standing technical barriers to fusion are soluble, at least in principle. If and when they are overcome — five, fifteen, or thirty years from now — man will then have available an inexhaustible, cheap, clean and safe source of energy. This could spell the end of man's grand-scale need for his ancient friend and enemy, combustion.

But the widespread deployment of fusion reactors is a long way off — perhaps half a century or more. Meanwhile, unless all the people of the world adopt new and unlikely attitudes that radically deflate the value of energy as an index of human advancement, we are likely to see fossil-fuel consumption continuing in its recent trend, at least doubling every twenty years. Even at present, some 15,000 cubic miles of air are fed into the flames of combustion each year, emerging greatly depleted in oxygen and poisoned as well. The time has come when the earth's atmosphere can no longer be regarded as limitless, but must be regarded rather as an exhaustible resource.

The traditional goals in engineering have been maximum performance and minimum cost in the objects being engineered. Now the objects being engineered must often include the very biosphere itself, the earth's thin, life-supporting peel of rock, soil, water and air. All costs must be refigured, and many will increase. The costs may be paid in the form of nonproductive capital or operations, in compromised performance and sometimes perhaps in simple self-denial. But if the payments are not made early, mankind will end up paying far greater penalties later — of property, of peace of mind, of health, or of life itself.

Gordon Smith — National Audubon Society

RESCUING THREATENED ANIMALS*

89 American Species Are Near Extinction

BY PETER T. CHEW

MANY species of America's fish and wild-life are disappearing. This fact is made clear each year when the Bureau of Sport Fisheries and Wildlife of the Interior Department— which operates the Endangered Wildlife Research Station — publishes a red-jacketed volume entitled *Rare and Endangered Fish and Wildlife of the United States.* The "red book," as it is known among naturalists, numbers 89 forms of fish and wildlife in danger of extinction, including 14 mammals, 46 birds, 8 reptiles and amphibians and 21 fish; it

* Reprinted by permission from *The National Observer,* January 12, 1970

The bald eagle, emblem and symbol of the United States. Its numbers are steadily decreasing as people disturb its nesting areas and kill it with pesticides and bullets.

also provides data on several hundred more that are listed in the "rare" category.

In almost every situation, *Homo sapiens Americanus* is named as the root cause of the animals' perilous situation. As Americans have increased in runaway numbers, they have pressed in upon and either befouled or destroyed the habitats of fish and wildlife.

There is, however, evidence at every hand that an increasing number of Americans — preoccupied as they now are with the rapid deterioration of their own habitat — are becoming aware of the plight of their diminishing fellow creatures.

A notable example: The signing by President Nixon of the Endangered Species Act "to prevent the importation of endangered species of fish and wildlife into the United States; to prevent the interstate shipment of reptiles, amphibians, and other wildlife taken contrary to state law; and for other purposes."

There is little evidence, on the other hand, that Americans yet realize how costly and complicated a business it is to rescue animals from the brink. Nor has it been shown that they are willing to pay the high price, or that they even have any conception of how high the price will be.

"Just as no single factor has been responsible for the decline of most of the species and subspecies that have become endangered or extinct, so it is recognized that no single remedy is likely to alter such trends in the future," says Dr. Ray C. Erickson, chief of the Endangered Wildlife Research Station. "Preservation and management of habitats, enforcement of protective regulations, and development of an informed and sympathetic public are important. These measures surely have prevented the complete disappearance of species which otherwise would have been lost. They have not, however, been adequate to cause a reversal of the downward trend or increase to safer numbers for some species."

The red book list

The red book's list of endangered species includes:

The bald eagle, the nation's emblem and symbol, continues to decline steadily, especially the Southern bald eagle which is found primarily along the East Coast of the United States. The Northern bald eagle, a larger bird found in Alaska and elsewhere, is in somewhat better shape. Among the reasons given for the eagle's decline: "Increase in human population in primary nesting areas. Disturbance of nesting birds, illegal shooting, loss of nest trees, and possible reduced reproduction as a result of pesticides ingested with food."

The whooping crane, standing nearly five feet, is the country's tallest bird, one of its most instinctively aggressive, and next to the bald eagle, one of its most publicized. With its long legs and long neck, the whooping crane has been likened to "an after-dinner speaker in a swallow-tail coat." When fully grown, the whooper has white plumage with black wingtips and bright yellow eyes. Known for its trumpetlike call that can be heard a mile away, the whooping crane breeds in the marshlands of Canada's Northwest Territories not far from the Arctic Circle, and flies 2,500 miles to winter in the Aransas Migratory Waterfowl Refuge on the Texas Gulf Coast. As of early 1970, there were 55 wild whooping cranes in existence (5 more than the year before) and 23 in captivity: 17 at the Endangered Wildlife Research Station in Maryland, and the remainder in zoos in New Orleans and San Antonio.

THE ENDANGERED SPECIES

MAMMALS

Indiana Bat
Utah Prairie Dog
Delmarva Peninsula Fox Squirrel
Eastern Timber Wolf
Texas Red Wolf
San Joaquin Kit Fox
Black-footed Ferret
Florida Panther
Caribbean Monk Seal
Guadalupe Fur Seal
Florida Manatee or Florida Sea Cow
Key Deer
Columbian White-tailed Deer
Sonoran Pronghorn

BIRDS

Hawaiian Dark-rumped Petrel
California Least Tern
Hawaiian Goose (Nene)
Aleutian Canada Goose
Tule White-fronted Goose
Laysan Duck
Hawaiian Duck (or Koloa)
Mexican Duck
California Condor
Florida Everglade Kite
 (Florida Snail Kite)
Hawaiian Hawk (or Io)
Southern Bald Eagle
American Peregrine Falcon
Attwater's Greater Prairie Chicken

Masked Bobwhite
Whooping Crane
Yuma Clapper Rail
Light-footed Clapper Rail
Hawaiian Gallinule
Hawaiian Coot
Eskimo Curlew
Hawaiian Stilt
Puerto Rican Plain Pigeon
Puerto Rican Parrot
American Ivory-billed Woodpecker
Northern Red-cockaded Woodpecker
Southern Red-cockaded Woodpecker
Hawaiian Crow (or Alala)
Small Kauai Thrush (Puaiohi)
Nihoa Millerbird
Kauai Oo (or Oo Aa)
Crested Honeycreeper (or Akohekohe)
Molokai Creeper (or Kakawahie)
Akiapolaau
Kauai Akialoa
Kauai Nukupuu
Maui Nukupuu
Laysan Finch
Nihoa Finch
Ou
Palila
Maui Parrotbill
Bachman's Warbler
Kirtland's Warbler
Dusky Seaside Sparrow
Cape Sable Sparrow

REPTILES AND AMPHIBIANS

American Alligator
Blunt-nosed Leopard Lizard
San Francisco Garter Snake
Puerto Rican Boa
Santa Cruz Long-toed Salamander
Texas Blind Salamander
Black Toad, Inyo County Toad
Houston Toad

FISHES

Shortnose Sturgeon
Longjaw Cisco
Piute Cutthroat Trout
Greenback Cutthroat Trout
Montana Westslope Cutthroat Trout
Gila Trout
Arizona (Apache) Trout
Desert Dace
Humpback Chub
Moapa Dace
Colorado River Squawfish
Cui-ui
Devils Hole Pupfish
Comanche Springs Pupfish
Owens River Pupfish
Pahrump Killifish
Big Bend Gambusia
Clear Creek Gambusia
Gila Topminnow
Maryland Darter
Blue Pike

The American alligator has long been the victim of predators that attack its nests and human poachers after its valuable skin. By placing heavy penalties on those engaging in interstate shipment of alligator hides, the Endangered Species Act should go far toward improving the alligators' chances of survival. In addition, Mayor John V. Lindsay of New York signed a law prohibiting, as of July 1, 1970, the sale there of articles — handbags, shoes, and the like — made from the skin of American alligators. "The alligator should soon be in pretty good shape," says the Smithsonian Institution's Dr. James A. Peters, who looks to a day when alligators will become plentiful enough to be killed legally for their hides.

The Eastern timber wolf and Texas red wolf have both been the victims of heavy hunting and trapping as well as the encroachment of civilization upon their habitats. An NBC-TV program devoted to the plight of the wolf resulted in thousands of letters to the Interior Department demanding that more effective measures be taken to protect the animal. Interior's reply: The management of fish and wildlife is the responsibility of the separate states, except for Federal wildlife refuges within the states.

The Florida manatee or sea cow, one of God's homelier creatures, is a 1,000-pound aquatic mammal with a blunt, whiskered face, rotund body, and rounded tail. Although still thriving in waters off Latin America, the manatee has been disappearing from the Southern coast of the United States. In the past, the manatee was the victim of overkilling by hunters; of late many have fallen victim to the keels and propellers of boats.

The blue pike, once one of the most important commercial fish in Lakes Erie and Ontario, has all but disappeared because of water pollution.

The Atlantic salmon, like the blue pike, is the victim of pollution; in his case, of the New England rivers, streams, and coastline where he once thrived as an important game and commercial fish. Damming of streams and rivers also has

been a factor. Elsewhere in his range, in Canadian waters, the Atlantic salmon is holding his own.

The red book lists, as well, many other lesser-known endangered species such as the Aleutian Canada goose, Puerto Rican parrot, Texas blind salamander, black-footed ferret, and Arizona Apache trout. Among the species which have disappeared forever: the passenger or wild pigeon, heath hen, great auk, Merriam elk, plains wolf, Badlands bighorn sheep, sea mink and many others.

The fish and wildlife situation elsewhere in the world is no less critical.

The International Union for the Conservation of Nature and Natural Resources (IUCN) in Morges, Switzerland, names more than 550 fish and wildlife in its red book, a number which the World Wildlife Fund, for its part, considers far too conservative.

"For some reason, scientists are reluctant to list an animal as endangered unless it is about to take its last cough," says Herbert H. Mills, executive director of the World Wildlife Fund. "In our view, for example, all the spotted cats are in great danger of being wiped out, yet the IUCN lists only a few subspecies such as the Moroccan leopard."

On the IUCN's list of severely threatened species are the orangutan of Borneo and Sumatra, which brings $4,000 on the animal black market; Indian rhinoceros; vicuna; and Galapagos tortoise, to name just a few.

"There is, to say the least, a notable lack of uniformity in wildlife-management practices around the world," says Russell Train, Undersecretary of Interior, and a prominent conservationist. "The Republic of South Africa has a fine tradition; some other countries don't seem to care whether any animal is left crawling, or any fish swimming."

Even the British, noted for their love of animals, evidence vagaries. "The British import somewhere between 500,000 and 1,000,000 European tortoises every year," says a Smithsonian biologist. "Now why, in God's name? Apparently every

The California condor, a species of large vultures. This bird is nearly extinct; members of the species are found almost exclusively in the coastal mountain ranges at the southern end of the San Joaquin Valley in California.

Englishman likes to see a tortoise wandering around his lawn; must be some sort of ornament. And, of course, these tortoises have a high death rate."

British animal lovers, on the other hand, were disturbed when, early in 1970, Italian actress Gina Lollobrigida appeared in a maxi-coat of tiger skins. Lady Muriel Dowding, head of a conservationist group called Beauty Without Cruelty, sniped: "Gina shows her age" in the fur maxi-coat.

And U.S. Secretary of Commerce Maurice H. Stans came under fire with rumors that he and Emperor Haile Selassie of Ethiopia were planning to shoot an Ethiopian wild ass and a nyala mountain antelope for eventual display in Mr. Stans' African museum in Rock Hill, South Carolina.

The worldwide traffic in animals is tremendous. In 1968, the United States alone imported 150,000 mammals; 500,000 wild birds, exclusive of parrots and canaries; 170,000 amphibians; 64,000,000 live fish; 180,000 mollusks and crustaceans; and 2,000,000 reptiles ranging from tiny chameleons to huge boa constrictors. Just what effect the Endangered Species Act will have upon this traffic cannot yet be determined, but the legislation calls upon the Secretary of Interior, in consultation with the IUCN and other world conservationist bodies and individuals, to draw up a list of endangered species whose importation (except in certain circumstances) will be prohibited. By taking the lead in this way, the United States hopes to in-

spire other nations to follow suit, and plans are afoot for an international wildlife conference to work out the complicated details.

Conservationists contend that this country has contributed its share to the dismal saga of mankind's treatment of wild animals, the passenger pigeon being an oft-cited example.

The passenger pigeon was a remarkable bird, capable of flying at speeds up to 60 miles per hour according to the researches of John James Audubon, who also credited the bird with phenomenal eyesight. The pigeon traveled in sky-blackening flocks, and this contributed to his undoing, for he was killed by the millions, sold in markets, eaten by farmers, or fed to livestock. Audubon once described a typical pigeon-killing spree which took place in a forest along the banks of Kentucky's Green River in the early 1800's.

"As the period of their (the pigeons') arrival approached, their foes anxiously prepared to meet them," said Audubon. "Some were furnished with iron pots containing sulphur, others with torches of pine-knots, many with poles, the rest with guns. . . .

"Here they come"

"Suddenly there burst forth a general cry of 'Here they come!' The noise which they made, though yet distant, reminded me of a hard gale at sea, passing through the rigging of a close-reefed vessel. As the birds passed over me, I felt a current of air that surprised me. Thousands were

191

knocked down by the pole men. The birds continued to pour in."

The men fell upon the birds with poles and torches. The rifle fire continued all night long. Foxes, lynxes, and other wild animals snatched their share of the dead birds. Next day, wrote Audubon, "the authors of all this devastation began their entry amongst the dead, and dying, and mangled. The pigeons were picked up and piled in heaps, until each had as many as he could possibly dispose of. Then the hogs were let loose to feed upon the remainder."

One day, to everyone's apparent surprise, there was only one passenger pigeon left on earth. Her name was "Martha," and she lived out her days in the Cincinnati Zoological Gardens. You can see her today, sitting lifelike in a glass case in the Smithsonian Institution.

"Martha, the last of her species, died at 1 P.M. September 1, 1914, aged 29," says the attached card.

"The extinction of a species, no matter how alien to us the creature may be, is an awesome thing," says Faith McNulty in *The Whooping Crane*. "In its presence, we experience a sort of shiver, perhaps an instinctive (should I say premonitory?) awareness that this is a death quite different from the death of an individual; that it has a different finality. This extinction of something that will never, in all eternity, be duplicated, is an occurrence that seems to break the strand of life itself."

A latter-day Noah

In an effort to snatch at least a few imperiled species from the abyss, the Endangered Wildlife Research Station was established five years ago on the grounds of the Patuxent Wildlife Research Center, which occupies several hundred acres of open country between Washington, D.C., and Baltimore. The station puts one in mind of a land-borne ark, except that, unlike Noah, Dr. Ray Erickson must work within the confines of a tight budget. Consequently, only a few endangered species are lucky enough to walk up Dr. Erickson's gangplank.

"There is a tremendous amount of emotion involved in our work," says Dr. Erickson, a shy man, renowned in his field for his work with whooping cranes. "There is a sense of urgency about it that tends to make us take conservative approaches because we simply cannot afford to make any mistakes."

Before the final decision was made to pick up the first whooping-crane egg in the Canadian wilds, for example, Dr. Erickson and his assistant, Glen Smart, spent five years cautiously retrieving, transporting by air, and incubating the eggs of three varieties of sandhill cranes, a species closely related to the whoopers. With that background, Dr. Erickson and Mr. Smart flew to Fort Smith, Northwest Territories, in the spring of 1967 where they were met by biologist Ernie Kuyt of the Canadian Wildlife Service, who spots the whooping-crane nests every year. From Fort Smith, the three scientists flew northward in a little bubble-nosed helicopter to the nesting grounds in the remote marshlands.

At the helicopter's approach, the adult whooping cranes stalked away from the nests, and the scientists picked up six of the brownish-buff eggs. Five of the birds survived the flight to the research center, and each year since that time, Dr. Erick-

The American alligator. Is it doomed to extinction because of the commercial value of its skin?

Allan D. Cruickshank — National Audubon Society

son has made successful egg retrievals. Today, a number of lovely young cinnamon-colored whooping cranes are thriving in outdoor pens at the research center, the nucleus of breeding stock that one day may produce whoopers in quantity to be returned to the Canadian wilds.

There have been problems, however, intriguing ones. When a crane pops out of its egg, it tends to identify with the first animal it sees, a psychological process known to biologists as "imprinting." Hence if a crane sees a man, it tends to think of itself as a human being and will eventually refuse to mate with one of its own kind. To forestall this possibility, Dr. Erickson cloaks his bird-handlers in formless white sheets, and makes certain that the cranelings, when they emerge from their shells, see other cranes or movable cutouts of cranes.

The aggressiveness of the whoopers is another problem. Whooping cranes in the wilds lay two eggs at a time, and after they hatch, the parents separate the nestmates lest the young birds kill one another, which is their habit until they mature. In captivity, the first baby cranes also tried to savage one another, and hence were placed in separate pens. This was costly and time-consuming, however, and, as an experiment, the young cranes were eventually placed in a pen with some domestic turkeys. As the biologists suspected, the cranes worked off their aggression by attacking the turkeys.

"The cranes couldn't hurt the turkeys, though, because they couldn't catch them," says Dr. Erickson. "They all ran around a lot which was good for them. It was a tremendous breakthrough."

Just as sandhill cranes serve as stand-ins or prototypes for whooping cranes, the Andean condor stands in here for the California condor; a common form of European ferret stands in for the black-footed ferret of South Dakota, and so forth.

The mission of the endangered wildlife station often carries its staff members far afield. Thus biologists W. E. Banko and John L. Sincock are at work in Hawaii studying twenty varieties of endan-

The Florida panther. The unspoiled areas that are his home are being replaced by roads, homes and shopping centers.

gered birds; Dr. Cameron Kepler is stationed in Puerto Rico devoting much of his time to the lovely Puerto Rican parrot, now reduced in numbers to less than two dozen; and Paul W. Sykes, Jr., is ranging the southeastern United States, concentrating on the vanishing Florida Everglades kite and other endangered birds.

Inevitably, the men who have devoted their lives to such work are asked variations of the question: "How can you justify the expenditure of money on mere animals when there is so much human poverty in the world?"

During the U.S. Senate Commerce Committee hearings on the endangered-species legislation, Dr. Peters of the Smithsonian Institution was asked why he felt it was so important to save the Texas blind salamander, a species whose sole survivors now occupy a cave in Hays County, Texas.

"As far as I am personally concerned," replied Dr. Peters, "the Texas blind salamander has just as long an evolutionary history behind it as I have. Therefore, it has an equal right to the opportunity to survive as I have."

PESTICIDE POLLUTION*

Ecologists Attack Use of DDT

BY CLARENCE COTTAM

LIKE a spaceship the planet earth has a finite air supply, vast and subject to being refreshed and recycled. Even man's immense use of oxygen over the past highly industrialized century has made only a dent in the available total; the recycling system has been able to produce almost as much elemental oxygen as man has used.

As any good spaceship must be, earth has also been self-sufficient in many other ways. Working solely with light and heat from the sun, its system has provided a renewable food and shelter supply for a pyramid of living organisms, at the top of which man has elected to place himself. But the ship has been sabotaged.

In 1874 a German chemistry student named Othmar Zeidler unwittingly dropped a rock into the planet's intricate living machinery. The rock rattled around harmlessly for 65 years. Then it jammed and began to chew up the gears, and today our spaceship's life support systems are showing signs of breaking down. Under heavy stress in any case from other human activities, living organisms are disappearing in droves, leaving great gaps in the pyramid. Some of these gaps serve, as far as we know, "only" to impoverish the human mind and spirit; others threaten the entire biological structure.

Perhaps the least published effect of Zeidler's discovery — now known the world over by the acronym DDT — will be the most damaging in the long run. Scattered scientific reports seem to indicate that the air-freshening system of the earth, consisting mainly of green plant plankton in the oceans, is breaking down. Although at one time oxygen production from the

* Reprinted by permission from *National Parks & Conservation Magazine*, November 1969, which assumes no responsibility for its distribution other than through the magazine.

194

Joseph Smith

Pesticides such as DDT have saved millions of dollars worth of crops from being eaten by insects. But the cost has been the dangerous, often lethal increase of these chemicals in the bodies of fish, birds and mammals, including mankind.

oceans was almost able to keep up with oxygen consumption by man, now there are strong signs that production is declining even more under the influence of DDT and a half dozen much more poisonous relatives.

By far the majority of synthetic organic chemicals was synthesized more in an effort to learn the mechanics of organic reactions than to develop a new substance. So it was with Zeidler's synthetic. Zeidler learned how to make DDT, described its basic properties, then put it on a dusty back shelf along with other useless curiosities.

In 1939 the Swiss chemist Paul Mueller was taking part in a concerted effort to find an insecticide that could halt the ravages of the imported Colorado potato beetle. Zeidler's creation was one of thousands of chemicals tested for insect-killing properties. Mueller found it potent. Either on contact or after ingestion, minute quantities scrambled an insect's nerve endings and caused death. The small amounts that could be expected to reach a human through a treated crop proved unable to strike the human dead on the spot; and as far as the researchers were concerned, these two considerations meant that their hunt for an ideal pesticide was successful.

Shortly after Mueller's discovery the U.S. armed forces began to use the chemical to control insect disease vectors, and the popularity of DDT was assured. By 1948, when Mueller was awarded the Nobel Prize for his work, one of mankind's greatest assaults on his environment was well under way.

At first satisfaction with DDT knew no bounds. During World War II it generated wild enthusiasm. It controlled malaria-carrying mosquitoes, typhus-carrying lice, and the arthropod vectors of some two dozen other diseases. It has been extravagantly estimated that the use of DDT in this war averted about 10 million deaths and 200 million cases of pest-borne illness. To many people after the war, DDT seemed the final answer to control of agricultural pests. It was cheap, effective in microscopic amounts, and, most important of all, it was persistent.

No one knows precisely how long DDT takes to break down in nature, but it has been estimated that it has a half-life of at least 15 years. This means that half a given application will have broken down in 15 years, half the remainder in another 15 years, and so on. One application indeed goes a long way — just what a tragically long way should have been realized, but no one wanted to be a Jeremiah. With the combination of childish enthusiasm and arrogance typical of the technological revolution in America, DDT by the thousand tons was spewed over the surface of our planet.

Few bothered to ask what effect a chemical with such demonstrated biological potency could have on living organisms other than insects or considered that not all insects harm man — that some, in fact, are beneficial. If such simple questions were so poorly considered, it could hardly be expected that DDT's effect on the "balance of nature" would be seriously weighed. The fledgling science of ecology was then only beginning to publish the idea that no member of a community of life, or ecosystem, is independent of the others; that no matter how useless or annoying the smallest creature might seem, it has a function in the planet's system; that before eliminating any organism, therefore, it might be wise to consider what that function is. Meanwhile, DDT in dust, spray and fog continued to blanket the land. If in a year or so an application washed into the soil out of range of target insects or ran off into drainage ditches, more DDT was applied. If mosquitoes bothered suburban taxpayers, out came a fogging truck to spread DDT. By the time the first small sign of trouble appeared in 1949, DDT had been applied to every crop from tomatoes to timber and was treated around people's homes almost as carelessly as oatmeal. Then someone detected DDT in milk.

Now, inasmuch as milk involves children, it constitutes a sensitive part of the American political anatomy. So people paid some attention to this small fact. How did DDT, an insecticide, get into cows? In a demonstration of several of its more obvious faults, traces of DDT dust and spray intended for fields under crops had drifted to neighboring pastures. Dust from croplands blown into pastures carried more DDT. There its persistence allowed it to accumulate on alfalfa, and cows ate the alfalfa. DDT is practically insoluble in water, but it is soluble in various hydrocarbons and in animal fat. Traces of DDT, not detectable on the alfalfa, are concentrated by the cow in fatty tissues and, of course, in the butterfat of its milk.

After a few such early instances it was decided that perhaps DDT should be used more carefully — "in moderation on crops, only in amounts sufficient to get the job done," as one agricultural bulletin advised in 1950. No one suggested not using it at all.

In the two decades since, while bits of evidence have shown DDT to be a global pollutant, production of DDT in the United States has grown to an industry with a sales peak in 1962 of nearly $30

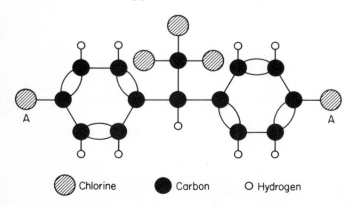

Chlorine   Carbon   Hydrogen

DDT molecule. Related pesticides (other chlorinated hydrocarbons such as dieldrin and lindane) are made by substituting such atoms as fluorine and bromine at point A.

The American eagle and several other species of birds are threatened with extinction by DDT. DDT in the liver of a mother bird causes an excess production of an enzyme that breaks down steroid hormones. These hormones are essential to the manufacture of calcium. Without sufficient calcium, the bird's eggs are thin-shelled and flaky, offering little protection for the developing embryo.

Michigan Dept. of Natural Resources

million, declining to about $20 million in 1969. Chemists, following the lead of DDT's molecular structure, went even farther by developing a whole class of DDT-like compounds called chlorinated hydrocarbons, many of which are much more poisonous than DDT. All these poisons pose substantially the same problems as DDT even though they are not yet used on the same scale.

The evidence was assembled for the public by the late Rachel Carson in her bestseller *Silent Spring,* published in 1962. This book, which in the light of more recent evidence and discussion seems a model of reason and restraint, sparked hysterical denunciations of the author, her scientific credentials, conclusions, and even writing style. Her basic message was: Man's assault on the living environment with chemicals, principally DDT but including a large supporting cast, had succeeded in poisoning the environment for higher creatures such as birds, fish and mammals (presumably including man).

This assault had succeeded in tearing askew the delicate ecosystems of the earth that ultimately keep man alive. But — a cruel irony — it was on the verge of failing utterly to control insect pests.

Complex higher animals have generation periods ranging up to man's 20-odd years and generally produce few offspring per female. So the trial and error of evolution can proceed only slowly. Insects, on the other hand, may have generation periods of only a few days or weeks, each female producing huge numbers of offspring. Consequently, if 99 per cent of a population of flies is killed by DDT, the 1 per cent surviving because of a slight inborn resistance can produce a new crop of flies very quickly. The new crop, all stemming from resistant flies, may have up to 2 per cent able to survive a DDT application. And so it goes — each generation a bit more resistant. By now scientists have been able to produce houseflies in the laboratory that can stand wetting down with a concentrated DDT solution!

Since the attacks on Miss Carson 8 years ago, action on a wide front has vindicated her. Michigan and Wisconsin have banned the use of DDT except in a few minor circumstances. Many other states have restricted it and probably will ban it. In November 1969, both the United States and Canadian Governments ordered that its use be virtually banned by the end of 1970. Australia has banned its use on pastures because Australian meat was not meeting residue requirements of the U.S. Food and Drug Administration. Sweden, which had given Mueller the Nobel Prize, has banned it.

It is too late to avoid serious consequences, however, and no one really knows what the final biological outcome will be. Enough DDT already has been released to play all sorts of havoc, yet there is even more lying in the soil to eventually seep into water supplies; therefore, even if the use of DDT were to halt tomorrow, concentrations of the poison in the water of the world would continue to rise before falling.

Affects both friend and foe

The various properties of DDT (and the chlorinated hydrocarbons in general tend to follow the pattern) may be summarized as follows:

● DDT is among the most pharmacologically active substances known. In many cases it behaves like hormones, those trigger chemicals secreted by organisms in tiny amounts to control their bodily functions.

● It is soluble in animal fat but not in water. Most of an organisms's fluids are aqueous; only its fatty tissues can dissolve and retain DDT, so DDT tends to be deposited in these tissues.

● It is chemically stable. Chemical and biological forces that may encounter DDT in the environment break it down only with difficulty, and it breaks down spontaneously only very slowly.

● It is not easily metabolized in the systems of animals (an extension effect of its stability and its insolubility in most body fluids). Thus, once deposited in fat,

it tends to stay there (half-life 15 years!). With continued ingestion of polluted food by an animal, DDT accumulates to ever higher levels. This leads to the phenomenon of biological magnification, discussed later.

● It is nonspecific. This potent substance hits friend as well as foe, often wiping out a predatory insect that has been able to control a pest better than DDT ever could. Consequently the target pest's population rises instead of declines. Even DDT's side effects share the shotgun approach, striking not at species or genera but whole orders of creatures.

The biological potency of the chlorinated hydrocarbons means that, whereas a particular dose may not poison an organism outright, it is capable of altering living systems in several harmful ways. Early signs indicate that chlorinated hydrocarbons, including DDT, can cause cancer and mutations. Autopsies of people dead of blood and liver diseases have shown higher than normal DDT residues. However, as the pesticide industry never fails to point out, no human deaths have been proven to be due to the direct effects of DDT under prescribed controls. But "prove it!" seems the most childish of arguments in the face of a possible link.

The chemical's potency, its affinity for fat, its ability to accumulate, and its persistence all combine to suggest that there is no safety in tolerance levels set by the U.S. Food and Drug Administration (FDA) unless these levels are zero. There is no such thing as a sensible degree of poisoning.

One fallacy in FDA tolerance levels is due to the fact that the effects of the chlorinated hydrocarbons may be additive. Tolerances for each are set, but a farmer often uses more than 1 chemical on a particular crop. Thus a vegetable may carry half the legal limit of 4 different chlorinated hydrocarbons — say, DDT, dieldrin, chlordane, and lindane for a hypothetical example. Animal tests have demonstrated that the effect is roughly like having twice the legal limit of any 1 chemical on the product. When a diet containing theoretically harmless levels of 2 parts per million

Pesticides affect friend and foe alike. Russell Train, chairman of the U. S. Council on Environmental Quality, after mentioning that pesticides have wiped out butterflies in most of Europe, once asked, "I wonder if your grandchildren will ever see a butterfly? Does it make any difference?"

Paul M. Tilden

A living pesticide, one that doesn't poison the environment. The ladybird beetle, shown eating an aphid, has an enormous appetite. When present in sufficient numbers, these beetles, sometimes called ladybugs, will easily keep aphids and scale insects under control.

Jerome Wexler — National Audubon Society

(ppm) each of DDT, lindane, toxaphene, chlordane and methoxychlor — a total of 10 ppm of chlorinated hydrocarbons — was fed to laboratory rats, liver damage resulted.

The phenomenon of biological magnification underlies another fallacy of "acceptable" tolerance levels. Americans who eat normal amounts of the normal American high-fat diet produced from farms using normal practices of insect control ingest "normal" levels of DDT in their food. These levels are not permitted to exceed the FDA's tolerances, so the food is "safe." Yet DDT accumulates in fatty tissues, and mother's milk, for example, is made from fatty tissue. A nursing baby receives a concentrate of the DDT its mother ate and thus ingests even higher levels. The FDA would consider mother's milk unsafe for human consumption were

it a marketable item, so high is its content of DDT.

A clear illustration of biological magnification comes from the Green Bay area of DDT-laced Lake Michigan. There the bottom muds were found to contain 0.014 ppm of DDT. But tiny crustacea living in and on the mud absorbed and concentrated DDT in their bodies to a level of 0.41 ppm. Fish eating the polluted crustacea in large volumes accumulated 3 to 6 ppm of DDT in their bodies. Herring gulls eating large amounts of these fish accumulated the DDT from their diet until it reached *99 parts per million.* This amount is enough to kill them during times of food scarcity when they are forced to draw on their own poisonous fat reserves.

Biological magnification has economic effects, too, although other effects are much more serious. In the 1930's the people around the upper Great Lakes ate fish — beautiful big lake trout, whitefish and other species; and commercial fishing was their livelihood in some places. Then sea lampreys and alewives appeared, let in around formerly impassable Niagara Falls by the Welland Canal, an ecological blunder in its own right. The parasitic lampreys wiped out the whitefish and trout industry. The alewives' population exploded to fill the void, nothing checking their increase but the physical size of the lake. Killed finally in millions by overcrowding, stinking windrows of alewives rimmed the lake as a memorial to man's meddling.

Years went by, a way to deal with the lamprey was found, and the lakes were safe again for commercially valuable fish and sport fish. Lake trout, coho salmon and Chinook salmon were stocked. As expected, the stocked fish found the environment empty of predators and competitors and full of prey in the form of alewives. All 3 species did well, but the coho waxed incredibly fat. The Lake Michigan fishery was reborn. It was estimated that the influx of sport fishermen alone would net the state $100 million a year. Released as fingerlings in the spring of 1966, the coho had grown to 15 or 20 pounds by the fall of 1967. Anglers went on something like a piscatorial gold rush. State officials dreamed rosy dreams. The 1968 fall season was anticipated with the eagerness usually reserved for Christmas by lakeshore dwellers, who were eating well again.

But DDT got there first. The FDA, finding DDT levels as high as 20 parts per million in coho harvested from the lake by commercial fishermen, seized the fish and forbade the sale of Lake Michigan coho. Few anglers wanted to go after fish the FDA said were poisonous. If the FDA's interim tolerance level of 5 ppm becomes permanent, it will eliminate the sale of about 80 per cent of the commercial coho catch and severely limit sport fishing. Moreover, fingerlings apparently are killed by 20 ppm of DDT in their bodies, so natural spawning of all 3 stocked fish probably will be prevented until DDT levels in the lake fall considerably. With DDT's 15-year half-life, it could take 35 to 40 years before the residues in the fish get down to 5 ppm. The coho, Chinook, and lake trout are at the top of a food chain that passes through the alewives from the microorganisms in the mud of the lake.

Areas of concern

The principal arguments against DDT and its relatives must rest on their drastic alteration of the living environment. These alterations are subtle but profound and in the long run may threaten man's survival.

One of the most dangerous areas of concern is the effect of DDT on oxygen production. Marine biologists subjected 5 common species of oceanic plant plankton to roughly the DDT levels found in the surface waters of the open ocean. Addition of the DDT was followed by a severe reduction in the rates of photosynthesis and cell division in all species. In one case the reduction in photosynthesis was more than 50 per cent. Photosynthesis is the process by which green plants convert carbon dioxide, water and the energy of sunlight into food for their own growth. Oxygen is a by-product of this process. Between 50 and 70 per cent of the earth's oxygen is produced at sea by phytoplankton (plant plankton). Even without considering DDT, oxygen production is lagging behind oxygen consumption because of man's vast demands. If the effect found in the laboratory is widespread — and it is reasonable to believe it is — the results could be more disastrous than a nuclear war. Decreased conversion of carbon dioxide to oxygen, accompanied by the buildup of carbon dioxide from air pollutants, could result in planetary overheating due to the greenhouse, or heat-trapping, effect of this gas in the atmosphere. As a result, polar caps would melt, and sea levels would rise perhaps 200 feet. It can be hoped only that there is enough flexibility in the oxygen cycle to prevent such drastic consequences until the DDT in the oceans decomposes.

Even supposing that this long-term effect does not occur, a relatively short-term consequence probably cannot be avoided. Zooplankton (animal plankton) also is highly susceptible to DDT. Reduced amounts of zooplankton along with reduced photosynthesis and cell division in phytoplankton means a decrease in the amount of plankton available for organisms that eat it and a consequent drop in their population, a drop in the population of organisms that feed on *them,* and so on. Plankton lies at the bottom of almost every marine food chain. It is unfortunate that this basis of marine productivity is being eroded just when optimists are proposing to feed ocean products to the increased billions of human population predicted in the next few decades.

A second area of concern, DDT's effect on hormones, has been receiving some publicity lately, due mainly to the fact that the bald eagle is America's symbol. Raptorial birds, of which the eagle is one, have been the first victims of the hormonal effects of DDT pollution because of their position at the top of food chains. In concentrations of a very few parts per million — in mammals and birds at least and perhaps in other animals — DDT stimulates the liver to produce enzymes that destroy many other enzymes and hormones. Among the destroyed substances is estradiol, which in birds regulates the withdrawal of calcium from bone for the manufacture of eggshell in the oviducts. Consequently these birds lay thin-shelled eggs — in some cases eggs with no shell at all. Such thin-shelled eggs cannot be incubated properly, so a potential eagle, hawk or fish-eating bird is lost. Because of their position in their food chains, raptorial birds in the United States have been reduced to desperate straits by chlorinated hydrocarbon pollution. The once-numerous peregrine falcon is now extinct as a breeding bird in the East and is surviving only precariously elsewhere, partly because of breeding success depressed by DDT and its relatives and partly because of direct effects on these birds. The Everglades kite, pushed to the brink by man anyway, may be doomed to rapid extinction by pesticides. The Southern bald eagle is endangered, with perhaps only six hundred birds surviving. The American osprey or fishhawk, once numerous, because of its feeding habits is especially liable to ingest DDT, and its population is in sharp decline and already at the danger point. The osprey feeds on fish; and fish, of course, are prime biological magnifiers.

Too many farmers dislike hawks and as a group are not inclined to mourn their demise. What once again goes unrealized, however, is the importance of the falconiforms in maintaining ecological balances. Birds of this order that do not eat mostly carrion, one valuable service, likely include rodents as a major item of their diet as another valuable service. One team of writers has estimated that, were the rodent control performed by these birds removed, mice would cover the United States from coast to coast 2½ inches deep. This example is a statistical trick, but it indicates the important service that if not done by hawks and other predators, would have to be done by some agency of man's devising.

Hawks and eagles are merely the first birds to be affected by DDT's action on the liver. Brown pelicans are now in a dangerous decline, and other birds with less DDT in their diet must follow suit to some degree as they accumulate the chemical. Then there are the mammals to worry about. (Man, of course, is a mammal. What effect might DDT accumulation have on human biochemistry?)

The third area that greatly worries scientists is the possible mutagenicity of DDT. Whether DDT can cause mutations is not definitely known. It is known that many chemicals, including some that are widespread as pollutants, can cause changes in the gene structures of certain organisms, so biologists keep a sharp eye out for this phenomenon. (What effect might chlorinated hydrocarbons have on human genes?)

Obviously there are many unanswered questions about persistent pesticides, as well as demonstrable harmful effects.

HEALTH
AND DISEASE

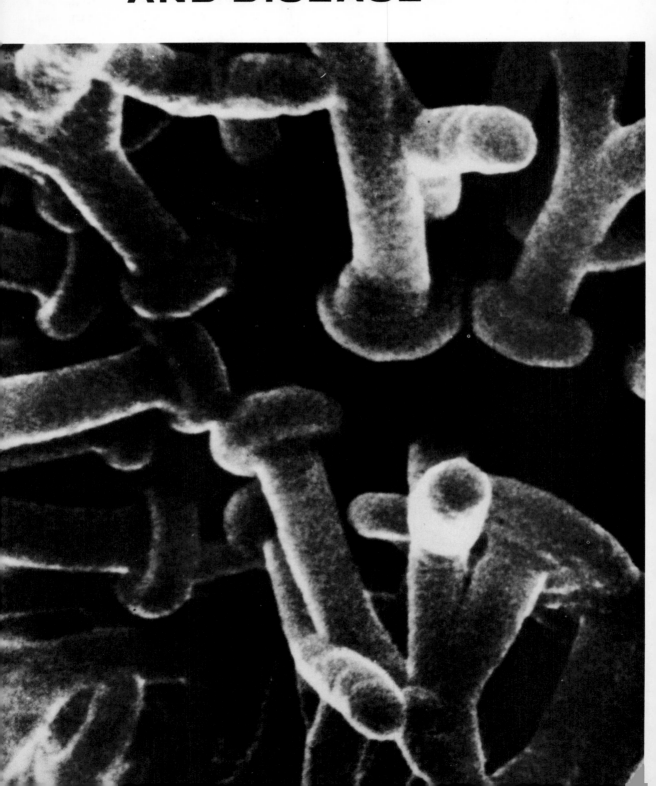

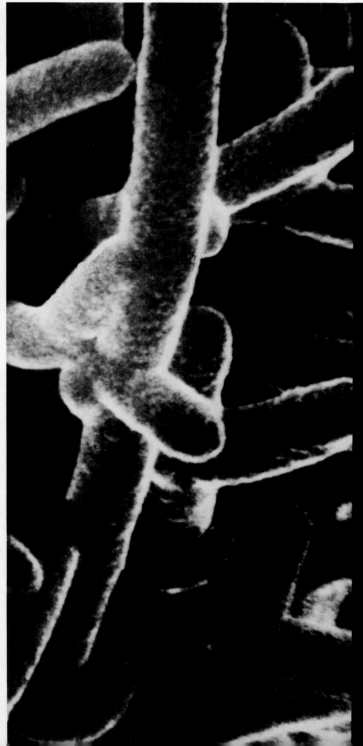

CONTENTS

The incredibly small fibers and synaptic knobs that link together the nervous system of an animal. Scientists believe the knobs pass nerve impulses from one cell to another in the neural communications network. (Magnification: about 5,000 times.)

UPI

REVIEW OF THE YEAR-
HEALTH AND DISEASE

Transplants. The most spectacular medical achievement of 1969 was the successful implantation on April 4 of a complete artificial heart into the chest of a 47-year-old man. But the feat was clouded by controversy and accusations of improper conduct. Dr. Denton A. Cooley of St. Luke's Episcopal Hospital in Houston, Texas, used the 8-ounce, 4-chambered plastic device as a temporary measure until a heart donor could be found. The prosthesis worked perfectly for 65 hours and was then replaced by the heart of a 31-year-old woman; 32 hours later, the patient died. The controversy centered on whether use of the device had violated National Heart Institute guidelines about clinical trials of new cardiac devices developed with Federal funds. Although the experiment has not been repeated, many surgeons consider the artificial heart more promising than a transplant from another person as a substitute for a diseased human heart. (For one thing, there will never be enough donor hearts to meet the need, even if the problem of rejection is solved.)

Heart transplants, meanwhile, were on the decline. Of the total of 148 patients who underwent heart transplants (23 of whom were still alive at the end of 1969), 2 received their new hearts in 1967, 99 in 1968 and only 47 in 1969. On August 17, 1969, the longest-surviving heart recipient, Dr. Philip Blaiberg, died — 19½ months after transplantation. Such operations, which reached a peak of 26 performed during November 1968, dropped to 2 in the month of Dr. Blaiberg's death, 4 the following month, 1 in October and no more until Christmas morning, when Dr. C. Walton Lillehei of New York Hospital transplanted the heart and both lungs of a 53-year-old woman into the chest of a 43-year-old construction worker. After 3 hours and 13 minutes, all 3 organs began to function. By the third day the patient was walking and talking. But the seemingly inevitable rejection set in and he survived only 8 days. Another lung recipient, the only one of 23 who survived more than a month, died in September 1969, ten months after receiving the transplant. He was Alois Vereecken, a 23-year-old Belgian steelworker, who had been given a new right lung by Dr. Fritz Derom of the University of Ghent hospital. Another team at the same hospital, headed by Dr. Paul Kluyskens, performed the world's first larynx transplant in February 1969. It worked well, but the patient died of cancer 10 months later.

Kidney transplants, of which more than 3,000 have been done, have reached a stage where nearly half of all those who receive cadaver kidneys survive at least a year, while 90 per cent or more of those who receive kidneys from blood relatives live a year or more. Liver transplants have been less successful, but Dr. Thomas E. Starzl of the University of Colorado, who has performed about half of these operations, points out that the survival rate is about that of kidney transplants six years ago.

Virology. In the fight against viral diseases, 1969 was a notable year. The new vaccine against German measles (rubella) was licensed and a campaign to vaccinate 50 million children by 1971 was begun. Progress was made against another viral disease, hepatitis, as blood banks began screening their stocks for Australia antigen in the hope of detecting hepatitis carriers among donors. Discovered in 1963 by Dr. Baruch S. Blumberg and his colleagues at Philadelphia's Institute for Cancer Research, the antigen is closely associated with hepatitis and may be the hepatitis virus itself. At the New York Blood Center, a group led by Dr. Alfred M. Prince has begun using an automated testing system that can screen donor blood for the antigen in an hour. According to Dr. Prince the system should be able to detect up to 90 per cent of the hepatitis carriers among donors; older tests took at least 24 hours and could detect only 1 in 4 carriers. The development will be none too soon: the National Communicable Disease Center announced that there were 52,587 hepatitis cases in 1968–69 compared with 44,261 the year before, a rise in incidence from 22.3 to 26.2 per 100,000 population. Between 1,500 and 3,000 persons are believed to die each year from hepatitis contracted during blood transfusions.

Cancer. Dr. Robert J. Huebner, chief of the National Cancer Institute's viral carcinogenesis branch, told an international leukemia symposium that C-type RNA viruses, found in cancers in ten animal species and in some 20 per cent of human leukemia patients, had become the chief viral suspect in human cancer. He has developed a general theory of viral cancer around the hypothesis that the virus lives in body cells from the moment of conception, but its action is repressed unless and until a specific gene is somehow activated. Then it transforms normal cells into cancer cells. Another elegantly inclusive theory linking a virus to cancer was developed by Dr. James T. Grace, Jr., director of Roswell Park Memorial Institute in Buffalo, New York. Noting that the Epstein-Barr (EB) virus, which was first associated with Burkitt's lymphoma, then with infectious mononucleosis, then with a particular type of nasopharyngeal cancer, had recently been linked to leukemia, he theorized that which, if any, of these conditions a person develops depends on the strength of his immune system's reaction to the virus. In other words, mononucleosis may be a comparatively mild, reversible form of leukemia.

Leukemia appears to be coming under a certain amount of control. A combination of drugs and supplementary treatment has steadily raised the survival rate. About 30 per cent of treated patients now survive at least 5 years; patients who live more than 5 years have a 50 per cent chance of indefinite survival. Some experts have begun to use the formerly taboo word, "cure," in discussing leukemia survival. The latest antileukemia agent to be cleared for clinical use, cytosine arabonoside, received Food and Drug Administration (FDA) approval in 1969. The drug, which blocks synthesis of deoxyribonucleic acid (DNA), is the most effective known for acute granulocytic leukemia; in one fourth of the cases in which it has been used, the disease has receded into remission. Another promising leukemia treatment is immunotherapy, pioneered by Dr. George Mathe of France.

Smallpox. Drs. J. Michael Lane and J. D. Millar of the National Communicable Disease Center in Atlanta, Georgia, published a paper pointing out that smallpox is now so rare in the United States that the risk of death from vaccination is far greater than from the disease. They calculated that at least 210 deaths from smallpox vaccine reactions could be expected in the next 30 years, while if only high risk groups (travelers to smallpox-prone areas, military recruits and so on) were vaccinated, the vaccine deaths would number about 60. Other experts, however, recalling when the entry of 3 smallpox cases from Canada in 1924 led to 74,000 cases and 1,270 deaths in the United States, called the report "a numbers game" and contended that the risk of a disastrous epidemic far outweighed that of vaccine complications.

Food additives. In a speech early in May, 1969, Charles C. Johnson, Jr., of the Consumer Protection and Environmental Health Services said "the use of food additives to impart flavor, color or other qualities has increased 50 per cent in the past 10 years, and each of us now consumes an average of 3 pounds of these chemicals yearly. Pesticides leave residues on food crops, and traces of veterinary drugs occur in meat, milk and eggs — all this in addition to the chemical barrage that reaches us from other parts of the environment." The use of several food additives has since been banned or curtailed. Cyclamates, 30 times as sweet as sugar and with almost no caloric value, had been widely used since they gained FDA approval in 1950. But after experiments showed that they could cause bladder cancer in rats, cyclamate-sweetened beverages were ordered off the market and new labeling rules were laid down for their use in dietetic foods. In October 1969, the major producers of baby foods announced that they would no longer use monosodium glutamate (MSG), a flavor-enhancing chemical, in their products. This decision came after Dr. John W. Olney of the Washington University Medical School reported that he had produced brain damage in infant mice and in an infant rhesus monkey by giving them large doses of the chemical. In January 1970, the FDA ordered food manufacturers to restrict the use of brominated vegetable oils in soft drinks and other products. This action followed a Canadian report that high doses of these oils (which are used as stabilizers in foods) caused heart damage in rats.

Birth control. Findings indicate that oral contraceptives, already used by some 8.5 million American women, increase the user's risk of developing blood clots, and may be associated with some forms of cervical and breast cancer. While some experts feel that the Pill should be taken off the market until additional studies are made, most agree that the risks involved in unwanted pregnancy are far greater than those faced by Pill users. Meanwhile, newer birth control methods are almost ready to replace the Pill. An injectable contraceptive, medroxyprogesterone acetate, is before the FDA for approval. Clinical tests indicate that a single shot of the new drug gives almost 100 per cent protection against pregnancy. The same drug can be used to impregnate a vaginal ring made of Silastic (silicone rubber). Looking much like the spring-reinforced ring of a diaphragm and inserted similarly, it remains in place during the 21-day reproductive cycle and is then thrown away. A fresh ring is inserted five days after the next menstrual period begins.

Sight. From the world of electronics comes promise of an almost miraculous development — artificial sight for the blind. A British physiologist, Dr. Giles S. Brindley, has found that artificially-stimulated flashes of light perceived within the brain's "visual space" can be used to produce visual images. When he implanted 80 electrodes in a blind woman's head, 37 of them produced these phosphenic light spots. Meanwhile, at Albert Einstein College of Medicine in New York, biophysicist Herbert Schimmel is working on a mini-TV camera using the same principle; this apparatus could be worn by a blind person much like a miner's headlamp. A different principle is used by Drs. Paul Bach-y-Rita and Carter C. Collins at the University of the Pacific in San Francisco. Their device changes visual images from a small TV camera to electrical impulses, which in turn activate 400 tiny vibrators mounted on the back of a wheelchair. When the subject presses his back against the vibrators he receives skin sensations that his brain eventually learns to accept as visual information. The researchers have trained 40 blind subjects to "see" shapes, movement, color and even to read type. Next step is a miniaturized version to be worn as a headlamp, with an undershirt containing 10,000 electrodes to carry images to the skin.

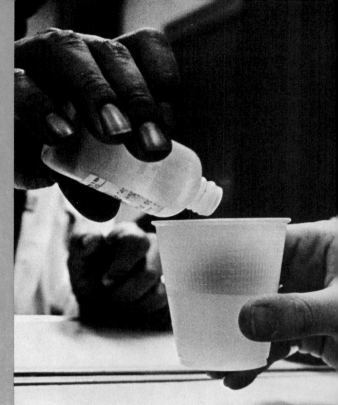

A glass a day. . . . A former heroin addict receives his daily dose of methadone in a glass of fruit juice. This synthetic drug blocks the patient's desire for heroin.

METHADONE THERAPY FOR HEROIN ADDICTS*

The Problem: Methadone Is Addictive, Too

BY HUGH SPITZER

JOSEPH X, formerly a heroin addict, says he has kicked the habit — with a daily glass of orange juice.

Joe's orange juice has a special additive: a dose of methadone. This is a synthetic narcotic that blocks the craving for heroin but has no serious side effects itself. Joe says it makes him feel "like a human being instead of an animal," in contrast with heroin.

Each morning on the way to work, Joe stops at the San Francisco Health Department's Center for Special Problems and takes a carefully measured dose. The center runs 1 of about 30 methadone maintenance programs in the nation. Advocates of this therapy say methadone is 80 per cent effective in treating heroin addiction.

But methadone presents a problem. It is itself habit-forming — meaning that a user may have to rely on it for life — and its employment is provoking vehement criticism. "It's about as effective as switch-

ing an alcoholic from Old Crow to gin," says a California narcotics official. A spokesman for Synanon, which treats addicts with rigorous group therapy and group living, calls the use of methadone "like giving babies to child abusers."

Cautious approval

Controversial it may be, but some authorities say methadone seems to offer an approach to heroin addiction that merits consideration. A committee from the Federal Bureau of Narcotics and Dangerous Drugs recently visited several methadone clinics to judge just how effective the medicine is. A spokesman says the committee concluded that the treatment is legitimate, and the committee soon will recommend regulations to govern future methadone research. (Doctors now administering methadone welcome official acceptance of the drug, but they express apprehension about regulations that might restrict their treatment methods.)

Debate on the effectiveness, method and morality of methadone treatment comes at a time of mounting concern over

* Reprinted from *The Wall Street Journal*, September 9, 1969.

The fight against addiction: educational programs are trying to make people, especially youngsters, aware of the dangers of heroin, amphetamines and other drugs.

heroin addiction. The FBI says annual arrests for heroin violations have risen more than 120 per cent since 1965. Law-enforcement agencies manage to seize only a fraction of the illegal drugs entering the country each year. Federal sources estimate the number of addicts at a minimum of 50,000 people, and some officials put the figure at several hundred thousand. Addiction-related crime runs to many millions of dollars a year and results in untold physical violence.

Amid such doleful statistics, methadone advocates express impatience with their critics. Physicians administering the drug say the procedure is simple enough to treat most of the nation's addicts. And, they point out, it is inexpensive, costing about 9 cents a day per patient. Drs. Vincent Dole and Marie Nyswander, a husband-and-wife team working at Rockefeller University in New York City, say the methadone regimen has proved successful with 83 per cent of addicts treated over 5 years of experimentation.

Taking out the kicks

An addict embarking on treatment goes either to a hospital or a carefully controlled outpatient clinic for daily doses of methadone that are steadily increased to a "maintenance" level that permits him to function normally. Each patient provides regular urine samples for analysis to check if heroin is being taken at the same time.

But the urine tests soon prove superfluous, methadone users say. The desire for heroin simply dissipates. The methadone patient who continues using heroin no longer gets any "kick" from the illicit drug. And the methadone doesn't produce the mental dislocations and lassitude associated with heroin "highs" (however, withdrawal symptoms accompanying the need for methadone can be as powerful as those with heroin). Physicians dispensing methadone say it "blocks" the influence of opium-derivative drugs without having ill effects itself.

"Then these people can act like normal human beings," says Dr. Barry Ramer, who directs the methadone program

Illus: National Institute of Mental Health

in San Francisco. Methadone, he says, enables former heroin addicts "to keep out of trouble, get a job or go to school, and stay off dope."

Reports of successful treatment, from the original methadone clinic in New York and others, are spurring formation of new programs. Dr. Ramer says that if his results continue to prove favorable, San Francisco may start 5 neighborhood centers using the synthetic drug.

The worst cases

Many desperate heroin addicts apparently have decided that methadone is the answer to their problem. When the San Francisco center announced its pilot program in June 1969, it received hundreds of inquiries from people with drug habits. "We're still getting 20 to 30 inquiries a day," says Dr. Ramer. Patients for the program were carefully selected, he says. "We took the worst kind of criminal addicts, the most challenging cases, so we could prove to the Federal and state narcotics people that this is the right treatment."

One patient acknowledges that he is "scared about being on methadone for the rest of my life." But, says another, "You gotta face that fact, and we all think it's better than heroin."

"I had a few side effects when I first started on methadone," says one former heroin user, "but now I feel fine. I can relax for the first time in my life." Another addict offers this comment: "Being clear is a trip all by itself." (Reported side effects of methadone usually involve a skin rash that disappears within a week or so. Some methadone patients who experience sweating, sleeplessness and other discomforts are simply reacting to the change in their habits, researchers say.)

An addict who had a 7-year habit suggests the cost of heroin addiction to society. "Figure it this way," he says. "I used to illegally hustle anywhere from $100 to $300 a day on an average when I was on dope. Now, you multiply that by 365 days and again by the 5,000 addicts in San Francisco, and that accounts for a hell of a lot of money and crime."

Another former addict, who previously "hustled" in what he calls the "dog-eat-dog scene" of San Francisco's Haight-Ashbury district, says, "Addicts fill the jails in most cities. They would save the Government money by staying home and keeping their wives happy." His remark produces laughter among a group of former addicts: most heroin users are impotent, while methadone users have normal sexual capabilities.

Encouraging reports from physicians dispensing methadone haven't persuaded critics that the drug is useful. Some of the strongest opposition comes from officials of Synanon, former addicts themselves. "Methadone is insidious. It's immoral. It treats the symptoms but not the disease," says Chester Stern, director of Synanon in Oakland, California.

Dr. Dole, who runs a data center compiling statistics on about 1,600 methadone patients in several New York City programs, has this reply to Mr. Stern: "The people at Synanon make irresponsible statements about the effects of methadone without even looking at our clinics. They think our patients are going around high all the time, and that simply isn't true."

Critical views of methadone often focus on what Dr. Victor Vogel of the California Narcotic Evaluation Authority calls "moral qualms about giving people narcotics on a continuing basis instead of withdrawing them from narcotics." Mr. Vogel's chief worry about methadone is its long-range effects. "I have my fingers crossed about methadone," he says. "I recall historically when heroin was introduced, it was promoted as a cure for opium and morphine addiction. I fear that history may be repeating itself."

John Storer, chief of the California State Bureau of Narcotic Enforcement, is a harsh critic of methadone therapy. "It's not a treatment, it's a substitution, a sociological experiment by physicians out of their field," he says. "But it's a fraud to call it a cure, because people have to keep taking it all their lives."

Many state and Federal officials advocate keeping methadone in the "experimental" category of drugs for the time being, rather than authorizing it for widespread use. "You have to remember that methadone use is still a research undertaking," says Gene Haislip, a lawyer with the Federal Bureau of Narcotics and Dangerous Drugs and one member of the four-man committee investigating the drug. "This is an unconventional use of a narcotic drug with addicts, and there is a need for regulation to ensure a professional, scientific manager."

Dr. Dole is apprehensive about the Federal activity. "What you call research is a vague thing," he says. "This is the most documented treatment for addiction and should be available to any qualified physician. But a Federal agency still calls it research, and a doctor without an elaborate program is under pressure if he prescribes methadone for a small number of patients."

In New York City, Mayor John V. Lindsay vetoed a bill in 1969 that would have provided for methadone treatment of addicts in city prisons. The Mayor said he had decided that the bill wasn't consonant with Federal regulations on the administration of methadone. Mr. Lindsay noted, however, that the city is operating a methadone-research program for five thousand addicts with Federal approval and Federal funds. He has spoken of the drug as a hopeful approach to the narcotics problem.

Dr. Dole believes the methadone method has been unjustly scored by its critics. He challenges those urging other methods of rehabilitating heroin addicts "to publish their statistics as we have and give an honest cost-benefit accounting so we can learn from their mistakes and see what works and what doesn't."

Dr. Avram Goldstein, a Stanford University pharmacologist, believes that needless biases have been generated against methadone. "It is a safe drug, and it puts people back into society," he says. "Does it cure addiction? No one asks if insulin cures diabetes. We have to get rid of the notion that there are moral and immoral molecules."

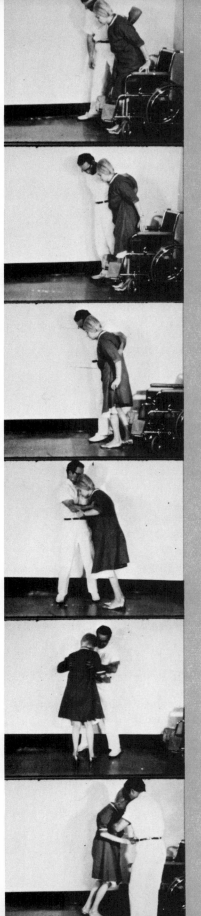

THE REMARKABLE EFFECTS OF L-DOPA*

Drug Brings Parkinson Victims Back into Life

BY ISRAEL SHENKER

"MY FIRST night here was a nightmare, and when they gave me the L-Dopa pill in applesauce, I thought they were trying to poison me, with camouflage. Finally I agreed to take the pills.

"Now I walk around the terrace 3, 4, 5 times after dinner. I jog around once or twice. I might say I'm a human being. Before I took the pills I was something questionable; what would be the stage below depression?"

When Mike arrived at Beth Abraham Hospital, in New York City, he went into a psychotic depression, convinced he was in a slaughterhouse. His expression was rigid, his hands clenched. He was unable to speak and could rise only with difficulty, and his balance was poor.

Drug brings improvement

Now he came striding into the doctors' conference room with his arms swinging, his balance perfect.

Mike (the names of patients have been changed in this account), like many other patients suffering from Parkinson's disease, has shown remarkable improvement after treatment with the drug L-Dopa (Levo-Dihydroxyphenylalanine). In the last few years, researchers have been using the drug to relieve the disease and restore the more fortunate patients to considerably better health.

The films show a patient suffering from Parkinson's disease. Left: before the administration of L-Dopa, the woman can walk only if assisted. Right: after receiving L-Dopa the woman can easily walk unaided.

All photos: Brookhaven National Laboratory

211

About a million Americans suffer from Parkinson's disease. For some of them, the ailment stems from the encephalitis pandemic that raged between 1916 and 1927. Many of those stricken experienced extreme drowsiness and stupor lasting up to six months.

In a few cases, the disease produced not lethargy, but abnormal insomnia and restlessness. Of those who recovered, many went on to develop parkinsonism.

The onset of parkinsonism, which is named after the 19th-century London physician James Parkinson, who published a paper identifying the disease, is sometimes delayed until 10, 20, even 30 or more years after the disappearance of every symptom of encephalitis.

Treating this variety of parkinsonism has been even more frustrating than dealing with the more common, so-called idiopathic parkinsonism, which rarely occurs before the age of 50. In idiopathic cases, physicians have often managed, with surgery and belladonna-type drugs, to ease the characteristic rigidity and tremors.

Postencephalitic patients, however, are especially prone to a trancelike immobility involving depression or apathy, severe difficulty of speech, very poor balance, crises of staring and panting and sweating. These symptoms have resisted the conventional treatment.

Many of these symptoms are caused by a deficiency of a chemical called dopamine, which is necessary for the transmission of nerve impulses in the brain. L-Dopa raises the level of dopamine in the brain.

The Food and Drug Administration (FDA) now permits more than 200 clinical investigators and hospitals across the country to use L-Dopa in treating patients.

The synthesis of the drug is not difficult, and a representative of the Nutritional Biochemicals Corporation of Cleveland, which furnishes most of the world's L-Dopa, said supply was no problem. He predicted that the drug's price would drop by at least ½ by mid-1970.

Wider use expected

Even before then the FDA is likely to receive an application from 1 or more suppliers to authorize the general marketing of L-Dopa for prescription by all physicians.

In mid-1969 L-Dopa cost $500 a kilogram (2.2 pounds), down from $5,000 some years ago. It cost up to $1,000 to treat a patient for a year. Like severe diabetics who must get regular doses of insulin, those who benefit from L-Dopa regress immediately if they give up the drug.

Doctors warn against overoptimism about L-Dopa. "There are complications which can be serious," said Dr. Jack Sobel, chief of medicine at Beth Abraham.

In some cases it does not help patients at all. Even for those it helps, there are sometimes side effects, such as nausea and dizziness, and the drug must be used with extreme care.

Film of patient shown

Beth Abraham is one of the hospitals whose experiments will help guide the eventual decision on general release of L-Dopa. This institution for the chronically ill has one of the largest groups any-

Dr. George C. Cotzias, recipient of the 1969 Albert Lasker Award for Clinical Medical Research for his "dramatic demonstration that large daily doses of L-Dopa can reverse most of the crippling effects of parkinsonism."

where of postencephalitic-parkinsonism patients.

In mid-1969, 25 severely disabled postencephalitics, some of whom had been institutionalized for more than 40 years, were included in the group being treated with L-Dopa.

Dr. Oliver W. Sacks, the neurologist who supervised the treatment, said:

"Close to 90 per cent have benefited. It's been spectacular in about 30 per cent, of very substantial help in about 30 per cent and of modest help in about 30 per cent. A minority appear either refractory to medicine, or have adverse reactions."

As he showed a group of his colleagues a film of one patient, Dr. Sacks provided a running commentary:

"Drooling, eyes closed much of the time, motionless posture in the chair. Swallowing is very difficult. To communicate he has to point to a letter at a time, though he is a man of superior intelligence, with three college degrees. He showed the first signs of parkinsonism when he was 15, and from age 30 until now — age 50 — he has been completely incapacitated.

"Now," Dr. Sacks continued, as the film showed the patient, called Abe, after treatment with L-Dopa, "he's writing the 10th chapter of his autobiography. He demonstrates quick head movement, claps his hands vigorously and — most remarkable of all — walks without assistance.

"When he was on a higher dose of Dopa, there was a tendency to repeat entire sentences. The patient said it was 'like an effortless hoop of words' going through his mind.

"In some cases the sexual arousal is remarkable, though many of these people had little childhood and no adolescence. Abe is now an avid fan of Philip Roth, though he can't do anything about it yet. He calls himself the parkinsonian Portnoy. And he writes endless letters which he never posts, so he also calls himself the parkinsonian Herzog."

One of his letters was a love poem to his therapist, in which he boasted: "I'm out of the custody of my symptoms."

"I've had a rather interesting life," said Abe, after wheeling himself into the room. "In my autobiography I'm talking about my thoughts and the things that happened to me in the 33 years I was ill — how my personality has now changed. I was mild, meek, and couldn't get angry about anything. Now I get angry, get aggressive — against everybody."

In addition to drug therapy, patients require occupational and physical therapy.

Patients need guidance

"These patients are also bound to need guidance when recalled from a mummified state," Dr. Sacks said.

Dr. Sacks observed the patients night and day — watching them as they slept, questioning them by day. "If one is going to rehabilitate a patient," he insisted, "it is not enough simply to give Dopa. One should know as much as possible about him: his background, skills, goals, wishes and fears.

"Otherwise one may simply have an absurdly activated cripple who is tormented by a physiological change which he is not equipped to exploit."

Because sensitivity and reaction to L-Dopa can fluctuate, all patients, but above all the postencephalitics, have to be watched closely. Dr. Sacks spoke of a "Yo-Yo effect" in which some patients alternate between sudden restless excitements and a reversion to their original immobility. The Yo-Yo effect has been controlled by giving smaller doses more frequently. One patient at Beth Abraham takes a dose an hour.

Theodore, a Talmudic scholar, used to spend most of each day standing immobile in a corridor. He recalls that before using L-Dopa his "thoughts were glaciated."

From summer camp he wrote Dr. Sacks:

"I was bathing every day. I won the first prize for poetry. Everyone showed me the highest respect. I walk better, I eat better, I speak better. I know that I'm well enough to live in the community like a normal American citizen."

PAIN*

Your Body's Early-Warning System

BY WEBB GARRISON

"I'VE never felt labor pains," the mother of seven explained to Dr. Richard Sternbach. "If I hadn't heard about other mothers," said Mrs. X, "I wouldn't have known that childbirth is supposed to be an uncomfortable experience.

"Years ago I took a bad tumble and my playmates asked if I had been hurt. I told them 'Not a bit.' But after I took a bath and tried to put my shoe back on, I found that I had broken my ankle."

The spasmodic, cramplike abdominal pains of colic are well expressed in this engraving by George Cruikshank.

* Reprinted by permission from *Today's Health*, published by the American Medical Association

Mrs. X paused. "I could go on like this for hours. Honestly, I've never felt pain. After I started cooking my friends had to warn me not to take casseroles out of the oven with my bare hands."

Pain is foreign to Mrs. X because she is one of the rare individuals of normal intelligence who has congenital analgesia (inborn immunity to pain). As her case history unfolded in the "pain lab" at Massachusetts General Hospital several years ago, it became apparent she would provide exceptionally interesting data about one of medicine's oldest enigmas. In tests to measure intensity of pain, she demonstrated that short of brutality she really couldn't be hurt. Her sister is also free of pain, and their aunt died of cancer without suffering enough to need drugs.

All seven children of the X family were tested. Two proved to be as free of pain as their mother. Two others could feel pain, but not at levels ordinarily experienced. Three children showed normal responses to pain-producing stimuli, but said that they seldom notice any pain.

A splendid inheritance with which to face life's challenging and often traumatic situations? Not at all!

Despite repeated warnings the youngest son was continually burning himself on stoves and radiators. His oldest brother was taken to the hospital when he said his stomach felt "stiff"; examination showed that his appendix had ruptured without pain. Had he not received emergency treatment, peritonitis would have developed. Mrs. X once developed eclampsia (a complicated and sometimes fatal disorder associated with pregnancy) and was in an advanced stage before her condition was recognized. It was not recognized earlier simply because Mrs. X hadn't felt a typical symptom: excruciating headache.

PATH OF PAIN

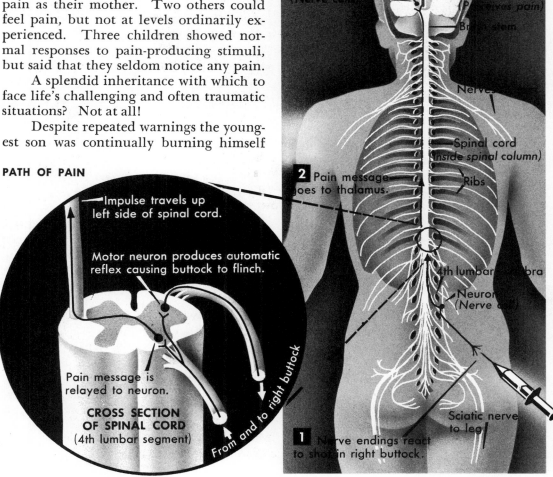

Time magazine

3 Message reaches part of brain where pain is interpreted.

Cortex

Neurons (Nerve cells)

Thalamus (perceives pain)

Brain stem

Nerve

Spinal cord (inside spinal column)

Ribs

2 Pain message goes to thalamus.

4th lumbar vertebra

Neuron (Nerve cell)

Sciatic nerve to leg

1 Nerve endings react to shot in right buttock.

Impulse travels up left side of spinal cord.

Motor neuron produces automatic reflex causing buttock to flinch.

Pain message is relayed to neuron.

CROSS SECTION OF SPINAL CORD (4th lumbar segment)

From and to right buttock

When you have a toothache, do you hurt more, or less, than other members of your family?

Why do some persons moan and groan over sufferings from minor disorders, while others remain cheerful and buoyant during periods of intense pain?

Does the capacity to experience pain have any long-range significance for the development and perpetuation of life . . . or is it a bodily state "full of sound and fury, signifying nothing"?

Questions like these have engaged the minds of some of the world's best thinkers. Current research has yielded many insights and a cluster of physiological and neurological data but we still don't understand pain in all its form and dimensions.

Three things, however, are certain. Pain is infinitely complex. Pain is as variable as human nature. And pain is an utterly solitary experience.

No matter how hard he tries, your physician cannot feel your pain. His understanding of it is limited to a professional interpretation of how you act and what you say about how you feel. Your report, never objective, is conditioned by many factors: your biological inheritance, your past experiences, cultural attitudes concerning pain, other stimuli that compete with pain for your attention, plus current emotions and goals.

No wonder that a generally satisfactory definition of pain has never been framed! "Let a sufferer try to describe a pain in the head to a doctor," said word-artist Virginia Woolf, "and language runs at once dry."

Attempts to measure and to classify pain, until recently regarded as promising areas of investigation, have run into unexpected difficulties. Electrical stimulation of the nerves of the teeth (feasible only with volunteers whose teeth have metal fillings) was once regarded as a sure way to establish an objective scale by which to measure pain. Pressure on a tender part of the body, such as a nail bed, has been carefully applied to determine the "pain threshold," or the exact point at which pain is first felt.

At Cornell University a variety of electrical, mechanical, and chemical stimuli have been tried. Light from a 1,000-watt lamp, focused by a lens and passed through a small hole to shine on a portion of the forehead blackened with India ink, seemed to offer the most reliable results.

Using this method, neurologist Harold G. Wolff and his colleagues devised a dolorimeter or "pain measurer." With this system they hoped to arrive at a set of objective standards, applicable to all or most situations. A unit of pain was termed a *dol,* with the scale running from 1 (threshold pain) to 10 (maximum pain a person can experience).

Few modern American mothers will be surprised to know that on this scale the pain of childbirth was rated at 10, while coronary thrombosis rated only 4 to 6 dols. Pain of stomach ulcers was judged to range from 2 to 3.5 dols, while an "ordinary" headache registered 0.5 to 1.5 dols.

Though these results were achieved since World War II, they are now regarded as suspect: not because tests weren't conducted with scrupulous care, but because experimental pain has been shown to differ in quality from real-life pain. Apprehension and dread, major factors affecting the way pain is experienced in ordinary situations, are missing from the laboratory context. And though a stimulus can be measured accurately, the reaction cannot.

All attempts to measure the intensity of pain rest on use of controlled methods applied to volunteers. And since these findings don't carry over to your migraine headache or the shoulder your son sprained at football, for practical purposes we're back where the ancients found themselves: incapable of measuring pain, and able to talk about it only in general terms.

Emotional factors account for part of the difference between induced and clinical pain, but not all of it. By necessity, experiments have tended to focus upon the body's exterior covering. In everyday life, however, many pains originate deep within muscles and joints or inside our body cavities.

In 1846 a Boston dentist, William T. G. Morton, made a surgery patient unconscious of pain by having him inhale ether. The surgeon braced himself for the familiar screams, but the patient was silent. After the operation the surgeon declared: "Gentlemen, this is no humbug." Within the year, ether was being used in hospitals all over the world.

Severe internal (or visceral) pain seems more diffuse than exterior pain. Unlike the pain that stems from burning or pricking the skin, internal pain is produced by inflammation, chemical irritation, pressure, stretching, or squeezing. Most surface pains are localized; those that come from deep within your body may be felt at considerable distances from their sites of origin. After a heart attack one's heart doesn't hurt; instead, there may be pain in the left shoulder and arm. Clues that seem to signal a stomachache may actually stem from the large bowel — separated from the stomach by twenty feet of intestinal tract.

In spite of the fact that pain can neither be defined nor measured, research workers have devoted a great deal of effort to the attempt to find out just how and why we feel pain.

Scientific inquiry into the problem began about 1846, when German physiologist Ernst H. Weber announced that he had succeeded in separating pain from the sense of touch. For nearly a century his ideas were accepted and pursued.

It came to be taken for granted that your body has not only receptors for touch, sight, and the other senses, but also a special system of pain receptors. Prac-tically any expert who worked a few decades ago would have told you that the palm of your hand has 40 to 70 "pain spots" in each square centimeter of skin. But an equal area of the armpit was said to have at least 200 such sensors.

According to this view, the human body is more sensitive to pain in parts equipped with a higher concentration of pain receptors. "The logic of this is obvious," one authority declared. "Without such a highly functional distribution of pain receptors, developed through ages of natural selection, the act of walking would be utter agony to our feet, while the delicate structures of our eyes would be far more vulnerable to destruction without their multiplicity of pain receptors."

Sounds convincing (and very scientific), doesn't it? Contemporary research has disturbed this neat picture, however.

Many physiologists now doubt that there are special receptors in our bodies that register pain, and only pain. As though this skepticism were not confusing enough, present-day analysts think that (no matter how it is registered and transmitted by the body) a sensation that you or I label painful is actually a fruit of personal interpretation as well as physiological reaction.

218

Long before anyone thought of trying to identify specific pain receptors, anatomists and philosophers took for granted the notion that the body has a definite "pain center." Aristotle reached that judgment 24 centuries ago. "The motions of pleasure and pain, and generally of all sensation plainly have their source in the heart," he said, challenging earlier views which held the liver as the organ in which pain is felt.

Discovery of the central nervous system, about 300 B.C., caused physicians to shift their attention to the brain and spinal cord. Eventually the thalamus (a specialized structure in the posterior of the forebrain) was identified as *the* pain center — this in spite of evidence pointing to registration of pain at various sites in the brain's cortex.

Today's specialists tend to minimize the concept of a single pain center. Mounting evidence indicates that (at least) the frontal cortex, parietal cortex, thalamus, hypothalamus, and brainstem reticular formation are involved in pain perception. Add to these the physiological structures involved in remembering, feeling emotions, and working toward abstract goals and you reach the conclusion that many sensory systems and information-processing structures are involved in even the simplest experience of pain.

Small wonder that so complex a problem has caused man to turn to religion and philosophy as well as to science for an explanation of pain.

Much evidence supports the view that some of the first major operations were performed to relieve headache. Almost everywhere that early remains of man are found, are skulls showing that medicine men were skilled in the art of trepanning, or piercing the skull. Possibly (but not positively) the operation was performed, not to ease cranial pressure and reduce pain caused by it, but to make a hole so that the evil spirit thought responsible for the headache could exit.

Until recent times many Christian theologians held that pain is inflicted as a divine punishment. Because Eve sinned in paradise, all women were considered doomed to bear children "in labor and sorrow."

General acceptance of this view hindered the progress of anatomy, surgery, and internal medicine: If a person believes God ordered every mother to suffer as a consequence of Eve's guilt, it becomes impious to interfere with the divine will by relieving pain.

Doctors, midwives, and expectant mothers inevitably experimented with herbs and other remedies despite dire warnings from the clergy. In 1591, Dame Euphanie Macalyane of Edinburgh managed to secure a bitter medicine supposed to relieve her from the pangs of labor. King James VI learned of her at-

The Bettmann Archive

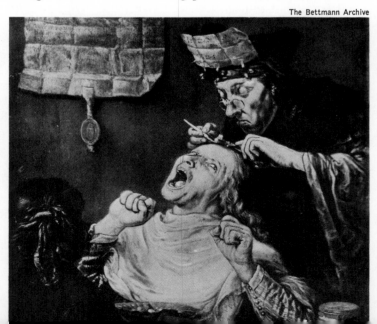

Even prehistoric man practiced trepanation to let demons or evil spirits escape from the brain or to relieve skull fractures and other injuries. This process consisted of boring holes in the skull. This painting shows a 17th-century doctor pretending to remove stones from a peasant's head in order to relieve his headache.

tempt to cheat providence and righteously ordered the culprit burned alive as a warning to all women who might seek to evade suffering.

Another Scot, Dr. James Y. Simpson of Glasgow, introduced the use of chloroform in childbirth. Simpson first employed the recently discovered anesthetic on November 4, 1847; as soon as he announced its superiority to ether, in use since 1842, he was subjected to a torrent of abuse. Fellow physicians joined clergymen in attacking him as a blasphemer and heretic. In 1853, Queen Victoria brushed aside theological arguments, took chloroform from her obstetrician, and made "painless labor" respectable.

Whatever else it may be, there is no doubt that much pain really is a distress call that sounds within a fully automated biological alarm system. Many analysts think capacity to feel pain increases with complexity of the central nervous system, so that humans are more sensitive to it than other creatures. This theory doesn't lend itself to laboratory testing, but one aspect of pain's protective role is clear. It is pain (an elaborate symptom) rather than illness or injury underlying pain that sends most persons to their physicians. Check your own record over the past few years. You're about average if pain sent you seeking professional help in 9 cases out of 10.

Total analgesia, first described clinically in 1932, is rare and is usually associated with mental retardation or severe mental disorders. A person who doesn't feel pain often experiences great numbers of burns, cuts, and bruises during childhood. He is likely to bite his tongue frequently while eating, may not recognize that diseased teeth are damaged until they are past saving. In one bizarre case a pain-free attorney who had a finger crushed refused medical help and bit off the injured member.

A person with congenital analgesia, like Mrs. X, has some chance of surviving and living a fairly normal life in today's highly developed society. But in earlier periods, insensitivity to pain would have

greatly reduced life expectancy. Without capacity to suffer, it is questionable whether or not our primeval ancestors could have survived in sufficient numbers to produce modern man. Even in the space age, pain enhances one's capacity to survive.

But in many illnesses, suffering lingers for days or weeks after its warning function has been performed. Long-lasting or "intractable" pain of high intensity tends to disrupt personality. A person who was once gentle and happy can become irritable and depressed during years of suffering. No utilitarian result is apparent in such a case. Lord Morgan, a noted British physician, bluntly challenged the "warning" theory of pain by insisting that "a person passing a kidney stone is hardly better off because he passes it in torment."

In terminal illnesses such as those brought about by cancer or stroke, physical anguish long seemed to have no positive value whatever. Such pain does not serve to preserve or even to prolong life. But brutal as it sounds at first thought, pain may play a constructive role in a terminal illness by causing the sufferer to lose the fear of death and look for it as a welcome friend.

So pain has many facets. Interpretation of even the simplest ache or dull internal throbbing involves many variables. Some of these variables are individual; others are social.

In laboratory situations, threshold pain (or the first perceptible pain produced) is experienced in about the same way by most normal persons. With rare exceptions, experimentally applied heat will cause a young woman or an old one, a male or a female, a neurotic executive or a tough Eskimo fisherman to "hurt" from approximately the same stimulus.

Even in the laboratory, once the threshold level has been passed, reactions vary widely. One person will smile and say, "Keep turning up the heat!" Another will break into sweat and struggle to avoid fainting. Presumably the two are receiving the same sensory input, but are mak-

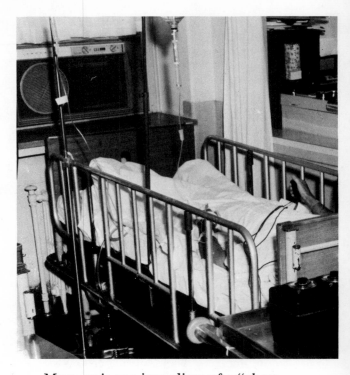

Dr. Philip H. Sechzer, director of Anesthesiology at New York's Maimonides Medical Center, notes the progress of a patient using his push-button pain-control unit. By pushing the button an electronically controlled pump is activated. This flushes one milliliter of a pain-killing solution through an intravenous tube and into the patient's vein. The patient repeats the process until the pain is eased.

ing different interpretations of that input in higher centers of their brains.

Regardless of whether it is barely perceptible or at an intense level, pain fluctuates. Intensity of the pain-producing stimulus may remain constant, but the pain felt by the persons reporting it tends to waver up and down as well as to "radiate." In the latter case, pain is not felt in the affected body part. Instead, it is "referred" to a different site.

This is a major reason for the fact that though pain remains one of the physician's most important diagnostic aids, it is often deceptive. Inflammation of the liver may be experienced as pain in the right shoulder. A woman who suffers from a uterine disease may go to her physician seeking relief from what she thinks is lumbago. Through such radiation and "eccentric projection," incipient hip-joint disease may cause a child to complain of pain in the knee.

Phantom-limb phenomena, or "ghost pains," are even stranger. Most amputees continue to "feel" the missing limb for a period; in about 30 per cent of cases, pains are felt in definite parts of the phantom member.

Memory is one ingredient of a "ghost pain," for a person born without a leg or hand doesn't experience pain in the missing member. Many physicians think this clue points to an important variable. Your past experiences, and the vividness with which you remember them, probably pay a major role in determining the amount and quality of pain that you feel in a particular situation. Since your experiences and memories are highly individual, your experience of pain may be quite different from that of a friend or relative with a different set of memories and experiences.

Part of one's evaluation of pain, whether remembered from the past or experienced in the present, consists of responding to stimuli in the fashion considered "proper" by standards of the culture. Some observers think American Indians were from infancy "conditioned" to show a stoical attitude toward stimuli that persons in other cultures have labeled as painful.

Ready availability of nonprescription analgesic agents in modern U.S. life (as a nation we consume more than 45,000 pounds of aspirin a day) may foster a

Maimonides Medical Center

tendency to be "sissy" about pain. If that's the case, such cultural magnification has not produced imaginary pain; it is real, but much of it might be ignored by Eskimos or by tribesmen who live in South American rain forests.

For centuries, Westerners have taken it as axiomatic that childbirth involves as much pain as a woman can endure. But anthropologists have studied numerous cultures in which most women show little or no sign of suffering at the time of labor. Perhaps the weirdest cultural impact upon pain is that exhibited in the ritual of the *couvade* (named from French for "brooding" of a fowl over its eggs).

In societies where the *couvade* is an accepted practice, women work in the fields until labor begins. Once the child is delivered the mother returns to her work, while her husband goes to bed and receives the attentions that in other cultures would be shown to a woman after childbirth. Numerous analysts have reported that in such situations the husband is likely to wince and groan.

Early students thought these responses were phony; today, some psychologists believe many of them are genuine, that the father may really hurt despite the fact that his body has experienced none of the physical effects of childbirth. Since there's no way to know whether the mother actually feels no pain or only says she doesn't and acts as though she doesn't, the *couvade* remains an enigma.

But an observer doesn't have to look far to see that different persons react in quite different fashion to the same sets of stimuli. A professional hockey player or veteran football pro may not even ask for time out after receiving a blow that would send a spectator to the hospital. Part but not all of the difference in response can be linked with training. Much of it stems from attitude; the player tends to take his bruises casually, while the frightened spectator may be in genuine agony.

Life-absorbing goals and values may so dominate attention that pain cannot be felt. During World War II, Dr. Henry K. Beecher of the Harvard Medical School noticed that only 25 per cent of soldiers who suffered serious wounds complained of pain. Their "insensitivity," Beecher concluded, stemmed from the fact that a wound was regarded as desirable — a badge of heroism that meant an end to combat.

Fantastic as it sounds, there is a possibility that some ancient Christian martyrs who were burned alive or boiled in oil experienced no pain. Totally absorbed with life-shaping goals, they may have been incapable of perceiving the sensations that ordinary persons interpret as pain. This view is supported by eye-witness reports of Buddhist priests and nuns who have burned themselves to death in Vietnam. In some instances, photographs of the immolation show the victim in what appears to be a state of ecstasy rather than a state of excruciating pain.

But it doesn't take a Buddhist with a martyr complex to demonstrate that pain may be eliminated or reduced by attention to another set of stimuli. Have you ever suffered toothache for hours or days, then walked into the dentist's office to find that the pain had ceased? Or have you been in agony until told your child needed you in an emergency — acting swiftly in response to the plea for help and becoming oblivious of your own pain until the crisis was over?

Fluctuating power of attention probably accounts for the fact that a pain of which you've been vaguely conscious all day may suddenly become unbearable after you retire for the night. With no other stimuli competing for your attention, those which you interpret as "ouch!" may so dominate your consciousness that you actually do hurt much worse than you did all day. Hence you may be tempted to try to reach your doctor at midnight despite the fact that you didn't call during office hours.

In several U.S. medical centers, experiments are under way with push-button administration of analgesics by postoperative patients. At Brooklyn's Maimonides Medical Center, Houston's Methodist Hospital, and at Baylor University's College of Medicine, physicians have developed a variety of devices with one common denominator. Within limits established by his physician, the patient self-administers pain-killing drugs — at intervals and in quantities he determines.

Already, tentative findings suggest that self-medication (under controlled conditions) fosters the work of drugs. Surprisingly, many patients give themselves smaller doses than surgeons ordinarily would prescribe. Part of the plus factor from self-medication seems to result from the patient's feeling that he is in control of the situation; part of it may stem from the fact that attention given to self-dosage reduces the degree of attention that can be centered on perceiving pain.

Hypnotism, long a controversial means of reducing or eliminating pain in some circumstances, works well with some patients. But recent experiments indicate that a distracting task such as trying to listen carefully to a recorded narrative may reduce the intensity of experimental pain about as much as does hypnotism. One girl tested was found able to direct her attention to a spot on her skirt in such fashion that she effectively prevented pain from reaching consciousness.

Self-inflicted pain is experienced differently from pain that descends uninvited. In many tribal societies, self-mutilations are inflicted in the process of initiation into adult life or as a means of gaining status. They seem to cause little or no pain. On a different level of experience, very ticklish persons in highly developed societies find it difficult or impossible to tickle themselves.

At McGill University, tentative results from experiments with Scottish terriers suggest that animals feel no pain until they have been in situations that acquaint them with it. Even the most firmly established findings from use of animals as experimental subjects can't be carried over into human life. Still, the very notion that one may have to learn to experience pain is intriguing. Does a baby suffer in the process of being born? No adult could endure so traumatic an experience — but there is a possibility that a newborn hasn't yet acquired the capacity to hurt.

A journey around the moon presents less difficulty than the attempt to probe the full meaning of pain. Essentially a mental state that is affected by physical, mental, and social variables, it is so highly private that you can never be sure your description of a headache causes others to know precisely how you feel.

Recognizing its complexities and granting that some kinds of pain seem to have no warning or survival value, for most of us most of the time pain is much more than discomfort to be avoided or shut off. Pain is a major defensive weapon in nature's arsenal. We are equipped to experience it so that we can respond by seeking not simply relief from pain, but life-guarding treatment for the condition that causes pain. When you experience significant pain for any duration, recognize it as nature's call for help — and see your physician.

THE SMOKING BEAGLES*

Another Link between Cigarettes and Lung Cancer

FOR the first time, scientists have produced lung cancer in a significantly large experimental animal as a result of heavy cigarette smoking. The lung cancer was produced in a group of purebred male beagle dogs by having them smoke non-filter cigarettes.

The findings of this experiment were reported early in February 1970 by Dr. E. Cuyler Hammond, the American Cancer Society's vice-president for Epidemiology and Statistical Research, and Dr. Oscar Auerbach, a pathologist at the Veterans Administration Hospital in East Orange, New Jersey.

Teaching dogs to smoke

A tracheotomy was performed on each of the dogs. In this simple operation a small incision was made through the front of each dog's neck into his trachea; a tube, placed into the trachea, could then be connected to a cigarette holder. Except for 8 control animals, the beagles were gradually trained to smoke. And, unlike most nonhumans, the beagles liked the habit. Eventually, said Dr. Auerbach, "they wagged their tails and whined for cigarettes."

* From information provided by the American Cancer Society

The study involved 94 dogs. The 38 heaviest beagles were put into a special group; these would continue to smoke until they eventually died. By the time of the report, 12 of these dogs had died (11 of pulmonary diseases, 1 possibly from acute toxic effects of smoking).

The remaining 56 dogs were divided into 4 groups:
(1) controls (nonsmokers)
(2) filter smokers
(3) light nonfilter smokers
(4) heavy nonfilter smokers.

Work with these dogs continued for approximately 2½ years (875 days). During this time, 16 of the 48 smokers died, 12 of lung diseases such as emphysema and bronchial pneumonia. At the end of this period, the beagles were put to death (except for the heavyweight dogs). Autopsies were performed on all the dead dogs.

Although dogs smoking filter cigarettes experience less extensive damage to lung tissue — in the form of emphysema, fibrosis and so on — than the nonfilter-smoking dogs, those that were still alive and smoking filter cigarettes to the end of the study demonstrated significant lung damage at autopsy. According to Dr. Hammond, "since the degree of such damage progresses with duration of smoking, the evidence indicates that lung parenchymal [tissue] damage advances less rapidly with the smoking of filter-tip cigarettes than with the smoking of nonfilter cigarettes." He referred to this phenomenon as a "dose-response relationship."

RESULTS OF THE EXPERIMENT

GROUP	NUMBER OF DOGS	NUMBER OF CIGARETTES SMOKED BY EACH DOG	NUMBER OF DOGS WITH TUMORS	PERCENT OF DOGS WITH TUMORS	PERCENT OF AUTOPSY SLIDES WITH EMPHYSEMA	DEATHS BEFORE DAY 875
CONTROLS	8	0	2 — BENIGN 0 — MALIGNANT	25.0	0.0	0
FILTER SMOKERS	12	6,143	4 — BENIGN 0 — MALIGNANT	33.3	12.9	2
LIGHT NONFILTER SMOKERS	12	3,103	7 — BENIGN 0 — MALIGNANT	58.3	24.3	2
HEAVY NONFILTER SMOKERS	24	6,129	9 — BENIGN (only) 10 — MALIGNANT	79.2	98.8	12

THE CHEMICALS YOU EAT

Are Some Food Additives
Harmful?

BY SUSAN WERNERT

CHEMICALS that have long been accepted as safe additives to the foods we eat are now the target of increasing criticism. According to Charles C. Johnson, Jr., of the U.S. Public Health Service, "each of us now consumes an average of three pounds of these chemicals yearly." They include substances that add flavor; others that improve color; still others that preserve the food. Approximately 2,500 additives are currently being used in the United States. According to a report released by Ralph Nader's Center for Study of Responsive Law, in April 1970, half of these have never been adequately tested for safety.

Prior to 1958, no Governmental agency in the United States had the power to provide advance clearance of food additives. Food processors could add any substance to their products that they felt would enhance the products. These substances could only be removed from the market by court order; but first, the Food and Drug Administration (FDA) had to prove them "poisonous or deleterious." This, assuming adequate manpower and testing facilities, might take several years.

In 1958 the FDA was given authority to control the additives; new chemicals now had to receive FDA approval *before* they could be used in foods. But the many substances already in general use were exempted from testing. Those "generally recognized as safe" were placed on the GRAS list. This list, which now numbers about 680, includes such diverse

substances as cloves, salt, sodium bisulfite, aluminum calcium silicate and pipsisswa leaves.

A sweetener turns sour

Until last year cyclamates were just one type of GRAS chemical listed on food packages in households across America. They are white, odorless powders that are entirely man-made. Produced from an acid and either sodium or calcium, they have no calories and no nutritional value. They were used as an additive because they have about 30 times the sweetening power of sugar.

In a report on cyclamates issued in November 1968, the National Academy of Sciences-National Research Council said that, although eating large amounts of the substances caused diarrhea or light sensitivity in some people, there was no evidence that they were hazardous to human life.

But on October 1, 1969, Dr. Jacqueline Verrett, an FDA research scientist, reported that she had injected cyclamates into approximately 4,000 chicken eggs. At hatching, about 600 of the chicks had deformities such as missing legs, twisted spines and underdeveloped eyes. Notification of these results, Dr. Verrett said, had been given to FDA officials almost a year earlier.

Another FDA report described chromosome breaks in the sperm-producing cells of rats injected with cyclohexylamine. In some people this substance is a product of the body's metabolism of cyclamates. The implication of both this and Dr. Verrett's study was that offspring of people using cyclamates might be harmed, as they had been by thalidomide. The FDA requested a new evaluation of cyclamates.

A week later, the evaluation was no longer important. Abbott Laboratories, the world's largest producer of cyclamates, reported that bladder tumors had developed in rats receiving cyclamates; the tumors in at least 4 rats were malignant.

In 1958 the U.S. Congress had approved the Delaney Amendment, which prohibited the use of food additives that were found "to induce cancer in man or in animals." On the basis of this amendment, Secretary of Health, Education, and Welfare Robert H. Finch ordered a gradual withdrawal of cyclamate-containing products. Low-calorie soft drinks, the most widely used of these products, would be the first to go.

The scientific basis of the withdrawal and the inflexibility of the Delaney Amendment drew much criticism. The main attack was on the large amounts of cyclamates used: the dose that produced the malignant tumors in rats was equivalent to 50 times that recommended for adult-human consumption. "You would have to drink a bottle of diet cola a minute for eight hours straight to achieve that dosage," said Michael Sveda, the inventor of cyclamates. Critics wondered how many other substances taken in that amount could cause cancer.

Another argument against the ban was that cancer was induced not in man but in rats — and only in rats that had been fed large doses of the cyclamates for 18 months.

Medical workers cited the advantages of cyclamates. They help keep down weight, decrease the incidence of tooth decay, and permit diabetics to eat a wide variety of food. Some critics felt that the consumer should be given a choice between cyclamate and noncyclamate products and that the Government should not make the choice for him. There were

charges that the Government was giving in to the sugar lobby. Secretary Finch delayed some of the withdrawal steps for cyclamate-sweetened foods.

Meanwhile, soft-drink manufacturers rushed to place new low-calorie drinks on the market. They used sugar, saccharin (a synthetic on the GRAS list) and new chemicals. People wondered if these would be any safer than cyclamates.

Tasty baby foods

Meanwhile, another additive controversy simmered. Monosodium glutamate (MSG), a flavoring agent on the GRAS list, was first used thousands of years ago in the Orient. It is a naturally occurring salt of a protein compound. In some people it causes the "Chinese restaurant syndrome": an adverse reaction including headaches, sweating and other symptoms, and usually occurring after an MSG-rich Chinese meal.

Until late 1969, MSG was used in certain kinds of baby food, primarily to please the taste of the infants' mothers. But the three largest baby-food manufacturers in the United States stopped using the substance after experiments indicated that it might harm infants.

The experiments were conducted by Dr. John W. Olney of the Washington University School of Medicine in St. Louis. In his first experiment, he injected a large dose of MSG beneath the skin of newborn mice. Electron-microscope examinations showed that certain nerve cells in the brain had been killed. Later in their lives the mice became excessively fat, and the females were incapable of reproducing.

The arrows point to breaks in human chromosomes. The breaks were produced in a test tube to which large amounts of cyclamates were added.

Dr. David Stone

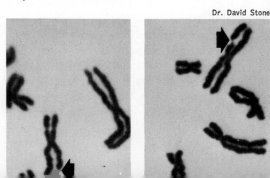

After I quit smoking—you will remember—I developed hyper,—

tension + heart trouble from the weight I'd gained—so my doctor...

...put me on a diet which contained many artificially......

... sweetened things and now, well, I know that you'll understand

Haynie in *The Louisville Courier-Journal*

A similar experiment was conducted with an infant rhesus monkey. Again the subcutaneous injection of MSG caused acute nerve-cell death.

Human beings, of course, do not inject MSG into their body; they take it orally. Thus a seemingly more relevant experiment by Dr. Olney was one in which he fed MSG to 9 young mice. Brain damage occurred in 7 of these animals. The dose of MSG was 0.01765 ounce (0.5 gram) per 2.2 pounds (1 kilogram) of body weight. According to Dr. Olney, this is about 5 times the amount of MSG commonly found in a jar of baby food (an infant often eats 2 such jars a day).

Again, critics felt the public was being unduly alarmed. As in the cyclamate experiments, scientists mentioned the small number of animals tested, the possibly unwarranted extension to human infants, and the lack of evidence from more than one laboratory. But critics could not defend the use of MSG in baby food.

Further study of the effects of MSG is being carried out by a National Research Council panel. In a report issued early in April 1970, the panel said it "considers it unnecessary to recommend any restriction at the present time in foods for [adults]." The panel had not considered the suitability or safety of using MSG in infant foods.

Additional restrictions

FDA scientists are now reviewing all experiments and data concerning the additives on the GRAS list. In January 1970 the FDA announced restrictions on brominated vegetable oils, GRAS products used in citrus-flavored drinks. This action resulted from findings that the oils caused heart damage in rats. The agency also banned the use of paprika in most fresh meat products, contending that the red color makes spoiled meat appear fresh.

But food additives are not on the way out. Americans used more than 700 million pounds of these chemicals last year, and indications are that usage will increase, not decrease. They add flavor, thicken foods and help preserve everything from poultry and seafood to cakes and potatoes. Additive-containing products have a ready market: cooks save time by using "just add water" mixes; people demand exotic-tasting foods; and calorie-conscious consumers would rather eat artificially-sweetened foods than simply eat fewer sweets.

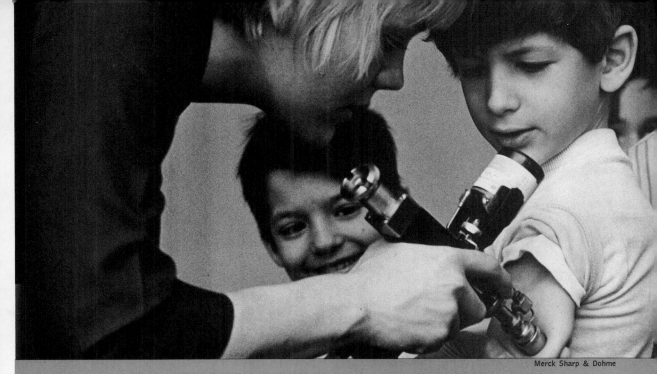

THE FIGHT AGAINST RUBELLA

Millions of Children Will Receive New Vaccine

BY JENNY ELIZABETH TESAR

GERMAN measles: most of us had it when we were young children. We "caught" it from a friend at school, an older brother or the playmate who lived next door. It really wasn't painful and the rewards often seemed greater than the inconveniences: we could stay home from school, our parents pampered us and perhaps we received a new toy or comic book to amuse us.

Rubella — more commonly known as German measles — is a viral disease that is contracted by most children before they reach puberty. A disease that occurs in cycles, its prevalence reaches epidemic proportions in the United States every 6 to 10 years. During the last major epidemic, which occurred in 1964–65, an estimated 10 to 12 million Americans developed the disease. For most of them, the course of the disease was relatively mild, consisting mainly of fever and a temporary rash. But for pregnant women who contracted rubella, results were often tragic.

If an expectant mother develops this disease, especially during the first three months of her pregnancy, the rubella viruses may pass through the placenta into the embryonic child where they attack the developing organs. Effects can be catastrophic. During the 1964–65 epidemic, approximately 30,000 fetal deaths occurred and some 20,000 babies were born with serious defects such as deafness, cataracts, heart disease and mental retardation.

Developing the rubella vaccines

The damaging effects of rubella in pregnancy were first recognized in 1941 by Dr. Norman M. Gregg, an Australian ophthalmologist. He traced a high incidence of cataracts in newborn babies to a rubella epidemic that occurred in New South Wales during the previous year. Other physicians and scientists, stimulated by Dr. Gregg's findings, conducted further investigations into the effects of the disease.

227

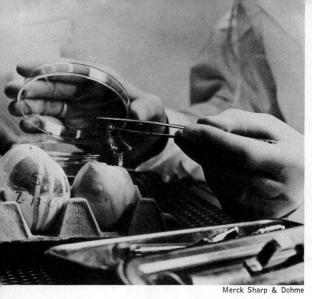

Merck Sharp & Dohme

The cell tissues of duck embryos are an ideal culture for growing viruses used in producing the rubella vaccine.

Twenty years later, in 1961, scientists reported that it was possible to develop a vaccine against rubella. Two research teams — Drs. Thomas H. Weller and Franklin A. Neva of Harvard University and Drs. Paul D. Parkman, Edward L. Buescher and Malcolm S. Artenstein of the Walter Reed Army Medical Center — reported that the rubella virus had finally been isolated. Following this isolation, intensive efforts were made to develop a vaccine that could eliminate rubella-induced birth defects. At first scientists tried to develop a vaccine from dead viruses that would be safe even in pregnant women. However, results of these efforts were disappointing and researchers shifted their attention to the production of a live virus vaccine. (*Live* vaccines contain living viruses that multiply in the body; *killed* vaccines contain viruses that have been inactivated and are not able to multiply. The latter are effective only if the viruses can be killed without losing their ability to give immunity.)

The first live attenuated (weakened) virus strain was developed in 1965 by two National Institutes of Health scientists, Drs. Harry M. Meyer, Jr., and Paul Parkman. They named this strain HPV-77 (for "high-passage virus"; the viruses had been passed through tissue cultures 77 times in order to produce a properly modified and weakened strain). Further re-

search by Dr. Maurice R. Hilleman and Eugene B. Buynak of Merck Sharp & Dohme led to the development of an HPV-77 vaccine. This vaccine underwent extensive testing, both in the United States and abroad. Then, in June 1969, the United States Government granted Merck the first license for marketing rubella vaccine in the United States.

Philips Roxane Laboratories and Smith Kline & French Laboratories have also developed rubella vaccines (HPV-77 and Cendehill strains, respectively). The United States licensed the Philips Roxane vaccine in December 1969; the SK&F vaccine, which is manufactured by their Belgian subsidiary, has been licensed in several European countries; the United States licensed it in March 1970.

Can pregnant women be vaccinated?

Once an individual has German measles, he develops an immunity that apparently persists for the rest of his life, even if the infection is mild or inapparent. The person's body builds up defenses, in the form of proteins called antibodies, against future exposure to the disease.

Approximately 85 per cent of the women in the United States had rubella when they were children. Thus they have a natural immunity and need not worry about contracting the disease while they are pregnant. However, the remaining women are susceptible. It has been estimated that fetal damage occurs in more than 50 per cent of the women who get rubella during the first three months of pregnancy.

The purpose of the vaccine is to stimulate production of rubella antibodies without giving the patient the disease. Can the attenuated vaccine virus cross the placenta and enter the embryonic child, causing birth defects as does the natural rubella virus? Until scientists can clearly demonstrate that the rubella vaccines are safe for expectant mothers, public health officials in the United States and other nations advise women of childbearing age against receiving the vaccine unless their doctors are certain that they are not pregnant and will not become pregnant for at least three months.

Meanwhile, scientists at the University of Helsinki in Finland and Nagoya University in Japan are studying the effects of the rubella vaccines on pregnant women. These studies involve pregnant women who are scheduled for therapeutic abortions (for reasons other than rubella infection). The women are inoculated with rubella vaccine at various stages of pregnancy; the fetal and placental tissues are then examined for the presence of rubella viruses. Initial results show that the weakened viruses in rubella vaccines seldom cross the placenta to reach the fetus. However, they may do so on rare occasions. Additional studies are needed to determine how often such "accidents" may occur. If it can be demonstrated that the chances of fetal infection after vaccination are small, then the vaccine could be given to pregnant women who are exposed to rubella during the first months of pregnancy.

Pregnancy is not the only condition which should prevent a person from receiving the vaccine. Active infections and diseases such as leukemia, lymphoma and generalized malignancy can interfere with the effectiveness of the rubella vaccine. In addition, the vaccine should not be given to infants less than one year old.

Massive vaccination of children

According to Dr. William H. Steward, Surgeon General of the Public Health Service, "the most effective use of the vaccine would be the immunization of children in kindergarten and the early grades of elementary school, because they are commonly the major source of virus dissemination in the community." Children transmit the disease to each other at school and in the playground; they bring it into their homes, exposing brothers and sisters and, perhaps, their pregnant mothers.

Thus health officials will concentrate on vaccinating this age group, hoping that by reducing this pool of the disease, they will decrease the chances of infection in susceptible pregnant women.

It is estimated that 50 to 60 million children in the United States should receive the vaccine. Some of these have already had the disease and have thus acquired a natural immunity. However, because rubella often occurs unnoticed or is confused with other illnesses, it is advisable that these children receive the vaccine.

The first massive immunization program in the United States was held in September 1969 in central New Hampshire; approximately 3,700 elementary school children were vaccinated. In late October 1969, Dr. F. Robert Freckleton, Chief

Roy Perry

Dr. Harry Meyer, Jr., who helped develop the HPV-77 strain, is shown with children born with physical defects resulting from the 1964–65 rubella epidemic. Both children received early speech training from an agency in their community.

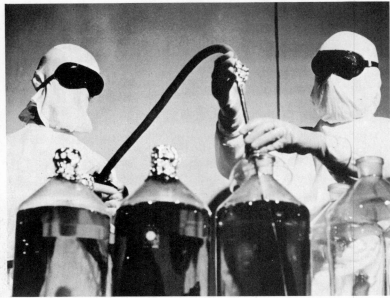

Clothed in anticontamination garb and wearing goggles as protection against germ-killing ultraviolet rays, technicians pool virus harvests during the production of rubella vaccine.

Smith Kline & French

of the Immunization Branch of the National Communicable Disease Center in Atlanta, Georgia, predicted that 15 to 20 million children would be vaccinated by the end of 1970.

Children who received the HPV-77 vaccine during field trials have maintained fairly high antibody levels for three years or more. Similar results are being obtained with the Cendehill strain. This is encouraging evidence that vaccine-induced immunity may last a long time. However, it does not guarantee lasting immunity. As Dr. Frederick C. Robbins, Nobel Laureate and Dean of the Case Western Reserve School of Medicine, pointed out, if the immunity wore off "we might prevent infection in childhood, but develop a pool of susceptible adults. This in the long run could be a much worse situation that that with which we are now faced."

Multipurpose vaccines

Vaccination programs are expensive and time-consuming. To simplify the administration of vaccines, laboratories are developing multipurpose vaccines capable of preventing several diseases. Such a combination—the DPT vaccine — is designed to prevent diphtheria, whooping cough (pertussis) and tetanus. Other combinations include a mixture of smallpox with yellow fever vaccine and a combined smallpox and measles vaccine.

Scientists are currently working on a trivalent (three-in-one) vaccine that would give combined immunity against rubella, regular measles and mumps. Twenty thousand Soviet children have received such a vaccine developed at the State Research Institute of Influenza in Leningrad. A similar vaccine is being tested in the United States and may be on the market in 1971. A bivalent vaccine for mumps and rubella has also been developed; this is expected to be licensed soon.

Will there be another epidemic?

The occurrence of German measles, as mentioned earlier, tends to reach epidemic proportions at intervals of six to ten years. The next nationwide epidemic in the United States could be expected as early as the 1970–71 winter. However, it is hoped that widespread vaccinations will substantially reduce or possibly even prevent this, and future, epidemics. But cooperation between physicians, health agencies and private citizens is needed if the new rubella vaccines are to protect the unborn from the crippling effects of one of the most tragic of all viral infections.

WILL CANCER SOON BE AN EXTINCT DISEASE?*

Hunt for Cancer Vaccine Closes In

At 90,000 magnification these Rauscher leukemia viruses are detected in the blood of leukemic mice. Note the tails and the outer shells surrounding the dense inner nucleoids — all of these characterize the leukemia virus.

Photos: Chas. Pfizer & Co., Inc.

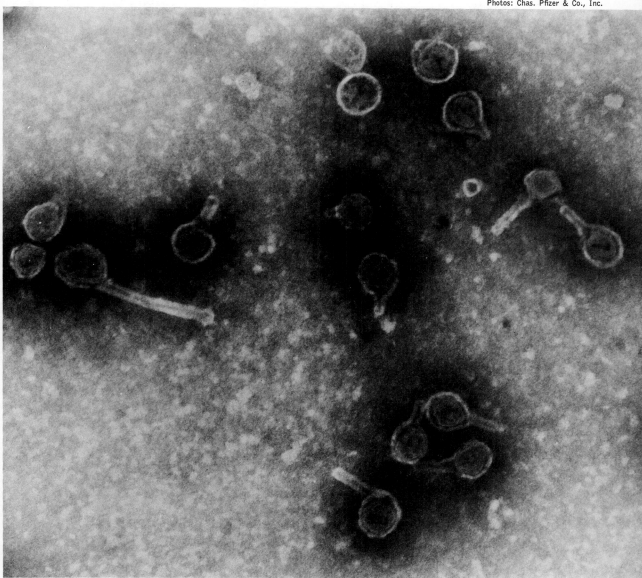

SCIENTISTS used to scoff at the idea of a human-cancer vaccine. They scoff no longer. The reason: they know that viruses cause many, if not most, forms of cancer and that if they can isolate a virus, they can make a vaccine to protect against it.

Already they are far beyond the theory stage. They have made a vaccine

* Reprinted by permission from *Business Week*

231

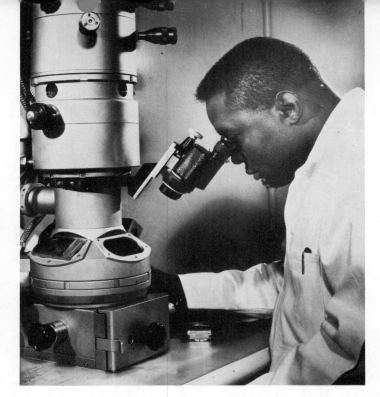

As deadly as they are small, the viruses of leukemia are brought to view only by the tremendous power of the electron microscope. This researcher is studying the mouse leukemia virus. Photographs can be made of the actual leukemia virus in the blood of infected mice, or in tissue cultures, where the virus is grown in large quantities and purified prior to further research.

that prevents a form of leukemia (blood cancer) in mice. They have developed another vaccine to prevent a chicken leukemia that causes huge poultry losses each year. And they believe that within two years they will be able to offer for public use a vaccine that will act against leukemia and some other cancers in humans.

Speedup

Exciting as these prospects are, cancer researchers are stimulated by yet another fact. For the first time, the technique of systems analysis developed in the aerospace industry is being focused on a single goal in a major health project. Cancer research labs throughout the United States, and some abroad, are conducting the vaccine hunt as one giant team, coordinated by National Cancer Institute virologist Dr. Frank J. Rauscher. The technique speeds the flow of scientific information, points up where new research projects are needed and — it is hoped — will cut by years the time needed to get results.

Of all projects now under way in this concentrated search, the brightest hope today centers on a lab in Buffalo, New York, and on a virus known as EBV (Epstein-Barr virus).

Cancer vaccine researchers have picked two or three likely virus candidates to work with out of eighty known to be involved in human cancer. But their heaviest betting is on EBV, because this virus either causes or is implicated in a wide spectrum of cancers. Among these are chronic lymphocytic leukemia, Hodgkin's disease, postnasal cancer, and Burkitt lymphoma — a cancer found mostly in tropical Africa. But EBV apparently also causes infectious mononucleosis, or "mono."

Type of leukemia

Known to thousands of stricken college students as the "kissing disease," mono is a blood disease which is seldom thought of as related to cancer. But scientists today believe that mono may be a reversible, far less virulent type of leukemia. That being the case, they reason that if they can develop a vaccine against mono, then the same vaccine may act against other EBV cancers too.

They acknowledge that the EBV virus may not work alone in producing the cancers in which it has been found. Other factors, from cigarette smoke to the effects of combinations of viruses, are believed to be involved in causing different forms of cancer. But they figure that if they can defeat the root cause — in this case EBV — then they may be able to beat a whole group of cancers at once.

Timetable

Development work on the mono vaccine is being spearheaded at Roswell Park Memorial Institute in Buffalo, by a team headed by virologist James T. Grace. Despite a struggle for funds — a problem shared by most U.S. medical researchers — Dr. Grace feels that his group will have its first experimental vaccine by late 1970. And as a highly cautious prediction — it may be ready by the end of 1971 for protection against mono.

Once the EBV vaccine is developed, researchers expect to be able to check its effectiveness against other EBV-caused cancers in humans in two ways:

• If the vaccine is used in mass mono vaccination programs, the scientists would observe patients receiving it over a period of years. If the rate of EBV cancers in this group is lower than in the general population, this would be strong evidence that the vaccine is a true protector against these types of cancer, as well as against mono.

• They would probably try the vaccine in treating EBV cancer patients who otherwise face early death.

Both these uses, however, may still be several years off. So far, Grace's team has isolated from EBV-infected cell cultures an antigen — a substance that, when injected into animals, produces antibodies in the bloodstream — and started tests to confirm that these antibodies actually kill the EBV virus.

Researchers still do not know, however, what their basic antigen is. It may be part of the protein component of the EBV virus itself. Or it may be a protein made by the cultured cells in reaction to exposure to the virus. Either way, it does not fit the classical definition of a vaccine: that is, dead or weakened whole virus or bacteria. But as a protein, unable to spread disease like a live virus, the antigen should have a much easier time getting

U.S. government approval than a virus vaccine would.

Grace's project springs from the research of Dr. Verna Henle of Children's Hospital in Philadelphia, who isolated EBV from mono patients, and Dr. Paul Gerber of the U.S. Division of Biologics Standards, who demonstrated that EBV can make healthy cells appear to become cancerous. The work of all three is part of the huge systems approach directed by Rauscher at the National Cancer Institute (NCI).

Anticancer vaccines for animals

Rauscher himself started a chain of events in 1962, when he isolated the Rauscher leukemia virus in mice. A vaccine against this was developed in 1964 at the John L. Smith Memorial for Cancer Research, a nonprofit lab run by Charles Pfizer & Company under NCI contract. The vaccine gives well over 90 per cent protection, Pfizer reports. Its usefulness is limited to research on mice, and it is not an EBV vaccine. But the company hopes its experience will help it develop a comparable vaccine further up the animal scale, for cats.

Meanwhile, the first anticancer vaccine expected to hit the marketplace — by the end of 1970 — will almost certainly be for nonhumans. Its target is chick leukosis, more commonly called Marek's disease, which is responsible for about $200 million in poultry losses every year.

Field tests of this vaccine are in progress on hundreds of thousands of chickens on U.S. farms, following its development by a team headed by Ben R. Burmester of the Agriculture Department's laboratories at East Lansing, Michigan.

Chickens, however, may not be the only beneficiaries of the Marek's disease vaccine. The virus is a variety very similar to EBV, and Burmester and other scientists are now checking it in cell cultures for its relation to human cancer. If there is a connection, it would give a clearer picture of factors linking EBV to many forms of human cancer — and further hope for a vaccine to defeat it.

ORAL CONTRACEPTIVES

How Safe Is the Pill?

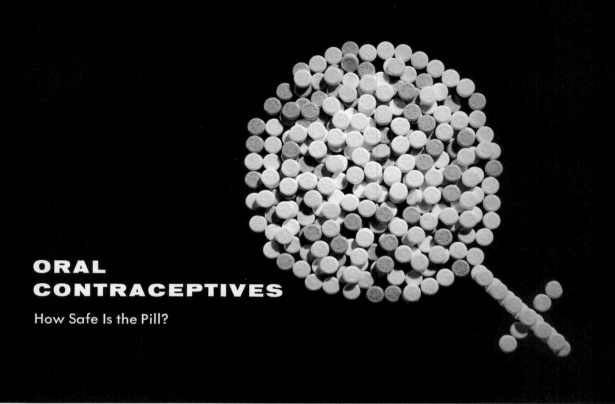

ONE of the most revolutionary medical developments of the 1960's was the worldwide introduction and use of the "Pill." "This modern, effective and very popular means of fertility control has," says Dr. R. T. Ravenholt of the Agency for International Development in Washington, D.C., "received more publicity, affected more people, and had a greater impact on health and society than any other medical innovation during the past ten years."

Much of the publicity has centered on the safety of the oral contraceptives (OC's). OC's cause a number of metabolic changes in a woman's body. These include changes in weight, water retention, thyroid function, blood-sugar levels and menstrual functions. These changes appear to be reversible: when a woman stops using OC's, these conditions revert to their pre-OC state.

There is, however, one serious disorder that has been linked with OC's: thromboembolic disease. This is the formation of blood clots in the vessels of the circulatory system. Such clots are potentially lethal. If they block a major blood vessel in a limb, amputation may be necessary; if they block a vessel to the lungs or brain, death may result. Studies done in Great Britain and the United States indicate that the risk of death from blood clotting is approximately 6 times greater in women using OC's than in women who do not use these pills. This averages out to about 3 deaths per 100,000 users each year.

OC's contain 2 major ingredients: the hormones progesterone and estrogen. Evidence indicates that the estrogen is responsible for clotting. Early OC's contained 100 milligrams of estrogen; these are apparently more likely to cause clots than the currently available pills that contain only 50 milligrams of estrogen.

Most doctors believe that women who have histories of blood disorders should not take OC's. Many physicians also refuse to prescribe the pills to women whose medical histories include migraine headaches, liver diseases, diabetes and certain types of cancer.

All women who do use the pills should have medical checkups at least once every 6 months. The examinations should include blood pressure and a Pap test (for detection of cervical cancer).

Do OC's cause cancer? After 10 years of increasingly widespread usage, there is no conclusive evidence that OC's are carcinogenic. Nor is there evidence that they cause diabetes, sterility, eye disorders, mental illness or any of a number of other diseases to which they have been linked by critics. However, the latency period for cancer is thought to range from 10 to 20 years. Therefore it seems probable that if OC's do cause cancer, this will become evident during the 1970's.

"If the Pill had to be absolutely safe, it would be off the market tomorrow," said Dr. Louis M. Hellman, chairman of the Department of Obstetrics and Gynecology at the State University of New York's Downstate Medical Center. "Safety must be weighed in accordance with the benefits derived."

The major benefit, of course, is the prevention of unwanted pregnancies. OC's are the most effective method of con-

traception currently available (other than continence and sterilization). An estimated 8.5 million women in the United States use the Pill. A survey of gynecologists and obstetricians showed that OC's were the contraceptive method most frequently requested by patients. Family-planning organizations report similar findings. There is no doubt that the Pill has had an important impact on American fertility patterns — and that it will continue to have this effect until (a) something safer or more convenient is marketed, or (b) it is proved to be harmful to a large percentage of users.

Numerous studies on the Pill are currently being conducted. Dr. James H. Nelson, Jr., at Downstate Medical Center will try to determine if OC's make women more susceptible to cancer of the cervix. "The main point when you get through matching the cancer patients and their controls is to find out whether the number of Pill users in the cancer group is out of proportion to the number in the control group where there is no cancer," explained Dr. Nelson.

At the University of Pennsylvania, researchers are studying the behavioral effects of the Pill. "There's been no good research on the subject," said project director Dr. Harold I. Lief, "but most people in my field have the impression that the Pill hasn't changed sex behavior."

In developing countries that have instituted birth-control programs, the Pill, if made available to women, appears to be as popular as in the United States. Studies of continuation rates (length of time a woman uses the Pill), national birthrates, and medical and social problems are being carried out in each of these nations.

Perhaps the major problem facing our world is the population explosion. During this decade, mankind will have to decide how this problem will be solved — and what part contraceptive pills will play in the solution.

Because oral contraceptives may cause harmful side effects, it is important that a woman use these pills only under the continued supervision of her doctor.

MAN AND
HIS WORLD

CONTENTS

"The true test of civilization is, not the census, nor the size of cities, nor the crops, — no, but the kind of man the country turns out."

Ralph W. Emerson

Tom McCarthy

REVIEW OF THE YEAR— MAN AND HIS WORLD

Throughout most of his history on earth, man maintained a close relationship with his natural surroundings. The land and waters were an integral part of his world: their plants and animals provided for his needs; he was well aware that changes in this environment closely affected him. But as he moved into cities, man gave up this close association: his appreciation of the natural world diminished or was forgotten. Now, increasingly, he lives in a world of artifacts, surrounded not by the beauty and serenity of quiet hills and trout-filled streams but by millions of fellow human beings.

Privacy. As technology pervades more and more of our lives, alarmed individuals fear that our rights to liberty and privacy will vanish. One target of criticism is the proposed central data bank in Washington, D.C., which is to contain important facts on all residents and citizens of the United States. Birth, residential, educational, vocational, familial, and related information would be stored in computers, which would release any or all of the data to government officials should the need arise. Although the Federal Government claims that the information would be strictly confidential, opponents of the plan feel that this might not be the case. According to the critics, facts about individual citizens can always be "leaked," secretly or even openly, to persons and organizations with ulterior motives. The critics also point to the fact that data on a person's financial status, occupation and activities from any number of sources have always been made available to interested parties who have had the money to pay for them. Proponents of the data bank claim that these critics are confusing anonymity with freedom and privacy. To study the question, the National Academy of Sciences is sponsoring a 23-man investigating group, consisting of scientists, government officials, businessmen, lawyers and professors. The investigation is under the direction of Dr. Alan F. Westin, professor of public law and government at Columbia; the study will continue until late 1971.

Population. The world's inhabitants continue to increase at an alarming rate. At its current annual growth rate, the world will gain 72.6 million people in 1970. In a few decades, China and India may each have a billion (1,000,000,000) citizens; world population may double from the present 3.6 billion to 7.2 billion by the year 2000. This increase is hampering attempts to improve living standards in underdeveloped countries. But the problem is becoming serious even in the United States. Wayne H. Davis, professor of biological sciences at the University of Kentucky, has written: "If our numbers continue to rise, our standard of living will fall so sharply that by the year 2000 any surviving Americans may consider today's average Asian to be well-off."

Programs to "stabilize" world population—that is, to maintain growth at a reasonable rate (1.5 per cent or less annually) or even to keep it stationary— have not been highly successful. Birth control is resisted by many people, who consider it an infringement of their religious and political rights. But the problems of overpopulation are being appreciated, and attacked, by an increasing number of governmental and private groups. In October 1969, representatives of conservation organizations met in New York City with leading proponents of birth control. The attitudes of many experts in these disciplines were well expressed by Dr. Hudson Hoagland of the Worcester Foundation for Experimental Biology: "So serious is the question of pollution of land, air and water, the consumption of irreplaceable metals, fuel and natural resources that competent scientists believe the world cannot indefinitely support the 3.6 billion people we have on earth today, let alone the horrendous numbers anticipated in the relatively near future."

Food is a major problem. Writes Dr. Georg A. Borgstrom, professor of food science and geography at Michigan State University, "If all food in the world [today] were equally distributed, and each human received identical quantities, we would *all* be malnourished. If the entire world's food supply were parceled out at the U.S. dietary level, it would feed only about one third of the human race. The world as a global household knows no surpluses, merely enormous deficits." In spite of the fact that the world is unable to feed satisfactorily 3.5 billion today, many scientists confidently talk about feeding twice or three times as many people in the coming century. As a result, there is increasing conflict between those scientists who are predicting sufficient food in the decades to come and those who feel that widespread famine will soon be commonplace.

The consequences of research. The responsibilities of scientists to the rest of society have been subject to increasing debate. Students have been especially critical of some of the actions and attitudes of researchers. In February 1970 it was announced that 25 leading scientists had formed the Council for Biology in Human Affairs. This organization, headed by Dr. Jacob Bronowski of the Salk Institute, will try to make scientists more aware of the social and political consequences of their work. That scientists can influence public opinion is obvious: society's current awareness of environmental problems is a prime example. But, as Philip H. Abelson, editor of *Science,* has written: "The goal of opinion-making should be constructive action. . . . Scientists can make imaginative contributions to planning, and they can help ensure that the factual bases for decisions are as sound as possible."

The academic community in the United States has, since during World War II, cooperated with the government in arms research. This "militarization of science" has sparked numerous protests in the past two years. As a result, a number of universities have stopped or are phasing out defense-oriented research. One area that had been particularly abhorrent to critics was research on biological-warfare agents. In November 1969, President Nixon pledged that "the United States shall renounce the use of lethal biological agents and weapons, and all other methods of biological warfare." In addition, he said that the nation renounced first use of both lethal and incapacitating chemicals.

Federal funding of research has declined in recent years, and, judging from President Nixon's budget proposals for 1971, the trend will continue. NASA is incurring major cutbacks, forcing a phasing down of the Apollo program and closing of its electronic-research facility in Cambridge, Massachusetts. In addition, NASA announced in January 1970 that it will cut 50,000 jobs from its programs by mid-1971. Medical researchers are also feeling the financial squeeze. Nineteen of the 93 clinical-research centers associated with major universities are scheduled for closing due to Federal cuts. National Institutes of Health (NIH) training grants for doctoral candidates in the biomedical sciences decreased from 6,200 in 1969 to 5,500 in 1970. No one is immune: the 3 winners of the 1969 Nobel Prize for Physiology or Medicine had their NIH grants cut by 4 to 15 per cent. Complaints are loud and numerous. Said Dr. Carl Leventhal of the American Society for Clinical Investigation: "We could have the Dark Ages of medical science. We're not there yet — but the potential is there."

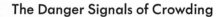

CAN WE SURVIVE THE MADDING CROWD?*

The Danger Signals of Crowding

BY BERNARD ASBELL

ONE of the engaging superstitions of our time, a three-part myth, is that overpopulation is just around the corner, that a shortage of food will do us in by the millions, and that only mass reduction of births (especially among the proliferating poor) will prevent disaster.

This is not an essay to encourage complacency about our rapidly growing population. The dangers facing us are real, perhaps more imminent than most of us think. But to deal with them properly, we need to catch up on some newly emerging scientific research that contradicts widely-held assumptions.

First of all, while there must be some level of population that would constitute *over*population of our finite-size planet, none of us has any idea what this level is. What will threaten us in advance of overpopulation is *crowding*, a wholly different idea. We are starting to learn something about crowding, thanks to a handful of scholars who are pooling an unlikely mixture of insights ranging from anthropology to biochemistry. One thing they are finding is that under some circumstances millions, perhaps scores of millions may live in densely packed harmony (say, in stacked dwellings of well-designed apart-

* Reprinted by permission from *Think* Magazine, published by IBM, Copyright 1969 by International Business Machines Corporation.

ment houses in a Boston-to-Washington megalopolis). But under other circumstances the old saw, "two's company but three's a crowd," may be a sound scientific warning.

Second, food supply is, at best, only indirectly linked with our possible doom. If we were to die of crowding by the millions, that would happen long before the food supply ran out. We would die not of hunger, but of shock, lowered resistance, rampaging disease, nervous breakdowns and, possibly, mass mayhem and widespread murder. Of the last, we are already

Ira Mandelbaum, Scope Associates

witnessing early-warning signals in our cities — collections of humanity that are not overpopulated but, in certain neighborhoods, dangerously crowded.

Finally, campaigns for birth control may do little to lessen the oppression of crowding, at least in the short run. In fact, there is evidence that a runaway birthrate among the poor is not so much a cause of crowding as a result of it.

Crowding is a specific happening, clinically observable and definable. In simplified terms, crowding occurs when organisms are brought together in such manner and numbers as to produce *physical* reactions of stress. Important among these reactions is stepped-up activity of the adrenal glands. When these reactions to stress are widespread and sustained, they are followed by physical weakening, sometimes rage and violence or extreme passivity, a rise in sexual aberrations, and a breakdown of orderly group behavior. What may follow is a tidal wave of deaths, ending when the population is no longer crowded.

These things have happened time and again, in various combinations, to all kinds of animals, from lemmings in Scandinavia to deer trapped on an island in Maryland. Ethologists — those who study group behavior of animals — have been cautious about projecting their findings on man. But Dr. Edward T. Hall, prominent Northwestern University anthropologist, and some colleagues in psychiatry are stitching together evidence that the animal in man may be governed by somewhat the same system of stress reactions. Hall discusses this in *The Hidden Dimension*, his definitive book on the subject of crowding.

"If man does pay attention to animal studies," says Hall, "he can detect the gradually emerging outlines of an endocrine servomechanism not unlike the thermostat in his house. The only difference is that instead of regulating heat the endocrine control system regulates the population."

Crowding, an everyday occurrence in New York subways, often produces physical and emotional reactions of stress.

242

UPI

John J. Christian, an ethologist also trained in medical pathology, was a pioneer in discovering that population buildup, leading to stress, brings on an endocrine reaction and finally population collapse — which he calls a "die-off."

What killed the sika deer?

About a mile out in Chesapeake Bay lies a small patch of land, half a square mile, called James Island. It is uninhabited, or at least was until 1916 when someone adorned the island by releasing 4 or 5 sika deer. The deer were fruitful and multiplied until by 1955 they had procreated a herd of almost 300 — about 1 per acre, extremely dense for deer.

In that year, Christian visited the island, bringing a hypothesis and a gun. He shot 5 animals and made detailed examinations of their adrenal glands, thyroid, heart, lungs, gonads and other tissues. Their organs appeared normal in every way except one. The adrenal glands were immensely oversized, bulging like overused muscles. When animals are under frequent or sustained stress, their adrenals

— which are important to regulation of growth, reproduction and defenses against disease — become overactive and enlarged. If this abnormality was related to crowdedness — and if the herd population was still growing — clearly James Island was in for an interesting time. Christian waited and watched.

For the next 2 years, herd size stayed about the same. Then in the third year, 1958, more than ½ the herd inexplicably dropped dead. The island was strewn with 190 carcasses in 2 years, chiefly females and young, leaving 80 survivors.

What had killed so many? It was not malnutrition, for food was abundant. The coats of the dead deer shone healthily; their muscles were well developed; plenty of body fat. For that matter, if the epidemic of whatever-it-was was so severe, how come 80 survived it — and now appeared robust?

After the die-off, Christian revisited the island in 1960, shot a few more animals and examined them. For one thing, they were substantially — more than 30 per cent — larger in body size than those shot at the

Ken Regan, Camera 5

Music festivals, such as those on England's Isle of Wight (previous page) and at Bethel, New York (above), drew hundreds of thousands of happy youth. But crowded supermarkets with their long waiting lines (below) are not so joyfully received.

climax of the crowding. But the more striking thing was that their adrenals were *half* the size of those examined earlier — back to normal. In young deer, they were ⅕ the size of their overstressed counterparts.

"Mortality evidently resulted," Christian later reported to a symposium on crowding, "from shock following severe metabolic disturbance, probably as a result of prolonged adrenocortical hyperactivity. . . . There was no evidence of infection, starvation or other obvious cause to explain the mass mortality." Subsequently, he says, it was found that the hyperactivity had in all probability resulted in potassium deficiency.

A landmark study it was, finding out how those deer died. But it doesn't tell us how they *lived*, what their behavior was like just before the agonies of emotional and physical stress killed them. A search for clues brings us to another study, which by chance was taking place at the same time in the same state.

Why the rats went berserk

In a stone barn at the outskirts of Rockville, Maryland, John B. Calhoun be-

UPI

244

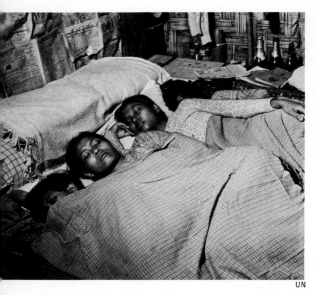

Part of a Burmese family, which shares one room. This kind of crowding helps increase Burma's high rate of tuberculosis.

gan breeding populations of Norway rats, a deliberate creation of crowding. In each of several rooms, Calhoun set up 4 pens, connecting them in a row by ramps arching over their separating walls. In the wild, these animals normally organize in sexually balanced groups of about 12. The penned rats soon multiplied to an adult population of 80, almost twice the comfortable number of 12 to a pen.

Rats are busybodies, and so got in the habit — at least at first — of scurrying over the ramps from pen to pen. Also they were conditioned to eat in the presence of others, cheek to cheek. So the 2 central pens, where they were most likely to find companions, became popular "eating clubs." Calhoun at times observed as many as 60 eaters crowding into a single inner pen.

This crowding soon led to what Calhoun calls a "behavioral sink." (A striking term. Webster's *New World Dictionary* defines the noun *sink* as: 1. a cesspool or sewer; 2. any place or thing considered morally filthy or corrupted.)

A single dominant male took charge of each of the less-populated end pens, preventing the entrance of other males, but freely permitting the comings and goings of his females. *His* females. The lord

rat of each end pen established a harem of a half dozen or more females.

Because of these end-pen harems, females were distributed among the 4 pens fairly evenly. Males, however, were overwhelmingly crowded into the middle pens. And their natural manners, under the stress of crowding and shortage of ladies, gave way to havoc. The more dominant males took to violence. They would suddenly go berserk, attacking females, juveniles and passive males, by biting their tails, sometimes severing them entirely. The floor was almost always bloody from these carryings-on, which Calhoun had never before seen among the species. Then there emerged a group of males that made sexual advances on unreceptive females, often those not in heat, and later on other males, and finally juveniles. Their ability to perceive appropriate sex partners seemed to have vanished.

Two other types of male emerged, almost opposite in levels of activity. "The first," Calhoun reports, "were completely passive and moved through the community like somnambulists. They ignored all the other rats of both sexes, and all the other rats ignored them. . . . To the casual observer the passive animals would have appeared to be the healthiest and most attractive members of the community. . . . But their social disorientation was nearly complete."

Perhaps the strangest type was what Calhoun called the "probers," who moved in packs of 3 or 4. They would confound a female by courting her as a group, harass lactating females and upset nests of pups.

End of motherhood

Under these strains, motherhood in the crowded pens began going to pieces. Mothers grew sloppy about nest building, often losing interest and leaving it incomplete. Litters got all mixed up, so no mother seemed to know whose babies were whose — nor seemed to care. Frequently, abandoned young were cannibalized by groups of male probers.

Of 558 born at the worst of the sink, only 1 in 4 survived weaning. Miscarriages were common. Autopsies of females revealed tumors of the uterus, ovaries, fallopian tubes and mammary glands. And, hardly surprising, adrenals were conspicuously enlarged. As on James Island, the stress took its greatest death toll on the young and the female, contributing heavily to halting the population growth.

There is reason to believe that the behavioral sink could have been prevented without increasing available space: if Calhoun had divided the same space into a greater number of smaller pens and closed them off from one another. Thus a small group of rats, say the instinctive group of about 12, although pressed for space, would have its own inviolate territory. An English ethologist, H. Shoemaker, tried this with canaries. First he placed a large number in a single large cage. A

Dangerously-crowded urban areas can lead to rampaging disease, nervous breakdowns and widespread aggression.

The New York Times

hierarchy developed in which the dominant birds interfered with the nesting of low-ranking families. Then he transferred them to small cages so that each adult male, including the low-ranking, was master over his family's territory. Brooding then proceeded more normally.

The canary experiment, simple as it is, may have vast significance in considering the development of — and prevention of — behavioral sinks in cities of human beings. Edward Hall, who as an anthropologist is chiefly concerned with human behavior, emphasizes the critical importance of architecture in avoiding the stress of urban crowding. He also emphasizes that architectural needs vary greatly from culture to culture: that one man's company may be another man's crowd. And the alarming thing is that, while some human populations are already showing clear signs of crowding stress, we are doing next to nothing about learning to design territories — proper homes and neighborhoods — to prevent behavioral sinks among the crowded poor.

One of the few studies linking human dwelling space with stress was made by a French couple, Paul and Marie Chombart de Lauwe, among working-class families of France. First they tried to correlate behavior with the number of residents per dwelling unit. This revealed little. Then they got the idea of considering the number of *square meters per person* in the home, regardless of the number who lived in it. They found that when each person had less than 8 to 10 square meters, instances of physical illness and criminal behavior were double those in less crowded homes. Thus human crowding was clearly linked with illness and violence.

Space and violence were linked in a different kind of study recently completed by a Columbia University psychiatrist, Augustus F. Kinzel. Small both in size and subject scope, the study was limited to 14 men in a Federal prison. Eight had histories of violent behavior; 6 were considered nonviolent. Standing his subject in the center of a bare room, Dr. Kinzel would say, "I'm going to step toward you.

Tell me to stop when you feel I'm too close." He would try this from several directions. It turned out that all the men seemed encircled by an invisible "buffer zone" which, when intruded upon, made them feel intensely uncomfortable. The violent men felt "crowded" at an average distance of 3 feet, the nonviolent at ½ that distance. Perhaps the most important finding of the study was that the violent men were more sensitive to approach from the rear. Their reactions were often clearly physical. Some reported tingling or "goose pimples" across their shoulders and backs. Some stepped away with clenched fists as Kinzel entered the buffer zone, even though he was hardly within touching distance. They accused Kinzel of "rushing" them. One commented, "If I didn't know you, I might be ready for anything."

Just as the violent and nonviolent prisoners felt crowded at different distances, the reactions of French workers establish no rule to measure what constitutes crowding in other ethnic groups, even other classes. Crowding differs from people to people, class to class. Hall describes customs of various national groups — particularly the Japanese, Germans and Arabs — to show the great variations in their sense of proper space between persons.

Most Japanese, for example, are happiest when family and friends are huddled together in the center of a room, or all making body contact under a huge quilt before a fireplace. They feel it is congenial for whole families to sleep close together on the floor. Their dwelling spaces are small but as variegated in purpose as the many rooms of a large American house. The Japanese change the size, moods and uses of their rooms by rearranging screens and sliding their doors open and shut. Their concepts of "togetherness" and "aloneness" are so different from ours that the Japanese language contains no word that translates into our word "privacy." Yet a Japanese has strong feelings against two houses having a common wall. If his house is not separated from his

neighbor's by a strip of land, no matter how narrow, he feels crowded. It is an important sign of his territorial integrity. When strangers are out of sight, Japanese are entirely untroubled by their sounds. In a Japanese inn, where a Westerner would toss and turn angrily at the sounds of a party in the adjoining room, a Japanese would sleep unmindful of it.

In contrast, Germans are especially sensitive to intrusion by sounds of strangers, one reason their hotels often have double doors and thick walls. A German has a strong sense of his own space — *Lebensraum*, another word not readily translatable — and is disturbed if that space is not respected. In an office, he keeps his door closed. American visitors often misread this trait as something unfriendly. On the other hand, Germans regard the American habit of leaving doors open as unbusinesslike. Hall tells of an American camp for German prisoners of war in which men were bunked four to a small hut. The men went to great lengths to find materials for building partitions to separate themselves. German families, too, require clear definitions of territory. During the postwar housing shortage, American occupiers blithely ordered Berliners to share kitchens and baths, having no idea of the extreme stress — and violence — their order invited. New arrangements had to be made, Hall reports, "when the already overstressed Germans started killing each other over the shared facilities."

Arabs are happiest amid crowds of people, a high noise level of conversation. They require great human involvement, closeness. Conversing, they look at each other piercingly, with much touching of hand to hand, hand to body. In his home, however, an Arab prefers spaciousness — large, high rooms with a commanding view — or he feels crowded. For all his love of involvement, the Arab needs privacy too. The way he gets it is by falling silent, retreating into himself. To talk to an Arab who appears conversationally withdrawn is to exercise bad manners in the extreme — an act of aggression certain to induce stress.

MAN AND HIS POLLUTED WORLD

Man, in his pursuit of ease and affluence, is covering the land with garbage, poisoning the oceans with pesticides and sewage, darkening the precious atmosphere with fumes from smokestacks and car exhausts.

Clayton J. Price

A throw-it-away society. Each year Americans discard 7 million automobiles, 26 million bottles, 20 million tons of paper and 48,000,000,000 metal cans. Meanwhile the resources from which such products are made become ever fewer.

All photos Steve Myers unless otherwise indicated

Noise is doubling in intensity every ten years. "It might be a good thing if people's ears would bleed," commented an environmental psychologist, "then people might get aroused."

"O beautiful for spacious skies. . . ." Millions of miles of wires are needed to distribute the massive amount of electricity used in the United States. In 1969 the nation's electric utilities produced 1.443 trillion kilowatt-hours (kwh) of electricity; the use of electricity in an average home rose to 6,550 kwh.

Undisciplined industries dump their wastes into rivers and lakes, making these bodies unsuitable as a habitat for aquatic life, as sources of drinking water or as recreational areas.

Advertisements, plastered on billboards and peeling from fences, proliferate along urban avenues and rural highways. Detroit city planner Gunther Weidle remarks: "Until citizens ask for stronger legislation, you have to say this is the will of the people."

Pollution is esthetically displeasing and psychologically demoralizing. But even more ominous, it is fatal . . . to plants, animals—and man. Air pollution is suspected of causing emphysema; DDT may be linked to cancer; sewage-filled water carries hepatitis and typhoid germs. Man, and only man, is responsible. As the cartoon-strip character Pogo once said: "We have met the enemy and they are us."

These examples provide the sketchiest of hints of how complex, delicate and explosive the matter of human crowding can be. Little is formally known about the elements of crowding that are at work in the impoverished ghettos of American cities — except that they *are* at work, rapidly creating behavioral sinks.

"It is fairly obvious," says Hall, "that American Negroes and people of Spanish culture who are flocking to our cities are being very severely stressed. Not only are they in a setting that does not fit them, but they have passed the limits of their tolerance to stress. The United States is faced with the fact that two of its creative and sensitive peoples are . . . being destroyed and like Samson could bring down the structure that houses us all."

Factories of stress

When the stress of newly urbanized Negroes is discussed, the solutions proposed are almost always limited to ending discrimination, improving education, providing jobs — and housing that is seldom described beyond being low-cost. Without these social improvements, clearly stress will not be eliminated. But Hall's thesis is that these alone cannot halt the growth of behavioral sinks. Space — and the architecture of that space — must be designed for the specific cultural needs of these urban newcomers. A great deal is now known about how *not* to design this space, but little about ways it should be designed.

For example, high-rise apartments, no matter how low-cost, for people recently of an agrarian tradition, are factories of stress. "It's no place to raise a family," a typical tenant complains. "A mother can't look out for her kids if they are 15 floors down on a playground. When I want to go up or down, I think twice because it may take me half an hour to get the elevator."

For a starting point in planning proper spaces for urban newcomers, Hall urges planners to consider that "Puerto Ricans and Negroes have a much higher involvement ratio than New Englanders and Americans of German or Scandinavian stock." As an example of architecture for "involvement," Hall recommends a look at the Spanish plaza and the Italian piazza, "whereas the strung-out Main Street so characteristic of the United States reflects . . . our lack of involvement in others."

One enterprising planner, Neal B. Mitchell, a professor of design at Harvard, has worked out a novel way of finding out what impoverished Negroes want in their housing. He consults with impoverished Negroes. Mitchell bought $80 worth of doll houses and furniture and invited poor people to arrange it according to their preferences. He found — contradicting the assumptions of almost all low-cost-housing architects — that nobody wanted a dining room. They wanted a kitchen large enough to eat in. They also complained that public-housing apartments they lived in were much too small. Yet, Mitchell reports, "every single person who played with our game wound up with a smaller square footage than the one they thought insufficient. It was just a question of design."

Next, Mitchell brought out blocks marked "house," "school," "church," "store" and so forth, and let people arrange their communities. Most people in the ghetto, he found, reject the suburban single-family house. One welfare mother told him, "That green front yard is useless. I want to sit out on my front steps and see all those neighbors. I want to be close enough to holler at them."

"I think we are going to pull through . . ."

Thus that welfare mother confirms Hall's suggestion of "architecture for involvement."

Mitchell is hopeful: "I think we are going to pull through because, you know, there is one thing about this country: it is flexible and it is willing to learn."

If Edward Hall and his "crowding" colleagues are more apprehensive, it is because they fear that our willingness to learn may lose in a race against the onrushing development of the urban sink.

Insecticides are helpful in raising crop yields. Here, a new compound is tested on sorghum in India.

THE WORLD FOOD SUPPLY

Will Man Have Enough to Eat?

BY ROGER REVELLE

LONG before recorded history, early man obtained his food by hunting wild game animals, fishing, and collecting the edible seeds, berries, nuts and roots of wild plants. Among the many types of animals hunted for their meat were the boar, elk, hippopotamus, reindeer, seal and sheep. The plant matter eaten by early man included acorns, barley grains, pine nuts, wheat grains and yams.

Just when early man began raising his own crops is not known, but he is believed to have started about 10,000 years ago. As man was cultivating food crops, he was also domesticating animals as a source of food. Sheep and goats were probably domesticated as early as 9200

B.C., providing man with a source of meat when game animals were scarce. Cattle, which were domesticated by around 4000 B.C., were valued as a source of meat and milk and were also used as work animals. By 3000 B.C., man had domesticated a number of other animals and was cultivating a variety of crops, including barley, beans, carrots, lettuce, onions and wheat.

Over the centuries many agricultural tools and techniques were devised and improved. Irrigation and selective breeding were only two of the many innovations that enabled man to increase both the quantity and quality of his food supply. Today, thousands of varieties of plants and animals are raised for food, and the food industry employs millions of people, from farmers and fishermen to food processors, manufacturers and suppliers.

Only a century and a half ago poverty and misery were the common lot of most of mankind. Some people were hungry all the time, and most people were hungry some of the time. Between A.D. 10 and 1846, for example, 201 famines were recorded in the British Isles, an average of one every nine years. In the late 1700's the English political economist Thomas Malthus thought about England and Europe as well as Asia when he wrote, "The power of population is so superior to the power in the earth to produce subsistence for man that premature death must in some shape or other visit the human race. . . . Sickly seasons, epidemics, pestilence and plague advance in terrific array and sweep off their thousands and ten thousands. Should success be still incomplete, gigantic inevitable famine stalks in the rear, and with one mighty blow, levels the population with the food of the world."

In the last few decades hunger has ceased to be a major threat to the peoples of Europe, North America, the Soviet Union, Japan and Oceania, but it is still a fearful enemy for the rest of mankind. Although the technological revolution has improved the levels of living in the rich countries, its principal effect in the poor nations has been to multiply misery by causing an unprecedented rise in population growth rates. In the poor countries population growth and the lag in social and economic development are interrelated — each worsens the other. They have created the specter that these nations will not be able to feed their peoples. This specter will be exorcized for coming generations only if population growth is drastically slowed and if there is an unprecedented increase in the world's food supply by the end of the 20th century.

Factors underlying the food problem

Of the 3.3 billion (3,300,000,000) human beings on earth in 1965, slightly more than 1 billion, or 31 per cent, were citizens of the developed countries and nearly 2.3 billion, or 69 per cent, lived in the poor countries of Asia, South America and Africa. On the average each person needed the energy and protein equivalent of 570 pounds of wheat and rice a year to meet his minimum physiological requirements. It is most likely that by the year 2000 the total world population will be over 6.7 billion people, slightly more than

twice what it was in 1965. About 5.3 billion people, close to 80 per cent of the total, will live in the presently less-developed countries. The minimum world food requirement will have increased from 935 million to 1,936 million tons of cereal equivalents.

In 1965 the total world cereal production was estimated at 968 million tons, slightly more than the required cereal equivalent for the world population. Because cereals comprise only about two thirds of the food eaten by humans, the average human diet safely exceeded the physiological requirements. However, the food supplies were very unevenly distributed. Cereals are the predominant food grown in most of the poor countries, but these nations produced only 40 per cent of the world cereal supply while the developed countries produced 60 per cent of all the cereals. Also, the per capita cereal production in the poor countries averaged less than 0.2 tons a year, equivalent to 1,860 food calories per day, whereas in the developed countries, each person's share was more than 0.5 tons, equivalent to about 5,000 calories per day. Because of their low per capita production, almost all the cereals harvested in the poor countries, beyond the amounts required for seed or lost to pests, must be used directly for human food. In the developed nations less than half the cereals produced are eaten by man; most of the remainder is fed to animals and consumed indirectly by man in the form of milk, meat and eggs.

During the period 1934–1961, the total cereal production in the poor nations increased by 42 per cent, but the per capita cereal production declined by nearly 3 per cent. The underdeveloped countries gradually changed from net exporters of 13.2 million tons of cereals a year to net importers of over 19.8 million tons.

Less than half of the annual increase in cereal production in the poor countries resulted from raising yields. More than half of the increase resulted from additions to the cultivated area. This was accomplished in three ways: increasing the proportion of the total sown area planted

250

with cereals at the expense of other crops and animal products; increasing the proportion of land planted with two or more cereal crops each year; and bringing new land under cultivation, usually at the level of subsistence agriculture. In contrast, the increase in cereal production in the developed countries since World War II was brought about almost entirely by raising crop yields. In many of the developed countries the area devoted to cereals was actually reduced.

Future food needs

Basing their views on such factors as the long-term downward trend of per capita food production, the low rates of increase in crop yields and the accelerating rates of population increase in the poor countries, some writers have predicted a food crisis in these countries during the 1970's and 1980's. Near-famine conditions in northeastern India in the drought years of 1965–1966 and 1966–1967 have been used to give credence to this view. However, there is good reason to believe that such a food crisis is by no means inevitable and that if effective measures are taken, it will not occur as a widespread phenomenon.

On the average the populations of most of the underdeveloped nations now obtain sufficient calories and protein supplies to meet their physiological needs. For example, average food supplies in India at the household level are equivalent to about 2,100 calories and 1.83 ounces of protein per person per day. While this seems small in comparison with the United States per capita daily consumption of 3,000 calories and 3.17 ounces of protein, it must be remembered that Indian men and women weigh about 40 per cent less than American adults, and their nutritional requirements are correspondingly smaller. Moreover, the proportion of children under 15 years is about 42 per cent in India, as compared to about 30 per cent in the United States, and the physiological food requirements for children are only three fourths those of adults. Taking these factors into account, the Panel

on the World Food Supply of the president's Science Advisory Committee (1967) has computed that the present per capita requirement for food calories in India is about 1,900 calories per day and the protein requirement for the types of protein available in the usual Indian diet is 1.70 ounces per day.

While present food supplies are thus sufficient on the average to meet the physiological requirements of persons carrying out normal physical activities, there are serious problems of food distribution. In the developed countries most people at all income levels obtain enough food to satisfy their needs for calories, proteins and other nutrients. In the less-developed countries, however, the poorest people are unable to obtain enough food to provide their needs for energy, let alone for proteins and other essential nutrients. These people are forced to compensate for this deficiency by living at a relatively low level of physical activity. Probably at least 20 per cent of the people of India obtain less than 80 per cent of their physiological requirements for calories and less than 90 per cent of their needed proteins. Data from Chile and northern Brazil show that the diets of the poorest classes of people in these areas are also far below their requirements for calories and protein. In all the poor countries many pregnant and breast-feeding women and many young children, after they have been weaned from their mother's breast, lack sufficient high-quality protein, that is, protein with a balance of amino acids similar to that of eggs or milk.

During the 1970's and 1980's food supplies in the less-developed countries should be increased by about 4 per cent a year even though the mean rate of population increase will probably be less than 3 per cent a year. There are four reasons why the rate of increase of food supplies should be greater than the rate of population increase. First, if the poorest classes are to obtain enough food, the per capita supply for the entire population must be raised above the level of minimum physiological requirements. This does not necessarily mean that persons of average income will obtain too much food in terms of total quantities of calories and proteins, but rather that the quality of the average diet must improve above the present subsistence levels.

Second, if children obtain a better diet, they will grow more rapidly and attain a larger adult size, increasing their food needs. Experience in the United States, Europe and Japan indicates that with improved diets, the rate of increase of adult body weight is about 6 per cent per decade. Third, if family planning programs are even partially effective, the proportion of children in the poor countries will diminish, and hence the average per capita physiological food requirements will rise.

Lastly, food production in a major part of the underdeveloped world cannot be increased much above present levels without overall economic development and a consequent rise in per capita income. As incomes rise, the demand for food will increase. Since 60 per cent to 70 per cent of income goes for food in the poor countries, a 2.5 per cent rate of increase in per capita income means a rate of increase in per capita food demand of about 1.6 per cent a year if food prices remain constant.

Increasing food supplies

Several ways of increasing future food supplies have been suggested: reducing crop and food losses from diseases and pests; increasing the harvest of food from the sea; increasing the industrial production of foods; greatly enlarging food aid from the developed countries to the poor ones; expanding subsistence agriculture on presently uncultivated land; and raising the crop yields per acre in areas that are now cultivated. Although the first five methods would be helpful, only the last one offers a satisfactory solution.

Reducing crop and food losses. The total world loss of stored cereals, for which rats are largely responsible, has been estimated at 36.3 million tons a year, less than 4 per cent of the total cereal production. The estimated crop losses to insects, diseases and weeds are much larger. Even in the United States, where preventive measures are widely used, the losses may be 15 per cent to 30 per cent of the total crop. Losses in the less-developed countries are

Thai farmers are counseled by an Indian agronomist of the Food and Agriculture Organization (FAO). Thailand has implemented a program of diversified agriculture in the former rice regions of the Central Plain.

FAO–Bunnag

Freshwater fish-farming has developed into a multimillion-dollar industry in the United States. Here, catfish are being harvested at a Louisiana fish farm.

USDA: SCS

unknown, but they may be larger than in the United States. Though substantial savings are possible by controlling diseases and pests, in many cases it may be as hard to save a bushel of wheat or rice from pests as to grow another bushel.

Increasing the harvest from the sea. The world's harvest from the sea increased about 6 per cent from about 1950 to the mid-1960's. In 1968, 60.5 million tons were harvested. Many marine biologists believe that the catch of marine fishes and invertebrates could be increased to 220 million tons before the year 2000. However, if this predicted catch materialized, and all of it were used for human food, it would provide less than 7 per cent of the food energy requirements of the expected population and about a third of the needed protein. The quality of fish protein is high, however, and the hoped-for harvest could be of great value in human nutrition.

Industrial production of foods. Some engineers and scientists have suggested that over the long term, the problems of revolutionizing agriculture in the less-developed countries could be avoided by the industrial production of foods. There are real possibilities for using bacteria and yeasts to produce supplementary protein foods from simple nitrogen compounds, with inedible plant materials or petroleum serving as sources of energy, hydrogen, and carbon.

Aid to poor countries. The present major food-exporting countries, notably the United States, Australia and Canada, might greatly increase their total agricultural production and sell or give their surplus to the underdeveloped countries. Aside from the obvious political and economic difficulties, such action on the part of the developed countries could at best be only a palliative or supplementary measure.

By increasing the acreage of land under cultivation to the maximum extent, food energy production in the United States could be raised 80 per cent by 1985 and nearly tripled by 2000. However, because of the growth of the American population and increased requirements for exports to western Europe and Japan, the fraction of this expanded production available for underdeveloped countries in 1985 would meet only about 10 per cent of their total requirements. Even if the rate of population growth in the underdeveloped countries markedly diminishes, the United States could provide less than 20 per cent of their total food requirements by the year 2000. Australia and Canada together could provide an additional 5 to 10 per cent.

Expanding cultivated land. At the present time about 3.4 billion acres of the earth's land area are under cultivation, but 7.9 billion acres are arable; that is, capable of being cultivated. Without irrigation, three crops could be grown each year on 1.2 billion acres in the humid tropics, and two crops could be raised on 0.4 billion acres in subhumid regions.

One crop could be grown without irrigation on 5.3 billion acres. Thus, without irrigation the potential gross cropped area (the cultivated area times the number of crops) is 9.7 billion acres. With irrigation, the gross cropped area could be as much as 16.3 billion acres. Irrigation is necessary to grow one crop on 0.85 billion potentially arable acres.

With appropriate technology and sufficient finances the potentially arable land area of the earth could produce sufficient food for a human population several times larger than that expected by the end of the 20th century. However, there are several grave obstacles to an expansion of the area of cultivated land. Much of the potentially arable land is of poor quality for use with present technological methods, and in other areas there is insufficient water. Even where the quality of the soil is adequate and water is easily available, a large capital investment, in the order of $500 to $1,000 per acre, would be needed for any major extension of cultivated area.

Most of the world's potentially arable but uncultivated land is in Africa and in South and North America, but most of the world's people live in Europe and Asia. In Africa, where only 22 per cent of the potentially arable land is now cultivated, and in South America, where 11 per cent of the potentially arable land is cultivated, much additional land could be brought under the plow at the level of subsistence agriculture; this could be a principal method by which the growing populations of these continents could obtain sufficient food during the next several decades.

In Asia nearly 85 per cent of the potentially arable land is already cultivated, and the remainder can be developed only through very large expenditures for large-scale irrigation projects. If the Asian people are to obtain sufficient food in the future, it will be necessary to increase their crop yields and, wherever possible, to grow 2 or 3 crops a year on each cultivated acre.

Increasing crop yields. Over the period from 1955 to 1970 crop yields rose at a rate of about 1.6 per cent a year, but recent developments in the field of plant genetics have completely changed the possibilities for the future. Largely through the work of the Rockefeller Foundation and the Ford Foundation new varieties of cereal crops, particularly wheat, rice and sorghum, have been developed. These new varieties are highly responsive to chemical fertilizers. Not only do they produce 2 to 3 times as much grain per pound of fertilizer as the previously used varieties, but they also give favorable results with very heavy fertilizer applications. Yields from the so-called "Mexican" wheat in Pakistan and northwestern India average more than 4,000 pounds per acre, in contrast to the average of about 0.66 tons per acre with the older varieties. The new rice has a short growing season and enables farmers to grow three crops a year on the same land if adequate water supplies are available.

Thus, in principle, about an 8-fold increase in crop production per acre per year can be obtained. Even if India's population were to increase to 1,200 million by the year 2000, 100 million acres under year-round irrigation (about half the potentially irrigable land and one third the presently cultivated land) could provide the dietary equivalent of 4,000 to 5,000 calories per person, more than twice the present per capita calorie supplies. There may even be a time in the not-distant future when India and Pakistan become major exporters of many staple crops.

The new wheat and rice varieties have already made a profound impact on Indian and Pakistani agriculture. During the crop year of 1967–1968, India's harvest of food grains was 110 million tons, 40 per cent higher than that of 1966–1967 and 13.2 million tons higher than it had ever been before. While most of this remarkable harvest must be credited to greatly improved weather conditions, at least 11 million tons resulted from the use of the new wheat and rice, which were planted over millions of acres.

Related factors

Economic requirements. If the potentialities of the new crop varieties are to be realized, major capital investments will be necessary for irrigation and drainage works, fertilizer plants, seed farms, pesticide factories, production facilities for farm tools, farm machinery and trucks, roads, warehouses, and marketing and food processing facilities. For India alone, the required capital investment for the years 1970–1990 is estimated at $30 billion dollars. For the underdeveloped world as a whole, close to $100 billion will be required. In the long run, there must be either considerable growth in incomes outside the agricultural sector — in other words, overall economic development — or an increase in export markets. Only the first alternative seems meaningful because markets for sugar, coffee, tea, rubber, jute and other agricultural exports from the poor countries to the rich ones are already nearly saturated and the rich countries will probably continue to be more than self-sufficient in cereal grains and other staple crops. Even if some poor countries could attain a comparative advantage in cereal production, the benefits would be doubtful because the resulting loss of agricultural export markets for the United States and other cereal exporters might seriously inhibit the flow of foreign aid for overall economic development.

The implications are clear. In order to grow enough food to feed even their own villages, the farmers must be able to sell a major share of their produce to customers in their own countries outside the agricultural sector. To gain incentives for sufficiently increasing their production they must be able to purchase consumer goods and services produced by these customers. The increase in crop yields, which is essential if the poor nations are to feed themselves, has now been made possible by the plant geneticists, but it can be accomplished only if there is overall economic development within these countries.

The capital investments required for overall economic development, including the foreign exchange component, are 5 to 10 times as high as the necessary investments for agricultural development. To attain the 5.5 per cent annual increase in national incomes needed to sustain a 4 per cent annual increase in the monetary value of food production, a capital flow of $10 billion to $12 billion per year is needed from the rich countries to the poor ones. This is nearly twice the present amount and, in the existing climate of foreign aid, may be impossible to accomplish.

Social consequences. The agricultural revolution that is being forced upon the poor countries by their population growth will probably result in a lowering of food prices, which will stimulate economic development; however, the social consequences could be highly disruptive. The larger, richer and more efficient farmers will gain an enormous advantage over the smaller and poorer ones who will be unable to benefit from the new technologies. Because irrigation agriculture must be intensive to be successful, much of the presently cultivated area may have to be abandoned. Many small farmers may be driven off the land, and others will become laborers. The flight to the cities of masses of illiterate, untrained, poverty-stricken people will be accelerated.

Pesticide dangers. The use of pesticides in future agricultural development may also present serious problems. Present pesticides are increasingly becoming recognized as dangerous poisons with unpredictable and possibly catastrophic long-term effects on human beings and other organisms. Although new pesticides have been developed, they have not yet been adequately tested and may prove unsatisfactory.

Research and education

Of all man's activities, farming is one of those most directly dependent on the environment. Much of the land area of the poor countries lies between the Tropic of Capricorn and the Tropic of Cancer. Consequently, the hours of sunlight and darkness are more nearly equal than in the developed countries of the temperate zone, where there are long summer days and short nights. Over large regions rainfall is heavy during most months, and the continuously wet soils are severely leached. Elsewhere, there is too little rain during part or all of the year. Only relatively small areas have a season of frost, and hence both crops and plant and animal pests, given enough water, can flourish throughout the year. In many poor countries the climate for months on end is debilitatingly hot. All of these environmental characteristics demand different agricultural technologies than those used in the countries of the temperate zone. To modernize agriculture in less-developed countries, new technologies must be developed through adaptive research. Even when these new technologies are developed, they must be taught to the farmers.

Research goals. Research in plant genetics and physiology is needed to produce new crop varieties that do not require long hours of sunlight, are resistant to native plant diseases and pests, are highly responsive to fertilizer, have a short growing season, and have high nutritional value. The crops include such staples as wheat, rice, maize (corn), sorghum, millets, potatoes, yams, peanuts and other oil seeds, and beans, soybeans, peas and other legumes. The development of new varieties must be a continuing process because the disease-causing bacteria and viruses and insect pests tend to become adapted to existing strains. One of the most important aims of plant geneticists is to raise the protein content and improve the balance of amino acids in new varieties of cereals and legumes.

Improved livestock varieties are also necessary. Here, the aim must not be only to obtain higher meat and milk production and produce disease-resistant varieties, but also to improve livestock nutrition without reducing the availability of edible plant products for human food.

Because of the scarcity of water throughout most of the year, research is needed on soil-water-plant relationships. Scientists must study how much water is required by different crops and at what time during their growth. They must also study how groundwater basins can be most effectively and speedily recharged and the water most profitably utilized. In addition, new methods of biological control must be developed as substitutes for chemical pesticides.

From a longer range point of view perhaps the greatest opportunity for expansion of tropical agriculture lies in the humid tropics. The potentially arable land in these areas, which are now largely covered by rain forests and underlain by highly leached soils, is equivalent to about 35 per cent of the world's presently cultivated land and the potential gross cropped area (acreage times the number of crops per year) is about equal to the present gross cropped area of the earth. Yet, except for the island of Java, and a few similar places with very deep, recently formed volcanic soils, and for certain tree crops in other areas, farmers in the humid tropics must still practice the ancient technique of "slash and burn" agriculture. A new technology for intensive food production may require the genetic development of food-producing trees that can retain and recycle fertilizers in a carpet of organic matter on top of the soil.

Attention must also be paid to human nutritional needs, methods of food preservation, storage and processing, fish culture, and food synthesis by industrial means. It is also important to learn about the acceptability of different foods by different peoples and thus find ways in which food habits can be changed.

The most obvious sources of high quality proteins — meat, milk, and fish — are scarce and expensive in the cities of the poorer nations, let alone in isolated villages. This is largely due to difficulties in preserving these foods. Much hope has been placed on such potential panaceas as fish protein concentrates, but much research and development remains to be done on the methods of processing and preservation. This is also true of producing protein extracts from soybeans, cottonseed, and other oil seeds. Better and cheaper methods of preserving, processing,

A.I.D.

Above: a Bolivian woman compares a small native potato with an improved variety now grown with assistance from the Alliance for Progress.

Below: a U.S. Department of Agriculture inspector examines scallions being harvested by Navajo Indians on an irrigated field near Phoenix, Arizona.

USDA

and storing fruits and vegetables are also needed, as are techniques for protecting stored cereals and legumes from destructive insects and other animal pests.

Education. At present, the developing nations lack the research and educational institutions and the trained personnel necessary for the sustained creation and application of agricultural technology. It has been estimated that in India, by 1985, the number of college graduates with B.S., M.S., or Ph.D. degrees in agriculture should be increased from the present 10,000 to 130,000. In addition, 50,000 engineers, nutritionists, food technologists and economists will be needed, as well as 75,000 in other professions. For the less-developed nations these numbers should probably be multiplied by two or three.

Education for modern agriculture means much more than teaching agronomy and animal husbandry. It involves engineering, economics, sociology, law, the humanities and all the sciences. Some education, particularly that of new faculty members, can be provided in the advanced countries, but most of the teaching should be done in the poor countries and aimed at their unique conditions and special problems.

Reducing population growth

In the long run the balance between world food supplies and human food needs will depend as much on the slowing down and eventually the stopping of population growth as on increasing the food supply. In the absence of catastrophe, population

USDA–Schreider

School breakfast and lunch programs help teach children good eating habits and help insure that they will receive the nutrients needed for good health and proper growth. Above: elementary-school students in Maryland.

changes are inevitably slow. Effective programs of fertility control must be undertaken as a matter of urgency today if human diets are to be above near subsistence levels at the end of this century. Even over the short term an early reduction of rates of population growth may be necessary because economic growth and social development are made much more difficult by rapid population growth.

There are good reasons to believe that the birth rates in most of the less-developed countries will decrease during the next few decades. Surveys show that many couples in these countries want to limit the number of children that they have; many couples in these nations are very interested in learning about methods of contraception.

The governments of many developing countries are now adopting population control policies at a rate and in a climate of world approval unimaginable even during the early 1960's. Among the governments that have already decided to foster family planning are those of India, Pakistan, China, South Korea, Ceylon, Singapore, Hong Kong, Malaysia, Turkey, the United Arab Republic, Tunisia, Morocco, Costa Rica, Trinidad and Tobago, El Salvador, Jamaica and Barbados. The role of a government in reducing population growth is difficult, requiring a high degree of organization, adequate financial and logistic support, great flexibility in meeting changing conditions, and the continuing objective evaluation of the results of birth control programs.

LOOK,
TOUCH
AND LEARN

At the Ontario Science Center

The children in these pictures are learning through participation. (1) The boy rolls the tip of his tongue. Can you do this? (The ability is inherited.) (2) Youngsters try to beat the computer in a game of ticktacktoe. (3) Playing with water in the Junior Museum: children manipulate an Archimedean screw, raising water from one level to another.

1

A FAMILY sits on low stools in the cramped laboratory of Sir Frederick Banting and Dr. Charles Best, the discoverers of insulin. A ten-year-old boy looks in a mirror, trying to roll the tip of his tongue. A miniskirted teen-ager separates the Apollo command ship from its lunar module, turns it 180° and prepares for docking maneuvers. An elderly lady plays ticktacktoe with a computer.

These people are discovering the exciting worlds of science and technology. They are learning the principles that govern biological, chemical and physical reactions. They are looking at the past accomplishments of science — and at its future promise.

The people are visitors at the new Ontario Science Center near Toronto, a multibuilding complex filled with exhibits designed to show that science and technology can be understood by the layman. Its motto: please touch.

A signal from outer space

The Ontario Science Center, officially named the Centennial Center of Science and Technology, was opened in September 1969, with the help of quasar 3C273. A signal from this distant, mysterious object, traveling through space for 1,500,-000,000 years, was received by a radio telescope in northern Ontario. The signal was relayed to the Science Center where, with the aid of a laser, photocell and relay, it turned on an electric current. The current caused the curtains behind the dais to part, thus revealing the Center's symbol: three overlapping balls of red, green and blue.

The Center is divided into nine major exhibit areas: the Halls of Life, Molecular Science, Earth Science, Space Science, Engineering, Communications, Transportation and Canadian Resources, and the Junior Museum. The designers of the Center, aware that they could not cover every aspect of science and technology, used the following criteria in choosing subject areas:

"a) The number of areas should be small enough so that each could be reasonably complete.

b) The areas should be significant and more heavily aligned to the present and future than to the past.

258

2

3

c) The areas should, if possible, be interdisciplinary, showing the contribution of several branches of science and technology to our overall understanding.

d) The areas should reflect closely-related technological applications, so that no hard-and-fast distinction is made between 'pure science' and 'applied science.'

e) The areas should have special relevance to Canadian and, if possible, Ontario circumstances.

f) Finally, each area should lend itself to illustration by participatory exhibits, appropriate to the Center's technical and financial means."

Within each area, basic concepts of science are explained: concepts such as relativity, magnetism, the nature of light, mass and acceleration. Heavy emphasis is placed on the direct, physical involvement of the viewers.

Exploring the unknown

A new era of scientific research began in mid-1969 when men took their first steps on the moon. Project Apollo captured the interest of people everywhere; children and adults of all nationalities be-

came familiar with the intricacies of landing men on another celestial body; the jargon of astronauts — EVA, lunar orbit insertion, PLSS — became the jargon of the layman.

Among the most popular exhibits at the Science Center are 4 space capsules in which visitors can simulate certain phases of an Apollo mission. In 2 of these capsules, visitors can simulate the separation and docking maneuvers performed during translunar coast; the other 2 capsules simulate the approach of a lunar module to the moon's surface and its subsequent return to the orbiting command ship.

In another part of the Center, another universe is explored: the worlds of atoms and molecules. Models of linear accelerators and cyclotrons are shown. An "atomic pinball machine" enables visitors to simulate a classic experiment first performed by the British physicist Ernest Rutherford. The machine fires projectiles at an invisible target; by studying the way the projectiles rebound, the visitor can determine the nature of the target.

The oceans of the earth are still another universe being explored by scien-

259

tists. In the Hall of Earth Science, exhibits describe desalinization techniques, the process of sedimentation and the theory of continental drift. A large rotating globe, 10 feet in diameter, shows the earth in relief; the continental shelves and suboceanic mountains and valleys are as dramatic as the more familiar Canadian Rockies and Swiss Alps. A prospecting game enables visitors to "discover" ore deposits using modern mining techniques.

The role of modern technology

The Science Center devotes a large portion of its space to the enormous contributions of modern technology to the solution of both basic scientific problems and the more practical problems of our daily lives. In the Hall of Engineering, waterway and hydroelectric exhibits illustrate how the Great Lakes-St. Lawrence River system helps meet the transportation and energy needs of Canada. A large diorama shows the huge Eisenhower-Snell lock complex; beside it is a working model of a lift lock. Other exhibits illustrate parts of a hydoelectric system: circuit breakers, control switches, transformers and so on. Another exhibit features a meter that is connected to the Ontario

power grid; here visitors can read the immediate, total power load on the system.

Located in the Hall of Communications are many exhibits on computers and their applications. Some of the basic mathematics involved in computer operations, including the binary numeral system, is explained; one exhibit allows viewers to convert Arabic numerals to their binary equivalent. A visitor wishing to perform various arithmetic calculations can use one of several electronic calculators (a type of simple computer).

Other groups of participatory displays in the Hall of Communication explain the principles of television, telegraphy and telephony. Visitors can even simulate the beacon fires used by ancient peoples to flash messages across the countryside.

Pedal your way to knowledge

Participation at the Ontario Science Center ranges from pushing a button to pedaling a bike (which, in turn, generates electricity). Viewers become actively involved in the exhibits, and as they play Indonesian percussion instruments or try their skill at mirror writing, they learn. As Douglas A. Penny, director of education at the Science Center, writes in an outline of the exhibits: "Each exhibit . . . provides a valid learning experience — through direct, physical involvement rather than exclusively through the eye or ear. Children may not be conscious of learning in the Junior Museum, but as they move from 'game' to 'game' they will be absorbing, physically and subliminally, a wide variety of experiences upon which their teachers can build a deeper understanding of many principles of basic science."

In a world that is increasingly governed by advances in science and technology, such an understanding by the lay public is essential. And at the Ontario Science Center, learning to understand is fun.

The Hall of Space includes a scale model of a Saturn V rocket and its gantry and an actual-size model of an Apollo Command Module in launch position.

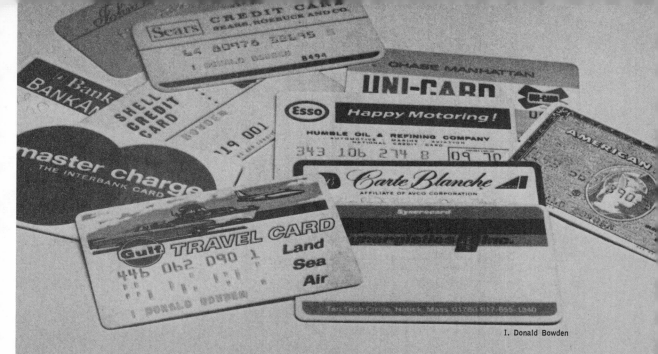

I. Donald Bowden

THE CASHLESS SOCIETY*

The Advent of Electronic Money

BY THOMAS J. GRADEL

LIKE it or not, the day is quickly approaching when the average American will use a computer to keep track of almost every cent he spends. He will do this without ever touching cash except for small change to tip the shoeshine boy or bellhop. In fact, the nature of his money will change from folding paper to electronic bleeps — or no bleeps — in the memory of a computer.

Life in this "cashless society" will be easier in many ways. However, the individual will be relieved of details but not of responsibility. He will not have to scurry to his bank, withdrawing cash for a weekend trip to the shore or depositing money to cover his wife's check written yesterday. Checks will be as obsolete as cash. His salary will automatically be deposited in his account, and he will be notified that he can begin using it at 9 A.M. Friday. Upon his authorization, regular bills, such as mortgage payments, will be transferred to his creditors' accounts.

Throughout the week, he will use an all-purpose identification and credit card to make food, entertainment, gasoline and many other purchases. (In the earlier years of the "cashless society," he would have utilized a change machine to obtain silver and small bills for vending machines and small merchants. But even this need will be eliminated.) Eventually every financial transaction will be initiated by the identification card, and every vendor, except the shoeshine boy, will have a credit-card terminal, linked to a nationwide computer system, that will instantly record all financial transactions. The system most likely will include personal computers, neighborhood time-sharing data-processing centers, and gigantic processors operated by banks and leading retailers.

Such a network will help eliminate a variety of financial headaches, ranging from the familiar backlogs on Wall Street to the annoying delays in receiving receipts and canceled checks. And with terminals in the home, it will be possible for computers to report on the financial status

* Reprinted from RCA *Electronic Age*

of individuals as well as businesses. The computer will display on a screen the balance in an account, payments due in the near future, and the number of loans outstanding, including the various interest rates on each. There will be no need to wait until the end of the month to find out exactly how much money is in an account. There will be electronic safeguards against unauthorized persons gaining access to the data, to protect the individual's right to privacy.

Many payments will be made immediately, by instructing the computer to subtract a charge from a consumer's account and add it to the grocer's account. Any deferred payment will become a charge-account sale and, after a certain period of time, will incur interest.

The average man's life will be simpler because he will have access to a computer to keep track of these financial transactions. It will be more complicated because virtually an unlimited number of opportunities to make loans or to borrow money will be open to him.

Despite objections from some quarters, there are definite signs that the coming of the "cashless society" is simply a matter of time. One authority points out that most of the technology needed to operate an "electronic" monetary system is already available. He further states that if the needed technology is available but not economically feasible today, it soon

will be. Yet, even today, there are holdouts against modern fiscal methods. Some people refuse to use banks, checks or money orders. Instead they hide huge sums in the mattress, send hundreds of dollars in cash through the mails, and consider it both sinful and foolish to borrow money or purchase goods with a credit card. Nevertheless, statistics are proving the popularity of credit cards and the coming of the "cashless society."

The Federal Reserve Board (FRB) reported that 699 commercial banks were operating credit-card programs by June 30, 1969, many with tie-ins with other banks. Of these 699 banks, 359 were national banks. A year earlier, only 416 banks had credit-card indebtedness on their books; 219 of these were national banks. The amount of credit outstanding under bank credit-card plans reached $2,300,000,000 at the end of 1969, compared with $1,300,000,000 a year earlier — an increase of more than 75 per cent!

Under most bank credit-card plans, cardholders can obtain merchandise or services on credit from local retail outlets and are billed through their banks. Interest on unpaid balances ranges from 1 to 1.5 per cent a month, or up to 18 per cent a year, depending on local usury laws. The average credit limit, according to the FRB, is $350.

Many of the nation's large retailers also have charge-card and credit-card

Above: Chinese shoe money.
Right: Money stone of Yap Island.

plans. People also carry travel, entertainment, and airline cards, and several banks even issue a card that triggers a money-dispensing machine. In addition, one of the nation's largest supermarket chains recently began an experimental credit-card program. The A&P, traditionally a cash-and-carry firm, introduced the program in six stores in Ohio and West Virginia.*

Credit-card plans are considered the first step toward the "cashless society," and their rapid proliferation is an indication that, someday, checks and paper money will not be able to compete with efficient "electronic" money. Other fiscal innovations in many industries are leading to the establishment of a national network for checking the credit and verifying the identity of the cardholder.

In an effort to reduce frequent hold-ups of bus drivers, the Philadelphia Transportation Company inaugurated an "exact fare" plan. Under this plan, passengers who do not have the exact fare deposit more than the cost of the ride in a locked box and receive a certificate. This entitles them to a refund for the difference, obtainable at centrally located refund centers. It is expected that, within a few years, buses in many metropolitan areas will carry devices that can read credit

---

* The total amount outstanding on all credit-card plans reached a staggering $15,000,000,000 by the end of 1969 (this includes bank credit cards, oil-company cards, department-store revolving-credit plans, travel and entertainment cards and so on).

cards. Fares charged against these cards will be recorded on magnetic tape or miniaturized magnetic disks. These records will be processed by computers, and, once a month, the passenger will receive a bill for all his bus and subway rides. Adapting to the exact-fare plan will help Philadelphians adjust to any computerized billing that might be introduced. A credit-card system would eliminate more fully the handling of money by the driver, while doing away with trips to collect the refund.

In another case, the Ripley Company will soon run tests to prove the feasibility of automatic utility-meter reading via public telephone lines. A spokesman claims that, when such a system is operable, a computer would be programed to interrogate the meters for each billing period and prepare the bill from the figures. With the customer's permission, the system could be tied to bank computers for automatic payment of utility bills.

The military is already using "cashless" money and computers to help curb black-market activities in Vietnam. The U.S. military command has issued plastic currency-control cards that must be used when a serviceman converts his military scrip into cash or when he spends it on certain higher-priced post-exchange goods. Data from these cards give officials a constant watch on the volume of converted scrip as well as on PX purchases. If, for example, a man should convert more than

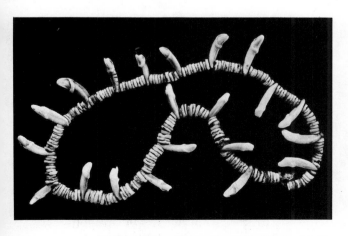

Photos Chase Manhattan
Bank Money Museum

Above: Dog-teeth currency of the Solomon Islands.
Right: A now-obsolete money tree from China.

the authorized amount of scrip, the computer "kicks out" a card identifying him and showing all his recent transactions.

A major factor in speeding the establishment of the "cashless society" is the continuing decline in data-processing costs and in the cost of transmitting information over telephone lines. In the late 1950's, it cost $1.35 to perform 100,000 multiplications on the most efficient computer available, according to a data-processing consultant. Today, the same function costs less than 3 cents.

Dr. James Hillier, RCA executive vice-president, Research and Engineering, frequently has stated that the "cashless society" is inevitable. In fact, he points out that, by reflecting on past economic and technological development, society might even be able to determine when it will be a reality.

A certain concept of this development, which he calls "the tyranny of numbers versus the constancy of humans," may hold the answer. This is explained by the fact that a department-store clerk is essentially a constant in regard to her ability to generate bills, manually verify credit authorization, or handle the transactions of the people who line up at her counter. On the other hand, the number of credit cards, volume of financial transactions, and degree to which individuals depend on others to produce food, clothing, and personal protection are expanding at a rate faster than that of the population. If this continues, there will not be enough people in the world to handle the financial transactions — buying, selling, and billing — generated by the people of the United States.

In the past, when the constancy of humans was violently coupled with the tyranny of numbers, the resulting explosions gave birth to technological breakthroughs and important innovations. An example can be found in the history of the telephone industry. The rapid increase in the use of telephones, combined with the geometric expansion in the number of possible connections that could be made by the operators, eventually produced direct dialing and computerized switching. If switchboards were still operated manually, there would not be enough girls in the world to handle all the calls made today. Thus, according to Dr. Hillier, it is only a matter of time before the number and complexity of financial transactions make it economically necessary to convert to "electronic" money. The reduced cost of communications and data processing, the public's growing familiarity with credit cards, computerized billing, and automatic meter reading, and the more efficient manufacture of computer terminals will combine to force the conversion.

In spite of these forces, there are still a few technological hang-ups that the nation's scientists and engineers have not completely solved. One is the need for a foolproof, inexpensive method of verifying the identity of the cardholder. No one looks forward to an "electronic" money system if it means that a thief will have unlimited access to all one's financial accounts. A lost wallet containing a code number could lead to total financial ruin. This is such a problem today that at least one company has sprung up to help protect consumers against lost or stolen credit cards. The company claims that within thirty seconds after notification, it can put a computer to work detailing the cards owned by a subscriber. Then the issuing companies are notified by telegram that the cards are missing and credit privileges should be canceled. Although this is a partial solution to the problem, it still puts the burden on the owners of cards to notify the firms. Any purchases charged on those cards are still their liabilities. What is really needed is a system that would deny credit privileges to the cardholder unless he could positively identify himself as the rightful owner.

Dr. Donald S. McCoy of the David Sarnoff Research Center in Princeton, New Jersey, has suggested a speech-recognition system that employs both code words and voice-signature prints to positively identify cardholders. A person would voice an assigned code phrase of easily identified sounds — "This is six one

VOICE PRINTS

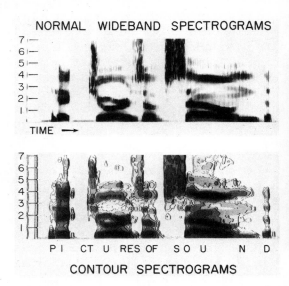

NORMAL WIDEBAND SPECTROGRAMS

TIME →

CONTOUR SPECTROGRAMS

The words "pictures of sound" are graphically displayed above on both normal wide-band and contour spectrograms. Lower frequencies (measured in hertz) appear at the bottom, and higher frequencies at the top of the spectrograms. Intensity is indicated by light and dark shading.

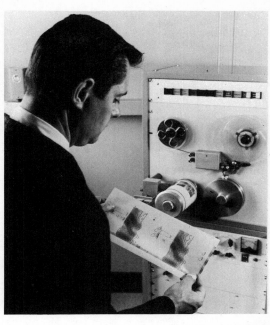

A. J. Presti examines a spectrogram — a "picture" of sound produced by the high-speed sound spectrograph that he designed. The device prints spectrograms in 80 seconds, producing them directly from standard magnetic recording tape.

Photos Bell Labs

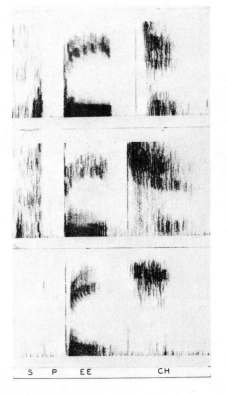

Patterns of the word "speech" by six different speakers. The spectrograms on the left were made by female voices. Upper: clear high-pitched voice; middle: "throaty" voice; bottom: Scotch-Irish accent. The spectrograms on the right were made by male voices. Upper: low-pitched, resonant voice; middle: midwestern accent; bottom: British accent.

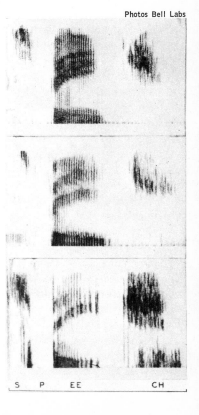

one tango" — and then speak his name. By means of the code phrase, the computer would be directed immediately to the place in its memory where that person's voice-signature file is stored. These voice-signature prints have been demonstrated to be as efficient and forgery-proof as are fingerprints. This speaker-identification system is already possible with the speech technology of today. The cost is still high, but it is rapidly approaching economic feasibility.

One of the first developments that must take place is the establishment of a large, computerized credit-card system. At the present time, one of the primary obstacles to such a pilot project is the high cost of terminals capable of reading credit cards. To attract widespread use, the terminals for the remote interrogation of credit files and the collection of credit transactions must be small and inexpensive. A credit-card system will not function properly unless a remote credit-card terminal is located wherever a charge can be made. Every hardware store, jewelry shop, grocery store, gasoline station, and restaurant must have at least one. These terminals must be small and easy to operate because they will be handled by proprietors and clerks who currently operate machines no more sophisticated than a cash register. The main function of these devices is to read and transmit the credit-account number and to accept variable data, like the dollar amount of the transaction. Also, these devices must have the capability of tactfully signaling the terminal operator that the sale has been approved and recorded, or that it has been rejected and not recorded.

One of the chief factors that will contribute to the practicality of on-line credit-card networks is the development of internal computer systems. A number of banks are developing computerized information networks linking all of their branches to a centralized computer. If banks develop central information files containing information on all their customers, it will become a relatively simple matter to add an automatic credit-card system. Actually, credit-card validation and purchase authorization require a very small fraction of computer time. Banks can continue to do batch processing and handle the credit-card system through the use of multiprograming and time-sharing techniques. It is then possible for credit-card terminals to interrupt the processor, request information, and receive it in only a fraction of a second. These techniques permit the processor to handle bulk processing and on-line communications at the same time.

However, many other problems must be worked out before the "cashless society" becomes a reality. For example, the competitive struggles between the banking industry, large retailers, the telephone companies and the Federal Government must be resolved. The lines separating the proper fields of activities for these industries begin to fuzz when their operations project into the age of "electronic" money. Many state and Federal laws will have to be modified to permit banks to engage in merchandising and also to allow retailers to perform some typical banking functions.

This would be only one of a variety of changes in the economic life of the nation. With the advent of the "cashless society," many new jobs will be created, while some pedestrian ones will be eliminated. It may even be a built-in answer to the problem of crime in the streets. Armed robbery would be obsolete if nobody carried money and a voice check was needed to use a credit card. A new breed of criminal would probably be developed, electronic embezzlers who could tamper with computer systems to inflate their accounts. Computer experts are already working on methods to foil this. In addition, Federal investigators would merely have to check employers' computers to discover the honest income of a suspect.

One thing is certain. A nationwide "cashless society" would provide everyone with his own electronic accountant: a computer that can handle almost all financial details but makes none of the critical decisions.

Wide World

Otto Stern

Pictorial Parade

Cecil Frank Powell

Baron — Pix

Bertrand Russell

Camera Press — Pix

Max Born

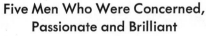

IN MEMORIAM

Five Men Who Were Concerned, Passionate and Brilliant

UPI

F. Peyton Rous

"THE independent scientist who is worth the slightest consideration as a scientist has a consecration which comes entirely from within himself: a vocation which demands the possibility of supreme self-sacrifice." These words, written by mathematician Norbert Wiener, well describe the five Nobelists in this article. Each was committed to the pursuit of science and knowledge. But even more important, each was committed to humanity.

Max Born

A brilliant scientist whose work in the "statistical interpretation of quantum mechanics" earned him the 1954 Nobel Prize for Physics,* Dr. Max Born was a man deeply concerned about the consequences of scientific discoveries and the responsibilities of scientists to society. In his autobiography, *My Life and My*

* Born shared the award with Dr. Walther Bothe.

Views, he wrote: "Science in our age has social, economic and political functions, and however remote one's own work is from technical application, it is a link in the chain of actions and decisions which determine the fate of the human race."

In the 1920's, Born developed mathematical formulas that described the behavior of electrons. These formulas, which stressed that the motion and position of electrons were matters of statistical probability, were more accurate than the original quantum theory. Born's formulas became the basis for all future developments in the field of quantum mechanics.

But Born's work was not universally accepted. His friend Albert Einstein was not convinced that such basic phenomena were matters of chance; in a letter to Born he wrote: "The Good Lord does not play dice."

It was perhaps the initial, slow-to-die skepticism about his work which caused so long a delay — 28 years — in the presentation of the Nobel Prize for this important contribution to science.

In the years following his work in quantum mechanics, Born studied crystallography and the kinetic theory of fluids and helped formulate the Born-Oppenheimer theory of molecules. He remained active in scientific research until a few months before his death.

Dr. Born was born in Breslau, Germany, on December 11, 1882; he died in Göttingen, Germany, on January 5, 1970.

Cecil Frank Powell

Recipient of the 1950 Nobel Prize for Physics, Dr. Powell was born in Tonbridge, England, on December 5, 1903; he died on August 9, 1969, in Bellano, Italy.

Dr. Powell was awarded the Nobel Prize "for his development of the photographic method in the study of nuclear processes and for his discoveries concerning mesons."

Powell coated photographic plates with a special emulsion. Using balloons made of a thin plastic, he sent these plates aloft. At sufficiently high altitudes, the plates were exposed to the cosmic rays that bombard our atmosphere from outer space. In one experiment, for example, Powell sent 660 pounds of emulsions aloft; they remained at an altitude of about 115,000 feet for 14 hours. Twenty tons of developing solution were needed to process these plates. It was in the study of such plates that Powell discovered the pi-meson, a subatomic particle that lives for only a fraction of a second.

Dr. Powell was a leading proponent of international cooperation among scientists. He was also very active in the British peace movement, where he occasionally worked with Bertrand Russell. In the 1950's, he often expressed his opposition to the development of the hydrogen bomb, which, he said, brought "the extermination of human life within the range of technical possibility."

F. Peyton Rous

Sixty years ago, a young pathologist at the Rockefeller Institute (now Rockefeller University) announced that cancer could be transmitted to healthy chickens by injecting them with cell-free extracts of malignant tumors. The man was Dr. Rous. His fellow scientists responded with disbelief, scorn and ridicule.

It has only been in the past 20 years that research has proved Rous correct. And it was only 4 years ago, in 1966, that the Nobel Committee recognized the significance of his work by naming him corecipient of the Nobel Prize for Physiology and Medicine. "The significance of Rous' initial discovery in 1910 has been enhanced with every passing year since the isolation of leukemia virus in mice in 1951," said the Swedish medical faculty, "and its real importance and bearings have only been comprehended in the last 10 years."

Dr. Rous was born in Baltimore on October 5, 1879; he died in New York on February 16, 1970. He remained at Rockefeller University until his death, working a full schedule even after his retirement in 1945. His major contributions to science were twofold: (a) his research, not only in cancer but in gallbladder and liver physiology and in the development of blood-preserving techniques; and (b) his superb training of dozens of students who went on to become leading scientists.

At the time of his death, Rous was doing tumor research with Dr. James S. Henderson. "He was a very eager liver," said Henderson; he was a man "who had the whole world as his laboratory."

Bertrand Russell

"Three passions, simple but overwhelmingly strong, have governed my life: the longing for love, the search for knowledge, and unbearable pity for the suffering of mankind."

The author of this passage, Bertrand Arthur William Russell, was perhaps best known as a philosopher and as a man keenly interested and active in social and political issues. He received the 1950 Nobel Prize in Literature "in recognition of his many-sided and significant writings, in which he appeared as the champion of humanity and freedom of thought."

But in his early life, his interest in philosophy was shared with a devotion to mathematics: "From that moment [at age 11] until Whitehead and I finished *Principia Mathematica,* when I was 38, mathematics was my chief interest and my chief source of happiness."

Russell and Alfred North Whitehead published the 3-volume *Principia Mathematica* between 1910 and 1913. As philosopher Brand Blanshard has written, it was "one of the most important and original works in the history of mathematics. Its aim was to show that logic and mathematics were a single discipline by demonstrating that virtually the whole of mathematics could be derived from a relatively few 'primitive propositions' of logic." The book removed mathematics from the worlds of magic and mysticism.

Russell was born on May 18, 1872, in Trelleck, Wales; he died at his home in Merionethshire, Wales, on February 2, 1970. During his extraordinarily productive life, he wrote numerous books on philosophy, science and mathematics.

And he was a fervent supporter of a number of controversial ideas. He had long been an atheist and, prior to the 1939 German invasion of Czechoslovakia, an ardent pacifist. In recent years, he strongly condemned American involvement in Vietnam and opposed nuclear testing: "If people could learn to view nuclear war as a common danger to our species and not as a danger due solely to the wickedness of the oppressing group, it would be possible to negotiate agreements which would put an end to the common danger."

Otto Stern

Physicist Otto Stern was born in Sohrau, Germany, on February 17, 1888; he died in Berkeley, California, on August 17, 1969. During his early career he worked in Germany, leaving that country in 1933 "because of the manner in which my [Jewish] colleagues were treated by the German authorities." He came to the United States, joining the Carnegie Institute of Technology as a research professor of physics. At the time of his retirement in 1945 he moved to California.

In the 1920's, Stern and his colleague Walter Gerlach explained the important principles of molecular beams (streams of neutral particles moving through a vacuum). They produced molecular beams by heating the element to be tested. This caused some of the atoms to evaporate, much as water evaporates into steam. These evaporated atoms were passed through an evacuated tube (a tube in which a vacuum had been created) and between the 2 poles of a magnet. Stern and Gerlach found that the beam split into 2 equal parts, indicating that the atoms went through the magnetic field with their axes all pointing in the same direction (and with ½ the atoms spinning 1 way and ½ the other). Later, scientists would explain this orderliness.

For his work in the development and application of the molecular-beam method of measuring the magnetic momentum of atomic particles, Stern was awarded the 1943 Nobel Prize for Physics.

PHYSICAL SCIENCES
AND MATHEMATICS

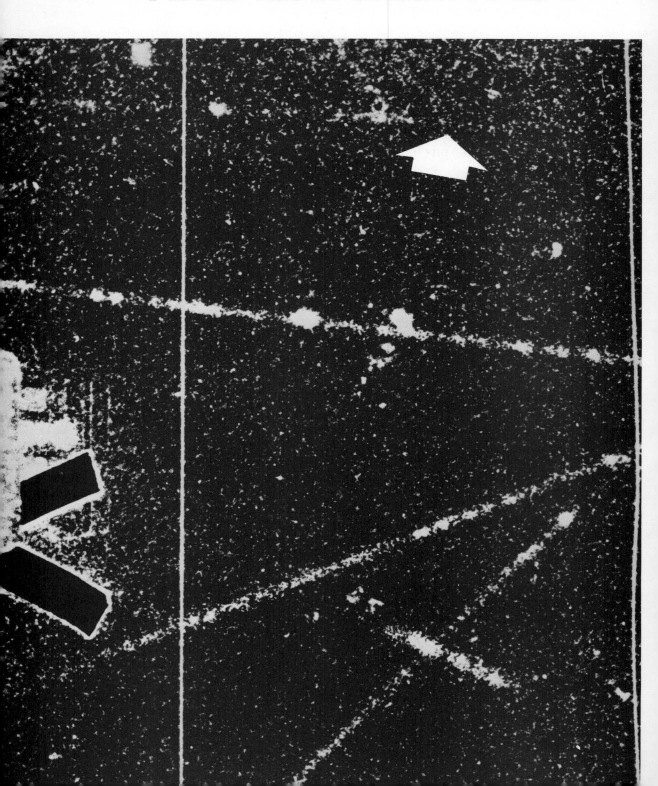

CONTENTS

Cosmic-ray tracks in a cloud chamber. Australian physicists claim that the arrow points to a track left by a quark, a previously undiscovered particle.

University of Sydney

REVIEW OF THE YEAR-
PHYSICAL SCIENCES
AND MATHEMATICS

Plasma physics. For twenty years scientists have tried to control nuclear fusion. This process, in which hydrogen nuclei join to form helium, releases stupendous amounts of energy. (Nuclear fusion is the basis of the hydrogen bomb.) This power is cheap, since it comes from commonly available materials (the heavy hydrogen contained in 1 gallon of water could produce as much heat as 300 gallons of gasoline). And it is "clean," with none of the evils of radioactivity and thermal pollution that result from nuclear-fission plants. But until recently scientists were unable to control the process so that it would proceed slowly, without fizzling out or, at the other extreme, creating a devastating thermonuclear explosion. The source of energy for controlled fusion is plasma, electrically-charged gas heated to millions of degrees for a short time. The stumbling block has been to keep the plasma at 180 million degrees F. for 1/10 to 1 second. Soviet scientists have developed a machine, the Tokamak, that has achieved the greatest success; the Soviets report maintaining plasma at 18 million degrees F. for about 1/50 of a second. In the United States, the Atomic Energy Commission is experimenting with a machine called Scylla IV; they reached a plasma temperature of 36 million degrees F. but could not maintain it so long as the Soviet device. In France, physicists reported making small fusion reactions by means of lasers acting on heavy hydrogen that had been cooled to almost absolute zero ($-460°$ F.).

Solid-state physics. In their investigation of solid crystalline materials, physicists at the Massachusetts Institute of Technology and New York University found that when electrons penetrate a crystal they set up units of vibrations called phonons; phonons and electrons then pair together to form energy packets called polarons. It is believed that the activities of traveling polarons will explain many phenomena in solid matter and will form the basis of new applications in electronics. Another energy packet that may be produced in both organic and inorganic crystals is the exciton. This consists of an association between an electron and positively-charged spaces, or "holes," in the crystal structure. The exciton travels through a material, from molecule to molecule, dispersing its energy. In organic crystals this energy is in the form of light. Early in 1969, New York University scientists reported that the weak fluorescence in tetracene, an organic compound related to naphthalene, is due to the behavior of excitons. Researchers believe that excitons may help them understand energy transfers in photosynthesis and other biochemical processes.

Subatomic particles. In 1964 two California Institute of Technology scientists independently proposed the existence of a fundamental, massive particle from which other subnuclear particles could be built. This particle was named the quark; it was proposed that quarks were the building blocks of heavy particles such as protons and neutrons. Since then, physicists have searched for evidence that such a particle exists. In September 1969, an Australian team claimed it had detected quarks. Dr. Charles B. A. McCusker of the University of Sydney and his colleagues reported that they found evidence of quarks in cosmic-ray showers. Scintillation counters were used to trigger four Wilson cloud chambers which, in turn, showed vapor trails of cosmic-ray particles. The supposed quarks left faint tracks that indicate their charges average less than half that of a proton (which has a charge of one). Some scientists are skeptical of the dramatic Australian findings. However, if the report is confirmed, it will be a major advance in physics.

Neutrons are subatomic particles that are, on the whole, electrically neutral. But within each neutron are both positive and negative charges that produce tiny electric and magnetic fields. Thus it is conceivable that a weak chemical bond could be formed between a neutron and a charged particle. In October 1969, Drs. T. J. Grant and James W. Cobble of Purdue University reported evidence of chemical bonding between neutrons and electrons in lithium fluoride that had been cooled to approximately 8 degrees above absolute zero. Other scientists have been unable to confirm these findings; if they do, "it would have to revolutionize some aspect of neutron physics," says Dr. Donald W. Connor of Argonne National Laboratory.

Muons, produced by bombarding a beryllium target with protons, are being used by physicists to study the nuclei of atoms. Scientists have found that when a muon enters a nucleus, the nucleus shrinks in size. Normally, the like charges of protons within the nucleus drive the protons apart. When a negative muon nears a proton, some of the positive proton charge is neutralized, and the nucleus compresses.

Antimatter. Theorists have long speculated that the universe is symmetrically composed of ordinary matter and antimatter. Dramatic proof of this theory came in 1966 when nuclei of antideuterium were discovered: these are the antimatter equivalent of heavy-hydrogen nuclei. Early in 1970 a team of Soviet physicists directed by Professor Yuri D. Prokoshkin reported the creation and detection of antihelium nuclei. Each consisted of two antiprotons and one antineutron (antiprotons carry a negative charge; antineutrons differ from ordinary neutrons in their magnetic properties). This was termed a "major achievement," since it proved that antimatter can exist in elements more complex than antihydrogen.

Chemistry. Scientists at Argonne have been using computers and mathematical "models" to study chemical processes. Many of these processes are difficult to analyze in a traditional laboratory because they may involve exceptionally high temperatures, very corrosive materials, short-lifetime particles or other extreme characteristics. For example, the technique has been used in studies of high-temperature properties of alkali-metal vapors (alkali metals are used to cool nuclear reactors). According to Dr. Arnold C. Wahl, "we are getting to the point, on simple chemical systems, where our results are better than experiments, because many experiments are difficult to perform. . . . We see an important future for this numeric instrument to complement the traditional tools of the chemist."

Which freezes faster, hot or cold water? Surprisingly, under certain conditions the answer is hot water. This was noticed in 1969 by Erasto Mpemba, a Tanzanian student who placed two ice-cream mixtures, one warmer than the other, into a refrigerator. The warmer mixture froze first. This result was later confirmed by C. S. Kell of the National Research Council in Ottawa, Canada. He explained that the phenomenon was due to the more active evaporation of the warmer substance. Evaporation cools the evaporating substance; under certain conditions, this cooling easily overcomes the temperature differential, and the warmer mass may freeze in about half the time required to congeal a cold mass. In a closed container, little or no evaporation occurs; thus, in this situation the colder liquid will freeze faster than the same liquid at a higher temperature.

THE HUNT FOR ELUSIVE NEW ELEMENTS*

Expanding the Periodic Table

IN THE depths of the ocean off Fiji, in balloons high in the earth's atmosphere, in the lead of 16th-century church windows, and in the debris of nuclear explosions, scientists are engaged in a worldwide quest. They are searching for heavy elements, those heavier than uranium, which ranks No. 92 in the periodic table of the elements. Now they are even

Opening gun

By 1940, scientists had identified all but one of the 92 elements — ranging from hydrogen, the lightest, to uranium — in the periodic table. That year, Dr. Edwin M. McMillan, now director of the Lawrence Radiation Laboratory at the University of California, Berkeley, and Philip H. Abelson, now editor of *Science* maga-

Photos: Lawrence Radiation Laboratory

The main accelerating chamber of the HILAC at Berkeley, California. The pattern on the end plate is formed by the cooling apparatus.

probing rock samples from the moon to see if they can find traces of heavy elements that once may have existed there.

Governments have sponsored most heavy-element research and are still spending millions on it. What will come out of it in the future isn't all that certain. But in the past 30 years, 13 heavy elements have been found, and one of them, plutonium, has decisively changed the world. This is what is driving researchers on. And, of course, there's also the chance of finding a commercial use for some new element that is discovered.

zine, synthesized No. 93, the first of the heavy, or transuranium, elements. They named it neptunium. The 12 transuranium elements isolated since then bring the periodic table up to 105. And the end is not in sight. Several of the heavy-element discoveries — in the form of isotopes — already have found applications:

• Plutonium 238 is being used as a heat source for auxiliary power supplies in space flight. It also is being tried out as a power source for an artificial heart now under test in dogs.

* Reprinted by permission from *Business Week*

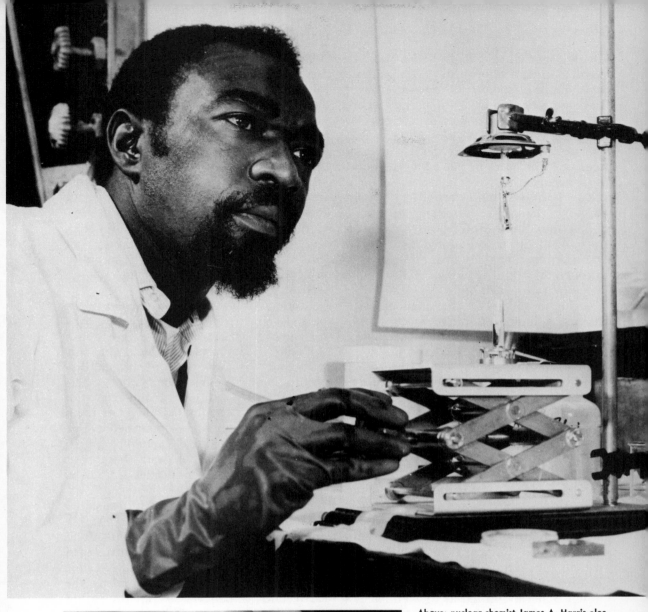

Above: nuclear chemist James A. Harris electroplates two-millionths of an ounce of californium-249 onto a thin foil. This target will be placed in the HILAC to produce element 104.

Left: a uranium target ready for positioning in the HILAC. This target is typical of those used in the production of heavy (transuranium) elements. The target material is located in the center of the frame.

275

• Americium 241 is being used to monitor industrial processes. The gamma rays it emits are being put to work in gages that measure material thickness where smoothness and even flow are critical, as in cigarette paper.

• California 252 is a dense source of neutrons which can be placed on the point of a needle and used to destroy cancer cells. It also is being tested for use in checking the characteristics of oil wells; and it may have applications in agriculture, for the mutation of seedlings; and in construction, for ascertaining the density of concrete.

The isotopes of other heavy elements — synthetic forms of the element with slightly different atomic weights — probably will be put to work, too, once all of their properties are uncovered and they can be produced economically in reactors.

Production of heavy-element isotopes currently is concentrated at the Atomic Energy Commission's Oak Ridge National Laboratory and their Savannah River Plant.

Continuing search

When Dmitri I. Mendeleev presented his periodic table of the elements to the Russian Chemical Society in 1869, 63 elements were arranged in groups (or families) based on similarities he had observed in their properties. Even then, several of the elements existed only in theory, their presence merely hinted at in Mendeleev's calculations.

Scientists have since built on Mendeleev's theoretical foundation. There's the shell theory — traditionally used as the basis for chemical research — which holds that the number of electrons revolving in shells or layers around an atomic nucleus determines an element's physical properties, such as its density and boiling and freezing points.

In 1944, just as elements 95 and 96 were being discovered, Dr. Glenn T. Seaborg, now chairman of the Atomic Energy Commission, predicted that elements up to 103 would exist; he codiscovered 9. In 1969, Seaborg said that elements up as high as 168 are theoretically possible. No. 168 may exist only as a "noble gas," he said, but it also may have a half-life — the time it takes for half of an element's energy to leave it — of 100 million years.

Building blocks

Basically, a heavy element is formed when its nucleus, which contains a stable number of protons, is bombarded with an ion that adds some of its protons or electrons to the target element. If they stick and the element remains stable, this pushes it up in number in the periodic table, either as a higher element or as an isotope.

Some of these higher elements are believed to exist in nature, and the search for them is what is taking scientists into the field. Seaborg predicts that physicists will find "islands of nuclear stability within seas of spontaneous fission." The stable elements will have arrangements of protons and electrons that will let them live long enough to be identified. The first of these could be element 114, which is tentatively called "ekalead" because it is believed to have properties similar to lead.

Dr. P. Buford Price and his associates at General Electric's Research and Development Center are hunting for this island of stability. Price is searching for traces of 114 that may be hitchhiking inside cosmic rays that are constantly bombarding the earth, and he believes he can find other traces in the radiation being generated by quasars and pulsars — distant objects in the universe which also are the source of radio waves.

Over the last few years, Price and others have sent several huge balloons into the atmosphere carrying stacks of a special plastic to trap cosmic radiation.

Other scientists are searching for the tracks of heavy elements that may be emanating as decay products from old gold, platinum and lead. The theory is that they may have been trapped in these dense materials. Soviet physicists, with the same intent, are examining the lead in old cathedral windows, and are testing

This large plastic ring, lined with mica detectors, was used at Berkeley to identify two new isotopes of element 104 produced when a californium-249 target was bombarded with carbon-12 and -13 nuclei. Fissioning atoms of element 104 produced stress patterns in the mica.

manganese nodules taken from the Pacific Ocean deeps near the Fiji Islands.

Using conventional techniques

Most of the new heavy elements, however, have been found as a result of nuclear research: in the atom-smashing cyclotrons, in research reactors, or in the radioactive debris of nuclear explosions. The most productive period for discovery was in the 1940's and 1950's, when 10 of the 13 transuranium elements came to light. The pace slowed in the sixties as the elements got tougher to find and isolate.

Now physicists are confident they can again make great leaps forward. They credit three factors for their confidence:

• Computer simulations have allowed them to work out the theoretical structure of the elements that they are looking for.

• New measuring techniques, satellites, and the Apollo program have pushed the search into new areas.

• New accelerators are going to be built, and old devices modified, to give physicists a powerful new tool: the ability to hit a uranium target with uranium ions.

Modification to permit the uranium-vs.-uranium experiment will be made on the Heavy Ion Linear Accelerator (HILAC) at Berkeley's Lawrence Radiation Lab, which has developed a reputation for being where the action is in the U.S. Heavy Element Research Program. This program, begun in 1954, now involves 3 AEC labs in basic research and 2 others in research and isotope production. AEC's fiscal-1970 budget for heavy-element research and isotope production is about $11.5 million.

The modifications to HILAC may give a boost to the program, which, some scientists say, has been muddling through compared with the resources available to their opposite numbers in the Soviet Union. The Soviet search for heavy elements is estimated to involve some 400 people, 4 or 5 times the money AEC is spending, and the use of 2 accelerators.

The team at Berkeley, considered the spearhead of the U.S. effort, employs 55 technical assistants and is funded at about $2 million. It is led by Albert Ghiorso, 53, a senior nuclear chemist at Lawrence Lab and part-time artist who whiles away his downtime with a sketch pad.

The competing Soviet team is headquartered at Dubna on the Volga River, at the Laboratory of Nuclear Reactions. It is led by Georgi N. Flerov, 56, a shy-looking, almost impish physicist who in 1969 was awarded the highest scientific title the Soviets can bestow — that of Academician.

Debate over elements 104 and 105

The Soviet Union formally instituted its heavy-element-research program in 1960. In 1964 its scientists claimed to have discovered element 104, which they immediately named kurchatovium, after Igor V. Kurchatov, a famous Russian chemist. The claim rocketed Flerov to fame. Then, in early 1969, Soviet officials announced that Flerov and his group had isolated a few atoms of an isotope of element 105.

On the American side, Ghiorso and four associates announced in April 1969 their discovery of element 104 — which the effervescent Ghiorso describes as the "hippie" element, because of what he called its somewhat hairy characteristics. Others on the team were: James A. Harris, a nuclear chemist who is believed to be the first Negro prominently involved in heavy-element research; and three Finnish physicists: Matti Nurmia and his students, a husband-and-wife team, Kari and Pirkko Eskola.

Ghiorso and his team have proposed the name rutherfordium for the element (in honor of the British physicist, Ernest Rutherford).

Whether the United States or the U.S.S.R. discovered element 104 first probably will be settled by the International Union of Pure and Applied Chemistry at its 1971 meeting. Meanwhile the Soviets also are questioning U.S. research data substantiating the discovery of two other transuranium elements: nobelium and lawrencium.

Late in April 1970, the Berkeley team reported that they had synthesized element 105. Again, a controversy. "We take the position that they [the Soviets] have not proved finding 105, whereas we have," said Ghiorso. The Berkeley scientists proposed that element 105 be named hahnium, in honor of the late German physicist, Otto Hahn.

New tool

Ghiorso is well aware of the intense competition offered by Flerov's team. But he bases his optimism that the United States can stay ahead in heavy-element research on the $2.65 million upgrading of HILAC.

What has the Berkeley team excited is the new capacity they will have when they can hit uranium with uranium. Ghiorso has no idea what other elements may result from the collision, but he hopes that the initial result will be element 114. In addition, the alterations will allow the scientists to carry on three experiments at the same time.

One of the keys to the new work is a technique known as "stripping," whereby each uranium ion is stripped of some of its negatively charged electrons before it is fed into the HILAC. This will produce a charged particle that will have some of its magnetic resistance reduced, thus making it easier to accelerate to extremely high speeds.

Until the HILAC is modified, however, Ghiorso and his colleagues are moving ahead with the painstaking search for the elements 106 and 107. They also are attempting to duplicate the work that Flerov claims to have done in his effort to produce element 104, but so far they haven't succeeded.

Back road

One of the large-scale research approaches to heavy-element synthesis has been somewhat neglected of late. This is the collecting and sifting of the debris of a specially tailored nuclear explosion, which in the early 1950's led to the discovery of two transuranium elements, einsteinium and fermium.

Several other attempts to find additional elements by this method failed. But Seaborg thinks if the atomic-explosion route could be worked out, it might be competitive with conventional reactor production techniques for the heavy isotopes. Dr. Paul Fields of Argonne National Laboratory, near Chicago, agrees. But he complains there has been no money around for three years to tie heavy-element experiments into underground nuclear testing.

Seaborg also worries about money for heavy-element research. Says he: "I believe the Soviets are funding it to a much greater extent than we are. They want to catch up so they can get into the business of naming elements. There is a prestige factor in heavy-element research just as much as there is in high-energy physics or space."

Lawrence Lab's McMillan adds: "We in the United States are on top [in heavy-element research] today. We're doing on a large scale the things that scientists know are important. But tomorrow — will we be obliged to yield the leadership to others?"

THE BINARY NUMERAL SYSTEM

In Which 1 + 1 = 10

BY IRWIN K. FEINSTEIN

THE binary numeral, or numeration, system offers an interesting glimpse into the world of mathematics. It is the simplest system in which addition and multiplication can be performed, for there are only 4 addition facts and 4 multiplication facts to learn. By contrast, in the decimal system there are 100 addition facts and 100 multiplication facts to learn.

The significance and power of the binary system in modern mathematics, however, lie in its practical application in computer technology. Most computers today are binary computers; that is, they use binary numerals in computing and in processing data. With binary numerals, modern computers can perform up to 1,000,000,000 additions each second.

Before going into the binary numeral system, we shall take a closer look at the Hindu-Arabic numeral system and the concept of place value in it. An understanding of place value is vital to an understanding of the binary numeral system.

The Hindu-Arabic system

The numeration system in use throughout the civilized world today is called the Hindu-Arabic system, probably because it originated with the Hindus and was carried to the western world by the Arabs. It is the only numeration system most of us have ever known, and it fits most of our commercial and technical needs very well.

The Hindu-Arabic system is often called a *decimal,* or *base-ten, system* because it needs only ten symbols to represent any number. These symbols, which are called *digits,* are: 1, 2, 3, 4, 5, 6, 7, 8, 9 and 0. These ten symbols stand for the

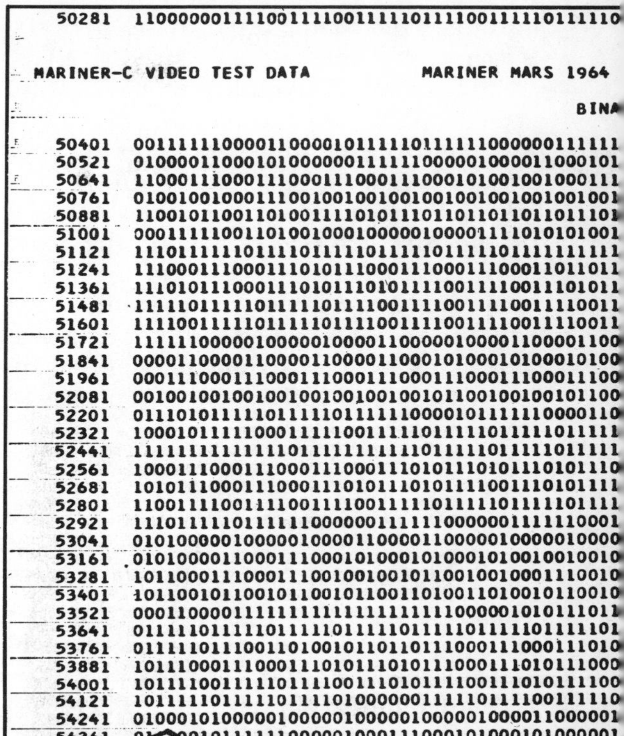

NASA

The binary numeral system is used to transmit photos from a Mariner space probe to receiving stations on earth. The pictures are transmitted as a series of radio signals, representing the zeros and ones of the binary system of calculation. At this stage therefore the photos are in the form of a pattern of zeros and ones, as illustrated in the upper picture. The digits are fed into an electronic computer to produce images consisting of a series of dots of varying darkness, somewhat like the dots of halftone pictures in newspapers. The lower picture, showing a part of the Martian surface, was obtained in this manner. Pictures from the moon are also relayed in this way.

numbers one, two, three, four, five, six, seven, eight, nine and zero respectively.

The Hindu-Arabic system is also called a *positional decimal system,* because the number each digit represents depends on its "position," or "place," in the numeral. The far-right place in any numeral is the unit, or one, position; the place value of the next position to the left is ten. In general the place values from right to left, in any decimal numeral, are: ones, tens, hundreds, thousands, and so on. For example, the place values represented by 4,081 are:

$$4,081 = (4 \times 1000) + (0 \times 100) + (8 \times 10) + (1 \times 1)$$

Another way of looking at a positional decimal system is through the idea of grouping. Suppose we have a set of 13 dots marked on a sheet of paper; we draw a ring around 10 of these dots. There will be 3 dots remaining. We have 1 set of 10 dots plus 3 remaining single dots. This fact may be expressed as $13 = (1 \times 10) + (3 \times 1)$.

Now suppose we have 37 dots, and that we "ring" them in groups of 10. We will have 3 sets of 10 dots plus 7 single dots. We could write this as $37 = (3 \times 10) + (7 \times 1)$. Similarly if we had 128 dots we could have 1 set of 1 hundred or 10 tens, 2 sets of 10, and 8 dots remaining. We could write $128 = (1 \times 100) + (2 \times 10) + (8 \times 1)$. All this emphasis on "tens" seems quite natural to us. After all, we do have ten fingers and ten toes. But how do you suppose man would be counting today and what sort of a numeration system would he be using if he did not have his anatomy structured as it is?

The binary numeral system

Imagine all of us with one finger on each hand and one toe on each foot. Suppose further that all the numbers we use could be expressed with the "digits" 0 and 1. Since we are going to use only two symbols to write any number, we can call this a *binary,* or *base-two, system.* In a binary system the value of any place in a numeral is twice as large as the place to its right. Thus the place values — from right to left — in a binary system are: ones, twos, fours, eights, and so on.

The number 1 expressed in the binary system would be written as 1 $_{two}$. Thus the number represented by 1 $_{ten}$ and 1 $_{two}$ is the same. But how would we indicate 2 $_{ten}$ as a binary numeral? Let's try to discover the answer to this question.

Suppose we have a set of 2 stars. If we draw a ring around them, we have 1 set of 2 stars, and no single stars remaining. We would write 2 $_{ten}$ = 10 $_{two}$, which is read as "1 two plus 0 ones." If we begin with a set of 3 stars and draw a ring around 2 of them, we would have 1 set of 2 stars plus 1 set of 1 star. This would be indicated as 3 $_{ten}$ = 11 $_{two}$, read as "1 two plus 1 one."

How would 4 $_{ten}$ be expressed? Notice that we have been making pairs of equivalent sets wherever possible. Thus if we had a set of 4 stars, we could first form 2 sets of 2 stars each. Now draw a ring around these sets. This approach suggests that 4 $_{ten}$ may be thought of as 1 four, no twos and no ones, and written as 100 $_{two}$. In similar fashion 5 $_{ten}$ = 101 $_{two}$, which is "1 four, no twos and 1 one."

TABLE I

Place-Value Chart — Binary and Decimal

8 eights	4 fours	2 twos	1 ones	10 tens	1 ones
			0		0
			1		1
		1	0		2
		1	1		3
	1	0	0		4
	1	0	1		5
	1	1	0		6
	1	1	1		7
1	0	0	0		8
1	0	0	1		9
1	0	1	0	1	0
1	0	1	1	1	1
1	1	0	0	1	2
1	1	0	1	1	3
1	1	1	0	1	4
1	1	1	1	1	5

Note how 6 would then be treated. We would first have 3 sets of 2 stars in each set. Then we could pair up 2 of these sets, and wind up with 1 set of four, 1 set of two, and no ones. We write 6 $_{ten}$ as 110 $_{two}$.

Using the same development, it is clear that 7 $_{ten}$ = 111 $_{two}$, interpreted as 1 set of four, 1 set of two, and 1 one. We can analyze 8 $_{ten}$ in the same way. First we have 4 sets of 2 stars in each set. Then we have 2 sets with (2 × 2) or 4 stars in each. Finally, we have 1 set with (2 × 2 × 2) or 8 stars in it. This would be written as 1000 $_{two}$ and interpreted to mean 1 eight, 0 fours, 0 twos and 0 ones.

We now summarize what we have learned so far about binary numeration in Table I, and see if we can extend our ideas.

How would we express 106 $_{ten}$ as a base-two numeral? Remember: the place values in binary numeration are ones, twos, fours, eights, sixteens, thirty-twos, sixty-fours, one hundred twenty-eights, and so on. The largest place value contained in 106 is sixty-four. There is 1 sixty-four in 106, and 106 − 64 = 42. There is 1 thirty-two in 42; 42 −32 = 10. There are 0 sixteens in 10. There is 1 eight in 10; 10 − 8 = 2. There are 0 fours in 2. There is 1 two in 2; 2 − 2 = 0. There are 0 ones in 0. We conclude that 106 $_{ten}$ = 1101010 $_{two}$.

How would 47 $_{ten}$ be expressed in the binary system? There is 1 thirty-two in 47; 47 − 32 = 15. There are 0 sixteens in 15. There is 1 eight in 15; 15 − 8 = 7. There is 1 four in 7; 7 − 4 = 3. There is 1 two in 3; 3 − 2 = 1. There is 1 one in 1. So 47 $_{ten}$ = 101111 $_{two}$. But this method is tedious. There is another process that saves much of this labor.

To convert any decimal numeral into its binary form, divide it successively by 2. For example, if we divide 47 $_{ten}$ successively by 2, we obtain:

$$\begin{array}{r} 23 \\ 2\overline{)47} \\ 46 \\ \hline 1 \end{array}$$

$$\begin{array}{r} 11 \\ 2\overline{)23} \\ 22 \\ \hline 1 \end{array}$$

$$\begin{array}{r} 5 \\ 2\overline{)11} \\ 10 \\ \hline 1 \end{array}$$

$$\begin{array}{r} 2 \\ 2\overline{)5} \\ 4 \\ \hline 1 \end{array}$$

$$\begin{array}{r} 1 \\ 2\overline{)2} \\ 2 \\ \hline 0 \end{array}$$

$$\begin{array}{r} 0 \\ 2\overline{)1} \\ 0 \\ \hline 1 \end{array}$$

The remainders, in inverse order, make up the binary equivalent of 47 $_{ten}$. Reading from bottom to top, the remainders are 1, 0, 1, 1, 1, 1. So 47 $_{ten}$ = 101111 $_{two}$. This checks with the result we obtained using the longer process.

A puzzling excursion

Another way of obtaining the binary numeral for any natural number is through a rather interesting game. Suppose we construct a table in the following way. In the extreme right-hand column, we start with 1, skip 2, write 3, skip 4, write 5, skip 6, and so on, stopping arbitrarily at 15. In the second column from the right, we start with 2. Write 2 and 3, skip 4 and 5, write 6 and 7, skip 8 and 9; and so on, until we reach 15. In the third column, we start with 4. Write 4, 5, 6 and 7, skip 8, 9, 10, 11, and write 12, 13, 14, 15. In the fourth column, we start with 8 and write the numerals for 8 through 15.

What this amounts to is a pattern: in the first column (going from top to bottom), the pattern is "write one number, skip one number, write one number, skip one number," and so on. In the second column, starting with 2, the pattern is "write two numbers, skip two numbers," and so on. In the third column, starting with 4, the pattern is "write four, skip four." In the fourth column, starting with 8, the pattern is "write eight, skip eight." This table could be extended indefinitely. The fifth column would start with 16, and the pattern would be "write sixteen, skip sixteen," and so on. For our purposes, Table II will be adequate.

Now ask someone to think of a number from 1 to 15, and not to tell you what it is. Ask him to tell you if his number is in the first column, second column, third column, fourth column, going right to left. Each time he says "yes" remember the number represented at the top of that particular column. The sum of all these *yes* numbers is the number he was thinking of. Why does this work?

Suppose he chose 13. This number is in the columns headed 1, 4, 8, and the sum of these, $1 + 4 + 8$, is indeed 13. If he chose 11 he would have said yes, yes, no, yes, and his number would be represented by $1 + 2 + 8$, or 11. Let us look at 13 and 11 written in binary form. $13 = 1101_{two}$; $11 = 1011_{two}$. If we let "1" stand for "yes" and "0" stand for "no," we see why this trick works. The pattern used to construct the table forms a "binary scrambler." It takes any natural number and represents it in binary form.

If Table II were extended to five columns, one could get binary forms for

numbers up to and including 31; for six columns, up to and including 63; for seven columns, 127. How many columns would one need to represent numbers up to 511? If you said "nine columns" you were correct.

Suppose, now, that a merchant has only an old-fashioned balance scale with which he wishes to weigh packages whose weights in pounds can be expressed in terms of a natural number. What would be the least number of weights he would need to be able to weigh packages whose weights are any number of pounds from 1 to 50? (It is assumed that the weights would be placed in one pan and the packages in the other.) Clearly he would need a 1-lb. weight and a 2-lb. weight. He would not need a 3-lb. weight, but he would need a 4-lb. weight. He would not need a 5-lb. or a 6-lb. or a 7-lb. weight, but he would need an 8-lb. weight. Clearly he would need a 1-lb., a 2-lb., a 4-lb., an 8-lb., a 16-lb. and a 32-lb. weight. These weights correspond to the binary place values 1, 2, 4, 8, 16 and 32.

Addition with binary numerals

Suppose we wish to add 11_{two} and 110_{two}. We expect the sum to represent the same natural number as if the numbers were expressed in base ten. As in base ten, addition in base two is always possible, the sum of any two numbers is unique, addition is commutative and associative, and 0 names the identity element.

With these structural properties in mind, it is relatively easy to develop addition in base two. (In the examples that follow, we shall at times discard the subscript "two" to avoid cluttering up our notation.) We begin:

$$1 + 0 = 0 + 1 = 1$$

and

$$0 + 0 = 0$$

The only remaining fact we need is $1 + 1$. But we have already found out that $1 + 1 = 10$ in the binary system. We therefore write:

$$1 + 1 = 10$$

TABLE II

8	4	2	1
9	5	3	3
10	6	6	5
11	7	7	7
12	12	10	9
13	13	11	11
14	14	14	13
15	15	15	15

We can summarize our addition facts in the form of a matrix for easy reference.

+	0	1
0	0	1
1	1	10

Now let's add 100 + 10, we have:

$$\begin{array}{r} 100 \\ +\ 10 \\ \hline 110 \end{array}$$

Now try 10 + 11:

$$\begin{array}{r} 10 \\ +11 \\ \hline 101 \end{array}$$

Discussion: $0 + 1 = 1$, so we write 1 in the ones' place in the sum. Then $1 + 1 = 10$. Write 0 in the twos' place in the sum, and 1 in the fours' place.

Now we shall do two more-difficult examples, using only the conventional addition algorithm.

(a) $11010 + 10111 = \square$
(b) $110100 + 1111001 = \square$

Solution (a):

$$\begin{array}{r} 11010 \\ +10111 \\ \hline 110001 \end{array}$$

Discussion: $0 + 1 = 1$; write 1 in the ones' place in the sum. $1 + 1 = 10$; write 0 in the twos' place and remember 1 four. $1 + 0 + 1 = 10$; write 0 in the fours' place and remember 1 eight. $1 + 1 = 10$; write 0 in the eights' place and remember 1 sixteen. $1 + 1 + 1 = 11$; write 1 in the sixteens' place and 1 in the thirty-twos' place.

Solution (b):

$$\begin{array}{r} 110100 \\ +1111001 \\ \hline 10101101 \end{array}$$

Discussion: $0 + 1 = 1$; write 1 in the sum. $0 + 0 = 0$; write 0 in the sum. $1 + 0 = 1$; write 1 in the sum. $0 + 1 = 1$; write 1 in the sum. $1 + 1 = 10$; write 0 in the sum and remember 1. $1 + 1 + 1 = 11$; write 1 in the sum and remember 1. $1 + 1 = 10$; write 0 and then 1 in the sum.

Here are two more examples for you. See if your sums agree with these.

$$\begin{array}{r} 110101 \\ +1100011 \\ \hline 10011000 \end{array} \qquad \begin{array}{r} 1101 \\ +1001 \\ \hline 10110 \end{array}$$

Subtraction in the binary system

Subtraction in the binary system is treated essentially the same as in the decimal system. What is needed is some additional flexibility with binary notation.

From 110 let us subtract 101.

$$\begin{array}{r} 110 \\ -101 \\ \hline 1 \end{array}$$

Discussion: We cannot subtract 1 one from 0 ones, so we take 1 unit from the next base position (twos) and think of it as '10' ones. 1 one from '10' ones leaves 1 one; write 1 in the ones' place in the difference. 0 twos subtracted from 0 twos leaves 0 twos; 1 four subtracted from 1 four leave 0 fours.

Here is another example:

$$1001 - 11 = \square$$

$$\begin{array}{r} 1001 \\ -11 \\ \hline 110 \end{array}$$

Discussion: 1 one from 1 one leaves 0 ones; write 0 in the ones' place in the difference. We can't subtract 1 two from 0 twos. The base position to the left of twos is fours, but there are no fours either. So we go to the eights' place. We change 1 eight to '10' fours. We take one unit from the '10' fours, which leaves 1 four, and change that to '10' twos. Now 1 two from '10' twos leaves 1 two; write 1 in the twos' place in the difference. We still have 1 four remaining, which we show by writing 1 in the fours' place in the difference.

Let us do a more difficult example:

$$10110 - 111 = \square$$

$$\begin{array}{r} 10110 \\ -111 \\ \hline 1111 \end{array}$$

Discussion: 1 is greater than 0. Change 1 two into '10' ones. 1 from 10 is 1. Change 1 four into '10' twos. 1 from 10 is 1. Change the 1 sixteen into '10' eights.

Take 1 of these eights, which leaves 1 eight, and change it to '10' fours. Now we complete the subtraction. 1 from 10 is 1. 0 from 1 is 1. The difference is 1111.

Here are two more examples:

```
 10011100      10101101
 -110101      -1111001
 --------     ---------
 1100111       110100
```

Multiplication with binary numerals

Suppose we wish to multiply 10 and 11. We expect the product to represent the same number as if the multiplication were performed in base ten. As in base ten, multiplication in base two is always possible, the product of any two numbers is unique, multiplication is commutative and associative, and 1 $_{two}$ names the identity element. Also we assume that the distributive laws hold; that is, multiplication is distributive over addition.

Keeping these assumptions in mind, let us develop multiplication in the binary system. We have:

$$1 \times 0 = 0 \times 1 = 0$$

and

$$1 \times 1 = 1$$

Our multiplication matrix would then be quite simple.

×		0	1
0		0	0
1		0	1

Let's multiply: 11 × 10.

```
    10
  × 11
  ----
    10
   10
  ----
   110
```

Discussion: 1 × 0 = 0; write 0 in the product. 1 × 1 = 1; write 1 to the left of 0 in the first partial product. 1 × 0 = 0; write 0 under 1, in the second partial product. 1 × 1 = 1; write 1 to the left of the 0 just written. Now add.

Now we are ready to try a more difficult multiplication example.

$$110 \times 1101 = \square$$

Solution:

```
      1101
  ×    101
  --------
      1101
     0000
    1101
  --------
  1000001
```

Discussion: For the first partial product: 1 × 1 = 1, 1 × 0 = 0, 1 × 1 = 1 and 1 × 1 = 1. Every entry in the second partial product is zero. The entries in the third partial product are the same as in the first. The addition is involved but not overly difficult.

Here are a few more examples for you. See if your products agree with these.

```
      10111            11100
  ×    1101         ×    111
  ---------         --------
      10111            11100
     10111            11100
    10111            11100
  ----------         --------
  100101011         11000100
```

Division with binary numerals

To be able to divide with binary numerals, you must be very familiar with binary multiplication and subtraction. The first few examples that we shall work will be done by repeated subtraction. Then we shall resort to the more conventional algorithm.

Let's divide 11011 $_{two}$ by 11 $_{two}$.

```
        1001
  11/11011
       11
      ----
       0011
         11
         --
          0
```

Discussion: 11 is contained in 11 just 1 time. 1 × 11 = 11. Subtract and get 0 for the difference. Bring down 0. 11 is contained 0 times in 0; write 0 in the quotient. Bring down 1. 11 is contained 0 times in 1; write 0 in the quotient. Bring down 1. 11 is contained 1 time in 11. The remainder is 0.

Let's look at another example:

```
        110
101/11110
    101
    ---
    101
    101
    ---
     00
```

Discussion: 101 is contained in 111 just 1 time. $1 \times 101 = 101$. Subtract and get 10. Bring down 1. 101 is contained in 101 also 1 time. $1 \times 101 = 101$. Subtract and get 0. Bring down 0. 101 is contained in 0 zero times.

Here are two more examples for you. See if your quotients agree with these. You may check your work by multiplying the divisor by the quotient to get the dividend.

```
              1110
10011/100001010
      10011
      -----
      11100
      10011
      -----
      10011
      10011
      -----
```

```
           1101
1101/10101001
     1101
     ----
     10000
      1101
     -----
      1101
      1101
      ----
```

Binary fractions in decimal form

Converting fractional numbers in binary notation to equivalent decimal numerals is not particularly difficult. The position to the right of the "binary point" has a value of $\frac{1}{2}$; the next position has a value of $\frac{1}{4}$; the next a value of $\frac{1}{8}$; and so on. In each position, the numerator is 1, and the denominator is a power of 2 that depends on the position: for example, the third place to the right of the binary point is $\frac{1}{2^3}$, or $\frac{1}{8}$. We consider now an example.

Example: $1.1011_{two} = \underline{\ ?\ }_{ten}$

Solution:
$$1.1011 = 1 \times 1 + 1 \times \tfrac{1}{2} + 0 \times \tfrac{1}{4}$$
$$+ 1 \times \tfrac{1}{8} + 1 \times \tfrac{1}{16}$$
$$= 1 + \tfrac{1}{2} + 0 + \tfrac{1}{8} + \tfrac{1}{16}$$
$$= 1\tfrac{11}{16} \text{ or } 1.6975_{ten}$$

Decimal fractions in binary form

Any decimal fraction can be converted to its binary equivalent as follows:

First write the fraction down; then multiply it by 2 using base-ten multiplication facts. For example, if the decimal fraction is 0.721, we write:

$$0.721$$
$$1.442$$

Then remove the integer to the left of the decimal point and record it, say on the right:

```
0.721
1.442
0.442   1
```

Repeating, we have:

```
0.884   0
1.768   1
0.768
1.536   1
0.536
1.072   1
0.072
```

The process is repeated until the decimal fraction is reduced to zero, or until the desired number of places in the binary fraction is obtained. The binary equivalent is obtained by reading the recorded digits from top to bottom.

Thus $0.721_{ten} = 0.10111_{two}$.

Converting to octal numerals

A number expressed as a binary numeral is readily expressed as an equivalent in base eight. For a natural number the technique is simple. Since $2^3 = 8$, we begin with the smallest unit and group the "digits" in clusters of three "digits" each.

Example: Convert 10110111_{two} to the equivalent base-eight numeral.

Solution:
$$(10)\quad(110)\quad(111)_{two} = 267_{eight}$$
$$\uparrow\qquad\uparrow\qquad\uparrow$$
$$2_{eight}\quad 6_{eight}\quad 7_{eight}$$

Example: Convert .1101101 $_{two}$ to base eight.

Solution:
.(110) (110) (100) $_{two}$ = .664 $_{eight}$

Summary

The binary numeral system offers an interesting glimpse into the world of mathematics. Addition and multiplication, at first glance, appear to be very simple operations in the binary system because there are so few facts to learn. A more careful study reveals that numbers of any sizable magnitude require an almost endless sequence of 0's and 1's for their representations. Operations very quickly become bogged down in these long and labored numerals. But computers, because of their tremendous speed, can utilize binary notation to great advantage; the binary system has many advantages over other numeration systems for computer circuit design.

There are many interesting phenomena that lend themselves to binary explanation. If a question can be answered by "yes" or "no"; if a circuit is either "closed" or "open"; if a light bulb is either "on" or "off"; if a choice involves either "male" or "female"; if the issue is either "binary odd" or "binary even" — these are the kinds of situations to which mathematicians apply binary notation.

All the "new mathematics" programs treat binary numeration in depth. The greatest gain from such study is the increased ability to understand and appreciate the Hindu-Arabic (decimal) system.

NIM: AN INTERESTING GAME BASED ON BINARY NUMERALS

AN INTERESTING game for two persons, called Nim, is based on binary numeration. In this game the players take turns drawing chips from three stacks before them. A player may draw as many chips as he chooses from any stack in a single move. In his next move he may take chips from the same stack or any other stack as he wishes. The player who takes the last chip left from the three stacks is the loser.

If this game is played by an experienced player and a novice, the beginner will rarely win. The secret of the game is to select the proper number of chips from the correct stack so your arrangement will be "binary even," forcing the other player to be "binary odd."

Here is what is meant by "binary even" and "binary odd." Suppose the stacks of chips, designated as A, B and C, contain 9, 11 and 15 chips respectively. Represent 9, 11 and 15 in binary form. 9 = 1001 $_{two}$, 11 = 1011 $_{two}$ and 15 = 1111 $_{two}$.

A →	1	0	0	1
B →	1	0	1	1
C →	1	1	1	1

After this is done, focus your attention on the columns of numbers instead of on the original row representations. If the sum of each column is 0 or 2, then your position is "binary even." If not, your position is "binary odd." (When it is your turn to move, hope that the position you are in is "odd"; if it is even, any move you make will force you into an odd position and may cause you to lose — if your opponent knows the game.)

Suppose you are faced with the situation depicted in the illustration: 9, 11 and 15 chips. Your position is clearly "odd," so you must make a move which will leave your position "even." With a little practice you will see that you should remove 13 of the chips from stack C. If you do, your position will look like this: Quite clearly, the sum of every column is either 2 or 0.

A →	1	0	0	1
B →	1	0	1	1
C →			1	0

Once you reach a safe (even) position, no matter what your opponent does you will win, provided you make an "even" move every time.

Recipients of the 1969 Economic Science Prize: Dr. Jan Tinbergen (left) and Dr. Ragnar Frisch (right). They were honored for their development of mathematical models that can be used to analyze economic activity.

Swedish Information Service

Norwegian Information Service

MATH PENETRATES THE SOCIAL SCIENCES*

Computers and Game Theory Provide Insights into Human Behavior

"TEN years ago we were looked upon as something crazy," recalls Professor Robert W. Fogel, who teaches economic history at the University of Chicago and the University of Rochester. "But from being the Young Turks back then, we've become the Establishment."

Professor Fogel was describing the rising academic status of the "cliometrician," the name honoring the Greek Muse of history that is applied to economic historians who rely heavily on mathematical analysis to reconstruct past movements and conditions of the economy.

Cliometricians, econometricians, polimetricians, psychometricians, jurimetricians are all rapidly proliferating species of a genus of mathematically minded scholars who are infiltrating the academic

world armed with computers and many of the analytical tools of higher mathematics.

Honored by prize

Their triumph in the field of economics was underscored in October 1969 when the first Economic Science Prize in honor of Alfred Nobel was awarded to Dr. Ragnar Frisch of Norway and Dr. Jan Tinbergen of the Netherlands for their work in econometrics, the mathematical expression of economic theory.

In addition, the mathematizers — whose ranks have grown rapidly since World War II and at an accelerated pace in the last decade — have established wide beachheads in psychology, biology and political science and somewhat narrower ones in sociology, anthropology, linguistics, law and literature.

One result of the mathematizing trend has been an expanding need for a

* © 1969 by The New York Times Company. Reprinted by permission.

287

high degree of mathematical competence in higher education, a need that has already reached a level that was only dimly foreseen a decade ago.

"It's a problem," says Paul A. Samuelson, the Massachusetts Institute of Technology economist, who has been one of the principal American mathematizers in his field, "for that girl who says she doesn't have a mathematical mind — and she isn't always a girl."

Political calculations

She, or he, would find it impossible these days to get through the *American Economic Review* without firm grounding in at least calculus and linear algebra. The *Review* rarely carried articles with mathematics in them before World War II; it now rarely carries an article that is not replete with ornate equations, formulas and tables, many of them on a higher mathematical level than those found in *The Physical Review*.

Physical scientists and engineers are no longer the only scholars who use computers and higher mathematics. The mathematizers now include sociologists, lawyers and so on.

IBM

Even the *American Political Science Review* presents high hurdles to the non-mathematically inclined, including articles such as that by Manfred W. Kochen of the University of Michigan and Karl W. Deutsch of Harvard: "Toward a Rational Theory of Decentralization — Some Implications of a Mathematical Approach."

Social-science and life-science departments in American universities are increasing the math requirements for students and encouraging mathematics courses for professors who got their schooling before the new mathematical tools were developed.

At least 2/3 of the country's psychology departments now require their students to take statistics courses. A decade ago most refused to give degree credit for such courses. One to 2 years of advanced mathematics are required for entrance to nearly all major graduate schools of economics.

In the last half dozen years graduate departments in the life sciences have also begun to make college-level mathematics a prerequisite. Among them are departments at Purdue, Stanford, the University of North Carolina and Dartmouth. Graduate departments of political science are not far behind: Temple, Tulane and Michigan State are among dozens that have instituted requirements in quantitative methodology in the last 4 years.

Graduate social-science departments generally used to require 2 foreign languages of incoming students until recently. Now grounding in higher mathematics often supplants 1 of the language requirements, sometimes both.

Mathematics is becoming, in effect, the imperative foreign language of the social sciences. "A young man coming into economics today," says Professor Fogel, "would have as much difficulty without math as someone going into Classics without Greek. The language of economics is now largely mathematics."

It is the computer that primarily accounts for the headlong mathematization of academia, though the trend can be traced to the precomputer excursions into econometrics in the thirties.

Physicians try a computer system that diagnoses mental and emotional disorders. The process of diagnosis by computer is similar to the process that takes place in a doctor's mind as he marshals the evidence for a final diagnosis. The differences are that the computer is able to store a larger body of knowledge and can respond almost instantaneously.

Professor Robert M. Thrall of Rice, chairman of a panel on mathematics in the life sciences for the Mathematical Association of America, reports that the panel has recently drawn up recommendations that students in the life sciences be required to include a computer course in their curricula.

The possibilities as well as the mathematical demands that the computer has posed are illustrated by a current undertaking at the University of Michigan.

Hundreds of years of data

Two computers are busy at Ann Arbor digesting and correlating all election results throughout the country at the county level, for president, Congress and state governor, since the early 19th century; all Congressional roll calls since 1775 (starting with the Continental Congress) and census data since 1790. This is an immense amount of raw information whose analysis would have been unthinkable without the computers, says the project's director, Dr. Warren E. Miller, professor of political science at Michigan.

In the 4 years since Professor Miller's group, the Inter-University Consortium for Political Research, began collecting and computerizing the data, it has sent out approximately 1 million punch cards of coded information to other researchers for analysis.

Beginning in 1970, the consortium will also start putting its data in print, in 15 500-page volumes. Professor Miller calls these publishing plans "ironic" because getting away from the cumbersomeness of print was one of the predicted virtues of computerizing the data to begin with. But he says one of the main reasons for publishing the data is that many scholars still aren't used to dealing with computers.

In fact, there remains a considerable generation gap between older scholars, who often feel uneasy with the new mathematical modes of analysis and the computer, and younger academicians who have been schooled in the use of these tools. Historians of all ages are probably most resistant to the trend.

Schlesinger "skeptical"

Arthur Schlesinger, Jr., now teaching at the City University of New York, describes himself as "skeptical" about approaching history by the numbers, and points to a speech he made before the

American Sociological Association in 1962. In it, he said: "As a humanist, I am bound to reply that almost all important questions are important precisely because they are not susceptible to quantitative answer."

Professor C. Vann Woodward of Yale, president of the American Historical Association, tends to be somewhat more receptive to the infusion of mathematics into historical interpretation, but he has some doubts. "It tends to coerce the selection of subjects," he says, "to select out those aspects of history that are susceptible to quantifiable analysis."

Whether or not "coercion" was involved, Dr. Fogel of the University of Chicago has cliometrically calculated that railroads were not so crucial to industrial growth as the traditional wisdom has pictured them. And Dr. Fogel, as well as Dr. John R. Meyer of Harvard and Dr. Alfred H. Conrad of the City University of New York, has concluded that slavery was not a dying institution in the South when the Civil War erupted, but was economically alive and quite well at the time.

Some are unenthusiastic

So, like it or not, historians are finding that they, too, must heed the new mathematical influence. If some don't like it, they may find some comfort in what appears to be a small countercurrent to the mathematization of the social sciences — among younger students and professors who find social sciences humanistically appealing, but the pressure to quantify dehumanizing and something of a drag.

"Many students are attracted to social sciences because of warm hearts," says Professor Samuelson, whose widely used basic undergraduate textbook of economics makes him a Dr. Spock of sorts to economics students. "But they get a cold shower when they face half a dozen years of mastering math."

Younger economists nowadays, he says, are pleading for "relevance." "They think things are rotten and you don't need to be Isaac Newton to know it."

There is little evidence, however, that the mathematizing trend is being stopped or even slowed down. Indeed, one potentially vast frontier in the mathematizing of the social sciences has only begun to be explored. This is the application of game theory to economic, sociological, political and anthropological analysis.

Game theory, so called because of its evolution from the study of actual games, such as bridge and poker, is concerned with strategy and the strategic alternatives a game-player chooses. By looking at slices of life as complicated games, game theory is able to provide a mathematical handle for what long have been considered subjective, unmeasurable motives.

Game theory is already heavily employed in economics, and one of the fathers of game theory, Dr. Oskar Morgenstern of Princeton, expects to see it "expand very greatly" into political science and sociology. The effect will be to open up wide new areas in the study of human behavior for the mathematizers.

Is there a limit?

Are there any areas of human life and behavior that are unsusceptible to mathematical analysis? Dr. Roy G. d'Andrade of Rutgers, an anthropologist, doesn't think so. Some anthropologists are working on an algebraic analysis of kinship systems, for example. And Dr. d'Andrade expects that other areas will eventually fall to new kinds of mathematics, nonquantitative and symbolic. "What mathematics will look like 20 years from now," he says, "we don't even know."

Dr. B. F. Skinner of Harvard, the behavioral psychologist, has similarly suggested that all human behavior can ultimately be interpreted in the rigorous language of mathematics.

But the late Dr. Norbert Wiener, the communications theorist, who died in 1964, disagreed with such notions. Dr. Wiener was as responsible as anyone for the flood tide of mathematics in academia today, but he also cautioned: "There is much we must leave, whether we like it or not, to the 'unscientific.'"

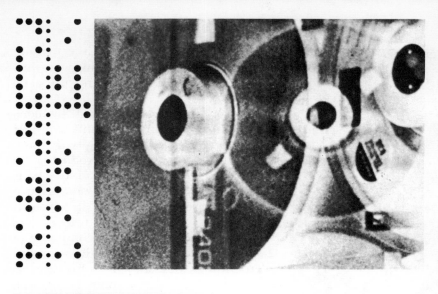

The Science Teacher

CYBERNETICS*

A New and Fast-expanding Science

BY V. G. DROZIN

ABOUT twenty years ago a new science was born and given the name "cybernetics." Its father was an outstanding American mathematician, Norbert Wiener, who in 1948 in *Cybernetics or Control and Communication in the Animal and the Machine,* introduced the name. He derived it from the Greek word "kybernetes" which means steersman or pilot; the Latin version of this word is "governor." In selecting this term, Wiener wanted to give recognition to the paper by T. C. Maxwell, "The Theory of Governor" (1868), which he considered as the first contribution to cybernetics because it dealt for the first time with feedback mechanism. Wiener also wanted to stress the fact that a ship can be considered as an example of a cybernetic system. We will discuss this example later.

Cybernetics has experienced a spectacular development. Within the first 17 years after its inception, 81 international symposia, conferences and meetings devoted to cybernetics or related problems were held; half a dozen periodicals devoted to cybernetics published; research institutes founded in a number of coun-

Reprinted from *The Science Teacher*

tries; and chairs in cybernetics established at some universities and military academies. Though cybernetics was originally concerned primarily with problems of biology, psychology, physics and engineering, it is now making an impact on other fields such as political science, sociology, medicine, linguistics, philosophy and even the arts.

How can one explain the unprecedented progress of cybernetics? The answer to this question can be found in the history of our technological civilization. The First Industrial Revolution originated in England in the textile industry in the second half of the eighteenth century. The water mill, steam engine, internal combustion engine, diesel engine, water and steam turbine, electrical generator and nuclear reactor are milestones of this revolution, which is still in progress. This Revolution has resulted in the tremendous amplification of our physical power. One needs only to think of the amount of energy we are using in our cars, home utilities and factories. Naturally, physics, as the science dealing with energy, emerged as the basic science.

Technological and scientific development in the twentieth century caused an

291

UPI

Norbert Wiener (1894–1964), the father of cybernetics.

exponential increase in the amount of information. For example, the number of physics publications referenced in the *Science Abstracts* since 1898 has doubled every 13 to 15 years. The "avalanche" of information produces more and more narrow specialization in science and the humanities, making communication between people more difficult. Complexity is the key word characterizing our present-day civilization.

Now we are witnessing the Second Industrial Revolution, which can be dated from 1944, the year when the first workable computer was built. This Revolution brings with it the amplification of our intellectual power — the power to solve problems which require a tremendous number of reliable computations and to manipulate a great amount of information. In the broad sense of the word, cybernetics deals with information. Since information is the major commodity of the Second Industrial Revolution, cybernetics emerges as the basic science of this revolution. One may call cybernetics the "physics of information." Indeed, everything which a physicist does with energy,

a cybernetist does with information; namely, he studies receiving, storing, transmitting, transforming and using information.

In a world characterized by complexity, it is important to find a proper frame of reference in dealing with information. This is done by introducing the concept of a *system* as one of the basic concepts of cybernetics. A system is anything which consists of at least 2 interrelated parts. For example, teacher and student represent a system consisting of 2 subsystems; school and family represent surroundings for a student or his external subsystems. The most complex artificial system created so far is probably the Apollo 11 which consists of more than 2,000,000 parts. The most complex natural system we know is the human central nervous system which consists of something like 100,000,000,000,000 nerve cells.

Every system can exist in a number of *states*. Any action on a system is called its *input*. As a result of an input, a system is transferred into another state. The result of the input is called *output*. For example, a switch in a circuit can be in two positions, off or on. The switching is input, the effect on the circuit is output. A student is a learning subsystem. Exposing him to one teaching lesson (input) transfers him into another state as a result of learning (output). One subsystem is *acting* on another if the output of the first system is the input of the second. If the output of the second subsystem is at the same time the input of the first, then we say both subsystems are *interacting* with each other.

Controlled systems

Not every system is treated in cybernetics. Cybernetics is only concerned with controlled systems. To illustrate, let us consider a ship as a cybernetic system. It consists of (1) a captain, who sets the destination and communicates it to the pilot, (2) the pilot, who compares the destination with the present position of the ship, (3) the surroundings which provide the pilot with feedback information about the position of the ship and about dangerous points to be avoided, (4) a steersman, who follows the steering commands of the pilot, and (5) the oarsman (the engine), which provides the energy for motion. The feedback information received by the pilot from the surroundings, which requires a change in course of the ship to reach the destination, is called negative feedback information.

If the course of the ship should not be changed, but because of wind, waves, or currents the ship deviates from its assigned course, the steersman gets feedback information about this deviation and corrects it. In an oceangoing ship a cybernetic system of servomechanisms between helm and rudder automatically corrects the course of the ship. A similar cybernetic system based on negative feedback information is the system thermostatically controlling the temperature of a room. If the thermostat is set at a temperature higher

than the actual temperature in the room, the discrepancy is reported as negative feedback information to the executive system — heater — which starts to operate until the desired and actual temperatures equalize.

The interest of cybernetics in controlled systems stems from two sources, the theory of automatic control and the study of control in living organisms. The similarity of these two control mechanisms inspired the idea that there are general laws of control in all systems independent of their nature. The existence of a general model of a controlled system operating on the feedback principle supports this idea. Communication between the parts of a controlled system (the flow of information between the subsystems of a given system) is the basic process of any cybernetic system. This allows us to define cybernetics as the study of the flow of information between the subsystems of a

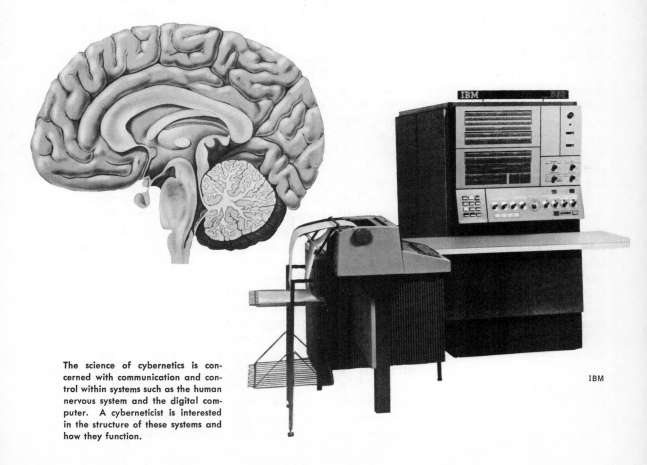

The science of cybernetics is concerned with communication and control within systems such as the human nervous system and the digital computer. A cyberneticist is interested in the structure of these systems and how they function.

IBM

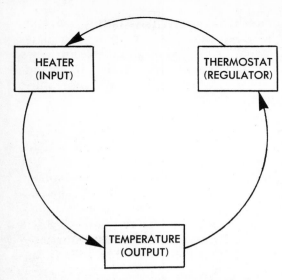

A simple controlled system: a thermostat-controlled heating system. The basic subsystems are the regulating unit (thermostat), the producing unit (heater) and the output (heat). The thermostat records the output and transmits this information to the control valve of the heating unit.

controlled system. During this flow the information may be received, transformed, stored, used, or transmitted in any of the subsystems.

The theory of information

While the natural sciences deal with matter and energy, cybernetics deals with information. What is information? In a broad sense, information is everything which is new to a person. The theory of information was created by an outstanding American mathematician, Claude E. Shannon, in his book *The Mathematical Theory of Communication,* published in 1949. In this theory, information is treated quite generally, independent of its meaning. The message informing which of 2 equally possible events actually occurred contains 1 unit of information called 1 bit (abbreviation of "binary unit"). For example, the message delivered to a father "you have a son" contains 1 bit of information (excluding the possibility of multiple births and stillborn babies). The measure of information is determined by its probability. The less probable the message, the more content it carries. We should not blame our newspapers for sensationalism since sensational information is less probable and, therefore, carries more content. The message about the birth of quadruplets has more information content than a message about a single birth. A murder, an earthquake, or a student riot are statistically less probable than the absence of these events, therefore, they carry more information and receive more coverage. No one is interested that 2,000 other colleges did not have any riots, since no rioting is more probable.

Studying a system

Let us consider now the methods used in cybernetics. Any system under study can be considered a cybernetic system because it is under control in the process of study. To learn a system means to find out its structure and its functioning. If one knows the structure of the system, he may explain its functioning. However, a reverse problem does not allow unique solutions since systems of different structure may operate in the same way. A cybernetist considers an unknown system a "black box." He studies the inputs and resulting outputs and by comparing them tries to build a model of the unknown system. If the system as a result of its inputs can be transformed into a finite number of states (outputs) the cybernetist would try to describe this in terms of Boolean algebra, or algebra of logical operations. Every statement is expressible in terms of three basic logical operations, "and," "or," and "not." Each of these operations in its turn can be modeled by simple electric circuits. This allows a system under study to be represented as an electric model, the output and input of which correspond to that of the original system. A cybernetist may use a physical or mathematical model of a system. He treats as the same model such diverse processes as, for example, transfer of mechanical energy by application of Newton's law to frictional forces, transfer of heat according to Fourier's law, diffusion of matter (Fick's law), and transfer of electricity (Ohm's law), since all of these equations contain corresponding gradients. Since such electrical quantities as current and voltage are easier to measure than are any others involved in these laws, one can model the first four laws by Ohm's law. This is done in so-called analog computers. More opportunities for creation of cybernetic models are offered by a digital computer.

As stated above, our epoch is characterized by increased complexity. Cybernetics has a quantitative expression for the range of complexity. It is called entropy. This is a rather difficult concept, so we will try to introduce it only in a qualitative way. Entropy is a measure of the degree of disorder of a system. The less organized the system, the more entropy it has. The more structured the system, the less entropy it has. Civilization's progress is accompanied by a decrease of entropy. However, there is a law in cybernetics which states that decrease in entropy in one part of the system is always accompanied by a larger increase in entropy in other parts of this system. Translating this law into practical language means that the artificial technological systems are created at the expense of destruction of natural systems in the form of pollution of our air and rivers, for example. Cybernetics puts the problem of conservation into a proper perspective.

Finally, we should show an aspect of cybernetics which distinguishes it from other sciences. Every science deals with a particular branch of knowledge and develops a special terminology usable only in this science. A cybernetist dealing with information as such can communicate with anybody. For example, he would ask a physicist or a sociologist exactly the same set of questions; namely, What system do you study? What are the external and internal subsystems of this system? What inputs and outputs do you have in your system? What channels do you use for their delivery? What is the relation between inputs and outputs? What model do you suggest for your system? These questions are nothing else but the inductive part of the scientific method. The final question would be: How did you verify the correctness of your model? This question corresponds to the deductive part of the scientific method. The universal character of the terminology used in cybernetics allows its use as a meta language, that means as a language in which other sciences and humanities could be described. This may help to overcome the semantic barrier between the people of different professions. Indeed cybernetical conferences seem to be the only ones where the representatives of such diverse professions as engineers and biologists, linguists and mathematicians, psychologists and economists come together and are able to communicate with each other.

Within the frame of a single article, it is impossible to convey more than general ideas of cybernetics. We must omit most interesting applications of cybernetics in biology, medicine, economics, psychology, pedagogy and other branches of knowledge as well as mathematical apparatus used there, such as the theory of games and the theory of optimization of systems. Cybernetics is a new and fast-expanding science. Therefore, a word of warning is appropriate. One should critically evaluate its claims in an objective spirit of free inquiry.

Cybernetics certainly cannot compete with any other science since it is not concerned with particular systems treated in each of them but rather with general laws of flow of information in all controlled systems.

One often reads advertisements in larger newspapers in which a firm is looking for a system analyst. A system analyst or an operations researcher uses the same mathematical apparatus and terminology as a cybernetist does. He has, however, a practical purpose: to find ways to improve the efficiency of operation of a firm. As such he is related to a cybernetist as an engineer to a scientist. For example, a city having a traffic problem may invite a system analyst, who, after studying the problem, may suggest installing additional traffic lights or making some streets one-way or letting a computer control the traffic through light signals.

THE 1969
NOBEL PRIZES
FOR PHYSICS
AND CHEMISTRY

California Institute of Technology

Right: Dr. Murray Gell-Mann.

BEFORE a gala audience in the Stockholm Concert Hall, King Gustaf VI Adolf of Sweden presented the distinguished scientific and literary awards, the Nobel Prizes. The date: December 10, 1969.

Among the 9 recipients was a brilliant young scientist who helped bring order to the world of subatomic particles. Dr. Murray Gell-Mann, 40, of the California Institute of Technology (Caltech) was awarded the Nobel Prize for Physics.

The Nobel Prize for Chemistry was shared by 2 men: British organic chemist Derek H. R. Barton, 51, of the Imperial College of Science and Technology in London, and retired Norwegian physical chemist Odd Hassel, 72, formerly of the University of Oslo. These 2 men were honored for their contributions toward understanding the complex structures of organic compounds.

Order out of chaos

Murray Gell-Mann was born in New York City on September 15, 1929. A precocious child, he developed an early interest in mathematics and the natural sciences. He retains this love for the world of nature; when asked how he would spend his Nobel Prize money he said, "I'd

like to buy a small stretch of wild land somewhere." He is an avid bird watcher and camper, and in recent years has been very involved in environment problems.

Why, then, did he major in physics? It "just happened," he said. Graduating from Yale University with a Bachelor of Science degree in 1948, he entered the Massachusetts Institute of Technology. There he received his Ph.D. in physics in 1951 — at the age of 21. Dr. Gell-Mann taught and studied at Columbia University and the University of Chicago before moving to Caltech in 1955, where he has remained ever since.

In the years following World War II, new, powerful atom smashers enabled physicists to greatly expand their knowledge of the atom. Unusual new subatomic particles were discovered, and as the number and types of particles increased, so did the mystification and bewilderment of the physicists. Existing "laws" of physics could not explain the behavior of these newfound particles: they interacted and transformed themselves into other particles in ways that seemed to violate some of the most fundamental concepts of physics. For example, some of these particles took much longer to decay into other particles

Dr. Derek H. R. Barton in his laboratory at the Imperial College of Science and Technology in London.

UPI

than predicted by existing theories; others exhibited unexpected properties of mass, charge or spin. In other words, the particles were "strange." The once orderly world of subatomic physics had become a chaotic "zoo."

Order was restored by Dr. Gell-Mann when, in 1953, he formulated his Theory of Strangeness. He assigned "strangeness" values to the subnuclear particles, based on their rates of decay. Later, going one step further, he classified the particles into groups of 8; the particles in a particular group have similar masses but have different charges and are able to transform into other particles of the same group. In any change, however, the strangeness value of the particle remains the same.

There were gaps in Dr. Gell-Mann's groups of 8, and to fill them, he predicted the existence of particles that have since been discovered by other physicists.

Dr. Gell-Mann's next major contribution came in 1961 when he theorized that subatomic particles consist of still-more-fundamental particles. All matter, he said, is actually made of 3 basic building blocks. He called these building blocks "quarks" (from a line in Jame Joyce's *Finnegans Wake:* "Three quarks for Muster Mark!"). A quark, if it exists, would have a fractional electrical charge, something previously unheard of in physics. Scientists around the world have been hunting for proof that these particles exist. In 1969, four scientists from Australia's Sydney University claimed that they detected quarks. If this discovery is substantiated, the field of atomic physics will be revolutionized.

Below: Dr. Odd Hassel of Norway.

Norwegian Information Service

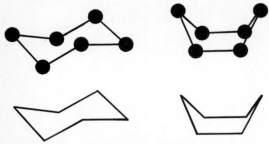

Configurations of cyclohexane that are free of angle strain. Left: chair shape; right: boat shape.

The different shapes of things

Odd Hassel was born in Oslo, Norway, in 1897. He studied at the University of Oslo and at Berlin University, receiving his Ph.D. in chemistry from the latter in 1924. In 1925 he accepted a position at the University of Oslo and remained there until his retirement in 1964. Today, Dr. Hassel is still active in chemical research, concentrating mainly on the structure of halogen compounds.

Derek Barton was born in Gravesend, England, in 1918. He attended the Imperial College of the University of London where, in the 1940's, he received Bachelor of Science and Ph.D. degrees. He also holds a Doctor of Science degree from the parent University of London. Dr. Barton taught and did research at several institutions in England and the United States in the forties and early fifties; since 1957 he has been a professor of organic chemistry at the Imperial College.

Drs. Hassel and Barton, who worked independently of each other, were awarded the Nobel Prize for their work on the three-dimensional structure of certain carbon compounds. Prior to 1930, relatively little was known of the detailed spatial structure of these compounds. Empirical formulas, giving the numbers of atoms in compounds, and structural formulas, representing the arrangements of atoms in molecules in flat, two-dimensional schemes, do not convey accurate impressions of the enormous complexity of many organic compounds.

The development of new analytical methods using X rays and other kinds of radiation enabled scientists to study the three-dimensional structures of compounds. Beginning in the 1930's, Dr. Hassel applied these new techniques to the study of a type of hydrocarbon called cyclohexane. Chemists had long believed that the atoms of the cyclohexane molecule were arranged in a ring. But what kind of ring? A ring can be twisted into an almost infinite variety of shapes. In addition, the atoms in the ring exert forces on each other that may distort or strain the entire molecular framework.

In the absence of outside forces, a molecule will take a certain preferred shape. What would this be for cyclohexane? The two most favored configurations were a form resembling a boat and one resembling a chair. Dr. Hassel found that the cyclohexane molecule was most commonly found in the chair shape.

Dr. Barton read Dr. Hassel's papers, and extended research in this field to other ringlike organic chemicals. Whereas Dr. Hassel was primarily concerned with the shape of isolated molecules, Dr. Barton's main interest was the shape of molecules during the course of a reaction.

The work of these two chemists formed the basis of modern conformational analysis. In the words of Dr. Barton, this is "the correlation of preferred shapes or conformations of molecules with their physical and chemical properties." For many substances the shape of a resting molecule is not the same as the shape of a molecule during the course of a reaction.

Conformational analysis has revolutionized man's understanding of the structure of compounds. The properties of substances yet to be synthesized can be predicted with far more accuracy than previously. The molecular structure of many chemicals can be determined spatially with a great degree of certainty. The advent of computers has simplified the complicated mathematical procedures that are involved in conformational analysis. The way has been opened to elucidating the nature of biological molecules which are often enormously complex, consisting of millions of atoms.

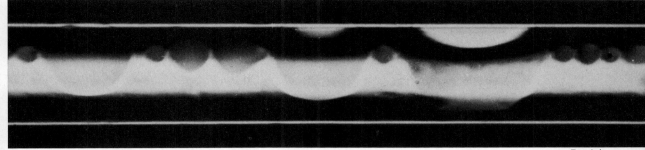

POLYWATER*

Newly Discovered Form of Water Intrigues Scientists

BY MORT LA BRECQUE

Globules of polywater inside a hair-thin capillary tube. This strange form of water is about 15 times more viscous and 40 per cent denser than ordinary water.

IT APPEARS that even the most endearingly familiar substances are not sacrosanct in a changing world. The first announcement, in 1961, of the discovery of anomalous water by a team of Soviet chemists was greeted by Western scientists with stony silence. Could a form of the commonest liquid really remain undiscovered, they wondered, until now? Apparently it could, because both British and American teams finally confirmed the discovery in 1969. Anomalous water is indeed a highly individual kind of H_2O with unique and striking characteristics of its own, according to researchers at England's Unilever Research Laboratories and at the University of Maryland.** It has lower vapor pressure, 40 per cent greater density and as much as 15 times higher viscosity than run-of-the-tap water: anomalous water has been observed crawling stealthily up its container's walls. Considerably more stable under temperature change, it won't boil below 932° F. and won't freeze above −40° F. Because it expands substantially less than normal water when frozen, the ice it forms looks like glass. These unusual properties are those of a water polymer, say the Maryland team, and they have coined the name "polywater" for anomalous water.

The discovery of anomalous water came about when Boris V. Deryagin and his Soviet colleagues observed secondary water columns forming at both ends of small, sealed glass capillaries. Later they prepared the liquid by condensing water vapor in glass and fused-quartz capillaries under reduced vapor pressure. Western scientists ignored their reports in the Soviet literature until Professor Deryagin himself visited Britain and the United States in 1966 and 1967 to explain his findings. Repeating Deryagin's experiments, E. Willis, G. K. Rennie, Colin Smart and B. A. Pethica of the Unilever Research Laboratories in Port Sunlight, Cheshire, reported, "we have been able to confirm several of Deryagin's findings but have not succeeded in identifying the entities responsible for the anomalous behavior. We conclude that the 'anomalous' water we have obtained in Pyrex glass is composed chiefly of normal water and that some of its properties are consistent with those of a gel. It is possible that a gel could be formed by the leaching of silicates from the glass."

Anomalous no more

The Port Sunlight team had some reservations about accepting the water as a stable and distinct molecular entity be-

* Reprinted from *The Sciences*, published by the New York Academy of Sciences, © 1969
** This team includes scientists from the University and the National Bureau of Standards.

299

NORMAL WATER

H–O–H

HEXAGONAL POLYWATER STRUCTURE

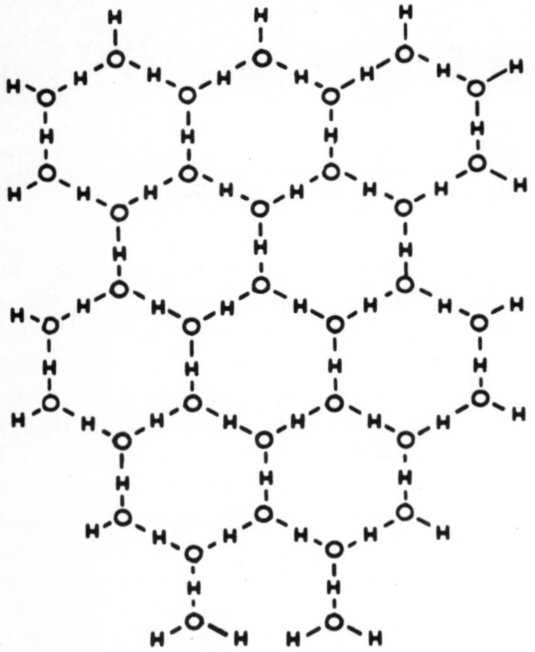

BRANCHED CHAIN POLYWATER STRUCTURE

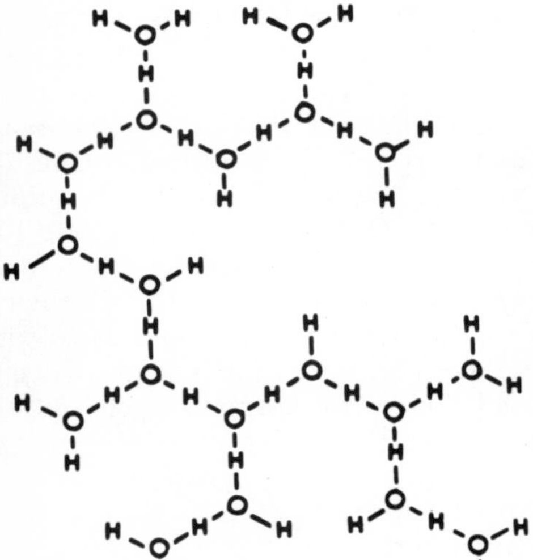

The diagrams show the structure of ordinary water and two possible structures for polywater. Dr. Deryagin suggests that something in the glass capillary tubes, perhaps silicon, acts as a catalyst, causing unusual forces to bind ordinary water molecules together.

cause only minute amounts of it could be formed for study; however, the team of chemists at the University of Maryland are unequivocal about their experimental results. From an interpretation of infrared and Raman spectroscopic studies of anomalous water, "the material is a true high polymer, consisting of H_2O monomer units," say Drs. Ellis R. Lippincott, Robert R. Stromberg and Warren H. Grant and Mr. Gerald L. Cessac. "The properties, therefore, are no longer anomalous but, rather, those of a newly found substance — polymeric water or polywater."

For the first time, the Maryland team studied the new liquid outside of the capillaries in which it had been formed. Disagreeing with the Port Sunlight team's speculations about silicate-leaching, the University of Maryland group observed "no strong absorption which would indicate the presence of such substances as hydrogen peroxide, silica gel, silicic acids, or silicates. Indeed, there is no evidence in the [infrared] spectrum for any contamination by silicon-containing compounds, oils, greases, and the like."

The Raman and infrared spectra indicate to Dr. Lippincott and his colleagues that polywater is composed of a previously unrecognized bonding for a system containing only hydrogen and oxygen atoms, and that it is formed when normal water is restructured by a catalytic effect of the surface of fused-quartz or Pyrex tubes. Polywater is spectrally similar to bifluoride-ion solutions, which form strong bonds of F–H–F atoms with both bonds exactly equivalent. They suggest an extremely strong, symmetrical three-center polywater bond of O–H–O units, arranged in a network of hexagons or highly branched polymer chains. A polymer, like the plastics polyethylene, polyvinyl and polystyrene, consists of giant molecules bonded together. The properties of polymers are distinct and separate from those of the molecules that form them, so polywater "should not be considered to be or even called water."

Ubiquitous potential

The most striking evidence that polywater has been accepted by the American scientific Establishment is a new project undertaken by the Pentagon's Advanced Research Project Agency, a study of ways to isolate and gather polywater more efficiently. Salt is relatively insoluble in polywater, and the substance might be used to desalt seawater. Polywater may also find employment as a corrosion preventive in metals, as an antifreeze, and as fuel for proposed automobile steam engines.

Polywater may be found naturally in clays, and other mineral systems whose water density is greater than normal; another possible natural source of polywater is man — and every other living organism.

Solid surfaces in living cells may order intracellular water, in the same way that fused-quartz capillaries restructure columns of ordinary water so that it assumes the semicrystalline structure of polywater, according to Freeman Cope of the Aerospace Medical Center in Warminster, Pennsylvania. After feeding rats heavy water so that their tissue H_2O was partially replaced with D_2O, Dr. Cope examined the electric quadrupole moments of the deuterium (D) nuclei in muscles and brain. Using nuclear magnetic resonance to probe the electric fields surrounding water molecules in these tissues, he found that the intracellular water had a structure more like ice than water. Cellular water may not be an inert solvent but an integral part of a solid-phase system, says Dr. Cope, and biologists may have to rethink their ideas about the nature of cells.

NBS

NBS

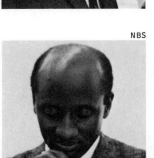

Industrial Research

Below: with the aid of a microscope, Dr. Grant examines samples of polywater in three capillary tubes. These capillaries are about ten micrometers in diameter (10/25,000 of an inch).

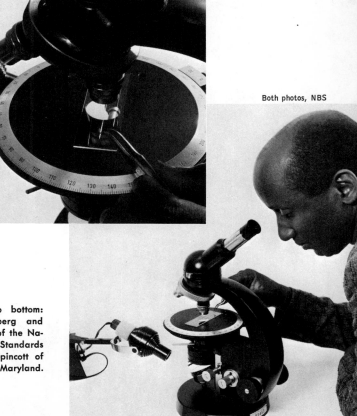

Both photos, NBS

Left, from top to bottom: Robert R. Stromberg and Warren H. Grant of the National Bureau of Standards (NBS); Ellis R. Lippincott of the University of Maryland.

SPACE
EXPLORATION

CONTENTS

Imaginative men have been landing on the moon for centuries. Some of their methods of travel have proved to be closer to fact than fiction. (This scene is from a 1902 movie, "A Trip to the Moon.")

The Bettmann Archive   **303**

REVIEW OF THE YEAR-
SPACE EXPLORATION

"That's one small step for a man, one giant leap for mankind." These historic words — the most memorable ones of 1969 — were spoken by astronaut Neil A. Armstrong as he stepped onto the moon. For the first time in human history, man visited another body in this vast universe. The implications of this achievement are not yet clear and, in fact, may not be completely apparent for decades or even centuries. One thing, however, is probably certain: man will never again be limited to earth; he will travel ever farther into space, visiting objects not only in our solar system but also planets and stars tens or hundreds of light-years away. Yet as man journeys to these distant bodies, he may confirm a thought expressed by Dr. Wernher von Braun: "the more we go into space the more we'll find that the most interesting planet to study from space is earth."

Manned space flights. Apollo 9 was the first of 4 manned craft launched by the United States in 1969. The major task of this 10-day mission in March was to give the 16-ton lunar module (LM) its first flight test in space. Apollo 10, launched on May 18, was the last rehearsal for landing men on the moon. During this 8-day mission, astronauts Thomas P. Stafford and Eugene A. Cernan rode the Apollo 10 LM to within 9.4 miles of the moon's surface; John W. Young remained behind aboard the command module (CM). Shortly after splashdown on May 26, NASA Administrator Thomas O. Paine, enthusiastic at the success of the mission, said, "we will go to the moon."

And so, on July 16, Apollo 11 lifted from its launch pad at Cape Kennedy. Approximately 108 hours later, Neil Armstrong and Edwin E. Aldrin, Jr., were leaving man's first footprints in the lunar "soil." Their 2¼ hours of extra-vehicular activity (EVA) passed quickly as they collected rocks, set up experiments, took photographs, and so on. Meanwhile, the third Apollo 11 crew member, Michael Collins, circled the moon in the CM, one of the few Americans unable to watch Armstrong and Aldrin. The astronauts' return to earth on July 24 was followed by 18 days of quarantine as a guard against spread of possible lunar contamination. (Although there was no evidence of such contamination, the crew of Apollo 12 underwent a similar period of isolation.)

Four months later, on November 14, men again left earth for the moon. The Apollo 12 mission was far more complex than that of Apollo 11. It lasted 2 days longer; more time was spent on the moon; and EVA time was increased to approximately 8 hours. Astronauts Charles Conrad, Jr., and Alan L. Bean set up a nuclear-powered scientific station that was expected to radio data to earth for at least a year. They brought back approximately 140 pounds of lunar rocks and soil, and several parts of Surveyor 3, a lunar soft-landing vehicle launched on April 17, 1967 (indications are that a dust shower generated by the Apollo 12 LM as it landed caused more damage to the Surveyor 3 television camera than 950 days of exposure to the space environment). After rejoining Richard F. Gordon in the CM, the men jettisoned their LM, sending it back toward the moon where its impact triggered a type of seismic activity never recorded on earth. Surprised scientists called this "a major discovery."

The Soviet Union launched five manned space vehicles in 1969: Soyuzes 4 and 5 in January and Soyuzes 6, 7 and 8 in October. The tests conducted on these flights appeared to be directed toward the establishment of a space station; several Soviet spokesmen have indicated that the U.S.S.R. plans to construct such a station within the next five years.

Planetary probes.   The most outstanding achievement of unmanned space exploration in 1969 was the closeup viewing of Mars provided by Mariners 6 and 7.   These American probes sent back valuable data and television images when they flew past the planet in, respectively, late July and early August. ◆ In January 1969 the Soviet Union sent two probes toward our other neighboring planet, Venus.   The descent capsules of Veneras 5 and 6 entered the atmosphere of Venus on May 16 and May 17 respectively.   Results of the flights corroborated previous estimates of the high density and temperature of Venus' atmosphere, which apparently consists almost entirely of carbon dioxide, with small amounts of nitrogen and inert gases and mere traces of oxygen. ◆ The Soviet Union also launched two lunar probes in 1969.   Luna 15 was sent toward the moon on July 13 on an unspecified mission that may have been related to the Apollo 11 voyage; eventually it crashed onto the moon.   Zond 7 was launched on August 8; as had its predecessors in the Zond series, it successfully circumnavigated the moon and returned to be recovered back on earth on August 14.

Earth satellites.   The United States and the Soviet Union launched about 100 satellites in 1969.   (This box score diminished in the latter half of the 1960's as different programs drew to a close or were deferred because of budget cuts.) ◆ Other nations are increasingly participating in space exploration.   On January 30, 1969, Canada's ISIS 1 (International Satellites for Ionospheric Studies) was launched from Vandenberg Base, California, as part of a Canadian-U.S. project.   The ten experiments carried by the craft included an electrostatic probe that measured temperature and concentrations of electrons near the satellite; instruments to measure ionospheric and extraterrestrial radio noise; a receiver for measuring radio signals produced by lightning flashes; and detectors of energetic particles that determined their production, entrance and distortions within the magnetosphere.   Ionospheric phenomena were also studied by ESRO 1B, a European Space Research Organization satellite launched on October 1, 1969.   A West German AZUR spacecraft launched on November 8, 1969, carried seven experiments designed to study various aspects of the earth's space environment.   And on February 11, 1970, Japan launched a research satellite aboard a solid-fuel Lambda rocket.   Four previous Japanese attempts to launch a satellite failed; the most recent of these had been on September 22, 1969.

Among the important scientific satellites sent aloft by the United States in 1969 were OSO 5 (Orbiting Solar Observatory), launched on January 22; OSO 6, launched on August 11; OGO 6 (Orbiting Geophysical Observatory), launched on June 5 — a partial success and the last entry in the series; Explorer 41, launched on June 21, and returning radiation data from space between the earth and the moon; and Biosatellite 3, launched on June 29 — the third of four in NASA's biological-experimentation series. ◆ There were numerous scientific entries in the Soviet Union's series of Cosmos satellites, but few details are available.   Another Soviet program, Intercosmos, represents an international effort in which several Eastern European countries took part.   The first two craft launched in this series (on October 14 and December 25) were instrumented to study the atmosphere and solar radiation.

Applications satellites launched by the United States in 1969 included environmental-survey satellite ESSA 9, orbited on February 26, and meteorological satellite Nimbus 3, launched on April 14.   (It might be noted that early in 1970 Nimbus 3 began tracking a Montana elk that had been geared with electronic equipment so that its migration route might be studied.

◆ On January 23, 1970, ITOS 1 was launched by NASA. Expected to operate for at least 12 months, this 682-pound satellite provides global weather information every 12 hours. In addition to 4 television cameras and 2 infrared scanning radiometers that produce daytime and nighttime pictures, the craft carries instruments for measuring proton energy from the sun and for monitoring the earth's heat balance. ◆ The U.S. Communications Satellite Corporation successfully orbited two communications satellites, Intelsats 3C and 3D on, respectively, February 5, 1969, and May 21, 1969, for the International Telecommunications Satellite Consortium. Intelsat 3C was positioned over the Indian Ocean; the identical Intelsat 3D was placed over the Pacific.

◆ Numerous Soviet Cosmos satellites also fell into the category of applications satellites. In addition, the U.S.S.R. launched meteorological satellites Meteors 1 and 2 (March 26 and October 6) and communications satellites Molniyas 1K and 1L (April 11 and July 22).

Rocket engines. NASA is experimenting with several new types of rocket engines. Ion engines, one kind of electric thruster, may be used in the future to position spacecraft or to propel them to distant planets. Although they produce relatively small amounts of thrust, they are potentially more efficient in space than either chemical or nuclear rocket engines. On February 3, 1970, NASA launched Sert 2, an earth-orbital spacecraft with two electron-bombardment ion engines. These engines generate thrust by ionizing a vaporized propellant, mercury, electrically accelerating the ions, neutralizing these ions and expelling them at extremely high speeds — on the order of fifty thousand miles per hour.

For several years NASA and the Atomic Energy Commission have been working on a nuclear rocket. "What we are attempting to make," said Commission Chairman Glenn T. Seaborg, "is a flyable compact reactor, not much bigger than an office desk, that will produce the power of Hoover Dam from a cold state in a matter of minutes." Technicians have successfully tested an experimental engine called XE in a ground test; 55,000 pounds of thrust were produced. Design and engineering studies are now under way on a 75,000-pound-thrust engine.

Space in the 1970's. NASA has scheduled two Apollo missions in 1970, two in 1971, one in 1973 and two in 1974. Plans are also under way for a preliminary three-man space station in late 1972 as part of Skylab, the Apollo applications program. This program has been designed to make maximum use of space hardware developed for the Apollo moon missions. Flight tests of a space "shuttle" are scheduled for 1975. As visualized, such a ferry would have two main sections: a booster capable of returning to earth for reuse after launch, and an orbital stage that also could reenter the atmosphere, making an airplane-style landing. There has been talk, as well, of a manned flight to Mars, perhaps in 1986 — a possibility strongly urged by Vice-President Spiro Agnew in his role of chief space adviser to President Richard M. Nixon (who agreed to the 1986 plan, but not as a program to be conducted on a high-priority basis).

Planned unmanned missions include a "grand tour" of the outer planets in 1977. Such a mission, possible because of the unusual alignment of the planets, would take from 8.5 to 11 years, depending on the route of the spacecraft. Other unmanned missions planned by NASA include two orbital flights around Mars in 1971 and the landing of two craft on Mars in 1976; flights to Jupiter in 1972 and 1973; and flights to Venus and Mercury in 1973.

Thomas P. Stafford, Apollo 10 commander. Born in Weatherford, Oklahoma, on September 17, 1930. B.S.—U.S. Naval Academy, 1952. Selected by NASA in 1962. Pilot of Gemini 6; command pilot of Gemini 9.

THE MEN OF APOLLOS 10 AND 11

John W. Young, Apollo 10 command-module pilot. Born in San Francisco on September 24, 1930. B.S.—Georgia Institute of Technology, 1952. Selected by NASA in 1963. Pilot on Gemini 3 and Gemini 10.

Eugene A. Cernan, Apollo 10 lunar-module pilot. Born in Chicago on March 14, 1934. B.S.—Purdue University, 1956; M.S.—U.S. Naval Postgraduate School. Selected by NASA in 1963. Pilot on Gemini 9.

Photos NASA

The crew of Apollo 11. From left to right: Edwin E. Aldrin, Jr., Neil A. Armstrong and Michael Collins peer out of the window of the Mobile Quarantine Facility after their triumphant return from the moon. Since their mission two of the men have left the astronaut corps. Collins is now assistant secretary of state for public affairs; Armstrong is deputy associate administrator of aeronautics in NASA's Office of Advanced Research and Technology.

Astronaut Charles Conrad studies the Surveyor 3 craft in the Sea of Storms. On the horizon is the Apollo 12 LM, *Intrepid*.

RETURN TO THE MOON

The Flights of
Apollos 12 and 13

BY STEVEN MOLL

NASA

THEY were the best of flights and the worst of flights, to paraphrase Charles Dickens. Apollo 12 exceeded the scientific and technological achievements of its predecessor; Apollo 13 fell just short of condemning three astronauts to death in space. And yet, because the astronauts did return safely, Apollo 13 was itself a triumphant mission.

The Apollo 12 mission

With the visual if sometimes inarticulate poetry of Apollo 11, the first manned lunar landing, out of the way, the more prosaic exploration of the moon could begin in earnest. The scientific community of NASA, which had been chafing at what it considered its second-rank voice in U.S. manned space planning, could look forward to three or four years of serious investigation by Apollo astronauts into the nature of the moon.

The Apollo 12 mission began on the morning of November 14, 1969. The men aboard the spacecraft were Charles (Pete) Conrad, Jr., Richard F. Gordon, Jr., and Alan L. Bean, a rookie astronaut. (Conrad and Gordon had both flown previous missions in the two-man Gemini spacecraft.) Heavy clouds lay over Cape Kennedy that morning, and as the Saturn V rocket lifted the astronauts from Launching Pad 39-A, lightning discharges temporarily knocked power systems of the

Apollo out of commission. For a few moments there was real concern that the mission might have to be aborted. Fortunately, power was soon restored. But NASA came under criticism for permitting the launch to take place under storm conditions for no very justifiable reasons.

Down to the sea of storms. Tracking a hybrid trajectory to the moon — a flight plan that would not send them back toward earth without large course corrections (if injection into lunar orbit proved impossible) — the astronauts neared their destination three days later. Conrad and Bean climbed into the lunar module (LM) and carried out maneuvers to separate themselves from Gordon in the command module (CM) and descend to the moon's surface. Thenceforth the LM was referred to by its code name, *Intrepid;* the command/service modules (CSM) had been christened *Yankee Clipper.*

Given the go-ahead by Mission Control back on earth, Conrad and Bean began their descent to a site on the Sea of Storms, 110 miles west of Apollo 11's Tranquility Base where Neil A. Armstrong and Edwin E. Aldrin, Jr., had landed 4 months earlier.

Until the last few moments, the descent proceeded smoothly. Conrad commented with increasing excitement on the way their guidance systems were taking them right down the planned flight path.

They landed on target, only 600 feet from the Surveyor 3 probe, which had soft-landed on the moon in April 1967. This pinpoint landing was quite an improvement over that of Apollo 11, which was a few thousand feet off course. (An ability to make precise landings is of great importance to future Apollo missions, which are scheduled to come down in rough terrains.)

The final seconds before landing, as Conrad later described them, were very tricky ones: the craft's engine raised large quantities of obscuring dust, making a visual landing impossible. But *Intrepid* set down safely at 1:54:43 A.M. Eastern standard time (EST) on November 19. The moon was again inhabited by man.

Setting foot on the moon. As quickly as the donning of life-support equipment would permit, Conrad and Bean got to work. The struggle to get into their gear proved as laborious as it had for Armstrong and Aldrin, a difficulty perhaps inherent in the cramped size of the LM interior.

Conrad set the tone for the transmissions to follow when he stepped down from the ladder of *Intrepid*. Referring to that oft-quoted phrase from the Apollo 11 landing, Conrad (who is several inches shorter than Armstrong) said: "That may have been a short step for Neil, but it's a long one for me!" Thereafter he interspersed his commentary with humming, giggles and exclamations — a matter of personal style, but also indicative of the more relaxed atmosphere of this second landing mission. Bean, who soon joined Conrad outside the LM, also provided spirited descriptions of his stay on the moon.

The only — but major — disappointment of the flight came as Conrad was wheeling the portable camera to a position several yards from *Intrepid,* to provide live television images of their activities on the surface. The picture on home screens was suddenly replaced by a stark abstract pattern. Apparently Conrad had inadvertently pointed the camera at the sun, thus burning the image tube and putting the camera permanently out of commission. Thereafter home viewers had to be satisfied with voices only (together with realistic simulations of the astronauts' activities).

Chores of the astronauts. The men had 3 main tasks to carry out during their 2 ventures onto the surface. (Their first period of extravehicular activity lasted 4 hours, and the second more than 4½ hours, separated by a rest interval of 12½

Charles Conrad, Jr., Apollo 12 commander. Born in Philadelphia, Pennsylvania, on June 2, 1930. B.S. — Princeton, 1953. Selected by NASA in 1962. Pilot, Gemini 5; command pilot, Gemini 11.

Richard F. Gordon, Jr., Apollo 12 CM pilot. Born in Seattle, Washington, on October 5, 1929. B.S. — University of Washington, 1951. Selected by NASA in 1963. Pilot of Gemini 11 mission.

Alan L. Bean, Apollo 12 LM pilot. Born in Wheeler, Texas, on March 15, 1932. B.S. — University of Texas, 1955. Selected by NASA in 1963. This was Bean's first mission in space.

Photos, NASA

hours.) They conducted a geological-sample-gathering survey of the environment; set up an impressive array of instruments; and trekked over to the Surveyor to examine its condition.

Sample collecting went well. By the time they were through with their delighted examination of surface wonders, the men had gathered about 140 pounds of lunar rocks and soil (earth pounds, that is; on the moon the combined samples weighed less than 25 pounds). The men later revealed that in the course of their work they had fallen to the ground several times, then easily pushed themselves upright with one hand. This dispelled the concern, aroused by the inflexibility of the moon suits, that an astronaut might not be able to get to his feet again if he fell over.

The trip to Surveyor 3 was carried out with equal ease. Conrad and Bean photographed the surface around the probe to record any changes that might have occurred since the probe's cameras had observed the scene many months earlier. They also removed the Surveyor's scoop and camera and portions of tubing to take back for study on earth.

In addition, the astronauts took many excellent photographs and set out an aluminum foil to collect solar-wind particles, as had the men of Apollo 11.

The ALSEP instruments. The most important instruments deployed by Conrad and Bean were contained in the Apollo Lunar Surface Experiments Package (ALSEP). Included in the assembly were a seismometer, a magnetometer, a solar-wind spectrometer, a lunar-ionosphere detector and a lunar-atmosphere detector. It might seem odd to speak of a lunar atmosphere or ionosphere, but any celestial object the size of the moon is likely to maintain at least a very thin, if continually changing, "shell" of atoms and ions; the lunar ionosphere and atmosphere detectors were to observe and report on such stray particles.

A central station in ALSEP served to gather, process and transmit the instruments' data to earth and to relay earth commands to the instruments. The package was powered by a SNAP-27 nuclear battery, which produces electricity by thermoelectric means from the heat of the radioactive decay of plutonium 238. Thus equipped, ALSEP was expected to send data for at least one year.

The voyage home. With ALSEP deployed and operating, and with rock, soil and Surveyor samples safely stowed away in the ascent stage of *Intrepid,* Conrad and Bean left the moon on November 20. Rejoining Gordon in lunar orbit, they spent one more day photographing the moon before starting home. They also sent the ascent stage hurtling back onto the lunar surface in order to create a seismic event for the seismometer to record; the magnitude and duration of the tremors were a surprise to scientists back on earth.

During the return trip to earth, the men conducted the first live news conference from space. On the afternoon of November 24, the CM splashed down in the southern Pacific, only three miles from the waiting carrier *Hornet.* After recovery, the astronauts were quickly hustled into quarantine. Their precious cargo was flown to Houston and the eager scientists who would spend many months studying the lunar rocks and soil.

The Apollo 13 mission

Five months after Apollo 12 had set out for the moon, another landing mission got under way. The flight offered exciting scientific opportunities: Apollo 13 was to land in the hilly Fra Mauro area where the astronauts would deploy a large array of instruments and drill holes in the lunar surface.

The measles crisis. For many months, three-time space veteran James A. Lovell, Jr., had trained with rookies Fred W. Haise, Jr., and Thomas K. Mattingly 2d for the Apollo 13 flight. Then, days before launch time, one of the backup pilots for the flight came down with German measles, exposing his fellow trainees to the disease. NASA, unable to risk illness during the mission, tested the Apollo 13 crew. Lovell and Haise were found to

EXPLORING THE MOON

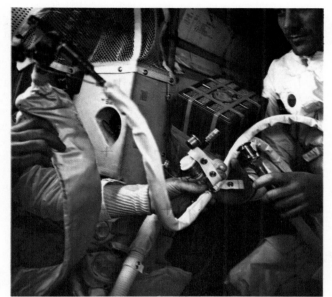

The anticipated thrill of watching Apollo 13 astronauts explore the moon was denied mankind when an explosion aboard their craft prevented a landing on the lunar surface.

Left: John L. Swigert, Jr., holds the jury-rigged arrangement the astronauts built to remove carbon dioxide from the lunar-module atmosphere. *Below:* The severely damaged service module, photographed after it was jettisoned. As seen here, an entire panel was blown away by the explosion of an oxygen tank.

All photos NASA

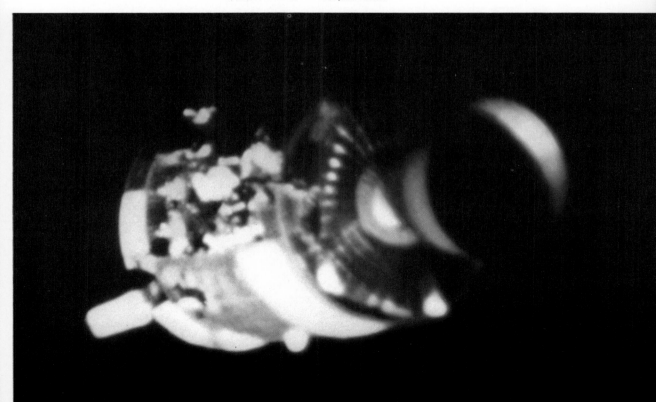

Right: Personnel in the Launch Control Center at Kennedy Space Center monitor prelaunch activities prior to the lift-off of Apollo 12 on November 14, 1969. Aboard the craft were Charles Conrad, Jr., Richard F. Gordon, Jr., and Alan L. Bean.

Below: An Apollo 12 astronaut, "glowing" in the sun's glaring light, walks on the Sea of Storms. Behind him is the central station of the Apollo Lunar Surface Experiments Package.

Below: Launched during a thunderstorm, Apollo 12 suffered a brief loss of electrical power shortly after lift-off. "I'm not sure we didn't get hit by lightning," said Conrad.

Left: A remote camera located at the 360-foot level of the mobile launcher photographed this fiery scene of the Apollo 12 lift-off at Kennedy Space Center, Florida.

Below: Working on the moon. Scientific instruments are unloaded from the lunar module and carried to their sites of deployment. On the horizon: the blackness of space.

July 20, 1969. Edwin E. Aldrin, Jr., who together with Neil A. Armstrong placed man's first footprints on the moon, poses beside the American flag—239,000 miles from home. The third member of the Apollo 11 crew, Michael Collins, remained in the command ship.

Tranquility Base. Aldrin deploys an aluminum-foil sheet designed to collect solar-wind particles. Before the end of the astronauts' "moonwalk," the sheet was reeled up for return to the earth where scientists studied the solar particles trapped within it.

John L. Swigert, Jr., Apollo 13 CM pilot. Born August 30, 1931, in Denver. B.S. — Univ. of Colorado, 1953; M.S. — Rensselaer Polytechnic Institute, 1965. Selected by NASA, 1966. First space mission.

James A. Lovell, Jr., Apollo 13 commander. Born March 25, 1928, in Cleveland. B.S. — U.S. Naval Academy, 1952. Selected by NASA, 1962. On crews of Gemini 7, Gemini 12 and Apollo 8.

Fred W. Haise, Jr., Apollo 13 LM pilot. Born in Biloxi, Mississippi, on November 14, 1933. B.S. — University of Oklahoma, 1959. Selected by NASA in 1966. This was his first mission in space.

be immune to German measles. But Mattingly was not. Hurriedly, backup CM pilot John L. Swigert, Jr., ran through practice sessions with Lovell and Haise to see whether they worked well together.

The final decision came only one day before launch: the Apollo 13 mission was "go."

An engine shutdown. On April 11, 1970, at 2:13 P.M. EST, the flight began. The first stage of the giant Saturn V booster rocket performed well and separated according to schedule. When the five engines of the second stage were fired, however, the central engine shut down more than two minutes ahead of schedule.

The astronauts readily compensated for this partial loss of thrust by firing the other engines for a longer period of time. Soon the spacecraft was safely in orbit, and shortly thereafter it headed toward the moon. Traveling on a different lunar trajectory was Saturn's third stage, destined to impact on the moon and create a seismic event for scientists back on earth to study.

The explosion. On April 13, 56 hours and 200,000 miles into the flight, all was proceeding smoothly on Apollo 13. The astronauts had changed their "free-return" trajectory to a path that would help them in their lunar maneuvers, and they had just completed a telecast that the networks had not bothered to broadcast live. Lovell and Haise, who had been checking the systems aboard their landing craft, *Aquarius,* were crawling back into the CM (*Odyssey*) shortly after 10 P.M. EST when a sharp "bang" was heard. A little shudder ran through the ship.

What happened? Swigert called Houston: "Hey, we've got a problem here!" Matters rapidly worsened: the CM's electrical system began to fail; two of the three fuel cells ceased to provide power; and the pressure in first one and then the other of the main oxygen tanks

North American Rockwell

This artist's conception shows the configuration of the Apollo 13 modules during the flight home. From left to right: SM, CM, LM. The LM, and then the CM, were jettisoned before the CM, containing the astronauts, reentered the earth's atmosphere.

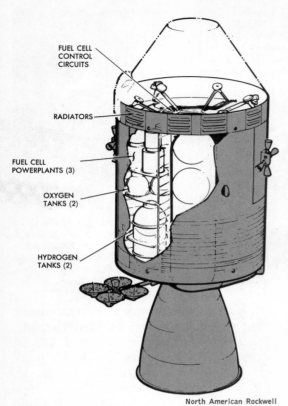

FUEL CELL
CONTROL
CIRCUITS

RADIATORS

FUEL CELL
POWERPLANTS (3)

OXYGEN
TANKS (2)

HYDROGEN
TANKS (2)

North American Rockwell

Cutaway view of the service module, showing the compartment where the Apollo 13 explosion occurred.

free-return trajectory and to speed them toward an earlier landing. And the astronauts had to set aside a reserve supply of oxygen in the CM for use during the atmospheric reentry maneuver — one task that the LM definitely could not perform because it did not have a heat shield.

The astronauts settled down in their linked LM-CM quarters, working closely with Mission Control throughout the remainder of the flight. Using flight-simulation facilities, ground crews checked out possible courses of action and then relayed detailed instructions to the astronauts. Meanwhile, Lovell, Haise and Swigert did their own share of improvising. For example, they had to jury-rig an air-purification system from the equipment in both modules. Because power use was kept at a minimum, the astronauts also had to endure an uncomfortably damp and chilly shipboard environment. And navigation by means of the LM provided a host of difficulties. Yet the men never panicked during those four perilous days — days during which the entire world watched, listened, prayed.

Safely home. On April 17, shortly after 1 P.M. EST, it ended happily after all. The astronauts jettisoned the SM as they neared the earth, managing to photograph the explosion damage as the module drifted past. Shortly before reentry, Lovell, Haise and Swigert climbed into the CM and cast off their lifeboat LM — the *Aquarius* lunar lander that had served them so well. They descended to the Pacific Ocean, near American Samoa, within view of television cameras and only four miles from the waiting carrier *Iwo Jima*. The journey was over.

Investigating the accident. With the men home, engineers began analyzing the data from the Apollo 13 mission. They determined that the "most probable cause" of the accident was an electrical short circuit inside oxygen tank No. 2. The resulting combustion caused a rise in temperature and pressure, thus rupturing the tank. This, in turn, caused a pressure increase in SM bay No. 4 and the panel covering this compartment blew out.

in the service module (SM) plunged toward zero.

All thoughts of a lunar landing were soon abandoned. The only task of the mission now was to keep its crew alive and to get these men back home.

The days of Aquarius. The SM's engine and life-support equipment were unusable. One of the module's oxygen tanks had exploded; the astronauts could see debris and gas venting from their craft. The LM and its descent engine would have to serve as a "lifeboat" on the trip back to earth; the CM had to be shut down immediately to conserve whatever supplies it had left.

There were several immediate crises to meet. The CM's navigation system had to be kept in operation until its data could be transferred to the activated system in the LM, so that the ship could "know" where it was. The LM had to perform two crucial burns, to get the men back to a

EARTH

JUPITER

SATURN

URANUS

PLUTO

NEPTUNE

FLY BY

OUT OF ECLIPTIC

Photos, NASA

A planetary "grand tour" of the outer planets is planned by NASA for the late 1970's. This unmanned flight will be possible because of the favorable alignment of the planets.

AFTER APOLLO, WHAT?*

A Balanced Program of Space Exploration

BY WERNHER VON BRAUN

ONE of the greatest goals of the manned space-flight program is that earth-orbital flight will eventually become safe enough and low enough in cost to facilitate a first-hand scientific investigation from that vantage point.

Current manned space flights are complex missions that involve thousands of people. Someday, however, space vehicles will fly in and out of earth orbit in a more routine manner, and the usefulness of space to science and to all people will have reached a highly desirable plateau.

The ability to fly nonastronauts on space missions will allow the research scientist, whether his field be medicine, chemistry, metals, geology or what have you, to pursue the potential of his discipline as a space passenger without having to master the techniques of space flight.

The day may eventually arrive, although exactly when is unforeseeable, when selected science classes can take field trips to earth orbit for a firsthand look at the scientific processes unique to the weightlessness of earth orbit.

While the moon landing is one of the more glamorous goals of Project Apollo, another, perhaps even more important goal is simply to advance our capability to fly in space. In future manned-flight projects, then, we will build on Apollo experience, and our space-flying ability will get better and better until it becomes as routine, almost, as air travel. When this happens, science will have at its disposal an invaluable tool for further enrichment of the lives of all mankind. This

* Reprinted from *The Science Teacher*

313

low-cost space transportation will bring the mind of man into a direct daily confrontation with the space frontier.

In my opinion, the current debate over the merits of manned and unmanned missions too often presupposes that the current high cost of manned-flight missions is a permanent part of the space-program picture. It is therefore argued that more emphasis should be placed on unmanned, automated missions that are currently less costly, since they do not require life-support systems, return and recovery of payload, higher reliability and safety standards, and more elaborate ground-support equipment necessary for manned trips.

While I support and strongly advocate a balanced space program within the National Aeronautics and Space Administration (NASA), it is my belief that man is an essential ingredient in space exploration. Man can perform a vital role in the development of complex earth-orbital systems that later may operate satisfactorily unmanned, with only periodical calibrations and repairs by man. In this manner, the manned and unmanned programs supplement one another.

Plans for the future

What exactly is the nature of this new tool that the space program hopes to make available in our long-range future beyond Apollo? What are the visions within NASA for the period beyond the landing of astronauts on the moon?

First, it should be emphasized that manned space-flight plans beyond Apollo lunar explorations are mostly just that, plans and studies. The only approved and funded program currently in progress involves an embryonic space station called the Saturn I Workshop, scheduled to fly in 1972. This will be discussed later.

Concerning the future of manned space flight, it has been recommended by an influential committee that the program concentrate in the 1975–85 period on:

(1) Continued exploration of the moon, leading to the possibility of manned colonization.

(2) Exploration of Mars, first with unmanned spacecraft but leading to a manned expedition, with the mid-1980's as a tentative target date. This will be followed by exploration of other planets.

(3) Broad use of earth-orbiting space stations for the observation of earth's resources, for meteorology, as laboratories for research in the natural and life sciences, and as laboratories for solar and stellar astronomy.

Exploring the moon

Lunar exploration will be directed toward obtaining answers about the moon and from that, clues to further knowledge of the earth and the solar system. While the first lunar landing put man on the moon's surface, it did not answer many of our questions about the moon's history, gross composition and overall degree of chemical differentiation — especially whether variations in different parts of the lunar surface are great. Studies of the lunar surface over wide areas and in several different locations are needed.

To achieve this extended type of lunar exploration, we are currently studying dual launches of the Saturn V in which one of the giant Saturns would be launched unmanned with a payload consisting of a shelter, equipment, supplies, and vehicles for exploring the surface away from the original landing site. These vehicles might include small lunar flyers and lunar-surface wheeled vehicles. After the unmanned Saturn has carried the equipment to the moon, another Saturn would then be launched sending astronauts and spacecraft to a landing near the equipment vehicle. By use of dual launches, our ability to explore the moon will be increased substantially.

A grand tour

In a vigorous program of planetary exploration, consideration must be given to investigation of all the other planets, asteroids and phenomena within the solar system with the broad objectives of increased understanding of them and attainment of the new discoveries that await the first men who travel these great distances.

Increasing man's understanding of the dynamic processes that shape the terrestrial environment is of vital scientific and practical importance here on earth. This should be enhanced tremendously in the planetary program.

There are at this time firm plans to pursue unmanned exploration of Mars. Two Mariner spacecraft flew past Mars in late July and early August 1969. Their objectives were to study the surface and atmosphere of Mars to establish the basis for future experiments in the search for extraterrestrial life and to develop technology for future Mars missions.

Missions to Mars are also planned for 1971 and 1975. In 1971 two Mariner-class vehicles will orbit Mars for three months; and in the 1975 missions, Project Viking, two spacecraft will orbit Mars and detach soft landers to descend to the planet's surface.

An exciting and much discussed opportunity to explore the outer planets will occur in 1977 and 1978 because of the configuration of the solar system at that time. There is considerable interest in the scientific community in this so-called "Grand Tour" mission of Jupiter, Saturn, Uranus and Neptune, for these planets will not be lined up in similar fashion for another 179 years. Studies have shown that a spacecraft could be launched into a swing-by trajectory around Jupiter, using the gravitational assist from that giant planet to speed it up, like a rock released from a sling. The increased speed would greatly reduce both the flight duration and launch energy required for a flyby mission to the other 3 distant planets. The curving

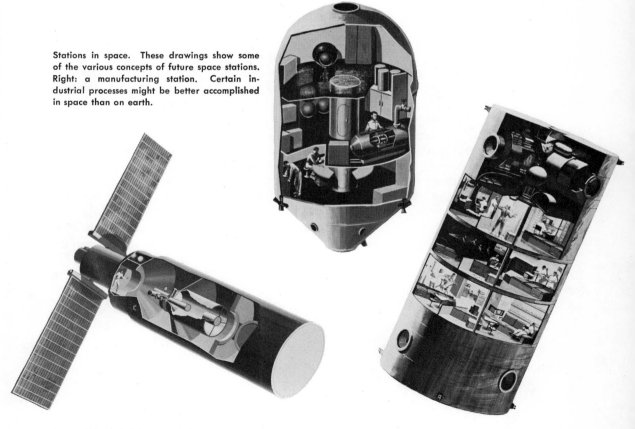

Stations in space. These drawings show some of the various concepts of future space stations. Right: a manufacturing station. Certain industrial processes might be better accomplished in space than on earth.

An astronomical laboratory with a powerful telescope. The earth's atmosphere distorts and obscures observations of distant bodies; in the near vacuum of space this could be avoided.

A 12-man space station. Each man would spend from 3 to 6 months at the station, carrying out experiments and observations.

journey to Neptune, 2,700,000,000 miles from the sun, will probably take more than 8 years, even given these advantages.

Of course, it is my opinion that flights by man to the planets are inevitable. The alternative manned flights most discussed at this time include a Mars flyby with surface-sample return; orbital reconnaissance of Venus; and a Mars landing and return. Excellent opportunities occur in the 1980's because of the positions of the planets. It is believed that the automated, unmanned planetary probes will have provided enough preliminary information by the mid-1970's to begin the design of a manned Mars system in plenty of time to be ready for planetary flight by man in the 1980's.

Space stations

Other than Apollo, the only U.S. manned-flight program currently active is the Saturn I Workshop; it is scheduled for flight in about 1972. Our first step in space-station evolution, the Workshop will contain 10,000 cubic feet of interior space and will include bath, bedroom and kitchen facilities. Flights of 28 and 56 days are scheduled.

In the Workshop program, we hope to learn many of the things necessary to the design of a permanent space station. We want to know the type of accoutrements needed for long missions in space. We want to determine the best means of

A full-scale model of a Dual Lunar Rover Vehicle designed to operate at speeds up to 10 miles an hour.

waste management and food preparation. And we want to know the effects on the human body of really long staytimes in space.

But the Workshop program also envisions a long list of scientific experiments designed to acquire more knowledge about the universe, the space environment and the solar system. Perhaps the most ambitious of these is the Apollo Telescope Mount, a large package that will be orbited and attached to the Workshop. It includes accurate pointing equipment and a number of astronomical instruments for studying the sun. These instruments are the largest and most complex ever designed for performing solar research from an orbiting spacecraft. Special emphasis will be placed on observations of those portions of the sun's emissions which are invisible to astronomers on the ground because of absorption in the earth's atmosphere.

If it is eventually the decision of the American Congress and public to follow the Workshop with larger, more permanent and more sophisticated space stations, a host of meaningful scientific and medical experiments can be performed.

One of the most important features of future space stations is that they will have plenty of room for a variety of activities. Indications are that there will be early emphasis on materials research and the potential for manufacturing in space. Looking back in history, we see that the vacuum was discovered during the 17th century. It paved the way for the technical period of the steam engine and the vacuum tube. Compare that with the space-age achievement of a permanent zero-gravity environment in earth orbit, and the new potential has exciting possibilities for the future.

In addition, biological research, conducted by medical teams rather than purely space-trained technicians, faces a new phase of discovery.

Heart-transplant surgeon Christiaan N. Barnard has suggested that experiments should be carried on in earth satellites to learn more about the human body's rejection mechanism. He noted that data from the U.S. Biosatellite program indicate that cellular changes occur in a gravity-free environment. Dr. Barnard says: "If cells in weightlessness lose some of their discrimination in regard to their own character, it is possible that they will discriminate less sharply against cells from another organism. If we can solve this problem in space, it will help us solve the problem of rejection here on earth."

Weightlessness itself will be scrutinized for potential medical benefits. Right now, only "superhealthy" astronauts have experienced orbital flight. Someday it will be interesting to find out what happens if people with diseases or other abnormalities are subjected to the weightlessness of orbital flight. It's entirely possible that no medical benefits will occur. But the entire scope of the idea of placing the human body outside the gravitational influence it encounters day by day deserves much thought.

In the large space stations of the future, there will in all probability be room for both doctor and patient. There may be a treatment or an operation that would lend itself to the space environment, and lives could be saved through processes not available on the earth's surface.

I want to make it clear that I am not an expert in the medical field. The main point that I want to emphasize is that there is room for all scientific disciplines in America's space future and that consideration will be given to all ways in which life can be enriched and bettered through science and its practical applications. NASA is a service organization with the mandate to perform research and investigations in aeronautics and space and to make the results available for applications by the public for the benefit of mankind.

Service to mankind

There remains no reasonable doubt that we can explore space. The great task now lies in the wise selection of the course of future space programs. Naturally, we must pursue the programs that promise immediate practical applications. These appear to be (in the area of space near earth) in the fields of communications, meteorology, navigation, and the observation and management of earth's resources. But we should also continue our thrust into the outermost reaches through energetic planetary programs.

Although I might be oversimplifying, it could be said that the various features of NASA's space program fall into three general phases: reconnaissance, exploration and utilization.

Such programs as Explorer, Pioneer, Ranger, Mariner, and even Project Mercury, when we learned that astronauts could fly in space, eat and sleep there, and return without serious ill effects, provided our first steps in exploring the many avenues of space.

After the preliminary phase of a particular endeavor, we moved forward into the exploration phase. After we prove, beyond a shadow of a doubt, that we can mount expeditions to land on extraterrestrial surfaces in Project Apollo, we shall begin the phase of detailed exploration of the moon.

Some NASA programs have already entered the third, or utilization, phase. This phase occurs when the program is put to daily use. Examples are in the communications and meteorological fields where satellites have become a part of our daily lives.

The sum total of the NASA space program is the role of service, to the community of science and technology, to the community of industry, and to the entire community of individual citizens whose personal investment of faith and resources makes our whole program possible and worthwhile. This is the nature of NASA's complete role in space.

For the future beyond Apollo, then, we are planning for the continuity of a balanced program of space exploration. While the discussion here has centered on manned space flight, the part of the space program in which I am most involved, we should be diligent in all aspects of exploring the new space frontier.

PORTRAIT OF MARS

Mariner Program Provides New Information about Our Neighboring Planet

BY JENNY ELIZABETH TESAR

Mars, photographed from a distance of 293,200 miles.

DRAMATIC photographs of the Martian surface, telemetered to earth in mid-1969 from Mariners 6 and 7, greatly increased man's knowledge of his neighboring planet. But while the mass of data and pictures provided tentative answers to many age-old questions about Mars, it also raised a multitude of new questions.

The flights confirmed the presence of vast fields of craters photographed by Mariner 4 in 1965. However, other distinctive types of terrain were photo-

graphed for the first time: broad, featureless terrain and chaotic, ridged terrain.

A number of excellent photographs showed the south polar ice cap. The composition of the cap is still in doubt; another puzzle is the darkening of the cap near both the limb and the terminator.

In addition to photographing the planet, the Mariner craft performed five other experiments that have provided valuable data on the composition of the atmosphere, the surface temperature and

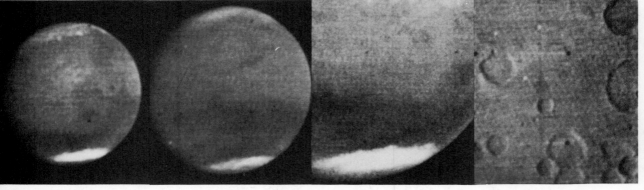

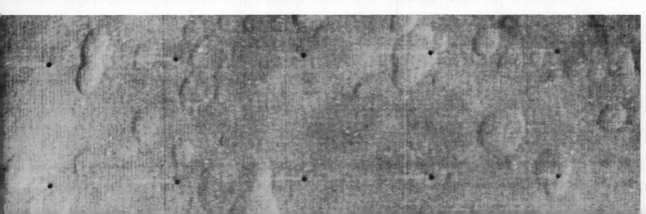

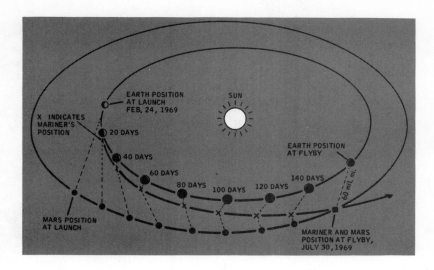

EARTH POSITION
AT LAUNCH
FEB. 24, 1969

SUN

X INDICATES
MARINER'S
POSITION

20 DAYS

40 DAYS

60 DAYS

80 DAYS

100 DAYS

120 DAYS

140 DAYS

EARTH POSITION
AT FLYBY

60 mil. mi.

MARS POSITION
AT LAUNCH

MARINER AND MARS
POSITION AT FLYBY,
JULY 30, 1969

This diagram shows the relative positions of the earth, Mars and Mariner 6 between the launch date and the date when the craft flew past Mars.

so on. But here, too, questions were raised. Is there any nitrogen in the Martian atmosphere? Why are the atmospheres of Mars and Venus largely carbon dioxide, while earth's consists mainly of nitrogen? Why doesn't the observed flattening of Mars produce a comparable distortion of the planet's gravitational field?

The Mariner spacecraft

The Mariner program, designed to gather information on Venus and Mars, is

These five pictures (left) were taken by Mariner 6 from distances ranging from 771,500 miles down to 2,150 miles. Note the highly irregular terrain and the crater within a crater in the nearest photograph.

The cratered area on the right of this Mariner 7 photo is part of the Hellespontus region; the smooth area to the left is the Hellas region (see map on page 320).

managed for NASA by the California Institute of Technology's Jet Propulsion Laboratory in Pasadena, California. To date, there have been five successful Mariner launches: Mariners 2 and 5 flew to the vicinity of Venus; Mariners 4, 6 and 7 swept past Mars.

Mariners 6 and 7, each weighing 850 pounds, were boosted into space by Atlas-Centaur rocket combinations. Once in space, four 19-foot-wide solar panels were extended from each craft. Two television cameras and other instruments were mounted on a large, rotating platform. The cameras were equipped with red, blue and green filters to provide finer surface details.

Mariner 6 was launched from Cape Kennedy on February 24, 1969; it took 156 days to travel approximately 241 million miles to the vicinity of Mars. Mariner 7, launched on March 27, had a shorter distance to travel; it took 130 days to travel 197 million miles.

The craft neared Mars five days apart, on July 31 and August 5 respectively. Their flight paths varied, enabling them to cover different parts of the planet. Mariner 6 concentrated on the equatorial region while Mariner 7 primarily photographed the south polar region.

Seventy-four complete television pictures of Mars were received from Mariner 6. Forty-nine of these were far-encounter photos, taken at distances of 771,500 to

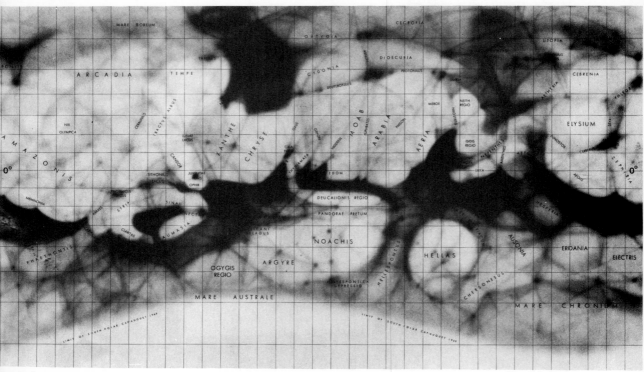

This map of Mars is based on telescopic observations (the Equator is at 0° latitude).

126,500 miles. The remaining 25 were near-encounter pictures, taken at distances of 4,600 to 2,280 miles above the Martian surface.

Mariner 7 relayed 126 photographs of the planet; 93 of these were far-encounter (1,140,000 to 81,700 miles) and 33 were near-encounter (5,800 to 2,370 miles).

The near-encounter photographs from Mariners 6 and 7 identified objects as small as 900 feet across. In comparison, the 1965 Mariner 4 mission radioed back pictures showing features no smaller than two miles across. The best earth-based telescopes take pictures showing features no smaller than 100 miles in size.

When Mariner 4 reached Mars, the planet was 135 million miles from earth. At the time Mariners 6 and 7 reached the planet, it was approximately 60 million miles from earth. The decreased distance for these recent flights greatly improved communications between the craft and stations on earth. Increased broadcasting power, better antennas, more rapid transmission of photographs (5 minutes versus 8 hours for one photo), a different system of message coding and other factors enabled us to receive a great deal more information from Mariners 6 and 7 than we did from Mariner 4.

The surface of Mars

Information received from Mariners 6 and 7 confirmed earlier evidence that much of the Martian surface is heavily cratered. Two types of craters can be distinguished: (a) large and flat-bottomed and (b) small and bowl-shaped. Some of these have very marked features while others show much evidence of erosion. Such erosion is to be expected since Mars has an atmosphere. Wind, rather than liquid water, is probably the main erosive agent. According to Dr. Robert Sharp of the California Institute of Technology, another important weathering process is "creep" — the movement of material "too coarse to be carried by winds."

Although the Martian craters resemble lunar craters in a number of ways, there appear to be differences. For example, rays, a characteristic feature of large impact craters on the moon, have not been seen on Mars. This, however, may be due to greater erosion on the latter body. The craters are believed to have been formed by meteorites and asteroids; there is little, if any, indication of volcanic origin.

The nature of Nix Olympica was one of the most interesting discoveries of the recent missions. This large surface feature, visible even through earth-based telescopes, is located at about 20° N latitude. Mariner photographs indicate it is a giant bright-rimmed crater approximately 300 miles in diameter. For reasons still unknown, this crater brightens periodically.

Other large, circular features were also noted. Perhaps the most significant is Hellas, a bright area centered at about 40° S latitude. This is one of the areas called "deserts" by early astronomers. Essentially featureless, with no noticeable craters (that is, craters with a diameter of 900 feet or more), Hellas is unlike anything previously observed, either on Mars or on the moon. It is possible that other bright circular "deserts" on Mars will also prove to be smooth and featureless. Dr.

Sharp has suggested that wind storms could have eroded or filled in craters in these areas.

In contrast, Mariner photographs also indicated the presence of a very chaotic terrain in an area about 20° S, between the darkened regions known as Aurorae Sinus and Margaritifer Sinus. Consisting of an irregular pattern of short ridges and depressions, the area is practically uncratered. This suggests rather recent surface activity (more recent and of greater intensity than any surface processes occurring on the moon). However, nothing indicates that the depressions resemble water-eroded valleys here on earth.

The most prominent region seen on the Mariner photos was the south polar cap. The terrain is moderately cratered and covered by a layer of "snow." The thickness of this cover is unknown, though it obviously varies in depth. However, it is quite thin in comparison to the ice caps on earth. The latter are a mile or more in depth at some places; the Martian caps are believed to be only inches thick. The northern edge of the south polar cap is very sharp, but irregular. This "ragged" appearance may be due to topographical features such as craters and rilles.

Putting the pieces together. The photographic mosaic (left) was fashioned from 7 wide-angle pictures taken by Mariner 6 as it moved past Mars. The 3 individual frames (left bottom) are high-resolution narrow-angle pictures that fall within the wide-angle photos (see map, right). The 4 middle frames cover an area 450 miles wide and 2,500 miles long.

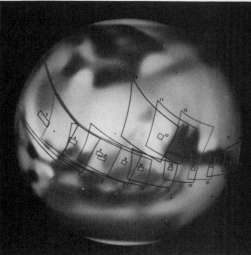

Indications are that the "snow" consists of carbon dioxide — the main component of the Martian atmosphere. Slight amounts of water may be present; the possibility that water is the main constituent of the cap, however, is doubtful. An infrared radiometer aboard Mariner 7 measured surface temperatures of the south polar cap. The average reported temperature was −193° F. This is approximately the freezing point of carbon dioxide in the low Martian air pressure (the freezing point of water on Mars is about −117° F).

Wide range of temperatures

Both Mariner spacecraft carried infrared radiometers that measured temperatures on the Martian surface. The dark areas on the planet, including the region of chaotic terrain, were found to be several degrees warmer than the lighter, brighter "deserts." This was to be expected, since a dark area would absorb more of the sun's heat than a bright area, which would reflect the heat. The maximum temperature recorded by Mariner 6 in bright areas on the day side was 41° F; the highest in dark areas was 57° F. Mariner 7 recorded temperatures of 61° F in dark areas on the day side. Temperatures on the nightside of the planet were very low, dropping down to −85° F.

The Martian atmosphere

The atmosphere of Mars is much thinner than the earth's. Air pressure on the surface of Mars is comparable to that on earth at altitudes of from 100,000 to 150,000 feet. Radio signals transmitted through the Martian atmosphere indicated that the surface atmospheric pressure is about 6.5 millibars. At sea level on earth, the atmospheric pressure is 1,000 millibars. In other words, the air pressure on the Martian surface is less than one per cent of the atmospheric pressure on the earth's surface.

Because the atmosphere is so thin, the Martian surface is exposed to direct ultraviolet radiation from the sun. Such radiation would be fatal to organisms here on earth.

The composition of the atmosphere was studied with instruments called spectrometers. These detected the presence of hydrogen, oxygen, carbon dioxide and carbon monoxide. Carbon dioxide is the most abundant substance in the Martian atmosphere. The spectrometers found no indication of nitrogen, an element essential for life here on earth. "If additional intensive analysis substantiates this conclusion," says Dr. Charles A. Barth of the University of Colorado, "a very key chemical compound is missing from the Martian environment. If this is true any life chemistry on Mars will have to be much different from what we know on earth."

An unusual atmospheric feature is the so-called "W" cloud located near the equator in the Tharsis region. Astronomers on earth have observed this cloud for many years; it is also seen on far-encounter pictures taken by Mariners 6 and 7. Occurring only in the Martian afternoon and varying in brightness from day to day, it is reminiscent of the afternoon development of large thunderhead clouds in equatorial regions here on earth. Some scientists propose that deposits of underground ice are located in the area; as the ice melts, the resultant water moves to the surface, evaporating and forming the cloud. Other scientists suggest that the "W" cloud is actually a variable spot on the surface rather than in the atmosphere.

There are indications of clouds, as well as fog and haze, over other parts of Mars, including the southern polar cap.

Future trips to Mars

Two major Mars missions are planned within the next few years. In 1971, when Mars is again relatively close to earth, two Mariner craft will be placed in orbit around the planet. They will be operational for several months, telemetering photos of approximately 70 per cent of the Martian surface from an altitude of 1,000 miles. These photographs will aid in locating the best sites for the first unmanned landings.

In 1975, NASA plans to launch two unmanned Viking spacecraft. As each craft orbits Mars, it will release a capsule that will make a soft landing on the planet, using a retrorocket system similar to that of the Surveyor moon vehicles.

The landing craft will conduct a number of investigations and experiments. These will include:

a) detection of photosynthesis and respiration, as well as the presence (if any) of microbial life

b) determination of the composition and structure of the atmosphere; recording variations in atmospheric pressure, atmospheric temperature, wind velocity and water vapor

c) measurement of the magnetic properties of surface particles

d) detection of seismic activity

e) photographing the landing site.

The orbiting mother ship will photograph the planet, measure the abundance of water vapor in the atmosphere and record surface temperatures.

In September, 1969, President Nixon's Space Task Group made public their recommendations for the United States' long-term goals in space. They proposed that the United States "plan and move forward as a nation toward the objective of a manned Mars landing before the end of this century."

According to rocket scientist Dr. Wernher von Braun, "the round trip would take over a year. It's pretty obvious, due to the duration of the flight, you have to plan the whole thing on a somewhat grander scale than Apollo. I don't believe one would want to send [only] three men to Mars. You would probably want to send along, for instance, a doctor and a cook.

"The exact timing," he said, "depends on the funding level after such a program is officially accepted and endorsed as a national objective." Dr. von Braun believes if the space program "continues to be supported at the present rate it would appear [that] we would have the capability to land a man on Mars by 1982 to 1985."

The men would probably travel to Mars in a vehicle with a nuclear-powered rocket system. Such a system, called Nerva, should be ready for flight-testing by 1977. According to Dr. Thomas O. Paine, NASA administrator, the program to land men on Mars "should be no more expensive than the program to go to the moon."

Is there life on Mars?

The 1969 Mariner flights provided much information about our neighboring planet. But many questions remain unanswered. Perhaps the one that most interests us is that concerning the possibility of life on Mars.

At the beginning of the 20th century, astronomers believed that Mars was quite similar to our own world. They thought the dark regions were oases, farmed by Martians who irrigated their land with water transported from the polar caps via a system of canals. Percival Lowell, the famous astronomer who founded the Lowell Observatory in Arizona, wrote that "a mind of no mean order would seem to have presided over the system we see — a mind certainly of considerably more comprehensiveness than that which presides over the various departments of our own public works."

Photographs taken by Mariners 5, 6 and 7 show no evidence of the canals. Nor is there any other proof that life exists on Mars. But neither is there proof that life does not exist there. Evidence overwhelmingly indicates that Mars does not have, and never did have, advanced life forms. The chances of finding higher plants and animals are very slight. But it *may* support a primitive life — microorganisms of various types. Therefore it is important that any flights to the Martian surface do not introduce contamination from earth. If earth organisms are introduced to the Martian environment, they may proliferate to such an extent that the existence of native life forms could never be definitely established. The discovery of life on another planet would be one of the greatest discoveries of our century; it would be a shame if man's carelessness prevented this event.

View from the Cosmos Pavilion in the U.S.S.R.'s Economic Achievements Exhibition. The major exhibit shows the docking performed by Soyuz 4 and 5 in January 1969.

THE SOVIET YEAR IN SPACE

Preparing for Cosmodromes in the Cosmos

BY JENNY ELIZABETH TESAR

DURING the past decade, man has witnessed the beginning of a new age — an age that has extended man's frontiers far beyond his home planet.

The birth of the space age is usually given as October 4, 1957. On this day the Soviet Union launched Sputnik 1, the the first artificial earth satellite. Since then progress has been surprisingly rapid, due at least in part to a competitiveness between the Soviets and the Americans.

In 1969 the Americans stole the spotlight when they landed men on the moon. But the Soviets were also active, launching approximately seventy spacecraft during the year. On the following pages, we will look at some of the more newsworthy of these missions.

Sharing headlines with Apollo 11

On July 13, 1969, three days before Apollo 11 blasted off on its historic mission, another spacecraft headed for the moon: Luna 15. Rumors and speculation were as numerous as they were varied. Tass, in an announcement shortly after the launch, stated that "the aim of the flight is to check the systems on board the automatic station and to conduct further scientific exploration of the moon and space near the moon." Such vagueness is customary: the Soviets release little or no information until a mission has achieved its objectives or ended.

In the weeks preceding the launch of Luna 15, unofficial sources in the Soviet Union raised the possibility that the country would soon send an unmanned craft to the moon. Its mission would be to land, pick up soil and rock specimens and return to the earth ahead of Apollo 11.

Was Luna 15 this mission? Sir Bernard Lovell, head of the Jodrell Bank Observatory, said he expected "an attempt either to land the whole of the spaceship or part of it to try to get some rock."

But NASA official Dr. George Mueller doubted that Luna 15 would return to earth, although it might land on the moon and pick up specimens. The main argument against return was the problem of propulsion. If Luna 15 descended directly to the moon's surface, an enormous propulsion system would be needed to blast off from the moon and return to earth.

If instead Luna 15 entered a lunar orbit and then detached a smaller craft to the moon for soil samples, the weight would be less. However, the subsequent rendezvous and docking between the two craft would be very tricky, requiring extremely accurate timing.

On July 17, Luna 15 entered an orbit around the moon. On the following day the Soviet Union hinted that the craft would not attempt a landing but would simply orbit the moon.

The spacecraft's orbit was altered several times; its minimum altitude above the lunar surface varied from approximately 150 miles down to 10 miles. Jodrell Bank, which was tracking both Luna 15 and Apollo 11, indicated that the Soviet craft was relaying large quantities of data but no photographs.

On July 21 a retro-rocket was fired; four minutes later the craft apparently crashed into the Sea of Crises, about 500 miles from the newly established Tranquility Base. A crash rather than a soft landing was suggested by the fact that the craft ceased to transmit as soon as it touched the surface.

The mission apparently was a failure. The Soviet press, after announcing its end, did not refer to it again.

Soviet men on the moon?

Several days later, as Apollo 11 splashed down into the Pacific Ocean, NASA Administrator Dr. Thomas O. Paine predicted that the Soviets would land men on the moon by early 1971. "My guess," he said, "is it'll be much sooner than most people think."

However, statements by Soviet scientists and officials indicate that plans to put men on the moon have been abandoned for the time being. One of the strongest confirmations of this was made by Dr. Mstislav V. Keldysh, president of the Soviet Academy of Sciences. In October 1969, while on a visit to Stockholm, Sweden, he said: "At the moment we are concentrating wholly on the creation of large satellite stations. We no longer have any scheduled plans for manned lunar flights."

Preparing for stations in space

The Soyuz* program, whose ultimate goal is the construction of a manned orbiting platform, has involved both manned and unmanned craft in earth-orbital missions. The program began on a tragic note with the fatal plunge to earth of Soyuz 1 in April 1967; cosmonaut Vladimir M. Komarov died when the braking parachute failed to function properly. The accident led to major design changes in the Soyuz craft.

In October 1968, Soyuz 3, carrying Georgi T. Beregovoy, rendezvoused within 650 feet of the unmanned Soyuz 2. Western experts believe the primary objective of this mission was to check out the redesigned spacecraft.

Information on the structure of Soyuz is sparse, but indications are that, beginning with Soyuz 2, the craft have been more or less identical. It consists of 3 sections and weighs approximately 14,000 pounds. (In comparison, the combined Apollo 12 command and service modules weighed more than 60,000 pounds.)

* Soyuz is the Russian word for union.

Artist's conception of the descent capsule of Venera 5 as it passes through the atmosphere of Venus.

Tass from Sovfoto

Soyuz is estimated to be about 34.3 feet long and between 7.5 and 9.75 feet in diameter.

Like Apollo, the sections are arranged one behind the other. Unlike Apollo, which has one crew cabin, a Soyuz vehicle has two compartments for crew members. The front section, the orbital compartment, is spherical and has a cylindrical collar for docking. This is where the cosmonauts live during most of a mission. They eat, sleep and exercise here; this is where they conduct research projects.

The middle section, the command module, contains the control panels. The crew is in this cabin for takeoff, reentry and craft maneuvers. This is the only section that returns to earth at the end of the mission. It is bullet-shaped and has heat shielding that protects against the high temperature of reentry.

The rear section is comparable with Apollo's service module. It houses a computer, atmospheric controls, instruments and two redundant rocket engines. These engines are liquid-fueled and provide about 880 pounds of thrust. They are used for retrofire and major changes in orbit.

During orbit, two large, winglike solar panels are deployed. These are attached to the service module. They convert sunlight to electrical energy.

When a Soyuz is ready to return to earth, one of the rockets in the rear section is fired. The rear and forward compartments are then jettisoned; the middle section, containing the cosmonauts, travels down through the atmosphere to a parachute-aided soft landing.

A cosmic troika

On two successive days in January 1969, Soyuz 4 and 5 were launched. Aboard Soyuz 4 was Vladimir A. Shatalov; on Soyuz 5 were Boris V. Volynov, Aleksei S. Yeliseyev and Yevgeny V. Khrunov. After a nose-to-nose docking of the 2 craft, Khrunov and Yeliseyev performed one hour of EVA and then transferred to Soyuz 4. The 2 craft separated but continued to fly in tandem, performing various additional maneuvers. Khrunov and Yeliseyev returned to earth with Shatalov aboard Soyuz 4; Volynov returned alone aboard Soyuz 5.

This was the first docking of 2 manned Soviet spacecraft and the first time that men transferred from one vehicle to another while traveling in space. The Soviet Union called the mission man's "first experimental space station."

In what appeared to be a test of techniques needed for the development of permanent space stations, the Soviet Union, beginning on October 11, 1969, launched three Soyuz craft on three successive days. Soyuz 6 carried Georgi S. Shonin and Valery N. Kubasov; aboard Soyuz 7 were Anatoly V. Filipchenko, Viktor V. Gorbatko and Vladislav N. Volkov; on Soyuz 8 were two veterans of the January mission, Vladimir Shatalov and Aleksei Yeliseyev.

Soyuz 7 and 8 were equipped for docking, and Western observers believed a docking was scheduled. However, although the two craft rendezvoused within 1,500 feet of each other and practiced a number of manual maneuvers, they did not actually dock.

Was docking prevented by unexpected manual-control problems? Following the mission, the deputy manager of the group that developed the Soyuz control system said that "unanticipated situations arose which were new for both the cosmonauts and the ground control station." But cosmonaut Konstantin P. Feoktistov, while visiting NASA headquarters in Houston, Texas, said that docking had not been planned for the mission.

Soyuz 6 had no docking capability. It was aboard this vehicle that the first welding experiments aboard a spacecraft were performed. On October 16, Kubasov, using an apparatus called the "Vulcan," tested three different techniques: electron-beam welding, consumable-electrode welding and compressed-arc-plasma welding. He apparently did not try cold welding, a process of great interest to American space scientists. Tass reported that the electron-beam method "works normally" in space;

no comment was made about the other two methods. Gordon Parks, of NASA's Marshall Space Flight Center in Huntsville, Alabama, doubts the latter methods were successful — "unless they know something we haven't discovered."

The Soviet experiments, using steel, aluminum and titanium, were performed in the forward section of the craft. The compartment was depressurized; the resultant conditions of vacuum and weightlessness thus simulated conditions in open space. Kubasov controlled the experiments from the middle section of the spacecraft.

Welding is preferable to mechanical bonds in joining space structures together. A permanent space station would be quite large—certainly much larger than a linkup of two Soyuz craft. Thus the need for rigidity and airtightness would be proportionately greater, and insufficiently met by the use of mechanical clamps such as those now used in Apollo and Soyuz dockings.

A number of other experiments were planned for the triple mission. These included geological-survey work, biomedical testing of the cosmonauts and basic physical research. Aboard Soyuz 6 were instruments that studied the density of micrometeorites.

The vehicles returned to earth five days after they lifted off the pads at the Baikonur launching center in Kazakhstan. They soft-landed in an area north-northwest of the city of Karaganda, not far from Baikonur.

Another Soviet first?

The Soyuz 6–7–8 mission showed that the Soviet Union is able to launch 3 manned vehicles from the same site within a 48-hour period. Such a feat requires expert ground crews to prepare and check out the spacecraft; a mission-control center capable of handling 3 separate but overlapping countdowns; and detailed flight-planning that will coordinate the activities of 3 vehicles and 7 crewmen.

Such precision launchings are necessary for the deployment of a space station. That an earth-orbital station is the ultimate goal of this program was reiterated by Leonid I. Brezhnev, general secretary of the Soviet Communist Party, at a cere-

Tass from Sovfoto

Cosmonaut Vladimir Shatalov in training prior to the launch of Soyuz 8 in October 1969.

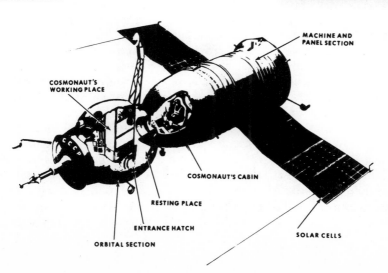

MACHINE AND PANEL SECTION

COSMONAUT'S WORKING PLACE

COSMONAUT'S CABIN

RESTING PLACE

ENTRANCE HATCH

ORBITAL SECTION

SOLAR CELLS

A Soyuz spacecraft. The cosmonaut sits in the middle cabin during launch, re-entry and certain maneuvers during orbit.

Novosti from Sovfoto

mony honoring the seven cosmonauts of the October mission. "Our science," he said, "approached the setting up of long-term orbital stations and laboratories — the decisive means of extensive exploration of outer space. Soviet science regards the setting up of orbital stations, with crews that will be relieved, as man's main road into outer space. They can become cosmodromes in the cosmos, launching ramps for flights to other planets."

At a November 1969 press conference, Dr. Keldysh was asked when such a station will be built. He answered, "within a few years; it will certainly be within ten years, and I think less than five years."

The United States plans to launch its first space station in 1972. This "orbital workshop" will be a modified third stage of a Saturn V rocket. It will house 3 astronauts on missions lasting 28 to 56 days. A more-or-less-permanent American space station, housing up to 12 men, is tentatively planned for 1976.

Space stations will greatly increase man's ability to explore his universe. They will enable scientists to study the universe from above the earth's distorting atmosphere and will provide a new vantage point for the observation of the earth. They will also be used as launching bases for expeditions to the moon and the planets.

Voyage to Venus

The nearest planet to earth is Venus, a mysterious body hidden from us by its dense, cloud-filled atmosphere. Venus has been an item of priority in the planetary-exploration programs of both the Soviet Union and the United States.

The first probe sent to the vicinity of Venus was the Soviet Venera 1. Launched in February 1961, it passed within 62,000 miles of the planet. However, its radios were dead, and thus it did not return any data to earth. Venera 2, launched in November 1965, passed Venus in February 1966 but also failed to return planetary data. Venera 3, launched four days after Venera 2, crashed on Venus on March 1, 1966; no planetary data was sent.

During this time, the United States sent one probe toward Venus: Mariner 2. Launched in August 1962, it passed within 21,594 miles of the planet. It was the first craft to telemeter information about Venus back to earth. Perhaps its most startling data was that indicating the high temperature of Venus — 800° F. (hot enough to melt lead).

In June 1967, Mariner 5 and Venera 4 were launched. Mariner 5 passed behind Venus during a close-approach on October 19, 1967. Venera 4 had penetrated the Venusian atmosphere the previous day. It transmitted information for 90 minutes during its descent. At the time, the Soviet Union hailed the event, calling Venera 4 the first spacecraft to make a soft landing on another planet. However, it is widely believed that the craft was destroyed by the extreme atmospheric pressure before it reached the planet's surface.

Data transmitted by Venera 4 and Mariner 5 provided much of the information now known about the planet. But the two sets of data often contradicted each other, and many questions remained unanswered.

Scientists hoped that Venera 5 and 6 would provide answers to these questions. The craft, launched from Tyuratam on January 5, 1969, and January 10, 1969, had major design improvements. Each consisted of 2 main sections: a "command module" and a descent capsule. Each spacecraft weighed 2,491 pounds, the descent capsule making up 893 pounds of this. The descent apparatus, a sphere approximately 40 inches in diameter, was built to withstand pressures 25 to 27 times that at the earth's surface.

Shortly before reaching the Venusian atmosphere, the descent capsule was separated from the main module. Braking parachutes reduced the capsule's speed before the main parachute was deployed.

The U.S.S.R. explained that the missions were strictly atmospheric investigations: there were no plans to transmit from the planet's surface. The flight plans called for landings on the dark, or night, side of Venus. This was to prevent solar interference with radio transmissions.

The spacecraft entered the atmosphere of Venus on May 16 and 17; the instrument-laden capsules separated from their mother craft, and parachutes were released to slow their speed. Data telemetered from the capsules indicated that they descended to an altitude of approximately 15 miles before ceasing to function. Each capsule transmitted information for about 50 minutes during its descent.

The missions confirmed earlier findings that the major component of the atmosphere is carbon dioxide. They reported that the atmosphere consists of 93 to 97 per cent carbon dioxide, 2 to 5 per cent nitrogen and less than 0.4 per cent oxygen. Minute amounts of water vapor were also detected.

Since the atmosphere is mainly carbon dioxide, it seems probable that the clouds are composed of the same compound, probably as a solid (Dry Ice).

Extrapolation of measurements indicates that atmospheric pressure on the planet's surface is 140 atmospheres (Venera 5) and 60 atmospheres (Venera 6).* Soviet scientists have explained that this discrepancy is due to "the considerable unevenness of Venus' relief."

However, radar studies indicate that it is unlikely that extensive 50,000-foot mountain ranges exist; the Venusian surface is believed to be desertlike and fairly level. It seems likely that the altimeter results on Venera 6 are inaccurate and that the average pressure on the surface is above 100 atmospheres.

Recordings of surface temperatures also varied. Venera 5 indicated temperatures of almost 1,000° F.; Venera 6 readings were about 750° F.

Is there life on Venus? A definite answer requires further exploration. But because environmental conditions are so different from those on earth, Soviet Academician Anatoly A. Blagonravov believes "if there are any traces of biological life

---

* The pressure at sea level on earth is 1 atmosphere. This is equal to 14.7 pounds per square inch.

there, it is not similar to that found on earth."

A variety of missions

In addition to the above-mentioned programs, the Soviet Union is continuing to launch craft involved in other projects.

The largest program is the Cosmos series, a space-applications program that includes a large number of military satellites. These satellites, launched into low orbits around the earth, maintain an almost continuous watch on targets of Soviet interest; many are routinely recovered about eight days after launch. More than fifty Cosmos satellites were launched in 1969.

The Intercosmos program began on October 14, 1969, when Intercosmos 1 lifted off the launching pad at Kapustin Yar. Its primary purpose was to study solar X-ray and ultraviolet radiation and the effects of this radiation on the upper atmosphere of the earth. A second craft, Intercosmos 2, was launched on December 25, 1969. It was designed to study the earth's ionosphere, including the concentration of positive ions and electrons. Both vehicles contained instrumentation built in East Germany and Czechoslovakia as well as the Soviet Union; Intercosmos 2 also carried equipment from Bulgaria.

The Zond series is unmanned lunar probes. Zond 7, launched on August 8, 1969, circled the moon, photographing its surface and measuring various physical characteristics. It returned to the earth on August 14, making a soft landing in northern Kazakhstan. Zond vehicles are believed to be considerably larger than the Luna series of moon vehicles. They may be able to carry men on eventual manned missions to the moon.

Other Soviet space projects include the Molniya satellites, a television-distribution system, and the Meteor series, a weather-satellite system. These and other space projects will be greatly enhanced by the creation of permanent space stations. And in 1969, Soviet officials made it quite clear that they consider such stations to be the "main road" to space exploration.

TECHNOLOGY

CONTENTS

Computer terminals are an increasingly common sight in American schools. This young lady seems puzzled by the math problem that confronts her.

John G. O'Connor from Black Star

REVIEW OF THE YEAR- TECHNOLOGY

Standing at the threshold of the 1970's, we can look back at the technological developments of the 1960's and also look ahead at what technology may have in store for us in this new decade. The 1960's saw many startling innovations: the wide use of artificial satellites in weather forecasting, communications and resources surveying; the invention of the laser; the rise of a new generation of high-speed computers; new applications of atomic energy; small but significant advances in the control of nuclear fusion; major breakthroughs in solid-state electronics; and others too numerous to mention. Experts foresee a continuation of such wonders in the 1970's, but some voices are prophesying potential disaster. The antitechnology chorus, which includes many accredited scientists, is voicing concern in behalf of the "common man." At the December 1969 meeting of the American Association for the Advancement of Science, militants charged scientists and technicians with ignoring the environmental, social and political effects of their discoveries, and accused them of furthering the interests of business and government to the ultimate harm of ordinary people. The militant scientists further charged the technological Establishment with misapplying its talents to military and abstruse research projects, neglecting truly urgent problems such as hunger, urban decay, pollution and overpopulation. Young radicals even decried the stance of scientific objectivity, calling it a mask for indifference or even hostility to vital human needs. Older scientists defended their attitudes, asserting that scientific objectivity was more necessary than ever. But flexibility to meet the demands of a swiftly changing technology is needed. Many authorities believe the only way out of the "technology trap" is more technology — applied in new and more humane ways. Whether it is humane or not, there is no reason to believe that the rate of technological progress will decrease in the 1970's. In fact, evidence indicates that technology will continue to revolutionize our lives.

Nuclear energy. Atomic power plants and reactors are being built or planned in a number of areas, but not without opposition from local citizens and officials who fear possible explosions, radiation hazards and general pollution. The United States Atomic Energy Commission claims that modern atomic plants are equipped with many safety devices, making them almost entirely foolproof. However, many people are not convinced of their reliability. They believe, and a number of scientists agree with them, that the long-term effects of even slight radiation may be harmful to humanity. In addition, nuclear plants produce a great deal of waste heat in the form of hot water. This water is often discharged into nearby streams, raising the streams' temperature and killing or driving away many kinds of aquatic life. However, nuclear heat may have great economic value. It could be used to warm buildings and natural surroundings. At Oregon State University, Dr. Larry Boersma, a soil specialist, is experimenting with a system of heating the ground in order to increase crop growth. At present, electric cables do the job. In the future, however, the waste hot water from an atomic power plant could be circulated in underground pipes covering many acres of cropland; the water would be cycled back to the plant for reuse after it has cooled.

Despite its spectacular successes, Project Plowshare, the United States Government's program for peaceful uses of atomic explosives, is running into opposition from various groups. Conservationists and health officials oppose further blasts until the question of radiation hazards is examined more closely. They feel that the permitted levels of radiation are far too high. But nuclear scientists disagree: they believe the radiation hazards are minimal and greatly overshadowed by the resulting benefits. Since 1961, more than 20 subterranean nuclear blasts have been set off by Plowshare; most have been detonated on the Atomic Energy Commission's test reservation north of Las Vegas, Nevada. In September 1969 a 40-kiloton atomic device was exploded 8,400 feet below the surface in western Colorado. Known as Project Rulison, this test was the second Plowshare attempt to release natural gas from underground reservoirs. The earlier Project Gasbuggy created a reservoir that produced 214 million cubic feet of gas in the 15 months following the blast in late 1967 (in comparison, a nearby conventional well only produced 80 million cubic feet in 10 years).

Solar energy. High in the Pyrenees of southern France is the world's largest solar furnace. Sunlight hitting 63 flat mirrored panels, each with an area of 585 square feet, is reflected onto a gigantic paraboloid. This parabolic array, consisting of 9,000 mirrors and averaging 160 feet in diameter, is mounted on the side of a 10-story building. The paraboloid, in turn, focuses the beam upon the material to be heated. Results are dramatic. For example, less than a minute is needed to melt a hole in a ½-inch-thick steel plate.

Computers. Time-sharing computers are accounting for a rapidly increasing percentage of the computer market. In September 1969, RCA introduced a computer that can process the programs of up to 350 users at one time. For the 1970's, authorities predict that almost every home will have a computer that will provide the latest information on almost any subject in a few minutes. Or each home will have access to a central computer capable of doing the same thing.

The use of computers is spreading into every business and field of research. Even astrologers are using them: computerized horoscopes are now available at hundreds of department stores across the United States. In New York City, a computer system has replaced the hiring boss on the waterfront. The port's 22,000 dock workers are the input material for the computer. In turn, it makes up work gangs requested by employers; it keeps track of where each worker is today and where he will be assigned tomorrow. Also in New York City a computer at Police Headquarters is being used to quickly dispatch patrol cars to addresses where crimes are reported. Input consists of the address at which the crime is reported. Within 3 seconds the computer indicates the exact patrol beat and precinct in which the crime occurred, the closest cross streets, the nearest hospital and the 3 nearest available patrol cars.

Orthoferrites. Magnetic "bubbles" — tiny, movable magnetic domains each smaller than the diameter of a human hair — may one day perform much of the work of a conventional computer or telephone switching system within a piece of material the size of a 25-cent piece. These "bubbles" can be moved around in precise patterns so that they can represent coded information, do computations or switch signals — all on a small chip of solid material. Enormous amounts of information — a million bits — can be stored in one square inch. The "bubbles" are tiny magnetized regions in orthoferrites, magnetic materials composed of rare-earth iron oxides. When a pattern of magnetic fields is generated in the material, the "bubbles" can be made to race around at high speeds in patterns conforming to the magnetic field. This technology is being developed at Bell Telephone Laboratories. Much work still remains before these devices can be shown to be practical. One challenge is producing the orthoferrites in sufficient quantities. However, their potential for functional adaptability, physical simplicity, small size, low power and low cost may soon open the door to new methods of designing computers and telephone switching systems.

Lasers. Noteworthy research on lasers continued in 1969. A laser generates an intense beam of light that can do many things: cut steel, align sewer pipes, make three-dimensional photographs (holograms), profile the height of ocean waves, and so on. The most versatile and commonly used device of this kind is the gas laser, which produces the light in a column of gas. Unlike the solid laser, it can operate continuously and requires little power to activate. An important possible use of lasers may be in the fusion of hydrogen nuclei to provide a source of energy. In September 1969, French scientists reported that they produced very small thermonuclear explosions by shining a powerful laser beam through frozen hydrogen (deuterium). The oceans contain vast amounts of deuterium; unfortunately, however, the release of this energy, if perfected, could be used for military as well as peaceful activities.

In December 1969, Ovitron Corporation introduced a laser scanning device that can detect the size and position of flaws in plastics, acetate film, rubber, paper and other sheet materials. The device can detect discolorations, nonuniformities or flaws only .002 inches long; it categorizes the flaws not only by size but by position, type and density. A computer tied in with the inspection system gives instant readout and makes possible automation of the system. The laser scanner is capable of speeds up to 800 feet per minute.

Sputtering. The electronics industry has discovered sputtering, a coating process first observed 100 years ago. The process lays down metallic coatings as thin as $\frac{1}{1,000,000}$ inch. This seems almost nonexistent when compared with coatings produced by more conventional methods, such as electroplating, where the film may be $\frac{3}{1,000}$-inch thick. In the sputtering process, the material to be coated (substrate) and the coating material (target) are placed in a vacuum chamber with a small quantity of argon, an inert gas. The coating material is charged negatively, and the substrate material to be coated is given a positive charge. The argon molecules, moving very rapidly, strike the coating material, knocking atoms off its surface. These atoms fly through the argon gas and into the material to be coated, becoming imbedded in its surface. Makers of razor blades, optical instruments, electronic microcircuits and other items say the coating forms a tough shield that is much more resistant to corrosion than stainless steel. The surface is also freer of pinholes than conventionally produced coatings.

Textiles. Man-made fibers are cornering a rapidly increasing portion of the textile market. Anim/8, the first of a new family of "anidex" fibers, was introduced in October 1969 by Rohm & Haas, Inc. These fibers are made from an emulsion of butyl acrylate. Anim/8 will be used primarily to provide stretch for textiles requiring elasticity. Thus it will compete with spandex fibers (which are polymers of polyurethane). Many new synthetics possess qualities of appearance and wearability far superior to traditional fabrics. Among the most exciting to clothing manufacturers and consumers are the synthetic silks, modified nylon fabrics composed of polyamides. Best known is Qiana, produced by Du Pont. Allied Chemical also has a synthetic silk; called Source, it was first used in making luxury carpets. A silklike clothing fabric called K6 has been introduced by Toyobo of Japan. It is a combination of a synthetic (acrylonitrile) and a natural substance (protein from milk casein). The currently popular "wet look" vinyls are produced by applying a thin coat of urethane foam to a fabric backing.

Split screen. During the instant replay of an exciting pass play, the split-screen technique allows viewers to watch both the passer and the receiver (left) and to watch the receiver catching the pass (below).

Photos, Ampex Corp.

INSTANT REPLAY*

That Important "Second Look"
at Sports Spectaculars

BY J. PETER KANE

"NOW let's see that again on instant replay."

Familiar? Millions of sports fans have come to accept instant replay as a regular part of a sports telecast, like the half-time interview and the postgame rundown on scores from around the country.

Few, however, are aware of just how instant replay is obtained. Fewer still have any idea of the men and equipment needed to bring instant replay to the home television screen — in vivid color and often in slow motion or step-by-step stop action.

ABC Sports, which has pioneered many innovative techniques in sports coverage, has seen instant replay develop from a hit-and-miss, keep-your-fingers-crossed gimmick in the early 1960's, using the first portable video tape recorders, to a precise electronic recording function using magnetic disc recorders specifically designed for instant replay recording and playback.

A little bit of luck

One of the early ingredients still remains. Even with experts calling the

* Reprinted from *Electronics World*, courtesy of Ziff-Davis Publishing Company

plays to be covered and highly reliable disc recorders preserving the action, a little bit of luck is needed. With the isolated camera glued to the league's leading pass catcher as he runs through his pattern on a third and 10 situation, there will be no instant replay if the quarterback decides to send his fullback up the middle.

Success is frequent enough, however, to make instant replay a valuable part of the sports coverage of all three television networks. The fans expect it, crowding around the TV set more intently during the replay of an exciting touchdown gallop than for the game itself.

At least 35 men — 20 technicians and 15 production people and a minimum of 4 cameras, are needed to produce a Saturday afternoon college football game for national television. This number increases when additional cameras are employed. As many as 7 color cameras are used during important games.

Camera location is critical. Two cameras are located in the press area near the 50-yard line; 1 camera is placed on a platform or mobile dolly along the sidelines; and 1 camera follows the action from the end zone. Often a camera is installed in the announcer's booth to pick up interviews and diagrams showing offensive and defensive formations. Depending on the importance of the game, 2 additional cameras can be placed in strategic spots around the stadium. Pictures from all of these cameras can be recorded for instant replay.

Often the decision to record some particular portion of the action for instant replay is guided by a member of the TV announcing team. Generally one of them is a former coach, like the University of Oklahoma's Bud Wilkinson, or an ex-player, like former All-American Jackie Jensen of the University of California. These experts are thoroughly familiar with the game of football, the strategy patterns of the coaches, and the particular talents of the players in the game. Whether a team is a passing club that makes its critical yardage through the air, or relies on an explosive runner like the University of Southern California's (USC) O. J. Simpson,* is important in trying to guess what it (the team) will do in any given situation.

For instance, USC may face a third and 4 situation on its opponent's 20-yard line. Wilkinson, knowing that Coach John McKay favors Simpson in such spots,

---

* Mr. Simpson graduated from USC in 1969. He now plays professional football with the Buffalo Bills.

will write Simpson's jersey color and number "32" on a piece of paper. The associate director in the announcer's booth, who is in constant contact with the producer, notifies him that Simpson is the man to watch. The camera director is alerted, and he instructs one of the cameramen to cover No. 32 and at the same time tells engineering to record the output from the camera on the Ampex HS-100 disc recorder.

In more important games, 2 cameras and 2 recorders are assigned to instant replay coverage of a given play. Action from 1 camera is recorded on the HS-100 or on an Ampex VR-2000 color video tape recorder. Often one camera is focused on an offensive player, and the other on a defensive player. Both sources are available for instant replay. The picture from the disc recording is available within 4 seconds for on-the-air showing. On the video tape recorder, which records on reels of magnetic tape, the tape must first be rewound and the action located before it is ready for viewing.

Quick playback

Today's high quality color instant replay is possible because of the HS-100 disc recorder, designed by Ampex at the request of ABC Sports. It records up to 30 seconds of action on highly polished aluminum discs. Thus, the instant replay ma-

Operating the control panels for a HS-100 recorder. Time counters (center of picture) indicate when play began so the engineer can return to that point to replay a segment of action. The television screens show what is picked up by the television cameras and what is being aired. The lever in the engineer's left hand allows him to control the speed of an instant replay so viewers can watch maneuvers in slow motion.

chine enables the operator to cue-up any portion of the recording in just four seconds for immediate playback on the air and to play the recorded action as many times as necessary. The replay can be shown in variable slow motion or stop action and its output can be recorded on a video tape recorder and preserved for postgame highlights. A disc recorder is used instead of tape for instant replay because pictures are instantly available and because it has variable slow-motion capability and good color quality. The disc records pictures continuously, erasing old information as new information is being stored.

Whirling around at 60 revolutions per second, the 16-inch diameter magnetic discs record 60 fields each second (2 fields equal a frame). Individual television fields are recorded as circular tracks (channel width is 10 mils track-to-track center, with a 7½ mil recording track and a 2½ mil guard band) on the surface of the magnetic disc while the recording head stays stationary. Four head assemblies are required to record on the 2 surfaces of both discs. When head A has completed recording a single field, head B begins recording the next field and head A moves on. When head B completes recording its field, head C records next, then head D, and finally back to head A, which is now in a new location and ready to record again.

Thus, each head records its successive fields in rotational sequence. Heads A and C record odd fields; heads B and D, the even ones.

Head movement is accomplished by a stepping motor which actuates a steel band to which the head is attached. The incremental movement of each head is 0.020 inch along the radius of the disc. The inward motion of the head, that is, motion toward the center of the disc, is such that space is left between the recorded tracks for a subsequent set of concentric tracks to be recorded in an interleaved fashion during the outward motion of the head assemblies.

Recorded tracks are individually erased by means of a DC current applied to the head. During any given field period, 1 head is recording and 1 head is erasing; the 2 remaining heads are being repositioned.

Each individual recorded field may be reproduced any number of times, depending upon the mode of operation desired. A normal real-time playback will involve a single reproduction of sequential fields. Incremental slow motion is obtained through repeating the fields at a rate equivalent to the ratio of slow motion desired. Therefore, repeating the fields three times will produce ⅓ slow motion. Stop motion is accomplished by the continuous reproduction of an individual field for any period of time required to permit detailed study of the scene.

In normal record mode, 30 seconds of continuous action are recorded. A full minute of recording may be obtained by recording alternate fields.

The machine operator can select any of the following replay modes from a simple control panel (the control panel includes a cueing indicator time clock for locating any recorded segment precisely): Normal — when color television images on the disc are reproduced in real time as many times as desired; 3 ratios of slow motion control, 2 fixed and 1 variable; and freeze frame where the head motion is stopped so that a single image is repeated continuously. It also plays back in reverse motion.

According to Richard Kirchner, sports producer for the American Broadcasting Company, "instant replay enables us [the networks] to take people inside an event wherever good taste dictates. We think it helps increase the fans' enjoyment of the game through a better understanding of what exactly is happening on the scene and why.

"The disc recorder is more versatile than tape for this job," says Kirchner. "And surprisingly, it produces pictures equal to and sometimes better than the best tape recordings. So far," he goes on, "the 30-second time limitation has not been a problem in football coverage. Key action is completed in 30 seconds."

ART AND THE COMPUTER*

Modern Artists Are Experimenting with the
Ultimate Mathematical Tool

BY TOM SHACHTMAN

TODAY, computers are helping artists to create new and intricate works of art, many of which have received wide critical acceptance. Some critics view these works as logical developments in the history of art, citing the artist's traditional

* Reprinted from RCA *Electronic Age*

concern throughout the ages for mathematics — the focal point of computer art.

The Greeks were aware of mathematical perfection in nature and believed that great creations could be described by mathematics, even if the formulas were beyond their comprehension. However, the first treatises on mathematics and art

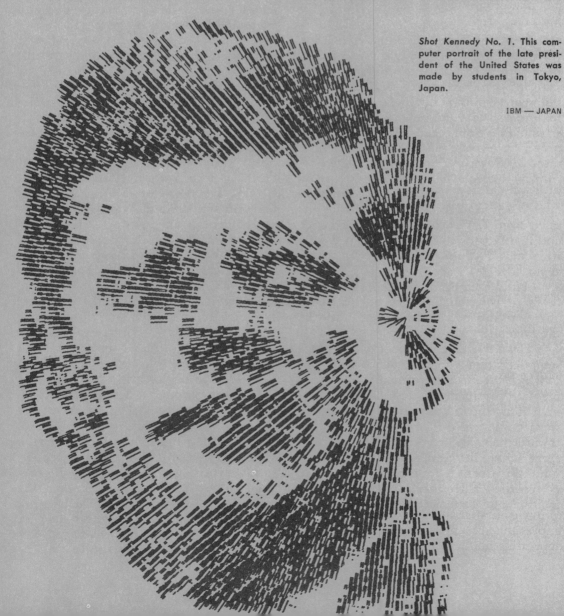

Shot Kennedy No. 1. This computer portrait of the late president of the United States was made by students in Tokyo, Japan.

IBM — JAPAN

were products of the Renaissance. Writers of that period discussed the importance of relative proportions in art, and artists tried to make their work conform to these descriptions. There were mathematically described relationships between the size of the torso, legs, head and arms and also among the various aspects of a painting such as the background, foreground and subject. It was known that certain repetitions within a painting produced generally pleasing effects. A line formed by the subject's arm might well be repeated in the curve of draperies or clothing, then show up again to good effect in the background scenery. Today, repetition and proportion are two of the tools of computer art.

Renaissance artists observed that the proportions for head to torso, legs to torso, or from any part of the body to another part changed when viewed from different angles. They recognized that reality and appearance were different and had to be painted differently, and developed techniques of foreshortening to give art the illusion of reality. Previously, art was representational. A painting depicted a girl with both arms in front of her in an anatomically impossible position, and convention helped the viewers know what was meant. With foreshortening and its outgrowth — perspective — paintings began to look more realistic. Perspective is essentially geometric: it is the way any object appears from a given point.

These developments were refined and continued through the latter half of the nineteenth century when Impressionism, a new, semimathematical development, took hold. The Impressionists noticed that points in space differed radically in the subjective eye of the artist, and they incorporated this phenomenon in their paintings. There were separate representations on the canvas for each point that they considered distinct. Thus, Impressionist paintings often reveal scenes of multitudinous colors that may either melt into one another and give one harmonious impression, or appear uniquely separate, depending on the perception of the viewer

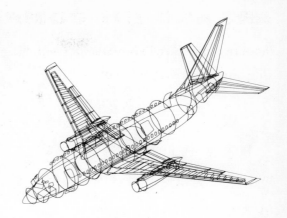

Computer graphics: new tool of industrial designers. Here the technique is used to visualize the Boeing 737 and to study human movements within the plane. The equipment used includes a keypunch, a reader printer, a computer and an automatic plotting machine (shown).

Photos, Boeing

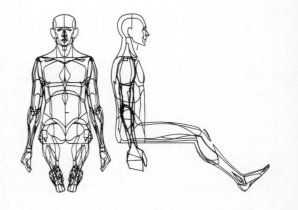

One hundred ninety-six micropatterns were used to make this picture. Place the page 12 to 15 feet away. Note that the small details of the micropatterns fuse together and the overall picture takes on the quality of a continuous-tone photograph. Compare the roundness and detail of the dial holes at the greater distance with the enlarged view of the same area (below).

Both photos, Bell Labs

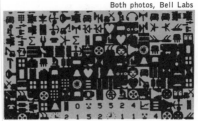

and his distance from the work. This use of substitution reached its apex in the pointillistic art of Seurat, whose paintings are made up of thousands of tiny dots that blend into a whole when viewed at a distance.

Substitution is also a major component of computer art and is quite mathematical in its precision and its technique. This use of optical illusion is basic to op art, which computer art sometimes resembles. Both depend on the cumulative effect of several points on the eye and the visual impression received in the mind.

The twentieth-century development that presaged computer art was the work of the futurists, a group of Italian and French artists who were obsessed with machines and the idea of introducing motion onto the still canvas. They experimented with repetition, permutation and substitution, and their paintings give impressions of fluidity and excitement, just as does the best computer art.

Marcel Duchamp, a leading figure of modern art, studied the treatises of French mathematician Jules Henri Poincaré as an aid to constructing optical illusions in his art. At about the same time, the faculty and students of the German Bauhaus school also were concerning themselves with mathematics. Artists Klee, Wassily Kandinsky, Lyonel Feininger and

Laszlo Moholy-Nagy as well as architects Walter Gropius and Mies van der Rohe all used mathematical relationships in their work. Feininger's subjects, for example, have cubical and trapezoidal shapes that ascend into the architectonic space above and about them — they exist only in a mathematical world. *Study for "The Triadic Ballet,"* by Oskar Schlemmer of the Bauhaus, shows ellipsoids and hyperbolic shapes for torsos and limbs and perfect spheroids for heads. The beauty of the shapes is almost totally dependent on their geometric perfection.

Mathematics continues to be important to the modern painter, and he is depending more and more on the ultimate mathematical tool. A computer, for example, can take a mathematically described figure and repeat it endlessly with much greater precision than a human hand can do. Through the simple addition of an equation to an existing program, the computer can distort or permute a figure as well as repeat a pattern with slight permutations randomly about a prescribed area. Guided by a relatively simple program, it can substitute one figure for another or produce a complicated figure for each point on a line. In addition, a computer can expand, contract, reshape, multiply or transform a figure or a series of lines. Various combinations of all these functions are at the heart of all computer art.

For example, Ken Knowlton and Leon Harmon of Bell Laboratories take conventional photographs and scan them electronically until they are broken down into 14 different shades of gray, white and black. For each shade, they program the computer to substitute tiny hieroglyphic symbols: faces, airplanes, animals, musical notes, telephones and automobiles. The effect is not unlike a Seurat painting: held close up, the hieroglyphs are seen separately; held at arm's length, a whole painting is perceived. This is simple substitution. More complicated are the works of programer John Mott-Smith of the Air Force Cambridge Research Laboratories. He works, as most computer artists do, by producing mathematical designs on a cathode-ray tube and modifying them with a light pen. He stresses duplication: a figure is repeated many times, another figure is superimposed on it, and so on.

A group of Japanese programers is using other techniques. In one recent show, they exhibited two dozen different variations on a basic photograph of President John F. Kennedy. In one version, the photograph is converted into a series of dashes, all of which converge with sinister impact on the left ear. Another shows him diffused, as if seen under water. The techniques used are deformations, metamorphoses or variations on a cubic pattern.

A second unusual effort by this group is called *Running Cola Is Africa*, in which a computer algorithm converts a line drawing of a running man into a bottle of cola. This, in turn, is converted into a map of Africa. One of the artists explains: "Computer art says something about time, space and existence. An object in space is transformed via magnetic tape into a set of units of information, or bits. These bits are conveyed throughout via two simple statements, 1 or 0."

Cyberneticist-artist Frieder Nake of the computer institute of the Stuttgart (Germany) Technischehochschule writes that the use of random patterns is "peculiarly suited to a computer's patience. An analogy may be drawn here to the artistic process of pursuing a theme through all of its possibilities, guided by intuition. Here, the concept of intuition refers to the choosing of possibilities from a given repertoire. The computer simulates intuition by the automatic selection of pseudorandom numbers."

Charles Csuri is an American artist who has used computers as a means of extending his art. For example, in his work *Random War,* he made a drawing of a toy soldier with a rifle aimed and about to fire, which was repeated in endless variations as dictated by the computer until it resembled a battlefield. A program that generated random numbers determined the distribution, rank and positioning of soldiers on the battlefield, and finally decided which of them should die (lying-down position); which should be wounded (half-down position); and which should

Studio International

Random War. A toy soldier, repeated in endless variation, eventually resembles a battlefield. The artist, Charles Csuri, says, "It's the potentiality that is offered by mathematics that is of special interest to me."

California Computer Products, Inc.

The Snail, an ink drawing created by programer Kerry Strand and produced by a computer-driven plotter.

survive (upright position). Csuri points out that the computer also could introduce such variables as terrain features, physical condition of the troops, weather factors and intelligence into the final print if he wished the program to be more sophisticated. Csuri also has weighed the possibilities of using the computer to obtain precise art effects. For example, a computer might transform a drawing of a head with uneven eyes so it looks anatomically right and then store the mathematical description of those eyes in its memory for future use.

Another variation — often the most beautiful type of computer art — is endless repetition of mathematically perfect or mathematically graceful forms, rotated slightly about an axis to produce delicate, appealing abstractions. Engineers at such diverse places as the University of Virginia, Carnegie-Mellon University, the Naval Ordnance Test Station at China Lake, Calif., McGill University and Princeton University have all experimented with such variations. Sometimes, the most startling results happen by serendipity, as in *Ellipse by Error,* a work pro-

duced by two engineers at the Sandia Corporation. One of them explains: "This elliptical figure was accidentally generated during a study of digitally generated Lissajous figures. The figure should have been an ellipse caused by a 45-degree phase shift, with sample points every 0.1 inches along the boundary of the figure." Such mathematical descriptions may be a part of art catalogs of the future.

Even though computer art is now widespread, the creation of such art generally has been confined until recently to engineers and scientists familiar enough with electronic data processing to take advantage of the machine's artistic capabilities. Now, artists are becoming more interested in using computers, and some engineers are attempting to help them by designing programing languages that they can use effectively. Ken Knowlton puts it this way: "The problem of providing an artist with good software involves the search for a comfortable compromise between the extremes of machine autonomy and machine stupidity. In the first case, we have a machine that works almost entirely automatically, producing great volumes of output over which the artist has little control except for culling the results. At the other extreme, the programer has complete spot-by-spot control, but far too much effort is required for specifying an interesting picture. . . . The outcome of present experimentation ultimately may be a number of relatively suitable languages for artists. Such languages may become sufficiently established and familiar — no longer a cute gimmick — that artists can use them to say something without the medium itself arousing such curiosity, acclaim or disdain as to distract severely from the artistic content of the work."

Although computers alone will probably never produce great works of art, they are becoming an increasingly important catalytic tool of the artist in producing beautiful things. For, as the late mathematician Norbert Wiener said: "The art of invention is conditioned by the existing means." And the computer is extending those means.

COMPUTER ART

Mathematically-programed art: an exciting creation of the computer age. This intricate work is by physicist John Mott-Smith. "Although I set the program," he says, "it's hard to predict what I will see. As I watch the screen, a sort of symbiosis develops between me and the computer."

Dr. John Mott-Smith

Right: Rocket by C. J. Fisk. Deep black backgrounds heighten the visual impact of computer pictures.

Above: Whirlpool by Mrs. Leigh Hendricks. Mathematical functions programed into the computer determine what appears on the display screen.

Below: Color Reflections by C. J. Fisk. An artist can change a design by telling the computer to "double the diameter of the circle," "remove this line" and so on.

Photos this page, Sandia Labs

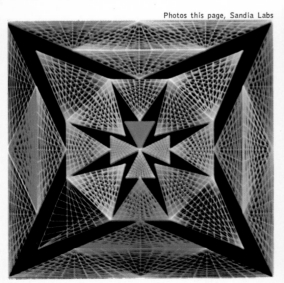

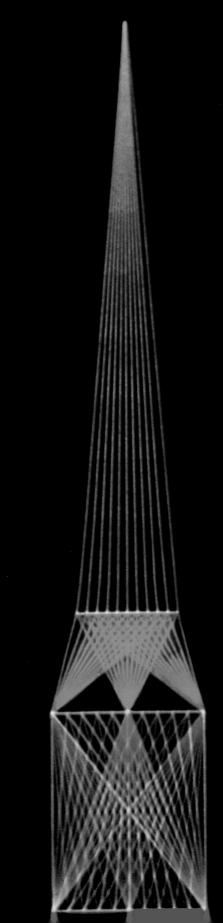

Sand Dollar. *This delicate design is reminiscent of a medieval stained-glass window.*

California Computer Products, Inc.

Right: David L. Caskey fed an American Indian design into a computer, instructing it to repeat the design 32 times. The result: Thunderbird.

Sandia Labs

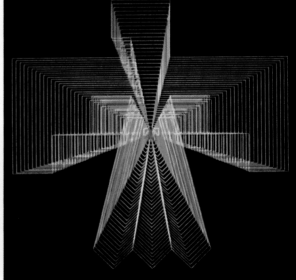

Sandia Labs

Left: Whirlpool *by Mrs. Leigh Hendricks. Computer art has attracted many scientists and engineers because of its emphasis on technology.*

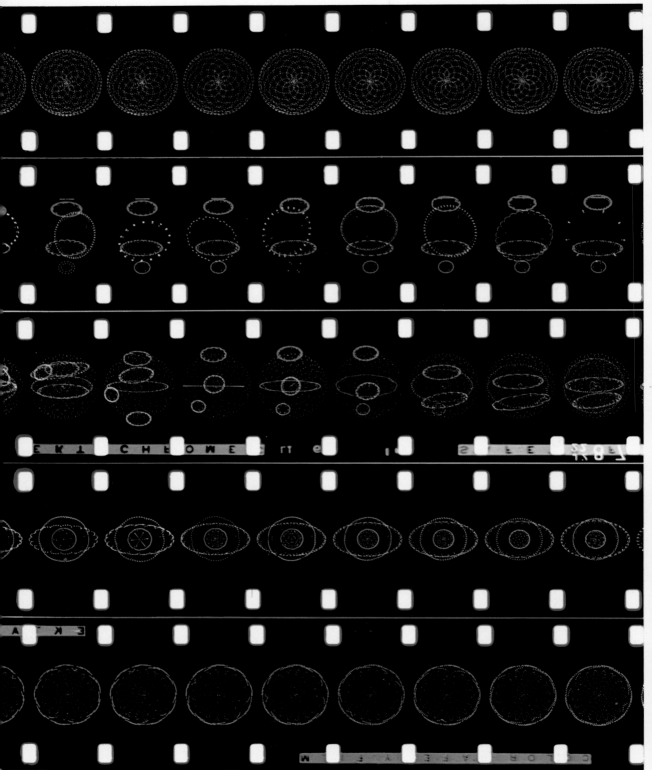

John Whitney

Sequences from the film Permutations by John H. Whitney. This film, writes Whitney, "repre-sents the first steps toward developing a compositional language of graphics in motion."

ELECTRONIC MUSIC

Sounds of the 20th Century

BY GERSHON KINGSLEY and JOHN WATTS

ONCE upon a time we thought of instruments such as violins, piccolos and harps as the sources of musical sounds. Today the sound sources on a phonograph record or in a concert hall may be oscillators, white-noise generators or modifiers. The sound source may even be a sneeze or a fire-engine siren, recorded on magnetic tape and subjected to various manipulations. These new "instruments" and sounds are part of electronic music, a field that has rapidly become an exciting frontier for both "serious" and "popular" composers and performers.

Recordings of electronic music range from *Switched-On Bach* by Walter Carlos and Benjamin Folkman to the Beatles'

The Buchla synthesizer is one of several electronic systems that have had a considerable impact on the music field. A wealth of records attests to the popularity of this new music.

Sgt. Pepper's Lonely Hearts Club Band. Electronic equipment is featured in concerts by rock groups and prestigious philharmonic orchestras. It is used for background music in movies and television commercials.

Composers of electronic music use electronic equipment as their instruments. They may generate sounds on these instruments, or they may take natural sounds and modify them electronically. The end result is a range of notes and sounds of, theoretically, infinite variety. No longer is the composer limited to the 70 or 80 pitch levels that can be produced by traditional instruments. Nor is he confined to relatively few frequencies; instead he can use the entire range of frequencies audible to man. Electronic music also makes available an infinite variety of rhythmic patterns, thus freeing the composer from traditional time values.

Historical development

Men have been interested in the idea of electronic or electromechanical musical devices for more than 200 years. But the field's history lies largely within the 20th century and has been dependent on technological developments in acoustics and electronics.

Early experimentation produced a wide variety of electronic concert instruments. These included Joergy Mager's Sphärophon, used in many theatrical productions, and Friedrich Trautwein's Trautonium, for which such well-known composers as Richard Strauss, Werner Egk and Paul Hindemith composed. In the 1920's, the Russian inventor Leo Theremin introduced a machine (named the Theremin), which a performer "played" by waving his hands in front of it. The machine consisted of two oscillators, one with a fixed frequency, the other with a variable frequency. The latter had a rod, or antenna, projecting from it. As the performer moved his hands in front of this rod, he changed the tuning of the oscillator. Music played on this instrument was used for the sound track of Alfred Hitchcock's 1945 movie *Spellbound*.

Instruments such as these were primarily designed to be used in conjunction with already existing musical instruments. With the exception of the vibraphone and the electronic organ, they have had little effect on musical practice. None of them signified the basic changes in the approach to music which are characteristic of today's electronic music.

In the early 1900's, the American inventor Lee De Forest presaged the present-day synthesizer with the development of the first electron tube, which he called the Audion tube. Although it is being replaced by the transistor, the electron tube

Composer Walter Carlos at his Moog synthesizer. Above the synthesizer's organlike keyboard is the system of generators, modifiers and controllers, interconnected to produce tones with any desired qualities. The composer's left hand rests on an 8-track recorder that tapes directly from the synthesizer's output.

Laura Beaujon

Robert A. Moog, developer of the instrument that bears his name, at the first live jazz concert that utilized synthesizers. Three synthesizers — polyphonic, bass and percussion — were used.

was the basis of today's huge electronic industry.

Another major advance on the road to electronic music was the development of sound-reproducing systems. The first such system was the phonograph; this was followed by magnetic-tape systems — first monophonic and, more recently, two- and four-channel stereophonic.

By 1930, composers such as Hindemith had already demonstrated the feasibility of using the recording medium itself as a creative device. Interesting sound montages could be constructed by changing phonograph speeds, transposing sounds and using various rhythms simultaneously.

The phonograph record, however, presented a limited medium: a groove in a record tends to be permanent. With the later advent of magnetic tape, new freedoms were possible. Because sound on tape is a kind of magnetic configuration, it can be erased (demagnetized) easily. Tape can be cut and spliced, records cannot. French engineer Pierre Schaeffer was one of the first experimenters in the use of tapes. One of his best-known works, *Étude for Railroad Trains,* is constructed

entirely from the recorded noises made by trains — changed, fragmented, recombined and structured in a hundred different ways to create a work of art. Another Schaeffer composition uses the sounds of a sneeze and a coin's coming to rest after being spun.

This process of using magnetic tape to record and recompose sounds gathered from "nature" is called *musique concrète.* Sounds from city streets, factories, beaches and bird-filled forests are treated electronically; the nonelectronic sounds are transformed into new, electronic sounds. In some cases the source of the new sounds can still be recognized; in other cases the sounds are so changed that the listener can no longer recognize them.

Working directly with sound sources on tape appealed to a number of composers. Research centers and studios sprang up, and electronic compositions quickly found their way to the theater, movie industry and recording studio. Today, *musique concrète* has become a characteristic feature of electronic music.

The first public concert of electronic music in the United States was presented at The Museum of Modern Art in New

345

York City on October 28, 1952. Composers Vladimir Ussachevsky and Otto Luening presented a program of tape-recorder music that included Ussachevsky's *Sonic Contours* and Luening's *Fantasy in Space*. Two years later their joint composition, *Rhapsodic Variations,* was premiered by the Louisville Symphony — the first instance of the use of the tape recorder as a "solo instrument" with an orchestra.

In 1955, engineers of the Radio Corporation of America experimentally built the first electronic system for synthesizing sound — the Olson-Belar Sound Synthesizer. This huge, wall-size "instrument" created the various properties of a musical sound, such as frequency, timbre (color), and attack and decay characteristics. With equal ease, it could produce sounds previously unheard by man. An operator could then assemble these sound "events" into musical phrases or their equivalents.

A second synthesizer, the Mark II, was built in 1959 and leased to the Columbia-Princeton Electronic Music Center in New York. As technical know-how accelerated, these early synthesizers became obsolete. Bulky, cumbersome and unduly complicated, they could be used only by the most skilled technicians.

Photographic International

Above: composer-pianist John Eaton stands beside a Syn-Ket. Used together with conventional instruments, it vastly expands the repertory of sound available to a composer. Below: the Mark II synthesizer. It is run by punching tape on a typewriterlike keyboard. Compare its size with the more-recent Buchla, Moog and Syn-Ket.

RCA

The development of the stereophonic record in 1958 enabled the development of much more highly sophisticated synthesizers. These new synthesizers, such as the Moog, the Buchla and the Syn-Ket (developed respectively by Robert A. Moog, Donald Buchla and Paul Ketoff), are transistorized and miniaturized. They are modular systems — many components may be interconnected — rather than closed systems.

The structure of a synthesizer

A synthesizer operates on the basic premise that any sound can be synthesized if you can control its pitch, timbre and envelope.

The pitch of a sound depends on the frequency, or number of vibrations per second. As the frequency increases, so does the pitch.

Timbre, or coloration, is the quality of a sound. This is chiefly determined by the overtones, and enables us to distinguish between the same note played on different instruments. For example, middle C played on a piano has the same frequency as middle C played on a violin or clarinet. But we can differentiate between these notes because they have different overtones.

The envelope of a sound describes the way a sound begins, progresses and ends. This includes the attack and decay characteristics of a sound. Attack is the speed with which a sound builds in volume; decay is the rate at which it decreases. The attack and decay characteristics of a sound can be more important than timbre in enabling us to recognize an instrument.

Voltage-control devices are used to regulate these characteristics. Three basic types of voltage-control components are found in a synthesizer: (1) oscillators and white-noise generators, (2) filters and (3) amplifiers. These and other components are connected according to the composer's requirements. The quality of the final sound depends largely on the components that are used to produce the sound. For example, different parts of the synthesizer are connected to produce harpsichordlike tones than are connected to produce trumpetlike tones; parts can also be connected to produce sounds never before heard by man.

The parts of a synthesizer can be considered in three general categories, according to their function: generators, modifiers and controllers.

Generators. These are the parts of a synthesizer that produce the initial sound signals. These signals are electrical and cannot be heard; only later (but within a

Part of the score for an electronic composition by Bulent Arel. (a) These 3 pentagrams indicate the pitch elements. (b) The envelopes of the sounds shown in (a). The wide black bands describe attack characteristics: the darker the band, the sharper the attack. The curved band in the middle pentagram represents the decay of a sound. (c) The length of the signals. (d) The acoustically created beat that results from (a) and (b). (e) The audible amplitude range, from very quiet (*pp*) to very loud (*fff*). (f) The timing in seconds. The music between 23 and 29 seconds was not notated because it was impossible to visualize.

348

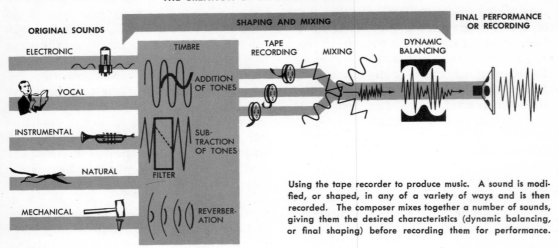

THE CREATION OF ELECTRONIC MUSIC

Using the tape recorder to produce music. A sound is modified, or shaped, in any of a variety of ways and is then recorded. The composer mixes together a number of sounds, giving them the desired characteristics (dynamic balancing, or final shaping) before recording them for performance.

tiny fraction of a second), are they transformed into audible sounds. There are various types of generators, each producing different types of signals.

Among the most commonly used generators are the oscillators. These instruments produce signals that have periodic or regularly repeating wave forms. The audible sounds are pitched and have a flutelike tone. As the voltage is changed, the frequency of the sound will also change. Thus, for example, a gliding tone can easily be produced.

In contrast, a random generator (also called a white-noise generator) produces a signal composed of all audible frequencies (as white light is composed of all colors of the spectrum). There is no predictable relation between any two parts of the wave form. The sound is completely pitchless and resembles a combination of escaping steam and a waterfall. However, by filtering the sound the composer can give it a definite pitch.

Between these two extremes are various transient generators that produce signals having definite but nonrepeating wave forms. A transient generator would, for example, be used to synthesize a trombone sound. This sound begins with a tone of low harmonic content (few overtones), which is then increased by applying a rising voltage. The opposite occurs in the synthesis of the sound of a plucked

cello or guitar string: the composer begins with a tone of high harmonic content (many overtones), which is rapidly reduced.

Modifiers. After the sound signals are produced they are fed into modifiers. These are instruments that change one or more characteristics of the sounds. They include amplifiers, filters, modulators and reverberation units.

An amplifier alters the amplitude, or intensity, of a sound signal. It controls the envelope of the signal. Thus, by adjusting the amplifier's volume-control knob, a composer can easily vary the attack and decay characteristics of a tone.

Filters modify sounds by emphasizing certain frequencies. They can cut out unwanted frequencies and mute others. Thus overtones can be made more prominent or can be entirely removed from a sound.

A modulator changes a given characteristic of one sound signal in response to variations of a second signal.

Reverberation chambers add echoes to a signal. This increases the timbre of the sound, often adding a sense of space to the material.

After the tone has been altered to the composer's satisfaction, it goes on tape. Further changes can be made by varying the speed of the tape recorder, recording notes on top of one another, and so on.

Controllers. The composer must have a way to control the amount of voltage entering the above-mentioned parts. On the Moog synthesizer these controllers are in the form of organlike keyboards. By playing different keys the composer not only varies the voltage but also triggers the sound impulse.

Syn-Ket, a small, portable synthesizer, is similar in conception to the Moog. It has several small keyboards. The Buchla synthesizer incorporates eight touch plates instead of a keyboard. Assuming the plates are set at frequency intervals similar to those of an octave on a traditional instrument, the composer must mechanically change octaves as he plays the Buchla.

The controls on all three synthesizers can be set at any frequency interval desired by the composer.

A further advance has been achieved by using a digital computer to produce the control voltages. The composer places his instructions on punched cards. These cards direct the computer, which produces a series of numbers. The numbers represent the shape of the desired sound wave (wave form). A digital-to-analog converter then changes these numbers to voltages.

The final composition

Electronic music is not, as you have seen, something composed by machines. A human being must specify every characteristic of each sound. Since there are so many more possibilities with, for example, a synthesizer than a piano, the demands of composing electronic music are in some ways greater than those involved in composing for traditional instruments.

The German composer Karl Stockhausen has been one of the leaders in the field of electronic composition. We now consider briefly one of his works, *Anthems for Electronic and Concrète Sounds.*

Like many electronic pieces, this work can be performed as a purely electronic work or in conjunction with live instrumentalists.

The basic source materials for the composition were national anthems. In addition, Stockhausen used other *concrète* sounds — recorded conversations, crowd noises, the christening of a ship, sounds in a Chinese store, and so on — as well as some purely electronic sounds.

The sounds were altered and distorted in a variety of ways. They were fragmented or combined. They were intermodulated: this combines a characteristic of one anthem (for example, its harmony) with a characteristic of a second anthem (for example, its rhythm).

Creating your own music

Perhaps you would like to experiment in this exciting field. If you have access to a tape recorder (or preferably two), it is possible for you to create an electronic composition.

You might begin by recording some *concrète* sounds: rainfall, the cry of a baby, the bark of a dog, the cheers at a football game. You can also tape sounds from a rock record, a radio commercial or your favorite television show.

These sounds can then be altered in a variety of ways. How, for example, does a cat's meow sound if played backward? By playing a tape backward, the sounds will occur in reverse, and each sound will also occur backward.

The faster a tape is played, the faster the sounds are heard. The increased speed will also result in higher frequencies. Test this by taping the sounds of a doorbell at 3¾ inches per second; then play the tape at 7½ inches per second. Experiment, too, with the reverse: record a dripping faucet at 7½ inches per second and play the tape at 3¾ inches per second.

If your tape recorder has two heads, you can create echo effects. The second head can pick up the sounds previously recorded on the tape; it feeds these back to the first head, which rerecords them over the original sounds with a slight time lag.

You can also alter the sounds by cutting the tape and then splicing the pieces together in a new order. The possibilities are endless, and your composition might be a great conversation piece at your next party.

From factory to homesite. Trucks carry modules to a vacation site where they are assembled and finished.

BUILDING HOMES WITH BUILDING BLOCKS*

A Possible Cure for the Nation's Housing Problem

BY CLAYTON R. SUTTON

BUILDING blocks, which have delighted children for years, are now seriously discussed by architects, contractors, steel companies and government agencies. They are not talking about a child's toy, but a new building concept which may help solve the problem of providing low-cost mass housing for the nation.

* Reprinted by permission from *Steelways*

The new concept calls for constructing homes or apartment houses in sections on a mass-production, assembly-line basis in factories. The sections (called modular units) would be shipped to home sites on flatbed trailer trucks and positioned side by side or one atop another to form complete homes or apartment houses.

This method is the latest step away from the traditional method of building

The finished vacation home: one of many purposes to which modular housing can be adapted.

Arbor Modules Inc.

Both photos Arbor Modules Inc.

homes toward more efficient, less costly methods. One of the earliest departures from the age-old procedure, in which materials are cut to size on the site and fitted together piece by piece, was the introduction of prefabricated components — building materials made in standard sizes — which reduce the amount of cutting and fitting required on the site. Today architects and contractors can select framing members, joists, wall panels, doors and frames made of steel to meet their particular design requirements and have them sent to the building site, where they are set in place during construction.

Another, more recent, step was the preengineered steel building introduced by steel companies and metal fabricators. Preengineered buildings consist of a complete package of steel components fabricated in a plant and assembled at the building site. They are widely used for homes, vacation dwellings, schools, colleges, motels, banks, offices and industrial buildings.

Although they have reduced construction costs, these modifications of traditional methods have not brought costs low enough to let most building contractors enter the low-income housing market.

Housing for low- and moderate-income families, however, has been supplied for many years by the mobile home, another departure from traditional home-building methods. According to the Mobile Home Manufacturers Association, mobile homes accounted for 33 per cent of all single-family housing starts in 1969 and 90 per cent of all homes valued under $15,000. Approximately five million people live in mobile homes.

Mobile homes, which evolved from the smaller travel trailers (now defined as recreational vehicles) that can be towed by an automobile, are complete homes. They are constructed in widths of from 8 to 12 feet and in lengths of from 29 to 65 feet; when finished, they are placed on wheels and towed over highways by tractors to the site they will occupy. Mobile homes are almost entirely "nonmobile," for about 98 per cent of them travel only from the factory to the home site.

These factory-built residences are completely equipped with major appliances, furniture, carpeting, draperies and lamps. The average retail price for the 12-by-60-foot model, which accounts for almost 85 per cent of total sales, is $6,000, or about $8.30 per square foot.

The mobile-home industry produces such low-cost homes by utilizing the same

Low-rise apartment units. A great variety of architectural treatments is possible in modular housing.

Stirling Homex Corp.

assembly-line techniques used in factories. One large Midwestern firm, for instance, has a quarter-mile-long assembly line that starts with a steel frame at the first station and ends with a completely furnished mobile home only one hour later.

To resist the stresses and strains that occur when mobile homes are transported over highways, steel is used extensively for structural framing and exclusively for underframes. Galvanized sheet steel is used for roofs, heating and ventilating ducts, and some exterior paneling. Including appliances and fixtures, there is nearly a ton of steel in the larger mobile homes.

The mobile-home industry, nearly 200 manufacturers, shipped more than 410,000 units in 1969 compared with 240,360 units in 1967. Conventional housing starts for 1969 amounted to about 1.5 million, up from less than 1.3 million in 1967. This year's burgeoning demand for housing, particularly in the low-cost market, is expected to boost mobile-home sales to around 490,000 units, according to the Mobile Home Manufacturers Association. The industry estimates that production will reach 560,000 mobile homes by 1973. The sales graph, going up since 1947, rose sharply in 1962, when the 12-by-60-foot home was introduced.

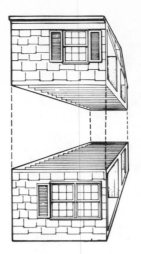
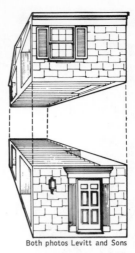

Both photos Levitt and Sons

Above: Four modules equal one two-story home. Below: Models of town houses. Components such as porches and projecting windows can be added to the basic modules.

Nashua Homes

Mobile homes no longer look like trailers; cabanas, carports and other additions change them into real homes.

In a further step toward the building-block home, the mobile-home industry is offering expandable and double-width units which are bolted together at the site to obtain as much as 1,440 square feet of living space for a total cost ranging from $8,000 to $13,000. Although these larger units account for less than 10 per cent of sales in the industry, they are opening previously untapped markets for some large manufacturers.

Commercial structures such as branch banks, radio stations, classrooms and recreational facilities are formed by the joining together of two or more of these units.

Similar but more conventional-looking units are being produced for more elaborate assemblies such as town-houses and apartments. With encouragement from the Federal Government, and in co-operation with a major steel company, a Detroit-based mobile-home firm is now developing an all-steel-framed modular residential building aimed primarily at the inner-city market. The prototype will emphasize the use of off-the-shelf standard components.

A company in College Station, Texas, using a technique developed for its mobile homes, has introduced a 12-by-40-foot modular unit that utilizes 1¼-inch standard black steel pipe in place of wood two-by-fours and uses ³⁄₁₆-inch steel plate in fabricating floors, walls and roof. Only 3 different lengths of pipe are required for the structure; they can be jigged and welded automatically on the assembly line in the factory.

These and other modular units can be placed side by side, stacked one above another, cantilevered, or inserted into a steel frame. For structures higher than three stories, however, a new set of conditions affects the economies achieved by mass-production. For example, some multi-story housing requires shafts for elevators and stairwells, which are not easily pre-fabricated. Structural and fireproofing requirements of buildings taller than three stories also add to the cost.

These problems are not insurmountable, however, and architects, engineers and steel manufacturers have come up with a profusion of ideas for modular construction of multistory buildings.

One of the most exciting and promising of these is the "plug-in" apartment concept, in which modular units, built at a plant or on the site, are hoisted by a crane and inserted into a larger structural steel frame. A large steel company will utilize the plug-in concept for the construction of two hotels in central Florida. Each module, designed to accommodate a family of 5, will be framed in structural steel and will measure 29 by 14 feet. It will be built with furnishings and utilities and hoisted into place between structural supports. One of the hotels, a steel A-frame building 10 stories high, will contain 360 rooms; the other hotel will consist of a main 12-story structure containing 250 rooms. The same room module will be stacked 3 high to make up motel annex buildings containing 840 rooms which will surround each hotel.

A series of imaginative designs for low-cost housing developed for a leading steel company by an architectural firm in Cleveland, Ohio, calls for individual homes, town-houses and small apartment clusters to be made of 12-by-36-foot steel-framed modular units which would be stacked either parallel or at right angles to form 4-story structures. The architects also propose using a 12-foot-square module to form 6-story structures. These modules would be constructed and shipped horizontally and tipped up on end at the site. Several of these units placed side by side would form an apartment house, with 1 unit serving as an elevator shaft.

Other modular concepts for high-rise buildings have been suggested, including stacking steel-framed modules in checkerboard fashion and suspending units from steel cables.

The concept of preengineered and modular construction is still in its infancy, but it has caught the imagination of architects, engineers, steel companies and government agencies. It has significant long-range implications as a possible cure for the nation's housing ills.

TRANSPORTATION AND COMMUNICATION

CONTENTS

Using neutrons to inspect the internal parts of a toy train. The neutron radiograph can be used to inspect welds and other components of aircraft, space vehicles, automobiles and so on.

General Electric   355

REVIEW OF THE YEAR-TRANSPORTATION AND COMMUNICATION

As more and more people move into already crowded urban areas and the surrounding miles of suburban communities, the need for improved transportation systems becomes increasingly obvious. The daily commuter spends more and more of his time in stalled trains, on clogged motorways or in planes stacked above an outdated airport. It is not uncommon for people working in New York City to spend three or more hours a day traveling to and from their offices. Air travelers often spend more time driving from their homes to the airport than they spend in the air. Whole communities are evacuated when derailed railway cars leak poisonous fumes into the atmosphere.

Rapid transit systems. Experts agree that new mass public transit systems must be built and present ones improved. They must be made attractive and convenient so that the public will prefer them to private automobiles. One of the most promising systems now under construction is San Francisco's Bay Area Rapid Transit System (BART), the nation's first completely new rail-transit system since 1906. This fully-automated system will have 75 miles of track and will connect downtown San Francisco to Oakland and Berkeley, communities on the other side of San Francisco Bay. The air-conditioned, carpeted trains will travel at speeds up to 80 miles per hour. They will be operated by a computer that will control starts and stops, monitor and adjust speeds, open and close doors and maintain safe distances between trains. The $1,400,000,000 system is scheduled to open in 1972; its designers claim that it will be able to carry 180,000 passengers an hour during peak traffic periods. Another system that may begin operating in 1972 is that in Washington, D.C. Ground was broken in December 1969 on this $2,500,000,000 line which will eventually cover 98 miles. A six-mile section in the downtown area should be completed in a few years; the entire system is scheduled to be finished in 1980. In August 1969, Mexico City opened the first line of its subway system — a system replete with marble floors, sculptured walls and superb architecture. In addition to filling a definite need in this auto-clogged city, El Metro has yielded a rich archeological treasure. Thousands of Aztec relics have already been found and additional finds are expected.

Air traffic. The construction of urban heliports and suburban landing strips for short-range flights has been recommended by a number of aviation authorities as an answer to overcrowded facilities at major airports. Aircraft companies are developing "air buses" designed for short city-to-city flights. In August 1969, the Federal Aviation Administration certified the Helio Stallion, the fastest and largest STOL (short-takeoff-and-landing) plane to be built in the United States. Capable of carrying 8 to 11 passengers, it can take off fully loaded from a 320-foot runway. But capacity is what catches the headlines. Boeing's 747, twice as massive as any other airplane, went into commercial operation in January 1970. The Pan American flight from New York to London was able to carry 362 passengers; however, the seating on a 747 can be arranged to accommodate up to 490 passengers. Two other jumbo jets are expected to be ready for commercial service in late 1971: the Douglas DC-10 and Lockheed's L-1011. Meanwhile, Boeing's development of a supersonic transport (SST) remained stalled as the United States Government debated the wisdom of appropriating additional funds for the construction of two prototypes. Two European SST's — the Soviet TU-144 and the British-French Concorde — have logged many hours of successful test flights. ◆ In April 1969, test pilot Robert Courter made the first manned free flight of the Jet Flying Belt. Developed by Textron's Bell Aerosystems Company, the 126-pound system burns standard kerosene-type jet fuel. It has a range of 10 miles and a speed of at least 60 miles per hour. The pilot controls his altitude and the direction in which he moves with twist grips and a pair of handlebar-like control arms. Uses of the belt could include fire fighting, rescue operations and traffic control; it might even be the commuter's vehicle of tomorrow.

Automobiles. The auto industry is under increasing pressure to develop vehicles that are essentially pollution-free. A variety of anti-fume devices are being tested and installed in automobiles. Early in 1970 New York City began testing catalytic mufflers. These contain various devices that neutralize carbon monoxide and hydrocarbons. It is expected that such mufflers will reduce these noxious gases by about 70 per cent of what is emitted from 1968 and 1969 cars. During 1970, more than 1,000 U.S. Government vehicles will be converted to use natural gas instead of gasoline. This is expected to cut noxious exhaust emissions by about 80 per cent. Some automobile manufacturers have announced that 1971 models will run on unleaded gas; this will decrease pollution but will also cut the performance of big-engine cars. ◆ Many companies are working on substitutes for the internal combustion engine. To date, battery-powered electric cars can travel only relatively short distances before needing recharging. Small models produced by a number of firms are primarily for use in urban areas. They could be used as taxis, postal vans and so on — vehicles that travel fixed mileage routes and return daily to a garage where they can be recharged. Another alternative, steam-driven cars, is potentially the best answer to the problem of vehicular air pollution. However, developers are facing a variety of problems. Engineers are also studying the feasibility of turbine-powered buses. Powered by an engine similar to those used in jet planes and experimental high-speed trains, the bus can use a variety of fuels. Not only does it produce less air pollution than a traditional diesel-engine bus, but it also provides a more comfortable ride and is more economical.

Shipping. Containerships — vessels designed to carry cargo in standard-sized containers — are revolutionizing the shipping industry. The first vessel of the new LASH (lighter-aboard-ship) design went into service in November 1969. Tugboats position preloaded LASH barges at the stern of the ship. Built-in cranes lift the barges from the water onto the ship. This system allows cargo to be loaded and unloaded quickly, independently of shore facilities. ◆ The Bell Aerospace Division of Textron is developing a surface-effect ship that moves over the sea at an incredible speed of 92 miles an hour. The company designed it for short-haul runs; it could carry 400 passengers on 50-mile trips.

◆ ◆ ◆ ◆ ◆ ◆ ◆ ◆ ◆ ◆

The most exciting communications event of 1969 was experienced by hundreds of millions of people all over the world as they watched Neil A. Armstrong step onto the moon. The clarity of the Apollo 11 pictures and the astronauts' voices attested to the exceptional technical quality of the intricate communications system. The system converts speech, pictures and other data into electrical signals. These travel through space in the form of electromagnetic waves, at the speed of light.   In 1.3 seconds the signals reach earth, where they are converted back into their original form.

Telephones.   A number of technical developments may prove to be alternatives to time-consuming business trips.   In February 1969, the Bell System demonstrated a new, improved picturephone (Model 11).   This has been tested in the New York and Pittsburgh areas and will soon be introduced to a limited number of subscribers.   A number of companies are marketing facsimile equipment capable of sending letters, sketches, computer-provided data and other printed matter over ordinary telephone lines.   Basically, these systems involve scanning the document with a photoelectric device.   The information is broken into thousands of tiny dots which are transmitted over the telephone as electrical signals.   The receiving unit converts the signals into a reproduction of the original document.

Television.   The first transmission of public television programming via satellite took place in February 1970 when the South Carolina educational television network transmitted a program to the West Coast via Applications Technology Satellite 3 (ATS-3).   The program was fed from Columbia, South Carolina, to a NASA ground station at Rosman, North Carolina, then up to ATS-3 in synchronous orbit 22,000 miles above the equator at 73° W. longitude.   From the satellite the program was transmitted to another NASA ground station at Mojave, California, and on to the public television network station at Los Angeles.   ◆   In September 1969, the United States and India signed an agreement that will enable millions of Indians to see educational television.   Under the agreement, an ATS launched in 1972 will receive television programs from a ground station at Ahmedabad and relay them to small receivers in about 5,000 Indian villages.   This will be the first time that use of a communications satellite will not require expensive ground relay stations.   Widespread use of such direct broadcast television from satellites is not expected for a decade or more, largely because of national and international regulatory problems.   ◆   Also in September 1969, RCA demonstrated SelectaVision, a home video system that, when attached to the antenna terminals of a TV set, will play prerecorded television programs on tape.   The system is built around laser holography.   A laser beam is used to transform images on a film into a series of holograms.   The master tape is then used to make thousands of copies on a thin plastic tape.   When a low-power laser beam in the player attached to the homeowner's television set strikes this tape, the original images are reconstructed.   In October 1969, Sony Corporation announced it would market a videoplayer that uses cassettes similar to those used in tape recorders.   An adapter will permit home recording in black and white or color on the cassettes.

Braille machine.   A new device smaller than a portable typewriter may one day vastly increase the amount of literature available to blind people who read braille symbols.   This device is being developed by engineers and scientists at Argonne National Laboratory.   The new instrument, when perfected, will take symbols recorded on ordinary magnetic tape and play them back as patterns of upraised dots — letters in the braille alphabet — on an endless plastic belt.   A blind person will read the information on the moving belt simply by touching the belt with his fingertips.   He will be able to vary the speed of the plastic belt to suit his desired reading speed.   At the end of each pass, the moving belt will be "erased" and new dot patterns will be impressed on it.   A conventional braille book, embossed on heavy paper, is about fifty times as bulky as its inkprint counterpart.   Recorded on magnetic tape for the braille machine, a braille book would require about as much space as a typewriter ribbon.

VOYAGE OF THE "MANHATTAN"

Conquering the Legendary Northwest Passage

THE climax of one of the biggest transportation stories of 1969 occurred in the late evening of Sunday, September 14. It was then that the SS *Manhattan* broke through the fog and ice of Prince of Wales Strait into Amundsen Gulf, becoming the first commercial ship in history to traverse the famed Northwest Passage.*

Motivation for the venture was born in 1968 when oilmen discovered on Alaska's North Slope what is probably the world's most inaccessible oil field. As subsequent wells more clearly defined the reservoir and its great potential, the inevitable question arose: how best can this petroleum be moved to market, particularly to the heavily-populated East Coast of the United States?

From a study of transportation alternatives — including various potential pipeline and shipping routes — came the reconsideration of a five-hundred-year-old

Humble Oil & Refining Co.

The *Manhattan*, followed by the icebreakers *Northwind* and *Sir John A. MacDonald* fulfills a 500-year-old dream.

dream. Using modern technology, could the famed Northwest Passage be opened as a commercial, year-round trade route? Was it possible for giant tankers to move oil from the Prudhoe Bay area of Alaska through the Arctic ice to the Atlantic?

After examining all available information, Humble Oil & Refining Company, one of the companies that had struck oil on the North Slope, decided to launch a large, powerful ship on a test voyage through the Passage.

Converting and equipping a ship

The first step was to find a suitable ship. After surveying the world tanker fleet, Humble selected the SS *Manhattan* as the best-equipped Arctic test vehicle

---

* The first navigation of the Passage by a single ship was completed by Norwegian explorer Roald Amundsen's *Gjoa* in 1906.

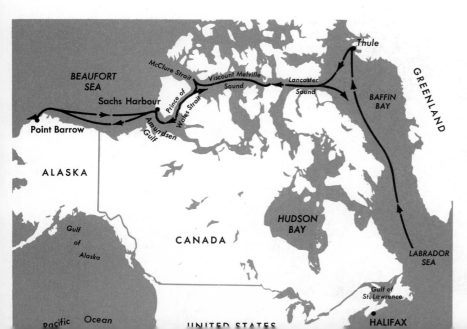

Route taken by the *Manhattan*. On April 3, 1970, the ship departed on a return voyage to the Arctic waters to obtain additional data on its performance and power requirements when operating in ice.

359

available. Built in 1961, the *Manhattan* is the largest merchant ship ever to fly the American flag. Her 43,000-shaft horsepower plant is nearly 1½ times more powerful than those on ships twice her size. The *Manhattan* also has twin propellers, making her more maneuverable and safer.

The next step was to refit the ship. No single shipyard in the country could complete all of the modifications in time for a 1969 sailing, so the *Manhattan* was sent to a yard in Chester, Pennsylvania, and sliced neatly into four segments. The stern and bow remained in Pennsylvania; the midship section — which included the navigating bridge — was towed to Mobile, Alabama; and the forward section was moved to Newport News, Virginia. Construction also began on an entirely new icebreaking bow at Bath, Maine.

Shipyard personnel strengthened the ship internally with steel braces and added a second "insurance" hull around the engine room. They toughened the outside of the vessel with an ice belt and added extra strong propellers and propeller shafts and ice deflectors for the twin rudders.

Designers utilized model test data in developing the new icebreaking bow. It operates on the downbreaking principle, moving the ship onto the ice at an 18-degree angle and increasing to a maxi-

mum of 30 degrees. The weight of the ship forces the ice down until it breaks.

To overcome the notorious Arctic radio blackouts, a communications network was installed that is effectively five hundred times more powerful than that normally found on commercial ships. The *Manhattan*'s navigation system used radio signals from four earth satellites placed in polar orbit as part of the U.S. Navy's Navigation Satellite System program. When a satellite dropped below the horizon, the ship's sonar system took over.*

As segments of the *Manhattan* returned to the Pennsylvania shipyard, workers fitted them together; other personnel began assembling supplies.

The *Manhattan*'s fuel order of 184,000 barrels of bunker oil went into the record books as the largest in commercial marine history. A partial list of provisions for the voyage included 5,600 quarts of fresh milk, 51,000 pounds of meat, 70,000 pounds of canned and dried food, 40,000 pounds of fresh fruits and vegetables and 51,000 fresh eggs. They even loaded 300 watermelons on board. Stores included 4,800 bars of soap, 1,500 light bulbs, jogging machines, a putting green, a portable

* The satellite system was not as useful as had been expected. Part of the Doppler-sonar speed-measuring device was damaged by ice moving under the ship. Thus, the satellite computer received false information and could not give the correct position of the ship.

Humble Oil & Refining Co.

Left: the *Manhattan* tests an ice pack in Baffin Bay. Heavy ice conditions with floes up to 15 feet thick presented little challenge to the giant tanker.

Right: the going is easy when the 1,005-foot-long *Manhattan* encounters a thin layer of new ice. The ship has a maximum speed of 17 knots.

X-ray machine, 100 full-length movies and 3 ice makers.

Setting sail

On August 26, the *Manhattan* steamed down the Delaware River, through Chesapeake Bay and into the Atlantic. Her voyage had begun.

The first stop was in Halifax, Nova Scotia, on August 28. After a few hours' visit, the *Manhattan* weighed anchor, steamed into the Gulf of St. Lawrence and through the Strait of Belle Isle into the frigid Labrador Sea.

Moving along the west coast of Greenland, lookouts kept a watchful eye, for this was iceberg country. As the *Manhattan* continued north, she was joined by the U.S. and Canadian icebreakers, *Northwind* and *Sir John A. MacDonald*. The *MacDonald* accompanied the *Manhattan* on the entire voyage, doing research work of its own and twice freeing the *Manhattan* when it became stuck in ice.

At dusk on the evening of September 1, the *Manhattan* approached the extensive ice pack in Baffin Bay. This was the first test of the vessel and its instrumentation. The ship moved easily through the pack, sometimes attaining speeds in excess of ten knots. On the morning of September 2, Project Manager Stanley Haas said, "We sliced through some floating ice with

forty-foot ridges and we're more than pleased with the outcome." Added Roger A. Steward, the ship's captain, "today's operations in ice proved that we have a very able vessel."

After a stop at Thule, Greenland, the *Manhattan* entered Lancaster Sound, the historic entrance to the Northwest Passage. The going was easy, and crew members watched schools of Belusa whales frolicking in the icy waters.

On September 8, the huge tanker stopped in the ice in Viscount Melville Sound to allow research parties to go out on the frozen waterway. The men clambered over the ship's side, laden with test gear, augers, drills, saws, measuring equipment and assorted markers. The ice parties were provided with sleds to carry the equipment; they also had two ski-doos, mechanized hot rods that can zip about all but the roughest floes with daredevil quickness.

The ice teams had three basic missions: to use drills to bore through the ice and measure thickness at given intervals; to use four-inch cores to gather samples for detailed laboratory analysis of salinity, a key factor in determining ice hardness; and to carefully mark a course for the *Manhattan* to break. These same missions were to be repeated more extensively later in the voyage.

Humble Oil & Refining Co.

Crewmen plant explosives to break out the *Northwind* when she became stuck in the ice. The 25-year-old ship left the expedition when it became obvious that she could not keep up with the other ships.

U.S. Coast Guard

Even with Arctic winds and the thermometer combining to produce an equivalent chilled temperature of twenty degrees below zero, the ice parties often found themselves involved in hot work. Gloves, hats and occasionally parkas were tossed aside when drilling got underway.

"We must use hand-powered tools," explained Dr. Elbert F. Rice, head of a ten-man contingent from the University of Alaska. "Engine-driven equipment is too fast, producing friction that would change the character of the ice. It's hard work, but it's interesting going through a twenty-foot piece of ice and finding out how it's put together."

Looking for trouble

On September 9, the *Manhattan* became stuck in ice when she slowed to allow the aged *Northwind* to keep up with her. The *Northwind* had fallen back several times and was considered the weakling of the convoy. Following this incident, the *Northwind* left the expedition and headed back to its home port. The *Manhattan*, unable to extricate itself, had to be freed from the ice by the *MacDonald*. (Although the *Manhattan* has 43,000-shaft horsepower in a forward direction, she has only 14,000 astern. This is not enough to drag her out of ice if she gets stuck. New tankers being planned for use in the Northwest Passage may have as much as 100,000-shaft horsepower in each direction.)

The most difficult part of the voyage lay ahead in McClure Strait. This strait, noted for its thick-formed ice and heavy ridging, has always been considered a major impediment to vessels attempting the Northwest Passage. "But," as Mr. Haas said, "unlike other ships which in the past have avoided ice up here, we're looking for it."

So, instead of heading southwestward for a relatively easy journey through the Prince of Wales Strait, the ship forged her way into McClure Strait. But 120 miles into the strait, the *Manhattan* was stopped by the ice. Side-looking airborne radar and infrared photographs provided by the Canadian Department of Transport and the U.S. Coast Guard overflights indicated that extremely rugged conditions lay ahead. There was a distinct possibility that the two ships might become stuck — a situation that would keep them there until the following summer. Thus, late on the 11th, Haas and Steward regretfully decided to retreat.

No major ice was encountered during the passage through Prince of Wales Strait, and on the night of September 14 the *Manhattan* slipped quietly into the waters of Amundsen Gulf — the first commercial vessel in history to traverse the formidable Northwest Passage. From there it was easy sailing to Point Barrow, Alaska, the final destination of the east-to-west segment of the 2½-month round trip.

On September 22, following ceremonies in Point Barrow, the *Manhattan* sailed back toward Melville Sound, where she remained until the end of October. During these weeks the ice scientists and engineers conducted extensive tests of the ice that covers these cold northern waters. The data they collected was important in determining the economic feasibility of using the Northwest Passage for shipping.

Ice tests were concluded on October 26 and the *Manhattan* headed for home. On November 12 she sailed into New York Harbor; the historic voyage was over.

Was it worth it?

Although the great dream of a new trade route moved closer to reality, the $40 million gamble had yet to prove itself. The voyage showed that moving commerce through the Northwest Passage is possible, but the economic feasibility of doing it could not be known until after the mass of technical data obtained during the voyage was analyzed.

Should the *Manhattan* prove the practicality of this Arctic trade route, the ultimate effects may be almost unlimited. An open Northwest Passage means not merely an oil route, but an international trade route that would have a profound influence on the rate of Arctic development and the patterns of worldwide trade.

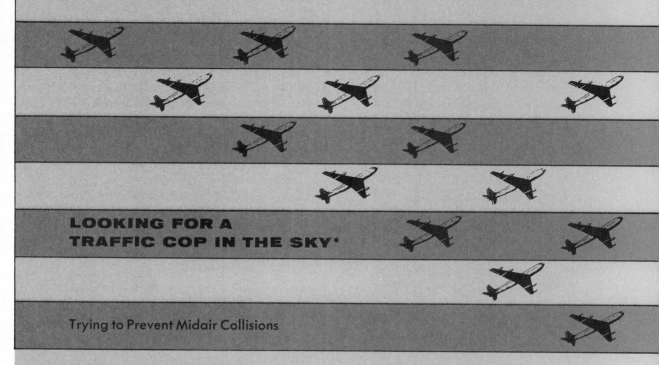

LOOKING FOR A
TRAFFIC COP IN THE SKY*

Trying to Prevent Midair Collisions

UNITED AIR LINES Flight 285 is a twin-engine Boeing 737 that routinely leaves Newark Airport at 8:30 every morning bound for Detroit. On Wednesday morning, November 5, 1969, though, United's 285 was anything but routine.

On that day, visibility was about a quarter of a mile, and Captain R. A. Lemmon was climbing through a light rain, toward his assigned altitude of 24,000 feet, when the second officer grasped his shoulder and shouted "Look!" There, just visible through the clouds was one of the most terrifying sights a pilot can see: another airplane on a collision course.

Lemmon practically stood his plane on its left wing as he desperately rolled away from the bigger plane — a huge DC-8 cargo jet. Later, the second officer said he vividly remembered seeing only the letters "EA" framed by his side window, the two jets were that close. The letters were the "EA" in the words Seaboard World Airlines lettered on the aircraft's fuselage. Later checking indicated the planes passed within 50 feet of each other. Captain Lemmon has since figured that he had only 4 seconds from the first sighting to the point of impact.

* Reprinted by permission from *Business Week*

The alarm

Flight 285 ended relatively happily. Only the 2 stewardesses were slightly injured. But the fright shook more than the crew and passengers. The entire industry was alarmed. The near-miss of November 5 was theoretically one that should not have happened. Both planes were under radar surveillance from air-traffic controllers on the ground; both pilots had filed flight plans; and the air through which they were flying was not the crowded, congested airspace found close to a terminal.

The areas of greatest danger from midair collisions are well known to the Federal Aviation Administration (FAA). Its figures for 1968 show that there were 327 reports involving air carriers where one or both planes had to take drastic evasive action within terminal areas. Of the planes involved, 40 per cent were below 2,000 feet; 83 per cent were below 5,000 feet; and virtually all were below 10,000 feet. Only 2.8 per cent of the near-misses were between air carriers; 14.4 per cent were between an air carrier and a military plane, and 82.8 per cent involved air carriers and private or business airplanes. And 73 per cent of the incidents were within 10 miles of the airport.

But the United-Seaboard near-miss served to point up the deficiencies in air-traffic-control equipment and procedures, and that air-traffic controllers are still overworked. More than that, it showed all too clearly that a much better collision-avoidance system is needed if ghastly crashes involving jumbo jets are to be avoided. That system may be ready soon.

In November 1969 the flight stage of a test and evaluation program of a new collision-avoidance system was completed. A final report was due around January 1, 1970, and the outlook is that the system will be approved for use in 1970.

The present

Right now, there are only two ways to keep planes a safe distance apart. One is visual. The pilot or cockpit crew is supposed to see other aircraft and take action to avoid them. At jet speeds, though, an airplane 20 miles away is only 1 minute from a jet going in the other direction. Even in perfect weather, relying solely on the eyesight of crew members, who have many other duties to perform, offers obviously inadequate protection for modern aircraft. And airline and business pilots often fly in conditions of less than perfect visibility.

The major role in preventing collisions today belongs to the air-traffic-control (ATC) system. This depends on radar surveillance and control of aircraft movement from the ground. But the ATC system tends to become overloaded near major air terminals and does not serve all of the country's airspace. Primarily designed for high-performance aircraft operating under instrument flight plans, ATC is provided only at altitudes above 24,000 feet, and around terminals.

The Air Transport Association (ATA) would like to see the ATC expanded to include coverage down to 18,000 feet nationwide, and down to 10,000 feet in the areas bounded by New York, Chicago and Washington and between Los Angeles and San Francisco. In "higher density terminal areas," ATA says, coverage should extend down to the ground. This is vigorously contested by many private pilots.

To accept the ATA recommendations, the FAA needs more manpower, equipment and money, all of which it would get under the proposed administration Airport/Airways Development Bill. In November 1969, President Richard M. Nixon asked Congress for 1,000 new controllers, in addition to the 2,800 new slots he asked for in the 1969 budget.

The bill passed the House of Representatives with provision for 3,800 controllers. But expansion of the ATC system will not by itself solve the problem. Really significant progress in improving the air-safety record will depend on adoption of some kind of collision-avoidance system (CAS) as a backup to the air controllers.

The system has been a long time coming. Given early impetus by the 1956 collision of two airliners over the Grand Canyon, CAS research got a big push from James S. McDonnell, chairman of the board and founder of McDonnell Company, now McDonnell Douglas Corporation. In June 1960, two test pilots were killed when a pair of McDonnell F-101B Voodoo fighter planes collided in clear skies while under ground control. McDonnell looked around for a collision-avoidance system. When manufacturers were unable to supply a workable CAS, McDonnell turned his own electronics experts loose on the problem. The result, in 1963, was the EROS — for Eliminate Range 0 (Zero) System.

Basically intended for high-performance fighter planes operating in an uncontrolled environment, EROS was a gratifying success. By 1968, more than 13,000 F-4 Phantom flights had been logged successfully with the EROS computer.

The planners

In 1966, the ATA created a group to draw up a commercial CAS. Several prospective builders sought to have their concepts and designs included in the final specifications. After months of negotiation and much tugging and pulling, the

COLLISION AVOIDANCE SYSTEM

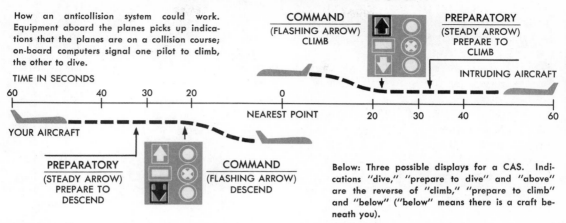

How an anticollision system could work. Equipment aboard the planes picks up indications that the planes are on a collision course; on-board computers signal one pilot to climb, the other to dive.

COMMAND (FLASHING ARROW) CLIMB

PREPARATORY (STEADY ARROW) PREPARE TO CLIMB

INTRUDING AIRCRAFT

TIME IN SECONDS

60 40 30 20 0 NEAREST POINT 20 30 40 60

YOUR AIRCRAFT

PREPARATORY (STEADY ARROW) PREPARE TO DESCEND

COMMAND (FLASHING ARROW) DESCEND

Below: Three possible displays for a CAS. Indications "dive," "prepare to dive" and "above" are the reverse of "climb," "prepare to climb" and "below" ("below" means there is a craft beneath you).

COCKPIT DISPLAYS

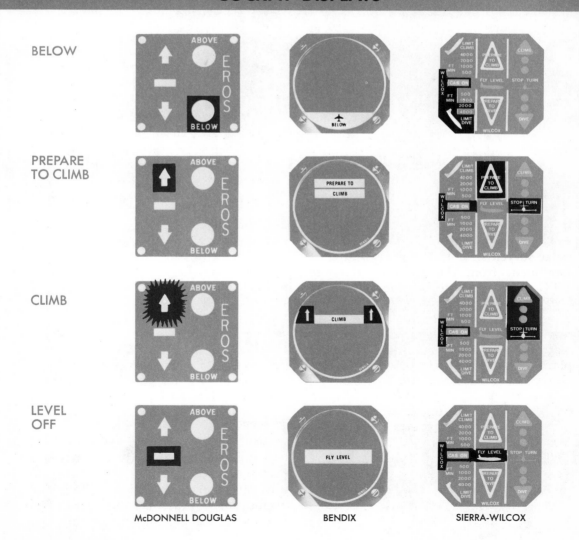

BELOW

PREPARE TO CLIMB

CLIMB

LEVEL OFF

McDONNELL DOUGLAS   BENDIX   SIERRA-WILCOX

MID-AIR COLLISIONS		
Year	Number	Fatalities
1960	26	152
1961	20	22
1962	19	27
1963	13	6
1964	15	12
1965	27	30
1966	27	33
1967	24	157
1968	38	71
1969	28	120

FAA

Left: A controller watches air traffic on a radarscope at the Leesburg, Virginia, traffic-control center. Twenty-two such facilities in the United States are responsible for preventing cross-country planes from colliding with one another.

Airport controllers must watch both the planes outside and the radar screens inside that show the overall pattern of moving air traffic in the area.

Dept. of Transportation

UPI

Above: A midair collision near Indianapolis in September 1969 killed 85 persons. The crash involved a twin-jet airliner and a small private plane. Below: A December 1960 midair collision over Brooklyn, New York, of 2 giant airliners resulted in 134 deaths. A CAS would help avoid such tragic accidents. But the only practical CAS is probably a cooperative system in which both aircraft are fitted with parts of the system.

UPI

ATA group came up with a system that resembles EROS but is simpler and thus cheaper.

The McDonnell Douglas commercial version is now called EROS II. Two other companies are participating in the flight-test and evaluation program. Bendix Avionics Division of Bendix Corporation, as well as McDonnell Douglas, is concentrating on a $30,000-per-unit CAS for airliners and other high-performance craft, based on EROS. And Sierra-Wilcox, a combination of Sierra Research Corporation and Wilcox Company, is aiming at the general aviation market with simpler equipment costing about $8,500, which would be compatible with the more expensive system.

The key to the airliner version is a time-reference system, or atomic clock. Timing is vital. Each aircraft must transmit a radio signal for a microfraction of a second at a precise and predetermined 3-second interval. The atomic clock, based on the known and steady oscillations of the electrons of the cesium atom, permits the exceedingly precise timing required. Ground stations synchronize the system.

How it works

Every plane in the system must be equipped with a CAS receiver, transmitter and miniature digital computer for the system to work. With knowledge of the altitude, distance, and closing range of other aircraft determined by its radio transmissions, a plane will be told by its computer whether a collision course exists. In such a case, a warning is flashed in the cockpit, and a visual display on the instrument panel advises the pilot on which evasive maneuver he must make. The system — designed to work if either plane or both take evasive action — can handle up to 2,000 planes at a time. When 1 plane transmits, all others receive, thus permitting the use of only 1 frequency and avoiding airwaves clutter.

Though collision-avoidance systems for commercial use probably will be ordered in 1970, the ATA system is not fully perfected. Probably the biggest problem is that it protects only similarly equipped planes from each other. And at $30,000 a copy, only airliners and the most deluxe business aircraft will have it. But most of the collisions are not among these types of aircraft.

Different approach

The Aircraft Owners & Pilots Association (AOPA), a trade group representing the light-plane part of the industry, wants a different — and cheaper — device called a proximity-warning indicator (PWI), which, so far at least, does not have that all-important compatibility with CAS. An AOPA spokesman says: "We have been pushing for a PWI for years. We think it is absolutely essential. But we are not pushing for the ATA-FAA collision-avoidance system. We think a proximity warning would be more helpful."

Several reasons are cited for this position. First is the "fantastically expensive" cost. The AOPA spokesman says: "From what we hear of CAS, it works well where it's not needed. It works well when there are a few planes around, but when you get it into a crowd, it goes mad. In a great amount of traffic, the thing just doesn't give the proper amount of indication without practically blowing its fuse." But the AOPA man admits, "The ATA system is a good start on the technology."

For its part, ATA insists that it is important to make a start with the system now while at the same time pushing research aimed at bringing down costs so that more light planes can come into the CAS net. Clifton F. Von Kann, ATA vice-president for operations and engineering, told the National Transportation Safety Board at hearings growing out of the September 9, 1969, collision between a DC-9 and a Piper Apache near Indianapolis, which killed 85 persons: "It is our firm belief that successful equipment for airline use and for private aviation will be produced in the next one to three years."

Chief complaint

A major criticism raised against the ATA system is that it was developed for relatively uncrowded air routes between cities and will not work in congested terminal areas. ATA says that initial testing of the system was purposely limited to "en route" situations; it has since modified the system to handle terminal congestion. Speeds are slower in terminal areas, ATA says, and the CAS can handle more traffic at slower speeds.

An airline captain worries that the vertical escape maneuvers required by the ATA system might not be safe if the plane was taken into altitudes assigned to other planes. ATA, on the other hand, insists that the vertical maneuver is the easiest to make, and points out that one plane should not be flying into another's space unless the second plane were way off course. And the maneuver would have less noticeable effect on passengers than a takeoff, ATA says.

In spite of the criticism, the preponderant reaction to CAS is favorable. Ted Linnert, director of the engineering and air safety department of the Air Line Pilots Association, says: "We are very interested in the ATA system and encourage any work toward collision avoidance. We are very much in support of their work. We are also very much in support of getting little aircraft equipped with compatible equipment."

Linnert would also like to see a PWI, or "horn in the sky" as he calls it, for general aviation. If such a device were compatible with the CAS, he says, "It would go a long way toward providing complete protection." But Linnert told the safety-board hearings: "Early solutions to the problem do not have to cover all possible conditions in order to substantially improve safety."

And an engineer who was involved in much of the development of the system now being evaluated claims it is a "conservative" one that should work well at the beginning and even better later. "A system is merely a communication and data-collection device," he says. "Once it works — once it collects data and communicates — the rest is software and is easy to change for different situations."

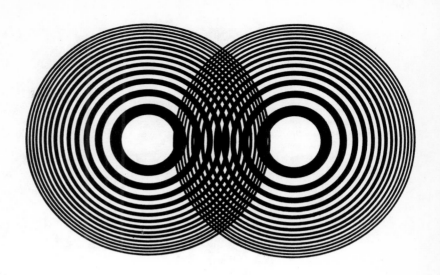

CASSETTES*

Not Either-or, but And!

BY CHARLES LINCOLN

THE people who promote tape recording as a home-entertainment medium have never been satisfied with the dent in the marketplace that tape has made since it was introduced about 20 years ago. Tape gave the recording and film industries a newfound freedom. And the ordinary mortal such as you or I could record and edit material in his own home without learning the skills of a machinist.

But that wasn't enough. Starting in the mid-1950's, tape has tried to compete with disc records as "the" medium for commercially packaged music. The battle was an uneven one from the start, and the odds are still weighted in favor of discs. For packaged music, tape has a few serious disadvantages that overshadow its advantages. Notably, tape costs more than a disc for the same program length; and finding a particular selection among the half a dozen or so on one track is more difficult than locating a selected band on a disc. The tape user also has "fumbling" prob-

* Reprinted from *Popular Electronics*, courtesy of Ziff-Davis Publishing Company

lems, and, to some extent, open-reel tape is best suited for use by people with nimble fingers.

In addition, there are technical problems involved in the quantity duplication of tapes, resulting in poorer audio quality than the best available from discs. Last, but not least, a boxed 7-inch reel of tape is heavier and somewhat bulkier than a 12-inch long-playing record in its jacket. (For the same content, a tape measures roughly 25 cubic inches and weighs almost a pound, while the disc is less than 20 cubic inches and about 8 ounces.)

With all that against it, what *is* the appeal of tape? The principal one is that reel-to-reel commercially recorded tapes are not so vulnerable as discs are to dust, dirt and scratches. There is less trouble with pops, clicks and crackle. The playing life of a tape, with minimum care in handling and occasional demagnetization of the tape heads, is indefinitely long. *But* the playing life of a disc, kept clean and played with a good stylus and cartridge with a 2-gram (or lower) tracking force, is also extremely long. In fact, you will probably get tired of the record before it wears out.

Enter the cassette

In 1964, Phillips, the Netherlands-based electronics firm, introduced a tape-

370

Cassettes are smaller than cartridges and easier to store. Experts believe that cassettes have a brighter future than cartridges and will become increasingly popular as sound qualities improve.

recording and playback system that overcame many of the disadvantages of tape. The tape was contained in a small functional package called a *cassette,* measuring 4 inches × 2 inches × ⅜ inch. Tape, cassette and all, simply snapped into the record/playback machine. The tape was 0.150 inch wide (a little more than ⅛ inch) and moved at 1⅞ inches per second.

At first, because of the limited audio quality, the cassette system was recommended for dictation and similar applications where fidelity was not the main objective. The machines were designed for 2-track monaural operation, and one could (and still can) get up to 2 hours of recording time (1 hour per track).

The cassette is a superbly ingenious piece of engineering. With improved tape-head design, it became possible to record 4 tracks instead of 2; and so the stereo cassette evolved, still offering the same program length as the mono cassette. The stereo cassette occupies only about 7 cubic

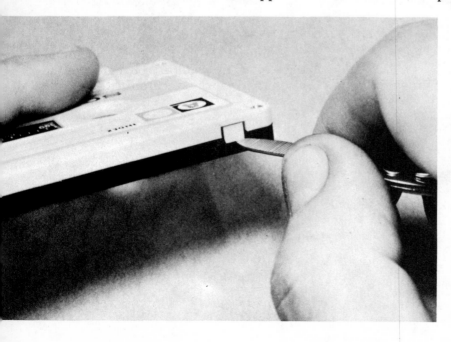

At the rear of each blank tape cassette is a plastic tab. When the tab is in place the erase-record function of the cassette recorder cannot be operated. Snapping out the tab will disable the lock.

inches and weighs only a few ounces, thus virtually eliminating the user's size and weight objections to tape.

What about fidelity? That's still the limitation. Even with the finest playback heads and the best duplicating techniques, the upper frequency limit at the tape speed of 1⅞ inches per second is between 10,000 and 12,000 hertz (Hz), compared with 15,000 to 20,000 Hz for many discs and the best open-reel tapes. Signal-to-noise ratio is limited to about 45 decibels (dB), which is comparable with good AM radio reception, but far short of good FM (65 dB). Distortion tends to run somewhat higher than on the other media, especially at high frequencies.

Still, except in direct comparison with discs or top-quality open-reel tapes, the stereo cassettes sound remarkably good, and their convenience and compactness make them very attractive.

Stereo cassettes are, in general, still about 25 per cent more expensive than

4 TRACK CASSETTE
(VIEW FROM COATED SIDE)

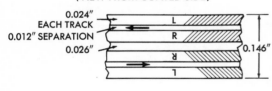

4 TRACK
REEL-TO-REEL

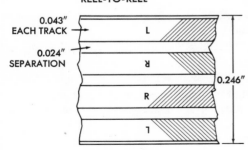

The magnetic tape used in cassettes (upper) is substantially narrower than tape in cartridges or on reels (lower). Note the track arrangement. In the cassette the left and right tracks are side by side; in a cartridge they are separated by a reverse track. This means that a cassette with a stereo recording can be played back in mono on a 2-track cassette player. One disadvantage of the narrow cassette tracks is an increase in the signal-to-noise ratio.

discs with comparable program material and playing time, and the variety of music available is sorely limited. So far, only certain cassette models include a means of locating a particular selection. Without this feature the cassette is less convenient than even an open-reel-tape machine.

In proper perspective

Each of the various sound-recording and reproducing media has its own peculiar advantages and drawbacks. It's a curious characteristic of American culture that when something new comes along, it is expected to conquer and replace all that went before. We tend to see competition in terms of a struggle for supremacy.

"Is tape better than a disc?" "Is a stereo receiver better than individual units?" "Is a ceramic cartridge better than a magnetic unit?" These are silly questions. There is no reason why two or more ways of doing something can't exist peaceably side by side forever. Sometimes a new development does deservedly supersede an older technique. For example, there is no good reason for designing new audio equipment with tubes. Transistors are simply superior in every way. But this is the exception, not the rule.

Tape has unquestioned advantages over discs *in certain areas,* which accounts for its complete acceptance for all original recording, whether the final form of the recording is disc, tape, or a film sound track. Its mechanical convenience, the ease with which synchronized multiple tracks can be recorded; the fact that it can be erased and reused; and, most of all, the simplicity of editing by physically cutting and splicing have put tape in a place all its own. For someone who wants to do original recording, especially if he wants to edit his material, there is nothing like the open-reel tape. But for someone who wants to purchase commercially recorded material in the widest possible variety with the best available fidelity and at the lowest cost, the disc record is still unsurpassed — and probably will remain so for a good many years. The universality of record-playing equipment assures that — if nothing else did.

The cassette falls somewhere in between. There are areas where it is better than anything else around: providing background music while you walk or drive and recording interviews, conferences, speeches or other spoken material with good fidelity, marvelous convenience and notable economy — these are two examples. Several radio stations and broadcast program services use cassette recorders extensively for on-the-spot coverage of news events or spur-of-the-moment interviews when it isn't practical to lure the subject into a recording studio. The raw material on cassettes is then dubbed off onto conventional ¼-inch tape for editing, and the cassettes are erased and reused.

It is not practical to edit cassette tape directly. Many cassettes cannot even be opened without damage, but even when they can, the tape is thin and narrow and difficult to handle. The spools inside the cassette have no flanges, and once the halves of the cassette are separated, the tape can too easily spiral off one of the spools until you have a hopeless tangle. Also, the 1⅞-inches-per-second speed makes any but the simplest editing difficult because the "sounds" are crammed tightly together. If you want to edit what you record, do it on conventional open-reel ¼-inch tape, preferably at 7½ inches per second.

Besides the battery-powered mono cassette recorders, there are now quite a few machines that record four-track stereo cassettes. Many "compact" audio systems include cassette facilities. This partly solves the problem of a limited variety of commercially packaged music. If you have a stereo cassette player in your car, you can record any disc or radio program on a cassette at home and then listen to it while you travel. Cassettes, incidentally, can be bulk-erased as easily as open-reel magnetic tape.

One inherent limitation in the cassette system is that it must use a combination record-playback head. (The degree of miniaturization of the design simply does not permit enough space for separate heads.) This not only limits top-end frequency response and signal-to-noise ratio, but also makes it impossible to monitor from the playback head while recording or to produce echo effects. For these reasons, cassettes will not supplant open-reel tape for serious recording.

There is no question that the cassette system is a brilliant contribution to the audio scene, but it must be considered on its merits, taking account of its own advantages and disadvantages. It *supplements* discs and open-reel tapes, but it won't replace them.

You may be wondering why we have said nothing about any of the "cartridge" tape systems. There is one good reason for this: cartridge systems are, at the moment, inferior to cassettes, discs and open-reel tape when all the factors of price, convenience, reliability and variety are considered.

So the word is: if you feel you can use cassettes to good advantage, by all means equip yourself to play them — and preferably to record them as well — but don't sell your turntable and/or tape recorder. Cassettes are good, but they won't make the other major home entertainment media obsolete.

A GLOSSARY OF TERMS

DECIBEL (dB)—unit that indicates the relative loudness of a sound

DISTORTION—an unwanted signal produced by the cassette system or on the tape

FLANGE—a protruding rim that holds the tape in place

FREQUENCY—the number of sound vibrations per second

FREQUENCY RESPONSE—the range of frequency that the machine is able to reproduce

HERTZ (Hz)—a unit of frequency equal to one cycle per second

PLAYBACK—reproduction of the program on the cassette tape

SIGNAL-TO-NOISE RATIO—ratio of the value of the recorded sounds to that of the noise produced by the cassette system

TRACK—recorded part of the tape

TRACKING FORCE—pressure exerted on a phonograph record by the needle (stylus)

THE JET FLYING BELT

A New Dimension in Individual Mobility

STRAP on the Jet Flying Belt and you're ready to fly over the Grand Canyon or the Mississippi River; able to avoid the congested highways between home and work; prepared to deliver medical aid rapidly to accident victims. "The scope of . . . applications," says Robert J. May, the Jet Belt's project manager at Bell Aerosystems Company, "is limited only by the imagination and ingenuity of its potential users."

Under development since 1965, the feasibility model Jet Belt logged its first manned free flight on April 7, 1969, when Robert F. Courter, Jr., lifted off a runway apron at Niagara Falls International Airport and piloted the system over a 300-foot elliptical course. He reached an altitude of 25 feet and speeds of 30 miles per hour.

Subsequent test flights have further verified vertical takeoff and landing, transition to and from horizontal flight, and coordinated turn and precise hovering maneuvers — some of which have been made in winds of up to 30 miles per hour.

Operation of the Jet Belt is similar to that of its rocket-powered predecessors. The turbine engine is mounted vertically, inlet down. It exhausts through twin ducts which distribute the thrust equally to nozzles located outward and pointing downward just behind the operator's shoulders.

The exhaust nozzles provide lifting thrust and, with proper position, also furnish forces for maneuvering in all axes of flight.

Operator controls consist of a pair of control arms and two motorcycle-type handgrips. Rotation of the right-hand grip controls engine speed throughout the entire engine-operating regime, from idle to full thrust. Manipulation of the control arms and rotation of the left-hand grip deflect the nozzles to provide movement in whatever direction desired.

During flight, air-to-ground and ground-to-air communication is maintained through two-way battery-powered field-radio equipment. A paratrooper's standard emergency parachute deployed by a drogue gun constitutes the operator-recovery system.

PROJECTS AND EXPERIMENTS

CONTENTS

"We should not pretend to understand the world only by the intellect; we apprehend it just as much by feeling."

Carl Jung

Lew Merrim — Monkmeyer

FUN WITH FIBONACCI*

An Unusual Set

of Numbers

BY DIANE SHERMAN

Count the clockwise and counterclockwise spirals of seeds on this pinecone. You should find 8 clockwise spirals and 13 counterclockwise spirals. Do these numbers look familiar?

Franklyn K. Lauden

IN THE thirteenth century an Italian mathematician named Leonardo Fibonacci discovered a most unusual set of numbers. They appeared as the solution to a problem in a book he wrote about

* "Fun with Fibonacci" by Diane Sherman, from the January 5, 1970, issue of *Nature and Science Magazine.* Copyright © 1970 by the American Museum of Natural History. Reprinted by permission of Doubleday & Company, Inc.

mathematics. Here is the problem. Can you figure out some way to go about solving it?

Suppose there are 2 baby rabbits in a pen, 1 male and 1 female. At the end of two months, they produce another male-female pair of rabbits, and they continue to produce a new male-female pair each month thereafter. After each new pair is two months old it too starts producing 1 new male-female pair a month, and so on. How many rabbits will there be in the pen at the end of a year?

Let's try keeping track. We'll let each line on the chart shown stand for one month. The first and second lines show A, the pair of rabbits we started with. The third line shows B, the pair born in the third month, making a total of 2 pairs of rabbits at the end of the third month. (Be careful not to count pair A twice.) The fourth line shows C, the pair of rabbits born in the fourth month. In the fifth month, pair A has another pair, D. Also in the fifth month, the B pair is two months old and has its first new pair, E.

On the chart you can see what has happened by the end of the seventh month. Run your eye down the figures

END OF MONTH	Nature and Science TOTAL PAIRS
1	1
2	1
3	2
4	3
5	5
6	8
7	13

showing the total number of rabbit pairs at the end of each month. Do the numbers seem to be related in any way? Keep looking until you figure out their relationship. Without drawing more rabbits, can you predict what the numbers might be at the ends of months 8, 9, 10, 11, and 12?

The numbers in the right-hand column are the first in a series that has come to be called "Fibonacci numbers." As you may have noticed, each number in the series (except the first two) is the sum of the two numbers before it. Fibonacci himself didn't investigate the series very thoroughly, but later mathematicians have found it fascinating. For one thing, they have discovered that Fibonacci numbers occur often in nature.

Flowers and Fibonacci

The next time you see a sunflower, notice its center part, made up of spirals of seeds. Some of the spirals curl in a clockwise direction, and some of them curl in a counterclockwise direction. If you count the number of clockwise spirals and the number of counterclockwise spirals, you will probably come up with two numbers that come one after the other in the Fibonacci series.

If you have chosen an average-size sunflower, you may find 34 counterclockwise spirals and 55 clockwise spirals. Larger sunflowers may contain 55 and 89 spirals, or 89 and 144. The record sunflower was found in Vermont, with 144 and 233 spirals. Can you find a sunflower to beat that?

You may also find Fibonacci numbers by counting the numbers of petals of different kinds of flowers. Irises and some lilies have 3 petals. Five-petaled flowers are the most common of all, and there are many species with 8 petals. Thirteen petals are common on such flowers as ragwort, corn marigolds, and mayweed. Garden and wild flowers often have 21 petals. Thirty-four petals is the commonest number for the daisy family, but some field daisies have 55 petals, and Michaelmas daisies may have 89 petals — all Fibonacci numbers.

If you play the piano, you may find another example of the Fibonacci series. The diagram shows an *octave,* or eight notes, beginning with the note C and ending with the C that is one octave higher on the musical scale. To make a C-major chord, you can play the third note of the octave (E), the fifth note (G), and the eighth note (C). So your chord is made up of notes 3, 5, and 8, a Fibonacci series. Perhaps you can find other ways in which musical scales and chords are related to Fibonacci numbers.

Some mathematicians have become real Fibonacci hunters. There is even a magazine called *Fibonacci Quarterly.* Brother Alfred Brousseau, who teaches mathematics at St. Mary's College of California, helped start the magazine. He claims that once people start looking for Fibonacci numbers, they find them everywhere.

Do you want to become a Fibonacci hound? Start looking around and counting. The numbers often pop up in some of the most unexpected places. Maybe you can find examples that no one has noticed before.

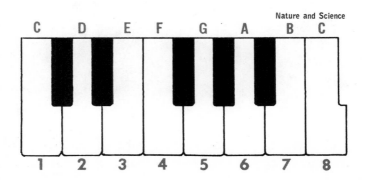

Nature and Science

HOW TO DO AN EXPERIMENT

Simple Guidelines to Help You Start Your Experiment

BY PHILIP GOLDSTEIN

When you do an experiment, it is necessary to keep accurate records of all your observations.

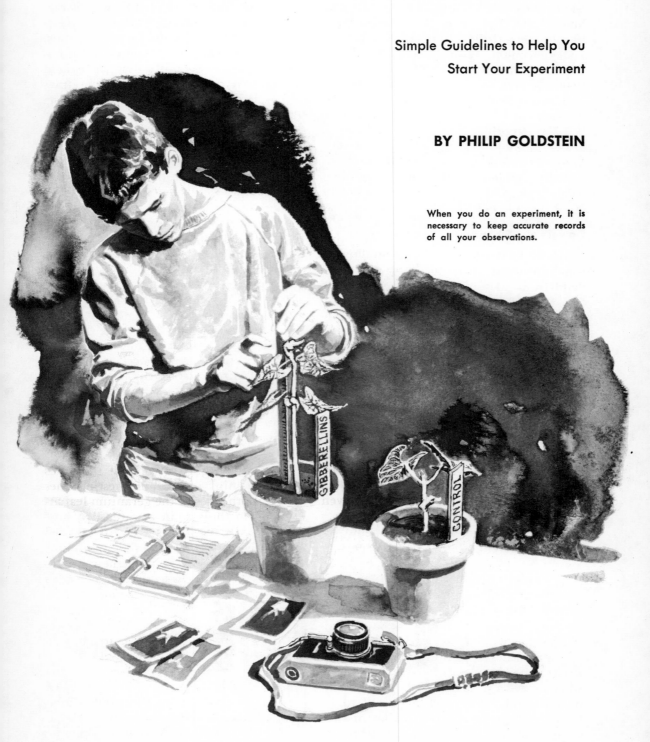

DOING an experiment is an exciting experience. True, it takes up lots of time that might be spent in other activities. It requires careful planning and hard work in carrying out. But it is worth the time and effort. The purpose of this article is to give you a little guidance in conducting an experiment. If you read this article carefully, and follow the advice it gives, you may save yourself a little sweat and a good many tears when you set out to do an experiment.

An experiment is *a planned effort to answer a question by making something happen under controlled conditions.* Usually a single experiment answers only a small, simple question that in itself may seem insignificant. But an accumulation of many experiments, each testing a little question, may ultimately give rise to something important. "Each adds a little to our knowledge of nature," said Aristotle, "and from all the facts arises grandeur."

How does an experiment begin? It begins in your mind. It begins when you ask yourself a question, or become curious about something. Curiosity and a desire to know lie at the bottom of all experiments.

How do problems originate?

Every experiment begins with a problem. Everyone encounters puzzling situations in the course of his everyday life. Few of us, however, recognize that a problem exists; even fewer are willing to do anything about solving the problem even if we do recognize its existence.

If you want to do an experiment, you must be different from the average person. You must give your curiosity free sway. Ask yourself questions about what you read, what you see, what you learn in school. Ask yourself why things happen, how they happen, and under what circumstances they will happen again.

Sir Ernest Rutherford, the Nobel Prizewinner in chemistry, often told how, when he was a youngster, he pushed a stick into a pond. The stick appeared to be bent. When he pulled it out it was straight again. He pushed it back, it was

bent. He pulled it out, it was straight. "This sort of thing makes you think," he commented. This story illustrates how curiosity leads to the discovery of scientific problems.

Don't worry if the problem seems to be a little one. Even an unimportant question can give you a start. If you set up an experiment to solve a little question, you are almost sure to be led into bigger and more-important ones. It is a well-known truth in science that every experiment raises more questions than it answers. Your little experiment most likely will not be an exception to the rule. Let us consider a case to see how this works.

In biology you learned that a geranium leaf has tiny pores called stomates (stomata). Your teacher explained that these pores allow the leaf to exchange gases with the outside atmosphere. Immediately questions begin to arise. What gases are exchanged through these pores? How do the pores work? Are they all the same size? What happens to a geranium leaf if its pores are clogged?

The last question interests you, and you decide to set up an experiment to find the answer. You realize that you must first find out where the stomates are located. Are they equally distributed over the whole leaf surface? Are there equal numbers of stomates on the upper and lower surfaces?

As you begin to work on this question, you think of other interesting questions. Both sides of the geranium leaf are exposed to the air; in a water lily, however, only one side of the leaf is exposed. Does this in any way affect the distribution of stomates? What arrangement of stomates is found in a plant such as elodea, which grows completely submerged underwater? And if a plant grows partly below and partly above the surface of the water, is the arrangement of stomates the same in both parts?

This line of questioning can lead you toward some exciting problems. Can environmental conditions affect the number and arrangement of stomates in a leaf? In other words, do plants adapt to changing environmental conditions by producing new stomates? Or by losing existing stomates? Or by rearranging them? Is there a seasonal change in the number and arrangement of stomates in a given plant?

This is only the beginning. The questions spread to cover wider and wider areas, like the circles in a pond when a pebble is dropped into the water. How do stomates open and close? Is there a daily cycle? A seasonal cycle? Does light affect their behavior? Sunlight? Moonlight?

Selecting a problem

If you ask questions about the things you see and hear, your mind will surely be bombarded with potential problems. But which problems should you select for your very own? Perhaps the following guidelines will help you make a decision.

1. Does the subject interest you? Pick a question that really excites you — one to which you are eager to learn the answer. Don't let anyone talk you into choosing a topic that bores you.

2. Is the proposed experiment suitable to your present level of maturity and knowledge? It is far better to select a relatively simple project that you can bring to a successful conclusion than to begin a complex experiment that is far too difficult for you to complete.

3. Do you have available the equipment, apparatus and laboratory space that your investigation requires? Obviously a ninth-grade student who is interested in astronomy could hardly hope to investigate the radio signals reaching earth from quasars lying far out in the cosmos — he does not have access to a radio telescope with which to detect them.

4. Do you have the technical skills that the project requires? For example, you may be interested in synthesizing DNA from its component parts. But do you have the chemical skills required to carry out such a complex chemical operation?

5. Can the experiment be completed in the time available to you? Remember, this experiment is not going to be your life's work. You probably have a rather

Curiosity often leads to the discovery and study of problems. Why does the stick appear bent when pushed into the water?

limited amount of time during which you must conduct your investigation. Therefore choose something that can be completed in a reasonable length of time.

6. Does the proposed experiment entail any danger to you? If it does, forget it. You should not consider an experiment dealing with pathogenic bacteria, explosives, dangerous drugs, or anything else that may do you injury.

7. Will your experiment cause harm or pain to the animal subjects you use? You are not an accomplished surgeon who can operate on an anesthetized animal under humane conditions. Thus you should avoid experiments that are apt to injure an animal or cause it pain. There are many possible experiments with small invertebrate animals or plants where these factors do not come into play.

Clarifying and stating the problem

When you first become interested in an area of research, you have a generalized idea that must be narrowed down and brought into sharp focus. Precisely what do you want to find out? You should begin by formulating a clear, concise statement of the specific problem that you wish to investigate. Let us consider an imaginary situation to see just how this works.

During a class discussion on adaptation, you learn that organisms are constantly adjusting to their environment. Various questions flash through your mind. Are organisms really aware of small changes in their surroundings? Can they detect a gradual change? Do they do anything when such a change occurs?

You decide to plan an experiment to test whether organisms respond to a changing environment. This is a fine idea for research, but obviously it is too broad. You would be wise to narrow your efforts to the effect of one environmental factor on a single species. You decide to use guppies because you are familiar with them, and you have many of them in your aquarium. But which environmental factor should you study?

At this point you may recall a recent television program. The commentator said that the increase in water temperature around a nuclear electric plant was killing fish in that area. He called the increase in water temperature "thermal pollution." You decide to study the effect of water temperature on guppies. More specifically, you want to see if guppies will move to that part of the water where the temperature is best suited for them. How do you state the problem?

How does "A study of adjustment to the environment" strike you? Or "How fish respond to changes in their environment"? Would either of these make it clear to anyone what you are trying to find out? Wouldn't it be better to include the name of the organism and the condition being tested? For example, "Thermal pollution and guppies." This is better, but not yet good enough. At last you come up with the following: "How do guppies react to a gradual change in water temperature?" This is a fine statement of the problem. It tells clearly that you intend to subject guppies to a gradual change in water temperature in order to see how they react. You are now ready to proceed to the next step.

Laying the groundwork

Before you begin the actual experiment, it is wise to take certain preliminary steps to lay the groundwork for your research.

1. Collect all the equipment and materials you will need. Answer questions like the following: If the school cannot supply a certain chemical, can I get it from another source? Can I afford to buy it? Does the school own such and such a piece of equipment? If not, can I build it?

2. Practice any new techniques that your experiment will require. The time

National Teaching Aids, Inc.

This is a thin slice across a green leaf. The arrow points to a small opening in the underside of the leaf. This opening is called a stomate. What is its purpose? Do all leaves have stomates? How can you learn the answers to these questions?

REQUIREMENTS FOR YOUR EXPERIMENT

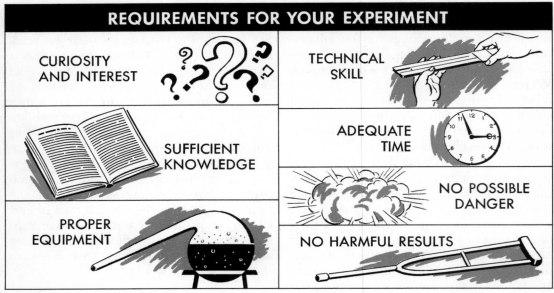

CURIOSITY AND INTEREST

TECHNICAL SKILL

SUFFICIENT KNOWLEDGE

ADEQUATE TIME

PROPER EQUIPMENT

NO POSSIBLE DANGER

NO HARMFUL RESULTS

to develop skills is *before* the actual experiment begins — not after it is under way.

3. Find out what other researchers have done in this and related fields. Long ago, Francis Bacon commented, "When a person prepares himself for discovery, he first obtains a full account of all that has been said on the subject by others." Bacon's advice is as good today as it was in 1620.

Reading about the work of others provides an insight into the best line of procedure. It gives you the opportunity to take advantage of earlier successes and failures. It tells what pitfalls may lie ahead, and what errors are to be avoided. It gives information on special apparatus and techniques that may help you in solving your problem.

Where do you find such information? Thomas Edison once said, "When I want to discover something, I begin by reading everything that has been done along that line in the past. That's what all those books in the library are for."

This is sound advice. The library has many sources of background information: college textbooks, magazine articles, original articles by research scientists, review articles, publications of Federal and state agencies, etc. In your search for background materials, enlist the help of an expert; the librarian can direct you to many aids that help locate materials bearing on your project.

Your school library is almost certain to have *The Readers' Guide to Periodical Literature.* This is an index, arranged like a dictionary, that lists the articles appearing in over one hundred magazines. Other, more technical, publications index special science articles. There are also periodicals like *Biological Abstracts* and *Chemical Abstracts,* which give brief summaries of important articles from the current science literature. These specialized journals are not likely to be in your school library, but they can be found in the libraries of almost all colleges and universities. (Most such institutions allow high-school students to use their library facilities.)

4. Record what you learn from your reading. Prepare yourself with a large notebook or a batch of file cards, and make your records as complete as possible.

If you find something in a book, summarize it in your notebook or on an index card. Be sure also to record the full name of the author, the complete title of the book, the date of publication, the name and address of the publisher, and the pages on which the information is found.

If your information comes from a magazine, note the full name of the author, the complete title of the article, the name of the magazine, the date of the issue, the volume number, and the pages on which the article appears. Once again, you should make a good summary.

5. Finally, prepare a preliminary plan of your experiment. Before you begin the actual experiment, you must have a clear picture of what you are going to do and how you are going to do it. Let us now see what goes into the planning of an experiment.

Planning the experiment

Whenever you are faced with a problem, it is logical to plan a line of attack. You should be certain that you have a clear picture of precisely what it is you are attacking — exactly what question you hope to answer.

If you are wise, you will think about the question for a while. You will turn it over in your mind and ask yourself what the answer might be. You should propose an answer that seems to make sense. Maybe you will even think of several possible answers. You should weigh them against each other, and form an opinion as to which is likely to be the most probable answer.

Being asked to guess at the answer may strike you as an unscientific procedure. But every research scientist makes such guesses. A guess of this type is called a *hypothesis*. It is an educated guess based on knowledge, background and experience. The task of the experimenter is to plan a test that will tell him whether his guess is reasonable and correct, or incorrect and unacceptable. Such a test is called a *planned experiment*.

A planned experiment is an attempt *to make something happen under controlled conditions where all variables except one have been eliminated or neutralized.* You hope that whatever happens in the experiment can be attributed to the single, remaining variable. Let's consider an imaginary case to see how this works.

You have read that growth substances called "gibberellins" cause certain plants to grow to two or three times their normal height. You decide that it would be interesting to try these substances on bean plants. You frame a clear question: "How do gibberellins affect growth in bean plants?" You realize that there are several possibilities. The gibberellins may make the plants grow faster and taller. They may have little or no effect. They may inhibit growth, so that the bean plants are dwarfed. They may kill the plants. You conclude that the third and fourth hypotheses can be eliminated because they do not seem logical in view of what you have read about gibberellins. This leaves two possibilities for testing.

How do you set up the test? How do you make bean plants grow under controlled conditions that will provide the answer to your question? You decide on the following plan:

Place a bean seed in a pot of good soil in a location favorable for growth. Moisten the soil daily; but, instead of using plain water, use a solution containing five parts per million (5 ppm) of gibberellins. As the seed sprouts, make daily observations and accurate measurements. Count the number of leaves, and measure their

Before beginning an experiment, read about the work of other researchers who have studied similar problems.

One method of recording what you learn from your reading is by placing the information on index cards. Summarize the material clearly and precisely. Label the cards and arrange them in an orderly fashion so that you can easily refer to the information.

R. E. Hudson

GIBBERELLINS – discovery

Gibberellins occur in several forms, of which gibberellic acid is one of the most common.

Discovered in 1926 by Japanese botanists who noticed that rice seedlings attacked by the fungus _Gibberella fujikuroi_ grew 2 to 3 times taller than non-infected seedlings.

Cronquist, Arnold, INTRODUCTORY BOTANY, Harper + Brothers, New York, 1961, pages 657-658

length and width. Measure the height of the flower stalk and the size of the flower when the plant blooms. In addition to recording these observations accurately in a notebook, make a series of dated photographs showing the plant in various stages of its development.

This sounds like a fine plan, doesn't it? You have made the bean grow under carefully controlled conditions, and you have made accurate observations. Therefore you should get an answer to the question. But no, this experiment cannot provide a definite answer. In certain respects, it is poorly designed. What is missing is a basis for comparison.

Without another bean plant for comparison, how can you be sure what caused the experimental plant to grow the way it did? Was it something in the soil? Some peculiarity of location? The gibberellins you added? Or was it simply the normal growth pattern of your particular seed?

Your plan would be improved if you added another part for comparison. This second part is called the _control_ or _check_. The object is to make the experimental part and the control part of your experiment _identical in every respect except one_. The one difference is the variable.

This, then, is your new and improved experimental design: Use 2 identical bean seeds planted in identical pots containing equal portions of the same soil. Put both pots in the same desirable location. Label one "CONTROL" and the other "GIBBERELLINS." Moisten the control pot daily with plain water. Moisten the gibberellin pot daily with a solution made from the same water, but containing 5 ppm of gibberellins. Be sure to give the same amount of water to each plant.

Again make daily measurements of growth and record them accurately in your notebook. Make side-by-side photographs of the 2 bean plants, so that any differences in growth pattern are clearly visible.

Now you surely have a good plan. The beans, the soil, the pots, the location, the water are all identical. There is only one variable: one pot was treated with gibberellins, the other was not. Surely any difference in growth must result from this one variable.

But there is still another factor to consider: the question of sampling. Your experiment is not testing all beans, but only 2. How do you know that the 2 you happened to choose are representative? How do you know that they will react like normal, average bean plants should?

The only way to be reasonably certain that your results are representative is to test as many bean plants as possible. You are in a better position to determine the behavior of the average bean plant if each half of your experiment has 10 plants or 50 or 100 or 1,000. The more times the experiment is repeated and the more subjects you have in your sample, the more reliable your conclusion will be.

Thus a well-designed experiment has 2 parts — experimental and control with a single difference between them. And there must be many subjects in each part. This describes a planned experiment in its simplest form; there are many complicating factors that make the design of an experiment much more complex. Let us go one step beyond the basic design. Suppose you want to know what concentration of gibberellins causes the greatest increase in the growth of beans. You decide to test 3 concentrations: 5 ppm, 25 ppm, and 50 ppm. Must you set up 3 parallel experiments, each having its own control? In each case the control would be a group of plants moistened with plain water. One control can therefore serve all 3 experimental parts. Thus the experimental design has 4 parts; 3 are experimental (5, 25 and 50 ppm gibberellins), and the fourth is the control (plain water).

It is impossible to cover all the complications of experimental design. The basic points that have been examined should be sufficient to give you a start. However, there is one more bit of advice. Before you begin work on the actual experiment, prepare a written plan. Such a plan should describe the experiment as you have worked it out in your mind. It should include one or more educated guesses as to the answer to your question, and proposals for testing them. It should detail the information you will need to determine whether your hypothesis is correct or incorrect, and how this information will be collected and analyzed. Once this plan of action is complete, you are ready to begin the actual experiment and collect the data.

Collecting the data

When you undertake an experiment, it is necessary to maintain complete and accurate records of all your observations. One way to do this is to keep a dated record of everything you do and everything that happens. Since you can never tell what may turn out to be important, it is wise to record every observation, no matter how trivial it may seem.

Observation is simply the use of the senses to discover what is happening. You see things, hear them, taste them, smell

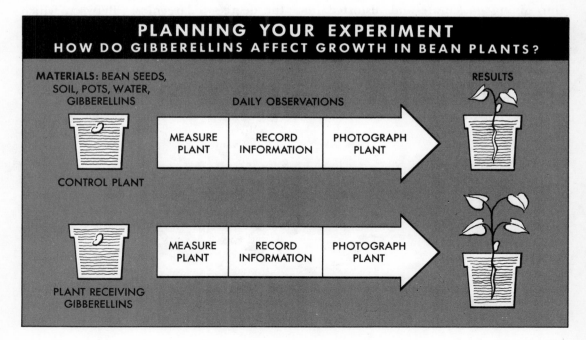

PLANNING YOUR EXPERIMENT
HOW DO GIBBERELLINS AFFECT GROWTH IN BEAN PLANTS?

MATERIALS: BEAN SEEDS, SOIL, POTS, WATER, GIBBERELLINS

RESULTS

DAILY OBSERVATIONS

MEASURE PLANT | RECORD INFORMATION | PHOTOGRAPH PLANT

CONTROL PLANT

MEASURE PLANT | RECORD INFORMATION | PHOTOGRAPH PLANT

PLANT RECEIVING GIBBERELLINS

them, feel them, sense them in a dozen different ways. Making observations is part of life itself. But observation becomes doubly important during an experiment: it provides the evidence on which you will decide whether or not your hypothesis is correct.

Although man has a variety of amazing sense organs, their power is comparatively limited. The environment is filled with things that our unaided sense organs cannot detect. For example, we cannot see the millions of tiny bacteria and viruses that exist all about us. Our universe is crowded with heavenly bodies too distant to see with the unaided eye. The atmosphere is filled with radio waves, but the human body has no way of detecting them.

But microscopes reveal the tiny bacteria and viruses. Telescopes bring the distant galaxies into view. Radio receivers change the radio waves into audible sound waves. These are but a few of the remarkable devices that man has invented to increase and extend the powers of his sense organs.

In addition, man has developed measuring devices with which he can substitute objective numbers for subjective observations. The human senses can be fooled into giving inaccurate and distorted impressions. Measurement can make observations accurate and objective. Since accurate observation is an absolute must in science, measuring devices are basic tools of the researcher.

The simplest measuring devices include rulers to measure distance; scales to measure weight; thermometers to measure temperature; manometers to measure pressure; voltmeters and ammeters to measure electricity; and so on. These basic tools have been refined in a hundred ways to make the measurements as accurate as possible.

Observation can be a very tricky business during the conduct of an experiment. There are many traps and pitfalls to be avoided. One of these is illustrated by the gibberellin experiment. The experimenter planned to see if treated plants grew larger than untreated plants. But what is meant by larger? Is a larger plant one that has more or larger leaves? One that is taller or thicker around the base? Is it one that weighs more? One with a taller flower stalk and a larger flower? There are many different aspects to being "larger."

It is not enough therefore to note that one plant is larger than another. You must tell in what way it is larger; how much it is larger; and how you determined the degree of largeness. Between which two points did you measure? From the

Before beginning an experiment, you should become proficient in the scientific skills needed for your project. The microscope is an important tool in many experiments.

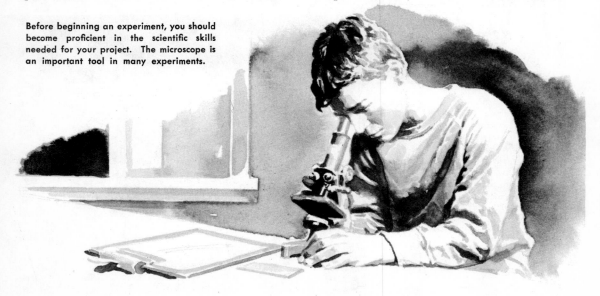

base of the stem to the top of the leaf? From the beginning of the flower stalk to the top of the flower? Obviously the comparison of two measurements is meaningless if a different basis was used for each.

Selection of the proper measuring instruments also requires good judgment. Would you use a yardstick to measure a salt crystal? An analytical balance to weigh out 100 grams of a chemical? Obviously these would be foolish procedures. A yardstick is much too coarse a measuring device for a tiny salt crystal. And the analytical balance is intended for weighing hundredths of a gram rather than a hundred grams.

Even when you use an appropriate measuring device, how accurate can you be? To how many decimal places can you measure? As a general rule, it is unwise to estimate more than one place beyond what the device measures accurately. Let us consider an example:

When you measure the length of a line with a ruler marked off in centimeters, you find it to be 9 cm long with a little left over. You estimate the extra piece to be just over half a centimeter, so that you write the observation as 9.6 cm. You can hardly say it is 9.58 cm or 9.62 cm. Your powers of estimation are not that good. But if you used a ruler marked off in millimeters, you might find that the line measures 96 mm plus a little extra that you estimate as two tenths of a millimeter. Now you can say that the line is 96.2 mm (9.62 cm) long.

There are also certain psychological factors that can distort your powers of accurate observation. It is easy to see only those things that favor your hypothesis and to overlook things that are opposed. Any person who consciously does this is dishonest. But often it can be a completely unconscious act on the part of the experimenter. Without being aware that he is doing so, he can favor observations that he hopes the experiment will produce. This is well illustrated by a research scientist studying the problem of lung blackening in coal miners. He said:

"One of our problems is the need to take elaborate precautions to prevent those examining the lungs from knowing where they came from. I don't care how dedicated a pathologist is, if he knows the history of the tissue he is examining, his findings are going to be influenced by that history. In our study those looking at the tissues know them only by a number. About 50 per cent of our subjects are miners; the other 50 per cent serve as controls."

This approach is known as doing an experiment "blind." Usually the term *blind experiment* describes a situation

R. E. Hudson

One of the most important phases of your experiment is keeping accurate records. These must be made at the time you make your observations. Drawings, charts and photographs are also important parts of records. Keep your records in a hardcover, permanent book or binder.

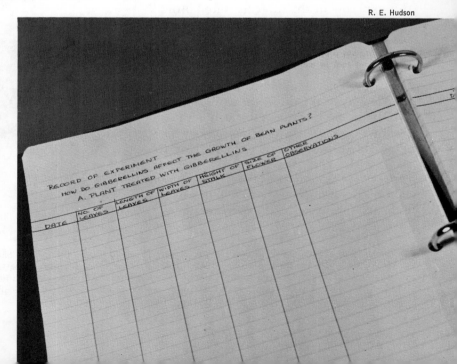

where the subjects are not aware whether they are in the experimental or control group.

Suppose a doctor is testing whether drug X causes blood pressure to rise. He divides his subjects into two equivalent groups. The subjects in the experimental group get a pill containing drug X. The controls get an identical pill without drug X. (In medical terminology this is called a "placebo.") To his great pleasure, the doctor finds that, on the average, blood pressure rose in the subjects getting the drug, but not in the controls. He concludes that the drug is effective.

However, this conclusion is not really valid. Blood pressure is affected by many psychological factors. Is it possible that the subjects reacted psychologically when they knew that they were getting drug X? Did their pressures rise merely because they knew that this drug was supposed to raise pressure, and not because of any action of the drug?

Experimenters try to avoid this problem by doing the test blind. The subjects are not divided into two groups. Each subject gets an identical-looking pill with a code number. Half the pills contain drug X, the other half do not. The subjects do not know what they are getting; only the experimenter knows.

Even this is not the final word. In this experiment the subjects were "blind," but the experimenter was not. He knew which subjects were receiving drug X and which were not. Perhaps he can still influence the outcome unconsciously by the way he looks, what he says, or what he does when he gives the subject the pill. This is avoided if neither the subject nor the experimenter knows which sample is which. The coded samples are prepared for the experimenter by someone else. The outcome of such a "double-blind" experiment cannot be influenced psychologically by either the subject or the experimenter.

M. J. Bukovac — Mich. State Univ.

These photographs show a time sequence of control and gibberellin-treated bean plants (the gibberellin was applied to the growing point, or apex, of the stem). (A) Control plant after 48 hours. (B) Gibberellin-treated plant, 48 hours after it was treated. (C) Control plant after 96 hours. (D) Gibberellin-treated plant after 96 hours. How has gibberellin affected the plant?

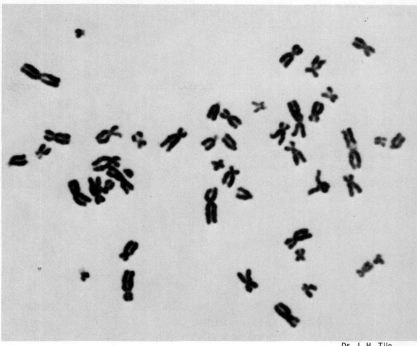

Careful observation is important in all scientific work. This is a microphotograph of human chromosomes. How many chromosomes are there?

Dr. J. H. Tjio

Let us return to the collection of data: In the planning stage of your experiment, you decided what observations and measurements you would require. You should also decide what method you will use to record the data. Choose a practical arrangement that is both convenient and understandable.

One practical device is a table or a chart. A table summarizes on a single page all the data that you collected during your experiment. It is much easier to see the figures all at once if they are organized in a table, than if they are scattered over the many pages of your record book. By looking at the table, you can get a good idea of where your experiment is heading. But you can only do this if you decide in advance what arrangement of columns will make the table most useful. When your experiment is complete, and you have collected all the data, you are ready to begin analyzing the results.

Analyzing the data

The data that you originally collected and recorded in your experiment are often referred to as the "raw data." This means that they are the original measurements without treatment or processing of any kind. Your next task is to prepare the raw data in such a way that they tell a meaningful story.

Sometimes a graph can be used to summarize the data. The most common types of graphs are bar graphs, pictographs, line graphs and circle graphs. Each type has its own advantages and disadvantages.

At other times it is necessary to analyze the data by applying a form of mathematics called "statistics." Statistics has been called the art of drawing inferences from the raw data of observation. An inference is something derived by logic and reasoning from a collection of evidence. In your experiment, your observations and measurements are the evidence. What you decide the evidence is telling you is your inference.

Statistics is a very useful tool for examining evidence. It can make a diffuse mass of data become a good deal more meaningful. While this brief article cannot possibly cover the science of statistics, there are certain fundamental ideas that you really should understand. Four of these concepts are explained here.

Communication is an important part of science. A person should share his discoveries and knowledge with other people. Here, a student explains his science project to teachers and fellow students.

1. If you measured or weighed a large number of specimens, you may need a figure that is representative of the whole group. For this you use a *measure of central tendency*. There are three to choose from: the mean, the median and the mode.

The "mean" is simply the arithmetic average. To determine the mean, you add the separate measurements and divide by the number of measurements. The "median" is the middle measurement of your series. To find it, you list all the measurements in order from the highest to the lowest and locate the one in the middle. There are always as many cases above the median as there are below. The "mode" is the measurement that occurs most frequently. It indicates that there are more cases at that level than at any other level.

2. If you need to know how variable or consistent your measurements are, you use a *measure of variability*. Such a measure tells you how far away from a central point your data may spread. There are three such measures: the range, the average deviation and the standard deviation.

The "range" is the spread from the highest measurement to the lowest. This tells you the upper and lower limits of your data. The "average deviation" is the average of the individual deviation from

the mean. To determine the average deviation, you must find the difference (deviation) between each individual measurement and the mean. Then you add the sum of the deviations and divide by the number of measurements. The mean, plus and minus the average deviation, always includes 50 per cent of the measurements in the series. Thus if the mean is 9 and the average deviation is 2.5, then 50 per cent of all the cases lie between 6.5 and 11.5. The "standard deviation" is a similar figure obtained by a slightly different calculation. The mean, plus and minus the standard deviation, includes about ⅔ of the measurements instead of ½.

3. To find whether there is a relationship between two series of events, you use some measure of correlation. Two things are said to be correlated if they occur together. This does not mean, however, that one of these things is the cause of the other.

Correlation can be positive, negative or zero. A positive correlation exists when a subject that is high on one series of measurements also tends to be high on a second series. A negative correlation exists when a subject that scores high on one series of measurements tends to score low on the second. Zero correlation is represented by the situation where there is no recognizable relationship between two events or two series of measurements.

4. An experimenter is always interested in knowing whether his results are accurate, and whether they would come out the same way again. For this he uses a *statistical measure of reliability,* such as the probable error. This is really a way of applying the "laws of chance" to the results. In simple words, it says, "the chances that a similar result will come out again are 100 to 1, or 10 to 1, or 1 to 1, or some such ratio."

Statistical reliability depends on two factors: the number of cases in your experiment and the variability of the sample. An experiment that includes a large number of cases is more apt to be reliable because it is more likely to be a true sampling of the total population. But if the sample you use is very variable, it may give unreliable results even though you use a large number of subjects.

Forming a conclusion

The conclusion is a final answer to your question. Early in the planning process, you proposed a hypothesis as a possible answer to the question. Now you must see whether the evidence produced by your experiment does or does not support this hypothesis.

Don't be upset if your hypothesis is unsupported. You will not be the first to face this situation. The English scientist Thomas Huxley made the point when he said, "The tragedy of all inquiry is that a beautiful hypothesis may be slain by ugly facts."

Your conclusion should be stated simply and clearly. It should be a natural outgrowth of your observations and the analysis of the data. Don't let your conclusion be tinted by your opinions or by what you had hoped to find. However, in discussing the conclusion, there is nothing wrong with offering an opinion as long as you label it such. It is often necessary to state that you are offering a tentative conclusion subject to further checking.

Your experiment was set up under precise and controlled conditions, and your conclusion is valid only within the limits of these conditions. Be careful not to state a conclusion not supported by the data. Mention if your conclusion is limited by factors you did not or could not control.

Accept the facts you discovered, even if they disagree with what you read. State your conclusion as the experiment in-

Science Talent Institute

Ten students whose science projects helped them win college scholarships: the winners of the 29th annual Science Talent Search (with Westinghouse representative, Marshall K. Evans). The winners were selected from 19,952 participating students.

dicates — not as authorities say it should be. Here is an actual case where an important discovery grew out of observations that ran counter to authority.

Until 1956 every biologist accepted 48 as the number of chromosomes in a human cell. This figure appeared in every biology textbook and in every medical book. In that year Joe Hin Tjio and Albert Levan claimed that the number should be 46. Their claim was based on chromosome preparations made with new and improved techniques. When the claim was checked and verified by other biologists, the figure of 46 was accepted, and Tjio and Levan were credited with the discovery. One of Dr. Tjio's photographs of human chromosomes is on page 389.

Several years earlier, however, a team of biologists working with human liver cells kept getting chromosome counts of 46. Instead of following up their curious observation, they dropped the whole project on the assumption that their technique was bad. They accepted the voice of authority over their own observations, thus losing the opportunity of being credited with making an important discovery.

What kind of conclusion can you reach if your results are negative? In science it is just as important to know what does not happen as to know what does happen. So state your negative result — it may be very worthwhile.

Perhaps your experiment fails completely, and you do not get any results. The same thing has happened before — even to great scientists. Like most human beings, scientists are more apt to advertise their successes than their failures. Thus, you are more likely to hear about experiments that worked than about those that failed. However, you can still form an honest conclusion under these circumstances. You can say that the experiment failed to answer the question for which it was proposed.

Once the conclusion is reached, you are ready to report the results of your experiment. This may be done in writing or orally. In either case, remember to make things clear and understandable for the benefit of people who don't know as much about the subject as you do. One of the values of reporting your results is that it gives other people the chance to repeat your experiment. A good experiment must be reproducible. If it cannot be reproduced, there is something wrong.

Summary

An experiment begins when you try to solve a puzzling situation. You would be wise to begin with a relatively simple problem that interests you. Be sure that you have the necessary time, space, materials, equipment and technical skills. Under no circumstances should you choose an experiment that is dangerous to you or to your subjects.

Your first step is to frame a concise statement of the problem, which gives a clear picture of the purpose of the experiment. Next, you must take care of the preliminaries. These include background readings, developing skills, gathering equipment and preparing a plan of action. The plan should include the hypotheses you propose to test by your experiment.

In its simplest form, the well-planned experiment consists of two parts that are identical except for the single variable that is being tested. There should be many subjects in the experimental and control parts of the experiment. All observations and data coming out of the experiment should be collected and recorded. Objective measurement is always preferable to subjective observation.

The raw data collected from the experiment must be organized and analyzed with the help of graphs and statistics. A simple, clear-cut conclusion is drawn from the inferences growing out of this analysis. The conclusion must be a direct outgrowth of the experimental results.

When it is completed, the experiment can be reported in the form of a written report or by a speech before an audience. If the experiment is valid, it is reproducible. When it is reproduced under the same conditions as the original, it should give the same results.

DOES HOT WATER FREEZE FASTER THAN COOL WATER?*

BY DAVID WEBSTER

A LONG time ago someone told me that hot water freezes faster than cold water. I really did not believe this, but I tried it anyway. On a winter night I set outdoors a glass of very cold water and another glass of hot water. As I expected, the cold water froze first.

Recently, however, I read another article about freezing hot water. Many skating rinks are flooded with hot water because it turns to ice more quickly. Hot milk is used in making ice cream for the same reason. Other people have found that warming water that is put out for birds in the winter only makes it freeze more quickly. And plumbers have reported that hot-water pipes freeze before cold-water pipes do.

Scientists have made careful experiments to test this idea. They have found that when water at room temperature (about 72° F.) is placed in a freezer, it takes longer to freeze than an equal amount of water that is either colder or warmer than 72° F. Even water that has been heated to boiling will freeze faster than an equal amount of water at room temperature under the same cooling conditions. You can test this finding yourself.

Get 2 alcohol or mercury thermometers and 2 drinking glasses of the same size and shape. Mix hot and cold water in a glass until the temperature of the water is 72° F. Have enough water so the level is 1 inch from the top of the glass. Put a little cold water into the second glass and slowly add hot water until the water has a temperature of about 110° F. (If the temperature goes higher, take the thermometer out and add a little cool water.) Be sure that the water levels in the 2 glasses are the same. (Why?)

Stick a thermometer into each glass of water, and place them in your freezer. Check the temperature every 15 minutes until the water in both glasses has begun to turn to ice. Record your measurements and when they were made.

Which froze first — the hot water or the water at room temperature? How much longer did it take for the slower-freezing water to begin to freeze? Did the water cool faster at the beginning or later on? What happens to water's temperature between the time when the water begins to freeze and when it is completely frozen?

If it takes longest for water to freeze when it starts out at a temperature of about 72° F., do you think that water at, say, 82° and 62° (10 degrees warmer and 10 degrees colder than room temperature) will take about the same time to freeze?

From your findings, can you guess why the cold water I set outdoors on a winter night long ago froze sooner than the warm water did?

* "Does Hot Water Freeze Faster Than Cool Water?" by David Webster, from the January 5, 1970, issue of *Nature and Science Magazine*. Copyright © 1970 by the American Museum of Natural History. Reprinted by permission of Doubleday & Company, Inc.

MORE INVESTIGATIONS

• When the air outdoors is colder than 32°F., you might repeat your investigations by setting glasses of water at temperatures of 72° and 110° outside. Do you get the same results as when you used the freezer? Does the water in either glass freeze faster or slower outdoors than it did in the freezer? How does the temperature of the air in the freezer compare with the temperature of the air outdoors?

• Can you think of any reason why hot water would freeze faster than cool water? Three possible explanations were given in the article I read:

1. Hot water circulates as it cools, and this water movement allows the colder water near the side of the glass to mix with the warmer water in the middle.

2. Cool water contains more dissolved air that would slow down the loss of heat.

3. The more rapid evaporation of the hot water helps to cool it faster.

What experiments can you perform to test each of these ideas? Can you put anything in hot and cold water that would enable you to see any circulation? Can you prepare cool water with less air in it by heating the water and then allowing it slowly to return to room temperature? What would happen if the containers of hot and cold water were covered, so that evaporation could not take place?

Chicago Natural History Museum

Smithsonian Institution

Smithsonian Institution

American Museum of Natural History

Smithsonian Institution

American Museum of Natural History

American Museum of Natural History

These photographs show some of the fossils you might find on your next collecting trip. (1) a trilobite, an early inhabitant of the sea that is probably related to the modern horseshoe crab; (2) crinoids, or sea lilies, plantlike animals; (3) an echinoid called the heart urchin; (4) dinosaur tracks in a dry stream bed; (5) another echinoid, related to today's sea urchins and sand dollars; (6) a brachiopod, an animal with two unequal shells; and (7) an ant preserved in amber, a fossilized resin.

DIGGING FOR FOSSILS

Unearthing Clues to Life's Beginnings

BY WILLIAM H. MATTHEWS, III

FOSSIL collecting is similar to most other hobbies in that the key to success lies in a certain amount of fundamental know-how. Although the fossil collector need not be an authority on fossils, it does help to know what equipment and supplies to use, where to look for fossils, and the best collecting and preserving techniques.

Equipment and supplies

Fossil collecting is a relatively inexpensive hobby, requiring a minimum of equipment and supplies. The basic tool in any collector's kit is the hammer. A beginner can use almost any hammer that

is strong enough to attack rock, but as he becomes more experienced, he may want to get a geologist's hammer or prospector's pick. These hammers are available in two basic types: one with a square head on one end and a pick on the other and one with a square head on one end and a chisel on the other — somewhat like a stonemason's or bricklayer's hammer. The square head is ideal for chipping or breaking harder rocks, and the pick or chisel end can be used for digging, prying, and splitting softer rocks.

Another important piece of equipment is a bag in which to carry tools,

394

supplies, and the fossils that have been collected. An army musette bag, a Boy Scout knapsack, a hunting bag, or similar leather or canvas container is generally inexpensive and convenient to carry in the field.

Although many fossils will be found free on the ground, some specimens will probably have to be chipped out of the surrounding rock (matrix). Many times, only the hammer need be used, but firmly embedded fossils may demand more selective chipping. Small chisels are very useful for this purpose, and two sizes — preferably ½ inch and 1 inch — will meet most collectors' needs. In addition, a small sharp punch or awl is effective in removing smaller specimens from soft rock formations.

Most collectors also carry a magnifying glass or hand lens — usually a Coddington or Hastings — to examine small fossils and to study the finer details of larger specimens. A 10-power magnification is satisfactory for most purposes, and several inexpensive models are available.

Often, fossil specimens that have been carefully collected in the field have been destroyed or badly damaged on the trip home. To avoid such mishaps the collector should carry an ample supply of wrapping material. Sheets of newspaper are essential and should be used to wrap each specimen. Fragile fossils should be wrapped in cotton or tissue paper and placed in small paper bags. Matchboxes or plastic pill vials filled with cotton will protect even the smallest and most delicate fossils. As a final precaution the collector should always place the heavier specimens at the bottom of the collecting bag and the lighter, more fragile specimens at the top.

It is not enough simply to collect fossils; one should also know where they were collected. A fossil without information on its location is hardly worth the paper it is wrapped in. Consequently, a small notebook should be taken along, and the collector should take notes at the time the material is collected. He should carefully and accurately record all that is known about the location, using a suitable county or highway map.

Small paper labels about 2 by 3 inches are also handy and should be used to record such information as the collector's name, the locality, the date, and the geologic formation, if it is known. A properly completed label should be placed inside each bag of fossils.

Paper or cloth bags can be used to separate specimens from different collecting areas. Use heavy-duty hardware bags for rough, heavy fossils and medium-weight grocery bags for smaller ones. Information about the collecting location may be written on the side of the bag or on a label placed inside with the fossils. Many collectors do both. The more advanced collector may prefer the cloth geological sample bags used by professional geologists. Available from geological supply houses, this type of bag has a drawstring opening and a cloth-backed label sewn on one side.

John W. Shrum

A fossil hunter's equipment. At the top left are field notes (with a pencil), a road map (folded) and a topographic map. At the bottom of the topographic map are magnifying lenses and a cold chisel, with a mason's hammer just below the latter. At the right, from top to bottom, are tissue paper, newspaper, masking tape and a knapsack, with pen and pencils attached to its side flap.

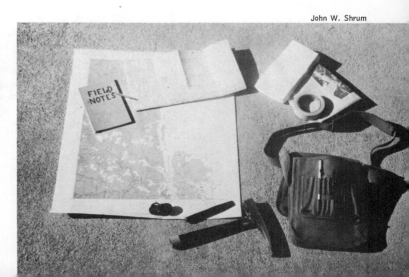

Where to look

A topographical map of the collecting area will help in accurately locating the places where fossils have been found. In the United States these maps are available for many areas and may be obtained at nominal cost from the United States Geological Survey in Washington, D.C., or Denver, Colorado. Another type of map, a geologic map, will help determine which formations may contain fossils, where they are exposed, and their geologic age. Fossil guides that describe prospective collecting sites and provide other valuable information are also available for many regions.

Before starting on a fossil collecting trip it is wise to do some advance planning. The collector who knows where he is going and what he is looking for is likely to be successful. Simply knowing where to look is an important part of fossil collecting. Because of their origin, certain rocks (lavas and granite, for example) are not likely to contain fossils. The collector should look instead for marine sedimentary rocks formed from sediments that were deposited in ancient seas, where conditions were favorable for life and facilitated preservation after death. Many limestones, limy shales, and certain types of sandstone have formed from sediments deposited under such conditions.

The collector should look particularly for places where rocks formed from marine sediments lie relatively flat and have not been greatly distributed by heat, pressure, and other physical and chemical

The great majority of fossils are found in sedimentary rocks. These are rocks formed from sediments laid down in seas and streams long, long ago. Above: geologists study fossil remains found in a creek bed in Canada's Northwest Territories. Right: a geologist examines a fossil sponge in Texas.

Both photos: Socony Mobil Oil Co.

A number of good books are available for identifying the fossils you collect. This student is using one such book to identify a shark tooth.

Most fossils require considerable cleaning before they are ready to be displayed. These students carefully prepare fossil ammonite shells (extinct mollusks).

Here, supervised by geologist Horace G. Richards, the boys clean the lower jaw of a Titanothere skull. Titanotheres were elephant-like creatures with long nasal projections resembling tusks. Their fossils are found in the Badlands of South Dakota.

Photos: Academy of Natural Sciences

changes. In areas where rocks appear to have undergone considerable folding, fracturing, and other types of deformation, it is very likely that fossils that were present have been destroyed or damaged by this action.

Quarries are good places to look because rock exposures in quarries are rather fresh but have still undergone some weathering. Special attention should also be directed toward railroad and highway cuts, since rocks exposed in this way are usually still in their original positions and are fairly well weathered. Construction excavations are likely to be more productive after they have undergone a period of weathering, since weathering helps separate the fossils from their enclosing rocks.

Gullies, canyons, and stream beds are also good places to look for fossils. Such places are continuously subjected to erosion, and new fossils may be recovered year after year. If there are abandoned coal mines nearby, check the dumps of waste rock around the deserted mine shafts. A careful search of this material may reveal well-preserved plant fossils. Beachcombing may also be profitable along certain parts of the Atlantic and Pacific coasts. There are stretches of beach in Delaware, Florida, Maryland, Massachusetts, New Jersey, Oregon, and Washington where large numbers of both vertebrate and invertebrate fossils have been found.

Collecting specimens

Once a likely collecting spot has been located, the ground should be examined carefully, preferably on hands and knees or while sitting. Be patient and search one spot thoroughly before moving to another. Look especially for pieces of rock that contain shell fragments, leaf imprints, or other traces of plant or animal remains. Such evidence of past life can be clues that will lead to larger and more complete specimens.

If the fossils have been freed by weathering, they can be easily picked up and placed in the collecting bag. If a fossil is still embedded in the rock, carefully chip the rock away or loosen the fossil with a chisel. The best way to do this is to chisel a narrow trough around the fossil, being careful to always point the chisel away from the fossil. When the trough is as deep or deeper than the fossil, carefully chisel beneath the pedestal that the fossil is resting on. The fossil should then break free. It is best not to risk ruining a good specimen by trimming it too closely in the field; the final cleaning and preparation of fossils is best done at home.

Although fossil collecting is not a dangerous hobby, certain precautions should be taken in the field. When collecting along the face of a cliff or quarry, be particularly careful not to dislodge rocks or boulders that might fall on someone collecting at a lower level. Also, the hammer should always be used cautiously to avoid producing flying rock fragments. If it becomes necessary to do a lot of hammering and chiseling, it is a good idea to wear safety goggles.

Before leaving a collecting locality, make certain that some record is made of the geographic location and the age of the rock in which the fossils were found. The place should be located and marked on a map, and the locality data (name of county and state) should be entered in the collector's notebook and on the label placed in with the fossils.

Preparing specimens for display

Most fossils brought in from the field require considerable cleaning and preparation before they are ready to be displayed. Before starting the final cleaning, it is helpful to soak the fossils in water overnight. This will loosen much of the excess rock material, making it possible to remove the softer material with a small scrub brush or toothbrush. Next, all excess rock matrix should be carefully chipped away with a hammer and chisel. Smaller tools, such as needles, tweezers, and awls, should be used in working with small specimens and around delicate structures of larger fossils.

When accidents do occur, broken specimens can be repaired with clear plastic household cement, and fossils that are crumbling may be coated with pure white shellac, thinned collodion, or clear nail polish. The nail polish is generally preferred since it is not likely to crack. Fragments of bone are particularly apt to crumble when they are uncovered and exposed to the air. Fossils of this type are normally quite fragile. Therefore, they should be excavated with great care and given a coating of shellac as soon as they are dry.

INDEX

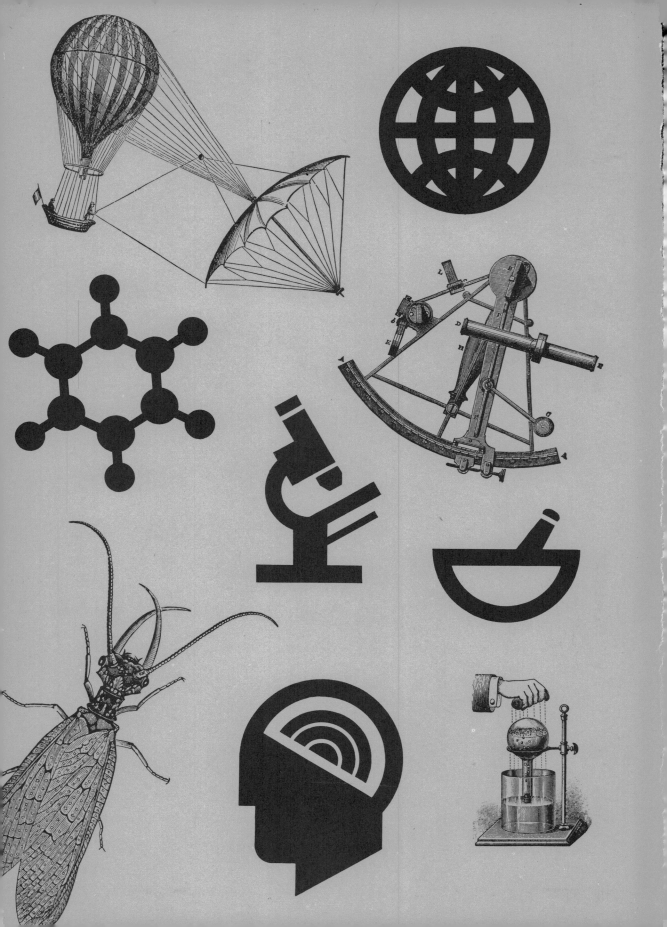